Becker Professional Education, a global leader in professional educatic  for the ACCA for more than 20 years. Thousands of students studying succeeded in their professional examinations studying with its Platinum Central and Eastern Europe and Central Asia.

Nearly half a million professionals have advanced their careers through Becker Professional Education's courses. Throughout its 60-year history, Becker has earned a strong track record of student success through world-class teaching, curriculum and learning tools.

Becker Professional Education has been awarded ACCA Approved Content Provider Status for its ACCA materials, as well as materials for the Diploma in International Financial Reporting (DipIFR).

We provide a single solution for individuals and companies in need of global accounting certifications and continuing professional education.

Becker Professional Education's ACCA Study Materials

All of Becker's materials are authored by experienced ACCA lecturers and are used in the delivery of classroom courses.

Study Text: Gives complete coverage of the syllabus with a focus on learning outcomes. It is designed to be used both as a reference text and as part of integrated study. It also includes the ACCA Syllabus and Study Guide, exam advice and commentaries and a Study Question Bank containing practice questions relating to each topic covered.

Revision Question Bank: Exam style and standard questions together with comprehensive answers to support and prepare students for their exams. The Revision Question Bank also includes past examination questions (updated where relevant), model answers and alternative solutions and tutorial notes.

Revision Essentials Handbook*: A condensed, easy-to-use aid to revision containing essential technical content and exam guidance.

*Revision Essentials Handbook are substantially derived from content reviewed by ACCA's examining team.

Becker Professional Education
is an ACCA approved content provider

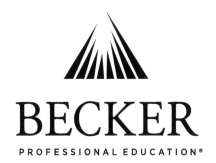

BECKER
PROFESSIONAL EDUCATION®

ACCA

ACCOUNTANT IN BUSINESS F1/FAB STUDY TEXT

September 2017 to August 2018 Edition

BECKER

PROFESSIONAL EDUCATION®

This training material has been prepared and published by Becker Professional Development International Limited: www.becker.com/acca

ISBN: 978-1-78566-367-3

LICENSE AGREEMENT

DO NOT DOWNLOAD, ACCESS, AND/OR USE ANY OF THESE MATERIALS (AS THAT TERM IS DEFINED BELOW) UNTIL YOU HAVE READ THIS LICENSE AGREEMENT CAREFULLY. IF YOU DOWNLOAD, ACCESS, AND/OR USE ANY OF THESE MATERIALS, YOU ARE AGREEING AND CONSENTING TO BE BOUND BY AND ARE BECOMING A PARTY TO THIS LICENSE AGREEMENT ("AGREEMENT").

The printed Materials provided to you and/or the Materials provided for download to your computer and/or provided via a web application to which you are granted access are NOT for sale and are not being sold to you. You may NOT transfer these Materials to any other person or permit any other person to use these Materials. You may only acquire a license to use these Materials and only upon the terms and conditions set forth in this Agreement. Read this Agreement carefully before downloading, and/or accessing, and/or using these Materials. Do not download and/or access, and/or use these Materials unless you agree with all terms of this Agreement.

NOTE: You may already be a party to this Agreement if you registered for a Becker Professional Education® ACCA Program (the "Program") or placed an order for these Materials online or using a printed form that included this License Agreement. Please review the termination section regarding your rights to terminate this License Agreement and receive a refund of your payment.

Grant: Upon your acceptance of the terms of this Agreement, in a manner set forth above, DeVry/Becker Educational Development Corp. ("Becker") hereby grants to you a non-exclusive, revocable, non-transferable, non-sublicensable, limited license to use (as defined below) the Materials by downloading them onto a computer and/or by accessing them via a web application using a user ID and password (as defined below), and any Materials to which you are granted access as a result of your license to use these Materials and/or in connection with the Program on the following terms:

During the Term of this Agreement, you may:

- use the Materials for preparation for the ACCA examinations (the "Exams"), and/or for your studies relating to the subject matter covered by the Materials and/or the Exams, including taking electronic and/or handwritten notes during the Program, provided that all notes taken that relate to the subject matter of the Materials are and shall remain Materials subject to the terms of this Agreement;

- download the Materials onto any single device;

- download the Materials onto a second device so long as the first device and the second device are not used simultaneously;

- download the Materials onto a third device so long as the first, second, and third device are not used simultaneously; and

- download the Materials onto a fourth device so long as the first, second, third, and fourth device are not used simultaneously.

The number of installations may vary outside of the U.S. Please review your local office policies and procedures to confirm the number of installations granted—your local office's policies and procedures regarding the number of allowable activations of downloads supersedes the limitations contained herein and is controlling.

You may not:

- use the Materials for any purpose other than as expressly permitted above;

- use the downloaded Materials on more than one device, computer terminal, or workstation at the same time;

- make copies of the Materials;

- rent, lease, license, lend, or otherwise transfer or provide (by gift, sale, or otherwise) all or any part of the Materials to anyone;

- permit the use of all or any part of the Materials by anyone other than you; or

- reverse engineer, decompile, disassemble, or create derivate works of the Materials.

Materials: As used in this Agreement, the term "Materials" means and includes any printed materials provided to you by Becker, and/or to which you are granted access by Becker (directly or indirectly) in connection with your license of the Materials and/or the Program, and shall include notes you take (by hand, electronically, digitally, or otherwise) while using the Materials relating to the subject matter of the Materials; any and all electronically-stored/accessed/delivered, and/or digitally-stored/accessed/delivered materials included under this License via download to a computer or via access to a web application, and/or otherwise provided to you and/or to which you are otherwise granted access by Becker (directly or indirectly), including, but not limited to, applications downloadable from a third party, for example Google® or Amazon®, in connection with your license of the Materials.

Title: Becker is and will remain the owner of all title, ownership rights, intellectual property, and all other rights and interests in and to the Materials that are subject to the terms of this Agreement. The Materials are protected by the copyright laws of the United States and international copyright laws and treaties.

Termination: The license granted under this Agreement commences upon your receipt of these Materials. This license shall terminate the earlier of: (i) ten (10) business days after notice to you of non-payment of or default on any payment due Becker which has not been cured within such 10-day period; or (ii) immediately if you fail to comply with any of the limitations described above; or (iii) upon expiration of the examination period for which the Materials are valid as specified on your order confirmation and in the title of the course package. For example, Materials marked, "For Examinations to August 2018," are valid for examinations from September 2017 to August 2018 and the license to these Materials terminates at the end of August 2018. All online packages and Materials will be removed after the relevant examination period and you will no longer have access to the online packages or Materials. In addition, upon termination of this license for any reason, you must delete or otherwise remove from your computer and other device any Materials you downloaded, including, but not limited to, any archival copies you may have made. The Title, Exclusion of Warranties, Exclusion of Damages, Indemnification and Remedies, Severability of Terms and Governing Law provisions, and any amounts due, shall survive termination of the license.

Your Limited Right to Terminate this License and Receive a Refund: You may terminate this license for the in-class, online, and self-study Programs in accordance with Becker's refund policy at https://becker.com/ACCA.

Exclusion of Warranties: YOU EXPRESSLY ASSUME ALL RISK FOR USE OF THE MATERIALS. YOU AGREE THAT THE MATERIALS ARE PROVIDED TO YOU "AS IS" AND "AS AVAILABLE" AND THAT BECKER MAKES NO WARRANTIES, EXPRESS OR IMPLIED, WITH RESPECT TO THE MATERIALS, THEIR MERCHANTABILITY OR FITNESS FOR A PARTICULAR PURPOSE AND NO WARRANTY OF NONINFRINGEMENT OF THIRD PARTIES' RIGHTS. NO DEALER, AGENT OR EMPLOYEE OF BECKER IS AUTHORIZED TO PROVIDE ANY SUCH WARRANTY TO YOU. BECAUSE SOME JURISDICTIONS DO NOT ALLOW THE EXCLUSION OF IMPLIED WARRANTIES, THE ABOVE EXCLUSION OF IMPLIED WARRANTIES MAY NOT APPLY TO YOU. BECKER DOES NOT WARRANT OR GUARANTEE THAT YOU WILL PASS ANY EXAMINATION.

Exclusion of Damages: UNDER NO CIRCUMSTANCES AND UNDER NO LEGAL THEORY, TORT, CONTRACT, OR OTHERWISE, SHALL BECKER OR ITS DIRECTORS, OFFICERS, EMPLOYEES, OR AGENTS BE LIABLE TO YOU OR ANY OTHER PERSON FOR ANY CONSEQUENTIAL, INCIDENTAL, INDIRECT, PUNITIVE, EXEMPLARY OR SPECIAL DAMAGES OF ANY CHARACTER, INCLUDING, WITHOUT LIMITATION, DAMAGES FOR LOSS OF GOODWILL, WORK STOPPAGE, COMPUTER FAILURE OR MALFUNCTION OR ANY AND ALL OTHER DAMAGES OR LOSSES, OR FOR ANY DAMAGES IN EXCESS OF BECKER'S LIST PRICE FOR A LICENSE TO THE MATERIALS, EVEN IF BECKER SHALL HAVE BEEN INFORMED OF THE POSSIBILITY OF SUCH DAMAGES, OR FOR ANY CLAIM BY ANY OTHER PARTY. Some jurisdictions do not allow the limitation or exclusion of liability for incidental or consequential damages, so the above limitation or exclusion may not apply to you.

Indemnification and Remedies: You agree to indemnify and hold Becker and its employees, representatives, agents, attorneys, affiliates, directors, officers, members, managers, and shareholders harmless from and against any and all claims, demands, losses, damages, penalties, costs or expenses (including reasonable attorneys' and expert witnesses' fees and costs) of any kind or nature, arising from or relating to any violation, breach, or nonfulfillment by you of any provision of this license. If you are obligated to provide indemnification pursuant to this provision, Becker may, in its sole and absolute discretion, control the disposition of any indemnified action at your sole cost and expense. Without limiting the foregoing, you may not settle, compromise, or in any other manner dispose of any indemnified action without the consent of Becker. If you breach any material term of this license, Becker shall be entitled to equitable relief by way of temporary and permanent injunction without the need for a bond and such other and further relief as any court with jurisdiction may deem just and proper.

Confidentiality: The Materials are considered confidential and proprietary to Becker. You shall keep the Materials confidential and you shall not publish or disclose the Materials to any third party without the prior written consent of Becker.

Severability of Terms: If any term or provision of this license is held invalid or unenforceable by a court of competent jurisdiction, such invalidity shall not affect the validity or operation of any other term or provision and such invalid term or provision shall be deemed to be severed from the license. This Agreement may only be modified by written agreement signed by both parties.

Governing Law: This Agreement shall be governed and construed according to the laws of the State of Illinois, United States of America, excepting that State's conflicts of laws rules. The parties agree that the jurisdiction and venue of any dispute subject to litigation is proper in any state or federal court in Chicago, Illinois, U.S.A. The parties hereby agree to waive application of the U.N. Convention on the Sale of Goods. If the State of Illinois adopts the current proposed Uniform Computer Information Transactions Act (UCITA, formerly proposed Article 2B to the Uniform Commercial Code), or a version of the proposed UCITA, that part of the laws shall not apply to any transaction under this Agreement.

F1

Contents

Contents

Introduction

ABOUT THIS STUDY TEXT

This Study Text has been specifically written for the Association of Chartered Certified Accountants' exam F1 *Accountant in Business* in the ACCA Qualification and FAB *Foundations of Accounting in Business* of Foundations in Accounting.

It provides comprehensive coverage of the core syllabus areas and is designed to be used both as a reference text and as an integral part of your studies to provide you with the knowledge, skill and confidence to succeed in your ACCA studies.

About the author: Keith Rye is Becker's lead tutor in international auditing, assurance, corporate governance and ethics and has more than 15 years' experience in delivering ACCA exam-based training.

How to Use This Study Text

You should start by reading through the syllabus, study guide and approach to examining the syllabus provided in this introduction to familiarise yourself with the content of this exam.

The sessions which follow include the following features:

Focus	These are the learning outcomes relevant to the session, as published in the ACCA Study Guide.
Session Guidance	Tutor advice and strategies for approaching each session.
Visual Overview	A diagram of the concepts and the relationships addressed in each session.
Definitions	Terms are defined as they are introduced and larger groupings of terms will be set forth in a Terminology section.
Illustrations	These are to be read as part of the text. Any solutions to numerical Illustrations are provided.
Exhibits	These extracts of external content are presented to reinforce concepts and should be read as part of the text.
Examples	These should be attempted using the pro forma solution provided (where applicable).
Key Points	Attention is drawn to fundamental rules, underlying concepts and principles.
Exam Advice	These tutor comments relate the content to relevance in the examination.
Commentaries	These provide additional information to reinforce content.
Session Summary	A summary of the main points of each session.
Session Quiz	These quick questions are designed to test your knowledge of the technical content. A reference to the answer is provided.
Study Question Bank	A reference to recommended practice questions contained in the Study Question Bank. As a minimum you should work through the priority questions after studying each session. For additional practice you can attempt any remaining questions.
Example Solutions	Answers to the Examples are presented at the end of each session.

SYLLABUS

Aim

To introduce knowledge and understanding of the business and its environment and the influence this has on how organisations are structured and on the role of the accounting and other key business functions in contributing to the efficient, effective and ethical management and development of an organisation and its people and systems.

Rationale

The syllabus for FAB/F1 *Foundations of Accounting in Business* introduces students who may not have a business background, to the business, which as an entity is made up of people and systems which interact with the environment and with each other.

The syllabus begins with examining the purpose and types of businesses which exist, the key stakeholders and the rights and responsibilities that businesses have in connection with them, exploring the external influences that affect the business in its environment, including economic, legal, social and technological factors.

It then examines the structure and functions of business, focusing on corporate governance and the specific accounting-related roles in this process, particularly in financial reporting, assurance, control and compliance.

It then introduces key leadership, management and people issues such as effective individual and team behaviour, motivation and personal effectiveness.

Finally, the syllabus examines how behaviour at all levels within business should be underpinned by accepted professional ethics and professional values.

Main Capabilities

On successful completion of this exam, candidates should be able to:

A. Understand the purpose and types of businesses and how they interact with key stakeholders and the external environment

B. Understand business organisation structure, functions and the role of corporate governance

C. Recognise the function of accountancy and audit in communicating, reporting and assuring financial information and in effective financial control and compliance

D. Recognise the principles of authority and leadership and how teams and individuals are recruited, managed, motivated and developed

E. Understand the importance of personal effectiveness as the basis for effective team and organisational behaviour

F. Recognise that all aspects of business and finance should be conducted in a manner which complies with and is in the spirit of accepted professional ethics and professional values.

Relational Diagram of Main Capabilities

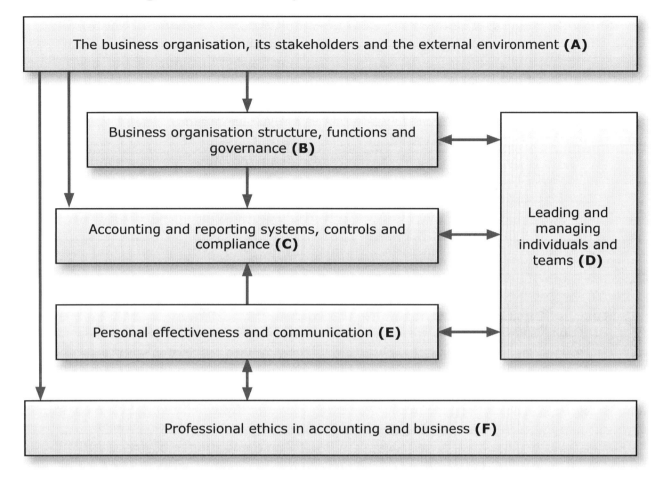

Position in the Overall Syllabus

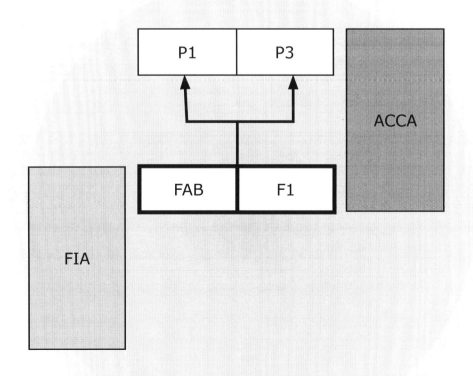

Detailed Syllabus

A. The Business Organisation, Its Stakeholders and the External Environment

1. The purpose and types of business organisation
2. Stakeholders in business organisations
3. Political and legal factors affecting business
4. Macro-economic factors
5. Micro-economic factors
6. Social and demographic factors
7. Technological factors
8. Environmental factors
9. Competitive factors

B. Business Organisational Structure, Functions and Governance

1. The formal and informal business organisation
2. Business organisational structure and design
3. Organisational culture in business
4. Committees in business organisations
5. Governance and social responsibility in business

C. Accounting and Reporting Systems, Controls and Compliance

1. The relationship between accounting and other business functions
2. Accounting and finance functions within business organisations
3. Principles of law and regulation governing accounting and auditing
4. The sources and purpose of internal and external financial information, provided by business
5. Financial systems, procedures and related IT applications
6. Internal controls, authorisation, security of data and compliance within business
7. Fraud and fraudulent behaviour and their prevention in business, including money laundering.

D. Leading and Managing Individuals and Teams

1. Leadership, management and supervision
2. Recruitment and selection of employees
3. Individual and group behaviour in business organisations
4. Team formation, development and management
5. Motivating individuals and groups
6. Learning and training at work
7. Review and appraisal of individual performance.

E. Personal Effectiveness and Communication

1. Personal effectiveness techniques
2. Consequences of ineffectiveness at work
3. Competency frameworks and personal development
4. Sources of conflicts and techniques for conflict resolution and referral
5. Communicating in business.

F. Professional Ethics in Accounting and Business

1. Fundamental principles of ethical behaviour
2. The role of regulatory and professional bodies in promoting ethical and professional standards in the accountancy profession
3. Corporate codes of ethics
4. Ethical conflicts and dilemmas

Approach to Examining the Syllabus

The syllabus is assessed by a two-hour paper-based or computer-based examination (CBE).

Questions will assess all parts of the syllabus and will test knowledge and some comprehension or application of this knowledge.

The examination will consist of two sections.

Section A will contain 30 two-mark objective questions and 16 one-mark objective questions. Section B will contain 6 four-mark multi-task questions, each of which will examine one of the six main sections of the syllabus.

ACCA Support

For examiner's reports, guidance and technical articles relevant to this exam, see www.accaglobal.com/gb/en/student/exam-support-resources/fundamentals-exams-study-resources/f1.html (also www.accaglobal.com/gb/en/student/exam-support-resources/foundation-level-study-resources/fab.html for FAB).

The ACCA's Study Guide which follows is referenced to the Sessions in this Study Text.

ACCA STUDY GUIDE

A. The Business Organisation, Its Stakeholders and the External Environment	Ref.

1. The purpose and types of business organisation

a) Define "business organisations" and explain why they are formed.   **1**

b) Describe common features of business organisations.

c) Outline how business organisations differ.

d) List the industrial and commercial sectors in which business organisations operate.

e) Identify the different types of business organisation and their main characteristics:

   i) Commercial

   ii) Not-for-profit

   iii) Public sector

   iv) Non-governmental organisations

   v) Cooperatives

2. Stakeholders in business organisations   **2**

a) Define stakeholders and explain the agency relationship in business and how it may vary in different types of business organisation.

b) Define internal, connected and external stakeholders and explain their impact on the organisation.

c) Identify the main stakeholder groups and the objectives of each group.

d) Explain how the different stakeholder groups interact and how their objectives may conflict with one another.

e) Compare the power and influence of various stakeholder groups and how their needs should be accounted for, such as under the Mendelow framework.

3. Political and legal factors affecting business   **3**

a) Explain how the political system and government policy affect the organisation.

b) Describe the sources of legal authority, including supra-national bodies, national and regional governments.

c) Explain how the law protects the employee and the implications of employment legislation for the manager and the organisation.

d) Identify the principles of data protection and security.

e) Explain how the law promotes and protects health and safety in the workplace.

f) Recognise the responsibility of the individual and organisation for compliance with laws on data protection, security and health and safety.

g) Outline principles of consumer protection such as sale of goods and simple contract.

4. Macro-economic factors

a) Define macro-economic policy and explain its objectives.   **4**

b) Explain the main determinants of the level of business activity in the economy and how variations in the level of business activity affect individuals, households and businesses.

c) Explain the impact of economic issues on the individual, the household and the business:

   i) inflation

   ii) unemployment

   iii) stagnation

   iv) international payments disequilibrium.

d) Describe the main types of economic policy that may be implemented by government and supra-national bodies to maximise economic welfare.

e) Recognise the impact of fiscal and monetary policy measures on the individual, the household and businesses.

(continued on next page)

	Ref.

5. Micro-economic factors   **5**

a) Define the concept of demand and supply for goods and services.

b) Explain elasticity of demand and the impact of substitute and complementary goods.

c) Explain the economic behaviour of costs in the short and long term.

d) Define perfect competition, oligopoly, monopolistic competition and monopoly.

6. Social and demographic factors   **3**

a) Explain the medium and long-term effects of social and demographic trends on business outcomes and the economy.

b) Describe the impact of changes in social structure, values, attitudes and tastes on the organisation.

c) Identify and explain the measures that governments may take in response to the medium and long-term impact of demographic change.

7. Technological factors   **3**

a) Explain the effects of technological change on the organisation structure and strategy:

    i) Downsizing

    ii) Delayering

    iii) Outsourcing

b) Describe the impact of information technology and information systems development on business processes.

8. Environmental factors   **3**

a) List ways in which the businesses can affect or be affected by its physical environment.

b) Describe ways in which businesses can operate more efficiently and effectively to limit damage to the environment.

c) Identify the benefits of economic sustainability to a range of stakeholders.

9. Competitive factors   **3**

a) Identify a business's strengths, weaknesses, opportunities and threats (SWOT) in a market and the main sources of competitive advantage.

b) Identify the main elements within Porter's value chain and explain the meaning of a value network.

c) Explain the factors or forces that influence the level of competitiveness in an industry or sector using Porter's five forces model.

d) Describe the activities of an organisation that affect its competitiveness:

    i) purchasing   iii) marketing

    ii) production   iv) service

B. Business Organisation Structure, Functions and Governance	**Ref.**

1. The formal and informal business organisation   **6**

a) Explain the informal organisation and its relationship with the formal organisation.

b) Describe the impact of the informal organisation on the business.

2. Business organisation structure and design   **6**

a) Describe Mintzberg's components of the organisation and explain the different ways in which formal organisations may be structured:

    i) Entrepreneurial

    ii) Functional

    iii) Matrix

    iv) Divisional (geographical, by product, or by customer type)

    v) Boundaryless (virtual, hollow or modular).

(continued on next page)

     xi

Ref.

b) Explain basic organisational structure concepts:

    i)   separation of ownership and management

    ii)   separation of direction and management

    iii) span of control and scalar chain

    iv) tall and flat organisations

    v)   outsourcing and offshoring

    vi) shared services approach

c) Explain the characteristics of the strategic, tactical and operational levels in the organisation in the context of the Anthony hierarchy.

d) Explain centralisation and decentralisation and list their advantages and disadvantages.

e) Describe the roles and functions of the main departments in a business organisation: **1**

    i)   research and development

    ii)   purchasing

    iii) production

    iv) direct service provision

    v)   marketing

    vi) administration

    vii) finance.

f) Explain the role of marketing in an organisation: **1**

    i)   the definition of marketing

    ii)   the marketing mix

    iii) the relationship of the marketing plan to the strategic plan.

3. Organisational culture in business   **7**

a) Define organisational culture.

b) Describe the factors that shape the culture of the organisation.

c) Explain the contribution made by writers on culture:

    i)   Schein—determinants of organisational culture

    ii)   Handy—four cultural stereotypes

    iii) Hofstede—international perspectives on culture

4. Committees in business organisations   **8**

a) Explain the purposes of committees.

b) Describe the types of committee used by business organisations.

c) List the advantages and disadvantages of committees.

d) Explain the roles of the Chair and Secretary of a committee.

5. Governance and social responsibility in business   **9**

a) Explain the agency concept in relation to corporate governance.

b) Define corporate governance and social responsibility and explain their importance in contemporary organisations.

c) Explain the responsibility of organisations to maintain appropriate standards of corporate governance and corporate social responsibility.

d) Briefly explain the main recommendations of best practice in effective corporate governance:

    i)   Executive and non-executive directors

    ii)   Remuneration committees

    iii) Audit committees

    iv) Public oversight

(continued on next page)

Ref.

e) Explain how organisations take account of their social responsibility objectives through analysis of the needs of internal, connected and external stakeholders.

f) Identify the social and environmental responsibilities of business organisations to internal, connected and external stakeholders.

C. Accounting and Reporting Systems, Controls and Compliance	Ref.

1. The relationship between accounting and other business functions   **10**

a) Explain the relationship between accounting and other key functions within the business such as procurement, production and marketing.

b) Explain financial considerations in production and production planning.

c) Identify the financial issues associated with marketing.

d) Identify the financial costs and benefits of effective service provision.

2. Accounting and finance functions within business   **10**

a) Explain the contribution of the accounting function to the formulation, implementation, and control of the organisation's policies, procedures, and performance.

b) Identify and describe the main financial accounting functions in business:

   i) recording financial information

   ii) codifying and processing financial information

   iii) preparing financial statements

c) Identify and describe the main management accounting and performance management functions in business:

   i) recording and analysing costs and revenues

   ii) providing management accounting information for decision-making

   iii) planning and preparing budgets and exercising budgetary control.

d) Identify and describe the main finance and treasury functions:

   i) calculating and mitigating business tax liabilities

   ii) evaluating and obtaining finance

   iii) managing working capital

   iv) treasury and risk management.

e) Identify and describe the main audit and assurance roles in business: **11**

   i) internal audit

   ii) external audit

f) Explain the main functions of the internal auditor and the external auditor and how they differ.   **11**

3. Principles of law and regulation governing accounting and audit   **12**

a) Explain basic legal requirements in relation to retaining and submitting proper records and preparing and auditing financial reports.

b) Explain the broad consequences of failing to comply with the legal requirements for maintaining and filing accounting records.

c) Explain how the international accountancy profession regulates itself through the establishment of reporting standards and their monitoring.

4. The sources and purpose of internal and external financial information, provided by business   **10**

a) Explain the various business purposes for which the following financial information is required:

   i) The statement of profit or loss

   ii) The statement of financial position

   iii) The statement of cash flows

   iv) Sustainability and integrated reports

(continued on next page)

	Ref.

b) Describe the main purposes of the following types of management accounting reports:

   i) Cost schedules

   ii) Budgets

   iii) Variance reports

5. Financial systems, procedures and related IT applications — **13**

a) Identify an organisation's system requirements in relation to the objectives and policies of the organisation.

b) Describe the main financial systems used within an organisation:

   i) purchases and sales invoicing

   ii) payroll

   iii) credit control

   iv) cash and working capital management.

c) Explain why it is important to adhere to policies and procedures for handling clients' money. — **15**

d) Identify weaknesses, potential for error and inefficiencies in accounting systems.

e) Recommend improvements to accounting systems to prevent error and fraud and to improve overall efficiency.

f) Explain why appropriate controls are necessary in relation to business and IT systems and procedures.

g) Identify business uses of computers and IT software applications:

   i) Spreadsheet applications

   ii) Database systems

   iii) Accounting packages.

h) Describe and compare the relative benefits and limitations of manual and automated financial systems that may be used in an organisation.

6. Internal controls, authorisation, security and compliance within business — **14**

a) Explain internal control and internal check.

b) Explain the importance of internal financial controls in an organisation.

c) Describe the responsibilities of management for internal financial control.

d) Describe the features of effective internal financial control procedures in an organisation, including authorisation.

e) Identify and describe the types of information technology and information systems used by the business organisation for internal control.

f) Identify and describe features for protecting the security of IT systems and software within business.

g) Describe general and application systems controls in business.

7. Fraud and fraudulent behaviour and their prevention in business — **15**

a) Explain the circumstances under which fraud is likely to arise.

b) Identify different types of fraud in the organisation.

c) Explain the implications of fraud for the organisation.

d) Explain the role and duties of individual managers in the fraud detection and prevention process.

e) Define the term money laundering.

f) Give examples of recognised offences under typical money laundering regulation.

g) Identify methods for detecting and preventing money laundering.

h) Explain how suspicions of money laundering should be reported to the appropriate authorities.

(continued on next page)

D. Leading and Managing Individuals and Teams	Ref.
1. Leadership, management and supervision	16

a) Define leadership, management and supervision and explain the distinction between these terms.

b) Explain the nature of management:

   i)   scientific/classical theories of management—Fayol, Taylor

   ii)   the human relations school—Mayo

   iii)   the functions of a manager—Mintzberg, Drucker.

c) Explain the areas of managerial authority and responsibility.

d) Explain the situational, functional and contingency approaches to leadership with reference to the theories of Adair, Fiedler, Bennis, Kotler and Heifetz.

e) Describe leadership styles and contexts: using the models of Ashridge, and Blake and Mouton.

2. Recruitment and selection of employees	17

a) Explain the importance of effective recruitment and selection to the organisation.

b) Describe the recruitment and selection process and explain the stages in this process.

c) Describe the roles of those involved in the recruitment and selection processes.

d) Describe the methods through which organisations seek to meet their recruitment needs.

e) Explain the advantages and disadvantages of different recruitment and selection methods.

f) Explain the purposes and benefits of diversity and equal opportunities policies within the human resources plan.	18
g) Explain the practical steps that an organisation may take to ensure the effectiveness of its diversity and equal opportunities policy.	18
3. Individual and group behaviour in business organisations	19

a) Describe the main characteristics of individual and group behaviour.

b) Outline the contributions of individuals and teams to organisational success.

c) Identify individual and team approaches to work.

4. Team formation, development and management	19

a) Explain the differences between a group and a team.

b) Explain the purposes of a team.

c) Explain the role of the manager in building the team and developing individuals within the team.

   i)   Belbin's team roles theory

   ii)   Tuckman's theory of team development.

d) List the characteristics of effective and ineffective teams.

e) Describe tools and techniques that can be used to build the team and improve team effectiveness.

5. Motivating individuals and groups	20

a) Define motivation and explain its importance to the organisation, teams and individuals.

b) Explain content and process theories of motivation: Maslow, Herzberg, McGregor, and Vroom.

c) Explain and identify types of intrinsic and extrinsic reward.

d) Explain how reward systems can be designed and implemented to motivate teams and individuals.

6. Learning and training at work	21

a) Explain the importance of learning and development in the workplace.

b) Describe the learning process: Honey and Mumford, Kolb.

(continued on next page)

	Ref.

c) Describe the role of the human resources department and individual managers in the learning process.

d) Describe the training and development process: identifying needs, setting objectives, programme design, delivery and validation.

e) Explain the terms "training", "development" and "education" and the characteristics of each.

f) List the benefits of effective training and development in the workplace.

7. Review and appraisal of individual performance	22

a) Explain the importance of performance assessment.

b) Explain how organisations assess the performance of human resources.

c) Define performance appraisal and describe its purposes.

d) Describe the performance appraisal process.

e) Explain the benefits of effective appraisal.

f) Identify the barriers to effective appraisal and how these may be overcome.

E. Personal Effectiveness and Communication in Business	**Ref.**
1. Personal effectiveness techniques	23

a) Explain the importance of effective time management.

b) Describe the barriers to effective time management and how they may be overcome.

c) Describe the role of information technology in improving personal effectiveness.

2. Consequences of ineffectiveness at work	23

a) Identify the main ways in which people and teams can be ineffective at work.

b) Explain how individual or team ineffectiveness can affect organisational performance.

3. Competency frameworks and personal development	23

a) Describe the features of a "competency framework".

b) Explain how a competency framework underpins professional development needs.

c) Explain how personal and continuous professional development can increase personal effectiveness at work.

d) Explain the purpose and benefits of coaching, mentoring and counselling in promoting employee effectiveness.

e) Describe how a personal development plan should be formulated, implemented, monitored and reviewed by the individual.

4. Sources of conflict and techniques for conflict resolution and referral	23

a) Identify situations where conflict at work can arise.

b) Describe how conflict can affect personal and organisational performance.

c) Identify ways in which conflict can be managed.

5. Communicating in business	

a) Describe methods of communication used in the organisation and how they are used.	25
b) Explain how the type of information differs and the purposes for which it is applied at different levels of the organisation: strategic, tactical and operational.	24
c) List the attributes of good-quality information.	24
d) Explain a simple communication model: sender, message, receiver, feedback, noise.	25
e) Explain formal and informal communication and their importance in the workplace.	25
f) Identify the consequences of ineffective communication.	25
g) Describe the attributes of effective communication.	25
h) Describe the barriers to effective communication and identify practical steps that may be taken to overcome them.	25
i) Identify the main patterns of communication.	25

(continued on next page)

F . Professional Ethics in Accounting and Business	Ref.

1. Fundamental principles of ethical behaviour   **26**

a) Define business ethics and explain the importance of ethics to the organisation and to the individual.

b) Describe and demonstrate the following principles from the IFAC (IESBA) code of ethics, using examples.
- i) Integrity
- ii) Objectivity
- iii) Professional competence
- iv) Confidentiality
- v) Professional behaviour

c) Describe organisational values which promote ethical behaviour using examples.
- i) Openness
- ii) Trust
- iii) Honesty
- iv) Respect
- v) Empowerment
- vi) Accountability

d) Explain the concept of acting in the public interest.

2. The role of regulatory and professional bodies in promoting ethical and professional standards in the accountancy profession   **26**

a) Recognise the purpose of international and organisational codes of ethics and codes of conduct, IFAC (IESBA), ACCA etc.

b) Describe how professional bodies and regulators promote ethical awareness and prevent or punish illegal or unethical behaviour.

c) Identify the factors that distinguish a profession from other types of occupation.

d) Explain the role of the accountant in promoting ethical behaviour.

e) Recognise when and to whom illegal, or unethical conduct by anyone within or connected to the organisation should be reported.

3. Corporate codes of ethics   **26**

a) Define corporate codes of ethics.

b) Describe the typical contents of a corporate code of ethics.

c) Explain the benefits of a corporate code of ethics to the organisation and its employees.

4. Ethical conflicts and dilemmas   **26**

a) Describe situations where ethical conflicts can arise.

b) Identify the main threats to ethical behaviour.

c) Outline situations at work where ethical dilemmas may be faced.

d) List the main safeguards against ethical threats and dilemmas.

EXAMINATION TECHNIQUE

General

- Divide your time in proportion to the marks on offer (1 mark = 1.2 minutes)
    - On average, a 2-mark question should take you just a little under 2½ minutes with 1-mark questions taking just over a minute.
    - Allocate 5 minutes to each 4-mark question.
- Keep to this time allocation. Your time spent on Section A must NOT exceed 90 minutes, with Section B taking no longer than 30 minutes.
- Answer all questions.

Objective Questions

- Section A will consist of 30 two-mark and 16 one-mark questions.
- The structure of these questions will be either:
    - multiple-choice questions (MCQs) where there is one correct option from two or three options (for 1 mark) or four options (for 2 marks); or*
    - multiple-response questions where TWO options should be selected.

*Two option 1-mark questions are typically of "true or false" type.

- MCQs mostly consist of:
    - "stem" (the question);
    - "key" (the correct answer); and
    - "distracters" (plausible but incorrect answers).

The average time per item should not be applied exactly to each individual question, as some will take longer than others. The following approach is recommended:

- Avoid spending too long on more difficult questions. Even with good knowledge, if you do not quickly understand a question move on to the next question. Leave these questions until the end—but do not forget to come back to them.

- Guess the solution to any questions that you do not have time (or the knowledge) to do. You may guess the correct answer, in which case you will get the marks for that question. If you leave any blank, you will not get any marks!

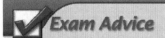

- The aim is to obtain a mark of at least 50%. Doing the easy questions first will maximise, within the time available, the probability that you pass. Cover up the options (A, B, etc) while reading the stem. If the answer that occurs to you is then an option—select it.
- When time is up, guess an answer. If one of the options stands out as the "odd one out" compared to the others, it is more likely to be a distracter than the key—so do not select it.

Illustration 1 Answering an MCQ

Which one of the following statements is correct in relation to monetary rewards in accordance with Herzberg's two-factor theory?

A Pay increases are a powerful long-term motivator

B Inadequate monetary rewards are a powerful dissatisfier

C Monetary rewards are more important than non-monetary rewards

D Pay can never be used as a motivator   (2 marks)

Solution

■ **Step 1**

Read and understand the stem (requirement).

■ **Step 2**

Write down what you know that is relevant to the stem (e.g. in this requirement—the two factors of Herzberg's two factor theory and how monetary rewards relate to them). If you are not sure, use Step 3 to jog your memory.

■ **Step 3**

Read **all** of the alternatives (A to D) and identify the one you believe to be correct.

■ **Step 4**

If you are not sure of the correct answer, eliminate the alternatives you believe to be incorrect—if one is left it must be correct. If you are still not sure, draw upon your practical experience and knowledge—how would you react to A, B, C and D? If you really cannot identify the correct alternative, then guess—never leave a question blank.

■ **Step 5**

Select the appropriate box on your answer sheet—the correct answer is B.

Multi-task Questions (MTQs)

Section B will contain six 4-mark MTQs; one on each of the six main areas of the syllabus.

Multi-task questions (MTQs) contain a series of tasks which relate to one or more scenarios. The following forms of MTQ will primarily be used in Section B:

▨ Multiple-response questions with more than four options. For example, a question may ask you to choose two correct responses from six choices, or perhaps four choices from eight. The question will state if partial marks are available.

▨ Questions requiring completion of sentences—"gap-fill" questions. Each "gap" requires a letter corresponding to single words or short phrase given (paper-based exam). In computer-based exams (CBE) the gap will offer responses in a drop-down menu.

▨ Multiple-response matching. These questions will ask you to select responses according to a grid of choices. Again, partial marks will be available.

▨ "Hotspot " questions (in CBE only)—click on the appropriate choices on a set of boxes or on a diagram.*

Commentary

*If taking CBE, you are strongly advised to work through the CBE Specimen Exam available at http://specimen.accaglobal.com/flk.html.

The Business Organisation

FOCUS
This session covers the following content from the *ACCA Study Guide.*

A. The Business Organisation, Its Stakeholders and the External Environment

1. The purpose and types of business organisation

a) Define "business organisations" and explain why they are formed.

b) Describe common features of business organisations.

c) Outline how business organisations differ.

d) List the industrial and commercial sectors in which business organisations operate.

e) Identify the different types of business organisation and their main characteristics:
   i) Commercial
   ii) Not-for-profit
   iii) Public sector
   iv) Non-governmental organisations
   v) Cooperatives

B. Business Organisation Structure, Functions and Governance

2. Business organisation structure and design

e) Describe the roles and functions of the main departments in a business organisation:
   i) research and development
   ii) purchasing
   iii) production
   iv) direct service provision
   v) marketing
   vi) administration

f) Explain the role of marketing in an organisation:
   i) the definition of marketing
   ii) the marketing mix
   iii) the relationship of the marketing plan to the strategic plan

Session 1 Guidance

■ **Note** that this session looks at the need for organisations to coordinate work in different ways. Focus on what organisations have in common, how they differ and the different types of organisations.

■ **Understand** the brief overview of basic business functions (s.2) which will be covered in greater detail in later sessions.

(continued on next page)

VISUAL OVERVIEW

Objective: To describe the basic concepts and functions of business organisations.

```
                    ┌─────────────────────────────────┐
                    │      BUSINESS ORGANISATION       │
                    │   • Concept                      │
                    │   • Purpose                      │
                    │   • Characteristics of           │
                    │     Organisations                │
                    │   • Types of Organisation        │
                    └─────────────────────────────────┘
```

BUSINESS ORGANISATION
- Concept
- Purpose
- Characteristics of Organisations
- Types of Organisation

BUSINESS FUNCTIONS
- Research and Development
- Purchasing (Procurement)
- Production
- Direct Service Provision
- Administration
- Finance (*Session 10*)

MARKETING
- Concept
- Basic Functions
- Elements

MARKETING MIX
- Concept
- The 4 Ps
- The 7 Ps

MARKETING STRATEGY
- Goals and Objectives
- Orientation
- Market Segmentation
- Product Life Cycle
- Boston Consulting Group (BCG) Matrix

Session 1 Guidance

■ **Recognise** the basic functions and elements of marketing (s.3).

■ **Know** the marketing mix (s.4) and how marketing integrates with business strategy (s.5).

1 The Business Organisation

1.1 Concept

Although there are many different types of formal and informal organisations, the common factor linking them is that they represent a collection of people using resources to reach a common objective.

According to Buchanan and Huczynski, the organisational "social arrangement" provides a structure that allows people:

■ to work together;

■ *toward* collective goals;

■ *through* controlled performance.

According to Brech, a business organisation is "an aspect of planning concerned with the definition of:

■ the responsibilities of the executive, supervisory and specialist positions into which the management process has been subdivided; and

■ the formal interrelationships established by virtue of such subdivided responsibilities."

1.2 Purpose

■ Formal organisations exist to:
  • achieve results collectively which individuals cannot achieve alone (e.g. through greater available resources);
  • create synergy (i.e. the collective output is greater than the sum of the individuals' output) and increase productivity;
  • save time through effective and efficient application of resources;
  • share knowledge and expertise; and
  • facilitate specialisation.

■ Structure is founded on specialisation. An organisation that has grown too big for control by an individual must:
  • group key activities;
  • establish roles, tasks and lines of authority and responsibility; and
  • specify relationships and lines of communication.

Illustration 1 One-Stop Shops

Consider the way international firms of accountants and auditors are organised to provide a "one-stop shop" of financial, assurance, taxation and related services to their clients.

1.3 Characteristics of Organisations

▓ Organisations are distinguished by:

- Activity
- Ownership
- Stakeholders
- Size
- Financing
- Objectives (see below).

▓ For example, industrial companies tend to be:

- of large size;
- diverse;
- organisationally complex;
- separately managed (by directors) and owned (by shareholders); and
- profit driven.

▓ Many organisations have the same basic component parts:

ENVIRONMENT

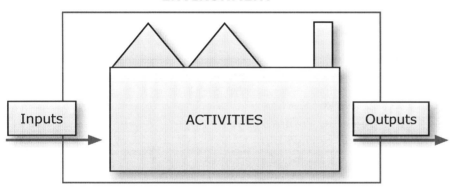

ENVIRONMENT

- Resource inputs (e.g. finance, labour, raw materials, services, time, space, information);
- Organisational activities (e.g. purchasing, manufacturing, selling, marketing, research and development, accounting, etc);
- Outputs (e.g. products/services, wealth, taxes, waste, employment);
- Environmental factors:
  - Political (e.g. government policy, the law, grants, etc)
  - Economic (e.g. inflation, exchange rates, competitors, etc)
  - Social (e.g. fashion, tastes, age, gender, etc)
  - Technological (e.g. production methods, new materials, use of IT, etc).

▓ Different organisations have different objectives or collective goals:

- Profit (e.g. commercial businesses)
- Health and welfare (e.g. hospitals, medical centres)
- Value for money (e.g. government departments, local authorities)
- For the benefit of members (e.g. clubs and associations)
- Effective collection and distribution of resources (e.g. charities).

1.4 Types of Organisation

1.4.1 Commercial

- Commercial organisations (businesses) are generally profit-seeking (i.e. they aim to maximise the wealth of their owners/shareholders).*
- Sub-classifications include:*
  - industrial (e.g. extractive, steel, pharmaceuticals, textiles, clothing, electronics, transport, construction, engineering, service);
  - manufacturing (e.g. specific divisions of industrial such as pipes, drugs, fabric, shoes, semiconductors, cars);
  - financial, which can also be considered as a service in managing money (e.g. banking, insurance, investment funds); and
  - service, where no goods or products are produced (e.g. audit and accountancy, consulting, entertainment, advertising, marketing).
- The primary objectives of businesses are to:
  - continue in existence;
  - maintain growth (or at least not decline); and
  - make a profit.
- Other objectives (as identified by Peter Drucker) for commercial organisations include:
  - market standing (e.g. to achieve market share);
  - innovation (e.g. to lead new product developments);
  - productivity (e.g. optimum allocation of resources);
  - managing and sustaining physical and financial resources;
  - manager performance and development;
  - worker performance and attitude; and
  - public responsibility (e.g. waste recycling and local employment).

1.4.2 Not-for-Profit

- Not-for-profit organisations do not consider profit to be their primary objective. They aim to satisfy particular needs of their members (they do not have shareholders) or of society in general, and usually consider financial objectives as constraints under which they have to operate.
- Examples include:
  - government departments, local authorities and agencies (exist to implement policy);
  - educational establishments (but note that private education has a profit motive);
  - hospitals (note that private hospitals would be classified as profit orientated);
  - charities (collect money and effectively distribute according to charity's aims);
  - pressure groups which raise money to follow a given agenda (e.g. Greenpeace); and
  - clubs and mutual societies that raise money directly from members to be able to provide common services to those members (e.g. golf clubs, tennis clubs, building societies, insurance, trade unions).

*"The business of business is business."
—*Milton Friedman*

*Primary industries are extractive industries; secondary industries manufacture products; and tertiary industries provide services.

The main characteristics of many charitable organisations include:

- separate entity and identity;
- primary objective to benefit others; and
- operation within a legal framework.

1.4.3   Cooperative

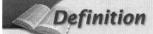

Definition

Cooperative—"an autonomous association of persons united voluntarily to meet common economic, social and cultural needs and aspirations through a jointly owned and democratically controlled enterprise."

—*International Co-operative Alliance*

- Cooperatives are not owned by investors/shareholders nor accumulate capital for investors, but are owned by individuals who use and benefit from the business.

- "Mutuality" (the concept that the users and beneficiaries are identical) is often used to distinguish cooperatives from private companies.

- Examples can be found in housing, retail, workers, agricultural, consumer, insurance, banking, building societies and car sharing (i.e. cars are purchased by the cooperative and then hired out for use by the members).

- They usually offer one vote per member (as opposed to the one vote per share in a company) and hence all members have equal rights.

- They may be for-profit or not-for-profit organisations.

Key Point

The main characteristics are:
- Voluntary association
- Mutuality
- Separate legal entity
- Equal rights
- Democratic management
- Service motive

Example 1   Banks

Identify the specific differences between a commercial bank and a cooperative bank in relation to borrowers, depositors, shareholders and members.

1.4.4   Public Sector

- The public sector is the part of the economy and the services provided which are controlled by governmental organisations. Typical examples include the police, military, fire and ambulance services, public roads, public transport, public utilities (gas, electricity, water, telephone—although in many countries these may have been privatised into commercial organisations with shareholders), primary healthcare, libraries, refuse collection and local authorities.

- Those facilities, businesses and services not controlled by government will be in the private sector.

1.4.5 Non-governmental Organisations (NGOs)

- Originally established by the United Nations in the 1950s, the concept of the NGO spread into general usage during the 1970s. Many diverse types of bodies are now described as NGOs.

- Generally accepted characteristics of an NGO include:
  - voluntary formation;
  - aim to improve circumstances and prospects of disadvantaged people;
  - independence from the direct control of any government;
  - not constituted as a political party;
  - non-profit-making; and
  - not a criminal group (in particular it is non-violent).

- However, some NGOs may be closely identified with a political party; many NGOs generate income from commercial activities (e.g. consultancy contracts or sales of publications); and a small number of NGOs may be associated with politically based protests.

- The World Bank classifies NGOs as either operational or advocacy:
  - **Operational** NGOs are primarily involved in the design and implementation of development (aid) related projects (both relief-oriented and development-oriented).
  - **Advocacy** NGOs defend or promote a specific cause, typically trying to raise awareness, acceptance and knowledge by lobbying, press work and activist events.

- For example, Oxfam, although a charity, is an NGO and establishes NGOs in many countries to enable funds raised to be disbursed to end recipients. Other NGOs may promote a country's culture and language in other countries or establish health education programmes (e.g. AIDS, birth control).

Definition

Non-governmental organisation—an independent voluntary association of people acting together on a continuous basis, for some common purpose, other than achieving government office, making money or illegal activities.

*Commentary

Many NGOs are small and horizontally structured with short lines of communication which enable them to respond quickly and flexibly to changing circumstances and clients' needs.

Example 2 Distinguishing Factors

Suggest FIVE factors which distinguish a professional body of accountants (e.g. ACCA) from a private water company (e.g. Thames Water, the largest water company in the UK).

Solution

Factor	Professional Body	Water Company
1. Legal constitution		
2. Ownership		
3. Control and management		
4. Principal objective		
5. Principal source of income		

2   Business Functions

2.1   Research and Development (R&D)

■ Without a formal process for developing new products and/or services, most organisations face decline and eventual failure. The role of R&D may therefore be considered as:
  ● improving and innovating existing products and services; and
  ● developing new products.

■ R&D may be:
  ● pure or scientific with no obvious commercial value;
  ● applied with a practical objective or application; and
  ● engaged in the development of existing and new products.

■ R&D is essential:
  ● New product development takes time and costs a substantial amount of money. The life cycle of many products has become shorter in recent years requiring effective innovation (to extend the useful life of a base product) and strong cost management (to ensure maximum contribution from current and new products).
  ● The failure rate of new products is very high. Failed products result in high write-off of costs to the income statement.
  ● New and innovative products can overcome entry barriers to existing industries and markets, especially if new technology is involved. They may also increase entry barriers to potential competitors.
  ● Management must plan when to introduce new products, how best to extend the life of mature products and when to retire products. R&D supplies a critical input to product life decisions.

■ Matching R&D with marketing is essential to maximise the anticipation of customer needs and generation of new ideas and products.

■ R&D leading to new product development involves:
  ● **Exploration**—of new ideas which will meet organisational objectives;
  ● **Screening**—a quick analysis to see which ideas warrant further study;
  ● **Business analysis**—development of the idea into a more concrete concept including product features and a programme for production and development (moving the "idea-on-paper" to a "product-in-hand");
  ● **Testing**—the commercial experiments necessary to verify earlier business judgements; and
  ● **Commercialisation**—launching the product into full-scale production and sales, committing the organisation's reputation and resources.*

■ R&D is not only concerned with products, but also with processes and emerging technologies. Process research focuses on how goods and services are produced. It examines:
  ● processes and planning;
  ● efficiency and productivity (cutting out non-essential and non-useful processes during production to save time and money and increase the overall productivity);
  ● quality; and
  ● uses of emerging technologies.

Commentary

*The launch point is often a crucial moment as it is the point where maximum costs have been incurred and no revenue has been generated.

2.2 Purchasing

Purchasing is a significant factor in any manufacturing organisation's strategy and a major contributor to cost and quality management in any business.*

■ The purchasing process covers:

- **Costs**—raw materials and services are a major cost for many firms.
- **Quality**—the quality of the material and services bought by a firm will have a big influence on the product(s) it produces and how efficiently it can do so.
- **Strategy**—the mix of cost and quality that will effectively address the target market's value proposition

■ Purchasing decisions are often based on four factors (the purchasing mix)—quantity, quality, price and delivery:

1. **Quantity**—holding sufficient inventory to ensure that production is not disrupted, while minimising costs of holding the necessary quantities (e.g. capital tied up, storage facilities, security, insurance, shelf-life, shrinkage).

2. **Quality**—high-quality raw materials (with high-quality production) can result in high-quality, high-cost products ("over engineered"). But is this what the market wants and is the market prepared to pay? Low-quality inputs will result in a product at low cost, but with the risk of high production rejection rates, high maintenance costs and rejection by the market.

3. **Price**—an obvious financial accounting element. Driving a hard bargain with a supplier may result in that supplier going bankrupt. Favourable short-term prices may lock in the customer to the supplier, who may then raise prices or demand a premium for any element that is outside of the contract (e.g. a quicker delivery time on a particular order). Obtaining value for money is a key element for all purchasing decisions.

4. **Delivery**—the lead time between ordering and delivery is often critical to efficient inventory control, production planning and minimising costs. It is not unusual for suppliers to have integrated access to an organisation's production and inventory control systems to be able to deliver raw materials "just-in-time".

■ Basically, with purchasing "you get what you pay for". So, knowing what and where to buy is the key task of the purchasing function. Purchasing decisions might require answers to questions such as:

- What sources are available; where are they located?
- Can existing suppliers supply what is needed, the quality needed and within the time frame?
- One source of supply or several to minimise risk of disruption to supply?
- Cost of supplies?
- Reputation of supplier?
- Is a long-term relationship with a supplier possible?

Purchasing— procurement (acquisition) of material resources and business services for use by the organisation.

*Parallels can also be drawn with service industries in that service employees would need to be "purchased".

2.3   Production

- Production uses resources (inputs) to create a commodity suitable for exchange (output).

- The production function includes responsibility for product and process design, planning (scheduling) and control issues (capacity, quality, inventory levels, wastage) organisation and supervision of the workforce.

- The main responsibility of production management lies in planning and controlling the process of production so that it moves smoothly at the required level of output while meeting cost and quality objectives. For example:

  - To ensure that operations are performed according to plan;

  - To continuously monitor and evaluate the production plan to see if modifications can be devised to better meet cost, quality, delivery, flexibility, or other objectives;

  - To control inventories including raw materials, component parts, work in process, finished goods, packaging materials and general supplies.

- As a key function, production has to be fully integrated with other business functions, for example:

  - Quantities which have to be produced will be specified by the sales and/or marketing department;

  - The product design is coordinated with R&D;

  - The human resources department ("HR") will be involved in providing and helping to manage the workforce;

  - The finance department will advise on the resources available for new machinery and production facilities.

2.4   Direct Service Provision

- "Direct service provision" is a service organisation's equivalent of production, with significant emphasis on human resources (experience, technical and personal skills) and the management of such resources (client matching, scheduling, time billing).

- Examples include financial advice, auditing, accountancy, taxation, consultancy, marketing, advertising, law and legal services.

2.4.1   Characteristics

- **V**ariability (i.e. heterogeneity)—maintaining consistency in the standard of output can be a problem. Unlike automated production, the quality of a service depends on:

  - who delivers the service; and

  - when it takes place.

- **I**ntangibility (i.e. lack of substance)—there are no material or physical aspects. By combining product and service elements a firm can exploit the service element in a value chain.

- **P**erishability (i.e. services cannot be stored for "later" use).

- **S**imultaneity, also called inseparability (i.e. many services come into existence and are consumed simultaneously). They are only a promise when they are sold.

- **O**wnership does not result in the transfer of property. Purchasing a service accesses or gives a right to use, but not ownership.

Service—"Any activity of benefit that one party can offer to another that is essentially intangible and does not result in ownership of anything. Its production may or may not be tied to a physical product."

—*Kotler*

For service characteristics remember the mnemonic "VIP SO".

2.4.2 Difficulties

✗ Lack of distinction between the service and its delivery.

✗ Poor service quality (i.e. waiting times, queues, staff rudeness/incompetence).

✗ Consistent reputation—it is difficult to maintain and promote an attractive image whether the service offers complicated future benefits or is consumed immediately.

✗ Complicated pricing structures, especially if large numbers of people are involved in providing the service.

✗ Human resources management, not just customer care, is a key ingredient in the services marketing mix, as so many services are produced and consumed in a specific social context. It is important that the firm have employees capable of delivering the service in an engaging manner. The human element cannot be "designed out" of a service.*

Commentary

*The reputation of many service organisations is based on its employees—in particular the senior employees/directors/partners. It is not unusual for clients to follow their main contact. For example, if a tax partner leaves, many clients may follow him to retain the personal service, knowledge and experience of their tax affairs.

2.4.3 Examples

▣ Business planning and analysis:
  • Development of business strategies and plans.
  • Financial analysis of activities.
  • Advice on legal issues.
  • Market testing.
▣ Productivity analysis and review:
  • Analysis of service requirements.
  • Assessment of productivity.
  • Comparison benchmarking of outputs and achievements.
  • Recommendations on service improvement.
▣ Tender analysis:
  • Tender assessment and preparation.
  • Preparation of competitive tenders.
  • Development of tendering strategies.
  • Resource scheduling.
  • Financial appraisal.

2.5 Administration

▣ Administration has many facets and definitions:
  • The process of organising resources—capital and human—to achieve common aims and objectives.
  • The process of decision-making to affect performance and manage business operations.
  • The department in an organisation that specialises in the collection of information, distributing it to decision-makers, processing and storing information.
  • The provision of support and service for the activities of the board of directors and other managers.

- In older, traditional organisations, the administrator would be the general manager or chief executive officer (CEO).

- More recently, the term has expanded to include departments such as personnel, HR, information systems, Web master and finance management. A company secretary also may be considered part of the administration function.

- In some organisations, routine and technical operational essentials come under the administration function. In others, it is the operational or bureaucratic accomplishment of daily office tasks (e.g. a director's administrative assistant would ensure that the director's office ran smoothly, keep the director's diary, make travel arrangements, sort out visas, remind the director of staff birthdays, etc).*

*Commentary

*Visit www.admin.cam.ac.uk for an interesting view on what constitutes an administration function (Cambridge University).

3 Marketing

3.1 Concept

Definition

Marketing

- Marketing—"the management process that identifies, anticipates and supplies customer needs efficiently and profitably."
  —*Chartered Institute of Marketing*

- The "right" definition of marketing is "getting the right goods and services to the right people, at the right price, at the right place, at the right time, with the right communication and promotion".

- A short and simple definition is "marketing is the process that sells goods that do not come back to people who do".

Marketing is the one function of management that is more concerned with what goes on externally than internally. An organisation is usually an open system with the various activities and people linked together in a structure to achieve the objectives of the organisation. Marketing activities not only cross internal boundaries but are conducted mainly throughout the environment in which the organisation operates.

3.2 Basic Functions

- **Customer analysis**—analysing the characteristics and needs of customers.

- **Buying**—procurement, analysis and selection of suppliers, terms of purchase and procedure for buying.

- **Selling**—advertising, sales promotion, sales force management, publicity and public relations, customer relations and interaction with consumers, dealer relations, warranties and displays.

- **Product and/or service planning**—new product development, product management, branding, packaging and removal of old products.

- **Social responsibility**—obligation to offer safe, useful and ethically sound products and services.

- **Price planning**—profitability, level and range of prices, terms and credit availability, cash flow, sales and reductions, budgeting and flexibility.

- **Distribution**—warehousing, wholesaling, retailing and retail site locations, physical distribution and method of transportation, stock management, service levels, allocation and vendor management.

- **Marketing research**—data, information, collection and analysis as a basis for further decisions and planning.

- **Opportunity analysis**—appraisal of risks and benefits associated with the decision-making.

Commentary

Responsibility for these functions can be moved to and shared between manufacturers, wholesalers, retailers, marketing specialists and consumers, but cannot be eliminated entirely.

3.3 Elements

Kotler (*Principles of Marketing*) identified five elements of a core marketing concept:

1. Needs, wants and demands.

2. Products.

3. Value, satisfaction and quality.

4. Exchange, transactions and relationships.

5. Markets.

3.3.1 Needs, Wants and Demands

- Maslow's hierarchy of needs (see *Session 20*) is a good tool for considering needs, wants and demands.

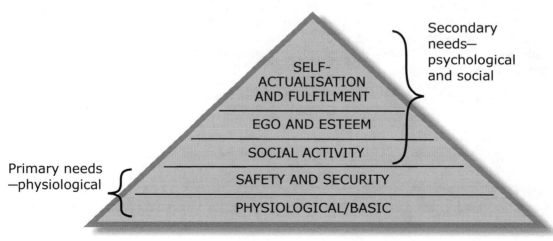

Secondary needs—psychological and social

SELF-ACTUALISATION AND FULFILMENT

EGO AND ESTEEM

SOCIAL ACTIVITY

SAFETY AND SECURITY

PHYSIOLOGICAL/BASIC

Primary needs—physiological

- According to Maslow, human needs include:
  - Physical needs (e.g. food, clothing, shelter, safety).
  - Social needs (e.g. belonging, affection).
  - Individual needs (e.g. knowledge, self-expression).
- If a need is not satisfied, an individual will look for a way to meet that need ("want") or will try to reduce the requirement for that need.
- "Wants" are needs shaped by culture and individual personality, usually described in terms of objectives that will satisfy needs. Certain aspects of marketing will concentrate on identifying the "wants" to produce more "want-satisfying" products and services.*

*Commentary

*Phrases relating to "wants" are the "I want" and "me too" cultures—"I want this, I want that, I want everything ... If they have that, then me too". Some marketing may be considered unethical because of its play on the "I want" and "me too" cultures. The "I want" culture was identified as one of the drivers of the looting that took place during the August 2011 riots in the UK.

- People attempt to purchase products and services with benefits which give them the highest satisfaction. Wants become *demand* when people are willing to buy a product and are able to pay for it.

3.3.2 Products

- A product is anything that can be offered to a market to satisfy needs, wants or demands. It includes:
  - Physical objects, services (intangible products) and experiences.
  - Organisations, people and places.
  - Information and ideas.
- A business may therefore not only sell a tangible product but will try to provide a solution to any need, want or problem including marketing and selling a lifestyle.

3.3.3 Value, Satisfaction and Quality

- Value is the difference between what a customer gets from having and using a product and the costs of obtaining the product. It is ensuring the right combination of Quality, Service and Price ("QSP") for the target market.
- In most situations, there will always be competing products. Customers will usually base their decision on what product to buy on their perception of the value that a particular product gives them.

- The concept of value is not always based on monetary concerns, but can just as easily be based on Maslow's hierarchy and cultural values (e.g. esteem, self-actualisation, ego, etc).

- Satisfaction depends on how customers judge a product's performance according to their own perceptions and expectations. This leads to the concept of quality.

- "Quality in a service or product is not what you put into it. It is what the client or customer gets out of it."

    —*Peter Drucker*

- Poor quality is where a product does not live up to the standard a customer expects. The customer will be dissatisfied—and tell everyone about the bad experience.

- Good quality is achieved when the customer's expectation of the delivered value of the product is exceeded. The customer most likely will make repeat purchases and, it is hoped, tell others about the product.

- Cheap quality is expensive; good quality is cheap.

Example 3 Value

Describe the value placed on a top-of-the-range prestige car (e.g. Bentley, Ferrari, Aston Martin) by its owner.

3.3.4   Exchange, Transactions and Relationships

- Exchange is the act of obtaining a desired product from someone by offering something in return—a transaction takes place.

- The transaction is a unit of measurement where at least two parties are involved. One party gives X to another party and gets Y in return.

- Relationship marketing looks into building long-term relationships with customers, suppliers and distributors to create and maintain customer satisfaction, on the basis that if a good network of relationships is built with key stakeholders, profits will follow.

3.3.5   Markets

- A market is a set of actual and potential buyers of a product. These buyers share a common need or want which they seek to have satisfied.

- Markets need not be physical locations where buyers and sellers meet and interact. Virtual markets based on the Internet are just as viable (e.g. eBay Inc).

4   Marketing Mix

4.1   Concept

- Successful businesses have a strong marketing orientation within their business culture (see *Session 7*). The way they think and the choices they make are all directed towards the satisfaction of customers' needs.

- As the business operates in an open and dynamic environment, it must monitor and respond to the changes in its operating environment. In doing so there are a number of variables it can control to influence buyers' decisions. Collectively these controllable variables are called the **marketing mix**.

- The marketing mix is concerned with how to influence consumer demand.

- The variables in the marketing mix are commonly grouped into four classes that Jerome McCarthy refers to as the 4 Ps—product, price, promotion and place (or distribution).

Definition

Marketing mix—"The set of controllable variables that the firm can use to influence the buyers' responses."

—*Kotler*

4.2   The 4 Ps

Product	Price	Promotion	Place
Brand name	Level	Sales promotion	Distribution channels
Packaging	Discounts	Personal selling	Distribution coverage
Features	Allowances	Publicity	Outlet locations
Options	Payment terms	Advertising	Sales territories
Quality	Delivery options		Inventory levels
Warranty	Inventory locations		
Service			
Style appeal			

4.2.1   Product

- The product relates to all aspects, whether tangible or intangible. It refers to anything offered for attention, acquisition, use or consumption that might satisfy a want or need. Products can be physical objects, services, persons, places, organisations or ideas.

- Products can be categorised into three elements:

  1. The base (core) product (e.g. a car), sometimes referred to as the product class.

  2. The actual product, brand or make (e.g. BMW 325) or product form, which can be subdivided (e.g. two door, four door, manual or automatic).

  3. The augmented product (e.g. a BMW 325 with 0% finance).

- General factors to be considered when taking a product from actual to augmented form include quality, packaging, branding, aesthetics, product mix, servicing, warranty and guarantee.

4.2.2 Price

- Price is different from the other Ps; the other Ps represent costs whereas "price" generates revenue.

- All businesses provide customers with an amount of value. Value is a combination of the functionality of a product or service in terms of the benefits that are offered to the customer and the price that is charged. Price is the revenue to be obtained from the customer, a part of the value proposition.

- Price must be consistent with other elements of the marketing mix (e.g. a high-quality, premium product should not have a low price as this may send a confusing signal to customers). A high price usually implies high quality (although not always the case) and exclusivity (often reflected in the brand name and high-visibility logo).

- When establishing price, the business must consider the general factors affecting price (e.g. capacity, cost, quality, competition, customer value), pricing techniques (e.g. cost-based, demand-based, competition-based) and pricing strategies (e.g. new product in a new market, new product in an established market, existing product, barrier to competitors).

4.2.3 Promotion

- For promotion, read communication. For communication, read advertising (communication to create awareness and interest); sales promotions (incentives such as special pricing or limited time offers); public relations (building goodwill, crisis management, monitoring feedback channels and press relations); and personal selling.

- Promotion is intended to move potential customers through four behavioural stages ("AIDA") so they become actual customers:
  - **Awareness** of the product.
  - **Interest** in the product.
  - **Desire** to buy the product.
  - **Action** through actually buying the product.

- Advertising requires the most effective media (e.g. published, visual or oral) to be identified in terms of cost, customer, and consumer penetration and impact.

- Sales promotion is designed to stimulate purchase in the short term. It is an immediate or delayed incentive to purchase, expressed in cash or in kind (e.g. buy one, get one free; money-off coupons; satisfaction or money back offers; contests; sponsored events).

- Public relations are critical. An image of reliability and/or good quality will have a long-term effect on sales. Brand names, logos and trade characteristics establish an image that can give a competitive advantage. A reputation that has taken a number of years to establish, can, however, be destroyed in just as many seconds (20/20 rule).

- Selling is a personal experience. Sales staff must consider the messages that they consciously, or subconsciously, give to customers to ensure that the product is portrayed as satisfying the appropriate needs.

4.2.4 Place

▓ By the time the product has been manufactured, packaged, advertised and promoted, decisions should have been made in two areas:

  ● How the product is distributed (i.e. logistics of storage and transportation).

  ● How the product is placed in front of the customer.

▓ These areas are frequently overlooked and yet are crucial to the success of the product. If a new product is to be launched and has undergone an extensive marketing campaign, then the product must be in the shop on the launch date. Having created interest, aroused desire, etc, non-availability of the product must be avoided unless creating shortage is part of the marketing strategy.*

▓ It is not uncommon for "the place" to be an exclusive outlet only selling that manufacturer's goods. This is most common in car retailing. Another way to block a competitor is to purchase the distribution chain and prevent the use of that chain by the competitor.

▓ The basic arrangements open to organisations in terms of distribution/point of sale arrangement are shown in the following diagram.

*Some manufacturers (e.g. of computer game consoles and programmes) deliberately create a "shortage" of a new product at the launch date to create exclusivity (for those who get it) and increased desire for those who do not.

DIRECT SUPPLY

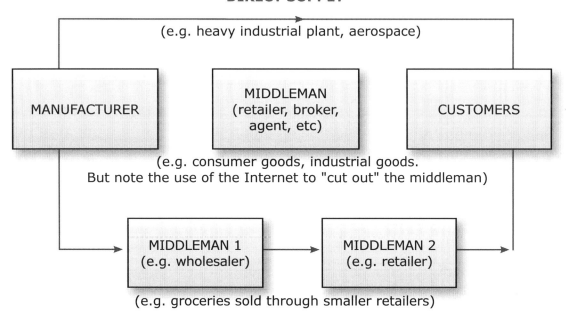

4.3 The 7 Ps

▓ In addition to the four Ps described above, three further Ps can be identified for service providers.

▓ The additional Ps have been added because in a modern business environment the service sector of many economies has come to dominate economic activity and marketing must clearly be customer-oriented.

People	Processes	Physical Evidence
Corporate culture	Procedures/policies	Environment
Job design	Information/ accessibility	Physical layout
Motivation	Capacity/volume	Facilities
Appearance/ behaviour	Automation/ mechanisation	Decoration/ furnishing
Attitude/ professionalism	Speed/timing	Packaging
Skills/knowledge	Access/queuing	Paperwork/tickets/ invoices
Commitment		Brochures
Discretion		Signage (uniforms, aircraft)
		Business cards

4.3.1   People

▨ Service providers are heavily dependent on their employees, as many of them will have direct face-to-face contact with customers (e.g. sales staff in a retail shop). Although many organisations consider that "their employees are their greatest asset", many may not identify with their employees as marketing the organisation.

▨ The first impression obtained by many customers of many organisations (not just service organisations) will come from, for example, the receptionist/telephonist, the entrance and reception areas and the organisation's website. Effective marketing of these areas is essential.

4.3.2   Processes

▨ The procedures by which customer service is managed and delivered may range from dealing with complaints, to delivering information to customers (e.g. websites, electronic tracking), to managing queues and to managing the whole customer experience (e.g. going on holiday; buying goods over the Internet; travelling by bus, train, boat or plane; going to the cinema; going shopping; going to the restaurant).

▨ Effectively, any process that deals with customers and consumers (internal or external) will have marketing overtones to some degree.

4.3.3   Physical Evidence

▨ Physical evidence is the material part of a service. As service is strictly intangible and there are no physical attributes, so a consumer tends to rely on material clues and signs.

Illustration 2 Failure to Deliver

In March 2008, the opening of Heathrow Airport's new Terminal 5 (T5) turned into a complete and utter marketing disaster following significant technical, staff and procedural failures on the first day of its public operation.

British Airways (BA) staff were ill-prepared for the opening because of poor training, low morale and unfamiliarity with the terminal layout and security procedures. This occurred despite the staff warning senior management of their concerns months before the official opening. Although BA is a service-oriented organisation, its staff morale is extremely low (e.g. many staff members feel that they can no longer support the firm when asked to give up rest days to "help out" in emergencies such as that at T5). This was reflected by reports from passengers of unhelpful and surly BA staff.

The baggage system (marketed as the most modern worldwide) failed, resulting in many flights being cancelled or leaving without passengers' luggage (in some cases, it took up to three weeks to reunite baggage with its owners).

Booking in and screening passengers took far longer than expected (again because staff were unfamiliar with the procedures, the broken baggage system and lifts) resulting in many passengers missing their flights.

Although passengers were waiting in a beautifully designed building with many shops, there was a distinct lack of seating and catering facilities.

Many passengers considered their experience to have been the worst of their lives, vowing never to fly BA again and to avoid Heathrow Airport if possible.

The full transfer of BA flights to T5 was delayed by several months and it was not until November 2008 that T5 finally became fully operational.

Example 4 Marketing Service Operations

Identify and comment on SIX factors that lead to the effective marketing of a service organisation.

Solution

Factors	Comments
1.	
2.	
3.	
4.	
5.	
6.	

5 Marketing Strategy

5.1 Goals and Objectives

■ A marketing strategy is designed to guide management towards getting products or services to customers and encouraging them to buy. Although it is subordinate to the overall business strategy, it makes a significant contribution to that strategy in that the marketing department inputs much of the information needs for the development of the corporate strategy.

■ The strategic element of the marketing strategy focuses on the direction the organisation wishes to take in relation to its products, services and markets.

■ The operational element, dealing with products and markets, defines the tasks and activities to be carried out in order to achieve the short-, medium- and long-term objectives.

■ In developing the marketing strategy, key questions must be asked:*

* By asking these questions and analysing the market, it will be possible to start to plan and determine a marketing strategy.

- What business are we in? For example, do we just provide a product, service or experience in which the product is incidental (e.g. do restaurants provide an evening meal or do they provide a dining experience, in which selling the food may be considered incidental)?

- What broad markets does the business wish to serve? Can the business serve them? What is the competition in each market?

- What specific market segments does the business wish to concentrate on?

- What proportion of total effort should be concentrated on each market and segment (and associated plans and services)? In other words, how many eggs and in what baskets?

- What are the basic customer needs, expectations and power of each market segment?

- What are the sizes of the markets the business is now in, or will be in? What is the likely growth pattern? How attractive are these markets?

- At what market standing does the business aim? (A "big fish in a small pond" or vice versa?)

- What are the business's strengths and weaknesses?

5.2 Orientation

■ Organisations produce, market and sell products. Four strategic orientations towards the customer have been identified and can form the basis of an organisation's philosophy:

1. Production orientation

2. Product orientation

3. Sales orientation

4. Marketing orientation

5.2.1   Production Orientation

▓ The Henry Ford approach—"they can have whatever colour they like, so long as it is black." Organisations can produce whatever they want with the expectation that customers will buy them.

▓ The implications of this orientation are that product lines are narrow; pricing is based on the costs of production and distribution; research is limited to technical product research; packaging is designed primarily to protect the product; and promotion and advertising are minimal.

▓ Its approach may serve businesses well when goods are in short supply or are undifferentiated commodities but, with a free choice and open supply, they will struggle to survive.

5.2.2   Product Orientation

▓ The organisation believes that it knows what the customer wants and produces accordingly. Even though its products may be exciting and interesting, and the organisation seeks to generate interest in the market for these products, if customers have no need or desire for them they will not buy them.

▓ Ultimately, the organisation may become out of touch with its customer base, which will shrink as customers go elsewhere and new customers fail to replace them in sufficient quantity.

5.2.3   Sales Orientation

▓ Customers are sales resistant, so products must be pushed onto customers by an active and aggressive sales force to persuade them to buy. Sales promotions and sales calling are two techniques used.

▓ Sales orientation may be a useful strategy for intangible products, such as life insurance, or tangible products, such as motorcars, where there are clear benefits to owning the product but little immediate incentive to purchase.＊

＊Commentary

＊Sales orientation together with a financial incentive (i.e. bonus) for the sales person to "push" the product onto a customer has often resulted in (usually financial) entities being accused (and found guilty in law or breach of financial regulations) of misselling products to customers (i.e. giving unsuitable advice about a product where the risks of the product were not explained or essential information was not provided). Infamous cases in the UK include misselling by banks of mortgage insurance products to house buyers and interest rate swaps to small businesses.

5.2.4   Marketing Orientation

▓ The organisation believes that to succeed and be profitable it must establish the needs, wants and values of a target market and deliver the required product more effectively and efficiently than its competitors.

▓ Its activities, products and services are organised around the needs and requirements of its customers.＊

＊Commentary

＊Product and marketing orientation should be seen as complementary rather than opposing. Many organisations use both.

5.3   Market Segmentation

Market segmentation allows an organisation to treat similar customers in similar ways, while distinguishing between dissimilar customer groups. Each customer group has slightly different needs, which can be satisfied by offering each group, or segment, a slightly different marketing strategy.

Segmentation can be based on:

Definition

Market segmentation— "the subdividing of a market into distinct subsets of customers where any subset may conceivably be selected as a market target to be reached with a distinct marketing mix."

—*Kotler*

- demographics
- geographical;
- value;
- psychological;
- lifestyle;
- purchasing characteristics;
- benefits; and
- family life cycle:
    - bachelor;
    - newly married;
    - full nest 1 (young children);
    - full nest 2 (older children);
    - full nest 3 (children as adults, but living at home);
    - empty nest 1 (children no longer at home);
    - empty nest 2 (pensioners).

5.4   Product Life Cycle

- The product life-cycle concept attempts to classify a product's sales, profits, customers, competitors and marketing emphasis from its inception until its removal from the market. It plays an important part in marketing and production strategies.

- Ideally, a business will possess a portfolio of products in different stages of their respective life cycles.

- The six stages of the product life cycle are:

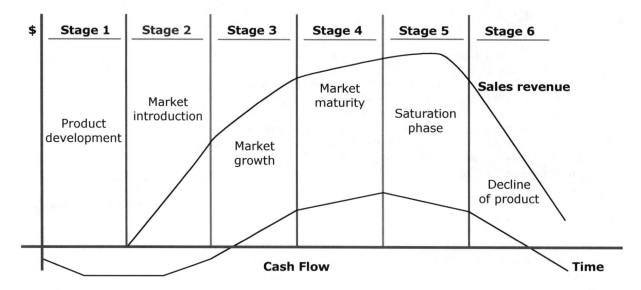

1. **Product development**—negative cash flow only as the result of design costs and the production of prototypes. After this comes the product launch.

2. **Market introduction**—there is not yet a proven demand for the product, sales are low and develop slowly. Cash flow is still negative.

3. **Market growth**—demand begins to accelerate and the total market size begins to expand quickly. This could be called "take-off stage". Unit production costs fall (due to increased volume of output) and so the product begins to generate profits.

4. **Market maturity**—demand levels off and increases usually only at replacement rate and new family-formation rate. Profits are still satisfactory, yet at the end of this stage, further acceleration is inhibited by competitive products.

5. **Saturation**—more products are available than the market can absorb. Competition is intensified and prices fall.

6. **Decline**—here few organisations can cope with competition and chronic overcapacity occurs widely. This may be when mergers are proposed. Production of the product is concentrated into fewer and fewer hands. Prices and profit margins are depressed.

5.5   Boston Consulting Group (BCG) Matrix

▓ Along with the product life cycle, the BCG matrix is a useful tool in marketing and production strategy. It shows the summarised performance of either individual products, a portfolio of products or an investment (e.g. division or subsidiary).

▓ The axes of the grid are market share and market growth, allowing four performance descriptions which broadly follow the product life cycle:

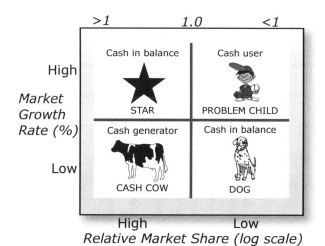

5.5.1 Problem Child

- Sometimes referred to as Question Mark products, these are low market share products, usually at the introduction phase of the product life cycle, which operate in high (potential) market growth areas. The business will invest heavily in these products to rapidly grow them in the hope they will eventually increase market share and generate cash returns in the future.

- They have low cash flow because of high investment demands and low returns due to low market share. If nothing is done to increase the market share, problem children will simply absorb great amounts of cash, effectively becoming "black holes" that will implode at some stage and become dogs.

- The business should either invest heavily or kill off, or invest nothing and generate whatever cash it can, before killing off. To avoid mistakes being repeated, the business needs to understand how a child star (i.e. a product under development with high potential) turned into a problem child when introduced to the market.

5.5.2 Star

- Stars have high market shares which operate in growing markets and are usually at the market-growth stage moving into market maturity in the product life cycle.

- They are products that, while requiring large amounts of cash, are leaders in the business so they will also generate large amounts of cash with the overall result of positive returns for the organisation.

- Businesses need rising and maturing stars in their product portfolio because these will become the next generation of cash cows.

5.5.3 Cash Cow

- These are products in the mature stage of the product life cycle (perhaps moving into the saturation stage) and are often considered the business's foundation products.

- They generate high amounts of cash, but as their growth rate is slowing there is little need for further development investment. Profits should be high for the company.

- Because there is a risk they may slip into decline, appropriate strategies need to be developed to ensure that they can be "milked" for as long as possible.

5.5.4 Dogs

- These are products which have low market shares and low (potential) market growth rates. The options for most would be to phase them out as soon as they slow down or stop providing positive cash flows.

- Some businesses may adopt a strategy of reinventing and injecting new life into the product. Doing so, however, may prove to be very expensive with the risk that the strategy will fail.

- As dogs tend to be products in the decline phase of the product life cycle, organisations need to avoid and minimise the number they keep alive, despite any sentimental attachment to the product.

Session 1

Summary

■ Business organisations achieve results collectively which individuals cannot achieve alone.

■ Different types of organisations have different goals:

● Commercial organisations—aim for continued existence and maximise shareholder wealth.

● Not-for-profit—satisfy member needs without profit as the primary objective.

● Cooperative—owned by individuals who use and benefit from the business.

● Public sector—provision of goods or services controlled by government.

● NGOs—independent from government and political parties; not-for-profit.

■ Direct service provision is effectively a service business's equivalent of production.

■ The marketing mix for a product includes product, price, promotion and place. A service has the additional classes of people, processes and physical evidence.

■ Four strategic orientations towards the customer which form the basis for the marketing strategy include production, product, sales and marketing orientation.

■ Market segmentation allows firms to develop different marketing strategies for different segments of their consumer base.

■ The six-stage product life-cycle model differentiates a product into various stages of sales growth and cash flow generation.

■ The BCG matrix helps firms identify the most valuable product types by analysing the rate of potential growth in the market and a firm's current low market share.

Session 1 Quiz

Estimated time: 20 minutes

1. Define "business organisation". (1.1)

2. Explain why formal organisations exist. (1.2)

3. List the primary objectives of commercial organisations. (1.4)

4. Explain why organisations have a purchasing department. (2.2)

5. Describe the characteristics of direct service provision. (2.4)

6. List the basic functions of marketing. (3.2)

7. Explain the link between needs, wants and demands. (3.3.1)

8. Briefly describe the additional THREE Ps. (4.3)

9. State a typical product life cycle. (5.4)

10. Describe the FOUR elements of the BCG marketing matrix. (5.5)

Study Question Bank

Estimated time: 40 minutes

Priority		Estimated Time	Completed
MCQ1	The Business Organisation	40 minutes	

EXAMPLE SOLUTIONS

Solution 1—Banks

A cooperative bank serves its members (it has no issued share capital thus no shareholders), while a commercial bank must maximise the wealth of its shareholders (who may not necessarily be customers of the bank).

To benefit members, a cooperative bank would attempt to minimise the interest rates charged to members for mortgages and loans, while maximising the rates paid for member deposits.

A commercial bank would attempt to maximise mortgage interest rates (income) and minimise the rates paid for deposits (costs).

Any surplus generated by the cooperative bank would be held purely for the benefit of its members. Commercial banks would be expected to earn sufficient profits to enable dividends to be paid to shareholders before retained profits are invested in the growth of the business.

If the members of the cooperative bank decided that the bank should change its status to become a commercial bank (this will usually allow the bank to raise additional capital on the markets for expansion), the bank will need to issue shares to raise the additional capital as well as distribute shares to its members in fair value to their "investment" in the net assets of the bank (this would be calculated based on deposits made, mortgages held and length of time as a member). Thus the members' investment in the cooperative bank would be converted to a shareholding in the newly commercialised bank.

Solution 2—Distinguishing Factors

Factor	Professional Body	Water Company
1. Legal constitution	■ Royal Charter of Association	■ Public limited company
2. Ownership	■ Members	■ Shareholders
3. Control and management	■ The Council (including Secretary, branches and committees)	■ Chief executive, board of directors and utility board
4. Principal objective	■ To advance the science of accountancy	■ To provide water and waste water services
5. Principal source of income	■ Fees and subscriptions	■ Water usage (e.g. metered) and waste disposal charges

Solution 3—Value

- Superior performance
- Reliability
- Reputation
- Looking "super cool"
- Crowd puller, showing off, ego, "mine is bigger/better than yours"
- Having the only one in the town/city/country (preferably the latter)
- "Flashing your wealth", "my wallet/private bank is bigger than yours"

Solution 4—Marketing Service Operations

Tangibles	The physical evidence, such as the quality of fixtures and fittings of the business's service area, must be consistent with the desired image.
Reliability	Getting it right the first time is important, not only to ensure repeat business but, in financial services, as a matter of ethics, if the customer is buying a future benefit.
Responsiveness	The staff's willingness to deal with customers' queries must be apparent.
Communication	Staff should talk to customers in non-technical language which they can understand.
Credibility	The organisation should be perceived as honest, trustworthy and acting in the best interests of its customers.
Security	This is especially relevant to medical and financial services organisations. A customer needs to feel that conversations with bank service staff are private and confidential. This factor should influence the design of the service area.
Competence	All service staff need to appear competent in understanding the product range and interpreting the needs of the customers. In part, this can be achieved through training programmes.
Courtesy	Customers (even rude ones) should perceive service staff as polite, respectful and friendly. This basic requirement is often difficult to achieve in practise, although training programmes can reinforce service skills.
Understanding customers' needs	The use of computerised databases can be very impressive in this context. Service personnel can call up a customer's records and use the data in the service process, thus personalising it. Service staff need to meet customer needs rather than try to sell products. This is a subtle but important difference.
Access	Minimising queues, having a fair queuing system and speedy but accurate service are all factors which can help prevent irritating the customer. A pleasant, relaxing environment is a useful design factor in this context.

Stakeholders in Business Organisations

FOCUS

This session covers the following content from the *ACCA Study Guide.*

A. The Business Organisation, Its Stakeholders and the External Environment

2. Stakeholders in business organisations

a) Define stakeholders and explain the agency relationship in business and how it may vary in different types of business organisation. ☐

b) Define internal, connected and external stakeholders and explain their impact on the organisation. ☐

c) Identify the main stakeholder groups and the objectives of each group. ☐

d) Explain how the different stakeholder groups interact and how their objectives may conflict with one another. ☐

e) Compare the power and influence of various stakeholder groups and how their needs should be accounted for, such as under the Mendelow framework. ☐

Session 2 Guidance

■ **Know** that classical theory (agency theory) considers that the duty of directors is to maximise the wealth of the shareholder (s.1). The current approach, stakeholder theory, considers that this maximisation cannot be achieved without taking into account the impact on and by stakeholders.

■ **Learn** the definition of stakeholders and understand the description and examples of the three main categories of stakeholder—internal, connected and external (s.2). **Expect a question in the exam on this area.** Be sure that you can identify/classify stakeholders in a given situation and/or identify what their particular interest might be.

(continued on next page)

VISUAL OVERVIEW

Objective: To explain the term "stakeholder" and stakeholder interactions with organisations.

```
                    ┌─────────────────────────────┐
                    │   AGENCY AND STAKEHOLDERS   │
                    │  • Development of Agency    │
                    │    Theory                   │
                    │  • Key Concepts             │
                    │  • Fiduciary Responsibilities│
                    │  • Stakeholder Theory       │
                    └─────────────────────────────┘
                       /                    \
        ┌──────────────────────┐   ┌──────────────────────┐
        │     STAKEHOLDER      │   │     STAKEHOLDER      │
        │     CATEGORIES       │   │     POWER AND        │
        │                      │   │     CONFLICT         │
        │  • Internal          │   │  • Risk              │
        │    Stakeholders      │   │  • Mendelow          │
        │  • Connected         │   │  • Stakeholder       │
        │    Stakeholders      │   │    Conflict          │
        │  • External          │   │                      │
        │    Stakeholders      │   │                      │
        └──────────────────────┘   └──────────────────────┘
```

Session 2 Guidance

■ **Understand** Mendelow's grid as a classic example of the Boston Consulting Group matrix, its structure and how it can be used to categorise stakeholders and their impact (s.3).

1   Agency and Stakeholders

1.1   Development of Agency Theory

> **Definition**
>
> **Agency**—Duties and conflicts which occur between parties who have a relationship in which one or more persons (the principals) delegate some decision-making authority to another person (the agent) in order for the agent to perform some service on behalf of the principals.

- Historically, the same individual owned, controlled and managed an individual company. As that company expanded and sought increasing finance through share issues to the general public, owners (the shareholders) found it more difficult to also manage (control) the business on a daily basis.

- The development of the market system (stock exchanges) in the UK and the US eventually resulted in shareholders delegating the running of the business to the company's management. The separation of ownership and control became evident.

- As stock markets became more active, owners became more passive, owning share certificates rather than assets of the business.

- Clearly, as the number of shareholders grew, the incentive and ability of individual shareholders to gather information and monitor managers decreased. Issuing shares and expanding share ownership may have been considered a "good thing to bring capitalism to the ordinary people" but it also gave managers greater potential to run the business as they wanted with little interference and accountability.

1.2   Key Concepts

Agents and principals: An agent is an individual hired or employed by another, the principal, to carry out a task on the principal's behalf.

Agency: The relationship between a principal and the agent.

Agency costs: The costs incurred in establishing and monitoring the agent by the principal (i.e. how the shareholder controls and verifies management's activities).

Residual loss: The reduction in shareholder value that results from excessive agency costs, e.g. directors awarding themselves other benefits beyond basic salaries and incentive schemes such as company cars, houses, planes, club memberships, etc.

Accountability: Under the agency relationship, the agent is accountable to the principal for the outcome of the work the agent carries out and the resources used. In theory, the directors are answerable to, and held responsible by, the shareholders for their actions.

Fiduciary duty: The duty imposed upon certain persons because of the position of trust and confidence in which they stand in relation to another.

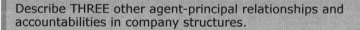

Example 1 Agency Costs

List FOUR types of agency costs in the shareholder-director relationship.

1.3 Fiduciary Responsibilities

Fiduciary duty is more onerous than duties which generally arise under a relationship of contract or tort. It requires full disclosure of information held by the fiduciary, a strict duty to account for any profits received as a result of the relationship and a duty to avoid conflicts of interest.

Under English law, fiduciary duties of directors to the company (now enshrined in company legislation) include:

▨ To act in good faith in the best interests of the company;

▨ To act within the powers conferred by statutory documents (e.g. memorandum and articles of association) and to exercise powers for proper purposes;

▨ Not to restrain discretion (must use independent judgement on the company's behalf);

▨ To avoid conflicts of interest and conflicting duties;

▨ Not to make a secret profit (includes accepting benefit or bribes from third parties);

▨ To exercise due skill and care in the performance of their duties.

Example 2 Agent-Principal Relationships

Describe THREE other agent-principal relationships and accountabilities in company structures.

1.4 Stakeholder Theory

▨ Freeman's definition implies the bi-directional nature of stakeholders—groups which can affect a firm or be affected by a firm.

▨ Typical examples of stakeholders include:

 ● the original capitalist institutions of shareholders and directors (agency theory);

 ● the more recently recognised stakeholders—managers, employees, customers, suppliers;

 ● the government, pressure groups, local communities, society in general; and

 ● in current thinking, the environment (incorporating animals, vegetables and minerals) and future generations.

Definition

Stakeholder—"Any group or individual who can affect or be affected by the achievement of an organisation's objectives."
—*Freeman, 1984*

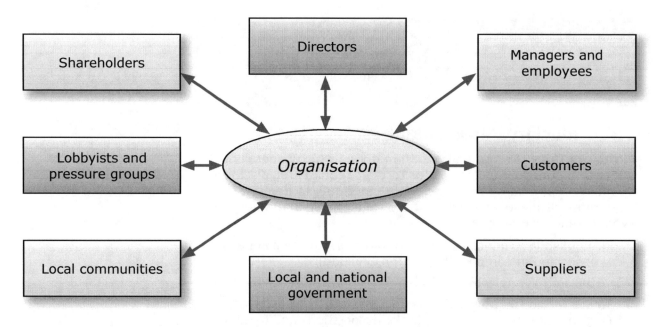

- Classical agency theory only considers the relationship between directors and shareholders with the need to maximise shareholders' wealth. It is based on the ideas of what shareholders (owners) must do to ensure that directors (agents) take into account the need to maximise shareholders' wealth when setting the direction and objectives of an organisation (rather than considering their own personal interests).

- Stakeholder theory has developed since the mid-'80s and establishes the need for the directors to consider the effect of all stakeholders (not only just the shareholders) in their decision-making to maximise the value of the company, thus effectively maximising the wealth of the shareholders. It has developed in parallel with corporate governance and corporate social responsibility.

- Put simply, if the concerns of a group of stakeholders are ignored, it may be possible that those stakeholders will be able to inflict economic damage on the entity (e.g. boycotts, bad publicity) and thus reduce the wealth being generated (e.g. profits or share price or both). Thus, failure to identify stakeholders and their concerns may result in the organisation failing to achieve its objectives.

2 Stakeholder Categories

There are many ways in which stakeholders are classified, but the initial classification relates to their "relative position" within the organisation, for example:

- internal;
- connected; and
- external.

2.1   Internal Stakeholders

▓ Internal stakeholders are intimately connected to the organisation. Their objectives are likely to have a strong influence on how it is run.

▓ They usually have an operational role in the company, will be involved in the corporate governance procedures of the company or will have a number of interests in being connected with the company.

2.1.1   Directors

▓ Directors are responsible and accountable to stakeholders for the strategic direction of a company, its day-to-day operations and for the company's moral and corporate social behaviour. Their powers are usually laid down in the company's constitution or articles and supported by relevant corporate laws and corporate governance codes.

▓ Under corporate governance, there is usually a distinction between executive directors (who manage the business on a full-time basis) and non-executive directors (who oversee and monitor the executive function).

▓ As stakeholders, their interest covers, for example, remuneration, bonuses, share options, retirement benefits, status, reputation and power.

2.1.2   Company Secretary

▓ The company secretary ensures that the company complies with relevant legislation and regulation and that the directors are kept informed of their legal responsibilities. He is usually the named representative of the company on legal documents and it is his responsibility to ensure that the company and its directors operate within the law.

▓ It is also the company secretary's responsibility:
  - to register and communicate with shareholders;
  - to ensure that dividends are paid;
  - to maintain company statutory records; and
  - to ensure the annual financial statements and all other statutory returns are appropriately filed with the relevant authorities.

2.1.3   Employees

▓ The significant majority of employees will carry out the instructions of management to achieve the short-, medium- and long-term objectives of the company, providing appropriate feedback to their supervisors, supervisors to their managers and managers to the board.

▓ They will comply with the various risk management and control systems within the corporate governance framework and culture of the company.

▓ As stakeholders, although their power is fairly limited, their interest (which can be high) will be in the performance of the company, pay, working conditions, job security and, for some, career progression.*

▓ Management may provide employees with feedback on the company's activities and performance—a form of "stakeholder report" specifically for employees.

Commentary

*Representation of employees at board level may be a legal requirement.

2.2 Connected Stakeholders

- Connected stakeholders, although external to the organisation, will (usually) have a form of contractual relationship with the organisation (e.g. employment contract, supply contract, loan contract). In some cases, the relationship can be crucial to the continued development of the organisation (e.g. key staff, suppliers of essential materials, reliance on a small number of customers).

2.2.1 Shareholders

Shareholders are usually classified into three categories—listed institutional, listed small and unlisted.

1. Institutional shareholders

It used to be that institutional shareholders (e.g. pension funds, insurance funds) were only interested in short-term dividend growth and capital value growth (market capitalisation) and they basically left the directors to run the business as they saw fit.

Now, those shareholders are also interested in exercising their responsibilities to actively participate. For example:

- to question the directors about policies;
- to use their voting power (rather than hand over a proxy vote to the directors); and
- to challenge directors' decisions.

In addition, institutional shareholders are beginning to look for long-term sustained growth in their investments.

Directors recognise this group's power to demonstrate its points of view. For example, voting against resolutions (e.g. to appoint a director), proposing their own directors and ultimately being able to sell their shareholdings, which are usually significant enough (e.g. 5%) to affect the market.*

Commentary

*Directors hold regular meetings with institutional shareholders to ensure open and clear communications between them.

2. Small listed shareholders

Small listed shareholders (in the UK they represent fewer than 20% of listed company shareholders) are becoming a rare breed. This means that they have very little power so their prime interest as a stakeholder will be in share value and dividends.

An individual shareholder is highly unlikely to be able to get a company board to take notice of a grievance. However, through the use of social networks it is relatively easy to find and contact other shareholders (including institutional shareholders) who may share similar concerns and put pressure on the board to notice.

In recognising this, most listed organisations have information pages and blogs on their websites to ensure that appropriate updates are regularly given to all stakeholders and that they can contact the organisation.

In addition, because of their relatively weak position, small investors may be abused by the majority shareholders. Most corporate governance codes, therefore, place strong emphasis on ensuring equal treatment by companies of all shareholders.

3. Unlisted shareholders

Unlisted shareholders usually are also the directors of the unlisted company. As the owner/managers of the organisation, their prime interest as stakeholders will be in the tax-efficient growth of their business. They will take a longer-term view of growth (e.g. passing on to their family through inheritance), plus they normally will arrange their affairs to be as tax efficient as possible—not only corporate profits tax, but also remuneration through dividends or salary, capital gains and inheritance tax planning.

2.2.2 Suppliers

- The suppliers of resources have an obvious stakeholder interest in an organisation.

- Ideally, the supplier wishes to establish a long-term relationship with an organisation. Suppliers require frequent and regular high-value orders at fair prices which are profitable for them to be able to reinvest. They also require prompt payment from their customers to be able to manage their cash flows. Lastly, they wish that their customers can grow, be successful and thus continue to do business with them.

- Businesses wish to have a consistent supply of high-quality resources from reliable suppliers. They wish to be able to manage their costs and not to become over-dependent on one resource or a limited number of suppliers of that resource. Many organisations aim to ensure that they have an appropriate number of reliable suppliers which can deliver the right quality at the right price at the right time.

- There is a fine balance between suppliers and their customers. Relationships have to be managed to the benefit of both.

Illustration 1 Price Cartel

Of recurring concern in the UK is the relationship between the supermarkets and farmers. Many farmers accuse the supermarkets of passing on the costs of price promotions (i.e. reduced selling prices) to the farmers, including asking/requiring the farmers to pay part of, or all of, the costs of the supermarkets promoting the product. If a farmer refuses, then he may easily lose his contract of supply with the supermarket—the farmer is effectively "locked-in" to supplying the supermarket.

In an ongoing case in the UK, the major supermarkets are being investigated on the possible operation of a price cartel (price fixing) on milk and dairy products. They have been accused of agreeing between themselves and the direct suppliers (i.e. the middlemen) what the prices to be charged to their customers should be. Although the consumer price has increased, it is claimed that the "farm gate" price (the price paid to farmers for the raw product, milk) has not increased. Although the end price has risen, none of that increase is supposed to have found its way back to the farmers.

2.2.3 Customers

■ The other side of the coin is the customer as a stakeholder (every supplier has a customer). Organisations should wish to maintain a strong and loyal customer base. They should aim to deliver what the customer wants, at an optimum price, of suitable quality and on time.

■ Customers look for low prices, value for money, high-quality products, good service, innovation, certain and regular supply, variety, and clear and accurate information on product choice.

- If they do not get the right mix of these elements, then the risk to the organisation is that the customer will go elsewhere (Internet searching is a successful price- and service-comparison tool).
- If there are a limited number of suppliers in the market for a particular product/service or if customers do not get the right service, they will turn to a competitor.

■ If an organisation fails to maintain good customer relationships and to deliver what the customer wants, the organisation will have no customers and will go out of business.

2.2.4 Finance Creditors

■ Finance creditors are primarily banks (loans, mortgages and overdrafts), but also include suppliers providing credit.

■ As stakeholders they are interested in prompt payment of debt and loan instalments, payment of interest, repayment at the agreed date, creditworthiness and assets that provide security.

■ Failure by an organisation to meet the interests of finance creditors can result in increased interest rates, withdrawal of credit facilities and the requirement to repay the loan. This may result in the going concern failure of the organisation (i.e. it must cease to trade).

2.2.5 Trade Unions

■ Trade unions are stakeholders through their relationship with employees in protecting and developing employee interests.

■ In some jurisdictions they are powerful entities supported by law, including the right to sit on the boards of companies.

■ Trade unions lobby in support of member interests when they may conflict with other stakeholder interests.

2.3 External Stakeholders

■ External stakeholders are individuals and groups which do not have core contractual connections with the organisation but are affected by the corporate and social actions of the organisation.

■ Many may, however, have dual classifications. For example, employees (internal) are likely to be members of the local community (external).

■ External shareholders are many and varied. The relationship and the claims an individual stakeholder will have with an organisation will cover a broad spectrum, from significant to virtually nil.

■ Examples of external stakeholders include government (national and local), lobbying groups (e.g. environmentalists), local communities, regulators and external auditors.

Exam Advice

If the examiner requires differentiation between connected and external stakeholders, then make the strict identification. Otherwise, include connected stakeholders within external stakeholders.

2.3.1 Governments

Governments are involved in just about all aspects of individual and corporate life.

- Taxes on sales, profits and capital gains are just a few of the taxes levied on companies. In most cases, companies are expected to also act as unpaid tax collectors.

- Tax structures and incentives—some governments deliberately establish favourable tax regimes to attract companies to their country, regions or cities or to encourage particular investment decisions.

- Regulatory environment—governmental laws and regulations which affect business have proliferated. Perhaps the major criticism of government by companies, especially small companies, is the amount of administration ("red tape") required by various government rules and regulations.

- Direct investment—in some jurisdictions, governments may purchase shares in a company to save it from closure, but this is more the rare exception than the norm. Any investment by governments in companies usually takes the form of loans or grants, especially in strategic companies and high-tech development.*

*Also banks in the UK and the US during the "banking crisis".

2.3.2 Local Communities

- No matter what type of activity an organisation undertakes, its presence in a community will leave a footprint on that community. The organisation will need at least offices and, at most, complete factory complexes. The footprint for offices may be fairly small; that for factories could be substantial.

- A community expects organisations to provide employment prospects; safeguard the local environment (e.g. minimal pollution, no rubbish, careful management of traffic); accept social responsibility (e.g. become involved in local community activities); and practice ethical behaviour (e.g. law abiding and fair treatment of employees).

2.3.3 Lobbyist, Interest and Pressure Groups

- Lobbying is the practice of trying to persuade legislators to propose, pass or defeat legislation or to change existing laws. A lobbyist may work for a group, organisation or industry, and presents information on legislative proposals to support the clients' interests.

*May relate to local community issues (e.g. increased traffic due to a company's expansion).

- Lobbying is not specifically aimed at an organisation, but may be used by the organisation to improve its position (e.g. to win government-backed tenders).

- An interest group is a group of individuals that forms because of some special topic of concern. Usually when the problem declines or the goals have been reached, the group disbands.*

- A pressure group is a specific interest group which endeavours to influence public policy and especially governmental legislation, regarding its particular concerns and priorities.*

*Concerning, for example, environmental pollution, animal testing and child labour.

■ The aim of all pressure groups is to influence the people who actually have the power to make decisions. That includes attempting to influence company directors, but may also take the form of consumer boycotts, or the withdrawal of supplies and services in an attempt to influence other stakeholders. Such direct action on other stakeholders does often achieve the required action by directors.*

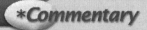

*Commentary

*Lobbying, interest and pressure groups can be seen in "action" in the current concern over the building of a third runway at London's Heathrow Airport. The Government is being lobbied to pass legislation both to allow and to prevent the building of the runway. Local interest groups have been formed to address concerns for effects of the runway on the local community. International pressure groups have been taking direct action against the company responsible for running the airport, BAA, primarily over concerns for pollution (noise and atmospheric).

2.3.4 External Auditors

■ External auditors have always been crucial to the shareholder-director relationship. They provide shareholders with assurance that management assertions in the annual financial statements show a true and fair view.

■ Although auditors are stakeholders and directly affect shareholders, they must also maintain an independent professional relationship with management. This can lead to conflicts of interest.

■ The auditor's interests and claims in the company (their client) include audit and other service fees, reputation, quality of relationship and compliance with audit regulations.*

*Commentary

*In many financial scandals, a common question asked was, "Where were the auditors"? This has resulted in a loss of confidence in the role undertaken by the auditors and the public perception that they are not independent of the management.

Example 3 Airport Stakeholders

For an international airport (e.g. Heathrow Airport in London), identify the potential stakeholders and their possible interests.

3　Stakeholder Power and Conflict

3.1　Risk

- **Business risk** is the risk that a business will not achieve its objectives. Such risks must be managed by the managers of all organisations.

- **Stakeholder risk** (as a subset of business risk) can be considered as the risk that the business will not achieve its objectives (e.g. maximise wealth and value) because of the lack of understanding of the effect of stakeholders on the organisation by its managers.*

- Under stakeholder theory, it is essential for all organisations to be able to identify all stakeholders, and assess their level of interest and power to hinder or support the organisation, when developing strategy and objectives.

Commentary

*Managers must identify stakeholders who may act negatively against the organisation, as well as those that can assist the organisation achieve its objectives.

3.2　Mendelow

Mendelow (1991) suggested that stakeholder influence on key strategic decisions could be "mapped" by looking at the relative strength of two aspects of their relationship with the organisation.

- **Power**—the ability to influence strategic objectives (how much they can).

- **Interest**—the stakeholder's willingness (how much they care) to influence.

As with similar grid approaches (e.g. the Boston Consulting Group matrix for risk analysis), the difficult part is identifying all of the stakeholders which have an interest in an organisation's strategy, their level of interest and the power they have to influence the strategy.

In addition, as most organisations operate in an open and dynamic environment, stakeholders will change and can easily move around the grid. It is important that once stakeholders are identified, they are continually tracked.

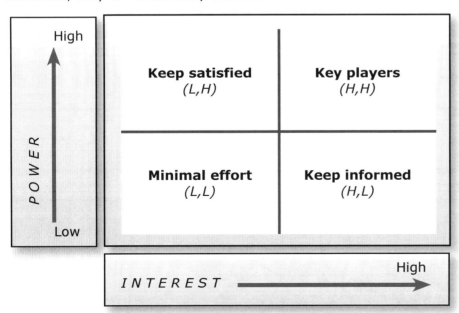

3.2.1 High Interest, High Power = Key Players

■ Most of the company's efforts need to be placed on the key players. The firm cannot manage without them. They have the ability (interest and power) to prevent the company from achieving its strategy (e.g. upsetting customers will drive them to competitors). Alternatively, a stakeholder may be in a position of power and have the interest to actively lobby for the benefit of the organisation.

■ A specific difficulty may be that there will be a number of conflicts between stakeholders in this category which have to be managed.

3.2.2 Low Interest, Low Power = Minimal Effort

■ Diametrically opposite are stakeholders with low interest and low power. Mendelow indicates that these stakeholders can be largely ignored when considering strategic objectives. However, from an ethical/moral view, they should still be considered because to ignore them may awaken their interest.

3.2.3 High Interest, Low Power = Keep Informed

■ High-interest, low-power stakeholders need to be kept informed and not underestimated. Because of their high interest they care a lot and can be useful to the company in forming positive lobby groups. Alternatively, they may join forces to form a stronger grouping and thus move towards the high-power sector and become lobbyists and pressure groups against the company.

3.2.4 Low Interest, High Power = Keep Satisfied

■ Lastly, the low-interest, high-power stakeholders need to be kept satisfied and stay dormant (often referred to as "sleeping giants"). If, for whatever reason they become more interested (woken up), they can easily become key players and, for example, frustrate the adoption of a new strategy.

■ Alternatively, their interest could be deliberately enhanced by the organisation so that their power can be effectively used.

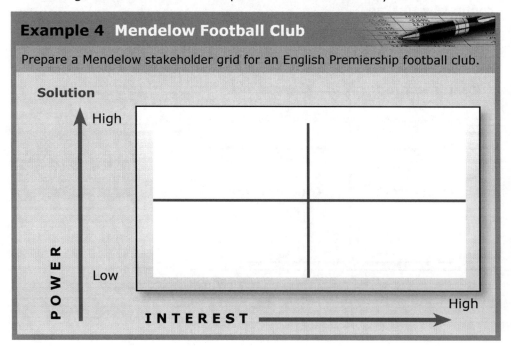

Example 4 Mendelow Football Club

Prepare a Mendelow stakeholder grid for an English Premiership football club.

Solution

3.3   Stakeholder Conflict

▦ Because each stakeholder group will have different objectives and interests in the organisation, they can easily be in conflict. For example:

- Employees requesting enhanced compensation benefits (e.g. retirement and health plans) when management are under pressure to keep costs under control due to price competition.
- Suppliers wishing to maximise price increases and management's desire to minimise them.
- Local residents' desire for a safe environment (e.g. no heavy traffic on roads) and the organisation's need for delivery of raw materials by heavy transport.
- Management's aim to minimise costs conflicting with an environmental group requesting costly procedures to minimise environmental damage.
- The government's plan to increase regulations although management wishes for greater relaxation of "red tape".

▦ The most common conflict relationship often arises between the managers of an organisation and its shareholders, especially where shareholders believe that management is acting in its own interest.

Illustration 2   Threats of Revolt

Following a takeover approach by Microsoft to Yahoo in early 2008 and the subsequent rejection of the approach by Yahoo's management, a major institutional shareholder of Yahoo threatened to instigate a shareholder revolt at the next Yahoo annual general meeting with the aim of replacing the board, specifically as the initial offer from Microsoft was some 40% higher than Yahoo's share price at the time it was made.

▦ By using Mendelow's framework and approach, an organisation can:

- Understand whether the current strategy is still in line with stakeholders' interests and power.
- Identify who will provide support to a strategic project, who has the ability and aim to stop it and, if conflict may arise between relevant stakeholders, the effect.
- Try to reposition stakeholders to increase support or reduce threats to a strategic objective and to minimise the risk of stakeholder conflict.
- Encourage stakeholders to stay in their appropriate category, or to avoid having them move across to another category.
- Identify changes in stakeholders which may imply that the current strategy needs to be re-thought with the possibility of a new strategy being developed.
- Develop an appropriate strategy to manage stakeholder groups.

Summary

- Shareholder agents (directors) have fiduciary duties to shareholders in addition to acting as their agents, but sometimes they fail to perfectly exercise this duty. The excess of agency costs over benefits can be to the detriment of shareholders.

- Management may have a duty to others with a stake in the organisation's operations (stakeholders) and, if not a duty, it may be in the organisation's interest to "reach out" to them.

- Stakeholders fall into three categories:

  1. Internal—work in the company, such as directors, the secretary, management and employees.

  2. Connected—usually have a contractual relationship with the organisation, such as shareholders, suppliers, customers, finance creditors and trade unions.

  3. External—affect or are affected by the organisation's actions, such as government, communities, lobbyists and pressure groups, and external auditors.

- Businesses which fail to comprehend stakeholder relationships run the risk of having their operations disrupted by angry stakeholders. Mendelow classified the influence of a stakeholder group by the interest it has in some aspect of the organisation's business, and the power it has to influence the organisation's strategy.

- Mendelow's approach can help organisations align their strategy with stakeholder interests and reposition stakeholders to encourage their support or reduce threats to the organisation's strategy.

Session 2 Quiz

Estimated time: 15 minutes

1. Define "stakeholder". (1.4)

2. Describe TWO duties which differentiate a fiduciary relationship from mere agency. (1.3)

3. Differentiate connected shareholders from internal shareholders. (2)

4. List SEVEN stakeholders of a company and identify at least FOUR who could be classified as connected stakeholders. (2)

5. Briefly describe each of the FOUR categories of stakeholder identified by Mendelow. (3.2)

6. Explain how Mendelow's grid can be used in attempting to avoid stakeholder conflict. (3.3)

Study Question Bank

Estimated time: 20 minutes

Priority		Estimated Time	Completed
MCQ2	Stakeholders in Business Organisations	20 minutes	

EXAMPLE SOLUTIONS

Solution 1—Agency Costs

1. External audit fees
2. Control and risk management systems
3. Governance procedures (e.g. internal audit)
4. Shareholder meetings (e.g. annual general meeting)
5. Risk sharing

Solution 2—Agent-Principal Relationships

1. **Shareholders and auditors**. Technically, the shareholders (principals) appoint the auditors (agents) who report to them on the financial statements produced by the directors. In practice, the directors may appoint the auditors, but the shareholders will approve the appointment at the following annual general meeting. Although the auditors work very closely with the directors, they are accountable to the shareholders for their work.

2. **Directors and employees**. Directors (principals) employ managers and other members of staff (agents) to carry out the day-to-day operations of the company. The staff are accountable to their immediate managers (and managers to the directors) for the work that is delegated to them.

3. **Banks and directors**. This relationship relates to the bank lending money to the company. The bank is the principal with the directors being the agents. The directors are accountable to the bank for the way they spend the money. Depending on the nature of the loan, a contract will be signed between the bank and the company. Terms of the contract will include how the loan will be used and how this can be monitored by the bank (the principal monitoring the agent).

Solution 3—Airport Stakeholders

- **Owner.** BAA directly owns most of the UK airports and is owned by a consortium led by Ferrovial, a Spanish international construction company.

  As owners, BAA will expect excellent returns on its investment in Heathrow. In return, many of the stakeholder groups will expect BAA to provide up-to-date facilities, services and security at Heathrow.

- **Airlines.** Heathrow is one of the world's busiest airport. All airlines expect to be able to land, turn around aircraft (e.g. unload passengers and baggage, service cabins, refuel, load baggage, board passengers and take off) within a minimum prescribed time. They expect to be able to land on time without waiting (delays cost money in burning extra fuel) and take off on time (delays have a domino effect for the aircraft's next flight).

- **Passengers.** Basically passengers expect to be able to deal with the formalities of arriving at the airport, checking in luggage, going through passport control and security and boarding aircraft as effortlessly as possible. They do not want to spend most of the time it takes travelling waiting in queues. They also expect polite, courteous and helpful airport and check-in staff.

In reverse, leaving the aircraft, going through passport control, picking up luggage and clearing customs should be as easy as possible. Passengers do not want to have to walk for 20 minutes to clear passport control (nor wait in a long queue to do so) and then wait a further 20 minutes to collect their baggage.

Getting to/from the airport must be easy:

- metro, train and road access must be relatively quick and convenient;
- drop-off points for car travellers (including parking); and
- metro stations should be as close as possible to the terminals.

While waiting at the terminal, passengers expect a minimum level of facilities to be available.*

*Commentary

*For example, seating, coffee shops, washrooms, duty-free shops, banks and ATMs, etc.

- **Employees.** Generally, the expectations of BAA employees at Heathrow would be the same as employees of any other similar organisation. Employees of the airlines and other organisations working at Heathrow (e.g. shops and restaurants not controlled by BAA) would be stakeholders of their employers as well as of Heathrow. They would expect Heathrow to provide an appropriate working environment.

- **Local community**. The local community has similar interests in Heathrow as any local community with organisations (e.g. employment). However, at Heathrow there are very specific interests with the local community (e.g. noise pollution of night flights, fume pollution, traffic congestion, terrorist attack, aircraft failure on landing/take-off).

- **Lobbyists, interest and pressure groups**. Airport expansion and the effect of increased air traffic (e.g. adding to the greenhouse effect) are currently "hot" topics for interest groups. BAA has recently proposed a third run way at Heathrow. This is being vigorously opposed by many pressure groups including Greenpeace (environment concerns), local authorities, the London Mayor's Office and local residents.

- Other stakeholders would include the many suppliers to the airport, transport systems (metro, train, taxis), the national government and the city of London (e.g. most tourists arrive through Heathrow so hotels, restaurants, historic sites, etc have an interest in Heathrow).

Solution 4—Mendelow Football Club

High	
Sponsors Taxman	Fans Shareholders Media Controlling regulators
Other clubs Public institutions Government Banks	Employees Players / coaches Players' agents Interest groups
Low	**High**

POWER — INTEREST

Notes: High/High

- Controlling regulators (e.g. FIFA, UEFA and Premier League) have significant influence over clubs through setting the rules, arbitrating disputes and punishing clubs who break the rules and "bring the game into disrepute".

- Fans, as for every customer, expect good quality and a high level of service for the price they pay. Fans are a critical commercial opportunity. Clubs need to attract and keep the fans. Fans often place managers and players under extreme pressure to perform. If managers or players do not meet the fans' expectations, then significant pressure can be placed on the club to release the manager/player.

- In football clubs, it is not unusual for one person to own a controlling interest. The individual, therefore, has significant power and interest. Often the interest is not financial but a passion. The individual bought the club because he or she is a lifelong fan of the club.

- Media can be divided into two elements—TV and press. TV has significant power and interest in the higher levels of football (e.g. the English Premier League). BSkyB invested significant money into buying the sole television rights to premier club matches. They assisted the clubs in developing a positive and "easy-to-sell" image and encouraged clubs to invest in key players (e.g. those who would win games and attract viewers).

The Business Environment

FOCUS

This session covers the following content from the *ACCA Study Guide.*

A. The Business Organisation, Its Stakeholders and the External Environment

3. Political and legal factors affecting business

a) Explain how the political system and government policy affect the organisation. ☐

b) Describe the sources of legal authority, including supra-national bodies, national and regional governments. ☐

c) Explain how the law protects the employee and the implications of employment legislation for the manager and the organisation. ☐

d) Identify the principles of data protection and security. ☐

e) Explain how the law promotes and protects health and safety in the workplace. ☐

f) Recognise the responsibility of the individual for compliance with laws on data protection, security and health and safety. ☐

g) Outline principles of consumer protection such as sale of goods and simple contract. ☐

6. Social and demographic factors

a) Explain the medium- and long-term effects of social and demographic trends on business outcomes in the economy. ☐

b) Describe the impact of changes in social structure, values, attitudes and tastes on the organisation. ☐

c) Identify and explain the measures that governments may take in response to the medium- and long-term impact of demographic change. ☐

7. Technological factors

a) Explain the effects of technological change on the organisation structure and strategy: downsizing, delayering, outsourcing. ☐

b) Describe the impact of information technology and information systems development on business processes. ☐

8. Environmental factors

a) List ways in which the business can affect or be affected by its physical environment. ☐

b) Describe ways in which businesses can operate more efficiently and effectively to limit damage to the environment. ☐

c) Identify the benefits of economic sustainability to a range of stakeholders. ☐

9. Competitive factors

a) Identify a business's strengths, weaknesses, opportunities and threats (SWOT) in a market and the main sources of competitive advantage. ☐

b) Identify the main elements within Porter's value chain and explain the meaning of a value network. ☐

c) Explain the factors that influence the competitiveness in an industry or sector using Porter's five forces model. ☐

d) Describe the activities of an organisation that affect its competitiveness: purchasing, production, marketing, service. ☐

(see ACCA Study Guide for expanded learning objectives)

VISUAL OVERVIEW

Objective: To understand elements of the external environment in which organisations operate.

```
                    ┌─────────────────────────────────────┐
                    │      ENVIRONMENTAL ANALYSIS          │
                    │  • Business Context                  │
                    │  • Physical Environment              │
                    │  • Business of Business              │
                    │  • Business Risk Environment         │
                    └─────────────────────────────────────┘
```

POLITICAL AND LEGAL FACTORS	SOCIAL AND DEMOGRAPHIC INFLUENCES	TECHNOLOGICAL FACTORS	COMPETITIVE FACTORS
• Government Influence • Legal Authority • Employment Law • Data Protection • Health and Safety • Consumer Protection	• Concept • Demographic Transition Theory • Organisational Impact • Government Measures	• Business Strategy • Competitive Advantage • Organisational Structure	• Porter's Five Forces Model • Generic Strategies • SWOT • Porter's Value Chain • Value Network

Session 3 Guidance

■ **Understand** the different meanings of environmental analysis, how the firm affects the physical environment and why businesses should consider the physical environment in maximising profit (s.1).

■ **Recognise** how political and legal factors influence business decisions (s.2), and the strategic implications of social and demographic influences (s.3).

■ **Know** the importance of technology to competitive advantage and thus to business strategy, and the effects of technology on business structure (s.4).

■ **Understand** how the PESTEL method of environmental analysis and SWOT method of strategic analysis integrate with Porter's five forces framework, and the implications for the value chain and the value network (s.5).

1 Environmental Analysis

1.1 In a Business Context

In a business context, environmental analysis can relate to:

- The physical environment (animal, vegetable, mineral, earth, water, wind and fire)—the negative/positive effect which an entity will have on that environment and the effect of the environment on the entity (e.g. global warming, weather, water levels and mineral resources).
- The business risks arise from the fact that entities operate in open and adaptive legal, political, economic, social and technological environments.

1.2 Physical Environment

- In the production and distribution of goods and services, a significant range of resources will be consumed (e.g. raw materials, power, fuel, water, labour) with resultant outputs (e.g. products, waste, packaging, pollution).
- The effect an entity has on the environment is referred to as its environmental footprint.*

*Commentary

*For an industrial setting, the quantity of depletable raw materials and non-renewable resources an organisation consumes to make its products and the quantity of wastes and emissions generated in the process determine its environmental impact. A subset of this is the carbon footprint.

1.2.1 Effect of the Entity on the Environment

- **Air pollution and quality**—airborne pollutant emissions (e.g. resulting in acid rain) and nuisance from odours.
- **Water quality**—availability of water supply, rational supply and use, pollutant emissions to water.
- **Soil protection**—soil erosion (e.g. deforestation can result in landslides), pollution and contamination, "land take" (i.e. the total area of land needed for a building or development).
- **Climate change**—emissions and concentrations of greenhouse gas ("GhG") and ozone depletion.
- **Noise**—noise emissions, noise nuisance and damage from noise.
- **Light**—light pollution affects the night sky, animal habitats and local communities.
- **Land and resource use**—depletion of non-renewable resources and irrational use of natural resources.
- **Biodiversity**—protection of endangered species (animal and plant habitats) and ecologically sensitive areas (e.g. rain forests).
- **Natural/cultural heritage**—protection and conservation of natural/cultural assets.
- **Waste management**—waste production/disposal, nuisances from waste and recycling.
- **Human safety and health**.

© DeVry/Becker Educational Development Corp. All rights reserved.

1.2.2 Effect of the Environment on the Entity

- Depletion of resources (e.g. extractive industries—coal, gas, oil, minerals, water).
- Weather (e.g. storms, tornadoes, snow, lightning strikes, landslides, flash floods).
- Geophysical activity (e.g. earthquakes, tsunamis, volcanic eruptions).
- Global warming and climate change.

1.3 Business of Business

- "The business of business is business" (Milton Friedman, 1970) implies that the sole responsibility of an entity's management is to maximise the wealth of its shareholders.
- There has always been a social contract between the entity and society (general public)— the entity will only exist at society's will. Customers will only buy the products they want—if they do not, the business will fail.
- Since Friedman's era, customer requirements in the way businesses are run and products/services produced have significantly changed.
- The ideas of social responsibility and the need for positive effects of business on the environment have firmly taken root through lobbying groups (e.g. Greenpeace), education and awareness of school and university graduates who progress into business and government, and the pervasive effect of the Internet and communications.*
- Although many businesses are very happy to show their "green" and "environmentally friendly" credentials, many laws and regulations have been implemented to protect the environment (e.g. factory emissions, car emissions, fuel consumption, noise at airports and the publication of environmental information in product specifications to help consumers make informed choices).
- Instead of businesses considering lobby groups as adversaries, many now consider the in-depth environmental experience and understanding of such groups to be vital in ensuring that the business is able to maximise the return from the environment in which it operates and the resources it uses.

*It can take 20 years to build a reputation and 20 seconds to lose it in a "CNN world". That is the power of investigative reporting and why many authoritarian governments and dictatorships (as well as similarly minded entities) loathe the Internet and social networks, as they cannot be controlled.

■ Actions commonly taken by firms in an industry to limit their environmental impact include:*

- Renewable/sustainable/recycled inputs in the production process.
- Sound quality-control procedures and training to reduce waste.
- Biodegradable materials (e.g. biodegradable plastics) for packaging.
- Renewable energy sources.
- Use of energy-efficient processes and investments in new equipment. The saving in energy costs will outweigh the cost of the investment (e.g. wing tips on aircraft to reduce fuel consumption).
- Insulation preventing heat loss.
- Cleaning, re-use and recycling of water used in a process.
- Scrubbing and cleaning techniques before effluent is released into the environment.
- Recycling and waste management programmes.
- Reducing packaging to the absolute minimum.
- Regular maintenance of equipment to ensure efficient use and to minimise potential damage caused, for example, by breakdowns and broken pipes.

*Commentary

*See www. greenpeace.org and www.wwf.org.uk for a broader view on environmental and climate-change impacts.

Example 1 Mitigating Strategies

Consider the following activities and environmental effects of a banking operation.

Required:

For each activity suggest TWO strategies to mitigate impacts.

(a) Paper usage:	**Office/copy paper; bank statements; direct mail; marketing; forms; financial paper; ATM envelopes and receipts.**
(b) Energy usage:	**Building heating and air conditioning; lighting; powering computers, servers, monitors.**
(c) Transportation:	**Employee commuter travel; business travel (air and ground); couriering (including armoured transport).**
(d) Buildings:	**Building construction; procurement of materials; carpet, furniture and office equipment (manufacturing/ distribution).**
(e) Water usage:	**Water usage and sewer usage.**

1.4   Business Risk Environment

▦ Effective corporate governance requires that organisations have in place a framework of prudent and effective controls which enable **business risk** to be assessed and managed. The responsibility for monitoring and controlling business risk rests with management.

▦ Such risks result from the way the entity is managed, its operating environment, information systems, products, production, finance, customer and supplier base, employee base, ownership, competitors, the economy, legal and regulatory regimes and the very fact that it operates in a dynamic and adaptive environment.

> **Business risk—**
> the risk that an organisation will not be able to achieve its objectives and execute its strategies.

▦ Although businesses face many risks, many writers categorise the basic business environmental factors relating to business risk into five categories:

- Political and legal
- Economic (see *Sessions 4* and *5)*
- Social
- Technological
- Competitive.

▦ Understanding and analysing the first four categories is often referred to by the collective term of a PEST analysis.*

> *Extrapolated to PESTEL by the addition of ecological/ environmental and legal factors.

2   Political and Legal Factors

2.1   Government Influence

▦ Government influence on an organisation varies considerably from country to country. In "free market" economies, governments believe in leaving businesses alone, arguing that they are better left unregulated, as the cost of regulation reduces economic success. At the other extreme, governments may own most of the organisations operating in the economy (especially where they are considered to be economically "strategic"—often used as a means of blocking foreign ownership).

▦ In addition, there are various layers of "government" (e.g. global (World Trade Organisation, European Union), national and local) each having its own set of laws and regulations which organisations have to analyse and apply.

▦ In mixed economies, the government is likely to influence companies in the following ways:

- **Laws and regulations:**
  - criminal law (e.g. relating to theft, insider dealing, bribery and corruption, competition and monopolies);
  - company law (e.g. relating to company registration, constitution, capital structure, registers, books and records, financial statements, auditors, directors' duties, resolutions, general meetings);
  - employment law (see s.2.3);
  - data protection (see s.2.4);
  - health and safety (see s.2.5);
  - consumer protection (see s.2.6); and
  - environmental protection (e.g. air/water pollution, waste disposal, dangerous substances, carbon emissions).

- **Taxation**—usually based on profits, capital gains, sales or sales-based (e.g. VAT) and payroll.
- **Economic policies**—all businesses are affected to some extent by the state of the economy. A well-managed, healthy economy is likely to help businesses prosper (e.g. low inflation, low interest rates, appropriate exchange rates, etc).
- **Government incentives**—governments often offer incentives to organisations to achieve key governmental objectives. For example, tax relief for creating jobs or investment (e.g. by overseas firms); subsidies for operating in sensitive industries or key locations (e.g. where there is high unemployment).
- **Trade policy**—the government's policy with regard to international trade may help or hinder organisations to develop export markets for their goods (e.g. member of the World Trade Organisation, customs unions, free-trade agreements, tariffs or import quotas, etc).
- **Infrastructure**—transport facilities (e.g. road, rail, air and shipping), appropriate buildings, relaxing necessary planning permission, local communities and facilities.
- **Education, training and development**—many emerging economies sell themselves to international investors on the basis of having a well-educated and trained workforce. Businesses operating in established economies will always need a well-educated and skilled workforce and depend on the government to ensure at least basic skill levels.

- In some countries, the government is actually a direct threat to business, for example misappropriating (nationalising) business assets without compensating the owners.

Example 2 Drugs

Describe FOUR ways in which a national government can directly influence a pharmaceutical company operating in that country.

2.2   Sources of Legal Authority

- **Statute law**—Acts created by national parliaments or equivalent bodies.*
- **Case law**—in some, mainly Anglo-Saxon countries, the courts may also have the authority to interpret the law or make decisions where the law is silent on certain issues. Such decisions become binding on future courts under the system of legal precedent. This leads to the development of "case law", which may become as important as statute law.
- **Delegated legislation**—parliaments may delegate the creation of detailed regulations to civil servants but maintain powers to veto such legislation. In the UK, such regulations are referred to as statutory instruments (e.g. an act is passed laying down the general principles of a new law). The specifics are then enacted over time through the issue of statutory instruments.

Commentary

*A statute is a written legal act of law. Statute law refers to primary legislation based on a country's constitution.

- **Supra-national bodies**—some forms of law also come from bodies outside of the national jurisdiction. Examples of supra-national bodies are:*
  - The European Union (EU)—the legal systems of member states of the (EU) are supplemented by various laws and regulations issued by bodies of the EU. A potential member must update its own laws to incorporate the EU supra-national laws and regulations.
  - The World Trade Organisation (WTO)—set up to promote free trade and resolve disputes between trading partners. The goal of the WTO is to help producers of goods and services, exporters and importers conduct their business. To join the WTO, a prospective member must reach agreement with every current member. This often results in prospective members being required to change business laws (e.g. stopping counterfeiting, protecting intellectual property, removing import barriers, removing protection of home industries).
- **Local governments**—regional/state governments pass regulations and may have the authority to levy taxes (e.g. the state and federal system in the US).

*Other examples include the United Nations, the International Court of Justice, the International Monetary Fund and the World Bank.

2.3 Employment Law

- The original idea behind employment law was to protect the interests of employees against "abuse" by employers, but now employers can also "benefit" from the changes made.
- The economic effect which employment legislation may have on employers (e.g. making it difficult to dismiss employees) should be balanced against the rights of the employee (e.g. fair pay for the work done, wage security, safe working conditions, no exploitation).
- Employment law typically covers the following areas:
  - Contracts of employment which set out the rights and duties of the employee and employer.
  - Basic remuneration (e.g. a legal minimum wage).
  - Working hours (whether part-time or full-time).
  - Working environment and conditions, including statutory breaks, protective clothing, medical facilities.
  - Holiday entitlement, maternity and sickness leave.
  - Termination of employment, including unfair dismissal, constructive dismissal and redundancy.
  - Equal opportunities and non-discrimination on the basis of gender, race, religion or age (see *Session 18*).
  - Trade unions (e.g. recognition by employers, employee rights not to join, trade union rights, strikes).
  - Appeals procedures and tribunals (e.g. for unfair dismissal).
- Managers should be aware of the main principles of employment law as breaches could result in legal action, fines and bad publicity.*
- Organisations should also have access to advice on employment law when necessary. In larger organisations, a Human Resources (HR) Department normally provides this function.

*Employers may settle out of court to avoid bad publicity.

2.4 Data Protection and Security

- With the development of powerful computer databases, organisations have the ability to store and access increasing volumes of data on individuals. There is concern that these individuals could be harmed (directly or economically) if the personal data is passed to, or captured by, unauthorised parties.

- Data protection concerns the potential damage and injury to individuals caused by the misuse of their personal data.

- Data security is concerned with protecting the integrity of the data so that it cannot be damaged or destroyed.

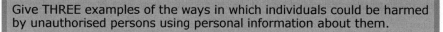

Example 3 Personal Data

Give THREE examples of the ways in which individuals could be harmed by unauthorised persons using personal information about them.

2.4.1 Data Protection Principles

- In order to minimise these risks, many countries have introduced specific data protection legislation often based on the UK's Data Protection Act (last updated in 2007).

- Personal data shall be **processed fairly and lawfully:**
  - The individual has given consent to the processing, usually by signing a form or declaration, or the processing is necessary:
    - for the performance of a contract or any legal obligation to which the individual is a party; or
    - to protect the vital interests of the individual (e.g. medical history after a serious road accident); or
    - for the administration of justice; or
    - as required for the legal purposes of the police or government; or
    - as required for the holder of the data to meet their legal requirements.

- Personal data shall be **obtained only for one or more specified and lawful purposes** and shall not be further processed in any manner incompatible with those purposes.
  - Data should not be used for any purpose other than the main reason it was collected (e.g. banks cannot pass on information about a customer to another organisation without that customer's consent).
  - The "specified and lawful purpose" should be made known to the individual.

- Personal data shall be **adequate, relevant and not excessive in relation to the purpose(s)** for which it is processed.
  - Information held should be the minimum necessary to enable the organisation to carry out its functions. Information cannot be obtained and held on the basis that it "might be useful in the future".

- **Personal data shall be accurate and, where necessary, kept up to date.***
  - If data is inaccurate, it may cause harm (e.g. if the personal information wrongly states that a person has a criminal record, they may be unable to find employment).

*How can ACCA ensure that the data it holds on you is up to date? Access MyACCA at www.acca.org.uk to find out.

■ Personal data processed for any purpose **shall not be kept for longer than is necessary** for that purpose.

- For example, when recruiting new employees, data on applicants who do not accept a job offer should be deleted or at least such data that identifies the applicant (e.g. name and address that makes the data "personal").

■ Personal data shall be **processed in accordance with the rights of data subjects** under the act.

- Individuals should be given rights to inspect the data that is held about them and to demand that any incorrect data held should be deleted.

■ Appropriate technical and organisational **measures shall be taken against unauthorised or unlawful processing** of personal data and **against accidental loss or destruction of, or damage to**, personal data.

- Physical controls to limit access to computer hardware.
- Logical controls (e.g. passwords).
- Firewalls and sentinel programs to prevent access to the data by hackers.
- Anti-virus software, encryption technology, secure backup of data.
- Fire protection systems, backup power supplies.
- Staff training.

■ Personal data shall **not be transferred to a country or territory outside the EU,** unless that country or territory ensures an adequate level of protection for the rights and freedoms of data subjects in relation to the processing of personal data.

- There are exceptions to this principle, for example:
  - where the individual has given consent to the transfer;
  - the transfer is necessary for reasons of substantial public interest.

2.4.2 Rights of Individuals

■ Individuals are entitled to be told whether an organisation holds personal data about them—the right of subject access. If so, the individual should receive:

- a description of the personal data;
- the purposes for which the data are being processed; and
- details of those to whom the data may be disclosed.

■ They can request (in writing) that an organisation:

- does not process data which might cause substantial damage or distress—if necessary a court order may be obtained to enforce the request;
- ceases (or does not start) processing data for direct-marketing purposes (e.g. mailing or electronic spamming)— if necessary a court order may be obtained to enforce the request;*
- ensures that no decision which significantly affects them is based solely on processing by automatic means (e.g. automatic credit rating).

*Commentary

*To block spamming, the source of spamming must be in the jurisdiction of the court which places the order.

■ Where an individual has suffered damage and/or distress because of the organisation's contravention of the act, damages may be claimed by the individual.

■ Individuals may apply to the court for an order requiring the organisation to rectify, block, erase or destroy any data or expression of opinion relating to them which is inaccurate.

■ The organisation also may be ordered to notify third parties to whom the data have been disclosed of the rectification, blocking, erasure or destruction.

2.4.3 Management

■ In view of the wide-ranging aspect of the data protection laws (and the potential liability should there be any breach), organisations should establish a data protection policy and appoint a particular individual with overall responsibility to ensure compliance with the relevant laws.

■ Employees should be made aware of the laws (and the consequences of breaches) through their contracts of employment, employee handbook and relevant training and updating.

2.5 Health and Safety

■ Employees are entitled to be able to carry out their work in relative safety and in conditions which are not detrimental to their health. Where their occupation exposes them to a certain level of danger (e.g. mining, chemicals, deep-sea oil drilling), they would expect their employers to provide appropriate safeguards to minimise the risk of injury.

■ Without health and safety legislation, some employers might be tempted to cut back on the expenses associated with health and safety to the detriment of the employees. The employees might not be in a strong enough bargaining position to demand that employers address these needs.

■ Initially employer (and employee) responsibilities for health and safety in the workplace were laid down in health and safety laws and regulations. With the increasing importance of corporate social responsibility, many employers consider health and safety to be a moral issue and provide a working environment which exceeds the minimum requirements of the current laws and regulations to achieve an appropriate work-life balance for their employees.

■ Risks to the health and safety of employees may come from many sources, and some are more obvious than others. Examples for a typical office environment include:
- Blocked fire exits or insufficient exits.
- Fire protection systems which do not operate correctly (or none at all).
- Poor ventilation.
- Low light in working areas, corridors and stairs.
- Sharp edges on equipment and furniture.
- Frayed electric wires, overloaded plugs, electrical equipment exposed to water.
- Trailing wires, cables and leads.
- Poorly designed seating which does not support the back.
- Top-heavy filing cabinets.

- Worn or torn carpets.
- Liquid on the floors.
- Untrained equipment operators.
- Lack of training in basic health and safety procedures.
- No first aid facilities.

2.5.1 Importance

It is crucial for organisations, their managers and the workforce to observe health and safety legislation for the following reasons:

- In many jurisdictions, health and safety is covered by legislation; thus breaches will be subject to criminal proceedings, fines and, in extreme cases, closure of the business (e.g. loss of licence to operate).

- Accidents and illness can be monetarily and reputationally costly (e.g. lost production, absence of key employees, low morale, legal fees if involved in a court case, bad publicity, difficulty in the recruitment of good employees, etc).

- Under civil law, it may be possible for employee (or visitors to an organisation) to sue for compensation if they are injured.

- Organisations have a moral obligation to protect others (including not only their workforce but customers, visitors and the local community*).

- Insurance cover is usually required by organisations. A poor health and safety record may invalidate any insurance cover, without which an organisation would not be allowed to operate.

Commentary

*If a health and safety breach affects the local environment (e.g. release of toxic fumes into the atmosphere or pollution into a river) then the organisation could be sued by the local community as well as face possible criminal proceedings.

2.5.2 Responsibilities

Employee	**Employer**
Take reasonable care of oneself and others.	Provide safe access in and out of a safe working environment.
Cooperate with anyone (including employer) in carrying out duties.	Provide safe and appropriate equipment and machinery.
Do not deliberately or carelessly operate or alter any equipment.	Arrange for the safe use, handling, storage and transport of hazardous substances.
Inform the employer of any dangerous situation.	Provide sanitation, washing facilities and fresh drinking water.
Consider the health and safety of others.	Maintain a suitable temperature.
	Provide regular information, instruction, training and supervision to all employees on health and safety procedures.
	Continually assess the risks to health and safety and to adequately investigate accidents, implementing necessary changes.

■ Management should promote health and safety practices by way of:

- a formal health and safety policy/manual;
- job descriptions;
- design of work systems;
- regular training and updating of employees;
- communication to employees (e.g. notice boards, bulletins, accident notes);
- disciplinary procedures;
- health and safety officers;
- employee counselling; and
- cascading management responsibility (e.g. awareness, attitude and actions).

■ A typical health and safety policy/manual setting out the organisation's rules, regulations and procedures should include:

- a statement of principles;
- detail of the various safety procedures (e.g. what to do in case of fire);
- good working practices for operating in a safer environment;
- instructions on how to use specific equipment;
- how to report an accident and where the accident book is kept;
- who are qualified first-aid personnel and where first-aid boxes are kept; and
- the names and duties of the official safety representative.

■ Employees should be required to confirm that they understand health and safety procedures.

2.6 Consumer Protection

■ Consumer protection laws (e.g. the UK's Sale of Goods Act) are primarily designed to ensure fair trade and competition and the free flow of truthful information in the marketplace. They give the consumer certain rights of action should they consider the product or service provided to be substandard.*

*Commentary

*Further detail on consumer protection can be found on the following websites:

■ www.direct.gov.uk/en/Governmentcitizensandrights/Consumerrights

■ www.which.co.uk/consumer-rights

Although this detail is outside of the scope of the syllabus, it does provide useful and interesting insights into the workings and form of consumer protection.

- When a product or service is purchased by a consumer, consumer protection legislation usually requires that it is:
  - of satisfactory quality—will last for the time expected and be free of any defects;
  - fit for purpose—fit for the use described and any specific use made clear to the seller/provider; and
  - as described—matches the description on the packaging or what the seller represented.
- If the goods or service do not meet the required standards, the consumer usually has the right to repair, replacement or refund:
- Consumer contracts must be:
  - Clear and unambiguous.
  - Contain no unfair terms or conditions (e.g. state that no refunds can be made).
  - Clearly state the work to be carried out, the cost, the time to be taken, the supplier's responsibilities and the consumer's responsibilities and rights.

3 Social and Demographic Influences

3.1 Concept

3.1.1 Social Structures

- The basic concept of social structures is that a society can be divided into broad strata (social class) comprising individuals who share common features (e.g. type of occupation, inherited wealth, income level, educational background).
- Some classes will have distinct advantages over other classes (e.g. access to power, educational opportunities, wealth, status and esteem).*
- The most common hierarchical social categories are "upper", "middle" and "lower" (or "working") classes.
- Other forms of class description include "old money" (inherited) and "new money" (earned through investment in business), and "blue collar" (shop-floor workers) and "white collar" (office workers and management).
- The concept of social influences also can be considered to be the values, attitudes and tastes of the population as a whole, of each individual social class or group. Examples include:
  - Sustainability, carbon footprints, recycling.
  - Work-lifestyle balances, including 24/7 lifestyles.
  - Professional careers for women with children.
  - Use of the Internet and online facilities.
  - The "me-too" and "compensation" cultures.
  - Fashions (not only just related to clothes).
  - Health and diet.
  - Political correctness.
  - Discrimination.

3.1.2 Demography

Definition

Demography—study of the human population, its structure and change.

Demographics—the selected characteristics of a population under study (and are frequently used in economic and marketing research).

■ Examples of **demographics** include:
  ● Population
  ● Location
  ● Age, gender and race
  ● Health
  ● Disabilities
  ● Disposable income
  ● Mobility
  ● Educational achievements.

■ One of the first writers to consider demographics was Thomas Malthus. Writing during the agricultural revolution in England, in 1798, he predicted that societies would always live at low subsistence levels. As agriculture incomes rose and living conditions improved, the birth rate would also rise, leaving income per person static.

■ The predictions of Malthus were proved to be incorrect by events such as the economic growth accompanying the Industrial Revolution and the advent of mechanised farming technology outweighing population increases.

3.2 Demographic Transition Theory (DTM)

■ Frank Notestein theorised, in 1945, that high birth/death rates will be replaced by lower birth/death rates as a society advances.

■ He initially identified four stages, with a fifth stage added at a later time to take into account later economic developments:

3.2.1 Stage 1—Pre-industrial Societies

■ Birth rates and death rates (particularly of young children) are both high and are approximately equal, so the population remains stable. Children start contributing to the household at a very early age and their net maintenance costs are minimal.

3.2.2 Stage 2—Early Developing Countries

■ Death rates fall due to improvements in food supply, sanitation and general health awareness and care. Birth rates do not fall, so population expands as far more children survive to become adults, thus generating more children.*

*Commentary

*For example, in sub-Saharan Africa (although death rates rise again as a result of epidemics).

3.2.3   Stage 3—Developing Countries

▨ Birth rates fall because not as many children need to be born
   to ensure adequate survival to an older age (thus supporting
   their parents); increased acceptance and use of contraception;
   increased wages; urbanisation; increased costs in raising
   children; and an increase in the status of women and the need
   for a second family wage. Population growth starts to level
   off. This group includes many countries from Central and
   South America and Central and Southeast Asia.

3.2.4   Stage 4—Fully Developed Countries

▨ During this stage, there are low birth rates and low death
   rates. The working portion of the population begins to shrink,
   meaning that the working population must support a growing,
   aged population. This stage applies to the US, Canada, most
   of Western Europe, Australia and New Zealand.*

3.2.5   Stage 5—Post-industrial Countries

▨ Recognises that some countries are in transition from
   industrial economies to post-industrial as they switch from
   manufacturing to service industries. The birth rate may fall
   significantly (i.e. not enough children are born to replace their
   parents' generation) and the population starts to fall. This is
   the case in countries such as Germany, Spain, Italy, Portugal,
   Greece and Japan.*

*Governments face
significant pension
fund and health cost
increases but with a
shrinking workforce
to fund the increased
costs.

*A declining population growth rate also may result from a sudden
economic crisis (e.g. the collapse of the former Soviet Union),
resulting in increased mortality (particularly among men), increased
emigration and a reluctance of others to immigrate into the region.

In addition, death rates may increase in Stage 5 because of health
problems (e.g. obesity, cancers and heart disease, caused by "the
way we live").

3.3   Organisational Impact

▨ Examples of the various social and demographic influences on
   organisations are discussed below. Remember that wherever
   there is an effect, there usually is an opportunity.

3.3.1   Population

▨ Population affects an organisation's supply of labour and hence
   its policies towards recruiting and managing human resources.
   It also affects the organisation's marketing, products and
   services provided.

▨ Growing populations offer a greater range of employment
   and selling opportunities. Decreasing populations offer
   greater challenges.

▨ Organisations may move their operations to areas of high
   population and may consider the use of bringing in foreign
   labour where the native population is declining.

3.3.2 Age

■ A country that primarily has a young workforce will be attractive to organisations seeking a large workforce which will be relatively cheaper, have greater flexibility and provide greater choice.

■ Where birth rates are falling, there will be skills shortages and fewer university graduates. Competition for this scarce resource will be higher, as will be the employment costs.

■ Where demographics point towards an ageing workforce, the higher cost of that workforce could be offset by individual skills, experience, customer orientation, loyalty and respect.

■ Although organisations obviously have to adapt to suit the age profile of their customers, they also must take into account the values, attitudes and tastes of those customers. Examples include:

- Older women requiring the same fashions and styles as their daughters.
- Older people being healthier and thus demanding more "exciting" holidays.
- Older people generally being wealthier and thus able to spend more on luxury goods and services.

Illustration 1 Baby Boomers

In the US, the "baby boomer" generation refers to the generation that was born in the period after the Second World War. This probably was the first demographic group which professional marketers actively targeted, because of their numbers and increasing affluence. In 2005, it was estimated that 50% of the population of the US was between the ages of 50 and 74. This "baby boomer" generation is clearly a major group in terms of the economy as a whole but could soon be replaced by younger generations with different tastes. This will affect demand for products and services.

Exhibit 1 OLD AGE DEPENDENCY

The following table taken from the *UN World Population Prospects* (2002 Rev.—Medium Variant) depicts the trends of old age dependency.

Source: *UN World Population Prospects* (2002 Rev.—Medium Variant); For EU25: Eurostat 2004 Demographic Projection (Baseline scenario); CC=BG, RO, HU, TR

3.3.3 Gender

▓ Women are rapidly increasing their participation in the workforce, especially in the professional and service occupations (accountancy, law and medicine). Many organisations are finding that female values are welcomed by their clients and customers.

▓ Many employers consider it cost effective to take the best of male and female employees and offer female employees (who start a family) child care facilities, career break schemes, homework schemes, part-time working, training and updating schemes and have them return to work, without any loss of effectiveness, when ready. The initial investment in recruiting and training female staff and the experience they obtain is not lost.

3.3.4 Health

▓ Poor health and unbalanced diet (e.g. smoking, excessive alcohol, fatty foods, lack of exercise) results in increased illnesses with the direct effect of absenteeism from work, lower productivity and increased costs.

▓ As obesity becomes ever more prevalent in many countries, health and safety procedures in organisations need to be reviewed (e.g. chairs or overhead walkways collapsing under the weight of a worker, gangways not being sufficiently wide on the shop floor).

▓ Growing markets for healthy foods with a corresponding decline in the markets for those foods considered unhealthy.

▓ Growing markets for health-related products (e.g. sports clothing and equipment).

3.3.5 Environment

▓ Companies are coming under ever-increasing pressure to develop technologies and products which are environmentally friendly or carbon neutral (e.g. cleaning agents that do not contain bleach, recyclable containers, aviation biofuels, etc).

3.4 Government Measures

▓ These include housing incentives to encourage builders to increase the number of affordable new-start housing, the release of government brownfield sites and easier planning permission. The cost of housing in the UK, even for a basic starter house, is now beyond the reach of most newly married couples. This places a severe restraint on individual mobility and the ability of organisations to attract people to their local area.

▓ Immigration laws which allow people of working age with required skills to migrate to countries with shortages. The EU allows freedom of movement between member countries.*

▓ Improvement in skills education and training for young people. Governments run skills training programmes and provide subsidies for organisations to provide necessary practical skills.

▓ Regulations to change the working environment to create a better "work-life" balance.*

*As Polish workers moved to the UK, Ukrainian workers filled the gaps in Poland and Turkish workers filled the gaps in Ukraine.

*More women may have children if they know they will be able to return to work.

- Introduction of more flexible pension schemes replacing the statutory retirement age with a more flexible approach, to encourage people to continue working beyond retirement age without losing state pension benefits.

- Health programmes to reduce the costs of treating illnesses and lower the cost to industry of sick leave.

- Pollutant tradable permits (e.g. Kyoto Protocol greenhouse gas emissions), which allow each country an agreed volume of greenhouse gases (e.g. carbon dioxide) with the aim of effectively reducing the amount of such gases emitted. A country or organisation that does not use (or need) its allocated permits can sell them to other countries that will not be able to keep below their agreed target.

- Capping levels of pollutant emissions from various industries (e.g. vehicle exhaust emissions).

4 Technological Factors

4.1 Business Strategy

- Investment in information technology (IT) and information systems (IS) is a strategic decision. A separate IT/IS strategy is therefore necessary but it must complement and fit in with the organisation's overall business strategy for the following reasons:

  - IS are adaptive and open and organisations exist in a dynamic environment.

  - Organisations must understand, as well as manage, the risks associated with implementing new technologies.

  - Executive management must gain an appreciation of the benefits, risks and constraints of IS to provide effective direction and adequate control.

  - IS are major functional areas of the organisation supporting all business operations to achieve their objectives.

  - Advances in IS outpace the ability of most organisations to keep up.

  - The information needs of managers and employees for effective decision-making are constantly changing.

  - There are very few organisations in which IS are not crucial to operations, survival and growth (e.g. operational efficiency, productivity, customer service).

  - Organisations require IS in order to provide the information to develop, monitor and update strategic and operational plans (critical to the success of the business).

  - IS require significant (and costly) investment and reinvestment. Duplication of systems and unnecessary expenditure must be avoided.

- Many examples exist of companies wasting huge amounts of money on new technology which did not really support the overall objectives of the organisation.*

*Commentary

*Business strategy should drive IS strategy. The IS strategy must not be allowed to dominate the business strategy.

4.2   Competitive Advantage

4.2.1   Business Strategy

Technology offers organisations significant opportunities for enhancing business strategy. Neumann suggested five ways in which new technology can be used to provide organisations with a competitive strategic advantage. Neumann's ideas were taken from the competitive strategies proposed by Michael Porter in the five forces model (see s.5).

1. **Cost leadership**—reduce costs below those of competitors, thus becoming a low-cost producer of products and services in an industry.

    *   The organisation focuses on cost control to find low-cost sources of supplies, establish centralised buying and stock control systems (e.g. just-in-time and continuous stock replenishment), reduce costs and time of production (e.g. computer-aided design), and establish customer management systems to reduce costs of administrating and servicing customers.

    *   By making investments in IS to improve operations, promote innovation or increase the complexity of the IS required to compete, an organisation can raise a cost barrier to existing competitors or new entrants.

Competitors may be discouraged to compete directly and potential entrants deterred.

2. **Differentiation**—making a product or a service stand out from those of a rival (e.g. perceived to be better); focus on particular market segments or niches; or reduce the potential differentiation of a competitor's product.

    *   IS are used for product differentiation by developing brand loyalty through creating unique new products and services which can be distinguished from those of competitors. For example:
        —customer online shipment tracking;
        —online ordering and support;
        —online insurance claim procedures;
        —personalised online shopping;
        —online check-in and boarding tickets for airlines.

    *   Focused differentiation develops products or services for identified market niches which can be delivered in a personalised way. For example, by analysing large volumes of data (e.g. spending of bank customers) to find patterns and rules (data mining), tailor-made services can be delivered to an individual customer or group of customers.

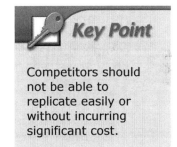

Competitors should not be able to replicate easily or without incurring significant cost.

3. **Innovation**—develop new ways of doing business; develop new products or services; identify new markets or niches; evolve the current business into a fundamentally different structure.

- Often the benefit of innovation is market leadership. For example:
  - ✔ the use of ATM technology to provide non-banking services (theatre tickets, mobile phone credit);*
  - ✔ customer access to in-house tracking systems;
  - ✔ online auction sites and bookshops;
  - ✔ short messaging service (SMS) and digital cameras incorporated into mobile phones;
  - ✔ online banking.
- Another benefit of innovation, for some organisations, has been survival (e.g. hard copy encyclopaedias evolving into online databases and search engines).

*The Automated Teller Machine (ATM) was first developed to dispense cash.

4. **Growth**—expand production and services; identify and enter new markets (location and buyers); produce new products.

- The use of IS has given many companies the capacity (production, time, resources) to expand, yet still maintain control. Central control is more effective with improved communications. Identifying and reacting to local market needs can be quicker and more effective using IS.
- The Internet has allowed many companies to reach new geographical markets and to have world-wide customers. Control of such a wide and diverse customer base is feasible with appropriate use of IS.

5. **Alliance**—forge strategic alliances through the Internet, extranet and other networks with customers, suppliers, competitors and other companies through the integration of systems, shared systems, joint ventures and mergers.

- Examples include suppliers accessing an organisation's inventory and production control system (through an extranet) to determine the need for stock deliveries; automobile manufacturers sharing online market places to allow them to place tenders for parts; non-competitive manufacturers (e.g. household goods, food and beverages) combining databases on customers to enable greater targeting of individual products; and e-travel agents allowing bookings to be made with different airlines, hotels and car hire companies all on the same website.

Illustration 2 BPR*

Business Process Reengineering (BPR) is the "fundamental rethinking and redesign of business processes to achieve dramatic improvement in critical measures of performance such as cost, quality, service and speed."

—Hammer and Champy

Rather than use technology simply to speed up bad processes, BPR aimed to replace the bad with the very good. For example:

- Shared databases, making information available to many users at the same time.
- Expert systems, allowing generalists to perform specialist tasks.
- Telecommunication networks, allowing organisations to be centralised and decentralised at the same time.
- Decision-support tools, allowing decision-making to be a part of everybody's job.
- Wireless data communication and portable computers allowing field personnel to work independent of an office.
- Automatic identification and tracking, allowing items to tell you where they are, instead of requiring to be found (e.g. radio frequency tags).
- High-performance computing, allowing on-the-fly planning, modelling and revision.

*Commentary

*Further detail on the use of IT and IS is provided in *Session 24*.

4.2.2   Relating to Society

- IS/IT is becoming more pervasive throughout society and society is becoming increasingly dependent on computer and communications technology. Examples include:
  - Internet commerce (e.g. call centres based in low-cost, highly educated countries);
  - Extensive websites for most organisations;
  - Internet shopping (e.g. Amazon, Tesco);
  - Internet banking;
  - Education and learning;
  - Entertainment (e.g. video streaming, interactive games); and
  - Teleworking/telecommuting.

4.3   Organisational Structure

- Organisational structures are covered in *Session 6*. IS has a significant effect on how organisations can be structured and managed. Specific examples include downsizing, delayering and outsourcing.

4.3.1   Downsizing

- Downsizing means reducing the number of employees on the payroll, without necessarily reducing the work or output of the organisation. It usually implies a permanent reduction, due to changes in the organisation, rather than temporary layoffs.

- It is typically accomplished through restructuring, which includes "spinning off" non-core activities (e.g. through outsourcing).

■ Examples of the role IS/IT has played in developing opportunities for downsizing:

- Fewer shop-floor workers and supervisors required in factories due to automated production techniques.
- Less support staff (e.g. typists and secretaries), as most professional staff are trained in using the programs they need (e.g. word processing, spreadsheets, databases).
- Fewer bookkeepers and accounting staff required as computerised accounting systems are used instead.
- Computerised inventory control and procurement systems (supply chain management) reduce the need for employees working in buying and warehousing.

4.3.2 Delayering

■ As the number of levels of management is reduced, the span of control increases and the scalar chain decreases. The organisational structure becomes flatter.

■ Benefits of delayering include:

✔ faster communication from top to bottom and vice versa;

✔ better morale of employees as they will enjoy more autonomy;

✔ increased responsiveness, particularly to the needs of customers, as decisions can be made more quickly;

✔ cost savings because with bureaucratic management systems, there is much overlap of roles.

■ Management information systems, decision support systems and executive support systems all help to reduce the need for middle and junior managers and so enable delayering.*

4.3.3 Outsourcing

■ Outsourcing involves subcontracting an activity to an external organisation.

■ The main purpose behind outsourcing is that non-core activities of an organisation can be performed by third parties, leaving management to focus on core activities of the business. Examples of commonly outsourced activities include:

- Cleaning
- Catering, staff canteen
- HR, payroll
- Accounting, bookkeeping
- Internal audit.

■ With IS, outsourcing can range from specific functions (e.g. maintenance of equipment, analysis, design and programming of systems, application service provider) through project management, network management and hosting of the organisation's website to the whole of the IS/IT function (hardware, software and people) being provided by a third party.

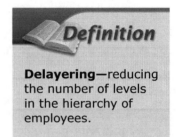

Definition

Delayering—reducing the number of levels in the hierarchy of employees.

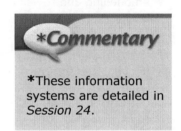

***Commentary**

*These information systems are detailed in *Session 24*.

Advantages of Outsourcing the IS/IT Function

✔ Enables the organisation and management to concentrate resources on key activities. The organisation's management effort can be focused on running a profitable and effective business rather than being distracted by events and needs of a department which is not perceived as being central to the delivery of the organisation's product.

✔ The service provided will be based on specific costs agreed in a contract (e.g. "pay as you use"). There will be greater certainty about running or development costs for the period of the contract.

✔ The organisation's planning and risk management is more assured as the service provider must deal with unforeseen changes or difficulties in maintaining the contract.

✔ Organisations for which it would not be cost effective to maintain a full or specialist IS function can obtain access to the services, specialists and support they need as and when they are required.

✔ From the service provider's view, they will specialise in providing a "start to finish" service to their clients. They will be able to benefit from costs of scale and 24/7 usage (e.g. instead of one costly system serving an in-house function, the system can be leased to many users).

Disadvantages of Outsourcing the IS/IT Function

✗ A key resource (i.e. information delivery) is passed to a separate, independent company. The provision of information is often a strategic element and thus too critical to be controlled by a third party.

✗ Key technologies, sensitive processes and core information may be placed outside of the company. Direct security over such items is not under the control of the company. Should the service provider also have contracts with the company's competitors, then there is always the risk that sensitive information may be lost to a competitor.

✗ By outsourcing the IS function, company management may lose the necessary knowledge to identify business opportunities through IS. If the service supplier only sees the provision of IS as a support function rather than a business development function, the company will be at a distinct disadvantage to its competitors.

✗ In any customer-supplier relationship there will be different objectives. The customer requires a high-quality service at a low price; the supplier wishes to meet the customer's requirements but at a higher price. The supplier also wishes to control costs and may thus reduce the actual quality of the deliverable.

✗ Outsourcing may be seen as an easy solution to a problem. If management cannot control in-house resources, however, can the external resource be managed correctly? The project must still be managed and controlled by the organisation.

✗ Poor negotiation of the original service contract often results in an organisation becoming tied into the service provider. They have failed to make the contract completely unambiguous in covering performance, productivity, accountability and escapability.

✗ Low bidding. Although a contract may be attained at a good price, this may be a deliberate policy of the service provider. Any further services which are required, or the renewing of the contract (of which the service provider is the only provider that can continue the contract) may be charged at a premium.

5 Competitive Factors

■ As part of an environmental analysis, it is crucial that organisations assess the degree and sources of competition and the effect such competition will have.*

■ Professor Michael Porter of the Harvard Business School engaged in extensive research into the competitive position and threats affecting major organisations. His theory of competitive forces, published in 1980, forced strategists to rethink their views on the nature of competition. He also proposed three generic strategies which organisations would need to consider to obtain a competitive advantage.

*Commentary

*Obviously, if an organisation does not understand who the competition is, what it is doing and how, the organisation will remain at a competitive disadvantage. The idea is to obtain a competitive advantage (taking into account, of course, that competitors should be doing the same).

5.1 Porter's Five Forces Model

■ Porter's five forces model focuses on the competitive nature of an industry and therefore attractiveness of a market. Attractiveness in this context refers to the overall industry profitability. They consist of forces which affect a company's ability to serve its customers and make a profit. A change in any of these forces normally would require a company to reassess the marketplace.

■ The five forces that influence the competitive environment in an industry are:

1. Competitive rivalry

2. Threat of new entrants

3. Bargaining power of buyers

4. Bargaining power of suppliers

5. Threat of substitutes.

5.1.1 Competitive Rivalry

■ Competitive rivalry within an industry will affect the profitability of that industry as a whole. Such rivalry puts pressure on companies to cut prices and/or improve quality and innovation to retain customers. In a highly competitive industry, companies continually fight for customers, thus lowering profits.

■ Porter suggests that rivalry is more powerful where:

● There are many firms with essentially equal market share. Where there are few firms, the rivalry is less intense.

● Industry growth is slow, such that firms compete for market share. High growth implies sufficient market share for all in that market

● Fixed costs are high resulting in firms cutting prices to marginal cost levels to maintain volume. Weaker competitors will be forced out of the market.

● There is little product differentiation and therefore little brand loyalty. Customers can switch between competitors easily.

● High strategic stakes (e.g. investment in factory or retail premises) exist so that the entity must stay in the market for as long as possible.

● There are high exit barriers (e.g. redundancy costs) requiring competitors to remain in the market until forced out.

5.1.2   Threat of New Entrants

▩ If an industry is experiencing high returns, new entrants will be attracted into the industry. A new entrant into the market will bring new capacity and greater competition, which may affect pricing structures.

▩ The number and quality of new entrants depends on the strength of the barriers to entry already established and the reaction of the current market players. Players already in the market will attempt to make it difficult for new competitors to enter and become established. This may have been through past strategies or as a reaction to the current threat. Either way, costs will be increased.

▩ Barriers to entry include:

  ● High capital requirements (e.g. investment in plant and machinery or marketing to establish a position in the market). For those players already in the market, such costs are historical.

  ● Economies of scale—high economies of scale, if already being achieved by those established in the market, will make it difficult for new entrants to be sufficiently profitable.

  ● Product differentiation—established firms should already have positive brand image and have built up customer loyalty. However, it may be because of customer dissatisfaction that a new competitor is being invited into the market by that customer.

  ● Regardless of size, experience can act as a barrier (e.g. patents, intellectual knowledge, favoured supplier status, etc).

  ● Limited availability of distribution channels, such as retail outlets or "prime sites" (as already taken by the current players), which restrict the ability of new entrants to compete effectively.

  ● Government regulations or government concessions, which may allow only one company to operate in a particular market.

  ● Established supplier and customer loyalty.

5.1.3   The Power of Buyers (Customers)

▩ Powerful buyers can exert influence on the market by, for example, demanding favourable prices or special service. Typically, customers/buyers want improved products at lower prices. Powerful buyers can force price cuts and/or quality improvements. This reduces profit for companies operating in the market.

▩ Porter suggests that buyers are most powerful when:

  ● The buyer is relatively large when compared to the supplier (e.g. takes a high proportion of the supplier's business).

  ● There are only a small number of buyers which will be more powerful than a large number of small consumers.

  ● The supplier provides an undifferentiated or standard supply, so the buyer may have alternative suppliers on hand with which to easily switch.

  ● There are few switching costs to prevent the buyer going elsewhere.

  ● The buyer sells at low margins so wishes to minimise buying costs, thus forcing down buying prices.

- The buyer is not quality or delivery-time sensitive, so can attempt to negotiate a lower price.
- The buyer has full information about the seller's cost structure and margins.
- Buyers have the opportunity for backward integration—that is they can buy the supplier, or buy a competitor of the supplier.

5.1.4   The Power of Suppliers

- Similar to the power of buyers, but where suppliers exert influence on the market. Suppliers will wish to increase prices and/or lower quality (e.g. lower costs of production).
- Suppliers are powerful when:
  - There are relatively few suppliers of the product or service, so that price can be controlled by dominant suppliers.
  - The supplier's product is an important component in the buyer's product or service.
  - The supplier provides a differentiated or unique product which is not available elsewhere, cannot be substituted and no new suppliers are due to enter the market.
  - Buyers are fragmented, so have little bargaining power.
  - Switching costs are high. The buyer is locked in to the supplier.
  - The supplier's service is required at short notice with no other source available.
  - The supplier perceives the buyer to be small or unimportant, thus charging whatever price it likes (the buyer takes it or leaves it).

5.1.5   Threat of Substitutes

- A substitute is a product or service which satisfies the same set of needs but originates in a different form or different state of technology. The threat posed by a substitute is that the market volume for an organisation's product or service might suddenly reduce as customers switch because of price differentials or a real/perceived improvement in quality.*

- Substitutes are powerful when:
  - Buyers prefer them to the original product/service.
  - There is a relatively higher profitability from the substitute.
  - Switching costs to the substitute are low.
  - The substitute is perceived to have a positive differentiation factor.
- Current market player defences against substitutes include:
  - To produce and control them.
  - To buy them out (governments may prevent this due to lack of competition).
  - To differentiate the current product to such an extent that customers perceive there is "no substitute" and thus no need to switch.

*Commentary

*Consider the options of getting from London to Paris—car/bus, rail or air. Eurostar is seen as a very viable alternative to air travel for many business people, as it runs from city centre to city centre and provides an appropriate environment for business to be conducted while on board.

- Which barriers exist?
- To what extent do they limit entry?
- Are we trying to get in or keep others out?

GREATEST WHERE
- Rivals are of similar size
- Slow growth in market
- High fixed costs
- Price wars to maintain turnover
- Lack of differentiation
- High exit barriers

BARRIERS TO ENTRY
- Economies of scale
- Other cost advantages
- Capital requirements
- Access to distribution
- Patents
- Government policy
- Reactions of existing firms

POWERS GREATEST WHERE
- Concentration of buyers
- Alternative sources of supply exist
- Cost of purchase is high proportion of total cost
- Threat of backward integration
- Low switching costs
- Buyers have low profits
- Buyer has full information

THREAT OF NEW ENTRANTS

BARGAINING POWER OF BUYERS

RIVALRY

BARGAINING POWER OF SUPPLIERS

THREAT OF SUBSTITUTES

POWERS GREATEST WHERE
- Few suppliers
- Few substitutes
- Switching costs are high
- Possibility of integrating forward
- Customers not significant
- Supplier's product differentiated

- Can we find new markets for our products?
- To what extent is there a danger?
- Can it be minimised by differentiation or low costs?

5.2 Generic Strategies

- Developed from the five forces model, Porter also proposed three strategic options (generic strategies) for organisations to achieve a sustainable competitive advantage.

5.2.1   Cost Leadership

■ This means being the lowest cost producer in the industry. This usually implies manufacturing excellence through, for example, the use of IS/IT (see s.4, previously). Being the cost leader in the industry gives a company the opportunity to:*

- set lower prices than competitors and so gain a higher share of the market; or
- set the same selling price as competitors and thus obtain greater margins.

5.2.2   Differentiation

■ This is establishing the product as being different or unique in comparison to competitors and offering a real or perceived advantage over competitors' products. This may be through design, brand image, technology, features, dealers or customer service.

■ Differentiation is likely to increase the costs of the organisation, which must be recovered through a premium pricing policy. Research has shown that a differentiation strategy is more likely to increase margins than a cost leadership strategy as differentiation creates a higher entry barrier to new products and organisations. The time frame in which differentiation can operate, however, can become shorter when IS/IT is a key differentiator (e.g. mobile phones). It is thus important that products are continually subject to innovation and/or replacement.

5.2.3   Focus or Niche

■ This strategy concentrates on a select few target markets. Often used by smaller firms (to be able to challenge the dominance of larger firms), the organisation focuses effort and resources on a narrow, defined segment of a market in the hope that it will be able to better serve the needs of that market.

■ With a focus/niche strategy an organisation could use either a cost focus (e.g. delivery at a lower cost than competitors) or a differentiation focus (by creating differentiation within the niche).

5.2.4   Risk in Selecting More Than One Strategy

■ Porter identified a particular risk in selecting more than one strategy. The organisation may become "stuck in the middle" without having achieved a competitive advantage (e.g. selecting both cost leadership and differentiation strategies but failing to achieve in both).

*In some cases, an organisation may not only be a cost leader, but also be able to set premium selling prices because of its perceived brand value and quality in the market place.

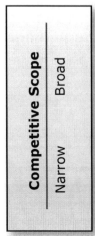

Competitive Scope		Competitive Advantage	
		Low Cost	Higher Cost
Broad		Overall Cost Leadership	Differentiation
Narrow		Cost Focus	Differentiation Focus

5.3   SWOT

▨ As discussed in section 1.4 and detailed throughout this session, the PEST (or PESTLE) analysis is a common approach to assessing a market. This was further enhanced above with Porter's five forces model, which also considers an industry and the market it operates within.

▨ As already discussed above, Porter derived a competitive advantage (generic strategies) model aimed at a particular business operating in a given market.

▨ As PEST is to five forces, so SWOT is to generic strategies.

▨ SWOT analysis is usually conducted through brainstorming or workshops. The process involves specifying the objective of the subject matter (e.g. business venture or project) and identifying the internal and external factors which are favorable and unfavorable to achieving that objective:*

> *Commentary*
>
> *Strengths/ weaknesses are paired, and look internally. Opportunities/threats look externally. Many of the paired criteria apply both ways (e.g. high level of skills is a strength; lack of skills is a weakness).

- Strengths: advantages, capabilities, competitive advantages, unique selling points ("USP"), enhancement, resources, experience, skills, financial returns, market reach, innovative, price, quality, processes, IT, philosophy, values.
- Weaknesses: disadvantages, capability gaps, uncompetitive, costs, vulnerabilities, deadlines, pressure, lack of supply chain robustness, effect on core activities, cash drain, lack of commitment or leadership.
- Opportunities: market, business and product development, import/export, competitor's vulnerabilities, setting trends, innovation, emerging markets, emerging technologies, developing USPs, global impact, niche target, partnerships, economies of scale, influences, tactics, contracts.
- Threats: politics, legislation, environment, economic, IT developments, competitors, declining market, emerging technologies, loss of partners, loss of key staff, loss of key customers/suppliers, sustaining key factors, lack of cash.

▨ In summary:
- Strengths: Develop, maintain, enhance, leverage.
- Weaknesses: Remedy, neutralise, exit.
- Opportunities: Prioritise, optimise.
- Threats: Defend, counter, neutralise.*

> *Commentary*
>
> *Remember that one man's threat is another man's opportunity in the realm of SWOT analysis.

■ Using a Boston Consulting matrix (2 × 2 grid) approach to matching SWOT outcomes can result in an action-based matrix:

	Strengths	**Weaknesses**
Opportunities	S/O	W/O
Threats	S/T	W/T

- Strengths/Opportunities—should clearly be the natural priorities and risks to take.
- Strengths/Threats—are easy to defend and counter.
- Weaknesses/Opportunities—potentially attractive options if weakness eradicated.
- Weaknesses/Threats—potentially high-risk combinations.

5.4   Porter's Value Chain

5.4.1   Introduction

■ To analyse the specific activities through which firms can create a competitive advantage, Porter developed a model of the firm as a "chain" of activities which add value to the product or service in the eyes of the customer.

■ The value chain provides a framework for analysing an organisation by breaking it down into "strategically significant" and support activities and understanding the linkages between these business activities.

■ The approach involves breaking down the organisation into five primary and four support activities. Each can then be looked at to see if they give a cost advantage or a quality advantage.

Key Point

The value chain is the chronological breakdown of all internal and external activities which lead to the supply of the product or service.

5.4.2   Primary Value Chain Activities

▨ The aim of these activities is to create value which exceeds the cost of providing the product or service, thus generating a profit margin. They are vital in developing a competitive advantage.

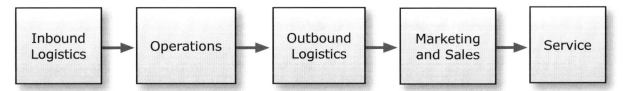

- Inbound logistics covers receiving, warehousing and inventory control of raw material inputs.
- Operations are the value-creating activities which transform the inputs (raw material and labour) into finished goods and services.
- Outbound logistics are the activities required to get the finished product to the customer including warehousing and distribution.
- Marketing and sales are those activities associated with persuading the buyers to purchase the product and enabling them to do so.
- Service activities maintain and enhance the product's value, including customer support, installation, repairs, training, spare parts, etc.

5.4.3   Support Activities

▨ The four support activities are:

1. **Firm infrastructure**—how the firm is organised, including head office, central planning, finance, legal, and quality management.

2. **Human resource management**—recruiting, training, developing, rewarding people so they contribute to competitive advantage.

3. **Procurement**—acquiring resource inputs, primarily purchasing the raw materials, equipment, subcontractors.

4. **Technological development**—R&D, process automation, use of IS/IT to support the value chain activities.

▨ Although support activities are often viewed as overheads, using the value chain can identify support activities which provide a competitive advantage (e.g. using IS/IT innovative MIS).

5.4.4 Diagram

▓ The value chain process is often diagrammatically summarised as follows:

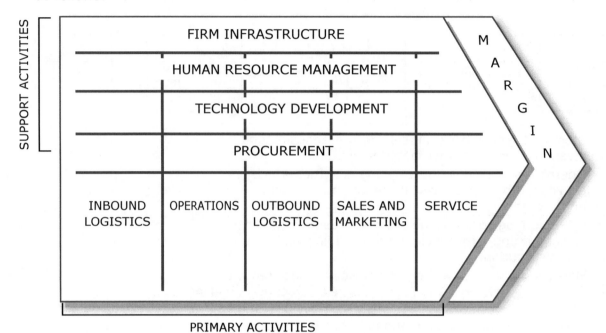

▓ Margin is the excess the customer is prepared to pay for the product (or service) over the cost to the organisation of obtaining resource inputs and adding value.

▓ The value chain deliberately takes a view of the organisation which cuts across organisational structure boundaries. For example, Porter stresses that procurement takes place throughout the organisation, not just in purchasing departments (e.g. recruitment of staff and the purchase of capital equipment).

5.4.5 Advantages

✔ The linkages between primary and support activities can be clearly understood.

✔ Can identify critical success factors.

✔ Can identify functions best outsourced (e.g. make-or-buy decisions).

✔ It provides a structure for identifying cost drivers for ABC.

✔ It can be used to analyse rivals, for comparison purposes.

Example 4 Value Chain

Suggest the content of each element of the value chain for:

(a) a food retail supermarket (e.g. Sainsbury, Tesco, Asda);

(b) a food discounter (e.g. Aldi, Lidl, Netto).

Solution

(a) Food Retail Supermarket (based on quality of product and service)

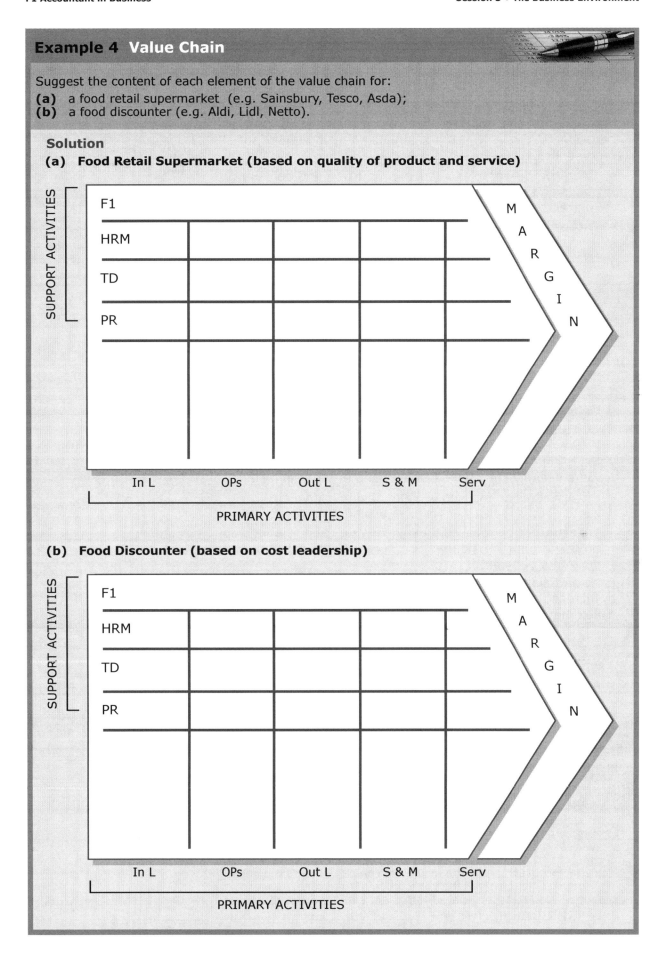

(b) Food Discounter (based on cost leadership)

5.5   Value Network

5.5.1   Meaning

■ A **value network** may be described as a web or map which describes the human and technical resources within and between organisations. The points in a value network represent participants or roles which are connected by interactions that represent tangible and intangible deliverables.

- **Tangible** deliverables support production and delivery of goods and services, revenue and funding. They include contracts and payments.
- **Intangible** deliverables take the form of knowledge or information exchanges and benefits that build up relationships.*

*Commentary

Intangibles are not paid for directly and rarely contractual but are critical to supporting the business.

Illustration 3   Deliverables

Anna pays for a revision course to help her prepare for her last ACCA examination, P7 *Advanced Audit and Assurance*. The tuition she receives is a tangible deliverable.

On passing the exam she becomes an affiliate member of ACCA and is invited to attend an ACCA graduation ceremony. Such recognition is an intangible deliverable; it is discretionary, not contractual.

■ Value is created through the relationships between roles. A value network may be external facing or internal facing:

- **External** facing focuses on relationships between customers, suppliers, investors, business partners, etc.
- **Internal** facing focuses on key activities and relationships across internal boundaries (e.g. order fulfilment and customer support).

■ Each participant in a value network relies on other participants to increase value (e.g. order fulfilment depends on production which may depend on product development).

5.5.2   Typical Components

■ A typical value network consists of:*

- A group of customers;
- A service that all customers use that enables them to interact;
- An organisation that provides the service;
- Contracts that enable access to the service.

*Commentary

Technology providers are obvious examples of value networks.

Illustration 4   Travel Insurance

A company provides travel insurance. Customers enter into a contract by paying an insurance premium for an insurance product to cover costs associated with unexpected events associated with international travel. Customers can go about their activities with reduced exposure to risk. The insurance company meets the costs covered under the terms of the contract (e.g. medical expenses, accommodation costs associated with flight cancellations, rental car hire, ransom payments in case of kidnapping).

Summary

- Environmental analysis involves determining the effect of the organisation on the physical environment or assessing business risks arising from the political, economic, social, technological and legal environments.

- Government influences an organisation through laws and regulations, taxation, economic policies, incentives, trade policy, infrastructure and education.

- Sources of legal authority include statute law, case law, legislation, supra-national bodies or local governments.

- Employers are expected to present employees with a safe working environment and mitigate potential harm to employees working in dangerous environments. Employees are expected to use care in carrying out their employment.

- Consumers are protected against false and misleading statements by producers and, if the goods don't meet required standards, consumers have a right to repair, replacement or refund.

- Social structures and demography can have extensive effects on the organisation's operating environment.

- Technological factors affect a firm's competitive advantage helping a firm to become the low-cost producer or differentiate the product in a way customers find appealing.

- Firms may match size to opportunities through:

  - Downsizing—reducing the number of employees.

  - Delayering—reducing the number of management levels and grades of staff.

  - Outsourcing—subcontracting an activity to an external organisation.

- Michael Porter identified five forces which help assess the attractiveness of a market: rivalry, threat of new entrants, buyer bargaining power, seller bargaining power and the threat of substitutes.

- A SWOT analysis matches an organisation's strengths and weaknesses with opportunities and threats to develop a matrix to help assess business strategies.

- Firms can use value chain analysis to determine ways to decrease costs and improve how they meet a client's value proposition.

- A value network extends the supply chain outwards from the organisation. It emphasises relationships and interactions in business activities.

Session 3 Quiz
Estimated time: 30 minutes

1. Define "business risk". (1.4)

2. List the ways in which governments can influence organisations. (2.1)

3. What is a "supra-national body"? (2.2)

4. Explain the difference between data protection and data security. (2.4)

5. Explain why personal data held by any organisation should be "adequate, relevant and not excessive". (2.4.1)

6. Describe FOUR responsibilities of the employer under typical health and safety legislation. (2.5)

7. List SIX examples of demographics. (3.1.2)

8. Describe FOUR measures governments can take to counter negative demographic trends. (3.4)

9. List the FIVE Neumann IS strategies. (4.2.1)

10. Explain the difference between "downsizing" and "delayering". (4.3)

11. Describe THREE advantages of outsourcing IS. (4.3.3)

12. State the circumstances in which competitive rivalry will be more powerful. (5.1.1)

13. Briefly describe Porter's THREE strategic generic strategies. (5.2)

14. List the support activities of Porter's value chain. (5.4.3)

Study Question Bank
Estimated time: 45 minutes

Priority		Estimated Time	Completed
MCQ3	The Business Environment	45 minutes	

3-**36**

EXAMPLE SOLUTIONS

Solution 1—Mitigating Strategies

Paper usage:

- Company-wide paper recycling policy.
- Increased recycled content of purchased paper.
- Only non-chemical bleached paper used.
- Printing and copying defaults set to duplex (two-sided) printing.
- Increased use of electronic reports, customer statements (which are not then printed off by recipients), Internet banking, etc.
- Shareholder information (annual reports, voting) communicated through the Internet (e-mails, websites).

Energy usage:

- Energy-efficiency enhancements in buildings (e.g. insulation).
- Green building techniques in new construction, materials and renovations.
- Lighting retrofits (e.g. replacing standard light bulbs with low-energy bulbs, adding reflectors and removing unnecessary lamps).
- Energy-efficient equipment purchasing policies (e.g. requesting environmental footprint information as part of tenders).
- Automatic shut-off of computers and other electrical equipment.
- Movement sensors to turn on lights when required.
- Green power purchasing. A green power resource (e.g. solar power) produces electricity with zero anthropogenic (i.e. human-caused) emissions.

Transportation:

- Employee car-pooling (sharing).
- Alternative fuel fleet vehicle purchasing.
- Increased use of video/teleconference meetings in lieu of travel.
- Employee working from home strategies.

Buildings:

- High-performance/green building.
- Materials recycling programs, including electronic waste.
- Procurement policies favouring energy-efficient and/or environmentally preferable equipment.

Water usage:

- Installation of water-saving fixtures (e.g. movement-activated water taps and flushers).
- Employee conservation awareness programs (would apply to all aspects, not just water usage).

Solution 2—Drugs

- Final certification of new drugs as being fit for use by humans. Without such certification the drug could not be issued.

- Provision of research and development monies (or through tax incentives) directly to the companies.

- Direct purchase of drugs for use in governmental health services (and therefore a significant customer of the company).

- Funding of universities to complement research programmes and deliver degree programmes which will be of direct benefit to the firms.

- Copyright protection and licensing laws preventing the exact copying, manufacture and selling of drugs.*

*Commentary

*The cost of providing patented drugs to patients in the UK's National Health Service is now considered to be virtually out of control. The government has been encouraging doctors and hospitals to purchase generic variations of drugs, which are much cheaper than the branded versions. The drug companies complain that they need higher prices to recoup their R&D costs and that consumers have faith in branded drugs. Consumers (and the government) maintain that the drug companies are taking a monopolistic opportunity on the patents issued for the drugs and thus charge higher prices because of lack of competition. The government threatened to make it easier for generic drugs to be sold in the UK and for branded drugs to be imported from overseas suppliers and not through the manufacturers (as this is usually cheaper). The drug companies have threatened to move their R&D and manufacturing base out of the UK as they consider the "investment climate" no longer favourable.

Solution 3—Personal Data

- Identity theft involving use of stolen credit card details, bank account details, passport details to obtain goods and services, to carry out sensitive transactions or to completely assume the identity of the individual.

- The information (e.g. political belief or religion) could be used to discriminate against individuals, blackmail them or embarrass them.

- The individual may be targeted for a specific purpose (e.g. SPAM, virus attack on a personal computer system, details changed on personal websites).

Solution 4—Value Chain

(a) Food Retail Supermarket

In the supermarket sector, retail stores (e.g. Sainsbury, Tesco) compete with the discounters in terms of service and choice.

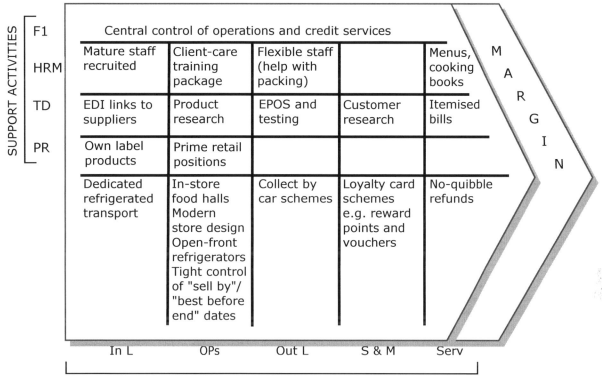

	In L	OPs	Out L	S & M	Serv
F1	Central control of operations and credit services				
HRM	Mature staff recruited	Client-care training package	Flexible staff (help with packing)		Menus, cooking books
TD	EDI links to suppliers	Product research	EPOS and testing	Customer research	Itemised bills
PR	Own label products	Prime retail positions			
	Dedicated refrigerated transport	In-store food halls Modern store design Open-front refrigerators Tight control of "sell by"/ "best before end" dates	Collect by car schemes	Loyalty card schemes e.g. reward points and vouchers	No-quibble refunds

SUPPORT ACTIVITIES

MARGIN

PRIMARY ACTIVITIES

(b) Food Discounter

In the supermarket sector, food discounters (e.g. Lidl) compete against retail food stores by using a cost leadership approach.

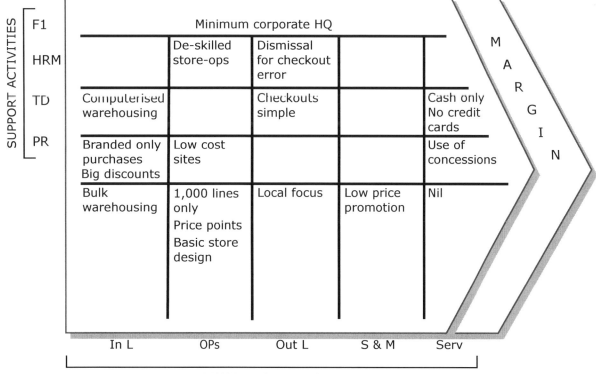

	In L	OPs	Out L	S & M	Serv
F1	Minimum corporate HQ				
HRM		De-skilled store-ops	Dismissal for checkout error		
TD	Computerised warehousing		Checkouts simple		Cash only No credit cards
PR	Branded only purchases Big discounts	Low cost sites			Use of concessions
	Bulk warehousing	1,000 lines only Price points Basic store design	Local focus	Low price promotion	Nil

SUPPORT ACTIVITIES

MARGIN

PRIMARY ACTIVITIES

The Macro-Economic Environment

FOCUS

This session covers the following content from the *ACCA Study Guide.*

A. The Business Organisation, Its Stakeholders and the External Environment

4. Macro-economic factors

a) Define macro-economic policy and explain its objectives.

b) Explain the main determinants of the level of business activity in the economy and how variations in the level of business activity affect individuals, households and businesses.

c) Explain the impact of economic issues on the individual, the household and the business:

    i)   inflation

    ii)   unemployment

    iii) stagnation

    iv) international payments disequilibrium.

d) Describe the main types of economic policy that may be implemented by government and supra-national bodies to maximise economic welfare.

e) Recognise the impact of fiscal and monetary policy measures on the individual, the household and businesses.

Session 4 Guidance

■ **Cover** this session in great detail as it is **highly examinable**. In this session you are presented with an overview of macro-economic policy concentrating on fiscal and monetary policy effects on demand and supply, investment, etc.

■ **Know** macro-economic objectives (s.1).

■ **Understand** measurement of business activity, including the business trade cycle, and factors which influence it (s.2).

(continued on next page)

VISUAL OVERVIEW

Objective: To understand the economic environment within which organisations operate and how governments may manipulate that environment.

```
                    ┌─────────────────────────┐
                    │    MACRO-ECONOMIC        │
                    │        POLICY            │
                    ├─────────────────────────┤
                    │  • Considerations        │
                    │  • Objectives            │
                    └─────────────────────────┘
```

MACRO-ECONOMIC POLICY
- Considerations
- Objectives

LEVEL OF BUSINESS ACTIVITY
- Gross Domestic Product
- Other Factors
- Business Trade Cycle

ECONOMIC ISSUES
- Price Inflation
- Unemployment
- Stagnation
- International Payments Disequilibrium

ECONOMIC POLICIES
- Monetary Policy
- Fiscal Policy
- Supply-Side Approach
- Taxation

ECONOMIC WELFARE
- Reasons for Intervention
- Competition Policy
- Privatisation

Session 4 Guidance

■ **Recognise** the relationships among unemployment, inflation and stagnation (s.3).

■ **Differentiate** monetary policy from fiscal policy, understand the strengths and weaknesses of each and how other schools, such as supply-side economics, integrate such policy tools (s.4).

■ **Understand** how governments use intervention and privatisation to maximise economic welfare (s.5).

1 Macro-Economic Policy

1.1 Considerations

■ **Macro-economics** focuses on the workings of the economy as a whole as opposed to micro-economics (see *Session 5*), which concentrates on the economic behaviour of individual consumers, firms and industries.

■ Policymakers focus on macro-economic analysis to determine how policy options and control mechanisms can help them achieve economic objectives. The policy can be designed to affect a national economy, a regional economy (e.g. the EU) or the global economy.

1.2 Macro-Economic Objectives

■ In many industrial economies, the government attempts to achieve the following objectives:*

● Full employment (or as low a level of unemployment as possible given that there will always be a core minimum of unemployable people).

● Real economic growth (as opposed to growth through inflation) leading to improved living standards and an acceptable distribution of wealth.

● Price stability and limited inflation.

● An acceptable balance between exports and imports to manage the balance of payments. Many economists believe that a continual external deficit (i.e. imports exceed exports) is unsustainable and is likely to lead to an exchange-rate crisis and currency devaluation.

Macro-economics—the study of economy-wide elements (e.g. employment, national income, rate of growth, gross domestic product, inflation and price levels).

*These may conflict (e.g. economic growth can lead to excess demand for resources and increasing prices).

2 Level of Business Activity

2.1 Gross Domestic Product

■ The level of activity for individual businesses will depend on specific PEST issues, including the overall activity in the economy—which can be predicted and explained by reference to mainly economic factors. This is primarily measured using the aggregate demand of a nation, its **gross domestic product (GDP)**.

■ GDP also may be considered as the sum of value added at every stage of production (the intermediate stages) of all final goods and services. This is the total output of goods and services during a year, measured at purchase price.

■ Gross domestic product is measured as follows:

Consumption + Investment + Government spending + Exports − Imports.

■ In considering all of the GDP elements, the general relationship is that if a factor reduces the ability to consume resources, the GDP reduces, thus the level of business activity also will have reduced.

Gross domestic product (GDP)—The total market value of all final goods and services produced in a country in a given period (usually a calendar year).

2.1.1   Consumption

■ Consumption is based on private (household) consumption (as it is the final end result of the consumption of resources by organisations) and is determined by three factors:

- the level of households' incomes;
- the rate of tax; and
- the portion of a household's income which is saved.

Exam Advice

Pay attention to the factors that determine the levels of consumption, investment, government spending and the balance of payments.

■ The higher the level of overall taxation in an economy, the lower will be the amount of net income for spending on consumption. Taxation includes both direct taxes (e.g. income tax) and indirect taxes (e.g. sales tax, VAT).

■ The portion of a household's income saved is likely to be proportional to the amount of income. People on lower incomes will find it harder to regularly save compared to people on higher incomes.

■ The portion of income saved also depends on interest rates. When interest rates are high there is an incentive for consumers to save more and so spend less.

■ John Maynard Keynes referred to the "paradox of thrift"—the fact that the more people save, the less will be the aggregate amount of consumption in the economy. As a result, business activity will decline and incomes will fall.

2.1.2   Investment

■ Investment is generally defined as the investment by organisations and households in capital items (e.g. buildings, construction works, plant and equipment and for households, new houses). GDP investment does not include the purchase of financial instruments as these would be classified as savings.

■ The level of investment in the economy will be determined by:

- The level of confidence in the economy. If businesses are confident that demand for their products will be high in the future, they will invest more.
- Interest rates. If interest rates are low, the cost of borrowing to finance investment will be low, so businesses may invest more.
- The availability of bank loans and other sources of finance. In the aftermath of the credit crunch, for example, many banks became risk averse and were lending less to businesses. As a result, businesses found it difficult to find the necessary finances to fund their investments.

2.1.3   Government Spending

■ Covers all government consumption (on final goods and services) and government investment (e.g. infrastructure). In most economies, government spending forms a large portion of the country's GDP and will be determined by the government's fiscal policy.

2.1.4   Balance of Payments

■ The balance of payments represents the value of exports minus the value of imports. If a country exports more than it imports, the balance of payments is favourable and thus increases net domestic production and thereby the GDP.

■ As GDP measures what is produced domestically, exports are included and imports are deducted.

■ As the world economy becomes more globalised, countries specialise in goods where they have a competitive advantage. This means they must import goods they do not manufacture, thus potentially creating a negative balance of payments.

■ Exchange rates influence the level of imports and exports in the short run. If a country's currency is strong, this means that imported goods become relatively cheap, so more goods will be imported and the balance of trade is likely to weaken.

■ In the longer run, the balance of payments depends on the abilities and resources that the country has at its disposal. Countries that have large oil or mineral reserves, for example, are likely to have a higher level of exports, which may lead to a balance of payments surplus.

2.2   Other Factors

2.2.1   Confidence

■ Greater consumer confidence will result in higher demand for products and services and thus greater business activity in the economy. When consumers believe that a recession is imminent (and their jobs are under threat) they will curtail their expenditure and only consider essential expenditures.

■ Low interest rates and rising house prices add to consumer confidence (i.e. borrowing money for consumption or capital investment is relatively cheap).

■ Higher business confidence generates greater capital investment, R&D, innovation and new products to sell.

2.2.2   Capital

■ Organisations need to raise new capital to invest in projects. This may be by way of internal funds, share capital or loans. As discussed previously, however, a lack of capital reduces the level of business activity in the economy.

■ An additional complication is that if an organisation seeks to raise additional capital, but shareholders do not provide the required level, the organisation will not be able to achieve its objectives and its business activity will not increase.

2.2.3   Exchange Rates

■ A weakening currency will make imports more expensive, thus decreasing the business activity of those organisations which rely on imported resources. Conversely, exporters will potentially find a greater demand for their goods as they will now be relatively cheaper in overseas markets.

2.3 Business Trade Cycle

2.3.1 Economic Activity

▦ The business trade cycle is a classic example of economies showing fluctuations in economic activity over a period of years, but with an underlying upward trend.

▦ The phases of the trade cycle are recession, depression, recovery and boom. Government policies often are devised to try to prevent, slow down or minimise "boom-bust" cycles (particularly crossing over into depression), but in a global economy events often are outside the control of national governments.

▦ The "classic" business trade cycle is explained below. But after the Great Depression of the 1930s and the recessions of the 1970s, 1980s and 1990s (data seem to show that there is a global recession about once every 10 years), governments thought they had learned from their mistakes.

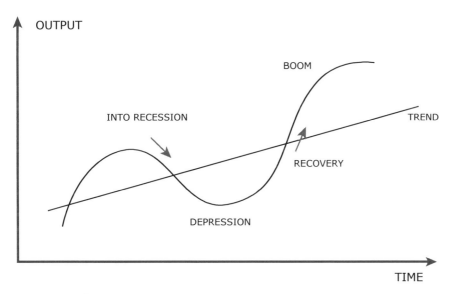

2.3.2 Recession

▦ A recession is more commonly known as a decline in a country's GDP for two or more consecutive quarters.

▦ Keynes believed that recessions are caused by a lack of demand in the economy. This could be due to a fall in consumption or government spending, for example. Governments can therefore stimulate demand by increased government spending.

▦ "Supply-side" economists disagree with Keynes' analysis, claiming that increased demand in the economy does not always lead to higher GDP. There may not be sufficient productive capacity in the economy to meet the extra demand, in which case prices will rise without a corresponding increase in GDP.

Recession—a period between an economic "peak" and a "trough". It is a significant, widespread decline in economic activity lasting more than a few months, normally visible in real GDP, real income, employment, industrial production and wholesale-retail sales.

—*National Bureau of Economic Research (NBER)*

2.3.3   Heading Into Recession

■ Specific events (very often a domino effect which gathers momentum and cannot be stopped) take place which result in a decline in consumer demand. Returns on investment will decline, with some projects being cut or put on hold. Orders will decline, inventory levels will increase, production and prices will fall and some business will face closure.

■ Layoffs and redundancies increase with the resultant decline in household income and an attempt to increase savings, leading to further reductions in demand.

■ If government measures (e.g. lowering interest rates, tax rates, injecting money into the economy to try to stimulate demand) fail to reverse the decline, business and consumer confidence will remain low and the economy may head into a depression (a recession which is deep and widespread throughout the economy over a long period).

2.3.4   Depression

■ Depression is a severe economic downturn which usually lasts several years. Annual GDP declines 5% to 15%.

■ The main driving factor is a loss of consumer confidence. Consumers do not buy, but try to survive on basic goods and services and save what they can.

2.3.5   Recovery

■ As and when consumer confidence returns, businesses will begin to re-tool, re-stock and employ more people. As more confidence returns, this effect multiplies leading to rising production, sales, profit levels, employment, investment in new capital equipment, products and hence GDP.

■ The recovery could be triggered by a series of "good news" events, or as in the case of the Great Depression of the 1930s, creating war and the need to prepare for war.

■ As recovery continues, the output level will rise above the general trend line, entering into the boom phase.

2.3.6   Boom

■ Capacity and labour become fully utilised. This will lead to increasing costs as competition for limited resources intensifies or demand is met through importing. Increasing the sales price may also result from trying to control demand.

■ Households will have higher incomes due to higher salaries, a higher share of profits and higher dividends.

■ As the demand level peaks, the expansion reaches an unsustainable level and a correction occurs in the economy (e.g. stock market values begin to fall). This may be a short-term consolidation as the economy "catches its breath", or it could trigger the start of a decline into recession.*

 *Commentary

It is not uncommon to consider a fall in the value of the stock market one of the triggers of a decline into recession, although some commentators believe that it is a symptom of recession rather than a cause.

3 Economic Issues

3.1 Price Inflation

▦ The maintenance of a low level of price inflation may be one of the government's key economic objectives.

3.1.1 Measurement

▦ A consumer price index (CPI) is a common way of measuring price inflation. A CPI attempts to measure changes over time in the monetary cost of a statistically weighted representative "basket" of goods and services. It is used as a benchmark across a broad range of government and consumer activities (e.g. wage negotiations, pension payments, benefit payments, etc).*

*Commentary

*In the UK, a retail prices index (RPI), which is the CPI plus housing costs (as a significant proportion of the UK population owns houses), is used as the benchmark for wage negotiations, pension payments, benefit payments, etc. The RPI is used by the UK government as its inflation target rate, as this is the measure adopted by the EU.

▦ Alternative measures of inflation exist to describe price increases of specific items. For example, the producer price index (PPI) measures two sets of inflation for manufacturing industry—the input price index (IPI = cost of raw materials and direct overheads) and the output price index (OPI = sales prices at the factory gate). Rises in the IPI would indicate increases in the OPI. Rises at the "factory gate" would normally indicate a future rise in the CPI.

Example 1 Types of Price Inflation

Explain the difference between demand-pull inflation and cost-push inflation.

Definition

Price inflation—the rate of increase of the general level of prices being a sustained increase in the aggregate or general price level in an economy.

Money will not buy as much today as it could yesterday.

3.1.2 General Consequences of Inflation

The general economic consequences of high inflation include the following:

- An increase in the prices of goods and services and a subsequent negative effect on the standard of living and health (e.g. being able to purchase healthy food, obtain medical treatment) especially for those on low or fixed incomes.

- The redistribution of income from those in a weak bargaining position (e.g. students, pensioners and others on fixed incomes) to those with economic power (a strong bargaining position) who are able to maintain the real value of their income.

- A disincentive to save as the purchasing power of investments may be reduced with interest rates unable to compensate for inflation (e.g. buy today or else it will cost much more tomorrow).

- An increase in bartering as money no longer maintains its role as a medium of exchange and store of value (especially in hyper-inflation).

- A fall in the exchange rate with countries where there is lower inflation, thus increasing the cost of imported goods, particularly for food and energy.

- The potential of a wage-price spiral as workers seek a higher-than-current-inflation pay raise in the expectation that inflation will rise over the next 12 months. This is a form of self-prophecy in that higher wage costs will be passed to consumers through higher factory gate prices.

3.1.3 Consequences on Organisations

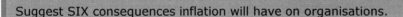

Example 2 Impact of Inflation

Suggest SIX consequences inflation will have on organisations.

3.2 Unemployment

Definition

- Unemployment may be measured in absolute terms (the number of people without a job) or as a percentage of the "working population". Alternative measures are the percentage of the population employed and the number of job vacancies. Decreasing unemployment, increasing employment and increasing vacancies are indicators of an improving economy.

- In the UK, people in employment, unemployed and economically inactive (e.g. students, pensioners, disabled) statistically make up the total household population aged 16 and over.

- "Hidden unemployment" is where unemployed people are not included in the statistics because they are not registered as unemployed and receiving benefits.

- Workers also may seek employment at occupations generally under their skill level ("underemployment").

Unemployment—the amount of joblessness in the economy. A person is generally unemployed if they are willing and able to work, but cannot find employment.

Unemployment rate—the unemployed as a percentage of those in the labour force (available for work or working).

3.2.1 Categories of Unemployment*

- **Real wage unemployment**—labour supply is greater than demand, but is not acceptable to employers as real wages remain high (e.g. under trade union resistance or a high minimum wage requirement).

- **Frictional unemployment**—occurs where job seekers are not aware of available jobs as the result of imperfect communication in the market about job opportunities. Friction is also caused by the difficulty of matching the right worker with the right job. This often will occur when employees move between jobs, careers or locations.

- **Seasonal**—certain industries have different demands for labour in the seasons (e.g. farming, tourism, sports, fair-weather building).

- **Structural**—arises because there is no demand for available workers with particular skills due to structural changes in an industry (e.g. closure of coal mines, steel mills, technology replacing manual procedures).

- **Cyclical**—when the unemployment rate moves in the opposite direction to the GDP rate. During a recovery and boom period, GDP would be increasing and unemployment decreasing. In a recession and depression, GDP would be declining and unemployment would be increasing.

> *Seasonal and frictional employment would be relatively short term, with structural and cyclical unemployment relatively long term.

3.2.2 Consequences of Unemployment

✗ Adverse social effects, sometimes referred to as "social blight". Individuals may rely on state unemployment benefits, take on debt or be forced into criminal activities in order to survive.

✗ A greater division in society, as the rich will (in theory) always have sufficient money to maintain their lifestyles, or at least avoid a noticeable decline. The poor will, without the monetary buffer, become poorer.

✗ Higher governmental costs through increased social and benefit payments.

✗ Loss of potential for maintaining or increasing national output and income. If people are not working they are unproductive.

✗ Loss of work skills and experience. The longer the period of unemployment, the greater the potential for a permanent loss of skills.

3.2.3 Direct Government Policies to Reduce Unemployment

- Establishing job creation schemes at the national or local government level.

- Granting assistance to employers (e.g. to create new jobs, to retrain older or long-term unemployed in new (employable) skills, establish apprenticeship schemes for school leavers).

- Encouraging labour mobility between regions.

- Offering incentives to "new technology" and overseas (e.g. car manufacturers) employers to establish production in areas of high unemployment.

3.3 Stagnation

"Stagnation" should not be confused with the term "stagflation", which is a condition of slow economic growth and relatively high unemployment accompanied by a rise in prices (inflation).

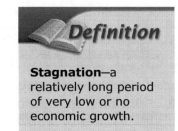

Stagnation—a relatively long period of very low or no economic growth.

- Economic growth of less than 2% to 3% is considered to be stagnation by some commentators.

- Although the economy is not actually in decline, slow or sluggish growth means that the economy is unable to reduce existing unemployment levels.

- Stagnation may lead to weak demand for goods and services, which hits the profits of companies adversely, leading to possible recession.

- Some commentators believe that periods of stagnation occur at both ends of the economic cycle (boom and recession).

- When investment declines, stagnation could set in.

3.4 International Payments Disequilibrium

- International payments disequilibrium occurs when a country's balance of payments is negative.

- The balance of payments is a record of a country's transactions with the rest of the world. It shows the net receipts from various aspects of trade and consists of the current and financial accounts.*

*A separate capital account shows the effect of the capital elements in the current and financial accounts.

- The current account is the record of payments (trade) in goods and services (the value of a country's exports less its imports—balance of trade) and is split into a number of sub-balances of payments (trade).

  - Balance of payments (trade) in goods. Sometimes referred to as "visibles".
  - Balance of payments (trade) in services (e.g. tourism, insurance). Sometimes referred to as "invisibles".
  - Net income flows (e.g. wages and investment income).
  - Net current transfers (e.g. government aid).

- The financial account is a measure of the net payments to and from other countries for investment purposes. This is a record of all transactions for financial investment.

  - Investment abroad (e.g. a UK firm buying a factory in Japan would be a debit item).
  - Investment from abroad (e.g. a Japanese firm establishing a manufacturing plant in the UK would be a credit item).
  - Net financial flows—mainly short-term monetary flows to take advantage of exchange-rate changes and interest rates (e.g. high interest rates cause money to stay or flow in; low interest rates cause money to flow out).
  - Reserves.

- The capital account is a summary of capital transfers in the balance of payments accounts, showing credits, debits and balances and including estimates of debt forgiveness and capital transfers (in the UK's case to/from EU institutions).

Exhibit 1   BALANCE OF PAYMENTS*

An extract from the website of the UK Office of National Statistics (www.statistics.gov.uk) states that:

The Balance of Payments is one of the United Kingdom's key economic statistics. It measures the economic transactions between United Kingdom residents and the rest of the world. It also draws a series of balances between inward and outward transactions, provides an overall net flow of transactions between UK residents and the rest of the world and reports how that flow is funded.

Economic transactions include:

- exports and imports of goods such as oil, agricultural products, other raw materials, machinery and transport equipment, computers, white goods and clothing;
- exports and imports of services such as international transport, travel, financial and business services;
- income flows such as dividends and interest earned by non-residents on investments in the UK and by UK residents investing abroad;
- financial flows, such as investment in shares, debt securities and loans; and
- transfers, which are offsetting entries to any one-sided transactions listed above, such as foreign aid and funds brought by migrants to the UK.

- A current account deficit implies that a country is importing more goods and services than it is exporting. This deficit has to be financed or offset, usually by borrowing from abroad, by encouraging foreign investment or by using reserves (not a good long-term idea).

- If a country operates a payments deficit, classical economic theory suggests that the exchange rate would automatically bring it into equilibrium again. Disequilibrium would lead to a fall in the country's exchange rate as demand for its currency fell below the supply. This would make imports more expensive, which would lead to a fall in the balance of payments deficit.

- Alternative direct action can be taken to make exporting easier and importing more difficult. For example:
  - influencing exchange rates to make exports cheaper or imports more expensive;
  - imposing tariffs and quotas on imports;
  - encouraging a reduction in aggregate demand in the domestic economy.

- A current account surplus may be considered a good thing for a country, but countries it trades with will have current account deficits and the consequential negative effects. Thus, countries running current account deficits will likely place pressure on the surplus country to reduce that surplus.

- A surplus implies more exports than imports. Deliberately undervaluing a domestic currency will make exports relatively cheap. This will increase employment. Low wage rates assist in making exports cheaper than those of competitors, as will government subsidies.

- Additional direct action (to maintain the surplus) includes making consumer imports expensive (e.g. tariffs, quotas) to encourage buying of domestic goods rather than foreign imported goods, and encouraging savings and investment (especially of foreign assets overseas).

■ However, running a long-term surplus can store up significant problems for the future (e.g. inflation, trading partner reactions, exchange rate appreciation).

4 Economic Policies

The primary types of policies designed to influence the economy can be described as either monetary policy or fiscal policy.

4.1 Monetary Policy

■ Methods to control the money supply include:

Definition

- Interest rates—an increase will increase the cost of borrowing and thus reduce the amount of money in the economy. Conversely, a decrease in rates can increase the demand for loans and thus increase the money in the economy.

- Open market operations—the central bank can sell government bonds and securities to remove money from the economy. By redeeming or buying back government securities, funds would be released into the market. The sale of government securities can also lead to a reduction in bank deposits which further reduces the money supply, as the banks' ability to lend is reduced. This is often referred to as a "multiplier effect".

Monetary policy— government or central bank actions designed to achieve economic objectives using monetary instruments. These actions may either directly control the supply of money in circulation (the money supply) or attempt to reduce the demand for money through its price (interest rates).

- Reserve asset requirements—banks are required to hold a minimum level of cash. Increasing the reserve requirement will decrease their ability to lend and thereby reduce the money supply.

- Special deposits required by the central bank reduce the banks' ability to lend and thereby reduce the money supply.

- Direct control by the central bank setting specific limits on the amount which banks may lend.

■ Difficulties with using a monetary policy include:

- there is often a significant time lag between the implementation of a policy and its effects;

- the ineffectiveness of credit controls in the modern international economy (can easily be circumvented through the fairly free international movement of funds);

- the relationship between interest rates, level of investment and consumer expenditure is not easily predictable;

- potentially undesirable side effects of increasing interest rates (e.g. strengthening currency exchange rates, making exports more expensive and imports cheaper); and

- less investment, leading to reduced industrial capacity and increased unemployment.

4.2 Fiscal Policy

Key elements of **fiscal policy** are:

Definition

■ government expenditures (e.g. education, health service, police, armed services, public buildings); and

■ government revenues raised through taxation and borrowing.

Fiscal policy—action by the government to achieve economic objectives through taxation, public spending and budget deficit or surplus.

4.2.1 The Budget

▨ In order to decide the level of expenditure, revenue raised through taxation and the amount of borrowing required, governments usually set an annual budget.

▨ Budgets can be in surplus (more revenue is raised than expenditure) or in deficit (more expenditure than revenues raised), in which case the government must borrow money to fund the shortfall—often referred to as the public sector "net cash requirement" or "borrowing requirement").

▨ Governments thus can use public expenditure and taxation (the budget) to regulate the level of demand in the economy. Those who view fiscal policy as crucial in the control of macro-economic activity are known as Keynesians (after John Maynard Keynes, who first advocated the use of these ideas and away from monetarism).

4.2.2 Using Fiscal Tools

▨ If the economy is in recession fiscal policy can be used to reflate the economy through the following actions:

- increase government spending to directly increase the level of demand in the economy (e.g. through public building programmes to increase the demand for goods and services, thus increasing employment (reducing unemployment) and boosting aggregate demand); and/or
- reduce taxation to boost both consumption and investment.

▨ However, problems can occur due to the following:

- government spending is an intervention into the free market and can easily lead to the misallocation of resources (e.g. support for inefficient industries);
- unemployment may be caused by a structural problem (e.g. workers in the wrong industry with the wrong skills, such that an increase in money will increase demand which cannot be met, thus increasing imports and inflation);
- there is often a significant time lag between the authorisation of additional spending, its actual occurrence and impact— thus the initial increase in spending may be over- or underestimated, with a consequential negative effect;
- tax cuts are not efficient at boosting domestic demand (as in times of recession, some of the extra disposable income made available will be saved and some of the extra monies spent will inevitably be on imports);
- a large budget deficit is likely to occur, which will lead to a large Public Sector Net Cash Requirement (PSNCR) and increased borrowing;
- the rate of inflation is likely to rise, as demand may increase for resources in limited supply and for which the prices will therefore tend to increase.

▨ If there is too much demand in the economy (it is overheating and inflation is increasing, as "too much money is chasing too few goods"), then fiscal policy can be used to depress demand or deflate the economy through the following actions:

- reduce government spending to decrease directly the level of demand in the economy; and/or
- increase taxation to reduce consumption and to assist with the redistribution of wealth.

■ However, problems can arise due to the following:

- it is not possible to cut government spending dramatically as some goods and services provided by government are unsatisfactorily provided for by the private sector;
- increasing taxation discourages enterprise.*

■ Although fiscal and monetary policies are interdependent, governments will use both to achieve their monetary and budgetary targets.

■ Which policies dominate depends on the economic theory preferred by the government of the day (e.g. in the UK there was a Keynesian approach to the management of the economy from the 1930s to the 1970s). However, this was believed to have contributed to the boom-bust economic cycles which were experienced. Hence recent governments have followed a more monetarist approach.

Commentary

*Pure Keynesians favour adjusting the level of government spending in preference to adjusting tax rates, as they believe it has a quicker and greater effect on the level of demand in the economy.

4.3   Supply-Side Approach

■ Supply-side policies focus on creating the right conditions in which private enterprise can flourish and thereby raise the capacity of the economy to provide the output demanded. The private sector, being driven by the profit motive, is deemed to be more efficient than the public sector at providing the output required.

■ Supply-side policies include:

- low tax rates to encourage private enterprise;
- the promotion of a stable, low-inflation economy with minimal government intervention;
- limited government spending;
- a balanced fiscal budget;
- deregulation of industries;
- a reduction in the rights of employees and the power of their trade unions;
- an increase in the training and education of the workforce;
- an increase in the provision of the infrastructure required by business (e.g. business parks); and
- a reduction in planning legislation.

■ Supporters of supply-side policies believe that, if business is to flourish, the economy must be in a stable condition and therefore fiscal policy should be in equilibrium. Thus, government spending should not exceed government receipts from taxation. Additionally, if the private sector is to be encouraged, tax rates should be kept to a minimum and government expenditure also should be kept to a minimum.

■ In order to provide the stable, low-inflation economy in which business can flourish, a monetary policy is used to control inflation.

■ Problems with using supply-side policies include the following:

- there is a time delay before the policies have any impact;
- the private sector will not provide all the goods and services required by society—for example, health provision.

4.4   Taxation

▨ Taxation is used to:

- raise revenues for the government (as part of its fiscal policy);
- raise barriers to activities considered undesirable (e.g. smoking, alcohol);
- price products at their social costs. For example, smoking (to discourage smoking and raise additional funding for the health costs created by smokers) and driving (fuel tax and car tax to discourage drivers from driving high-polluting vehicles and to use public transport, which is a "greener" process). Such money, however, often is used by governments for other reasons not related to the tax base (e.g. not in health services or improvement to public transport);
- tax profit "windfalls" of enterprises (e.g. oil company profits because of the price of oil being driven by supply, demand and speculative factors rather than production cost factors);
- redistribute income and wealth (e.g. higher rates on higher incomes, capital gains and inheritance); and
- protect industries from foreign competition and "dumping" (e.g. import taxes make the goods more expensive, so domestic goods appear price attractive).

▨ When setting the budget, a government must decide from what sources taxation can be raised and the form of that taxation (e.g. proportional, progressive, direct or indirect).

- Proportional taxation is based on a fixed proportion of the item base being taxed (e.g. a flat wages tax of 20%, sales tax at 15%).

- Progressive taxation increases as the wage band increases (e.g. wages tax of 10%, 15%, 20%, 15% and 40% at set wage bands). So the more an individual earns, the higher the effective tax rate will become.

- Direct taxes are paid directly to the government (e.g. wages tax, corporation tax, capital gains tax, death duties). They can be proportional or progressive and are usually unavoidable.*

- Indirect taxes (e.g. VAT) are not paid directly by the end user, but are collected by the government through an intermediary (e.g. the supplier). They usually are set at a fixed rate (e.g. 20% of the cost) but may be of a fixed amount (e.g. $100 per unit, regardless of the cost).

- Indirect taxes also are considered to be regressive in nature because they affect poorer or fixed-income individuals more than they do richer, higher-earning people (e.g. VAT on life essentials which will be purchased by everybody will be of a higher proportion of a poor person's income than of a rich person's).

*Remember Benjamin Franklin's words, "in this world nothing is certain but death and taxes."

5 Economic Welfare

Definition

Economic welfare—the level of prosperity and quality of living standards in an economy. It depends on many factors including levels of income (GDP per capita), the cost of living, the levels of pollution and congestion and security of income and jobs.

5.1 Reasons for Intervention

Monetary policy and fiscal policy influence the level of welfare through their effects on GDP, inflation and employment. Governments may also intervene in the economy for the following reasons:

▨ Where monopolies, mergers or restrictive practices operate against the public interest.

▨ Where there is a natural monopoly and competition is wasteful.

▨ Where the industry is of key national importance.

▨ Where the free market creates social injustice.

▨ Where companies fail to take account of the effects of their actions which are felt outside of the company; these are known as externalities (e.g. pollution that a company may cause).

▨ Where the free market fails to provide sufficient public or merit goods (e.g. healthcare or education).

▨ Where the free market is unable to provide the amount of capital required (e.g. when a large infrastructure project, such as the construction of a new tunnel or bridge, is being undertaken).

5.2 Competition Policy

▨ Governments develop competition policies in order to increase the efficiency of the economy by stimulating competition.

▨ The key components of competition policy in the UK have been:

● Monopolies and mergers legislation to prevent the development of monopolies which would have the power to act against the public interest.

● Restrictive practices legislation to eliminate practices such as setting retail prices by manufacturers.

● Deregulation in certain industries to remove regulations which restrict competition in the industry (e.g. deregulation of the UK stock market in 1986, causing dealing costs to reduce and therefore the volume of trade to increase greatly).

● The creation of internal markets in certain areas of the public sector (e.g. UK hospitals and schools must compete for limited government resources based on the services they provide and the results they obtain).

5.3   Privatisation

- A large number of state-owned firms have been sold to the private sector either by sale to the general public, direct sale to another company or management buyout. Examples in the UK include telecoms, gas, electricity, water and nuclear energy.

5.3.1   Arguments For and Against Privatisation

Arguments in Favour of Privatisation

✔ An increase in competition where a state monopoly is split into a number of operating companies prior to sale or where the monopoly position is removed.

✔ A short-term boost to government revenues which will reduce the PSNCR.

✔ A widening of share ownership, thereby increasing individuals' stakes in the economy as a whole.

✔ A reduction in the future PSNCR (as borrowings by the newly privatised industries are no longer public borrowings).

Arguments Against Privatisation

✗ Many privatisations just replace state monopolies with private sector monopolies, which require public regulation to ensure that their monopoly position is not abused.

✗ Breaking up large businesses into smaller companies results in the loss of economies of scale.

✗ The quality of service may deteriorate, especially to the small, less significant customer.

✗ Profit becomes a motive rather than social care (e.g. water, gas or electricity may be cut off for those customers who fail to pay their bills).

5.3.2   Official Aid

- Governments also intervene in the economy through official aid schemes. These aid schemes include the use of cash grants, consultancy advice and tax incentives to encourage investment in high technology or investment in areas of particularly high unemployment.*

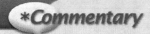

*Commentary

*The EU, as a supra-national body, plays a significant role in the economies of its national members through direct grant aid and loans, effectively redistributing wealth from the richer countries to the poorer ones.

Summary

- Macro-economic objectives include full employment, real economic growth, price stability and an acceptable trade balance.

- The welfare of people in a country will usually be measured by or related to the real per capita GDP for that country. GDP is the total market value of all final goods and services produced in a country in a given period. (Per capita means per unit of population or per person.)

- Confidence in a country's economy can play a huge role in whether it expands or declines over time.

- A recession occurs when economic activity declines; this is commonly defined as two consecutive quarters of negative GDP growth. An economic cycle includes recession, trough, recovery, boom.

- The CPI measures changes in the price level of a market-weighted basket of goods. Increases in CPI are known as price inflation.

- Unemployment will typically be measured as the number of unemployed or as a rate of unemployed against those in the labour force.

- Disequilibrium in the balance of payments can result in price inflation if the country runs a surplus versus its partners, and in unemployment if it runs a deficit.

- Tight fiscal policy attempts to slow the economy by increasing taxes and reducing expenditures.

- Tight monetary policy attempts to slow the economy by decreasing the supply of money or increasing interest rates.

- Both fiscal and monetary policy tools may not work well due to lags in establishing and implementing both types of policies.

- Supply-side policies focus on creating the right conditions in which private enterprise can flourish and thereby raise the capacity of the economy to provide the output demanded.

Session 4 Quiz
Estimated time: 15 minutes

1. Describe the objectives of macro-economic policies. (1.2)

2. Define "gross domestic product". (2.1)

3. Briefly describe the concept of a business trade cycle. (2.3)

4. Suggest FOUR consequences of inflation upon organisations. (3.1.2)

5. Describe the difference between seasonal and cyclical unemployment. (3.2.1)

6. List THREE fiscal tools used by governments to manage the economy. (4.2.2)

7. Describe how taxation can be used in the fiscal policy of governments. (4.4)

Study Question Bank
Estimated time: 40 minutes

Priority		Estimated Time	Completed
MCQ4	The Macro-Economic Environment	40 minutes	

EXAMPLE SOLUTIONS

Solution 1—Types of Price Inflation

Demand-Pull Inflation

- This arises from the excess of aggregate demand over the productive capacity of the economy. This usually will happen when an economy is healthy and consumer demand exceeds the economy's ability to supply.

- When consumer demand cannot be satisfied, the selling prices of products in the short term will increase in order to balance the demand.

- Organisations will attempt to meet the demand by increased output, thus requiring an increase in the factors of production (raw materials, labour, energy) resulting in an increase in input costs (which will feed through to higher output prices, thus inflation).

Cost-Push Inflation

- This arises when higher input costs to the production process result in higher output prices. The costs of factors of production rise regardless of whether demand exceeds supply, as in demand-pull inflation.

- Import cost-push inflation occurs because the cost of imports increases, regardless of whether they are in short supply. This may be because of political reasons (e.g. the rise in the cost of oil in the 1970s) or through a weakening currency making imports more expensive.

Solution 2—Impact of Inflation

- Higher input prices which will need to be passed through to the output price in order to avoid decreased profitability on a like-for-like basis.
- Reduced entrepreneurial activity (i.e. capital investment) as it is harder to estimate the likely returns from a new venture, thus increasing uncertainty.
- Higher cost of capital (e.g. borrowing interest rates) and returns expected by other investors (e.g. shareholders and debenture holders).
- International competitiveness suffers where domestic prices rise faster than those of foreign competitors.
- Higher interest rates (as part of government policy to reduce the increases in money supply believed to cause inflation) reduce the number of profitable investment opportunities and therefore the level of investment.
- In periods of rapid inflation the need to search for the best price currently available for the purchases required and the need to be constantly updating selling prices adds significant costs to industry.
- Inaccurate costing and management information. Income and expenditure is measured at historic cost. Yet if raw materials costing $100 are replaced at a cost of $120, what is the true cost of sales and the true profit? Current Purchasing Power (CPP) and Current Cost Accounting (CCA) have attempted to eliminate the distortions caused by high inflation and ensure the maintenance of capital.
- In addition, capital assets measured in historic terms do not reflect their fair value. Key ratios (e.g. return on capital employed) are distorted and do not provide management with an accurate picture.

The Micro-Economic Environment

FOCUS

This session covers the following content from the *ACCA Study Guide.*

A. The Business Organisation, Its Stakeholders and the External Environment

5. Micro-economic factors

a) Define the concept of demand and supply for goods and services. ☐

b) Explain elasticity of demand and the impact of substitute and complementary goods. ☐

c) Explain the economic behaviour of costs in the short and long term. ☐

d) Define perfect competition, oligopoly, monopolistic competition and monopoly. ☐

Session 5 Guidance

■ **Note** that this is a relatively short session on micro-economics.

■ **Understand** the difference between macro- and micro-economics.

■ **Know** the difference between supply and demand and the quantity demanded or supplied (s.2.1 and s.2.2), as well as the effect of substitute and complementary goods on elasticity of demand (s.2.3).

(continued on next page)

VISUAL OVERVIEW

Objective: To understand the micro-economic factors relating to supply and demand.

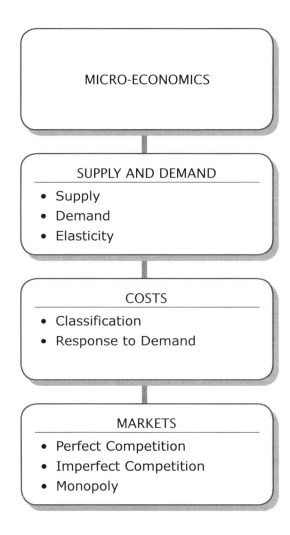

■ **Recognise** the different costs a business might encounter (s.3) and how costs respond to changes in demand in ways which might cause a business to alter its resource mix.

■ **Understand** the definitions for perfect competition, oligopoly, monopolistic competition and monopoly (s.4).

1 Micro-Economics

- Micro-economics is the study of how individuals and firms make economic decisions; how the interaction of buyers and sellers determines prices; and how prices determine the production, distribution and use of goods and services.
- It analyses the market behaviour of individual consumers and entities in an attempt to understand the decision-making process of those consumers (households) and entities.
- It focuses on patterns of supply and demand and the determination of price and output in individual markets.

2 Supply and Demand

2.1 Supply

- **Supply** describes the total amount of specific services or goods available to consumers. It represents how much the market can offer.
- It can relate to the amount of goods/services available at a specific price or the amount available across a range of prices, usually shown by way of a graph.
- The **quantity supplied** refers to the amount of a certain good which producers are willing to supply when receiving a certain price.
- The correlation between price and quantity of a good or service supplied to the market is known as the **supply relationship**.
- All else being equal, the supply provided by producers will rise if the price rises because all existing firms will be able to receive greater profits as they increase production and new firms will be able to profitably produce the good or service at the higher price. This direct relationship between price and quantity supplied is known as the **law of supply**.

2.2 Demand

- **Demand** describes consumers' cumulative willingness and ability to pay a price for specific services or goods.
- It refers to how much (quantity) of a product or service is desired by buyers. The **quantity demanded** is the amount of a product people are willing and able to buy at a certain price.
- The correlation between price and quantity of a good or service demanded by the market is known as the **demand relationship**.
- The quantity demanded of a good decreases as the price increases. This inverse relationship between price and the quantity demanded is known as the **law of demand.**
- In practice, a firm may not precisely know the demand curve for a product. However, the level of demand will still influence pricing. If demand is high, a firm would be able to charge a higher price for a product or service.

2.2.1   Influences on Demand

▣ **Income**—demand for most goods rises when consumers' incomes rise. The demand for inferior goods (e.g. cheap meat), however, might fall as incomes rise.

▣ **Price of substitute goods**—if substitutes are available for a much lower price, consumers may buy substitutes instead.

▣ **Price of complementary goods**—complementary goods are goods bought together, for example, petrol and cars. Car manufacturers have noticed a fall in demand for large 4 × 4 vehicles because of the increasing price of petrol.

▣ **Consumer tastes and fashion**—for example, in Western Europe, there is a trend towards buying organically grown vegetables, so demand for these products is high.

▣ **Advertising**—spending on advertising can increase demand for a product.

2.2.2   Demand Curve

▣ As demand is the total quantity of a product or service which the buyers in a market would wish to buy in a given period and depends on the price charged by suppliers, then for most goods, demand for the goods rises as the price falls.

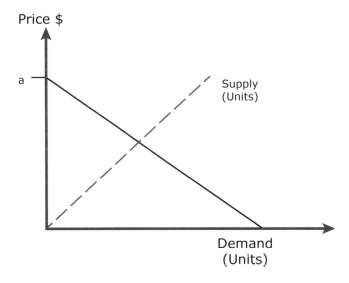

2.2.3   Equation for the Demand Curve

▣ A simplistic demand curve can be expressed as a straight line. $P = a + bQ$, where:

● P is the price which would achieve a given demand, Q;

● a is the price at which quantity demanded would be zero;

● b is the gradient (slope) of the demand curve. It shows how much the price must change to achieve a given increase in demand.*

$$b = \frac{\text{change in price}}{\text{change in quantity}}$$

*b is normally negative due to the inverse relationship between quantity demanded and price; that is, demand rises as price falls.

▣ Similarly, a supply curve (simplistically shown as a straight line) also can be drawn showing the relationship between the unit price and the unit quantity produced.

- The model of supply and demand predicts that for given supply and demand curves, price and quantity will stabilise at the price which makes quantity supplied equal to quantity demanded (a point of equilibrium).
- Supplying more than the equilibrium quantity means excess production expense; supplying less means lost revenue.
- If new demand and/or supply equations evolve, then a new equilibrium will be reached. For example:
  - If demand were to increase, then both the equilibrium price and quantity would increase (and vice versa).
  - If supply were to increase, the equilibrium price would decrease with the equilibrium quantity increasing (and vice versa).

2.3 Elasticity of Demand

2.3.1 Meaning

- **Price elasticity of demand** (PED) is the sensitivity of demand of a product/service (Q) to a change in price (P) of that product/service.*
- The more sensitive demand is (i.e. the more it changes) to a price change, the more elastic it is said to be.
- PED is the degree of sensitivity of demand for a good to changes in the price of that good.

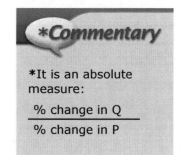

Commentary

*It is an absolute measure:

$$\frac{\% \text{ change in Q}}{\% \text{ change in P}}$$

2.3.2 Calculation

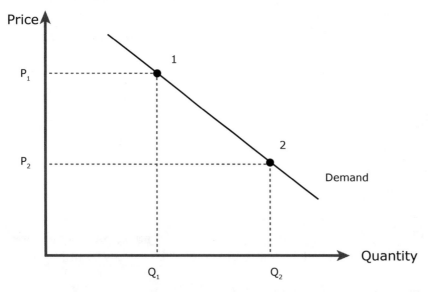

- PED at point 1 $= \dfrac{(Q_2 - Q_1) \div Q_1}{(P_2 - P_1) \div P_1}$

  - If PED is between 0 and 1 (i.e. the percentage change in demand is smaller than the percentage change in price), then demand is inelastic.
  - If PED = 1 (i.e. the percentage change in demand is exactly the same as the percentage change in price), then demand is said to be unitary elastic.
  - If PED > 1, then demand is elastic.

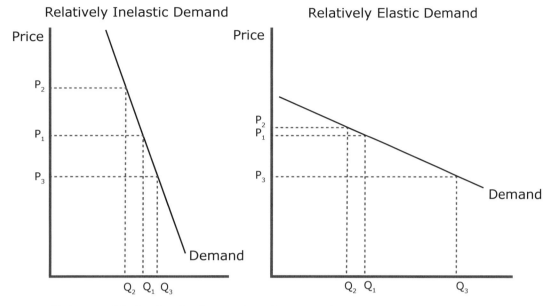

- If demand is inelastic then price rises can increase revenue as the expenditure is essential (e.g. necessity goods).
- If demand is highly elastic then increasing the price may lead to reduced revenue, especially if cheaper substitutes are available.
- When the price falls, expect to see an expansion of demand and when the price rises, expect to see a contraction of demand (the law of demand). Thus, PED is usually negative although the negative sign is often ignored.

2.3.3 Determinants of Price Elasticity of Demand

- Availability of substitute goods—the better the substitutes for a product, the higher PED will be. If the price increases, the demand will likely switch into an acceptable but cheaper substitute.

- Time—the longer the measurement period, the more price elastic is the demand for the product. This is referred to as the *second law of demand*.

- Where there are complementary products (e.g. computer hardware and software), the pricing strategy used for one of the products will affect demand for both products.*

2.3.4 Types of Goods

- **Normal goods** have a positive elasticity of demand. As consumers' incomes rise, more is demanded at each price level.

- **Necessities** that need to be purchased regardless of price will have an elasticity of demand of between 0 and +1 (i.e. relatively inelastic).

- **Luxuries** will have an elasticity of demand > +1 (i.e. the demand rises more than proportionate to a change in income).

- **Inferior goods** will have a negative elasticity of demand (i.e. demand falls as income rises).

*One product may be sold at a lower price to attract demand for the other (which is set at a normal or higher price).

3 Costs

3.1 Cost Classification

■ Organisations typically use fixed and variable resources when making products:

- Variable resources (e.g. labour) can be quickly changed;
- Fixed resources (e.g. plant and equipment) cannot be changed quickly.

3.2 Response to Changes in Demand

■ Demand for a firm's products usually changes over time. These changes consist of short-term cyclical movements within a longer-term trend.

■ To maximise profits, firms adjust production levels in response to demand (which can be changed by price movements).

■ Ideally, as production levels are adjusted in response to demand changes, the **resource mix** should also be adjusted to maintain economic efficiency.

■ It may be difficult, however, to make the ideal resource mix adjustment due to the mix of long-term and short-term cost factors. For example:

- If the change in demand is expected to be short-term, then short-term adjustments (e.g. labour) should be made. However, where demand increases, only so much new labour can be employed before costly additional capital investment will be required.
- Where the change is expected to be long-term, changes will need to be made to the fixed resources (e.g. investment in technology). This will need to be matched with changes to variable resources to optimise the economic efficiency over the course of the expected demand cycle.
- The risk with long-term fixed costs will be the possible reversal of the expected demand. The entity would then be left with expensive, inefficient long-term resources.

Definition

Resource mix—the quantities of various resources used as inputs to the production process.

4 Markets

4.1 Perfect Competition

- ◾ Characterised by:
  - ● Many sellers.
  - ● Many buyers.
  - ● Identical/homogeneous products.
  - ● No barriers to entry and perfect mobility of resources.
  - ● Perfect knowledge or complete information.
  - ● The selling price is set by the market—it is the market clearing price (i.e. the price at which the quantity supplied is the quantity demanded).
  - ● Individual firms are "price takers"—they must accept the market price.
  - ● The price is the firm's marginal revenue (MR) for all units sold and, thus, its average revenue (AR).
  - ● Firms do not have any decision to make regarding price, only output.

Commentary

There are no brand names or trademarks and consumers cannot distinguish which firm produced the product or service.

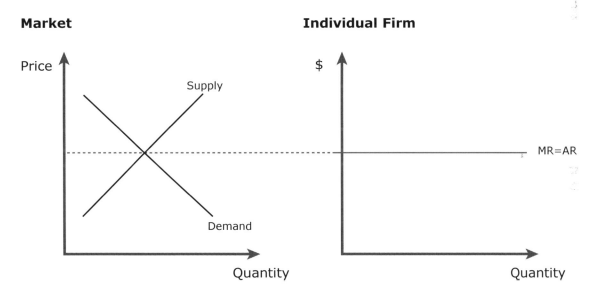

4.2 Imperfect Markets

- ◾ In an imperfect market, information is slow to be disseminated and the matching of buyers and sellers is not immediate. Generally speaking, an imperfect market is any market that does not adhere rigidly to perfect information flow and provide instantly available buyers and sellers (as described above).*

Commentary

*Imperfect markets include monopoly and oligopoly, with one or a few sellers controlling the market price. As most markets are highly unlikely to be perfect, most could be considered imperfect to some degree or another. Perfect markets could therefore be considered as a theoretical concept, with imperfect markets (to one degree or another) as reality.

4.2.1 Oligopoly

▓ An oligopoly is a market shared by relatively few producers or sellers. Each firm is therefore relatively large (e.g. in the car manufacturing industries). Oligopolies dominate their industry but may not account for all of it.*

- Products are almost identical but are usually differentiated (e.g. by brand names).
- Barriers to entry exist (e.g. reputations of established firms with significant advertising budgets can prevent new entrants).

▓ A characteristic of the market is the degree of high degree of inter-dependence between the decisions of the firms. A firm must take into account the likely response of competitors to changes in price, output and non-price competition.

- Firms can co-operate to charge higher prices and share profits.
- Firms can compete to pursue their own interest. Profits decline with a price cut as competitors may match them, leading to a fall in price but little increase in demand.

▓ Non-price competition is important in oligopolistic markets. It includes:

- advertising and marketing strategies to increase demand and develop brand loyalty;
- higher service level (e.g. guaranteed delivery, 24-hour customer support, etc);
- discounts on product upgrades.

*Commentary

"Duopoly" describes a market that is dominated by two industry "giants" (e.g. Airbus/Boeing, Coca-Cola/Pepsi, Procter & Gamble/Unilever).

4.2.2 Monopolistic Competition

▓ A large number of firms produce or sell similar products or services.

▓ Minimal barriers of entry.

▓ Products must be differentiated. Differentiation may be created by style, location or quality. It may be a real physical difference of perceived. Support services (e.g. extended warranties) also differentiate products.

▓ Producers have some control over price—they are "price makers" rather than "price takers". This is because differentiation means that the producer is a monopolist for the product that it produces.

▓ Many close substitutes limit the opportunity to set higher prices in the long run. Higher-than-average profits are only possible before competitors take effective counter measures.

Example 1 Market Type

Identify which of the following markets are examples of oligopoly:

(a) banking

(b) bottled beer

(c) breakfast cereals

(d) digital cameras

(e) film industry

(f) international airlines

(g) petroleum

(h) pharmaceuticals

(i) retail gas supply

(j) sports footwear

(k) telecommunications

(l) tobacco

4.3   Monopoly

■ A monopolist is a sole producer in an industry.

■ Barriers to entry are designed to block potential competitors from entering the market.

 ● Barriers therefore attempt to protect the monopolist's "supernormal" profits but there also must be no available substitute products.

 ● Barriers to entry include any aspect of a firm's cost structure which gives it a competitive advantage over potential entrants; protection of intellectual property rights owned by the monopoly which prevents other firms from producing the product or service; or government grants of a monopoly (as in electricity distribution).

■ A monopolist faces a downward sloping demand curve because the firm *is* the industry.

■ Assuming that the monopolist is a profit maximising firm, equilibrium output is where MR = MC, giving output Q_1 sold at price P_1 in the diagram below.

■ Where $P_1 > AC_1$ supernormal (abnormal) profits are made by the monopolist.

■ In competitive markets, this level of profit acts as a signal for new firms to enter the industry. But a monopolist is usually able to prevent this by using barriers to entry.

> ***Commentary**
>
> A monopoly is not necessarily large but must be the only supplier.

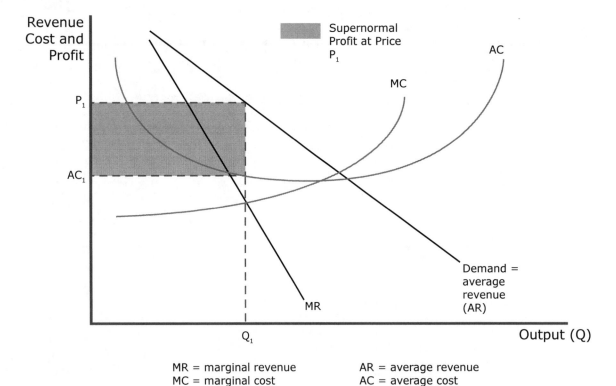

MR = marginal revenue   AR = average revenue
MC = marginal cost   AC = average cost

Summary

- *Supply* describes the total amount of specific services or goods available to consumers. It represents how much the market can offer.

- The *quantity supplied* refers to the amount of a certain good producers are willing to supply when receiving a certain price.

- The direct relationship between price and quantity supplied is known as the *law of supply*.

- *Demand* describes consumers' cumulative willingness and ability to pay a price for specific services or goods.

- The *quantity demanded* is the amount of a product people are willing and able to buy at a certain price.

- This inverse relationship between price and the quantity demanded is known as the *law of demand*.

- *Price elasticity of demand* relates to the sensitivity of demand of a product/service (Q) to a change in price (P) of that product/service.

- PED at point 1 $= \dfrac{(Q_2 - Q_1) \div Q_1}{(P_2 - P_1) \div P_1}$

  - If PED is between 0 and 1, demand is inelastic.
  - If PED = 1, demand is said to be unitary elastic.
  - If PED > 1, then demand is elastic.

- Fixed costs (plant and equipment) cannot be changed quickly; variable costs (labour) can be changed quickly. Over time, firms may vary their mix of fixed and variable resources used as inputs to accommodate changes in the underlying relative costs of the resources.

- Perfect markets have many buyers and many sellers, homogeneous products, no barriers to entry and perfect information.

- Imperfect markets comprise oligopolies and monopolistic competition.

- An oligopoly has a few large producers or sellers of an almost identical product.

- Monopolistic competition exists where a large number of firms produce or sell differentiated products.

- A monopoly effectively has only one supplier who controls the market and is a price maker.

Session 5 Quiz
Estimated time: 10 minutes

1. Describe the concept of micro-economics. (1)
2. Explain the difference between supply and demand and their relationship. (2.1, 2.2)
3. Differentiate between supply and quantity supplied. (2.1)
4. Explain the difference between perfect and monopolistic markets. (4.1, 4.3)
5. Describe the relationship between marginal cost and price for a firm in a perfectly competitive market. (4.1)

Study Question Bank
Estimated time: 15 minutes

Priority		Estimated Time	Completed
MCQ5	The Micro-Economic Environment	15 minutes	

EXAMPLE SOLUTIONS

Solution 1—Market Type

At a global level bottled beer, digital cameras, the film industry and international airlines are examples of monopolistic competition. However, at a national level these may be examples of oligopoly or even close to a monopoly (e.g. if a country is served only by its own national airline or has only one brewery). Public utilities (e.g. gas) may be oligopolies but can be monopolies (e.g. single, government-owned supplier). The other examples may all be considered oligopolies as the markets are dominated by a few giants. (Consider, for example, what names you can add to the list Kellogg's, Nestlé, Quaker Oats, for breakfast cereals.)

Organisational Structure

FOCUS

This session covers the following content from the *ACCA Study Guide.*

B. Business Organisation Structure, Functions and Governance

1. The formal and informal business organisation

a) Explain the informal organisation and its relationship with the formal organisation. ☐

b) Describe the impact of the informal organisation on the business. ☐

2. Business organisation structure and design

a) Describe Mintzberg's components of the organisation and explain the different ways in which formal organisations may be structured: ☐

   i) Entrepreneurial

   ii) Functional

   iii) Matrix

   iv) Divisional (geographical, by product, or by customer type)

   v) Boundaryless (virtual, hollow or modular).

b) Explain basic organisational structure concepts: ☐

   i) separation of ownership and management

   ii) separation of direction and management

   iii) span of control and scalar chain

   iv) tall and flat organisations

   v) outsourcing and offshoring

   vi) shared services approach

c) Explain the characteristics of the strategic, tactical and operational levels in the organisation in the context of the Anthony hierarchy. ☐

d) Explain centralisation and decentralisation and list their advantages and disadvantages. ☐

Session 6 Guidance

■ **Recognise** the importance of organisational structure (s.1).

■ **Understand** the basic forms of organisational structures and what influences such structures (s.2).

(continued on next page)

VISUAL OVERVIEW

Objective: To describe and understand the various types of organisational concepts and structures.

```
                    ┌─────────────────────────────────┐
                    │   ORGANISATIONAL STRUCTURE      │
                    │   • Description                 │
                    │   • Importance                  │
                    │   • Mintzberg                   │
                    └─────────────────────────────────┘
```

TYPES

- Influencing Factors
- Entrepreneurial Structure
- Functional Structure
- Product/Service Structure
- Geographical Structure
- Divisional Structure
- Matrix Structure
- Composite (Hybrid)
- Network Structures

CONCEPTS

- Ownership, Direction and Management
- Span of Control and Scalar Chain
- Tall and Flat Organisations
- Outsourcing and Offshoring
- Shared Services Approach
- Centralisation
- Decentralisation
- Informal Organisation

HIERARCHY OF LEVELS

- Anthony's Hierarchy
- Strategic Level
- Tactical Level
- Operational Level

Session 6 Guidance

■ **Know** the organisational structure concepts (s.3) and how different types of organisations use different concepts.

■ **Remember** the differences between strategic, tactical and operational levels of an organisation (s.4). You will come across the concept of Anthony's hierarchy often throughout your ACCA studies.

1 Organisational Structure

1.1 Description

■ The structure of an organisation (often represented in an organisational chart) shows relationships between its constituent parts and describes the:

- lines of authority;
- communication channels (vertical and horizontal); and
- reporting lines

> **Definition**
>
> **Organisational structure**—the established pattern or relationships among components or parts of an organisation.

1.2 Importance

■ To be effective in its operations, the organisation must have a working structure appropriate for its requirements and be capable of adapting to changes in its environment.

■ Without a structure, an organisation would have a difficult time controlling its resources and therefore achieving its objectives.

Example 1 Organisational Structure Advantages

Suggest FIVE advantages of a formalised organisational structure.

1.3 Mintzberg's Components

1.3.1 Five Generic Components

Henry Mintzberg suggested that all organisations have five components:

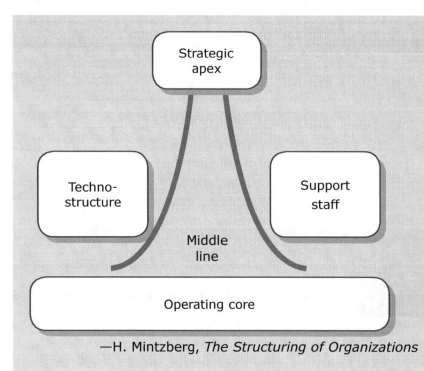

—H. Mintzberg, *The Structuring of Organizations*

1. **Strategic apex:** full-time top managers

2. **Operating core:** the operating group that makes products or delivers services

3. **Middle line:** the hierarchy between apex and core (middle management)

4. **Techno-structure:** is directed towards standardisation of the work (staff)

5. **Support:** indirect support of the operating core

■ The purpose of a **strategic apex** is to ensure the organisation follows its mission and manages its relationship with its environment. The individuals who comprise the apex (e.g. CEO) are responsible to owners, government agencies, unions, etc.

■ The **middle line** is concerned with converting the strategic objectives of the apex into operational plans that can be carried out by the staff (employees).

■ As organisations grow and become more complex, they usually develop a separate group of analysts who are concerned with the best way of doing a job—the **techno-structure**.*

*This will, for example, set quality standards and organise training programmes.

■ The organisation also adds other administrative functions that provide services to itself (e.g. legal advice, public relations, etc). These are the **support staff**.

■ Finally, at the bottom of the organisation is the **operating core**, which produces the products or delivers the services.

The relative influence of these elements to one another has a significant impact on the nature of the organisation and how it is coordinated. For example, the strategic apex will directly supervise operations in a simple structure.

1.3.2 Categories of Structure

Mintzberg suggested five categories of organisation structure, each of which depends on one specific component of his model.

■ **Simple structure**—this is centralised and often autocratic, with power coming from the **strategic apex**. Control is typically exerted by the chief executive or small, influential executive team.

✔ The structure can be flexible and sometimes informal, with a strongly defined sense of mission.

✗ However, it is vulnerable, as "one heart attack can wipe out the organisation's primary coordinating mechanism".

*For example, large-scale car manufacturing plants.

■ **Machine bureaucracy**—relies heavily on a strong **techno-structure**. Strategic planners and financial controllers create multiple layers of management, formal procedures and standardised production processes.*

✗ The tasks required of the operating core can be rigid, offering little discretion for the individual (and hence lacking motivation).

✗ The organisation can be unreceptive to the need for change.

*Examples include schools, hospitals and professional practices.

■ **Professional bureaucracy**—is similar to machinery bureaucracy, but the bureaucracy is imposed by external standards (e.g. set by law or regulatory or professional bodies).*

● The **operating core** has most influence on coordination.

✔ It is more democratic than machine bureaucracy and hence easier to motivate people.

*This structure is typical of multinational companies.

■ **Divisionalised form**—a small central core provides guidelines for business units that enjoy a high degree of autonomy. This extension of the machine bureaucracy may comprise several machine bureaucracies within a single entity.*

● The **middle line** has a strong coordinating influence.

■ **Adhocracy**—is task- or project-based. It has to respond quickly and flexibly to changing demands that are driven by the market or innovation.

- Research and development can be a primary driver.
- There is little formality, so direct supervision and defined processes are less important.

1.3.3 Separation of Direction and Management

Mintzberg's organisational model also illustrates an important principle of organisation structure: the separation of direction and management.*

■ Those who determine the mission and general direction of the organisation are different from those who implement plans and subsequently control operations to ensure that objectives are met.

■ Senior managers establish long-term organisational objectives and policies through which goals are to be achieved.

■ Middle managers:

- convert strategic plans into detailed action plans;
- specify managerial responsibilities for tasks and how resources are to be allocated;
- monitor activities and take action to ensure that resources are being used efficiently and effectively to achieve organisational objectives.

*Commentary

*Except in very small organisations.

2 Organisational Structure Types

2.1 Influencing Factors

■ Formal organisations are planned (i.e. deliberately created) to coordinate activities effectively. The type of structure often depends on:

- the history of the organisation;
- ownership (e.g. sole trader, partnership, private or public limited company);
- the size of the organisation;
- the products and services provided;
- the geographical distribution;
- the results needed to reach the overall objective;
- the activities needed to achieve the results;
- the best way to organise work;
- the best way each group of activities can be related to each other;
- the type of industry (e.g. manufacturing, service, not for profit);
- legal requirements (e.g. Companies Acts, partnerships, financial regulations, etc);
- the degree of specialisation in the organisation;
- the levels of authority and control; and
- whether decision-making is centralised or decentralised.

2.2 Entrepreneurial Structure

2.2.1 Features

- Owner-managed, with usually one or two top managers.
- The entrepreneur has a passion for excellence and success.
- The entrepreneur has an ability to organise available resources in new and more valuable ways.
- The entrepreneur has strong leadership, management and team-building skills.
- No formal reporting lines.
- Multi-skilled managers/employees.*
- Usually undefined roles.
- Changing tasks.
- Often related to initial start-up businesses.*

*Commentary

*Part-time tasks such as bookkeeping are taken on by whoever has time to do them.

*Commentary

*Entrepreneurs exist in all forms and types of organisations. Bill Gates and Microsoft started out in a garage, a typical entrepreneurial start-up. Richard Branson's success started (at the age of 16) by publishing a student magazine before expanding into record shops, recording studios, airlines, trains, mobile communications and space flight (to name but a few of his Virgin ventures). He is notorious for his sense of fun and self-parody and hatred of the rules and "straitjacket" attitude of city-based financial institutions. He was knighted (Sir Richard Branson) in 1999 for services to entrepreneurship.

*Commentary

*For example, to a functional structure in which responsibilities are clearly defined (s.2.3).

- Suitable for many small businesses.
- If lack of formality becomes unmanageable (e.g. through growth in business activity) the structure must change.*

2.2.2 Advantages and Disadvantages

Advantages

Small size should allow:

- ✔ Flexibility and good reaction to markets.
- ✔ Responsiveness to change.
- ✔ Easier decision-making/ implementation.
- ✔ Strong teamwork.
- ✔ Close bonding of owner to workers.
- ✔ Strong unity of direction.
- ✔ Ease of goal congruence between owner and workers.

Disadvantages

Small size means:

- ✗ Heavy dependence on capabilities of owner.
- ✗ Lack of career structure for workforce.

Growth leads to:

- ✗ Increased demands placed on the entrepreneur.
- ✗ Slower response to change as growth relates to increased complexity.
- ✗ Demotivation of entrepreneur and loss of "entrepreneurial" spirit.
- ✗ Risk that entrepreneur will wish to move on and look for new challenges.
- ✗ Dysfunctional decision-making.

2.3 Functional Structure

2.3.1 Organisation

▓ Based on the type (function) of work and usually divided by departments (e.g. procurement, production, finance, research and development, etc) this is the most common organisational model.

▓ It is usually the first formal structure following the entrepreneurial structure and is most appropriate to small businesses with few products and locations (e.g. one product made at one location).

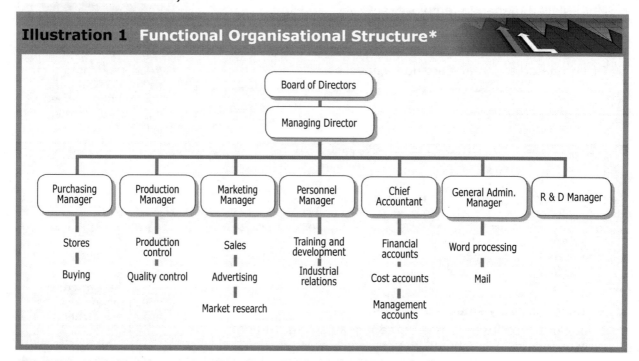

Illustration 1 Functional Organisational Structure*

*Commentary

*A small company may have only a production manager, finance manager, sales manager and IT manager (say) reporting to the CEO. A large company may have managers to whom other departmental managers report (e.g. managers for each of advertising, public relations and promotion all reporting to a general marketing manager). Individual departments may have similar organisation charts.

2.3.2 Features

▓ Board decides overall company policy (and is responsible to the shareholders for the company's success—although in most small companies the directors will also be the shareholders).

▓ Managing director has responsibility for running the company and is accountable to the board for implementing policy.

▓ Department heads are responsible for the smooth running of their departments and have authority to make day-to-day decisions. Each department head is directly accountable to the managing director.*

*Commentary

*In a small company:

● the managing director may be the majority shareholder;

● departmental heads may be on the executive board and could be family members.

- In each department, some authority is delegated to senior staff (e.g. supervisors in the production department, buyers in the procurement department).
- Usually a small team of directors, a larger (sometimes fairly substantial) lower management and supervisor layer and a large workforce.
- The organisation can be tall or flat: tall organisations have many levels (a long scalar chain), while flat organisations have fewer levels (see s.3.2 and s.3.3).
- In summary:
  - Formal job descriptions
  - Delegation of duties
  - Clear, single lines of authority and reporting
  - Logical division of tasks (i.e. each person has a set position).

2.3.3 Advantages and Disadvantages

Advantages	Disadvantages
✔ Simple, logical, well-accepted.	✗ Sectional interest rather than corporate thinking (e.g. functional managers look after their own best interests).
✔ Recognises and establishes specialists/ experts and encourages depth of skills.	✗ Inflexible—adapting to change may be difficult (e.g. all functions must move as one).
✔ Few top managers—maintains identity and authority of key functions.	
✔ Control and reporting lines logically based on functions.	✗ Demarcation lines drawn between functions make employees disinclined to do tasks that they do not consider their responsibility.
✔ Consistency of tasks, skills and roles of individuals working together.	
✔ Avoids duplication of tasks, therefore more efficient.	✗ Communication and coordination between functions becomes increasingly difficult (as number of functions increase).
✔ Economies of scale.	✗ Difficult to coordinate work of diverse specialists.
	✗ Inhibits development of general managers, as managers only have experience of their specific function.
	✗ Not specifically related to products or markets therefore too inward-looking. (Lack of focus on deliverables and customer needs.)
	✗ Not suited to organisations which are rapidly growing, expanding and diversifying.

2.4 Product/Service-Oriented Structure

2.4.1 Organisation

- A product (or brand) structure is based on individual products or services.
- A product or brand manager often has responsibility for the activities associated with the individual product (or brand).

2.4.2 Features

- Establishes each product (or group of products) as an integrated unit in the framework of the company, often structured as profit centres.*

- Reporting lines and control are based on each product or service.

- Primary/direct activities (for each product/service) which convert raw materials to finished goods include:
  - Inbound logistics
  - Operations
  - Sales and marketing
  - Outbound logistics
  - After-sales service and support.

- Support/indirect activities which assist primary activities are usually centralised and include:
  - Finance
  - Personnel
  - Research and development
  - Administration
  - Corporate planning
  - Information management.

Commentary

*Is suitable if products have distinctive brands and/or there is something distinctive about their design, production or marketing.

Illustration 2 Product/Service-Oriented Structure

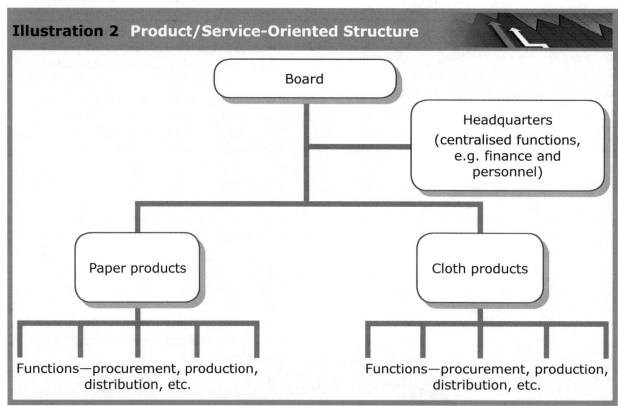

Example 2 Product/Service-Oriented Structure Advantages

Suggest FOUR advantages and FOUR disadvantages of the product/service-oriented organisational structure.

2.5   Geographical Structure

2.5.1   Organisation

▓ Organisation considers territorial boundaries (e.g. regions or countries) to have distinctive characteristics.*

▓ Ultimately, a geographical division may become a relatively complete administrative unit.

▓ Each geographical unit may be sub-organised by function or product. In *Illustration 3*, this is by function as there is only one service provided. For an international firm of financial advisers, the level below geographical may be by service (e.g. audit, tax, corporate recovery) as the service elements may be different for each region. Alternatively, a service-based structure may be preferable.

*This structure is especially important for large companies that operate across several continents.

2.5.2   Features

▓ Favoured among companies which have wide geographical areas—where it is important that activities in any area should be grouped and assigned to a manager.

▓ Not all functions will be split geographically (e.g. finance, management development and training may be centrally based at the head office).

▓ Usually indicated when customers' tastes/demands or product characteristics can best be satisfied on a local basis (e.g. coffee is given one brand name but its constituent elements are slightly different to meet local tastes) provided the product is not so complex or capital intensive as to make the establishment of regional operations too costly or impractical.*

*An estate agency chain is more likely to be geographically structured than an insurance agency.

2.5.3   Advantages and Disadvantages

Advantages

✔ Based in local markets, therefore can identify and respond quickly to local opportunities.

✔ Clearly assigns profitability for each region.

✔ Encourages delegation.

✔ Identity with the local community may provide opportunities not available to a more centralised approach.

✔ Provides a good training ground for general managers.

✔ Economic advantages of local operations (e.g. expanding production in low-cost economies).

Disadvantages

✗ Despite technological advances in communications, top management may have problems controlling an international company divided between various geographical areas.

✗ Strong central planning is often necessary to ensure overall group performance.

✗ Requires general management abilities.

✗ Difficult to maintain central services (e.g. personnel, management).

Illustration 3 Regional Road Transport Company

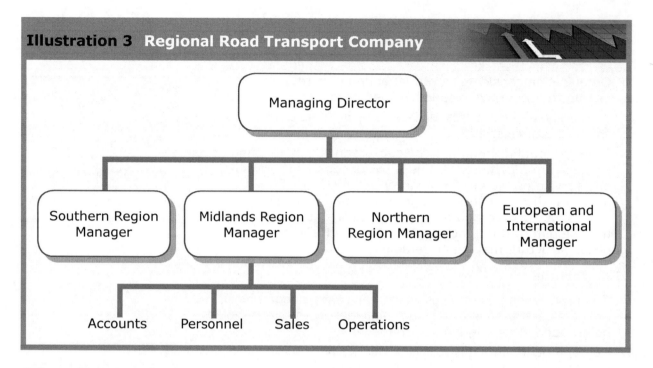

2.6 Divisional Structure

2.6.1 Organisation

Divisions are independent areas of the business operating
separately under the direction of a board of directors. Divisions
may be separate businesses owned by a parent company.
Divisions can be structured independently of each other.

Illustration 4 Divisional Structure

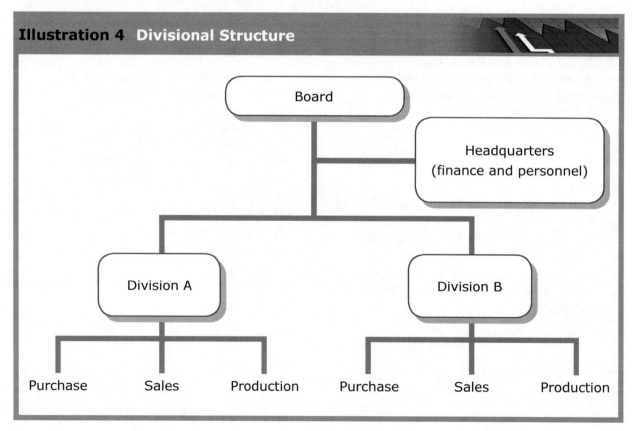

2.6.2 Features

▓ Divisions are created to serve different customers, products, market and/or geographical regions.

▓ Key functions are held centrally.

▓ Central control often is based on performance measures.

▓ Usually applied to large, international organisations.

2.6.3 Advantages and Disadvantages

Advantages	Disadvantages
✔ Enhanced career opportunities.	✗ Sub-optimisation.
✔ Local knowledge and flexibility applied.	✗ May be poor implementation of policies from headquarters. Greater control is needed.
✔ Facilitated customer dedication/ specialisation.	
✔ Allows diversification.	✗ Duplication of functions and resources e.g. employee roles.
✔ Autonomous and self-supporting business units suit larger organisations.	✗ Potential for increased overheads.
	✗ Potential inter-departmental competition for the same customers.

2.6.4 Types of Divisions

▓ The divisional structure consists of parallel divisions which may be responsible for:

   ● a product or service (s.2.4);
   ● geographic location (s.2.5); or
   ● customer type.

Example 3 Customer Type

Suggest THREE examples of industries which might be organised by customer type. For each industry suggest THREE divisions.

2.7 Matrix Structure

2.7.1 Organisation

This structure is a combination of product-oriented and functional structures. Employees from different departments often form a group to achieve a specific target, but they will report to different functional managers depending on their specific activities. This type of structure often is used in project-based businesses, such as the IT or aircraft manufacturing industries.*

*Matrix organisation started in the aircraft industry in the US, where it gained rapid acceptance in the construction, aerospace and computer fields. The majority of large companies in the UK have a matrix organisational structure.

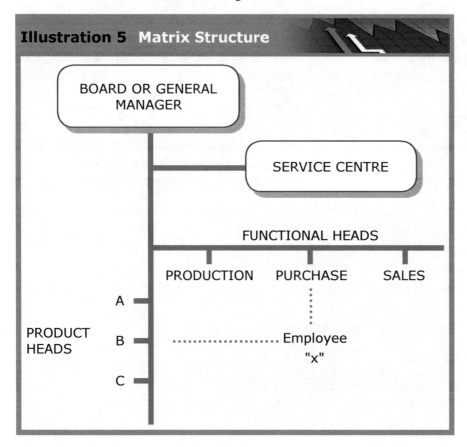

Illustration 5 Matrix Structure

BOARD OR GENERAL MANAGER

SERVICE CENTRE

FUNCTIONAL HEADS

PRODUCTION   PURCHASE   SALES

PRODUCT HEADS

A

B .... Employee "x"

C

2.7.2 Features

■ Combination of functional and divisional structures.

■ Many employees are accountable to more than one manager.

■ Only suitable where these conditions exist:
- long-term contracting business;
- peaks and troughs in demand;
- few major customers;
- highly skilled industry; and
- mature and professional employees.

2.7.3 Advantages and Disadvantages

Advantages

✔ Emphasis on product (project, process, etc) and customer orientation.

✔ Enforces communication and cooperation between heads of functions and heads of the projects, products, etc.

✔ Optimum resource allocation/flexibility.

✔ Close customer contact.

✔ Encourages teamwork and commercial awareness.

✔ Job enrichment may improve motivation.

✔ Individuals can exploit opportunities in pursuit of personal advancement.

Disadvantages

✗ Conflict between managers over allocation of resources.

✗ Recruitment problems in getting equally balanced management skills.

✗ Role conflict/ambiguity due to a lack of unity of command.

✗ Organisational inefficiencies may arise (e.g. slower decision-making).

✗ Much time is taken up in meetings and fire-fighting.

2.8 Composite (Hybrid)

▓ Divisional structure (usually) with mix of structures in each division. For example:

   ● marketing department by product;

   ● finance department by function.

▓ An appropriate mix will allow each division to be separately controlled for maximum effectiveness of the organisation as a whole.

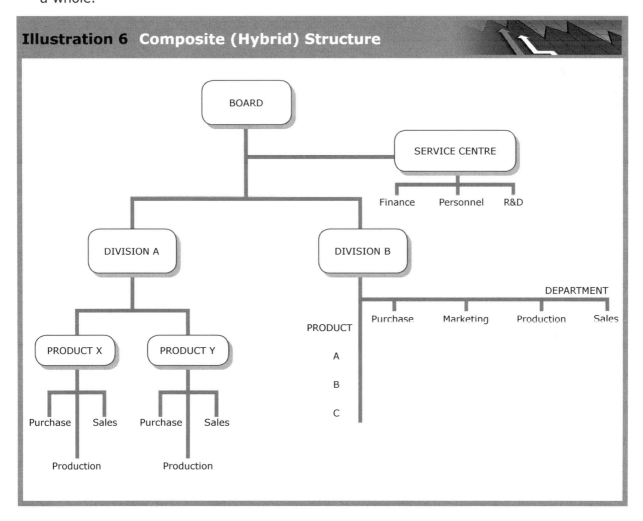

Illustration 6 Composite (Hybrid) Structure

2.9 New Network Structures

2.9.1 Boundaryless Organisation

- The boundaryless organisation replaces functional departments with cross-functional teams.
  - It reduces barriers (e.g. to customers and suppliers and between geographical regions).
  - It has limitless *spans of control* and seeks to eliminate the chain of command.
- Factors which contribute to such increasingly networked organisations include:
  - globalisation;
  - strategic alliances;
  - development of intranets (i.e. private nets);
  - telecommuting (i.e. working from a remote location rather than an office).
- The three models of boundaryless organisations are virtual, hollow and modular.

2.9.2 Virtual Organisation

- A virtual organisation creates networks of relationships that allow it to respond to an exceptional, and often temporary, market opportunity.*
- Temporary organisations are created with external partners and use technology to bring together people, assets and ideas.
- The organisation is driven by a small group of executives who bring their own expertise.
- The model can be adopted for:
  - an entire business (e.g. with a token physical presence at a registered office to meet statutory registration requirements); or
  - parts of a business (e.g. maintaining a large head office but with many staff working from home and rarely if ever needing to visit the office).

*This technology-based ("T-form") structure relies heavily on information technology.

Advantages

- ✔ The major advantage of the virtual organisation is its flexibility.
- ✔ It can respond quickly to changes in the market (e.g. to extend a range of products or services).
- ✔ As a temporary organisation it may be quickly disbanded or taken over by a larger organisation.
- ✔ Extending the virtual concept to customer relationships ("downstream"), dependence on retail premises and customer-facing staff is eliminated.*
- ✔ Costs can be greatly reduced (especially relating to premises).
- ✔ E-business solutions (e.g. automated re-ordering and seamless transaction processing) create efficiencies.
- ✔ Jobs may be more attractive (as no need for daily commuting).
- ✔ Modern image may appeal to stakeholder groups (including customers, suppliers and distributors).

*Amazon is often cited as the first major virtual business in this respect.

Disadvantages

✗ It requires intensive communication to avoid duplicating effort.

✗ A lack of trust among the various parties could decrease the benefits.

✗ Employees working in such a temporary environment may need additional motivation.

✗ Heavy reliance on IT can have a catastrophic effect when things go wrong.*

✗ Those who lack IT skills have no prospect of doing business with virtual organisations or working for them.

✗ Loss of "personal touch".

*Significant problems can arise from lack of connectivity, hardware and software failures, malware and security breaches.

2.9.3 Hollow Organisation

▦ A hollow organisation focuses on its **core** competencies and outsources peripheral processes.*
  ● It must identify activities that are critical to its growth.
  ● It uses the external market to supply non-core activities.
  ● Suppliers must have incentives to be aligned with the organisation's goals (i.e. there must be strong strategic links with trusted partners).

▦ It is most suitable when prices are competitive and a market exists to supply the non-core activities.*

*For example, Nike, a sports goods manufacturer, sub-contracts production activities while maintaining total control over design and quality specifications.

Advantages

✔ Advantages include cost savings as expenses are more variable than fixed.

✔ This also helps the organisation to survive in difficult economic times.

✔ Suppliers offer the latest technology or other developments available in the market.

Disadvantages

✗ Losing in-house capability and overall control.

✗ Innovation skills may potentially be lost.

✗ There is a risk of becoming too dependent on suppliers.

✗ It may be difficult to align the organisation and incentives for suppliers.

*For example, an organisation which simply "markets" products.

2.9.4 Modular Organisation

▦ Modular organisations order different parts from internal or external providers and assemble them into a product.
  ● The product must be divisible into manageable parts.
  ● Parts that can be manufactured more efficiently outside the organisation are outsourced to appropriate suppliers.
  ● Links between all the different providers are essential.

▦ This organisational model is useful when it is possible to separate the end product into modules and create links to facilitate effective assembly.*

*For example, Boeing has many suppliers, each of which is responsible for one component or assembly for producing the 787 Dreamliner aircraft.

Advantages

✔ It takes advantage of competencies beyond the organisation.

✔ It is contemporary and efficient. It eliminates complex ownership structures through parent companies and subsidiaries.

✔ It uses market forces to improve each part and force efficiencies.

Disadvantages

✗ Not all products can be divided into parts.

✗ Poor links can hamper assembly.

✗ External suppliers that fail to meet deadlines can delay delivery of the final product.

3 Organisational Structure Concepts

3.1 Separation of Ownership, Direction and Management

3.1.1 Ownership

▥ Business organisations may be owned by a sole-proprietor, partners, shareholders, government, co-operative members, etc (see *Session 1*). Shareholders of companies may be individuals, other companies, financial institutions, government, etc.

▥ Individual shareholders may also be directors of the company. "Family-run" companies may be large and even publicly listed (e.g. Walmart and Samsung).

▥ Many companies are, however, owned by shareholders but run by skilled managers. The problems of agency (see *Session 2*) have had a significant influence on the development of corporate governance.

▥ Most organisational structures are shown being headed by a board of directors. What often is not shown is the way the board is structured and the clear distinction between direction (strategy and objectives) and management of the company.*

▥ In general, the board sets the direction of the company and oversees/monitors the management of the company on behalf of the shareholders.

▥ Management implements necessary functions to ensure that the company's objectives (the direction established by the board) are achieved.

Commentary

*The roles of executives, non-executive directors and corporate governance are discussed in greater detail in *Session 9*.

3.1.2 Direction

▥ The King Report (South Africa) on corporate governance summarises the role of the board as:

"To define the purpose of the company and the values by which the company will perform its daily existence and to identify the stakeholders relevant to the business of the company. The board must then develop a strategy combining all three factors and ensure management implements this strategy."

- The UK Corporate Governance Code considers that the board:
  - Is collectively responsible for promoting the success of the company by directing and supervising the company's affairs.
  - Should provide entrepreneurial leadership within a framework of prudent and effective controls which enable risk to be assessed and managed.
  - Should set the company's strategic aims, ensure that the necessary financial and human resources are available and review management performance.
  - Should set the company's values and standards and ensure that its obligations to its stakeholders and others are understood and met.

3.1.3 Management

- The role of management is to ensure that objectives, as set by the board of directors, are achieved. Such objectives may be strategic, tactical, operational, financial and non-financial.

- Managers should use resources (e.g. money, people, material, equipment, information, time and space) in the most effective and efficient way to achieve the objectives set.

- Directors also may be managers. This is most common in owner-manager companies where the directors are also the owners (shareholders) of the company. However, only a few managers in any company also would be directors.

- For listed companies, corporate governance procedures usually require that company boards consist equally (as a minimum) of executive directors (who may also be managers) and non-executive directors (NEDs) who must be independent of the company and would not therefore be managers of the company.

- The separation of direction and management, together with the role carried out by NEDs, ensures that adequate time and resources are devoted to each function and that the potential for a conflict of interests is minimised. This is considered to be in the best interests of the company, its shareholders and other stakeholders.

3.2 Span of Control and Scalar Chain

3.2.1 Span of Control

- An individual manager's **span of control** can vary immensely and will depend on the following:
  - **Level of subordinate's skills and training**—the more trained and experienced a subordinate becomes, the more subordinates the manager can control in a given timeframe. The manager can increase his level of trust and reduce the effort and time he spends in controlling each subordinate.
  - **Clarity and effectiveness of delegation**—a subordinate who is uncertain about the levels of authority and responsibility that he or she can exercise inevitably will make demands on the manager's time for guidance and supervision, thus fewer subordinates can be managed in the time frame.

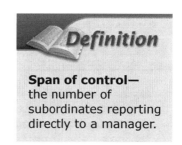

Definition

Span of control— the number of subordinates reporting directly to a manager.

- **Uniformity and clarity of plans**—where a manager can operate well-defined, workable plans and the subordinate understands what is expected of them, then little supervisory time per subordinate is needed.
- **Pace of change**—change can be slow in large, established organisations less exposed to competition (e.g. local government departments, public utilities, banks, etc) and managers can operate with a wider span of control. Where change is rapid or continuous, time becomes a scarce resource. Not only does the manager have to continually update subordinates, but the manager also has to take time to continually update himself.
- **Extent of use of objective standards**—given early warning of any deviation from the plan, this will reduce demands on management's time and so enable a wider span of control.
- **Effectiveness of communication**—where a manager can communicate plans and instructions concisely and there is prompt, meaningful feedback from subordinates (e.g. through the introduction of information systems, e-mail, groupware, video conferencing), then a manager can widen the span of control.
- **Amount of face-to-face contact necessary**—some aspects of a manager's job demand personal contact with subordinates (e.g. staff appraisal, personal matters, etc). The greater the contact needed, the narrower the span of control.
- **Complexity**—the more complex and fast changing the work, the greater the need for narrow spans of control.

3.2.2 Scalar Chain

- In any organisation there will always be a hierarchy of command and authority. This is essential for unity of direction (e.g. congruence of direction and objectives).

- The length of the chain is the number of levels of authority and responsibility which constitute an organisation's hierarchy, from the highest authority (e.g. the CEO) to the lowest level (e.g. a supervisor).

- In an entrepreneurial structure, this usually, by definition, will be short. In bureaucratic structures, this will tend to be longer. Fayol recognised that for each organisation there would be an optimal scalar chain—if too long, management would become bogged down and ineffective.

- As computer-based systems have become more pervasive throughout organisations, management layers have been removed and therefore the scalar chain has become shorter.

3.3 Tall and Flat Organisations

3.3.1 Tall Organisations

- A "tall" organisation is one that has a large number of levels in its management hierarchy and thus typically a long scalar chain and small span of control (e.g. governmental departments).

- Typically connected to centralisation, formal rule setting and division of labour (e.g. one man, one job). They are top-down, command-and-control structures.

Definition

Scalar chain—vertical arrangement of direct authority and responsibility; line of authority. (Attributed to Fayol.)

Advantages

✔ Roles and responsibilities clearly mapped out.

✔ Steady flow of promotion opportunities.

✔ Relatively smooth progression from one level to another (because there is only a minor increase in authority and responsibility).

✔ Spans of control can be kept small—increasing the opportunities for personal contact between manager and each subordinate.

Disadvantages

✗ Planning and coordination become more difficult as more levels are involved.

✗ Reaction to strategic changes in the marketplace may be too slow to gain full advantage.

✗ More expensive in terms of management overheads, as more management layers means more managers.

✗ Only minor increases in power and responsibility from one level to another—creates overlaps of responsibility and artificial, meaningless differences of status.

✗ The number of levels between senior management and shop floor creates remoteness, which is detrimental to staff motivation and performance.

✗ More levels of management mean more decision levels to be negotiated.

✗ Little scope for delegation, job enrichment or team building due to status barriers and responsibility overlaps.

✗ Tall-structure culture inhibits cultural dexterity, knowledge sharing and the diffusion of ideas.

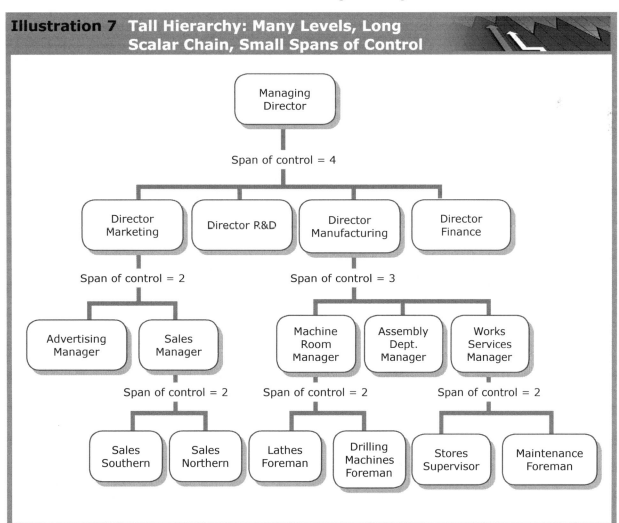

Illustration 7 Tall Hierarchy: Many Levels, Long Scalar Chain, Small Spans of Control

3.3.2 Flat Organisations

- A "flat" organisation has shorter scalar chains and wider spans of control. Such organisations are typically decentralised and task orientated.*

- They are structured around self-directed or self-managed, multi-disciplinary, cross-functional work teams where power flows from expertise, not position. Such teams are customer, problem and opportunity oriented.

- The leaders of flat companies espouse the values of collaboration. They see management as a reciprocal process between leaders and staff. Executives facilitate leadership skills in colleagues and make a priority of teamwork. Leaders influence the way work flows through coalition-building and finding consensus in the form of shared values. In flat companies the larger-than-life, omnipresent individual leader is replaced by executive teams.

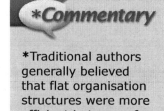

Commentary

*Traditional authors generally believed that flat organisation structures were more efficient in terms of cost, communications and motivation. Tall organisations tended to encourage bureaucracy and slow market response.

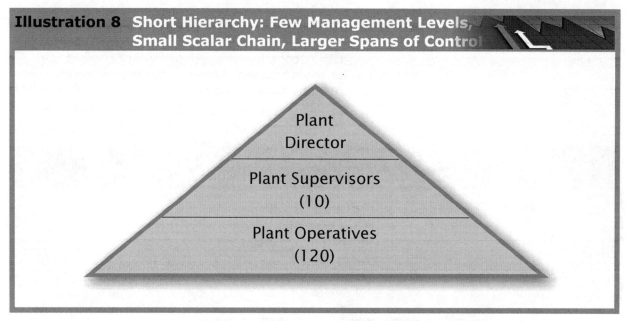

Illustration 8 Short Hierarchy: Few Management Levels, Small Scalar Chain, Larger Spans of Control

Plant
Director

Plant Supervisors
(10)

Plant Operatives
(120)

Advantages

✔ Wide span of control encourages delegation and greater flexibility.

✔ Usually lower management overhead costs, as there are fewer managers.

✔ Communications tend to be better as horizontal and lateral communication is encouraged.

✔ Less bureaucracy, easier decision-making, greater team spirit and motivation.

✔ Promotions are real and meaningful.

✔ Closer contact between top management and lower levels.

Disadvantages

✗ Wide span of control may lead to a lack of sufficient executive time being spent with each person directly reporting to the boss.

✗ Responsibilities between levels are widely different so promotion prospects are fewer and carry greater risk of failure.

✗ Greater control is needed as each worker may report to more than one manager.

Other factors influencing the choice of a flat or a tall structure include:

■ **Complexity of the product**—flat structures with wide spans are appropriate where there is mass production of a standardised product; one manager can control many workers with little need for individual supervision.

■ **Management style**—decentralised organisations with decision-making at lower management levels are likely to have flat structures and centralised organisations probably have tall structures.

■ **Use of information systems**—with greater use of information systems for reporting and control (e.g. decision support systems), more feedback can be received by one person. Thus, levels of control management can be removed with the subsequent movement to a flat structure.*

*Although flat structures often relate to small organisations, many large international organisations not only have survived but have grown because of their ability and willingness to throw off the shackles of a tall, command-and-control type of structure and implement the greater flexibility, customer- and team-oriented attributes of a flatter structure (e.g. GE, HP, Dell, Google, Apple and Yahoo!).

3.4   Outsourcing and Offshoring

■ As a result of increasing globalisation offshoring has become the fastest growing segment of the outsourcing market.*

*Offshore outsourcing (i.e. contracting with a vendor to undertake work offshore) has the advantages and disadvantages of both.

	OUTSOURCING	**OFFSHORING**
Definition	Contracting business functions out to an external organisation.	Relocation of production or other activities to a different country.
Examples	■ Legal work (e.g. review of contracts) ■ Internal audit ■ Marketing ■ Web design ■ Content writing	■ Call centres for customer service/support ■ Manufacture of electronic components ■ Airline reservations ■ Credit card processing
Advantages	✔ Access to specialist skills— increased capability may increase quality ✔ Usually cost savings ✔ Labour flexibility (avoids "hire and fire")	✔ Lower costs (increase investors' returns) ✔ More skilled people ✔ Greater efficiency (work done more quickly)
Disadvantages	✗ Increased reliance on third parties ✗ Lack of in-house expertise	✗ Transfers jobs to other counties ✗ Political risks ✗ Language and cultural differences ✗ Poor communication

3.5   Shared Services Approach

■ **Shared services** are used by many parts of the same organisation. Typical examples include:
- finance and accounting;
- human resources management (HRM); and
- information technology.

■ A shared service centre (SSC) may be a cost centre (i.e. responsible only for the costs incurred) or may charge for service provided.

■ Organisations may share their services centres with similar organisations or commission commercial shared service organisations to take responsibility for a service (i.e. outsource).

■ Shared services are being used more widely in the public sector (e.g. in local government, health and education).

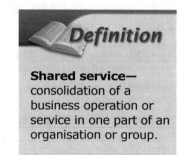

Definition

Shared service—consolidation of a business operation or service in one part of an organisation or group.

Advantages

✔ Cost savings and efficiencies (of time and resources) through centralisation. Duplication of effort is eliminated.

✔ Increased flexibility and responsiveness in a dedicated unit (e.g. through a helpdesk or hotline).

✔ Improvements in overall service though developments in technology and innovation.

✔ Business divisions can focus resources on primary business activities.

Disadvantages

✗ High start-up costs.

✗ Some loss of control over the service being shared.

✗ Unpopular with existing staff as it may result in redundancy or relocation or changes in culture or reporting lines.

✗ Centralisation may no longer tailor services to the needs of all users.

✗ Potential cost reductions may be over-estimated (e.g. if some specific needs cannot be so standardised).

3.6   Centralisation

Centralisation means that decision-making authority is held at the core of the company (e.g. at the head office rather than at local levels). As decisions are made at the higher levels of management, centralised systems tend to be found more within tall, bureaucratic structures or command-and-control structures.

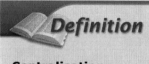

Definition

Centralisation—the practice of minimal delegation of authority by senior management.

3.6.1 Advantages and Disadvantages

Advantages	Disadvantages

Advantages

✔ Greater control over core resources.

✔ Greater coordinated decision-making.

✔ Better, uniform decision-making by top management.

✔ Quicker reaction to strategic decision-making.

✔ Standards for policies, products and services are easier to set and control.

✔ Organisational culture is easier to develop.

Disadvantages

✗ Overload and more pressure placed on higher levels of management as they have to be aware of all situations.

✗ Local (e.g. not head office) conditions and requirements may not be fully understood by central management.

✗ Decisions made centrally are likely to be of a "one-size-fits-all" nature.

✗ Slower reaction to local tactical or operational issues and inappropriate service to local customers.

✗ May encourage local entities to "do their own thing" if the head office cannot come up with a satisfactory solution to their requirements.

✗ Restricted career development and experience (especially as higher levels and experience will be at the head office).

✗ Discourages local initiative as most strategic and tactical decisions are made at the top.

3.6.2 Successful Centralisation

▦ The following requirements need to be met for centralisation to be successful:

● Control over strategic planning (e.g. major capital expenditure, transfer prices, research and development).

● Uniform product and services across all spectrums.

● Control and location of horizontal cross-sectional services (e.g. information systems, data warehousing, HR functions, etc).

3.7 Decentralisation

Decentralisation concerns the degree to which authority to act can be dispersed throughout an organisation and requires autonomous business units or divisions and a flat-structure management mentality.

3.7.1 Advantages and Disadvantages

Advantages

✔ Allows head-office management time to concentrate on strategic responsibilities.
✔ Speeds up local decision-making.
✔ Allows more flexibility for local conditions.
✔ Decision-making is more suited to local conditions.
✔ Responsibility and status is given to lower levels of management.
✔ Increased delegation improves management training at an earlier level.
✔ Focuses attention to cost/profit centres.

Disadvantages

✗ Potential loss of control by top (head office) management and loss of goal congruence.
✗ Can lead to inconsistent treatment of customers between locations.
✗ May encourage sub-optimisation and loose economies of scale.
✗ Requires more staff at higher levels.
✗ Increased information requirements to monitor divisional performance.
✗ Increased cost due to:
  - duplication of services (e.g. individual accounts departments);
  - duplication of management structure;
  - extra information processing; and
  - duplicated training requirements. (divisional and central managers).

3.7.2 Successful Decentralisation

▦ Several separate activities which require flexibility and specific decision-making.
▦ Independent products and divisions.
▦ Carefully designed strategic and performance evaluation systems to match local requirements.

3.8 The Informal Organisation

3.8.1 What It Is

▦ Most organisations have formalised ways of doing things (to enable managers to achieve objectives) which is described, for example, by company policies, rules, internal controls and job descriptions. The standard organisational chart is a typical form of showing the formal structure (as discussed above).

▦ Over time, however, an "informal organisation structure" will develop in most organisations which exists parallel to the formal organisation. The informal organisation is based on the reality of day-to-day interactions between managers and employees of the organisation and in some organisations has extended to include other stakeholders (e.g. customers, suppliers, local communities).

▦ It consists of "a dynamic set of personal relationships, social networks, communities of common interest and emotional sources of motivation. It evolves organically and spontaneously to changes in the work environment, the flux of people through its porous boundaries and the complex social dynamics of its members" (Katzenbach Partners).

3.8.2   Formal Compared With Informal

Katzenbach Partners identified the key characteristics of the formal and informal organisations as:

Formal	Informal
▓ Enduring, unless deliberately altered	▓ Evolving constantly
▓ Top-down	▓ Grass-roots driven
▓ Static	▓ Dynamic
▓ Excellent at alignment	▓ Excellent at motivation
▓ Plain to see	▓ Requires inside knowledge to be seen
▓ Equates "person" with "role"	▓ Treats people as individuals
▓ Hierarchical structure	▓ Flat structure
▓ Bound together by codified rules and order	▓ Cohered by trust and reciprocity
▓ Easily understood and explained	▓ Difficult to pin down
▓ Critical for dealing with situations that are known and consistent.	▓ Essential for situations which change quickly or are not yet fully understood.

3.8.3   Reasons for Its Existence

▓ There are many reasons why an informal organisation develops:

- **Informal standards**—personal goals and interests of workers differ from official organisational goals. Such standards often act as motivators as certain employees develop a pride in the work they do (over and beyond that formally expected) which becomes infectious in their formal and informal working groups.

- **Informal communication**—changes of communication patterns and methods from the formal to the informal (e.g. informal exchanges of information) due to personal relations between managers, between managers and employees, between employees and between the organisation and other stakeholders.

- **Informal groups**—certain groups of employees have the same interests or (for example) the same background. The patterns of interaction are shaped by friendship groups and other relationships.

- **Informal leaders**—due to charisma and general popularity, certain employees of the organisation obtain more influence and respect than their official position indicates. They will be the ones whom others turn to for help, resources, information, guidance or just plain mentoring to "get the job done".

- **Different status of employees**—in a hierarchical system, the formal structure may suppose that different levels of employees do not mix other than as required by the system. The informal organisation does not place such restrictions on employees.

- **Easier to use**—the formal structure may present barriers and be difficult to use. It is easier to work within informal structures to find new ways of doing things which are easier, save resources (e.g. time), yet still achieve the overall objective.

- **Lack of updating the formal structure**—quite often, once the formal structure and processes are documented, they quickly become out of date. Managers and employees develop processes "on the hoof" as needed.

3.8.4 Advantages and Disadvantages

Advantages

✔ Ability to innovate and achieve beyond the bounds of the formal organisation.

✔ Higher motivation, involvement and sense of ownership for employees.

✔ Opportunities for managers to facilitate the informal organisation to their and the organisation's advantage.

✔ Better communication between ALL stakeholders.

Disadvantages

✗ Clashes between the two forms may lead to inefficiencies and conflict.

✗ Opposition to change can be magnified through the informal organisation.

✗ Negative gossip and rumour may be difficult to control—"grapevine" effect.

3.8.5 Managing the Informal Organisation

■ Managers must be able to work with both the formal and the informal organisation. They cannot ignore the informal side of how the business operates.

■ The formal organisation has a strong role in business and is essential when strong command-and-control-based structures are required (e.g. in restructuring and turning around a failing business). Even then, informal elements can be crucial to the success of the process (e.g. using informal communication channels to motivate employees to accept and implement the changes needed). At a certain point in any business, the formal way will inhibit originality, intuition and motivation through imposing unnecessary bureaucracy and over-emphasising order over personal processes.

■ Managers need to understand what should be done (the formal way) and the actuality of what their employees do, why they do it and why it is successful. They must then balance and integrate the strengths of the two systems and counterbalance their weaknesses. They need to be able to use the informal organisation to fully achieve success and make sure that organisational objectives are aligned with the behaviours and work patterns of the informal organisation.*

*Commentary

*As "necessity is the mother of invention" (Plato), necessity also is the mother of informal organisations. In other words, what the formal organisation cannot achieve effectively and efficiently, the informal organisation will.

Illustration 9 — Informal Organisation

- In a study conducted by Steven J. Spear and H. Kent Brown for the Harvard Business Review, the pair concluded that the flexibility of Toyota's operations was due to the way the scientific method was ingrained into its workforce—not through a formal and structured training programme or use of manuals (the production system has never been written down) but through unwritten principles which govern how workers work, interact, construct and learn (part of Toyota's informal organisation).

- Part of Texas Instruments' (TI) informal organisation is referred to as "the Lunatic Fringe"—an informal and amorphous group of IT engineers (and their peers and contacts outside of the company) who are given free rein in what and how they innovate. Along with the formal research and development department, they are essential to the success of TI.

- eBay's business model is based on its informal community of well over 200 million buyers and sellers. Initially, the system relied heavily on the ethical transparency and collective trust of its customers—it was a non-hierarchical, democratic approach as there were few formal rules of doing business on eBay. As the business expanded, however, a more formal approach in laying down specific rules and enforcing them was required to counter growing incidents of fraud and behaviour not in line with eBay's values. The company provides an example of an organisation recognising the need to instigate formal procedures while maintaining a balance with the informal.

Example 4 — Informal Organisation

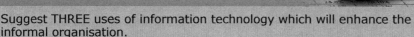

Suggest THREE uses of information technology which will enhance the informal organisation.

Illustration 10 — Properties of Informal Organisations

The informal organisation encapsulates Nike's marketing slogan, "Just do it!" and most of the eight themes of Tom Peters' and Robert Walterman's "In Search of Excellence":

- Bias for action, active decision-making—"getting on with it";

- Close to the customer—learning from the people served by the business;

- Autonomy and entrepreneurship—fostering innovation and nurturing "champions";

- Productivity through people—treating rank-and-file employees as a source of quality;

- Hands-on, value-driven—management philosophy which guides everyday practice (management showing its commitment);

- Simultaneous loose-tight properties—autonomy in shop-floor activities plus centralised values.

4 Hierarchy of Levels

4.1 Anthony's Hierarchy

■ Robert Anthony classified managerial responsibility and activities into a hierarchy, often referred to as the *Anthony hierarchy.* This neatly shows the separation of setting the direction of the organisation from the day-to-day management and supervisory processes at the operational level.

4.2 Strategic Level

■ Strategic (sometimes referred to as corporate-level) planning and decision-making is concerned with the whole business, not with a division of the business or one of the functional areas and is overseen by the board of directors and senior management.

■ Analysis will be made of political, economic, social and technological elements, including markets, competitors and the business environment, the use of resources and stakeholder expectations and influence. Thus, the information requirements are usually long-term, external and subjective.

■ Once the overall desired future has been envisaged, the organisational goals and objectives are broadly defined. Key business decisions are made, organisational programmes and policies established, control and risk objectives identified, overall organisational plans and budgets set (e.g. financial, capital, markets, information systems, structure, human resources) and critical success factors identified. Key performance indicators are also established so that they can be monitored.

4.3   Tactical Level

▨ This refers to the systematic determination and scheduling of mid- to short-term activities required in achieving the objectives of the strategic plan. Tactical planning and decision-making aims at achieving narrowly defined interim objectives (derived from the strategic plan) with predetermined means (e.g. resources budget). It translates the strategic plan into shorter-term goals and objectives to deliver the strategy.

▨ Managers at the tactical (business) level of the organisation utilise given resources to achieve divisional, departmental and sectional objectives established from the overall strategy— decisions are implemented, controls designed and operated, new procedures innovated, policies become reality, rules are applied and financial levels are confirmed (these actions often rely on the informal as well as the formal organisational structures).

▨ The required information will be a mix of internal and external medium-term data with the controlling emphasis on aligning tactical plans to achievement of the strategic plan.

▨ Significant feedback on performance indicators will be related upwards to the strategic level to enable an appropriate response. Business level managers must inform the strategic level (e.g. the board) of any divergence from their plans which will affect the overall business strategy.

▨ At the business level, decision-makers are more concerned with the immediate industry, product, market issues and the efficient and effective deployment of resources in the medium to short term. New product development and market segmentation will play a vital role in decision-making at this level.

4.4   Operational Level

▨ Supervisors implement short-term operational plans which deal with the day-to-day work of their teams. They interpret higher management plans (e.g. tactical business plans) for their particular area of responsibilities. Operational plans thus support tactical plans. They are the supervisor's tools for executing daily, weekly and monthly activities.

▨ Information needs are internal and short term (e.g. daily or weekly), allowing achievement of short-term objectives (e.g. procurement, materials, operations, warehousing, delivery, servicing, personnel, use of equipment and available finance).

▨ Information deliverables would be the day-to-day summaries of key performance indicators provided to tactical managers.

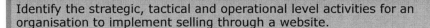

Example 5 Website

Identify the strategic, tactical and operational level activities for an organisation to implement selling through a website.

Summary

- An organisation's formal structure is delineated by lines of authority, reporting and vertical and horizontal communication channels.

- Organisational types include:

  - **Entrepreneurial**—multi-skilled workforce which in many cases reports directly to the entrepreneur. Undefined roles and changing tasks.

  - **Functional**—divided into units based on type of work. Clear, single lines of authority and reporting where delegation of duties follows a formal job description.

  - **Product/Service oriented**—reporting lines and control are based on each product or service. Primary/direct activities convert raw materials to finished goods; support activities assist primary activities.

  - **Geographical**—based on territories.

  - **Customer type**—to better meet their needs.

  - **Divisional**—independent business areas operating, often independently of each other, under board direction.

  - **Matrix**—combination of product-oriented and functional structures.

  - **Composite**—usually divisional structure with mix of structures across divisions.

  - **Boundaryless**—cross-functional, technology-based stuctures.

  - **Virtual**—primary functions are outsourced.

- *Scalar chain* concerns the number of levels of management; *span of control* concerns the number of a manager's direct reports.

- *Tall* organisations have many levels of management; *flat* organisations have few levels. Generally, a more complicated product or delivery process requires a taller organisation. IT adoption has somewhat flattened tall organisations.

- *Centralisation* implies that decisions are made only at the highest scalar level; *decentralisation* implies that they are made at the lowest practicable level.

- Although organisational structure describes the formal process of getting things done, the informal organisation describes how things really get done.

- Boards set strategy, management determines tactics in support of strategy and supervisors implement operational plans to implement tactics (Anthony).

Session 6 Quiz
Estimated time: 30 minutes

1. State how Kast and Rosenzweig described the organisational structure. (1.1)
2. List SIX factors which influence an organisation's structure. (2.1)
3. Describe an entrepreneurial structure, identifying its features. (2.2)
4. Identify FOUR advantages of a geographical organisational structure. (2.5)
5. Describe the virtual organisation. (2.9.2)
6. Explain the concept of the separation of direction and management. (3.1)
7. Describe FOUR factors which will determine a manager's span of control. (3.2.1)
8. Explain the concept of the "informal organisation". (3.8)
9. Distinguish between outsourcing and offshoring. (3.4)
10. State THREE examples of shared services. (3.5)
11. List and describe the THREE levels of Anthony's hierarchy. (4.1)

Study Question Bank
Estimated time: 35 minutes

Priority		Estimated Time	Completed
MCQ6	Organisational Structure	35 minutes	

EXAMPLE SOLUTIONS

Solution 1—Organisational Structure Advantages

✔ Clear reporting lines, structure and chain of control and command.

✔ Clear communication channels (vertical and horizontal).

✔ Easier to establish and maintain safeguards/internal controls in the organisation.

✔ Reduced risk of conflicts emerging.

✔ Allows managers to identify who does what in an organisation.

✔ Shows the scalar chain and span of control of each manager.

✔ Aids new employees and external consultants (e.g. auditors) to understand the organisation and how it functions.

Solution 2—Product/Service-Oriented Structure Advantages

Advantages

✔ Allows considerable delegation by top management.

✔ Clear profit accountability by division heads.

✔ Focus on product performance and profitability.

✔ Encourages growth and diversity of products (e.g. adding additional flavours, sizes, etc to capture other segments of the market).

✔ Promotes the utilisation of specialised equipment, skills and facilities.

✔ It provides a yardstick for future investment plans.

✔ General manager role is encouraged.

Disadvantages

✗ Support functions are duplicated.

✗ Centralised services (e.g. management accounting, research and development) become difficult to maintain economically.

✗ There is still a need for central co-ordination to ensure that an overall view is taken at company level not just at product level.

✗ Success depends on the ability of the people in the head of product positions (general managers, not specialist).

Solution 3—Customer Type

Generally industries will organise by customer type to meet specific customer expectations which require customised service approaches.

1. Healthcare: Outpatient, day-patient, in-patient (overnight stay), accident and emergency.

2. Colleges: Adult education, school leavers, children.

3. Telecommunications: Domestic retail (individuals), commercial retail (businesses), wholesale (other communication companies).

4. Fashion retail: Menswear, women's fashions; children's clothes.

Solution 4—Informal Organisation

- Instant messaging—this may be, for example, by way of mobile phone text messaging, standard e-mail messages or through the use of Yahoo!, MSN Messenger, Skype, etc for messaging and group verbal/text communications.
- Electronic networking and grouping (e.g. Facebook, Twitter, LinkedIn, MSN Groups).
- GroupWare (e.g. Lotus Notes).
- Blogs (Web logs)—many firms have established blogs as a way of quickly communicating with their customers (e.g. to inform them of particular events, new products, problems with products such as software programming errors, discussing customer issues, wish lists, etc). For example, Sony runs two blogs—one deals with its products and the other deals solely with PlayStation issues.
- Many blogs started as unofficial Web logs by company staffers (e.g. a senior programmer in Microsoft who gave his thoughts on the efforts by Microsoft to make its software more secure). In some cases, bloggers were fully supported (and trusted) by the company and a blog has now turned into a formal communication tool to be able to quickly contact appropriate parties and to obtain feedback on issues of interest to them. The view taken by many organisations was that it was far better to have the blog "in-house" and to be able to place a controlled reaction to what was being blogged about rather than have negative (and unexpected) press.

Solution 5—Website

- **Strategic**—making the decision to sell its products through a website.
- **Tactical**—analysing, researching, designing, programming and implementing the website.
- **Operational**—running, supporting, updating and maintaining the website on a daily basis.

Organisational Culture

FOCUS

This session covers the following content from the *ACCA Study Guide.*

B. Business Organisation Structure, Functions and Governance

3. Organisational culture in business

a) Define organisational culture.

b) Describe the factors that shape the culture of the organisation.

c) Explain the contribution made by writers on culture:

    i)   Schein–determinants of organisational culture

    ii)   Handy–four cultural stereotypes

    iii) Hofstede–international perspectives on culture

Session 7 Guidance

■ **Understand** the concept of "organisational culture"—it is important as it is the distinctive way an organisation does things, how it works and its particular style. Although Handy is usually considered to be the key theorist in this area, Schein and Hofstede cannot be ignored. The impact of national identity on organisational culture, as outlined by Hofstede, is relevant when discussing management in multinational and cross-cultural contexts.

(continued on next page)

VISUAL OVERVIEW

Objective: To describe and examine the role of culture within an organisation.

```
┌─────────────────────────────────┐
│           CULTURE               │
│   ─────────────────────────     │
│   • Types                       │
│   • Determinants                │
│                                 │
└─────────────────────────────────┘
                  │
                  │
┌─────────────────────────────────┐
│   CONTRIBUTIONS BY WRITERS      │
│   ─────────────────────────     │
│   • Edgar Schein                │
│   • Charles Handy               │
│   • Geert Hofstede              │
└─────────────────────────────────┘
```

Session 7 Guidance

■ **Learn** the difference between implicit and explicit culture types and their determinants (s.1).

■ **Recognise** the contributions of various writers in the organisational culture field, particularly Schein, Handy and Hofstede (s.2).

1 Culture

1.1 Types of Culture

■ Culture is very difficult to precisely define. Some definitions and explanations include:

- "In organisation basic concepts there are deep-set beliefs about the way work should be organised, the way authority should be exercised, people rewarded, people controlled ... these are all aspects of the culture of an organisation."

    —*Charles Handy*

- "A set of common understandings around which action is organised ... finding expression in language whose nuances are peculiar to the group."

    —*Becker and Geer*

- "A set of understandings or meanings shared by a group of people that are largely tacit among members and are clearly relevant and distinctive to the particular group which are also passed on to new members."

    —*Louis*

- "A system of knowledge, of standards for perceiving, believing, evaluating and acting ... that serve to relate human communities to their environmental settings."

    —*Allaire and Firsirotu*

- "A system of shared values and beliefs about what is important, what behaviours are appropriate and about feelings and relationships internally and externally. Values and cultures need to be unique to the organisation, widely shared and reflected in daily practice and relevant to the company purpose and strategy."

    —*Chartered Institute of Personnel and Development*

- "The way things get done around here."

    —*Deal and Kennedy*

■ Culture covers many levels, for example:

- **National culture**—nations, regions, ethnic groups;
- **Gender culture**—female/male and sexual orientation;
- **Social class culture**—lower class, middle class, upper class;
- **Occupational culture**—working class, professional class, blue collar, white collar;
- **Organisational culture**—for profit, not for profit, NGOs, entrepreneurial.

■ However, there are two basic views on culture—it is either implicit or explicit.

1.1.1 Implicit

■ Being implicit means that in social life, culture is what naturally emerges as individuals transform themselves into social groups such as tribes, communities and, ultimately, nations.

1.1.2   Explicit

▧ Being explicit implies that culture is a social product arising from social interaction either as an intentional or unintentional consequence of behaviour. In other words, culture comprises distinct observable forms (e.g. language, use of symbols, ceremonies, customs, methods of problem solving, use of tools or technology and design of work settings) that groups of people create through social interaction and use to confront the broader social environment. (Wuthnow and Witten, 1988)

▧ The explicit view of culture is most relevant to the analysis and evaluation of organisational culture and to cultural change strategies that leaders can employ to improve organisational performance.

1.2   Determinants

▧ The culture of an organisation is not something that is developed "overnight". It develops slowly over time and is the product of many influences and determinants.

Example 1   Determinants of Culture

Describe SIX determinants of culture within an organisation.

▧ The following can be used to describe or influence organisational culture:

 ● **The Paradigm**—what the organisation is about, what it does, its mission, its values.

 ● **Control Systems**—the processes in place to monitor what is going on. Role cultures would have vast rulebooks.

 ● **Organisational Structures**—reporting lines, hierarchies and the way work flows through the business.

 ● **Power Structures**—who makes the decisions, how widely spread is power and on what is power based?

 ● **Symbols**—these include organisational logos and designs, but also extend to symbols of power such as parking spaces and executive washrooms.

 ● **Rituals and Routines**—management meetings, board reports and so on may become more habitual than necessary.

 ● **Stories and Myths**—these concern people and events and convey a message about what is valued by the organisation.

▧ It has been recognised, since the 1980s, that organisational culture has a significant influence on how organisations operate.

 ● A strong organisational culture means everyone knows how things are done with little or no need for detailed formal plans and procedures to tightly structure activities.

 ● A tight or strong organisational culture implies that things will be done through social pressure and group commitment.

 ● A weak organisational culture implies the need for tightly structured activities through formal plans and procedures if the organisation is to survive economically.

2 Contributions by Writers

2.1 Edgar Schein

■ Edgar Schein (1928–), a professor at MIT Sloan School of Management, defined organisational culture as "the basic tacit assumptions about how the world is and ought to be that a group of people are sharing and that determines their perceptions, thoughts, feelings and their overt behaviour."

■ He believed that culture was the primary source of resistance to change. Managers who ignore the implications of an organisation's culture end up being managed by that culture rather than being able to manage and use that culture to their advantage. Cultural understanding is essential for leaders if they are to lead, especially if they deem it necessary to change the organisational culture to ensure the organisation's survival.

■ He classified organisational culture into three levels.

2.1.1 Level 1—Artefacts and Creations

■ This is the constructed physical environment (e.g. space and layout) and social environment (e.g. language and behaviour). These will usually be highly visual and can be seen in things such as the company dress code (spoken or unspoken), organisation logos and letterheads, greeting styles (handshakes, exchange of business cards, use of surname or first name), the office layout (open plan or private offices, size of offices, size of desks), the type of art chosen for the premises (modern or classic) or the use of elaborate decorative ornaments (e.g. fountains in the reception, fish tanks in the lifts).*

Commentary

*Although easily seen, artefacts may be hard to understand and decipher. For example, the tale of two executives sitting at a meeting where all executives are wearing black and white three-pointed hats, one saying to another, "I don't know how it started, either. All I know is that it's part of our corporate culture".

2.1.2 Level 2—Espoused Values

■ These are the conscious strategies, goals, values and philosophies held closely by management. In some cases, such values and beliefs may be overtly expressed in corporate slogans or in the mission statement.

■ These may be different from enacted values (the values reflected by employees' actual behaviour). For example, senior management might advocate an equal opportunity policy (espoused value), but middle management might disregard this in the recruitment process (actual behaviour).

2.1.3 Level 3—Basic Assumptions and Values

■ These are unconsciously held (taken for granted and therefore difficult to discern) learned responses. These may start as espoused values but become ingrained as problems are repeatedly solved and accepted such that the initial reason for doing so becomes lost. For example, how employees repeatedly deal with customers' problems (orientation towards customer satisfaction, informal procedures or formal company rules) can become a basic assumption.

■ These assumptions form because of the nature of humans, their relationships, activities, reality and truths.

2.2 Charles Handy

- Charles Handy (1932–), in his 1983 book *Understanding Organisations*, suggests four classifications of organisational culture based on the work of Harrison.

2.2.1 Power Culture

- Often described in terms of a spider's web with a central controlling spider (the "boss"). Those ensnared in the web are dependent on the central power source (i.e. there is one main source of power in the organisation).

- The controlling structure effectively radiates out from the centre with sideway links (the web). The control may be through a single individual (e.g. an entrepreneur) or through a small group (e.g. a family board of directors).

- There may be a specialist or functional structure but central control is exercised largely through appointing loyal key individuals who are expected to perform in accordance with the centre's wishes rather than on rules and procedures. Such individuals are often rewarded in ways that should they step out of line, the impact of losing their rewards and power will be significant and highly damaging to them.

- Power-based organisations can be strong, proud and dynamic. They will react quickly to external demands. Often, there is no need for formal rules and procedures, as decision-making is always referred to the centre or follows precedent previously set by the centre (i.e. there is only one rule—"Do as I say").

- Such organisations rely heavily on the ability and judgement of the central power—if they lose their touch (e.g. become weak, fail to recognise the need for change, react too slowly or make the wrong decision) the organisation will struggle.

- The organisation also may suffer from staff disaffection. Employees, especially management, may feel they have insufficient scope and freedom to use their initiative. The constant need to refer to the centre may create dysfunctional competition and jostling for the support of the boss. This will result in less cooperation and sharing of information between employees, as certain employees perceive a competitive advantage by not cooperating with others. They also may perceive that withholding resources will damage a potential "competitor's" position and status in the eyes of the centre (boss).

- As the organisation grows, the power culture may eventually break down as it becomes impossible for the centre to keep control over all aspects. The power is based on control over resources and personal influence over others who also may have created their own spider webs in the organisation (e.g. through divisionalisation).

2.2.2 Role Culture

- Role cultures tend to develop in relatively stable environments. Importance is given to predictability, standardisation and consistency. In a role culture, there is a highly formalised structure with clear job descriptions, well-defined rules and many procedures. It is characterised by a high degree of specialisation in job roles. Such organisations are effectively bureaucracies, working by logic and rationality.*

Commentary

*Typical examples of role culture are found in national and local government functions.

- Work is based on the position (role) rather than an individual. So long as somebody is capable of carrying out the required role, they are suitable. The structure of the organisation (and the roles within it) determines the authority and responsibility of individuals. Performance required is related to role and functional position. Performance over and above the role is not expected and may be disruptive.

- Individual views or personalities are unimportant. Entrepreneurial behaviour is regarded as dysfunctional. Decision-making and conflict resolution is taken up through the lines of authority until an appropriate response can be made.

- Efficiency stems from rational allocation of work and conscientious performance of defined responsibility. Application of rules and procedures are major methods of influence.

- Employees benefit from security and predictability in working patterns. Power is based on position not personal expression. Expert power is tolerated if it is in line with the accepted position.

- Because of the bureaucratic nature of role culture, such organisations may find it harder to adjust to change or to recognise that the rules, procedures and tested ways of doing things no longer fit the circumstances.

- Employees in a role-culture organisation may become frustrated and demotivated if they consider the work to be dehumanising or stifling initiative. Others may find it motivating in that they just have to follow the rules and know exactly what is happening and what needs to be done.

- Role cultures are managed rather than led.

2.2.3 Task Culture

- A task culture emphasises working in teams on individual tasks to get results and things done. Resources are given to the right people, at whatever level, who are brought together as a team and given decision-making powers to get on with the task. Individuals are empowered with discretion and control over their work.

- The task and results are the main focus and team composition and working relationships are founded on capability rather than status. Position in a hierarchy is usually irrelevant, with an individual's experience and knowledge being the key currency to successfully completing a task. However, in some organisations, an individual's experience will be an indicator of their position (e.g. assistant, senior, supervisor, manager, partner in a financial services/auditing firm).

- A team completing a task with a short timeframe (e.g. weeks) may be given further tasks or will be broken up with the individual members joining other teams (e.g. audit teams serving different clients). A task with a timeframe measured in months or years (e.g. a computer system development project) may change team composition as the project progresses and requires different capabilities.*

Commentary

*See Belbin's team role theory and the team-building theories of Tuckman (both in *Session 19*).

- Team-based organisations tend to have higher employment costs (e.g. more managers may be needed than in role-based organisations). Economies of scale may be difficult to achieve as each project may require different forms of resources at different times. If resources become scarce, then project managers may have to compete for such resources and a form of power culture may develop as individual priorities and objectives take over.

- Task cultures have team leaders or coordinators rather than managers.

- Other names applied to task cultures include:
  - Network organisations;
  - Matrix organisations.

2.2.4 Person Culture

- The individual is the central purpose of a person culture. If there is a structure, it exists only to serve the individuals within it. The culture only exists for the people concerned; it has no super-ordinate objective.

- This culture may be the only acceptable organisation to particular groups—such as workers' co-operatives or where individuals basically work on their own but find some backup useful (e.g. legal barristers, small partnerships, freelance consultants and professionals and other freelance workers who basically do all the work themselves and who may only require secretarial and similar support).

- Power is by consent. Influence is shared and the power base, if needed, is usually expert individuals who do what they are good at and are listened to on that basis.

- "Management" positions are often lower in status than those of professional individuals. In other cases, the professionals are "managed" by their personal assistants, secretaries and clerks.*

*Commentary

*Professionals can be persuaded, not commanded; influenced or bargained with, but not managed in the traditional sense.

2.2.5 Mix and Match

- Although Handy identified the above four classifications of culture, he also recognised that each could be found in an organisation at the same time. Taking Anthony's classification of managerial activity:
  - Strategic management, being concerned with setting direction, making policy and managing crisis, could be aligned with power culture.
  - Tactical management could be based on task culture in that it is concerned with establishing means to the corporate ends, mobilising resources and innovating.
  - Operational management, being concerned with routine activities to carry out the tactical plans, is aligned with a role culture.

In larger organisations it is possible that specific functions or divisions will be based on a person culture (e.g. consultancy and training).

As organisations are established and grow, the form of culture may also change. For example, a task culture may be best for establishing and managing the start-up of a set of activities. Once established (and the initial tasks have been completed), the organisation becomes more settled and homogeneous in carrying out its specific role. Thus a role culture may best be suited to running the business.*

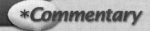

Commentary

*In a later book, *Gods of Management: The changing work of organizations*, Handy related each culture element to a Greek god— Zeus (power), Apollo (role), Athena (task) and Dionysus (person).

2.3 Geert Hofstede

Geert (Gerard) Hofstede (1928–) is a researcher from the Netherlands who looked at the influence national culture has on organisational culture. Between 1967 and 1973, Hofstede initially compared the cultural differences across the international offices of IBM in some 70 countries to develop his ideas.

His initial studies have been supplemented since 2001 by further studies covering commercial airline pilots and students in 23 countries, civil service managers in 14 countries, "up-market" consumers in 15 countries and "elites" in 19 countries.

From his initial studies, he identified four primary dimensions of national culture (see following). A fifth dimension, long-term orientation (LTO), was added following studies with Chinese employees by Michael Bond and a sixth in 2010, indulgence versus restraint (IVR), based on work by Michael Minkov.

Hofstede's ideas are crucial for firms opening divisions or pursuing merger activities in countries that may have a different cultural approach.

His website (www.geert-hofstede.com) contains data on his dimensions for some 55 countries and regions. The Singapore page also shows a world average graph giving:

- Power distance (PD) = 52
- Individualism (IDV) = 40
- Uncertainty avoidance index (UAI) = 61
- Masculinity (MAS) = 48
- Long-term orientation (LTO) = 44

2.3.1 Power Distance (PD)

▓ Power distance is the extent to which less powerful members of society accept and expect an unequal distribution of power ("all societies are unequal, but some are more unequal than others"). This is not so much taken from the viewpoint of the elite, but more from the "bottom of the pile". It suggests that a society's level of inequality is endorsed by the followers as much as by the leaders.

▓ A high PD index indicates cultures which accept higher inequalities of power:

- strong centralisation;
- power concentrated in the hands of the few (elite);
- a top-down chain of command;
- close supervision of the individual; and
- little opportunity given to individuals to influence decisions or progress to higher levels.

▓ A low PD index shows cultures in which equality and opportunity for everyone is stressed as being equal. Differences between power and wealth are not over-emphasised. Individuals are more likely to expect equality and equal rights in their society and have significant opportunities to reach the top in their chosen work or profession. An individual's abilities count for more than their parental background, educational establishment, class or wealth.

2.3.2 Individualism (IDV)

▓ The extent to which people form group ties and bonds. People in an individualistic society have looser ties between individuals and the boundary of care-giving is limited to immediate family. In a collectivist society, people have stronger extended families and the security knowing that extended families will be there for help when needed.

▓ High individualism implies a society in which the ties between individuals are loose. Individuals are expected to look after themselves and/or their immediate family. Autonomy, individual choice, individual initiative and accepting responsibility for self-actions are key elements. Fits well with flat-, group- and task-oriented organisations.

▓ Low individualism means collectivism-based societies in which people from birth onwards are integrated into strong, cohesive in-groups, often extended families (with uncles, aunts and grandparents) which continue protecting them in exchange for unquestioning loyalty. Fits well with organisations which offer a "job for life" approach to their employees.

2.3.3   Uncertainty Avoidance Index (UAI)

- The extent to which a society tolerates uncertainty and ambiguity (i.e. unstructured) or prefers security, order and control.

- A high UAI indicates that a country does its best to avoid uncertainty. It has a low tolerance for uncertainty, ambiguity, dissent and deviation. This creates a rule-oriented society which institutes laws, rules, regulations and controls to reduce the amount of uncertainty. People tend to be more emotional and motivated by inner nervous energy.

- A low UAI ranking shows less concern about ambiguity and uncertainty and more tolerance for unstructured situations, variety of opinions, dissent, conflict, change and deviations from the norm. This is reflected in a society which is less rule-oriented, more readily accepts change, and takes more and greater risks. Unstructured situations are novel, unknown, surprising or different from the usual. In such cultures, individuals tend to be more flexible and creative. They also may deliberately seek out change and take risk.

2.3.4   Masculinity (MAS)

- Refers to the distribution of roles between traditionally male or female values in a society. Male values might include competitiveness, assertiveness, aggressiveness, achievement, control, power and the accumulation of wealth. Feminine values include modesty, tenderness, compassion, consensus, relationships, quality of working life, caring and supportive behaviour.*

Commentary

*"Masculinity" does not mean to say that all males, and only males, have "male" values. There are many females who also display characteristics such as competitiveness, assertiveness, aggressiveness etc. Hofstede uses the terms "masculine" and "feminine" as reference points.

- A high MAS ranking indicates that the country experiences a high degree of gender differentiation. In these cultures, the male role dominates a significant portion of the society and power structure, with females being controlled by male domination. If females are to progress to higher levels in an organisation (e.g. breaking through the "glass ceiling"), they must use and display male role characteristics.

- A low MAS ranking indicates that the country has a low level of differentiation and discrimination between genders. In these cultures, females are treated equally to males in all aspects of the society. This does not mean that they develop 100% male characteristics but are more often accepted as they are and for what they do. Men take on more of the female characteristics as females take on more of the male characteristics.

2.3.5   Long-Term Orientation (LTO)

▓ Focuses on the degree the society embraces, or does not embrace, long-term devotion to traditional, forward-thinking values—the importance of the future versus the past and present.

▓ LTO societies will value thrift and perseverance. In short-term-oriented societies, respect for tradition and fulfilling social obligations and protecting one's "face" are valued more.

▓ High LTO ranking indicates that the country prescribes to the values of long-term commitments and respect for tradition. This is thought to support a strong work ethic where long-term rewards are expected as a result of today's hard work.

▓ However, business may take longer to develop in this society, particularly for an "outsider".

▓ A low LTO ranking indicates that the country does not reinforce the concept of long-term, traditional orientation. In this culture, change can occur more rapidly as long-term traditions and commitments do not become impediments.

▓ Both the positively and the negatively rated values of this dimension are found in the teachings of Confucius, the most influential Chinese philosopher, who lived about 500 BC. Hofstede's approach to this dimension ensures that it also applies to countries without a Confucian heritage.

2.3.6   Indulgence Versus Restraint (IVR)

▓ Indulgence stands for a society which allows relatively free gratification of basic and natural human drives related to enjoying life and having fun. This means freedom of choice, freedom of expression and the ability to control your life.

▓ Restraint stands for a society which suppresses gratification of needs and regulates it by means of strict social norms.

▓ A high IVR implies the freedom to have fun and show it. Low IVR implies that the state, religion or society has strong control over what behaviour is considered to be acceptable, when and how this may (if at all) be shown.

Summary

- Culture can be described generally as a system of knowledge, beliefs, evaluations and actions shared by a group.

- The belief that culture is implicit is that it is absorbed rather than taught.

- The belief that culture is explicit is that it arises from social interaction feedback and is taught by the positive and negative responses to a person's actions.

- A tight or strong organisational culture implies that there will be less need for formal plans and procedures; a weak organisational culture implies the need for tight structuring of activities through formal plans if the organisation is to survive economically.

- Schein classified organisational culture into THREE levels:

    1. Artefacts and creations

    2. Espoused values

    3. Basic assumptions and values

- Handy suggests FOUR culture types:

    1. Role culture—highly formalised structure, job descriptions, many procedures.

    2. Task culture—working on tasks, little emphasis on hierarchy (also called network organisations or matrix organisations).

    3. Person culture—individuals within the organisation are more important than the organisation itself.

    4. Mix and match—different cultures within the same organisation, usually found in different classifications of managerial activity (strategic, tactical or operational).

- Hofstede determined cultural differences across countries, which can be important for opening new businesses or mergers (power distance, individualism, masculinity, uncertainty avoidance and long-term orientation).

Session 7 Quiz

Estimated time: 15 minutes

1. Define "culture". (1.1)

2. List FIVE influences on culture. (1.2)

3. Describe Schein's THREE levels of organisational culture. (2.1)

4. Describe Handy's "person" culture. (2.2)

5. State the FIVE cultural dimensions identified by Hofstede. (2.3)

Study Question Bank

Estimated time: 25 minutes

Priority		Estimated Time	Completed
MCQ7	Organisational Culture	25 minutes	

EXAMPLE SOLUTIONS

Solution 1—Determinants of Culture

- Mission, aims and objectives of the organisation and clarity of direction given by management.
- History and values of the founder, including surviving family members active in management.
- Structure (e.g. private or public ownership).
- People—their background, nationality, sex, religion, age and how they interact.
- Management style (e.g. degree of formality, dominant individuals, communication channels, participation, contact, use and encouragement of the informal organisation).
- Degree of individual initiative, autonomy, responsibility, independence, risk and conflict tolerance allowed to individuals.
- Business values (e.g. professionalism, attitude to morals, ethical behaviour and social responsibility).
- Orientation towards quality in product, service and attitude to customers.
- Dynamism (e.g. entrepreneurialism).
- Reward systems (e.g. annual inflation, recognition of performance, promotions).

Committees in the Business Organisation

FOCUS

This session covers the following content from the *ACCA Study Guide.*

B. Business Organisation Structure, Functions and Governance

4. Committees in business organisations

a) Explain the purposes of committees.

b) Describe the types of committee used by business organisations.

c) List the advantages and disadvantages of committees.

d) Explain the roles of the Chair and Secretary of a committee.

Session 8 Guidance

■ **Note** that committees are one of the main mechanisms for organisational delegation, consultation and communication.

■ **Understand** committees' roles, types, composition, advantages and disadvantages (s.1).

(continued on next page)

VISUAL OVERVIEW

Objective: To explain the purpose, forms and composition of committees in business organisations.

```
                    ┌─────────────────────────────────┐
                    │          COMMITTEES             │
                    │  • Role and Purpose             │
                    │  • Advantages and Disadvantages │
                    └─────────────────────────────────┘
                      /                             \
                     /                               \
  ┌──────────────────────────┐       ┌──────────────────────────┐
  │          FORMS           │       │       COMPOSITION        │
  │  • Formal (Standing)     │       │  • Size                  │
  │  • Ad Hoc                │       │  • Make-up               │
  │  • Subcommittees         │       │  • Committee Chair       │
  │  • Joint Committees      │       │  • Committee Secretary   │
  └──────────────────────────┘       └──────────────────────────┘
```

Session 8 Guidance

■ **Recognise** the forms of committees and when they are appropriate (s.2).

■ **Know** the roles of the major players—the chair (s.3.3) and the secretary (s.3.4). Differentiate their responsibilities and basic skills required.

1 Committees

1.1 Role and Purpose

Definition

- **Committees** are formed to carry out specific functions which cannot be carried out effectively by the managing board (e.g. board of directors, board of trustees) alone because of:
  - the time commitment required (e.g. all of the directors cannot be involved all of the time in all business functions);
  - the specialisation of the subject matter (e.g. IS projects); or
  - the legal/regulatory requirement to establish specific committees (e.g. the Audit Committee under corporate governance regulations).

Committee—a group of people, to whom authority has been delegated by a larger group, to perform a particular function or duty.

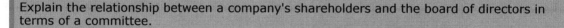

Example 1 Board of Directors

Explain the relationship between a company's shareholders and the board of directors in terms of a committee.

- In general, the purposes and roles of a committee are many and varied. Examples include:
  - Creating new ideas, research and development, brainstorming
  - Communication, disseminating information and obtaining feedback
  - Problem solving, task force or working party
  - Coordination of projects, departments, disciplines, organisations
  - Representing interests of others, stakeholders, environment
  - Overseeing procedures, roles, activities
  - Making formal recommendations (to do something or not to do anything).*

*Commentary

*Consider the various committees (working parties, task forces et al.) which operate in your own organisation and what objectives/ roles they have. In addition, research the structure of the International Federation of Accountants (www.IFAC.org) and the International Accounting Standards Board (www.IASB.org).

1.2 Advantages and Disadvantages of Committees

Advantages

✔ Decisions are based on the committee members' assessment of facts and ideas. Difficult decisions are not made by one individual.

✔ No one individual on a committee can be held responsible for the consequences of decisions made.

✔ Brings together talent and judgement and allows specialisation, combining abilities of the committee members. Multi-perspective approach to problem solving.

✔ Ability to undertake a larger volume of work than individuals working alone, including delegation to subcommittees.

✔ Maximises coordination between work groups represented by the committee members (who may have no other means of doing so).

✔ Provides a focal point for information and action in the organisation.

✔ Formalises important processes and improves communication.

✔ Can help managers to take time in making/announcing their decision (e.g. set up an investigative committee—that will take time to investigate and report).

Disadvantages*

✗ Slower decision-making, especially when committees are large.

✗ Decisions may represent compromise solutions rather than optimum solutions.

✗ Excessive procedural matters can reduce the time available for the discussion of substantive matters.

✗ Waste time and resources. Committees are time-consuming and expensive.

✗ Managers may abdicate their personal responsibility for decision-making.

✗ Some "experienced" committee members may be able to dominate and drive the decision-making process.

✗ "Groupthink" may easily develop.

✗ Cannot act quickly and flexibly to meet sudden changes in a situation.

✗ Can be used inappropriately as a "delaying tactic".

*Commentary

*"Design by committee" is a pejorative term used to describe the output from a design committee which fails to meet the original conception and ideas because they have been lost in the committee process (e.g. an IS project fails to meet the original specification from users because the project committee members consider that they know better than the users). Other examples include poorly designed or unpopular cars, household appliances and similar consumer goods.

The term has been popularised in the phrase "a camel looks like a horse designed by a committee".

2 Forms of Committees

2.1 Formal (Standing) Committees

- Established as part of the organisational structure (i.e. they are permanent).
- Usually have specifically delegated duties and authority:
  - A company's board of directors formed as a "committee" by the shareholders to run the business on their behalf.
  - The Audit Committee formed from members of the board to deal with specific matters as required under corporate governance regulations.
  - An Employees Committee (often referred to as a works council) formed to discuss employee-related matters (receiving input from employees) and to provide reports (feedback) to the board of directors.

2.2 Ad Hoc Committees

- Usually temporary, they are created for a specific purpose or to solve short-term problems.
- They are appointed to investigate some special matter or area of interest, report their findings, make appropriate recommendations and then disband:
  - IS project committees formed to deal with the implementation of a particular IS project and reporting directly to an IS steering committee (a main board committee charged with overseeing the IS strategy and resources).
  - An acquisition committee formed to oversee the acquisition of another company.
  - An investigative committee formed to investigate a particular event (e.g. a breakdown of quality control procedures resulting in contaminated produce).

2.3 Subcommittees

- Appointed by a committee to deal with a specific area of the prime committee's workload. Where the prime committee is known by another name (e.g. the board) the subcommittee will be referred to as a committee.
- An example would be risk subcommittees that consider specific areas of business risks identified by the Risk Committee.

2.4 Joint Committees

- As the name suggests, a committee comprising members from two or more committees, organisations or functions.
- As an example, a joint venture operating an oil pipeline formed by three companies would have a management board comprising directors from all three companies, effectively a joint committee.

3 Composition

3.1 Size

- In theory, the number of participants in a committee can be unlimited. The actual size of a committee depends on the terms of reference of that committee and the complexities of the matters to be considered by the committee.

- Small numbers (e.g. two or three) may be insufficient to ensure that the appropriate skills and knowledge are fully represented. If the matter is of a highly technical nature, however, one or two highly qualified members may well be sufficient.

- Large numbers (e.g. 20 or more) may result in greater complexity of interrelationships between committee members, more time required for debate and argument, increasing costs and sub-grouping with the result that decision-making may be hindered and ineffective (i.e. a compromise decision is reached rather than the one which is required). If each member of the committee represents a specific area of relevant interest, however, the size of the committee may be justified.*

*Commentary

*In 2012, the European Central Bank's Governing Council (another name for a committee) comprised 6 members of the bank's Executive Committee plus the central bank governors of the 17 euro area countries. Compare this to the 12-member committee in the US Federal Reserve System which makes the key decisions affecting the cost and availability of money and credit in the US economy. If based on the EU approach, there would be at least 50 members, one for each state.

- Considering the board of directors to be the primary committee of a business organisation, a search through the websites of major international companies indicates that their boards usually have 10 to 15 members. Subcommittees of the board, therefore, would have considerably fewer members. Unsurprisingly, on average, smaller companies have fewer board members.

3.2 Make-up

- The number and mix of individuals should be carefully considered to ensure that a strong yet well-balanced combination of individuals make up the committee (see Belbin, *Session 19*).

- The appropriate authority and responsibilities must be given to make decisions, to make recommendations, to deliberate and to provide feedback to a higher committee.

- The members of the committee must be selected based on the skills, knowledge, experience and expertise they can contribute to the committee's terms of reference.

- Two key members of the committee are the chair and secretary.

3.3 Committee Chair

■ Although there are many committees in business organisations, the chair's responsibilities and role within a board of directors can serve as those for the chair in any other business committee.

3.3.1 Responsibilities

■ According to the UK Corporate Governance Code and the related Higgs' Report, the committee chair's responsibilities are:

- leadership of the board;
- ensuring the board's effectiveness;
- setting the board's agenda;
- ensuring that all board members receive accurate, timely and clear information;
- ensuring effective communication with primary external parties;
- managing the board; and
- encouraging active engagement and participation by all members of the board.*

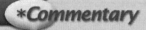

*Managing the board includes ensuring that sufficient time is allowed for appropriate discussion (includes arranging for informal meetings prior to the main board meeting to enable thorough preparation by the board members).

3.3.2 The Effective Chair

■ Upholds the highest standards of integrity and probity (moral correctness).

■ Sets the style and tone of board discussions to promote effective decision-making and constructive debate.

■ Promotes effective relationships and open communication.

■ Builds an effective and complementary board, initiating change and planning succession in board appointments.

■ Promotes the highest standards in corporate governance.

■ Ensures clear structure for and the effective running of board committees.

■ Ensures effective implementation of board decisions.

3.3.3   Skills Required of an Effective Chair

- A full and complete understanding of the formal committee procedures, how/when to apply them and the ability to apply informal procedures as needed.

- Persuasion, firmness and tactfulness to ensure that the agenda is followed and the "plot" is not lost or hijacked.

- Time management of the agenda and committee members to ensure appropriate time is allocated to each matter and each committee member.

- Communication—oral, visual and written—following the basic principles of high-quality information (timely, accurate, complete, concise, relevant, understood, confident, channel, volume). This includes the ability to summarise on a regular basis the thoughts of the committee to ensure a common understanding and direction.

- Being impartial to ensure that all members of the committee are given fair and equal treatment.

- Being objective and not allowing personal feelings or motives to dictate proceedings.

- Being discrete and tactful to avoid upsetting and making "enemies" in the committee.

- Being considered by the rest of the committee (and prominent stakeholders) to be the best person for the chair.

3.4   Committee Secretary

3.4.1   Primary Responsibilities

- To schedule committee meetings (with the chair).
- To prepare the meeting agenda (with the chair).
- To give notice of the meeting by sending out the agenda and relevant documentation.
- To take notes of the matters discussed at the meeting.
- To record decisions made and the allocation of responsibility for action.
- To draft the minutes for approval by the chair.
- To circulate approved minutes to all members.
- To ensure that members understand their responsibilities for action if appropriate.
- To generally assist the chair in running the meeting.
- To provide the chair with procedural support as necessary.
- To provide general administration between meetings (e.g. deal with correspondence).

3.4.2   Basic Skills Required

- Ability to organise
- Logical thinking
- Language and grammatical understanding
- Note-taking which captures the essence of what has been said
- Written communication
- Full understanding of committee procedures.

Summary

- Committees are groups of individuals who have been delegated authority to perform a particular function or duty typically aimed at solving specific problems or generating specific solutions.

- While beneficial, committees can become unwieldy in size, lack flexibility, delay important decisions and otherwise become ineffective at solving the problem for which they were formed.

- Formal standing committees have specific delegated duties and authority of a more permanent nature. Ad hoc committees, by contrast, are usually temporary and are formed to solve specific problems and then disband.

  - Subcommittees deal with some specific areas of the ad hoc committee's workload.

  - Joint committees may include members from various other companies or from other committees within the same company.

- Committee size should be appropriate to the subject of the committee's formation with specialists as required to address special issues.

- The committee chair sets the agenda and leads the board. The chair should have requisite experience, expertise and commitment to effectively lead.

- The committee secretary works with the chair to schedule meetings, prepare the agenda, take notes and draft minutes for the chair to have approved.

Session 8 Quiz
Estimated time: 10 minutes

1. Suggest FOUR disadvantages of committees. (1.2)

2. Explain the use of "ad hoc" committees. (2.2)

3. Describe TWO potential reasons for a joint committee. (2.4)

4. List THREE criteria for members who make up a committee. (3.2)

5. Explain the role of the committee "chair". (3.3)

Study Question Bank
Estimated time: 15 minutes

Priority		Estimated Time	Completed
MCQ8	Committees in the Business Organisation	15 minutes	

EXAMPLE SOLUTION

Solution 1—Board of Directors

- Shareholders own the business. In small companies, they probably also will form the board of directors and management. However, in larger businesses, especially listed companies, the number of shareholders is too large for all of them to be involved in running the business—communicating, meeting, discussing issues and understanding the business environment would be impractical.

- The board of directors is thus effectively a committee with delegated powers (albeit through laws and regulations) to make decisions on running the business on behalf of the shareholders.

- This "committee" meets on a regular basis, (usually) follows set procedures and reports to the shareholders on activities, findings and progress (i.e. annual financial statements, annual general meeting, shareholders' Web page).

Governance and Social Responsibility

FOCUS

This session covers the following content from the *ACCA Study Guide*.

B. Business Organisation Structure, Functions and Governance

5. Governance and social responsibility in business

a) Explain the agency concept in relation to corporate governance.

b) Define corporate governance and social responsibility and explain their importance in contemporary organisations.

c) Explain the responsibility of organisations to maintain appropriate standards of corporate governance and corporate social responsibility.

d) Briefly explain the main recommendations of best practice in effective corporate governance.

   i)   Executive and non-executive directors

   ii)   Remuneration committees

   iii) Audit committees

   iv) Public oversight

e) Explain how organisations take account of their social responsibility objectives through analysis of the needs of internal, connected and external stakeholders.

f) Identify the social and environmental responsibilities of business organisations to internal, connected and external stakeholders.

Session 9 Guidance

■ **Note** that there are a number of codes world-wide on corporate governance. The UK's Corporate Governance Code and the OECD code are used to illustrate good governance procedures.

■ **Understand** the *underlying principles* of corporate governance (CG) rather than the detailed provisions laid down in each separate code, especially the OECD definition (s.1.2).

(continued on next page)

VISUAL OVERVIEW

Objective: To explain the impact corporate governance and social responsibility have had on business organisations.

```
                    ┌─────────────────────────────┐
                    │   CORPORATE GOVERNANCE      │
                    │                             │
                    │   • Development             │
                    │   • Meaning                 │
                    │   • Underpinning Concepts   │
                    │   • Key Issues              │
                    │   • Rules- or Principles-Based │
                    └─────────────────────────────┘
```

```
┌──────────────────────────────┐        ┌──────────────────────────────┐
│      RECOMMENDATIONS          │        │     SOCIAL RESPONSIBILITY     │
│                               │        │                               │
│  • Development                │        │  • Concept                    │
│  • Board of Directors         │        │  • Factors                    │
│  • Non-executive Directors    │        │  • Stakeholder Considerations │
│  • Remuneration Committees    │        │                               │
│  • Audit Committees           │        │                               │
│  • Public Oversight           │        │                               │
└──────────────────────────────┘        └──────────────────────────────┘
```

Session 9 Guidance

◼ **Know** the key underpinning concepts (s.1.3) and the key issues in CG (s.1.4, s.1.5).

◼ **Recognise** "good corporate governance" (s.2). Read through a couple of times to understand the role of the board, non-executive directors, the various committees and the idea of "public oversight".

◼ **Understand** corporate social responsibility (CSR) and sustainability (s.3).

1 Corporate Governance

1.1 Development

- Organisations have existed for thousands of years, be they in the form of individuals (sole traders) or groups (merchant trader guilds).
- The way they operated (the way they were governed) was determined by the trading individuals, the regulations of any trade organisation (guild) they belonged to and the laws of the district/country they operated in.
- Financing of these organisations would have been provided by those who were directly involved in the organisation (i.e. the owner traders, craftsmen and merchants themselves). Where additional finance was required, this would have been obtained from individual (very rich) benefactors and appropriate contracts drawn up between the provider and user of the finance.
- In the early 1600s, governments started to issue charters to organisations which allowed them to form companies and raise public funding for ventures that required very significant funding (e.g. the East India Company formed to develop trade into the East Indies). Each investor was said to hold a "share" of the company and markets (stock markets) developed so they could trade their "shares".
- 1720 saw the first serious collapse of a company and its related stock market. This was referred to as the South Sea Bubble (after the name of the company involved). At one point in the trading of its shares, the company was worth more than £300 million ($500 million), twice the value of all of the land in England at the time.
- The outcome of the South Sea Bubble was the government effectively banning companies from raising public funds.*
- It was not until the mid-1800s that the UK passed laws allowing limited liability companies to issue shares. This helped fund the Industrial Revolution and, in particular, the building of a national railway network. Greater emphasis was placed on the rights and protection of the shareholder, as such shareholders (the owners) employed managers to run (control) the business for them (rather than run it themselves).
- The 14th Amendment to the US Constitution, ratified in 1868, gave corporations the same rights as an individual and, in the UK, *Solomon v Solomon* enshrined the same concept into case law—that corporations were separate legal bodies from their managers and owners. Thus commenced the so-called divorce of control from ownership.
- Throughout the early- and mid-1900s in the UK, various Companies Acts were passed incorporating some governance elements on regulating the requirement of companies to produce audited financial statements, concerning the duties of directors and the rights of shareholders. In addition, the London Stock Exchange placed further governance requirements on listed companies through their listing rules.
- From the 1970s–'80s, there has been a substantial growth in the number of corporations, their size, global trading and power. Many government-controlled utilities were privatised (especially in the UK), creating millions of additional shareholders, further widening the gulf between ownership and management.

Commentary

*More recent market collapses include the savings and loan crisis of the 1980s, the dot-com bubble of the 1990s, the sub-prime crisis of 2007/08 and the subsequent banking crisis and credit crunch.

▓ Initially this did not seem to be of concern to shareholders (many writers commented on an apparent malaise of shareholders at this time which allowed directors to gain greater control over companies). However, a series of UK corporate scandals in the early 1990s (e.g. Polly Peck, BCCI, Maxwell, British Gas and Barings Bank) acted as the spur to developing a detailed corporate governance code (the UK Combined Code) for listed companies. In the US, Enron and WorldCom had a similar effect, leading to the Sarbanes-Oxley Act (2002), and a review/update of the UK Combined Code in 2003, 2006 and 2010 (following the banking crisis) when it was renamed the UK Corporate Governance Code ("the Code").

1.2   Meaning

▓ A specific definition of corporate governance is difficult because of the many different legal jurisdictions, corporate structures, cultures, moral beliefs, application of ethics and conditions which affect organisations throughout the world.

▓ There is a wide range of definitions, from a classic narrow view that it is restricted to the relationship between a company and its shareholders (agency theory), to the modern view that corporate governance is a complex web of direct, indirect and ever-changing relationships between the entity and its stakeholders (stakeholder theory).

▓ Corporate governance has been defined and explained as:

 ● "The way in which organisations are directed and controlled."
—*Cadbury Report, 1992*

 ● "It is the relationship among various participants in determining the direction and performance of corporations."
—*Monks and Minow, 1995*

 ● "The *system* by which business corporations are *directed* and *controlled*. The corporate governance structure specifies the distribution of *rights* and *responsibilities* among different *participants* in the corporation ... and spells out the rules and procedures for making decisions on corporate affairs. By doing this, it also provides the *structure* through which the company objectives are set and the means of attaining those objectives and monitoring performance."
—*Organisation for Economic Co-operation and Development (OECD), emphasis added*

 ● "Corporate governance is concerned with holding the balance between economic and social goals and between individual and communal goals ... the aim is to align as nearly as possible the interests of individuals, corporations and society."
—*Cadbury Report, World Bank, 1999*

 ● "Corporate governance is the system by which companies are directed and managed. It influences how the objectives of the company are set and achieved, how risk is monitored and assessed and how performance is optimised. Good corporate governance structures encourage companies to create value (through entrepreneurism, innovation, development and exploration) and provide accountability and control systems commensurate with the risks involved."
—*Australian Securities Exchange 2003*

Key Point

Classic definitions stem from how the shareholders (principals) can influence managers (agents) to act in their best interests. The core of agency theory lies in the separation of ownership (by shareholders) and control (by management). The shareholders appoint the directors and delegate to them the responsibility for managing the company on their behalf. The directors are therefore accountable to the shareholders.

- "The system of checks and balances, both internal and external to companies, which ensures that companies discharge their accountability to all stakeholders and act in a socially responsible way in all areas of their business activity."

  —*Jill Solomon, 2004*

- "The ethical corporate behaviour by directors or others charged with governance in the creation of wealth for all stakeholders. It is the way of promoting corporate fairness, transparency, independence, integrity and accountability."

These definitions identify a number of critical elements that reflect corporate governance best practice:

- A framework through which strategic, tactical and operational objectives are set (taking into account both internal and external influences) and performance is optimised.
- Strong internal control and risk management procedures (the reduction and management of risk).
- Corporate strategies set and executed in an ethical and effective way taking into account stakeholders' interests.*
- Fairness, transparency, independence, integrity and accountability are essential to ensure market confidence and attract appropriate investment.
- Application of substance over form; the spirit as well as the letter of the law.
- The organisation and its managers are accountable not only to those who own the business (e.g. shareholders) but also to a wider range of stakeholders.
- Governance is top-down driven and pervasive throughout the organisation.
- No longer inward looking and no longer purely about current period earnings. Sustainable development and sustainability reporting have been evolving parallel to governance during the 1990s and both are now intrinsically linked.

*Best practice: A code of conduct should be established to guide executives in maintaining the company's integrity and preventing unethical practices.

1.3 Underpinning Concepts*

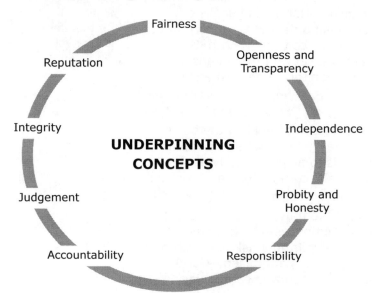

*See *Session 26, Ethics and Ethical Behaviour,* for further discussion of this area.

1.4   Key Issues

▦ A brief review of the contents page of the Code provides an insight into those areas considered to be key issues:*

- **Directors**—duties, functions, appointment, induction, continuing professional education and performance appraisal.
- The **Board**—composition, balance, committees, roles of the CEO and chairman, role of non-executive directors, appointment of new directors to the board, re-election of directors to the board and succession planning for board members.
- **Remuneration** policy (established by the remuneration committee)—appropriate to attract, retain and motivate directors, strong links to performance, service contracts, compensation.
- Reliability of **financial reporting** and external auditing (audit committee):
  - board to present a balanced and understandable assessment of the company's position and maintain a sound system of internal control (risk management);
  - audit committee to monitor the integrity of the financial statements, to review the internal financial controls, internal controls and risk management systems and to monitor the internal and external auditors.
- **Rights and responsibilities** of shareholders—satisfactory dialogue, communication of shareholder views to the board, constructive use of the annual general meeting (AGM), considered use of voting rights.

*Commentary

*Best practice:
- Functions reserved to the board should be formalised and disclosed.
- Roles of CEO and and chairman should not be exercised by the same individual.
- Directors' appointments should be in writing.
- Remuneration policies should be disclosed.
- Integrity in financial reporting should be independently verified.
- Shareholders should be able to exercise their rights effectively.

1.5   Rules- or Principles-Based

The two basic approaches to corporate governance are rules-based and principles-based.

1.5.1   Rules-Based

> **Example 1   Rules-Based Governance**
>
> Suggest FOUR elements of a rules-based governance system.

1.5.2   Principles-Based

▦ Developed as a set of guidelines rather than rules.

▦ Some flexibility given through a "comply or explain" approach. This allows companies to explain (in their financial statements) why they consider that a particular aspect of the governance code is not applicable to them.

▦ The market decides what financial penalty is applied to the company through discounting its share price in relation to those considered to have good corporate governance structure.

▦ Updated and modified through an operational and consultation process with all interested parties.

▦ Can react much quicker to emerging events than a rules-based system.

2 Corporate Governance Recommendations

2.1 Development

- Key factors in many of the financial scandals of the latter half of the 1900s and the first decade of 2000 led directly to the development of corporate governance codes:

  - Lack of oversight of key roles. For example, no effective control over the CEO (through, for example, an effective board of directors, independent non-executive directors, separate independent monitoring committees) led to a dominant CEO (Maxwell, Enron, WorldCom, Conrad Black, RBS) who tended to treat the organisation as a personal asset.*

  - No segregation of key roles (e.g. where the CEO and the chairman of the board of directors is the same individual, there is a significant opportunity for abuse of power).

  - Lack of effective supervision.*

*The respective roles and responsibilities of the board and management should be published.

*Commentary

*In some cases, unethical behaviour by employees is just ignored because they are making good profits for the business. In Enron, electricity traders deliberately engineered power shortages in California so they could sell higher-priced electricity to the state.

In other cases, such behaviour is directly encouraged (e.g. selling financial products the company knows is unsuitable for the client). Such "mis-selling" effectively crosses the line into corporate fraud.

  - Poor independent scrutiny. For example, external auditors may be reluctant to raise difficult questions because of the fear of losing the client and the (often larger) non-audit fees. Alternatively, the CEO/CFO may attempt to direct the scope of internal audit work (usually away from areas they do not wish the internal audit to see).

  - Ignoring or not seeking stakeholders' views.

  - Short-termism (e.g. policies based on short-term factors to increase profits to meet bonus targets/increase share price; share option schemes) rather than longer-term sustainability and growth.

  - Inappropriate compensation. For example, high increases in directors' salaries while the company is underperforming, termination payments which make it costly for shareholders to remove directors, use of "poison pills" to prevent takeovers (thus loss of jobs by the directors) which normally would be in the interests of the shareholders.

  - Misleading and contradictory financial information (e.g. providing different stakeholders with different, misleading and sometimes contradictory information in the hope that "at the end of the day, all will be well").

- Thus the vast majority of corporate governance code provisions attempt to minimise these risks.*

- The key recommendations are briefly discussed below using the UK Corporate Governance Code as an example.

*Corporate governance codes apply to listed companies but can be adopted by unlisted companies as best practice and applied to any form of organisation (e.g. public sector, partnerships, NGOs).

2.2   Board of Directors*

- Every company should be headed by an effective board with separate roles for the chairman of the board and the chief executive officer.
- An organisation's board:
  - is collectively responsible for promoting the success of the company by directing and supervising the company's affairs (this includes monitoring the CEO);
  - should provide entrepreneurial leadership within a framework of prudent and effective controls which enable risk to be assessed and managed;
  - should set the company's strategic aims, ensure that the necessary financial and human resources are available and review management performance (this includes succession planning, recruitment, training and development, appraisals, rewards); and
  - should set the company's values and standards to ensure that its obligations to its stakeholders are met, including effective communication to all stakeholders.

2.3   Non-executive Directors

- Non-executive directors (NEDs) are not involved in the day-to-day functions of the organisation (as are executive directors). Ideally, they should be independent of the organisation in that the only relationship they have (or have had) with the organisation is as NEDs compensated only with related salary (no bonus, no share options, no past business or directorship connections, no family connections, no material share holdings).*
- Where companies engage non-independent NEDs:
  - the independent NEDs should form a majority on the board;
  - this majority must be capable of self-policing at the strategic level; and
  - the non-independent NEDs' interests must be disclosed and any conflicts addressed.
- Their role is to:
  - provide advice and direction to a company's management in the development and evaluation of its strategy;
  - monitor the company's management in strategy implementation and performance;
  - monitor the company's legal and ethical performance;
  - monitor the veracity and adequacy of the financial and other company information provided to investors and other stakeholders;
  - assume responsibility for appointing, evaluating and, where necessary, removing senior management; and
  - plan succession for top management.

*Best practices:

- A board needs effective composition, size and commitment to adequately discharge its duties.
- Majority, including the chairman, should be independent.
- The process for performance evaluation of the board, its committees and directors should be disclosed.
- Shareholders should be encouraged to participate in general meetings.

■ They are expected to:
- contribute to and challenge the direction of strategic strategy;
- scrutinise executive management's performance;
- monitor performance reporting;
- represent shareholders' interests to avoid agency issues which reduce shareholder value;
- ensure robust financial and risk management systems;
- ensure accurate financial information;
- be responsible for determining appropriate levels of remuneration for executives;
- play a key role in appointing and removing senior managers and in succession planning;
- take direct responsibility for shareholder concerns; and
- link their role with that of institutional shareholders.*

■ Under current good practice, the board is expected to be composed of at least 50% NEDs.

2.4 Remuneration Committees

■ Directors' remuneration has been a major issue for many years, particularly with the increase in global international organisations.

■ An over-dominant executive who pursues personal objectives is just one example of an agency issue.*

■ Directors may "abuse" their position to reward themselves with what many consider to be excessive increases and perks in their compensation arrangements—rewarding themselves despite poor results and underperformance of share price.*

*Large investors can influence corporate governance by helping to ensure transparency and accountability and avoid conflicts of interest between owners and managers. Unlike small investors they can avoid being controlled by the will of the board by exercising their voting rights (e.g. in electing directors to the board).

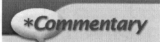

*Excessive remuneration is an obvious cost of the agency relationship which reduces shareholder value.

Commentary

*Contract length and termination payments were designed to make it very expensive to remove a director. Good corporate governance practice now recommends a one-year contract and that termination payments should only be triggered following specific events as determined by the remuneration committee.

■ Good corporate governance practice means an organisation needs to:
- establish a reward policy which attracts, retains and motivates directors to run the company successfully and achieve the long-term interests of shareholders;
- ensure that the performance elements of remuneration form a significant proportion of the total remuneration package;
- design remuneration packages to align director interests with those of the shareholders and to give executive directors appropriate incentives to perform at the highest levels;
- avoid paying more than necessary;
- ensure that benefits reflect performance and success; and
- ensure that full and transparent disclosure is made of the overall remuneration policy and detail of individual director's compensation arrangements.*

*Best practices:
- The structure of non-executive remuneration should be clearly distinguished from that of executives.
- Thresholds for payments of equity-based executive remuneration should be approved by the shareholders.

■ The Code recommends that organisations establish a remuneration committee to set remuneration, pension and compensation payments for the chairman and all executive directors.

- The committee should only consist of independent NEDs.
- The terms of reference made available (e.g. disclosed in the financial statements).
- The committee should also recommend and monitor remuneration for senior management.
- Independent consultants may be appointed to assist the committee.

■ Considerations to be taken into account by the remuneration committee when looking at each director's compensation include:

- the job itself;
- the skills of the individual;
- the past performance of the individual;
- overall contribution to company strategy;
- market rates;
- level of basic salary;
- performance-related elements;
- pensionable elements and retirement benefits;
- entry payments, length of contract and termination payments;
- position relative to other organisations; and
- motivation of director required.

2.5 Audit Committees

■ Audit committees aim to ensure market, public and stakeholder confidence in high-quality financial reporting.

■ The committee carries out a thorough and detailed review of audit matters, both internal and external, thus enhancing the environment for greater external confidence in the entity. Their role is divided into three areas—financial statements and control, external auditors, internal auditors.

■ As most corporate governance codes require the audit committee to comprise 100% independent NEDs (at least one of whom must have recent, relevant, financial accounting experience), the NEDs can contribute independent judgement on matters of critical importance (e.g. investment decisions, risk analysis) and play a positive role in areas that fit with their skills.*

■ The external and internal auditors will thus have a direct link with non-executive directors.*

*Commentary

*Best practice: The chairman of the committee should not be the chairman of the board.

*Commentary

*The chief executive and the chair of the audit committee must particularly develop a respected, transparent, trusted and professional working relationship.

■ Effective audit committees need to be able to investigate issues on their own initiative, rather than as directed by the CEO. They must be clear about what they need to know and determined to receive the information they require.

■ The audit committee should not seek to take an executive role but should aim to be satisfied that management has properly fulfilled its responsibilities.

■ As well as the risks and controls over the financial reporting process, the committee must consider the tax, environmental, legal and other regulatory matters that have a material effect on the financial statements.

■ Corporate governance codes will not change the mindset of a CEO/CFO determined to carry out a fraud. But an effective audit committee should act as a significant deterrent and minimise the opportunities for destructive fraud to remain undetected over time.

2.5.1   Financial Statements and Controls

■ Ensure that internal control properly protects shareholder interests and that financial reporting is accurate, timely and complete.

■ Provide oversight, assessment and review of the board and its functions.

■ Monitor the integrity of the financial statements and announcements relating to the company's financial performance, including review of significant financial reporting judgements.

■ Review the company's internal control, internal financial controls and risk management systems.

■ Monitor and review the effectiveness of the company's internal audit function.

2.5.2   External Auditor

■ Recommend to the board the appointment, re-appointment and removal of the external auditor. If the board refuses to accept such recommendations, it is required by the Code to explain why to shareholders.

■ Approve the remuneration and terms of engagement of the external auditor.

■ Review and monitor the external auditor's independence and objectivity.

■ Review the effectiveness of the audit process, including discussing the scope of the audit (strategy, risks, materiality, resources and work programmes).

■ Review of the representation and management letters and actions taken.

■ Discussing major issues arising from the audit, key accounting and audit judgements, levels of error identified during the audit and why unadjusted errors were not adjusted.*

■ Develop and implement policy on the engagement of the external auditor to supply non-audit services (e.g. approving or rejecting any additional services required).

Commentary

*Best practice: The external auditor should attend the AGM and answer shareholders' questions about the conduct of the audit and the content of the auditor's report.

2.5.3   Internal Audit

- Monitor and assess the role and effectiveness of the internal audit function in the overall context of the company's risk management system.
- Approve the appointment or termination of the head of internal audit.
- Ensure that the internal auditor has direct access to the board chairman and to the audit committee and is accountable to the audit committee.
- Review and assess the annual internal audit work plan.
- Receive a report on the results of the internal auditor's work on a periodic basis.
- Review and monitor management's responsiveness to the internal auditor's findings and recommendations.
- Meet the head of internal audit at least once a year without management's presence.
- Review arrangements which allow "whistle-blowing" by staff of the company.

> **Example 2   Audit Committee Disadvantages**
>
> Suggest THREE disadvantages of audit committees.

2.6   Public Oversight

- Control, supervision and oversight of the financial reporting and auditing process was originally carried out by various professional bodies which (as a group in their jurisdictions such as the UK and the US) also issued various financial reporting and auditing standards.
- As codes of corporate governance were developed (the UK's corporate governance codes were the first in 1992), independent oversight bodies were established to increase public confidence in implementation and effectiveness of the code.
- Public oversight means, in broad terms, the review, checks and balances over applicable procedures and application of rules by members of the public or independent officials representing the public interest.
- As an example of a public oversight role, the Financial Reporting Council (FRC) is the UK's independent regulator responsible for promoting confidence in corporate reporting and governance. The roles of the FRC include:
  - promoting high standards of corporate governance (through the Code);
  - setting, monitoring and enforcing accounting and auditing standards;
  - statutory oversight and regulation of auditors; and
  - operating an independent investigation and discipline scheme for public interest cases.

■ The bodies in the FRC charged with achieving these aims include:

- the Accounting Standards Board;
- the Auditing Standards Board;
- the Professional Oversight Board—oversight of the regulation of the auditing and accounting professions and monitoring of the quality of the auditing function; and
- the Monitoring Committee—seeks to ensure (through review of published financial statements and other information) that financial information reported by public and large private companies complies with relevant accounting requirements.

■ The FRC's strategic outcomes aim to ensure that:

- UK companies with a primary listing in the UK are led in a way that facilitates entrepreneurial success and the management of risk.
- Corporate reports contain information that is relevant, reliable, understandable and comparable and useful for decision-making (including stewardship decisions).
- Users of audit reports can place a high degree of reliance on the audit opinion, including whether financial statements show a true and fair view.
- Clients and employers of professionally qualified accountants and of accountancy firms can rely on them to act with integrity and competence and in the public interest.
- It is an effective, accountable and independent regulator which actively helps to shape the UK's approach to corporate reporting and governance and to influence EU and global approaches.

3 Corporate Social Responsibility

3.1 Concept

Definition

Corporate social responsibility (CSR)—the continuing commitment by a business to behave ethically and to contribute to economic development while improving the quality of life of the workforce and their families, the local community and society at large.

■ The idea of corporations having a responsibility to society has existed ever since they started to affect communities in which they operated. The "industrial revolutions" of the 1800s initially brought this concern to a national level by rallying for laws and regulations that changed, for example, the working conditions of employees.

■ As companies grew from having just a local effect to national and (eventually) global effects (especially from the 1960s), so the global awareness of their impacts on stakeholders (e.g. suppliers, customers, communities, societies and the environment) has grown beyond just local considerations.

- In most jurisdictions, CSR is not covered by laws, regulations or codes although guidelines exist (e.g. the Global Reporting Initiative). It is purely voluntary best practice driven by the fact that in a global environment, brands and business reputation are essential to an organisation's success.

- Organisations are vulnerable to reputation risk (e.g. bad publicity about a product or practice) which can result in damage to consumer (and other stakeholder) trust and thus shareholder value. Consumers will avoid what they see as irresponsible; CSR is seen as one way to minimise that risk.

- Thus many consider CSR to be enlightened self-interest on the part of organisations.
  - Ethically sound organisations attract better business. Those considered unsound are boycotted.
  - Employees are more attracted to work for socially responsible companies and are more committed to them.
  - Positive contribution to society will be a long-term investment in a safer, better-educated and more equitable community creating a more stable context in which to do business.
  - All of the above will result in greater long-term wealth generated by the business (e.g. a higher relative share price).

- Milton Friedman argued that a society determines and meets its needs and wants through the market place where the self-interest pursuit by business happens to result in society getting what it wants. Corporations have no responsibilities other than making a profit for shareholders. Only human beings have moral responsibility for their actions. Social issues are the province of the state and not corporations, thus corporate social responsibility as an end in itself is not appropriate—"The business of business is ... business."

3.2 Factors

- Archie Carroll (*The four faces of corporate citizenship, 1998*) suggested a four-part model of CSR covering the expectations placed on organisations by society:

- Economic—reasonable return to shareholders, safe and fairly paid employment, and quality products at a fair price.
- Legal—follow the letter and spirit of the law applicable to the organisations, its dealings, the environment and interaction with stakeholders.
- Ethical—doing what is right, just and fair over and above what is required by law or economic considerations.
- Philanthropic—the discretionary behaviour of organisations to improve the lives of others who have no direct stake in the organisation.
- In dealing with these, boards would need to consider and provide CSR reporting on:
  - ethical practices;
  - ecology, environmental impact and protection;
  - current and future needs of society;
  - product design and customer relations; and
  - employees, communities and human rights.
- Under the Global Reporting Initiative (www.globalreporting.org), sustainability is the key CSR concept.

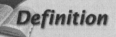
Definition

Sustainable development—development that meets the needs of the present without compromising the ability of future generations to meet their needs.

- Under the Global Reporting Initiative (GRI), sustainability reporting covers, for example, the following key performance indicators:*
  - Economic—customers, suppliers, employees, providers of capital.
  - Environmental—materials, energy, water, biodiversity, emissions, suppliers, compliance, transport.
  - Labour practices—employment, relations, health and safety, training, education, diversity, opportunities.
  - Human rights—strategy, development, non-discrimination, freedom of association, child labour, indigenous rights.
  - Society—community, bribery and corruption, political contributions, competition and pricing.
  - Product responsibility—customer health and safety, advertising, respect for safety.

*Commentary

*To fully understand the concept of CSR and sustainability reporting, it is useful to review an organisation's reports (e.g. www.btplc.com).

3.3 Stakeholder Considerations

▦ The CSR thesis is that companies will build shareholder value by engaging with and possibly satisfying the desires of stakeholders other than legal owners.

Illustration 1 Royal Dutch Shell

In 1995, Royal Dutch Shell (Shell) decided to dispose of an oil drilling platform, Brent Spar, by sinking it in the North Sea. After this had become public knowledge, Greenpeace activists occupied the platform. Following adverse international publicity, a major consumer boycott of its products and criticism from European leaders, Shell decided to abandon the idea of dumping the platform in the sea.

Also in 1995, the company was subject to further significant criticism because of its roll in Nigeria and relations with the military regime governing at that time.

In 1996, Shell undertook extensive market research and stakeholder consultation to establish how it was perceived. The resulting report was very unpleasant reading for the board of Shell—the organisation was basically considered as a corporate villain with very little public support.

The action taken by the board was considered to be radical—the board more or less completely re-wrote the company's General Business Principles to take into account a very broad range of ethical issues and stakeholders. The board recognised that the traditional model of scientific decision-making was no longer valid when dealing with the many and varied social, environmental and ethical issues of the world in which it operated.

The board thus committed itself to a very high level of stakeholder consultation, engagement, sustainability, CSR reporting, Web forums (e.g. "Tell Shell"), open meetings on key events and activities, Web discussion forums ("Shell Dialogue") and open websites where constructive criticism is encouraged. In doing so, the company moved from a DAD framework—decide, announce, deliver—to DDD—dialogue, decide, deliver. Shell has recognised that the company no longer lives in a "trust-me" world but one in which it needs to show stakeholders how and why Shell should be trusted, a "show-me" world.

And Brent Spar? In 1999, after an extensive consultation programme, the platform was recycled as the base for a quay in Norway—at twice the cost of disposal at sea. However, Shell shareholders found this well worth the money spent to have turned Shell into a company that improved shareholder wealth by making good sustainability decisions.

▦ As the Shell illustration shows, it is essential for organisations to identify the key stakeholders and establish their interests. *Session 2* discussed in detail the various categories of stakeholders, and *Illustration 1* shows that providing forums and communication channels for them may be a good way to understand their interests.

▦ Analysing the various stakeholders (Mendelow grid) and their claims will establish the potential sources of risk, influence (both negative and positive) and possible disruption. It also will be necessary to identify those stakeholders whose claims may be in conflict, as these will need to be closely managed.

■ The organisation should consider CSR issues which create business value (or at least minimise business loss), are linked to the company's core business and promote long-run sustainability rather than just reactively conceding to external stakeholder pressure.

■ CSR activities also should be linked to the core competencies of the firm and be systematically assessed, evaluated and communicated to stakeholders. The aim is to achieve social responsibility, sustainability and growth in profits.*

*Commentary

*In dealing with CSR, the GRI guidelines make it perfectly clear that reports should be balanced and report on matters which are of material concern to stakeholders—the good, bad and ugly should be reported, regardless of the fact that the overall picture may not be glowing.

■ Carroll suggested four strategies that organisations could take when dealing with CSR and stakeholder issues:

1. **Proactive**—a strategy which a business follows where it is prepared to take full responsibility for its actions (e.g. discovering a fault in a product and recalling it without being forced to, before any injury or damage is caused or providing full and transparent reporting and disclosure on its operations beyond any legal or ethical requirement to do so).

2. **Reactive**—involves allowing a situation to continue unresolved until the public, government or consumer groups find out about it.

3. **Defence**—minimising or attempting to avoid additional obligations arising from a particular problem.

4. **Accommodation**—taking responsibility for actions when, for example, encouraged to do so by special interest groups or the perception that a failure to act will result in government intervention.

■ In a "CNN world", being reactive and defensive are not acceptable options. Being accommodative in certain situations may well be too little, too late.

Summary

- Corporate governance addresses the means by which organisations are directed and controlled, involving a framework for decision-making processes.

- Nations typically address corporate governance through "codes" designed to protect stakeholders and typically it includes:

  - The composition, balance, committees and roles of various executive and non-executive directors.

  - Duties, functions, appointment, induction and appraisal of directors.

  - Remuneration policy established by the remuneration committee appropriate to attract, retain and motivate directors.

  - Financial reporting reliability, with special consideration towards a balanced and understandable discussion of the internal control system, as well as formation of an audit committee to control and establish risk and ensure accurate, complete and timely reporting.

  - Shareholder rights and responsibilities, including the AGM.

- Codes may be rules-based, meaning that the code determines the exact method by which companies will govern themselves.

- Codes may be principles-based, meaning that companies have some latitude over how they achieve the desired end result. If principles-based, the company may have a "comply or explain" requirement (as in the UK Code).

- The UK's independent regulator responsible for promoting confidence in corporate reporting and governance is the Financial Reporting Council (FRC). The bodies in the FRC are:

  - the Accounting Standards Board;

  - the Auditing Standards Board;

  - the Professional Oversight Board; and

  - the Financial Reporting and Review Panel (FRRP).

- CSR addresses the need for organisations to behave ethically and to consider stakeholder interests which extend past short-term financial gains.

- Sustainability is the key CSR concept with regard to the GRI. Sustainability concerns meeting the needs of the present without compromising the ability of future generations to meet their needs.

Session 9 Quiz

Estimated time: 15 minutes

1. Define "corporate governance". (1.2)

2. Identify FIVE of the nine key underpinning concepts in corporate governance. (1.3)

3. List the FIVE elements which form the key recommendations for most corporate governance codes. (2)

4. State FOUR internal audit requirements placed on the audit committee by corporate governance. (2.5)

5. Define "corporate social responsibility". (3.1)

6. Briefly describe the FOUR expectations suggested by Carroll which CSR places on the organisation. (3.2)

7. Define "sustainability". (3.2)

8. Describe a "proactive" CSR strategy. (3.3)

Study Question Bank

Estimated time: 30 minutes

Priority		Estimated Time	Completed
MCQ9	Governance and Social Responsibility	30 minutes	

EXAMPLE SOLUTIONS

Solution 1—Rules-Based Governance

- Incorporated into the legal structure of the country.
- Applies to all entities within its scope, regardless of the size of that entity.
- No exceptions are made.
- Can be considered as inflexible.
- Statutory penalties applied for non-compliance.
- Updated and modified through the legal process.

Solution 2—Audit Committee Disadvantages

✗ May be seen as an unnecessary legal or regulatory burden placed on the board—"we know how to run the company without anybody else trying to tell us what to do".

✗ Places an additional cost burden on the entity. The advantages offered by having an audit committee must be effectively utilised to ensure appropriate cost benefit (e.g. enhance public credibility, experienced sounding board for the executive directors).

✗ Audit committees will be effective only where they are able to operate as intended by the various codes. Anything less than respect, understanding of the role of the audit committee by the main board and access to all information will diminish that effectiveness.

✗ The demands now placed, for example by the UK Corporate Governance Code and the Sarbanes-Oxley Act, on the time and expertise of members of the audit committee are such that suitable candidates (e.g. experience and qualification) may be harder to find.

✗ The risks and burden of responsibilities being placed on members of audit committees may result in a feeling that the "reward is not worth the effort" or rather that the risks are too high. This may result in the overall ability of the audit committee being less than what it should be.

✗ It is not so much a disadvantage, more a fact of life, that what the audit committee does not know or is able to find out remains unknown—the "unknown unknowns". As when dealing with the auditors, if a CEO is sufficiently determined to withhold information from the auditors, other directors and the audit committee, it may be difficult for such information to be uncovered and determined.*

*Commentary

*Many objections to audit committees were put forward when the UK Corporate Governance Code was first introduced. However, the majority of organisations affected by the Code now recognise the significant benefits application has brought.

Accounting and Finance

FOCUS

This session covers the following content from the *ACCA Study Guide.*

C. Accounting and Reporting Systems, Controls and Compliance

1. The relationship between accounting and other business functions

a) Explain the relationship between accounting and other key functions within the business such as procurement, production and marketing. ☐

b) Explain financial considerations in production and production planning. ☐

c) Identify the financial issues associated with marketing. ☐

d) Identify the financial costs and benefits of effective service provision. ☐

2. Accounting and finance functions within business

a) Explain the contribution of the accounting function to the formulation, implementation and control of the organisation's policies, procedures and performance. ☐

b) Identify and describe the main financial accounting functions in business: ☐
   i) recording financial information
   ii) codifying and processing financial information
   iii) preparing financial statements.

c) Identify and describe the main management accounting and performance management functions in business: ☐
   i) recording and analysing costs and revenues
   ii) providing management accounting information for decision-making
   iii) planning and preparing budgets and exercising budgetary control.

d) Identify and describe the main finance and treasury functions: ☐
   i) calculating and mitigating business tax liabilities
   ii) evaluating and obtaining finance
   iii) managing working capital
   iv) treasury and risk management.

4. The sources and purpose of internal and external financial information, provided by business

a) Explain the various business purposes for which the following financial information is required: ☐
   i) the statement of profit or loss
   ii) the statement of financial position
   iii) the statement of cash flows
   iv) sustainability and integrated reports

b) Describe the main purposes of the following types of management accounting reports: ☐
   i) cost schedules
   ii) budgets
   iii) variance reports.

VISUAL OVERVIEW

Objective: To outline how the accounting function has developed over time and to explain the overall role and separate functions of the accounting department.

THE FINANCE FUNCTION

- Overview
- Financial Management
- Accounting
- Business Considerations
- Forms of Accounting

STRUCTURE

- Functions
- Finance Director/CFO
- Financial Accounting
- Management Accounting
- Comparison
- Finance and Treasury
- Other Business Functions

USERS

- Directors and Managers
- Employees
- Customers and Supplies
- Finance Providers
- Government and Tax Authorities
- Local Communities
- Analysts and Advisers
- Shareholders

INTEGRATED REPORTS

- Business Purpose
- Sustainability Reports

Session 10 Guidance

■ **Understand** the difference between finance and accounting functions (s.1.1).

■ **Know** the elements of financial management (s.1.2) and the forms of accounting (s.1.5).

■ **Know** the functions of the finance director/chief financial officer (s.2.2).

■ **Differentiate** the finance and treasury functions (s.2.6).

■ **Recognise** how different internal and external stakeholders use accounting data (s.3).

1   The Finance Function

1.1   Overview

■ The purpose of the **finance** function in an organisation is to:

- raise money;
- record and control money and related transactions;
- provide key information to managers on financing and accounting matters; and
- report to stakeholders.

■ Finance and accounting are terms often used interchangeably or transposed. Basically, finance is raising and applying money and accounting is recording and controlling what happens to that money.

1.2   Financial Management

■ Financial management describes managing an organisation's finances to achieve its objectives and consists of three elements:

1. **Financial planning**—ensuring the right amount and type of funding is available at the right time in the right place (e.g. short-term funding for purchasing inventory, payment of employees and supporting credit sales and longer-term funding of non-current assets to increase productive capacity or the acquisition of other businesses).

2. **Financial reporting and control**—ensuring that the organisation is managing income, costs and assets (financial and other) in relation to budgets. This process also may include ensuring that financial assets are secure and that management is utilising financial assets in the best way possible for the business and shareholders.

3. **Financial decision-making**—determining optimal choices regarding decisions about investment, financing and dividends. In terms of investment and financing, there are always alternatives available (e.g. through share issues, banks or credit from suppliers). How much of the profits earned should be retained and re-invested in the business or paid out to shareholders as dividends?

Finance—Finance is a branch of economics concerned with resource allocation as well as resource management, acquisition and investment. Finance deals with matters related to money and markets (e.g. raising money through the issuance and sale of debt and/or equity).

■ There are many different sources of finance including:

- the capital markets (long-term); for example, issue of shares (new shares, rights issues) and loan capital (e.g. debentures);

- money markets (short term); for example, bills of exchange, certificates of deposit;

- international money and capital markets (may be useful for international companies but need to take into account expected currency exchange fluctuations);

- retained earnings;

- bank loans, either long-term loans or current account overdraft facilities;

- working capital such as payables and receivables (short term);

- venture capital (usually in exchange for an equity stake and expected high short-term returns in small or start-up businesses); and

- government (e.g. capital or revenue grants which may or may not be repayable and tax reliefs).

Example 1 Public Sector Financing

State which of the previously listed sources of finance would not be available for government organisations.

1.3 Accounting

Accounting is concerned with providing economic information which will be useful to those directly (and to some extent indirectly) connected with an organisation. Although only part of the broader business system, all elements of the business system rely directly (to some degree) on accounting information.

Definition

Accounting—"the process of identifying, measuring and communicating economic information to permit informed judgments and decisions by the users of the information."

—American Accounting Association

■ The information provided by the accounting function should:

- assist management in planning, controlling and decision-making;

- assist business functions in achieving their objectives;

- assess performance of the various areas in an organisation;

- assess performance of the managers of the organisation; and

- enable compliance with various statutory requirements (e.g. annual financial statements).

■ The basic accounting function therefore involves:

- capturing and recording numerical transactions (data);

- analysing the transactions into a required format; and

- presenting the formatted data to a user for appropriate information and action (information).

1.4 Business Considerations

The detail and sophistication of the accounting function depends on a number of factors concerning the business.

1.4.1 Size

▓ Small businesses (e.g. a fruit and vegetable market stall) will have very simple accounting systems to record cash received (e.g. sales made), cash paid (e.g. for items to be sold, wages and services) and basic financial accounts (perhaps each month, but certainly each year for tax purposes).

▓ A large national supermarket chain will use very sophisticated management information systems to know exactly, for example, the cost of every item it sells, the profit margin on each group of products, the detailed costs incurred, inventory levels, sell-by dates, projected customer demand, actual sales per till for each location, available cash to be placed on deposit, cash on deposit, interest being earned, daily analysis and breakdown of sales, cost of sales and overheads.

1.4.2 Type of Activity

▓ **Manufacturing** organisations require basic accounting information relating to cost of raw materials, cost of production, inventory levels, sales, other overheads, assets and liabilities.

▓ **Service** companies may charge for their services based on labour hours, so they will need to account for employee time on a job/client basis. They would be less concerned with accounting for inventory as they are not manufacturers and thus have little inventory. Partnerships would need to account for each individual partner's activities, drawings and profit share.

▓ **Not-for-profit** organisations (e.g. charities) will not need accounting for raw materials, production or sales, but they need to know where their money is coming from, from whom, when and how much, and donations made (to whom, for what, when and how much) plus details of their running expenses.

▓ **Public sector** services, including the armed forces, police, fire and ambulance services, are more likely to be concerned with monitoring capital and revenue expenditure drawn down from their budget allocation and performance measures such as value for money. They will not be concerned with sales or with charging out employees.

1.4.3 Structure

▓ Functional, product, geographical, matrix and composite structures will all require accounting information to be captured, processed, analysed and reported in different ways.

▓ With a functional structure, the accounting may be centralised; with geographical it is more than likely to be decentralised (partially if not wholly).

1.4.4   Complexity

▥ The small sole trader (e.g. the market stall or corner shop) will need very little complexity in accounting function.

▥ The accounting function becomes ever more detailed and complex as businesses:

   ● grow to offer and take credit;

   ● increase the range of raw materials and services used;

   ● increase product ranges;

   ● increase the sophistication of the manufacturing process;

   ● increase suppliers and customers;

   ● trade overseas;

   ● need to buy/sell/hedge foreign currency; and

   ● need additional sources of capital.

1.5   Forms of Accounting

There are three basic forms of accounting—management accounting, cost accounting and financial accounting.*

Management accounting: the process of identification, measurement, accumulation, analysis, preparation, interpretation and communication of financial information that is used internally by an organisation's management to formulate policies, plan, forecast, direct, evaluate, analyse, make decisions and control the business.

Cost accounting: the process of identifying and evaluating production costs. It is one function of management accounting.

Financial accounting: the reporting of the financial position and performance of an organisation through the issue of periodic financial statements (in accordance with established concepts, principles, financial reporting standards and law) to specified external users.

Bookkeeping is the basic classification and recording of actual transactions in monetary terms and provides the underlying information used in financial and management accounting.

*Commentary

*Further detail on the forms of accounting will be covered in later sessions.

Example 2   Charge Out Rates
Detail the accounting information a partner in a major accounting firm would need to determine a charge out rate for a first-year student.

2   Accounting and Finance Structure

2.1   Functions

A typical company accounting and finance structure would be headed by a finance director (FD)—sometimes referred to as the chief financial officer (CFO)—with perhaps three separate functions—financial accounting, cost and management accounting and treasury (including a cashier). Following is an example of the structure of the accounting and finance function at Oxford University.

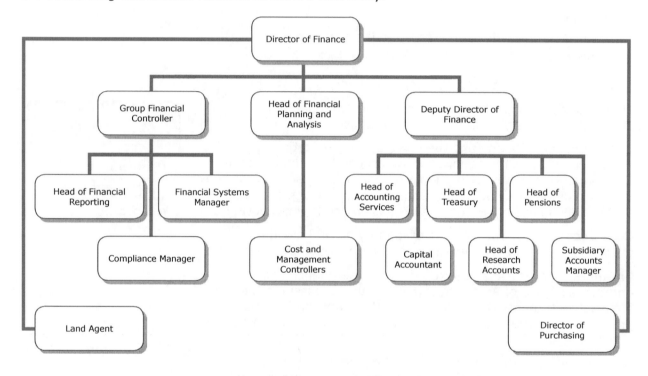

Example 3 Functions

List the main functional areas of financial, cost and management accounting.

2.2   Finance Director/Chief Financial Officer

■ A principal duty of the finance director (FD) or chief financial officer (CFO) is to ensure that the financial strategies support the broader corporate strategies crucial to the success of the whole enterprise. Roles include:

  • Ensuring a timely, full and accurate set of accounting books and records.

  • Implementing financial and management audit and control systems to monitor performance and adherence to budgets.

  • Providing appropriate and timely financial and budgetary statements to the board of directors.

  • Ensuring compliance with all statutory, regulatory and governance reporting, accounting and audit requirements.

- Preparing an annual management budget, financial plans, business plans, feasibility studies and all other financial and business documents as may be required by the board of directors.
- Coordinating activities of outside suppliers of financial services (e.g. financial consultants, banks).
- Developing and maintaining a working relationship with finance providers (e.g. to secure necessary funding).
- Developing a strong working relationship with all essential stakeholders for the benefit of the business (e.g. the audit committee).

2.3 Financial Accounting

As explained earlier, the basic accounting function involves:

- capturing and recording numerical transactions (data);
- analysing the transactions into a required format; and
- presenting the formatted data to a user for appropriate information and action (information).

2.3.1 A Simplified Diagrammatic Approach

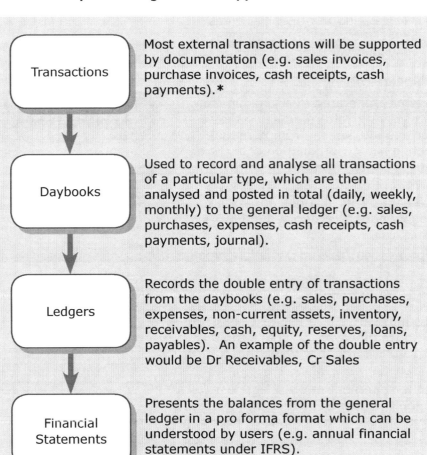

Transactions	Most external transactions will be supported by documentation (e.g. sales invoices, purchase invoices, cash receipts, cash payments).*
Daybooks	Used to record and analyse all transactions of a particular type, which are then analysed and posted in total (daily, weekly, monthly) to the general ledger (e.g. sales, purchases, expenses, cash receipts, cash payments, journal).
Ledgers	Records the double entry of transactions from the daybooks (e.g. sales, purchases, expenses, non-current assets, inventory, receivables, cash, equity, reserves, loans, payables). An example of the double entry would be Dr Receivables, Cr Sales
Financial Statements	Presents the balances from the general ledger in a pro forma format which can be understood by users (e.g. annual financial statements under IFRS).

*Commentary

*The various transaction cycles (sales, purchases, cash) are considered in greater detail in *Sessions 13* and *14* and the detail of double-entry bookkeeping and preparing financial statements is dealt with in F3 *Financial Accounting*.

Note also the extensive use of eXtensible Business Reporting Language (XBRL) for electronically communicating and reporting both internal and external business and financial data.

- Financial statements are historical with information being anything from 6 months to 18 months old (on the basis that they are presented to users 6 months after year end). As such, their practical use can be somewhat limited.

- Under International Financial Reporting Standards (IFRS), a complete set of financial statements comprises:
  - statement of financial position;
  - statement of comprehensive income;
  - statement of cash flows;
  - statement of changes in equity;
  - disclosure notes; and
  - comparative information.

2.3.2 Statement of Financial Position

- This statement shows the assets and liabilities at a given point in time.*

- Assets are presented to help users assess liquidity of available resources and the potential generation of future cash inflows. Liabilities show the potential for cash outflows in both the short term and long term.

- It provides information for calculating key financial ratios (e.g. gearing, return on capital, return on assets, inventory turnover, receivable days, payable days, etc).

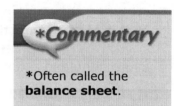

*Often called the **balance sheet**.

2.3.3 Statement of Comprehensive Income

- This statement shows revenue generated over a given period (e.g. one year), gross profit (after deducting the cost of sales—materials, labour and overheads—from revenue) and net profit after deducting all non-production costs (e.g. distribution, administration, finance) from gross profit.*

- Also shows **other comprehensive income**, usually as a separate part of the statement. This includes unrealised gains and losses which would not be recognised in profit or loss (e.g. a revaluation surplus).

- Gross profit percentage (gross profit/revenue) is a fundamental performance indicator.

*Usually referred to as the **statement of profit or loss**.

2.3.4 Statement of Changes in Equity

- This explains the changes in equity share capital and reserves over a period (e.g. retained profit, share capital issued, increase in asset values through revaluation).

- It brings together the key elements linking the statement of financial position with the statement of profit and loss. Sustainable increases in equity (increases other than by share issues) are of importance to investors as it indicates a strongly performing company.

2.3.5 Statement of Cash Flows

- Reports on cash flow activities are classified between operating (can be reconcilable to profit), investing (e.g. purchase and disposal of non-current assets) and financing activities (e.g. issue of share capital).

2.3.6   Accounting Policies and Explanatory Notes

▦ Financial statements are required to show a "true and fair view" of the performance of the entity. Figures alone would not provide sufficient detail required by users of the financial statements to understand them.

▦ Most notes are required by generally accepted accounting principles ("GAAP") such as IFRS or listing rules and legislation.

2.4   Management Accounting

▦ Management accounting concerns planning, controlling and decision-making concerning resources used and produced by an entity.

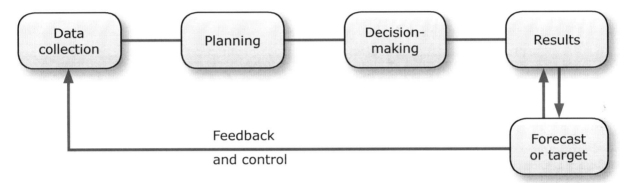

▦ In a modern computerised accounting system, the information required by cost and management accountants will be derived from the same sources as recorded for financial accounting. It is the preparation, presentation and use of the information which is significantly different.

2.4.1   Budgets

▦ Usually, a budget is a financial document used to project future income and expenses. In a manufacturing context, this may well incorporate items expected to be sold and produced and resources (materials, labour and overheads) purchased and consumed.

▦ Using a simplified production and sales model as an example, the initial phase of the budgeting process is to use historical accounting information and forecasts to produce a budget for sales units and price over a particular period (e.g. weekly, monthly, etc).

▦ From this primary budget, a budget for production (units) taking into account opening and closing inventory is produced leading to budgets for raw materials usage, labour usage and other direct overheads, and then required materials purchases and labour costs.

▦ Preparing budgets assists production planning and allows comparing budgeted detail with actual results to enable control over a production process (see s.2.4.3, *Variance Analysis*).

2.4.2 Cost Schedules

▩ Budgets usually will be based on standard costs (e.g. the estimated costs per unit—kg, hours—and usage per unit of production based on, for example, past actual accounting information plus inflation).

▩ Standard costs form the costing record of producing an individual unit (e.g. costing records for the manufacture of a motor car).

▩ A simplified production costing record would show:

- the direct production costs (i.e. those costs which vary directly with production) of materials, labour and direct overheads (e.g. power); and

- indirect production overheads including fixed production costs (management costs, heat, insurance) which either do not vary with units produced or are allocated based on units produced or direct labour hour in production.

▩ The non-production costs for each unit (e.g. post-production storage, distribution, selling, finance and administration) would then be added to give a complete costing record for each unit.

▩ Without the detailed costing structure, the entity would not be able to make pricing decisions factoring in the required profit and hence would be unable to estimate cash flows.*

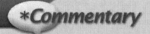

Commentary

*Costing and budgets also may be prepared on a marginal costing/ contribution basis; that is, looking at the contribution (sales price less all variable costs) made by each unit towards fixed costs. Once fixed costs are covered, the contribution is pure profit.

2.4.3 Variance Analysis

▩ Variance analysis is the process of comparing budgeted statements (e.g. sales, production, net profit) and costs with actual (e.g. unit sales, sales price, production costs) and then establishing reasons for the differences and taking appropriate action.

▩ For example, the actual time taken to produce a unit of production may have been greater than budgeted. The management accountant will establish the reasons for this and suggest changes to the production process (if necessary) to bring the time down to what was expected. If the actual time taken was less than budgeted, the accountant will establish why and suggest that production implement the same procedures to ensure that future unit production time is also reduced.

▨ A wide range of variances may be used to provide feedback and control over a production process. Typical variances include:

- **Sales price** variance (e.g. actual price less than budgeted which reduces budgeted profit—contract negotiation process to be reviewed to ensure discounts not freely given).

- **Materials usage** variance (e.g. actual kg used per unit less than budgeted thus increasing budgeted profit—variation made to one process resulted in savings and thus can be made to other processes).

- **Labour efficiency** variance (e.g. actual time taken to produce a unit was greater than budgeted thus decreasing budgeted profit—costing process needs to be reviewed to ensure that realistic timing is used in costing).

▨ Once all of the appropriate variances have been calculated, the budgeted profit can be reconciled to the actual profit.

▨ This is the basic process of planning and control—feedback from variance analysis will be used to (if necessary) modify planning, resources, inputs and/or processes.*

Commentary

*F2 *Management Accounting* covers in detail the specific management accounting requirements of planning, control and decision-making.

2.5 Comparison

	Management Accounting	Financial Accounting
Users of information	Internal management only	Shareholders, banks, creditors, potential investors, tax authorities, government
Format of information	Can take any form. No legal requirements. Best practice developed and used	Presentation regulated by law (e.g. Companies Acts) and the profession through accounting standards
Content	Financial and non-financial, predominantly current with future predictions (e.g. in budgets)	A summary of mainly historical financial information with supporting notes
Level of detail	More detailed (e.g. costs and revenues by department, product)	As prescribed by legislation, etc
Frequency of preparation	Quarterly, monthly, weekly, daily (MIS and ESS can produce on demand)	Usually annually (more frequently for certain types of "public interest" companies)
Purpose of information	Used to plan, control and make decisions	Stewardship and investment decisions
Bases of valuation	Standard costs, relevant costs, marginal costs, absorption costs	Historical costs (as modified by revaluation of certain fixed assets and fair values as required by IFRS)

2.6   Finance and Treasury

2.6.1   Treasury Management

■ Good treasury management is essential to business efficiency. The role of the treasurer is to ensure that a business has sufficient funds, in the appropriate currencies, to meet an organisation's operational, financial and strategic objectives.

■ To achieve these objectives, those involved in treasury management may need to borrow in the money markets, raise funds through long-term debt instruments or trade in foreign exchange.

■ Risk management is a key element in successful treasury management. Treasurers have to manage exposure to currency and interest rate fluctuations. They may use derivative financial instruments as treasury management tools to hedge against adverse movements.

■ According to the Association of Corporate Treasurers, treasury is concerned with four key issues:

- **Cash management**—monitoring the company's cash budgets and balances. For example, to decide if it is advantageous to give/take settlement discounts or to make overnight deposits of surplus cash.

- **Financing**—raising finance through the markets, monitoring the company's investment/borrowings to ensure they gain as much interest income as possible and incur as little interest expense as possible.

- **Foreign currency**—monitoring foreign exchange rates and managing the company's exposure to currency fluctuations.

- **Tax**—managing the company's affairs to legally minimise the tax payable by the company.

2.6.2   Taxation

■ As mentioned above, the treasury function, if not financial accounting, aims to legally minimise the organisation's exposure to taxation.

■ Legally minimising exposure to taxation is referred to as tax avoidance and is a perfectly acceptable business practice, provided the tools used are "in the spirit" of the tax legislation. Tax evasion is a criminal offence.

- **Tax avoidance**—the legal use of the rules of the tax regime to reduce the amount of tax payable by means that are within the law.

- **Tax evasion**—the use of illegal means to reduce a tax liability (e.g. not declaring overseas deposits, interest or earnings) and is therefore a criminal offence.

- **Tax mitigation**—the conduct that reduces tax liabilities without frustrating the intention of the legislation (i.e. in the spirit of the law).

2.6.3   Investment Appraisal

▨ For a company considering a long-term investment, one of the key questions to be asked is how the investment will be financed. For a public company, the options are either to issue new capital or to borrow.

▨ Reasons for issuing new shares:

- Dividends can be suspended if profits are low; loans, however, need to be repaid.
- Lending institutions usually require some form of security before advancing money.
- Does not increase the gearing ratio.

▨ Advantages of raising loan finance:

- Tax efficient—interest payments are tax deductible; dividends, however, come out of post-tax profits.
- No change of ownership, as with share issue.
- Shareholders normally expect a higher rate of return if new shares are issued.

2.6.4   Working Capital

▨ Working capital is the excess of current assets (e.g. inventory, receivables and cash) over current liabilities (e.g. trade payables and bank overdraft). The management of working capital can be vital to a company's success.

- **Inventory**—large inventory balances avoid stock-outs, but holding costs will be high. Inventory systems help to manage inventory levels and reduce inventory holding and obsolescence costs.
- **Trade receivables**—ideally the time frame in which customers settle should be as short as possible as this reduces the risk of bad debts (action to recover can be taken earlier) and improves cash flow. Customers, however, wish to take as long as possible to settle, unless beneficial settlement discounts are offered.
- **Trade payables**—suppliers wish to be paid as quickly as possible, while their customers wish to delay payment for as long as possible. Delayed payments may result in suppliers offering unfavourable terms or refusing to supply. It is often advantageous to the company to establish good relationships with its suppliers.
- **Cash**—attempting to strike a balance between having sufficient cash available for short-term needs while maximising investment opportunities for surplus cash.

▨ The finance function must establish appropriate guidelines and the balance to be struck for each component of working capital.

2.7   Other Business Functions

2.7.1   Purchasing (Procurement)

In considering the purchase cycle and the purchasing mix, further relationships between the accounting function and purchasing will include:

■ Providing suppliers with financial detail about the firm (e.g. financial statements) to negotiate and obtain a credit rating and payment terms from the supplier.

■ Establishing and advising the purchase department of the maximum purchase costs for raw materials and services to maintain budgeted financial margins.

■ Preparing overall financial budgets.

■ Advising purchasing of the economic viability of settlement discount terms when negotiating with suppliers.

■ Advising purchasing of the most economical way of settling with suppliers (e.g. electronic transfer of funds) such that this may be included in any contract with the supplier.

2.7.2   Production

The production function relies primarily on management accounting as opposed to financial accounting. Further relationships between the accounting and production functions include:

■ Cost measurement, allocation and absorption to produce budgets and actual costs, comparison and variance analysis.

■ Establishment of overall costs (capital and running, fixed and variable), expected income and expected returns in new product or business process development.

■ Advise on the financial viability of capital equipment proposals including an analysis of the financial feasibility of the project and the best option for financing the project.*

*Commentary

*May include estimated capital and running costs, estimated returns, payback period (time taken for the project to pay back its initial investment), discounted cash flow techniques (including net present value and internal rate of return), break-even analysis and return on capital employed.

2.7.3   Direct Service Provision

■ A key element of service provision related to the finance and accounting function is determining costs of providing the service and the price to charge for that service.

■ The management accounting function plays a key role in determining the elements of direct costs (e.g. salaries and perhaps materials) and the recoverable overheads which can be attached (and on what basis they are recovered). Their expertise in this area ensures all related costs have been identified and recovered in order to contribute to an organisation's profits.

■ Where a service charge is made, the financial accounting function will need to determine how that charge will be recognised as revenue in the financial statements.

■ In some cases, the service provided may be under a warranty clause such that there will be no charge to the end user. Under such circumstances, the costs of providing the service under the warranty must be estimated and an appropriate provision made in the financial statements.

2.7.4 Marketing

■ The basic functions of marketing (i.e. customer analysis, buying, selling, product/service planning, social responsibility, price planning, distribution, market research and opportunity analysis) share a strong relationship with accounting. (See *Session 1* for details of the marketing function).

■ Finance and accounting are embedded within most of these functions, for example:

- procurement, terms of purchase, discounts, warranties, etc;
- new product development, capital investment, profitability, etc; and
- customer credit plans, cash flow and inventory management, etc.

■ There are also the direct costs associated with marketing (e.g. advertising, employees, displays, packaging, branding, warehousing, distribution, after sales service, data collection and analysis).*

■ In addition, the marketing mix and the product life cycle have financing and accounting implications.

■ It is a common mistake to consider only the direct-marketing budget (e.g. the costs of the marketing department) as the financial issue. Because marketing affects most operational areas, it can be easy to underestimate its true financial effect (e.g. introducing a new product generates additional research and development costs, new capital investment, increased production costs, increased storage and distribution costs, etc).

*See *Session 13* for additional information on the marketing function.

■ The financial issues can broadly be divided into three areas:

- Raising finance
- Utilising finance
- Performance indicators.

■ When introducing a new product, sufficient finance should be planned to complete its life cycle. (The product life cycle indicates that there will be a negative effect on cash resources in the early stages followed by positive cash flows as the product enters and grows within its market.)

■ The initial effect on cash resources may include both revenue items (e.g. research and development) and capital items (e.g. buildings, plant and machinery). As the product progresses through its life cycle, the financial effect of innovation (e.g. upgraded versions) also must be recognised.

■ Utilising finance must ensure the most efficient and effective use of what usually will be limited cash resources (i.e. meeting the entity's benchmarks on financial performance).

■ The effect of marketing must be assessed to ensure that the resources used add value to the entity. Typical financial performance indicators include:

- increase/decrease in sales revenue
- return on investment
- market share (percentage and value)
- return on sales
- operating and net profit
- return on capital employed

■ One difficulty in measuring performance indicators is ensuring that all relevant marketing costs have been identified and accurately measured.

3 Users of Accounting Information

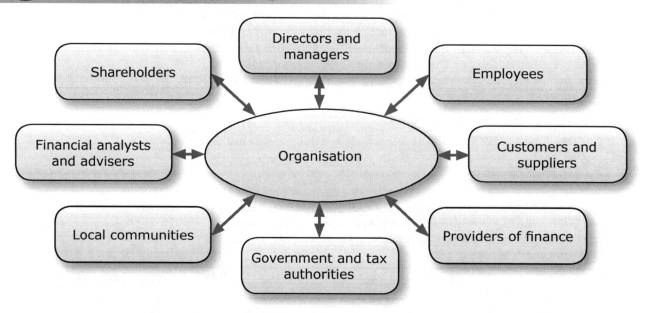

3.1 Directors and Managers

- Management is about planning, organising, commanding, coordinating and controlling (Fayol). It is effective utilisation and coordination of resources (e.g. capital, plant, materials and labour) to efficiently achieve defined objectives.

- Managers therefore need specific information to enable them to plan, control and make decisions. (Strategic, tactical and operational requirements for information are considered in *Session 24.*)

- Management information would be obtained through the internal cost and management systems.

Example 4 Decisions

Describe FOUR decisions requiring management accounting information related to production or sale of goods.

3.2 Employees

- As internal stakeholders, employees have a direct interest in wages, job security, career progression and so forth offered by their employer.

- Some employees below management level may be involved in decision-making and will therefore have access to relevant management information. In other cases they will be capturing, processing and reporting information to their managers.

- Companies which apply corporate governance and CSR principles may provide employees with regular "employee reports" summarising company performance (e.g. departmental sales compared to budget and prior year with explanations for any significant differences). In addition, they also will be given a copy of the full year-end financial statements.

3.3   Customers and Suppliers

■ Customers require financial information to assess whether the organisation will be a secure source of supply and will be able to continue to supply after-sales service. It is unlikely that they would be able to access management information and would thus need to rely on the annual financial statements and other external sources.

■ Suppliers primarily need to know that they will be paid for goods and services they deliver. Secondly, they may wish to establish a long-term relationship with their customers. As with customers, they are unlikely to have access to management information and thus would rely on annual financial statements and credit references. If suppliers are uncertain as to the creditworthiness of the company, they can require cash before delivery or take personal guarantees from the directors.

3.4   Finance Providers

■ Providers of finance basically wish to ensure that the company will meet its repayment schedule, including interest payments. Because of the critical nature of providing finance, many providers require security in the form of assets (e.g. land and buildings). Although providers can review the annual financial statements, many will carry out appropriate due diligence on the value of the assets proposed as security and will hold the ownership documents.

■ In addition, it is not unusual for banks which provide, for example, overdraft facilities to request monthly management accounts and budgets (especially cash flow forecasts). Failure to agree or produce this information on a timely basis will result in the bank withdrawing its facilities.

■ A further form of warning trigger will be the inclusion of financial performance benchmarks in the finance agreement. A typical performance indicator would be a liquidity ratio. While management accounts may provide that indicator, as the annual financial statements are audited, they will provide a more reliable source of information to the bank.*

*Commentary

*Auditors in some regulated industries (e.g. banking) are required to audit performance indicators throughout the year and report to the regulators if they were breached at any time.

3.5 Government and Tax Authorities

▨ Businesses are taxed on the basis of their taxable profits, as calculated through adjustments made to the annual profits. The tax authorities therefore take an interest in the annual financial statements.

▨ Governments can play an active role in the allocation of resources. They will, therefore, review the annual financial statements of companies in certain industries to establish whether any particular economic management is required.

▨ Information from companies also may be needed for regulatory purposes (e.g. information on costs and profits may be requested to consider whether a company or group of companies is adhering to competition policy, operating an illegal cartel or earning unfair profits). Such information will be sourced from management accounting information which, if the company refused to provide, could result in fines or the possible imprisonment of directors.

▨ Governmental contracts are often awarded on a "cost plus" basis (i.e. the cost of supplying the goods or service plus an additional profit element) and total costs to the government will therefore be based on the costs of the goods or services supplied by the contractor. This approach is often used when awarding defence contracts.

▨ The government also will be interested to learn whether businesses are making excessive profits as a result of their dealings with the government. Again, refusal to allow access to costing and management records may result in penalties.

3.6 Local Communities

▨ Local communities provide employees, suppliers and customers to organisations. They also take an interest in the organisation's impact on the local environment.

▨ They will not have access to management accounting information, but will be able to obtain copies of the annual financial statements. They may take great interest in any CSR information of direct relevance to them.

3.7 Financial Analysts and Advisers

▨ Financial analysts and advisers will require information from organisations to provide to their clients and, in the case of journalists, to the reading public. If the company is listed, then information will be provided through annual financial statements and half-yearly or quarterly interim financial statements. Listed companies also will have to provide specific reports to the stock exchange on particular events (e.g. a profits warning).

▨ Analysts and advisers do not have direct access to management information but rely on information provided to them through meetings with key management.

3.8 Shareholders

■ Shareholders have two primary interests in their "ownership" of a company—investment decisions and stewardship decisions.

3.8.1 Investment Decisions

■ Investment decisions are basically concerned with increasing the wealth of the owners through dividends and capital value growth. Shareholders will wish to assess the extent to which the business has generated financial benefits and the likely future prospects of the business.

■ Small shareholders in listed companies will be able to assess their investment through the annual financial statements (extensive disclosure requirements include detailed risk assessments), interim financial statements, stock exchange, the financial press and information provided through the company's website.*

*Commentary

*Although there are formal internal and external channels for obtaining financial information, most listed companies (in following best practice) also provide extensive information on their Web pages dedicated to investors and other stakeholders.

■ They also will wish to assess the degree of risk associated with their investment in the business. Information relating to associated risks and returns will be useful when deciding whether to hold or sell their shares in the business.

■ In unlisted businesses, the organisation tends to be owner managed. Thus, the primary shareholders are directors and will have access to full management information.

■ In listed companies where directors hold shares, they will have access to insider information (e.g. management accounts) and great care must be taken to ensure that insider trading does not take place.

3.8.2 Stewardship Decisions

■ As discussed in *Session 9*, institutional shareholders, under corporate governance requirements, will expect to have regular meetings with key management but will not be allowed access to management accounting information.

■ The stewardship decisions made by shareholders are served through the annual financial statements, CSR, annual general meetings, meetings with directors, company websites and press reports.

4 Integrated Reports

Definition

Integrated report—A report to stakeholders on the strategy, performance and activities of the organisation in a manner that allows stakeholders to assess the ability of the organisation to create and sustain value over the short-, medium- and long-term.

—*The Integrated Reporting Committee of South Africa*

4.1 Purpose

▓ The purpose of an **integrated report** is summarised by the definition. An effect report reflects the organisation's ability to create and sustain value based on:

- its financial, social, economic and environmental systems; and
- the quality of its relationships with its stakeholders.

Benefits

✔ It brings together the significant information about the organisation's strategy, governance, performance and prospects.

✔ It presents, in a single report, information from the following:
  - financial statements;
  - governance reports; and
  - sustainability reports.

✔ It reflects the commercial, social and environmental context within which the organisation operates.

✔ It provides a clear and concise representation of the organisation's stewardship and how it creates value, now and in the future.

Commentary

Currently these are separate reports although they may be combined in an Annual Report.

4.2 Key Components

▓ Report profile	The scope and boundary of the report.
▓ Organisational overview and Business model	What the organisation does. How it creates and sustains value in the short-, medium- and long-term.
▓ Governance and Remuneration	Governance structure. How governance supports the organisation's strategic objectives. Approach to remuneration.
▓ Operating context including: Risks and Opportunities	The circumstances under which the organisation operates including: • key resources and sustainability • opportunities faced.
▓ Strategic objectives and Strategies to achieve them	Where the organisation wants to go. How it is going to get there.
▓ Performance	How the organisation has fared over the reporting period.
▓ Future outlook	Opportunities, challenges and uncertainties and their implications for strategies and future performance.

4.3   Sustainability Reports

▨ A sustainability report* is about an organisation's capacity to endure or be maintained. It is based on performance in FOUR key areas:

   1. Economic

   2. Environmental

   3. Social

   4. Governance performance.

▨ It may be an intrinsic element of an integrated report or a separate report.

*Commentary

*Other terms for this non-financial report are the "triple bottom line" report and "corporate social responsibility" (or "CSR") report.

Purposes

▨ To assist organisations in making their operations sustainable by establishing a reporting process which:

   ● sets goals;

   ● measures performance; and

   ● manages change.

▨ To communicate positive and negative sustainability impacts to stakeholders.

▨ To monitor sustainability on an ongoing basis and provide management with information for decision-making about the organisation's strategy.

▨ To manage change towards a sustainable global economy that combines long-term profitability with social justice and environmental care.

Guidance

▨ The major providers of guidance for sustainability reporting include:

   ● the Global Reporting Initiative (The GRI Sustainability Reporting Framework and Guidelines); and

   ● the Organisation for Economic Co-operation and Development (OECD Guidelines for Multinational Enterprises).

▨ The GRI Guidelines contain three types of Standard Disclosures which identify information that is relevant and material to most organisations and of interest to most stakeholders:

   1. Strategy, Profile and Governance

   2. Management Approach

   3. Performance Indicators.

▨ Performance indicators provide comparable information about the organisation's economic, environment and social performance. (See *Session 9* for examples.)

Summary

- The finance function's purpose is to raise money, record and control the application of the money and provide information to key stakeholders, including management.
  - **Finance** is raising and applying money.
  - **Accounting** is keeping track of money.
- The three elements of financial management are planning, reporting and control and decision-making.
- The basic accounting function involves:
  - capturing and recording transactions;
  - analysing transactions into a usable format; and
  - presenting information to end users for their decision-making process.
- Management accounting formats accounting data to make decisions and control the business. Primarily used by internal management, it is concerned with cost schedules, budgets and variance analysis.
- Financial accounting reports financial position and organisational performance based on historical results, and generally presents data in a standardised form as required by law or listing rules.
- Cost accounting identifies and evaluates production costs; cost accounting data will likely be used in both management and financial accounting.
- The type of accounting information provided will depend on size, type of activity, organisational structure (functional, product, matrix, etc) and complexity.
- CFOs relate across the organisation at a strategic level and are often considered "partners" with the CEO.
- Treasury management attempts to:
  - ensure that a business has sufficient funds to meet operational, financial and strategic objectives;
  - determine how to acquire new funds required for expansion or acquisition;
  - manage exposure to currency and interest rate fluctuations; and
  - reduce the organisation's tax liability through legal means.
- Customers, suppliers, finance providers, government, financial analysts, shareholders and other stakeholders are all interested in a company's financial results.

Session 10 Quiz
Estimated time: 10 minutes

1. Describe the THREE elements of financial management. (1.2)
2. Explain the difference between management accounting and financial accounting. (1.5)
3. Describe the roles of a typical finance director. (2.2)
4. Explain the difference between treasury management and investment appraisal. (2.6)
5. Explain why customers require financial information. (3.3)

 Study Question Bank
Estimated time: 20 minutes

Priority		Estimated Time	Completed
MCQ10	Accounting and Finance	20 minutes	

EXAMPLE SOLUTIONS

Solution 1—Public Sector Financing

- Share issues on the capital markets, as public sector organisations do not have share capital. Government bonds would be issued instead on the national and international markets.

- Retained earnings as they are not profit/loss oriented.

- Venture capital as this relates only to the private sector.

- Tax relief—as such government organisations are not taxed.*

Solution 2—Charge Out Rates

- On the basis that charge out rates are based on the recovery of direct expenses (e.g. the cost of employment), of indirect expenses and a proportion for partnership profits:

  - Total hours available (hours per day, days per week, weeks in a year); less

  - Expected national and annual holiday hours; less

  - Expected hours of sick leave; less

  - Expected hours of training (examination and in-house); giving

  - **Annual chargeable hours available (from above).**

  - Annual gross salary; plus

  - Annual salary costs (wages tax, social tax, pension fund, car costs?); plus

  - Annual training costs (may be included in office overheads); giving

  - **Total employment costs.**

  - Office overheads (administration staff, rent, services, stationery, equipment, etc).

  - Partner profit share (as a percentage of the charge out rate).

- The first grouping would provide the charge out rate required to recover employment costs for the student, based on the expected chargeable hours.

- The second grouping would be based on total office overheads and total chargeable time for all grades.

- A very simplistic example would be that one third of a charge out rate recovers salary costs, one third recovers overheads and the remaining one third is the partner's profit share.

*Commentary

*The main source of financing for the public sector would be through taxation (national and local) and borrowings. Some public sector organisations will also raise money through fees (e.g. leisure centres, prescription charges, eye tests, dentistry).

Solution 3—Functions

Financial
- Sales ledger
- Debt collection
- Credit control
- Purchase ledger
- Suppliers
- Payroll
- General ledger
- Statutory statements
- Sales tax (VAT)
- Corporate tax

Cost
- Inventory
- Materials
- Labour
- Overheads
- Job, contract, process
- Variances

Management
- Budgetary coordination
- Analysis
- Investigation
- Project appraisal

Solution 4—Decisions

- Cost of goods produced
- Quantity of goods to produce
- Cost of goods purchased
- Appropriate mix of goods to produce
- Investment required in new equipment to produce the goods
- Amount of finance necessary to produce the goods
- Procurement of inventory (e.g. delivery times)

External and Internal Audit

FOCUS

This session covers the following content from the *ACCA Study Guide.*

C. Accounting and Reporting Systems, Controls and Compliance

2. Accounting and finance functions within business

e) Identify and describe the main audit and assurance roles in business ☐
   i) internal audit
   ii) external audit.

f) Explain the main functions of the internal auditor and the external auditor and how they differ. ☐

Session 11 Guidance

■ **Learn** all the definitions and key terms.

■ **Understand** the key differences between internal and external audit (s.1), although it is not crucial to learn the *detail* of the external auditor's report (s.3.2) or the audit process (s.3.3). These will, however, give you a good idea of what external audit is about.

■ **Know** the assignments of the internal audit function (s.4.5); this will help you differentiate internal from external audit.

(continued on next page)

VISUAL OVERVIEW

Objective: To describe the separate roles of external and internal auditors.

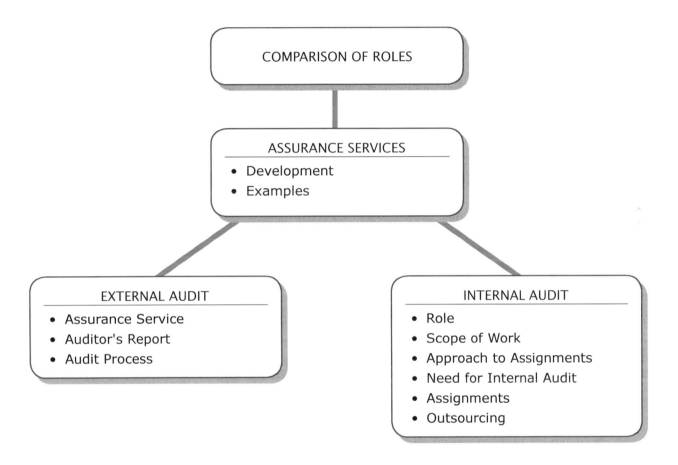

■ **Recognise** the principal agent relationships between external auditor, shareholders and management (s.3.1) versus the relationship between the internal auditor and management (s.4.1). These relationships identify the roles of external and internal auditors.

1 Comparison

Before considering in detail the separate roles of the external
and internal audit functions, the table below provides a useful
comparison of their differences.

	EXTERNAL AUDIT	INTERNAL AUDIT
Role	• To provide an independent opinion (in a report) on financial statements.	• To appraise, examine and evaluate organisational activities and assist management in discharging its responsibilities.
Required by	• Statute (typically).	• Management, usually in larger organisations, will be urged or required by best practice (e.g. governance codes) to continually review need for internal audit.
Appointed by	• Shareholders (usually at an Annual General Meeting) or directors on behalf of shareholders (must be approved by shareholders at AGM).	• Highest level of management charged with responsibility for internal audit (e.g. audit committee under corporate governance codes).
Reports to	• Shareholders (primary statutory duty) and management (professional responsibility).	• For listed companies, usually the audit committee under corporate governance codes. For other companies, the highest level of management charged with governance (e.g. the board).
Reports on	• Financial statements. Primary responsibility is of a financial focus.	• Organisational risk management, internal control and quality of performance. Focus is operational as well as financial.
Forms opinions on	• "True and fair view" (or similar) of financial statements.	• Effectiveness of risk management strategy and operations, operation of corporate governance, adequacy and effectiveness of internal control and other business functions as a contribution to the economic, efficient and effective use of resources.
Status	• Independent of client company.	• Employee (therefore potentially less objective).
Qualification	• Usually ACCA, ICAEW, ICAI or ICAS.	• May also be members of other professional bodies (e.g. IIA) or unqualified.
Scope of assignment	• Unlimited, to fulfil statutory obligation. Usually defined by legislation as well as International Standards on Auditing (ISA).	• Prescribed by management, those charged with governance or audit committee.
Conduct of audit	• In accordance with ISAs, for example.	• Similar, *Standards for the Professional Practice of Internal Auditing,* including ethics.

2 Assurance Services

2.1 Development

▓ Over the last 20 years or so, the auditing profession (both internal and external) has sought to broaden its role with external audit developing a wide range of **assurance services** (of which the financial statement audit is just one) and internal audit becoming an essential assurance element on the risk assessment necessary for strong corporate governance.

Definition

Assurance services—independent professional services which improve the quality of information, or its context, for decision-makers.

Assurance engagement—"... a practitioner expresses a conclusion designed to enhance the degree of confidence of the intended users other than the responsible party about the outcome of the evaluation or measurement of a subject matter against criteria."

—International Federation of Accountants (IFAC)

▓ Factors contributing to the increasing demand for assurance services include:

- The rapid expansion of information available, the changing information needs of businesses and consumers and the increase in demand for relevant information for decision-makers.
- Developments in IT and the growth of computerisation in businesses leading to more systems and risk-based approaches requiring assurance to be given to both internal and external users.
- Globalisation of businesses creating world-wide needs.
- Increasing corporate accountability demanding more relevant and reliable information.
- The accounting profession responding to the opportunity to position the professional accountant as a primary provider of non-audit services.

2.2 Examples

▓ Typical assurance services include:

- Audits of financial statements (can only be carried out by external auditors).
- Reviews of historical financial information (can be internal auditors, but usually an external auditor service).
- Business ethics audits.*
- Business risk assessments.*
- E-commerce assessments.*
- Performance measurement.*
- Systems and control reliability.*

*Commentary

*These are usually carried out by internal audit but may be undertaken by external audit.

3 External Audit

■ The independent **external audit** lends confidence to the integrity of corporate reporting for the benefit of shareholders, other stakeholders and society as a whole by providing an external, independent and objective view on the statutory financial statements and related reports produced by management.

3.1 As an Assurance Service

■ As noted above, the external audit is an assurance service. The responsible party (directors) prepare the subject matter (financial statements) for the intended users (shareholders). The auditor then provides assurance to the shareholders about those financial statements and related disclosures based on appropriate criteria (the directors' assertions, IFRS and other statutory requirements).

> **Definition**
>
> **External audit**—a periodic examination of accounting books and records by an independent auditor in order to express an opinion (whether the financial statements are prepared, in all material respects, in accordance with an identified financial reporting framework).

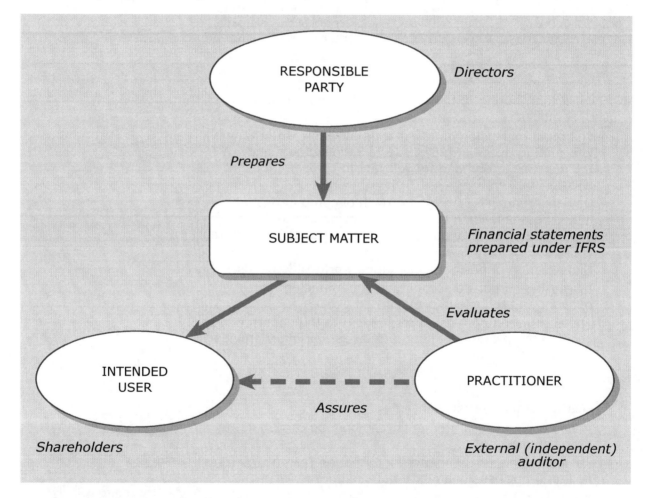

■ Generally, a company is owned by its shareholders (principals) but managed by its directors (agents). Shareholders appoint directors and then approve auditors to provide assurance on information presented by the directors (annual financial statements as required by law).

■ In most jurisdictions, the relationships between the directors, shareholders and auditors are described in terms of stewardship, agency and accountability.

3.1.1 Stewardship

▓ Stewardship is the practice of managing another person's property. Directors and other managers of an enterprise have the responsibility of stewardship for the property of that enterprise, which is owned by the shareholders.

▓ Responsibilities (e.g. duties embodied in statute and corporate governance requirements) include:

- keeping books of accounts and proper accounting records;
- safeguarding the assets of the enterprise;
- implementing appropriate business, financial and risk management controls;
- producing **financial statements** which show a true and fair view and the results of their stewardship; and
- producing a directors' report and other information consistent with the financial statements and containing certain specified information as required by listing rules.

3.1.2 Agency

▓ An agent is an individual (or another enterprise) employed or used to provide a particular service. The individual utilising the agent is referred to as the principal.

Example 1 Agents

Identify the agency relationships between auditors, directors and shareholders.

3.1.3 Accountability

▓ Directors of an enterprise are ethically accountable to the shareholders by the nature of their agency relationship.

▓ Many jurisdictions also place legal **accountability** requirements on directors and specify the way they communicate with shareholders and other stakeholders (e.g. director's reports, financial statements prepared under an appropriate framework such as IFRS).

▓ Directors of listed companies also will be subject to listing rules and corporate governance codes (e.g. interim financial statements, regular meetings with financial institutions, profit and going concern warnings, analysis and management of risk, audit committees, annual general meetings).

▓ The auditors of a company's financial statements are accountable to shareholders. Although auditors must act in the interest of the shareholders, they also must consider other stakeholders who may read their report.

Definition

Financial Statements—under IFRS these include statements of financial position, comprehensive income, cash flows and disclosure notes.

Definition

Accountability—responsibility for actions, products, decisions and policies within the scope of the role and encompassing the obligation to report, explain and be answerable for resulting consequences.

Key Point

Auditors are **not** agents of any other stakeholder; their report is addressed only to shareholders.

3.2   The Auditor's Report

■ The objective of an audit of financial statements is to enable the auditor to express an opinion whether the financial statements are prepared, in all material respects, in accordance with an identified financial reporting framework. This is done through the auditor's report.

■ The auditor's report presented is an example of a report with an unmodified opinion. Should the auditor materially disagree with any facts or figures presented in the financial statements or is unable to obtain all information required to form an opinion (limitation of scope) he must modify his opinion accordingly.

■ Note that the auditor only reports on the financial statements as defined by the relevant financial reporting framework. The auditor must, however, review any other information sent to shareholders with the financial statements (e.g. chairman's statement, CEO's review, directors' report, sustainability report) for inconsistencies with the financial statement. Any material inconsistencies must be reported to the shareholders by the auditor.

■ In addition, in most jurisdictions, the auditor is required to report, by exception, on certain matters if such matters have not been duly complied with (e.g. failure to maintain proper books and records). If the requirements have been adhered to they are not referred to in the auditor's report.

■ Although external auditors do not specifically report on the internal control of the company, they are required by ISAs to report to management (and the audit committee for listed companies) any material weaknesses in control design, implementation or operation they become aware of during their audit.

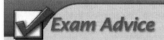 Exam Advice

The format and content of the auditor's report will not be examined in F1. It has been produced here to help in understanding the role of the external auditor.

Reference can be by page number →

INDEPENDENT AUDITOR'S REPORT TO ... ← On whose behalf audit is carried out

We have audited the financial statements of ABC Company, which comprise the statement of financial position as at 31 December 20X1, and the statement of comprehensive income, statement of changes in equity and statement of cash flows for the year then ended, and a summary of significant accounting policies and other explanatory notes.

Management's Responsibility for the Financial Statements

Detailed responsibilities including reference to internal controls and fraud →

Management is responsible for the preparation and fair presentation of the financial statements in accordance with International Financial Reporting Standards, and for such internal control as management determines is necessary to enable the preparation of financial statements that are free from material misstatement, whether due to fraud or error.

← Standards complied with

Auditor's Responsibility.

Our responsibility is to express an opinion on these financial statements based on our audit. We conducted our audit in accordance with International Standards on Auditing. Those standards require that we comply with ethical requirements and plan and perform the audit to obtain reasonable assurance whether the financial statements are free from material misstatement.

An audit involves performing procedures to obtain audit evidence about the amounts and disclosures in the financial statements. The procedures selected depend on the auditor's judgement, including the assessment of the risks of material misstatement of the financial statements, whether due to fraud or error. In making those risk assessments, the auditor considers internal control relevant to the entity's preparation and fair presentation of the financial statements in order to design audit procedures which are appropriate in the circumstances, but not for the purpose of expressing an opinion on the effectiveness of the entity's internal control. An audit also includes evaluating the appropriateness of accounting policies used and the reasonableness of accounting estimates made by management, as well as evaluating the overall presentation of the financial statements.

← Reasonable, but not absolute, assurance

Nature of audit examination (scope)

We believe that the audit evidence we have obtained is sufficient and appropriate to provide a basis for our audit opinion.

Opinion

Unmodified implies that, for example, changes in accounting principles have been properly determined and disclosed →

In our opinion, the financial statements give a true and fair view of the financial position of ABC Company as of 31 December 20X1, of its financial performance and its cash flows for the year then ended in accordance with International Financial Reporting Standards ... (and comply with ...).

or "present fairly, in all material respects"

Signature,

Date

Address

And/or applicable GAAP

Must include

Relevant statutes/law

3.3 Audit Process

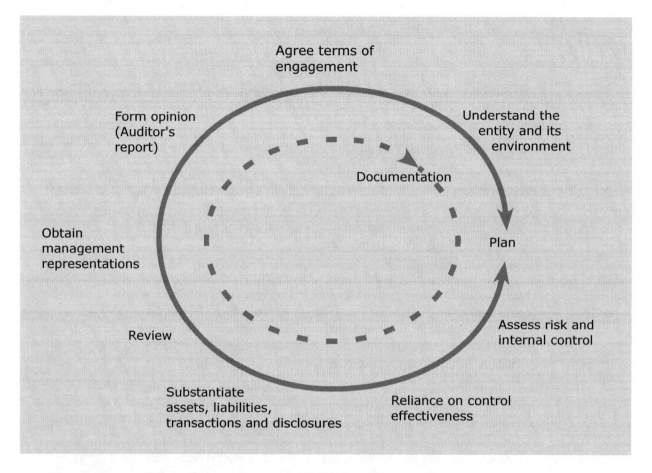

- ■ **Engagement letter**—sets out management's and the auditor's duties and responsibilities.

- ■ **Planning**—planning and controlling audit work is essential to performing work to the required high standard of skill and care. Includes understanding the entity, its environment and business risk, internal control and the risk of material misstatements in the financial statements.

- ■ **Reliance on control effectiveness**—the auditor must test the effectiveness of controls in order to obtain assurance of their operation. This is usually referred to as *control testing* or *compliance testing*.

- ■ **Substantiate (verify) assets, liabilities, transactions and disclosures**—the auditor tests substantive assertions (e.g. completeness, occurrence, measurement, rights and obligations, valuation, existence). Referred to as *substantive testing*.

- ■ **Review and finalisation procedures**—to ensure that the audit has been carried out in accordance with ISA and that the audit working papers fully support the audit opinion.

- **Obtain management representations**—the auditor asks management to formally confirm in writing that it:
  - is responsible for the financial statements and internal controls to prevent and detect fraud;
  - has recognised and carried out legal and governance responsibilities; and
  - approves the financial statements.*
- **Sign auditor's report**—after the directors have approved the financial statements, the auditor will sign the audit report.

*Representations may also be required to support audit evidence (e.g. that all liabilities have been recognised).

4 Internal Audit

4.1 Role

Internal audit—"An independent, objective assurance and consulting activity designed to add value and improve an organisation's operations. It helps an organisation accomplish its objectives by bringing a systematic, disciplined approach to evaluate and improve the effectiveness of risk management, control and governance processes."

—*Institute of Internal Auditors, IIA*

- This definition usefully outlines the relationship between **internal audit** and the management of an entity. Key elements are:
  - **Independent, objective**—although internal auditors cannot be fully independent because they are employees, they must still ensure that their objectivity is not impaired in any way. Under corporate governance procedures this is usually achieved through their relationship with the audit committee. (See *Sessions 8* and *9.)*
  - **Add value**—organisations exist to create value or benefit for their owners, other stakeholders, customers and clients by:
    - developing products and services; and
    - using resources to promote those products and services.

    When gathering data to understand and assess risk, internal auditors gain insight into operations and may spot opportunities for process improvements.
  - **Control**—actions taken by management, the board, etc to enhance risk management and increase the likelihood that established objectives and goals will be achieved.
  - **Adequate control**—this is present if management provides reasonable assurance that:
    - risks have been managed effectively; and
    - goals and objectives will be achieved efficiently and economically.
  - **Governance process**—procedures utilised by those charged with governance (e.g. the board of directors) to provide oversight of the risk and control processes administered by management (see *Session 9)*.

4.2   Scope of Work

- Understand key business risks (including fraud) and assess the adequacy of the processes by which these risks are identified, evaluated and managed.
- Review the sufficiency of the information, the adequacy of controls and whether they are actually used to manage those risks.
- Assess the reliability and integrity of key financial and operating information and the means used to identify, measure, classify and report such information.
- Review processes and systems to ensure compliance with policies, plans, procedures, laws and regulations which could affect the company.
- Review the means of safeguarding assets and other key resources, especially information in hard copy or on computer systems, including business contingency plans and the security of computer systems.
- Review operations or projects (including systems under development) to ascertain whether results are consistent with established objectives and goals and whether the operation or projects are being carried out as planned.
- Monitor corrective action plans to ensure management implements them promptly and effectively.
- Advise management on cost-effective controls for new systems and activities.
- Liaison with the audit committee and others charged with governance as well as the external auditors as necessary.

4.3   Approach to Assignments

- The general framework in which internal auditors will approach their assignments is similar to the approach used by external auditors (see s.3).
- Both require terms of reference—the external auditor in the letter of engagement; the internal auditor in the scope of instructions given by management/audit committee.
- Both need to understand the entity, its environment and internal control. In particular, the internal auditor will need to cover *all* controls (not just financial) which are relevant to the assignment.
- Both need to plan and document their work. Materiality, risk assessments, sampling, analytical review, use of computer assisted auditing techniques (especially in systems heavily reliant on information technology) are all aspects of the internal auditor's planning and work procedures.
- Both apply strong quality control procedures (e.g. IAASB and IIA requirements).
- Both will report on their work, although the nature, format and reporting audience are different (e.g. external to the shareholders, internal to the audit committee).

4.4   Assessing the Need for Internal Audit

▓ When the board and senior management is sufficiently close to the business and the systems are not so complex, the following sources of assurance about the way the business is operated may prove to be adequate:

- the views of, and representations from, executive directors and senior managers;
- results of management's internal confirmation procedures;
- regular information on financial and operational matters;
- performance indicators;
- early warning mechanisms;
- external auditors' management letters;
- reports of any relevant external regulators; and
- reports (if any) from relevant internal compliance functions.

In such cases there may be no immediate need for an internal audit function.

▓ However, management attention may become stretched as organisations grow and they:

- become more geographically diverse;
- undertake business in new environments (e.g. e-commerce);
- develop new products and competitive pressures increase;
- develop more complex systems; and
- must embrace change.

▓ In particular, when a company becomes listed, the demands placed on management for transparency and effective running of the business by the stakeholders increase significantly.

4.4.1   Key Issues

▓ Because many stock exchanges require listed companies to operate internal control functions (or explain why they do not in their annual reports), the key issues to consider mainly relate to larger, unlisted entities.

- Are the existing management processes adequate to:
  - identify and monitor the significant risks facing the company; and
  - confirm the effective operation of the established internal control systems?
- With ever increasing pressures on management at all levels, can those who are responsible for managing risks and operating controls always take a wholly objective and systematic view of their own performance?
- Does the board receive the right quality of assurance and information from management and is it reliable?

Example 2 Assessing Need

Suggest additional matters which directors might consider when assessing the need for an internal audit function.

4.4.2 Needs of the Board

▓ The board needs to obtain assurances that its risk and control processes are effective. Management, internal audit and others may provide such assurance. Objective assurance and advice is provided by an internal audit function, thereby assisting the board and senior management with their stewardship responsibilities.

▓ Boards, audit committees and senior management now recognise that what is of relevant value to their business is the internal auditors':

- knowledge of the organisation, its systems and its processes; and
- skills and experience (e.g. in independently reporting on their findings and making recommendations to improve effectiveness of the processes).

4.5 Assignments

▓ The various assignments which internal audit carries out for management include:

- Risk management
- Value for money
- IT/IS audit
- Financial processes audit
- Operational audit
- Functional (e.g. procurement, marketing, treasury, human resource, audits).

4.5.1 Risk Management

▓ The assurance role of internal audit is to deliver assessments of the adequacy and effectiveness of the processes by which business risks are:

- identified and prioritised;
- managed, controlled and mitigated; and
- reported.

▓ Internal audit can:

- provide advice on the design, implementation and operation of control systems;
- identify opportunities to control cost savings;
- promote a risk-and-control culture within the organisation;
- act as facilitators, guiding managers and staff through a self-assessment process (e.g. by leading workshops); and
- become a centre of expertise for managing risk by providing enterprise-wide risk management services (ERMS).

4.5.2   Value for Money (VFM)

▨ VFM auditing is the evaluation of management's achievements
in terms of the economy, efficiency and effectiveness (the
3 "Es") of operations.

   ● **Economy**—obtaining specified resources/inputs (e.g.
   material, finance, human, time) at the lowest cost.
   ● **Efficiency**—achievement of *either:*
      — maximum output (at a given quality) from a given input; *or*
      — a given output (at a given level of quality) from the
        minimum input.
   ● **Effectiveness**—achievement of outputs which meet
   management's objectives.

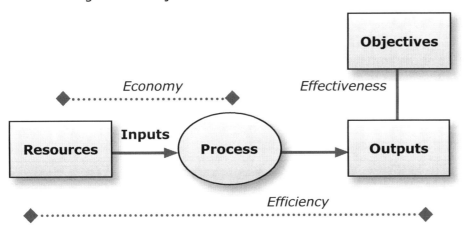

▨ For example, internal audit can report on:

   ● unnecessary spending (e.g. overtime guaranteed when work
   is completed in normal hours);
   ● misdirected spending (e.g. capital expenditure outlay on
   lower-quality assets requiring a higher level of revenue
   expense on quality control);
   ● over-priced spending (e.g. discounts are unclaimed); and
   ● under-recovered revenue (e.g. failure to collect on disposals
   of assets).

4.5.3   IT and IS Audits

▨ The primary role of internal audit will be to review and report
on all aspects of IS in the organisation (e.g. ensuring that the
controls and systems operate as intended).

▨ Where IT/IS systems are being developed, internal audit can
ensure that:

   ● adequate, effective controls are built into the system;
   ● complementary manual controls are designed to ensure
   adequate and effective internal controls over the business
   system as a whole;
   ● the most efficient combination of manual and automated,
   preventive and detective controls are designed and
   implemented;
   ● IS projects are being effectively and efficiently managed; and
   ● the firm carries out appropriate testing (e.g. static, dynamic,
   unit, system, performance) at each stage of the system's
   development process.

4.5.4 Financial Process Audit

▨ An examination of the appropriateness and accuracy of information for management and financial reporting to ensure:

- the completeness and accuracy of recorded transactions;
- that assets are safeguarded;
- that complete, accurate and relevant information is provided on a timely basis; and
- that accounting and finance functions are managed efficiently.

4.5.5 Operational Audit

▨ An audit of the operational processes of an organisation (its primary activities and support activities) ensures that management has:

- adequate controls and other risk management measures in place to achieve business objectives (risk management) economically and efficiently; and
- adequate routine assurances which inform them that the controls and risk management measures are effective.

*Commentary

Basically a compliance-based audit to ensure that controls are operating as intended.

4.5.6 Functional Audits

▨ Audits to ensure that individual functions are operating as intended.

▨ For example, the audit of the marketing function would ensure that:

- marketing processes are authorised and comply with company policy and relevant laws and regulations;
- complete, accurate, relevant and timely information is obtained from internal and external sources (e.g. market research) and is freely available to all involved;
- advertisements and promotions are planned, budgeted, cost-benefit analysed, monitored and controlled; and
- contingency plans are in place to limit potential image and reputation risk.

4.6 Outsourcing

▨ Some companies outsource their internal audit function to companies specialising in the provision of internal audit services or to their external auditors.

▨ In some jurisdictions, under corporate governance requirements for listed companies, the provision of additional services beyond audit by the external auditor is either specifically banned (Sarbanes-Oxley in the US) or has to be approved and justified by an audit committee (UK Corporate Governance Code).

Example 3 Outsourcing

Briefly suggest advantages and disadvantages for outsourcing the internal audit function.

Summary

- Assurance services are intended to engender confidence in the outcome of an evaluation or measurement against relevant criteria.
  - Internal audits perform this function for the highest levels of an organisation's management;
  - External audits perform this function for shareholders, other stakeholders and society at large. External auditors, however, perform such functions only for the benefit of shareholders.
- The organisation's shareholders appoint directors who then recommend external auditors for shareholder approval.
- The external auditors provide assurance on information presented by the directors of the organisation. External auditors do not report on internal control or risk management unless they uncover weaknesses during their engagement.
- Management uses the internal audit function to assure itself that internal governance, control and risk management processes are in place.
- Internal auditors must understand key business risks and all internal processes as well as assess the adequacy of methods to identify, evaluate and manage those risks and processes.
- Adequacy, accuracy and security of IT/IS systems and backups has become a primary role.
- Because of their intimate knowledge of operational processes, internal auditors may find themselves in the unique position of advising management on process improvements.
- Smaller firms with management close to the daily operations may have audits with only limited scope.

Session 11 Quiz
Estimated time: 15 minutes

1. Define "assurance engagement". (2.1)
2. Explain the concept of "accountability". (3.1.1)
3. List the NINE stages of the audit process. (3.3)
4. Define "internal audit". (4.1)
5. Describe the THREE elements of VFM auditing. (4.5)

Study Question Bank
Estimated time: 30 minutes

Priority		Estimated Time	Completed
MCQ11	External and Internal Audit	30 minutes	

EXAMPLE SOLUTIONS

Solution 1—Agents

- A director can be described as an agent having a fiduciary relationship (one of trust) with a principal (i.e. the company that employs them).
- Directors are similarly agents of the shareholders who appoint them to manage the company on their behalf.
- Auditors, as they are appointed by the shareholders in most jurisdictions, are also agents of the shareholders.

Solution 2—Assessing Need

- Corporate structure and the degree of autonomy of each of the business units.
- Overall corporate culture and management's philosophy.
- The company's appetite for risk or its ability to tolerate risk.
- Overall control environment.
- Changes in organisational structure (including delayering), reporting processes and/or underlying information systems.
- Changes in key risks arising from:
  - changes in internal processes (e.g. product or service lines or entry into new markets);
  - alterations in external factors such as regulatory requirements.
- Complexity of the company's systems, especially IT systems.
- The number of moderate- to high-risk areas that are not appropriately controlled.
- Deteriorating trends in internal control systems evident from the existing monitoring systems.
- Concerns about the level of "risk and control awareness" and the need to educate senior or middle management, or staff.
- An increased incidence of unexpected or unacceptable results or occurrences.
- The views of the company's external auditors.

Solution 3—Outsourcing

Advantages

✔ *Costs*—A company with an in-house internal audit service must pay salaries, training and overheads. By outsourcing, the company would pay only for resources when required and so overall the total cost may be cheaper.

✔ *Consistency with external audit*—There may be greater consistency in approach between the internal and external auditors. If external audit can place more reliance on internal audit work the company would benefit from a lower external audit fee.

✔ *Skills*—Contracting out internal audit allows the company to bring in new skills. External providers will have wider experience gained by auditing other companies.

✔ *New techniques*—Both the internal and external audit markets are very competitive. This encourages firms to develop new techniques which are more efficient and effective. The company therefore has access to these techniques without a high level of investment.

✔ *Management time*—Management time and resources can be freed to concentrate on core areas of the business instead of peripheral ones.

✔ *Liability*—Legal action may be brought against an external service provider if its standards are not acceptable.

Disadvantages

✗ *Skills*—An external contractor may lack the specialist skills relevant to a particular company which an in-house service will possess.

✗ *Constraints on service*—The service provider will need to act in accordance with the terms of reference. This may mean that they are unable to follow up suspicious circumstances outside their duties without first seeking permission from the company and re-negotiating the terms of reference.

✗ *Flexibility*—An in-house department will provide a permanent presence; contracted-out services may only be at the company for discrete periods. In-house staff may have more commitment to the company (e.g. willingness to work overtime, travel, etc). Outsourcing may result in reduced staff availability and flexibility.

✗ *Expectation gap*—An expectation gap has existed for external audit for many years. If the profession cannot meet public expectations for a narrow role defined by statute, then can they meet management expectations for a wider role? The company may discover too late that they are not getting what they want. If a contract has been agreed it may be difficult to change.

✗ *Standard of service*—Once an external provider has secured the contract the level of service provided may fall. The audit committee/board of directors must monitor and ensure that the quality of staff provided is satisfactory and work is completed according to the terms of reference.

✗ *Corporate culture*—Contracting out any service involves a change to corporate culture. Unless managed sensitively, outsourcing may lower employee morale, reduce performance, generate a negative cultural impact and create permanent job insecurity.

Regulatory Environment of Accounting

FOCUS

This session covers the following content from the *ACCA Study Guide*.

C. Accounting and Reporting Systems, Controls and Compliance

3. Principles of law and regulation governing accounting and audit

a) Explain basic legal requirements in relation to keeping and submitting proper records and preparing and auditing financial reports.

b) Explain the broad consequences of failing to comply with the legal requirements for maintaining and filing accounting records.

c) Explain how the international accountancy profession regulates itself through the establishment of reporting standards and their monitoring.

Session 12 Guidance

■ **Note** that if the purpose of accounting and audit is to engender trust that organisations handle affairs in a trustworthy manner, then accountants and auditors also must conduct themselves in a trustworthy manner. This session focuses on how the accountancy and audit profession regulates itself and how outside agencies regulate the profession.

(continued on next page)

VISUAL OVERVIEW

Objective: To describe and explain the basic laws and regulations governing accountants, accounting and financial statements.

```
┌─────────────────────────────────┐
│       LEGAL REQUIREMENTS         │
│  ───────────────────────────     │
│   • Regulation                   │
│   • Companies Acts               │
└─────────────────────────────────┘
                 │
                 │
┌─────────────────────────────────┐
│  INTERNATIONAL ACCOUNTANCY       │
│          PROFESSION              │
│  ───────────────────────────     │
│   • Accountancy Bodies           │
│   • IFAC                         │
│   • IASB                         │
│   • Regulation                   │
└─────────────────────────────────┘
```

Session 12 Guidance

■ **Understand** the UK Companies Act and various regulations which regulate accountants and auditors (s.1, s.2.4).

■ **Recognise** the types of regulation by various government agencies and accountancy bodies, including the IASB (s.2).

1   Legal Requirements

1.1   Regulation

■ In most jurisdictions, the terms "accountant" and "accountancy" are not reserved terms and it is therefore permissible that non-professional accountants may prepare accounts and financial statements for organisations.*

*Commentary

*Note that auditing is a reserved occupation and only appropriately qualified individuals can carry out the audit function.

■ However, specific organisations (e.g. limited companies, charities, pension schemes) are required to prepare their financial statements in accordance with specified laws and regulations. Other entities (e.g. sole traders, partnerships), although not specifically required to apply a legal format for their financial statements, usually will follow what is considered to be generally accepted accounting practice (GAAP).

■ In *Session 10*, the company finance director (FD)/chief financial officer (CFO) was identified as the individual most likely to be responsible for the accounting function and preparation of the company's financial statements in accordance with appropriate laws, regulations and standards.

■ The legal and regulatory accounting and financial reporting requirements are usually dealt with through:

  • Companies acts or equivalent (e.g. the UK's Companies Act 2006);
  • Specific statutory instruments (e.g. for charities and pension schemes);
  • Specific requirements of regulatory bodies (e.g. the Association of British Travel Agents, or ABTA);
  • Supra-national laws and regulations (e.g. EU directives which are usually incorporated into member states legislation);
  • Accounting standards (e.g. International Financial Reporting Standards, or IFRS);
  • Generally accepted accounting practice—GAAP (e.g. the extractive industries which are not yet fully covered by IFRS).

*Commentary

The remainder of this session deals only with the specific requirements of laws and regulations relevant to accounting and financial reporting for companies.

1.2 Companies Acts

Using the UK as an example, the Companies Act 2006 has many requirements related to accounting and financial reporting.

1.2.1 Adequate Accounting Records

- A company is required to keep adequate accounting records, which are records sufficient to:
  - show and explain the company's transactions;
  - disclose with reasonable accuracy, at any time, the financial position of the company at that time; and
  - enable the directors to ensure that any accounts prepared comply with the appropriate legal requirements.
- Accounting records must, in particular, contain:
  - entries from day to day of all sums of money received and expended by the company and the matters in respect of which the receipt and expenditure takes place; and
  - records of the assets and liabilities of the company.
- If the company's business involves dealing in goods, the accounting records must contain information regarding specific items in inventory:
  - statements of inventory held by the company at the end of each financial year;
  - all statements of inventory counting; and
  - statements (e.g. invoices) of all goods sold and purchased, showing the goods and the buyers and sellers in sufficient detail to enable all these to be identified. The sales detail is not required for goods sold through ordinary retail trade (e.g. supermarkets) but the purchase detail is required.
- Accounting records must be kept at the company's registered office or at a location considered appropriate by the directors and must be available to all directors. They must be kept for at least six years for a listed company and three years for all other companies.
- Failure to keep adequate records (by the applicable person or persons) is a criminal offence carrying a jail term of up to two years and/or a fine (limit not specified).
- In addition, a failure to keep adequate accounting records will result in the auditors modifying their audit opinion.
  For example:
  - If supporting inventory count records were lost, the auditors would be unable to form an opinion on the assertions (e.g. completeness, occurrence, measurement, carrying values, existence) of the financial statements and would thus qualify their opinion on the basis of limitation of scope (all other records are adequate).
  - If the company's computer systems crashed and corrupted all records with no backup to restore and rebuild the records, the auditors would not be able to form an opinion and would thus issue a disclaimer (as the inadequacy is both material and pervasive).

1.2.2 Preparing Financial Statements

▓ Directors of a company should approve the financial statements only if they are satisfied that they give a true and fair view of the assets, liabilities, financial position and profit or loss.

▓ The directors of every company must prepare accounts for the company for each of its financial years.

▓ The financial statements must be in accordance with the form and content of the statement of financial position and statement of comprehensive income and required additional information as laid down by the Companies Act or as required by IFRS.*

> ***Commentary**
>
> *In the UK, listed group company financial statements must follow IFRS and any *additional* disclosure requirements required by the Companies Act 2006 and the listing rules. In effect, the Companies Act and listing rules have been drafted to avoid conflict with IFRS requirements.

▓ The Companies Act does not specifically define "true and fair", but it is generally accepted that:

- True relates to factual accuracy, taking into account materiality* (in that the financial statements are not materially misstated) of the information provided and that the statement conforms to required standards, regulations and law (e.g. the Companies Act 2006 and IFRS).

- Fairness relates to the presentation of information and the view conveyed to the user. Such information is of appropriate quantity and quality, is free of bias and ensures that the financial statements reflect the commercial substance of the underlying balances and transactions.

> ***Commentary**
>
> *Note that the figures in most listed company financial statements are rounded to the nearest $m or even $b.

▓ As with the need to keep adequate records, failure to produce annual financial statements is a criminal offence punishable with jail and/or fines.

▓ In addition, failure to file financial statements with the appropriate authorities within the deadlines (e.g. six months for listed companies and eight months for unlisted) will again lead to fines and, if considered sufficiently grave, removal of the company's registration and ability to trade shares on a listed exchange.

2 International Accountancy Profession

2.1 Accountancy Bodies

■ The two main international accountancy organisations which directly regulate the accountancy profession (in virtually all countries) are:
- the International Federation of Accountants (IFAC); and
- the International Accounting Standards Board (IASB).

■ In most countries, there will be membership bodies of IFAC (e.g. ACCA in the UK and world-wide) which regulate their own members (in accordance with IFAC's requirements).

■ In addition, most jurisdictions will have a governmental or independent regulatory body overseeing the accounting and auditing profession, usually relating to publicly listed companies (e.g. the UK's independent Financial Reporting Council, or FRC).

2.2 International Federation of Accountants (IFAC)

■ The International Federation of Accountants (IFAC) is the global organisation for the accountancy profession (currently 2.5 million professional accountants in 133 member associations in 103 countries). Full details about IFAC can be found at www.ifac.org.*

*Commentary

*Remember that IFAC strives to serve the public interest by establishing standards in auditing, education, ethics and public sector financial reporting by advocating transparency and convergence in financial reporting, providing best-practice guidance for professional accountants employed in business and by implementing a membership compliance program.

■ In March 2004, IFAC issued the Statements of Membership Obligations (SMOs) to enhance the performance of accountants worldwide.

2.2.1 Statements of Membership Obligations

■ SMOs are designed to:
- provide clear benchmarks to current and potential IFAC member organisations to assist them in ensuring high-quality performance by professional accountants;
- cover a member body's obligations to support the work of IFAC and the IASB, and obligations regarding quality assurance and investigation and discipline;
- form the basis of IFAC's Member Body Compliance Program. Member bodies must perform self-assessments of their compliance with each of the SMOs including an assessment of actual standards in place in comparison to the relevant IFAC standards.

- There currently are seven SMOs in issue:
  - SMO 1: *Quality Assurance*—requires member organisations and firms to implement a system of quality control in accordance with the International Standard on Quality Control (ISQC 1).
  - SMO 2: *International Educational Standards for Professional Accountants*—deals with professional examination requirements, practical experience and continuing professional education.
  - SMO 3: *International Standards, Related Practice Statements and Other Papers issued by the IAASB*—sets out obligations in relation to auditing and assurance standards issued by the International Auditing and Assurance Standards Board (IAASB).
  - SMO 4: *IESBA Code of Ethics for Professional Accountants*—sets out obligations to apply a code of ethics at least as stringent as the IESBA code.
  - SMO 5: International Public Sector Accounting Standards.
  - SMO 6: *Investigation and Discipline*—sets out requirements for member firms in the investigation and discipline of misconduct by professional accountants.
  - SMO 7: *International Financial Reporting Standards*—requires member bodies to adopt and implement international standards established by the International Accounting Standards Board (IASB).

> **✓ Exam Advice**
>
> Although details of the SMOs are not examinable, they demonstrate the regulatory framework which IFAC expects its member bodies to implement (e.g. recruitment, training, examinations, education, ethics, quality control and disciplinary procedures).

2.3 International Accounting Standards Board

2.3.1 Objectives

- The objectives of the IASB are to:
  - develop, in the public interest, a single set of high-quality, understandable and enforceable global accounting standards;
  - promote the use and rigorous application of those standards; and
  - bring about convergence of national accounting standards.
- IASB standards are referred to as International Financial Reporting Standards (IFRS), although the standards issued before 2001 were referred to as International Accounting Standards (IASs).

2.3.2 Developing IFRS

- The IASB consists of 14 members who are appointed by the IASC Foundation based on their technical and practical expertise and experience. The IASB is supported by a team of technical researchers and authors.
- All IASB meetings admit public observers and most are podcast on the Internet. The IASB publishes regular summaries of its work with detailed analysis (including publication of comments received) of all projects undertaken.
- The Standards Advisory Committee (SAC) guides the IASB's work and provides a formal process for organisations and individuals to participate in establishing priorities and on major standard-setting projects. Its members have diverse geographical and functional backgrounds.*

> ***Commentary**
>
> *Full details on the IASB can be found at www.iasb.org.

2.3.3 Application of IFRS

▦ When preparing a set of general financial standards that will be issued to shareholders and the general public, finance directors should apply the appropriate laws and regulations (e.g. IFRS) of the jurisdiction.

▦ Where a particular form of transaction or event is not covered by a specific IFRS, the accountant should use judgement in developing a relevant and reliable accounting policy. This usually will mean considering the IFRS that applies to a similar transaction or event, relevant standards issued by other bodies (e.g. US GAAP) or accepted industry practice.

▦ Accountants may depart from the specific IFRS requirements for a particular transaction or event if following the standards will not show a true and fair view. The financial statements must then include full disclosure of reasons for the departure from standards and provide details of the effect of the departure.*

Commentary

*Departing from IFRS requirements in the event that following them does not fairly represent a transaction often is referred to as the "true and fair override".

▦ Where there is a direct conflict between IFRS and local law and the financial statements are to be issued under the requirements of local law, local law should always be followed. Full disclosure of the conflict and its impact must be made.

2.4 Regulation

2.4.1 Methods

▦ Examples of regulating the accountant (and auditor) are:

• IFAC educational requirements—professional accountants must follow a set educational and examination programme. After they have qualified, they must continue to keep themselves up to date (i.e. continuing professional development/education—CPD/CPE). For example, every ACCA member must confirm each year, in writing, that they have conformed to the CPD requirements.

• Investigation of complaints—this may be from another accountant, a client, a member of the public or a regulatory body.*

Commentary

*In the UK, the Monitoring Committee of the FRC (see *Session 9*) reviews the annual accounts of public and large private companies for compliance with the law and accounting standards. If Monitoring Committee disagrees with the application of an accounting standard or the law, it will discuss its concerns with the company's financial director and auditors and, if necessary, the financial statements will be withdrawn, adjusted and then re-issued. If appropriate, a report also will be made to the directors' and auditor's regulatory body.

▓ The review of auditors—carried out by their regulatory body (e.g. ACCA) and, for those who audited listed companies, by the FRC. Listed company auditors will be reviewed every year; other auditors, every three years.

The audit firm will be reviewed to ensure compliance with regulatory requirements (e.g. IFAC's SMOs, ACCA regulations and, for UK auditors, the UK's Audit Regulations).

Audit files will be reviewed to assess the quality control procedures applied by the auditor as well as the application of accounting standards and laws to the financial statements audited.*

2.4.2 Disciplinary Procedures

▓ All professional accountants are subject to the disciplinary procedures of their member body. Depending on the nature of the offence, disciplinary action can range from a fine ($5,000 through to $500,000 or more), being barred from practice (i.e. unable to have clients) or, ultimately, being barred from membership. In most cases, the name and details of the offence will be published.

▓ Although, for example, ACCA has jurisdiction over all of its members, where those members are involved (as employees, auditors or advisers) with a public listed entity, they also will be subject to disciplinary action by an independent oversight body (e.g. the FRC in the UK).

▓ As always, criminal and civil proceedings also may be taken against the accountant, depending on the nature of the offence.

*Further detail on ACCA's rules and regulations and the concept of public oversight of professional accountants is contained in *Session 26*.

Summary

- Although listed companies, charities, pension schemes and the like are required to follow legal reporting requirements, other companies will usually follow GAAP.

- The UK Companies Act 2006 requires that firms maintain accounting records adequate to show transactions, accurately show the financial position of the company, and enable directors to meet their legal requirements for disclosure.

- In the expression "true and fair", true relates to the accuracy given materiality and fair relates to information of appropriate quantity and quality that is free from bias and ensures that the financial statements reflect the commercial substance of the underlying balances and transactions.

- Regulations covering accountancy and audit generally will fall under IFAC members (such as ACCA) and the IASB. IFAC influences the profession through SMOs and the IASB through IFRS.

- If no specific IFRS covers the situation, then similar IFRS may be used. If no similar IFRS cover it, then relevant standards by other bodies or accepted industry practice will suffice. If an IFRS covers the situation, but the accountant recommends departure from the standard, financial statements should disclose the departure and indicate the effect of it (*true and fair override*).

Session 12 Quiz
Estimated time: 15 minutes

1. Explain the requirements for keeping adequate accounting records. (1.2.1)

2. Explain the concept of "true and fair". (1.2.2)

3. State the objectives of the IASB. (2.3.1)

4. Describe THREE levels of regulating professional accountants. (2.3)

5. List THREE methods of reviewing professional accountants. (2.4.1)

Study Question Bank
Estimated time: 20 minutes

Priority		Estimated Time	Completed
MCQ12	Regulatory Environment of Accounting	**20 minutes**	

Financial Systems and Procedures

FOCUS

This session covers the following content from the ACCA Study Guide.

C. Accounting and Reporting Systems, Controls and Compliance

5. Financial systems, procedures and related IT applications

a) Identify an organisation's system requirements in relation to the objectives and policies of the organisation. ☐

b) Describe the main financial systems used within an organisation: ☐
   i)   purchases and sales invoicing
   ii) payroll
   iii) credit control
   iv) cash and working capital management.

c) Explain why it is important to adhere to policies and procedures for handling clients' money. ☐

d) Identify weaknesses, potential for error and inefficiencies in accounting systems. ☐

e) Recommend improvements to accounting systems to prevent error and fraud and to improve overall efficiency. ☐

f) Explain why appropriate controls are necessary in relation to business and IT systems and procedures. ☐

g) Understand business uses of computers and IT software applications: ☐
   i)   Spreadsheet applications
   ii) Database systems
   iii) Accounting packages.

h) Describe and compare the relative benefits and limitations of manual and automated financial systems that may be used in an organisation. ☐

Session 13 Guidance

■ **Learn** the overall objective and activities of each accounting activity cycle (s.2, s.3).

■ **Understand** each stage of each cycle and the various controls required to minimise the risk that objectives will not be achieved (s.2, s.3).

(continued on next page)

VISUAL OVERVIEW

Objective: To describe the main financial systems, procedures and IT applications used in businesses.

```
                    ┌──────────────────────────────────────┐
                    │   SYSTEMS, POLICIES AND PROCEDURES    │
                    │   • Terminology                       │
                    │   • Background                        │
                    │   • Developing a System               │
                    └──────────────────────────────────────┘
```

ACCOUNTING SYSTEMS	FINANCIAL CONTROLS	PROCESS TYPES
• Procedures and Records • Purchases Cycle • Sales Cycle • Payroll Cycle • Inventory • Cash	• Internal Control • Accounting System Controls • Sales Cycle • Purchases Cycle • Payroll Cycle • Clients' Money	• Manual and Automated • Databases • Spreadsheets • Software Packages

Session 13 Guidance

■ **Note** that many of the IT applications (s.4) should already be very familiar to you.

■ **Read** through the session a couple of times to pick up on things you do not know. If you work in audit or in industry, you should be able to relate this session to your clients or to employer systems.

1 Systems, Policies and Procedures

1.1 Terminology

System: a group of interacting, interrelated or interdependent elements forming a complex whole. It is an organised assembly of resources and procedures united and regulated by interaction or interdependence to accomplish a set of specific functions.

Policy: a plan, a set of coherent decisions, a course of action or guiding principles intended to influence and determine decisions, actions and other matters with a common long-term purpose. It may be a specific programme consisting of desired objectives and the means to achieve them.

Procedures: a set of established forms or methods for conducting the affairs of an organised body such as a business, club or government. They are standard, detailed steps which prescribe how to perform specific tasks taken to accomplish an end.

1.2 Background

Organisations are open and dynamic and operate in an environment which is constantly changing and setting new challenges for those who operate in that environment.

■ In order to direct and supervise the company's affairs, the directors need to have in place a series of **systems** (including controls) to ensure that each business function (e.g. sales, purchases, inventory, finance, human resources, marketing, research and development, administration, communication to stakeholders) achieves its objectives and the business as a whole achieves its objectives.

■ This also means having systems which continually assess PEST and SWOT (see *Session 3*) in an open and dynamic environment.*

*Commentary

*Decision support systems (see *Session 24*), for example, must be able to deal with external and predictive data as well as non-financial data (e.g. environmental, sustainability information) to effectively run a business.

■ A system also must be considered as a collection of personnel, equipment and methods organised to accomplish a set of specific functions and will typically consist of:

- a physical, manual, mechanical and hardware (if IT based) infrastructure;
- software (if IT based);
- people;
- **procedures**; and
- data.

■ To ensure that business systems function and achieve their objectives, a whole series of policies and procedures should be formally developed by management to be applied in each system (e.g. human resource **policy**, health and safety policy, procurement policy, authorisation policy, payment policy, marketing policy).

Example 1 Policies and Procedures

Describe FIVE advantages for businesses having formal, documented policies and procedures.

1.3 Developing a System

■ Standard systems comprise an input, a process and an output. Inputs may be multiple (although more likely singular); the process is likely to be multiple sub-systems; and the output singular (or possibly multiple).

■ Analysts, designers and developers aim to establish the overall objective of a system and then the constituent parts (i.e. stages, steps and tasks). In doing so, the initial inputs and the inputs/outputs of each procedure in the system and how they relate to each other are established.

■ They must also consider what can go wrong with the procedures in the system and design the system to minimise the risk of processing errors (e.g. incorrect data and processing errors are detected, and then corrected or rejected).

2   Accounting Systems

2.1 Procedures and Records

■ The typical accounting system (e.g. sales, purchases) consists of procedures for, and records of, information necessary to satisfy financial reporting objectives.

■ Activities in an accounting system include:

● **initiation** (e.g. manually or by programmed procedures);

● **recording** (e.g. identify, capture and record valid transactions and relevant information on a timely basis, including information for disclosure);

● **processing** (e.g. edit, validate, calculate, measure, summarise, reconcile and classify);

● **reporting** (e.g. preparation of financial and other statements so that the transactions, disclosures and other information are correctly presented); and

● **maintaining accountability** (for the related assets, liabilities and equity).

■ These activities encompass recording the correct monetary value of transactions and ensuring that the transactions are recorded in the correct accounting period (i.e. cut-off).

■ A standard objective of accounting systems is to ensure correct recording and analysis of the various transactions.

The content covered in the remaining sections reflects the specific mention in the syllabus of the purchases, sales, payroll, credit control, cash and working capital management accounting systems.

2.2   Purchases and Liabilities (Purchase Cycle)

▧ The overall objective of the purchase cycle is to ensure that:

- payments are made only for goods and services received and required;
- purchases are not overstated (e.g. false); and
- liabilities are not understated (that all have been correctly recorded).

▧ A typical system and its general procedures would comprise:

Purchase requisition	• Departmental staff (e.g. production or inventory stores) decide what goods/services they wish to purchase (e.g. inventory level reaches the re-order level) and produce a purchase requisition (may be manual or electronic initiation). • This is authorised by the department manager/supervisor/budget and passed to purchasing/ordering department.
Purchase order	• Purchase department obtains several quotations from approved suppliers based on price, delivery time and quality. • Order placed with "winning" supplier. • Order would normally be authorised, especially if for a large amount.
Goods received	• A record is made of all goods received (e.g. using a goods received note, or GRN). • Goods received are inspected to ensure that they arrived in good condition and that the detail (quantity, quality) received agrees with the purchase order.
Purchase invoice received	• Supplier invoices the company for goods/services sent. • The invoice detail is checked against the GRN to ensure that the goods/services were received and that the price is the same as the order, contract or approved price list from the supplier. • Authorisation for payment made.
Invoice recorded	• Recorded and analysed in the purchases daybook and posted to the appropriate expense and liability accounts in the general ledger.
Payment made	• A cheque or bank transfer is raised for the amount owing to the supplier. • Approved for payment by a senior manager who should agree the payment details to supporting documents (e.g. purchase invoice). • Payment made is recorded as part of the cash payments system.

2.3   Sales and Receivables (Sales Cycle)

▩ The overall objective for sales is to ensure all goods and services despatched are correctly invoiced and processed.

▩ The objective for receivables is to ensure all receivables are collectable and will not result in bad debts.

▩ A typical system and its general procedures would comprise:

Sales order received	• Depending on the business, orders may be received by post, fax, telephone, in person or through an e-system (e.g. e-mail, website, electronic data interchange). • In all cases, a base record of all orders should be made to enable completeness checks to ensure that all have been correctly processed and dealt with.

Order processed	• Goods should only be approved for despatch if:
	  – customers are valid credit risks (i.e. have not exceeded their approved credit limits) or have paid cash in advance; and
	  – the goods are in inventory.
	• An order confirmation may be sent to the customer detailing when the goods will be despatched.

Goods despatched	• Goods selected, despatch note raised and agreed to order. • The goods are despatched to the customer, who confirms receipt (e.g. by signing a manual or electronic copy of the despatch note).
Invoicing	• An invoice is raised and approved (after agreement to the despatch note and authorised price list) and then sent to the customer.
Recorded in the accounts	• The invoice is recorded and analysed in the sales day book. • Posted to the sales ledger and receivables control in the general ledger.
Payment received	• Payment is received by cheque or credit transfer from customers. • Recorded as part of the cash receipts system. • Monthly statements sent to customers detailing invoices raised and payments received. • The credit controller reviews outstanding debts and takes appropriate action to collect.

2.4 Wages (Payroll Cycle)

■ Wages are an expense. As such, the overall system objective is to ensure that payment is only made to employees who have provided their services to the organisation.

■ A typical system and its general procedures would comprise:

Work carried out	• Hourly or unit-paid employees should record the work they carry out (e.g. through manual or electronic clock cards, timesheets, unit tags). • The hours/units should be approved by a manager. • Salaried employees will be paid monthly based on an approved contracted annual salary. • Any time worked beyond their contracted amount (e.g. 40 hours per week) should be approved before being claimed if payment or time off in lieu is allowed.
Pay calculated	• Pay rates should be approved. • Gross pay, tax and other deductions (e.g. social, pensions) will be manually calculated or programmed to arrive at net pay. • If manual, checks should be made to ensure correct calculations made. If programmed, checks should be made to ensure correct data entry.
Payroll approval	• Before payment is made to each employee, the payroll should be reviewed and authorised by a manager independent of the payroll function. • Analytical review and exception reporting (e.g. listing employees who have earned above a certain amount).
Payment to employees	• In most organisations, payment will be made directly to each employee's bank account. • If payment is made by cash, care must be taken to ensure that the correct employee receives the correct payment and provides signed documentary evidence of having done so. • The payment should be authorised and will be dealt with through the cash payments cycle.

2.5 Inventory

■ There are basically two forms of the inventory system:

1. **The classic form**, in which inventory is not part of the daily financial accounting double-entry system and its carrying value plus the cost of sales is only ascertained at the end of the financial period (a separate set of accounts is maintained for management accounting purposes).

2. **The full accounting system**, in which the balances (at any given point in time) on the purchases, work-in-progress and finished goods accounts represent the value of the inventory at that time. This system serves both financial and management accounting purposes.

■ Under the classic accounting form, inventory is counted and valued at the end of the financial period and used to calculate the cost of sales (e.g. opening inventory plus purchases less closing inventory).

■ With the more modern, full costing system, regular inventory counts take place—often referred to as a perpetual inventory system (e.g. high value items are counted every month, low value items may be counted every six months or just once per year).

- This system uses computerised inventory control accounts and the manual count checks the accuracy of these accounts (as well as quickly identifying inventory which may have been stolen).
- Inventory purchases, work-in-progress, finished goods and cost of sales accounts form part of the financial accounting double-entry system as well as provide information directly for the management accounts.

	Classic System	**Full Costing System**
Purchase raw materials	• Part of the purchasing system. No entry is made in inventory accounts until a full inventory count and valuation takes place at the end of the year.	• Charged directly to the raw materials account.
Raw materials	• Manual/computerised records of inventory levels are kept. • New orders are placed when a re-order level is reached. • Value only identified as part of a separate costing system for management accounting. • Value ascertained for financial statements at the end of the financial period. • Inventory only issued to production on the basis of authorised requisitions. • Appropriate security to prevent theft.	• On issue to production, "credit" raw materials account and "debit" WIP account. • The balance on the raw materials account represents the quantity and value of raw materials. • Further purchases are made when the re-order level is reached. • Similar accounting also takes place on overhead accounts (e.g. wages). • Regular counting of high value items agreed to accounts.
Work-in-progress	• Value of work-in-progress identified by management through separate management accounting system. • Value for financial accounts only ascertained at period end through full physical inventory count and valuation from management accounting records (e.g. costing records).	• Similar process to raw materials. • Debit entries are raw materials, labour and overheads as WIP progresses. Credit entries are transfers of completed WIP to finished goods. • Accounting for under/over absorption also made. • Balance on WIP account represents quantity and value of WIP at that point in time.
Finished goods	• Full inventory count and valuation only at the period end. • Double entry made through inventory account.	• When goods are sold, credit finished goods with value, debit cost of sales. • Balance on finished goods account represents quantity and value of finished goods at that point in time.
Inventory sold	• Normal sales system. • Cost of sales only identified for financial statements at the end of the year (i.e. opening inventory plus purchases plus production overheads less closing inventory).	• At the end of the financial period, the balance on the cost of sales account is transferred to profit or loss after taking into account cumulative effect of variances.

2.6 Cash Receipts and Payments

Cash receipts	• Cash receipts will come from different sources—credit sales, cash sales, non-current asset sales, bank loans, issues of shares. • On receipt, cash should be analysed in a daybook for posting to the general ledger. • Cash received directly (e.g. not through the organisation's bank account) must be closely controlled as it is highly liquid and can easily be misappropriated. • Cash received directly must be banked quickly, usually by an individual independent from those who first received and recorded the cash. A daily reconciliation between cash received and cash banked should be made to ensure timeliness and completeness of banking.
Cash payments	• As with receipts, payments will be made for many different reasons and may be in cash, by cheque or electronic transfer. To minimise the risk of fraud, any payments made in cash are usually of very low value and only made for sundry items. • All cash payments must be appropriately authorised and supported by relevant documentation (e.g. payment to suppliers supported by purchase invoices). • Cash payments will be analysed in the cash payments daybook for posting to the general ledger.
Bank reconciliation	• A reconciliation between the bank statement (usually monthly, but may also be weekly or daily for very large movements) and the cashbook will be carried out to identify timing differences (e.g. cheques issued but not yet paid into the bank), items not yet recorded (e.g. bank charges or electronic receipts made on the statement but not recorded in the cashbook) and errors. The reconciliation usually will be carried out by an individual who is not responsible for writing up the cashbook records.
Petty cash	• Similar system as cash receipts and payments, but used for "petty" (small) items paid or received directly in cash (e.g. stamps, office coffee, taxi fares). • All payments and receipts must be supported by appropriate evidence (e.g. taxi fare receipt and a petty cash voucher completed and signed by the claimant stating what the expenditure/income is for). • A maximum limit on the petty cash balance is set (e.g. $1,000) so that at any given time, the remaining petty cash plus vouchers will be equal to this balance (imprest system). • At regular intervals, the petty cash will be replenished by a transfer of cash from the main system. The transfer will be equal to the value of the expenses claimed, such that the petty cash balance will be reset to its maximum (e.g. $1,000). • In addition, regular, unannounced counting of the petty cash and the vouchers should take place by an individual not responsible for maintaining the petty cash system.

3   Financial Controls

3.1   Internal Control

▓ Controls placed over the financial information systems are part of the overall internal controls operated in an organisation. *Session 14* considers the overall framework of internal control in detail; this session considers only those internal controls directly related to the accounting systems.

Definition

Internal control—the process designed, and effected by, those charged with governance and management to provide reasonable assurance about:
- the achievement of the entity's objectives with regard to reliability of managerial and financial reporting;
- the effectiveness and efficiency of its operations; and
- the entity's compliance with applicable laws and regulations.
> —*Committee of Sponsoring Organisations (COSO)*

Internal control system—the policies and procedures (internal records) adopted by the directors and management of an entity to succeed in their objective of ensuring, as far as practicable, the:
- orderly and efficient conduct of the business;
- adherence to internal policies;
- safeguarding of the assets of the business;
- prevention and detection of fraud and error in the business;
- accuracy and completeness of the business accounting records;
- timely preparation of financial information.
> —*Auditing Practices Board (UK FRC)*

3.2   Accounting System Controls

▓ The basics of information systems were covered in *Section 1* and for each of the major accounting functions in *Section 2*.

▓ Internal controls over both manual and computer-based systems are also considered in greater depth in *Session 14.* *

▓ When considering internal controls, it is important to ask—"What can go wrong in the system to prevent the system objective being achieved?".

*Commentary

*Having a sound understanding of the business and best practice for effective and efficient controls enables management, as well as internal and external auditors, to identify weaknesses, the potential for error and inefficiencies. Internal/external audit in particular would be able to recommend improvements to prevent fraud and error.

Illustration 1 Control Objective

Consider the sales cycle. Identify the overall control objective (that all goods despatched are correctly recorded in the general ledger), break down the information system into its major components (i.e. the flow of documentation) and ask, "What could go wrong?" That is, what would be an appropriate control objective for that element (e.g. to ensure that goods cannot be despatched without the correct authorisation)? Effectively, devise control objectives at each stage.

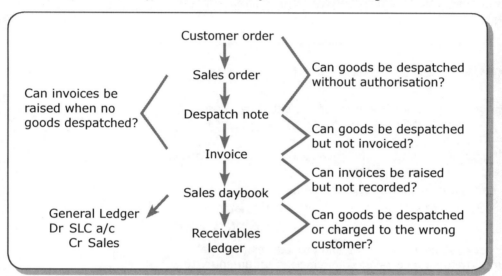

Then ask yourself what control activities need to be in place to achieve the control objective (e.g. authorisation, completeness checks, reconciliations, analytical review, pre-numbering of documents, segregation of duties, etc).

Example 2 Purchase System

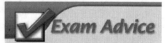

Break down the purchases cycle into components and generate FOUR key control questions.

3.2.1 Control Objectives

■ Control objectives are the expected outcome to be achieved by the financial accounting system. They aim to ensure that only:

- valid (**V**) authorised (**A**) transactions are
- accurately (**A**) and completely (**C**) recorded in the
- appropriate (**A**) accounts in the
- correct accounting period (cut-off, **C**) and that
- recorded assets exist (**E**).

> **✓ Exam Advice**
>
> Use the mnemonic "CAVE" to remember the control objectives of financial accounting systems.

3.2.2 Control Activities

■ Control activities are the specific controls required to achieve a control objective.

■ For the previous purchases example, the control objective would be "to ensure that payments are only made for goods and services received and required by the company". To achieve this overall objective, control activities over placing the order, receipt and acceptance of the goods/services, recording and analysing the invoice and settling the liability need to be operative.

▨ Controls may be manual or they may be electronic (e.g. sequence checks, credit limit checks, correctness of inventory codes input, password access).

▨ Examples of appropriate control activities include:

- Authorisation:
  - purchase or disposal of non-current assets
  - new suppliers
  - journals
  - payments
  - bad debt write-offs.

- Performance reviews:
  - actual against budget, prior year and variance analysis
  - analytical review, internal versus external data
  - functional or activity performance in that activities which should take place actually took place.

- Information processing (accuracy, completeness and authorisation):
  - checking arithmetical accuracy (e.g. of documents, records)
  - maintaining and reviewing accounts and trial balances
  - carrying out reconciliations (e.g. bank statements)
  - sequence checks of pre-numbered documents (e.g. despatch notes)
  - completeness checks (e.g. that all documents have been processed)
  - follow-up of error reports
  - IT application and general controls.

- Physical controls:
  - secured access to assets and records
  - password access to computer systems
  - comparing book to physical (e.g. inventory, petty cash, non-current assets).

- Segregation of duties:
  - separation of the authorising, recording and custody functions
  - actions of one employee are checked by another.

3.3 Sales Cycle

■ Control objectives would include:

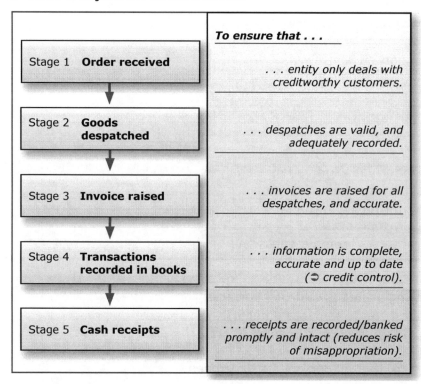

■ Control activities would include sales orders, despatches, sales invoices, recording and cash receipts.

3.3.1 Sales Orders

■ Authorised.

■ Serially numbered (i.e. pre-numbered or generated in strict numerical sequence).

■ Copy retained/register kept.

■ Validated (price, quantity, availability, customer creditworthiness).

3.3.2 Despatches

■ Creditworthiness check.

■ Matched to authorised order.

■ Goods despatched agreed to order.

■ Serially numbered despatch notes ("DNs").

■ DN authorised for despatch.

■ Sequence check for completeness.

■ Proof of delivery.

3.3.3 Sales Invoices

■ Matched with order/DN re address, detail of goods and quantity.

■ Explanations for unmatched DNs obtained.

■ Price checked to authorised price list/order/contract.

■ Calculation check (reperformance) to ensure accuracy.

■ Serially numbered and sequentially controlled for completeness.

3.3.4 Recording

▨ Pre-listing (e.g. in a sales day book)/batch control system.

▨ Sequence checks to identify invoices not recorded.

▨ Control account and reconciliation thereof.

▨ Monthly statements sent to customers.

3.3.5 Cash Receipts

▨ Mail opening procedures include two staff members.

▨ Pre-listing of receipts.

▨ Regular bank control a/c reconciliations prepared/reviewed.

3.4 Purchases Cycle

▨ Control objectives cover:

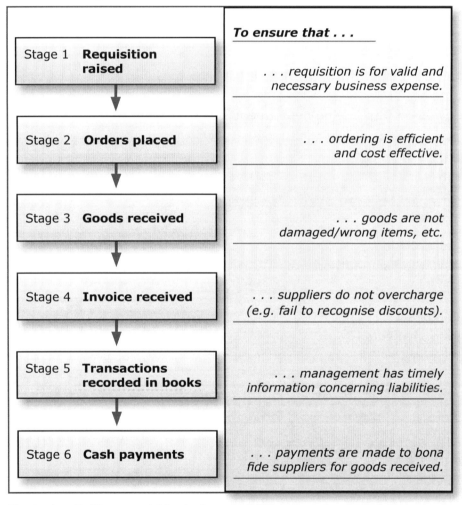

Control activities would include requisition, purchase orders, goods received, purchase invoices, recording and cash payments.

3.4.1 Requisition

▨ Authorised.

▨ Serially numbered for completeness.

▨ Inventory checks (to prevent overstocking).

3.4.2 Purchase Orders

- In writing.
- Serially numbered and sequence checked to ensure completeness.
- Competitive price using authorised supplier.
- Authorised.
- Outstanding orders followed up with supplier.

3.4.3 Goods Received

- Goods checked for quality.
- Quantity agreed to order.
- Serially numbered (completeness) and authorised (goods accepted) GRNs.
- Accounts notified (e.g. by copy GRN).

3.4.4 Purchase Invoices

- Recorded promptly (e.g. in purchase day book) and serially numbered on receipt.
- Agreed to GRN/PO for detail.
- Outstanding GRNs followed up with buying department.
- Prices agreed to PO, authorised price lists, contracts.
- Calculations checked.
- Authorised for payment.

3.4.5 Recording

- Batch control system.
- Control account and reconciliation.
- Supplier statements reconciled and authorised.

3.4.6 Cash Payments

- Authorised cheque signatories.
- Two signatures for larger payments.
- Review supporting documents.

3.5   Payroll Cycle

■ Control objectives cover:

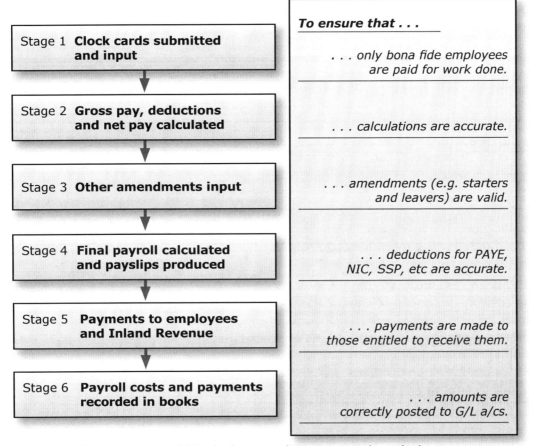

■ Control activities would include recording time and work done, payroll preparation, cash payments and recording.

3.5.1   Recording Time and Work Done

■ Safe custody and restricted issue of time cards (e.g. clock cards).

■ Pre-numbered recording documents and issue/receipt control.

■ Supervised clocking in/out.

■ Authorisation/overtime approved.

3.5.2   Payroll Preparation

■ Checked and approved.

■ Amendment forms authorised.

■ Authorised supporting documents for starters/leavers.

■ Independent review.

3.5.3   Cash Payments

■ Pay-out witnessed.

■ Wage receipts evidence.

■ Safe custody of pay packets.

■ Specific authority to disburse unclaimed wages.

■ Unclaimed wages re-banked intact.

■ Use of credit transfer facilities.

■ Control accounts for wages/salaries/PAYE, etc.

■ Payments for deductions reconciled to payroll.

3.5.4 Recording

▦ Referencing to general a/c codes on posting.

▦ Review of control a/cs.

3.6 Clients' Money

▦ Many businesses may receive money from clients, including banks, accountants, solicitors, estate agents, stock brokers and asset managers. The majority of these will be regulated (e.g. investment businesses by the Prudential Regulation Authority in the UK).

▦ Such businesses need to adhere to strict policies and procedures for handling clients' money to ensure, for example, that:

- it is segregated from the firm's money and adequately safeguarded;
- each client's money is separately accounted for (from other clients' monies);
- it can be used only for the intended (contractual) purposes;
- any interest accrued is paid to the client.*

*Client monies need to be "ring-fenced" to ensure that they are protected in the event of a firm becoming insolvent.

▦ Basic rules for keeping client accounts include:

- prohibiting custody or control of clients' money without their instruction;
- keeping detailed records of all transactions in accordance with legislation or regulation;
- providing receipts for all amounts received; and
- securing direct access to clients' accounts.*

*Handling clients' money also carries risks associated with money laundering (see *Session 15*).

▦ A robust system of internal controls must include, for example, a log of all errors and breaches and any corrective action taken.

▦ Other requirements typically include:

- an annual independent audit; and
- record keeping (e.g. for up to six years).

4 Process Types

4.1 Manual and Automated Systems

■ With a manual system, the operator must understand and complete the double entry (e.g. Dr Expense Cr Cash). With a computerised system, the operator will just enter the cash payments into a cash payments schedule presented on screen, select the name of the expense account and press enter—the system will then update the cash payments file and expense file as necessary.*

■ In terms of productivity, speed of processing, accessibility, analysis of data, report generation, quality of output, incidence of errors, volume and making corrections, automated systems are far superior to manual systems.

*Key functions, principles and procedures remain the same regardless of whether a system is manual or automated.

Example 3 Manual v Automated Systems

Explain why manual accounting systems are inferior to automated systems.

4.2 Databases

■ The financial accounting system and virtually all of the information systems discussed in *Session 24* will use databases as a core element of their functionality.

■ Where data is stored in multiple files (usually in the form of tables of rows and columns) with a matching field between two or more files (e.g. employee number) so the files can be queried simultaneously by a user, the database is referred to as a *relational* database (e.g. Microsoft Access®). Network, hierarchy and object are other database structures.

■ The database management system (DBMS) is the shell around the database which controls organisation, storage, retrieval, security and integrity of data.

■ The DBMS allows the data to be stored independent of the application using the data. Thus any application can request data from the database via the DBMS based on a specific identifier (e.g. the field name "Customer").

■ Typical functions of the DBMS include:

- Data security, protection from unauthorised access, viewing and editing.
- Data integrity ensuring that only one user can update a record at any one time and that records remain unique (e.g. no two employees can have the same name).
- Interactive query language and report writer allowing users to interrogate the database. These essential components give users access to all information as needed.
- Interactive data entry and updating.

Database—a comprehensive collection of related data organised for convenient access.

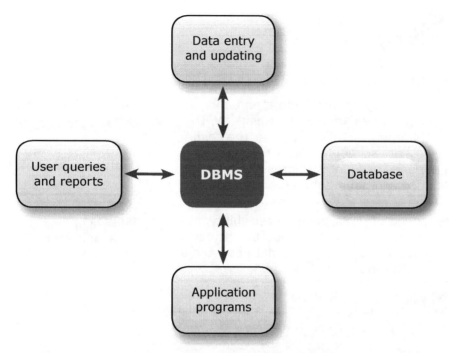

■ Many organisations design their database system as a central resource.

Benefits of Centralising the System

✔ One data set is available to all users, thus ensuring consistency of use and basis for decision-making.

✔ Only one database needs to be updated.

✔ Security is easier to maintain, including backing up the data.

Disadvantages

✗ If the DBMS fails, or the data becomes corrupt, the whole system may become inoperable.

✗ If the data is not kept up-to-date, inappropriate decisions may be made.

✗ The larger the system, the more expensive it becomes to operate and maintain.

✗ The more users that access the system at the same time, the slower the processing may become.

4.3   Spreadsheets

Definition

Spreadsheet—an electronic table used to store various forms of data. The data is arranged in rows and columns (in multiple worksheets) which make it easier to store, organise and analyse information. Functions programmed into the spreadsheet application include the use of formulaes, charts and data analysis tools.

- Use of **spreadsheets** in business varies considerably from simple record keeping, preparing management accounts, variance analysis and budgeting through to sophisticated forecasting models, bookkeeping, financial accounting systems and complete pro forma financial statements, including disclosures and notes.

- A significant factor contributing to their use is the ability (through the use of formulae) to change a figure and recalculate the spreadsheet (e.g. "what-if" analysis).

- Although spreadsheets are easier to programme and use than databases, their simplicity is also a danger. Far too many users prepare spreadsheets with little formal training and make mistakes in setting up their spreadsheets and formulae. Such mistakes often go undetected and have, for example, resulted in companies making incorrect investment decisions based on poorly programmed spreadsheets.

- For this particular reason, whenever auditors need to rely on information provided on a client's spreadsheet, they will very carefully audit the formula and assumptions built into the original spreadsheet.*

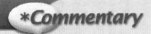

*Commentary

*One way to appreciate uses of databases and spreadsheets in a business organisation is to research Microsoft Excel and Access on the Internet.

4.4   Software Packages

▣ Most accounting system software contains a series of modules, with each module dealing with a specific part of the business function. Modules may be purchased separately or, more commonly, developed as a complete package suite.

▣ A typical accounting package will contain integrated modules covering:

- sales invoicing, daybook and sales ledger;
- purchase daybook and purchase ledger;
- payroll;
- cash book and petty cash;
- inventory;
- journals;
- costing;
- management accounting;
- general ledger;
- non-current asset register; and
- a report generator.

▣ An integrated system will store data in a central database and then use and share it with various modules as necessary. This allows both costing and management accounting functions to be fully integrated with the financial accounting functions using the same data sets.

▣ In addition, the data may also be integrated with spreadsheets, decision support systems, executive information systems and suppliers (through an extranet allowing suppliers to determine inventory delivery schedules based on inventory levels and planned production schedules of the organisation).

Summary

- Activities in an accounting system include initiation, recording, processing, reporting and maintaining accountability.

- Control objectives are expected outcomes from the financial accounting system.

- Control objectives follow the principle that only authorised transactions are accurately and completely recorded in the appropriate accounts in the correct reporting period and that recorded assets exist.

- Control activities are specific processes required to achieve a control objective.

- Centralised databases allow one set of data to be available to all users, thus ensuring consistency of data used for decision-making.

- Spreadsheets are electronic tables used to store various forms of data in rows and columns.

- Client money should be segregated from other firm assets to protect it from misappropriation, so that it will be used only for contracted purposes, and any interest accrued can be easily calculated and paid to the client.

Session 13 Quiz
Estimated time: 10 minutes

1. Explain the differences between systems, policies and procedures. (1.1)

2. List the contents of a typical purchase cycle. (2.1)

3. Explain the difference between control objectives and control activities. (3.2)

4. List SIX control activities appropriate to a sales cycle. (3.3)

Study Question Bank
Estimated time: 40 minutes

Priority		Estimated Time	Completed
MCQ13	Financial Systems, and Procedures	40 minutes	

EXAMPLE SOLUTIONS

Solution 1—Policies and Procedures

✔ Standardisation and consistency of approach to dealing with similar transactions, events and the preparation of management information and financial statements.

✔ All transactions and events can be captured, processed and recorded, thus assisting the directors in their legal duty of maintaining adequate accounting records.

✔ Best practice can be established, codified and used by all relevant employees.

✔ Training programmes can be implemented based on the formal documented procedures, thus ensuring effective and efficient use of human resources.

✔ Transactions and events not dealt with in accordance with the documented procedures and policies should be easily identifiable and investigated as to why they were outside of the standard procedures.

✔ Duplication of procedures, thus wasting time and effort, can be avoided.

✔ Documented procedures can easily be reviewed and updated in line with environmental changes and will assist external regulators and consultants.

Solution 2—Purchase System

■ Overall objective: To ensure that correct payments will be made only for goods and services received and required by the organisation.

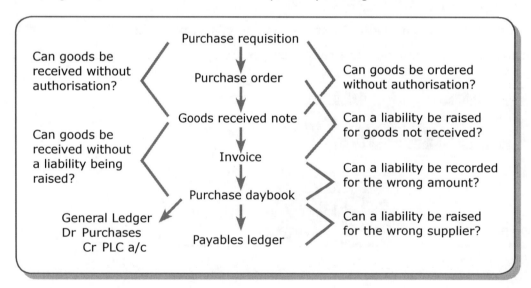

Solution 3—Manual v Automated Systems

- Productivity will be lower with a manual system, especially where the operation is routine and repetitive (e.g. for expenses, the detail is entered into a daybook, then added up and posted to the general ledger). With an automated system, expenses are entered into a single input document with drop-down menu selection—the system does the rest.

- Speed of processing is much lower in manual systems compared to automated systems (e.g. in analysing data and preparing reports).

- Accessibility. Only one user at a time can access manual systems. Automated systems will allow many users to access the same data at the same time. Individual items of data or data groups can be quickly found through search facilities in automated systems.

- Analysis of data. Finding data and sorting data is much more effective and efficient using an automated system (e.g. a data range is selected and mathematical functions such as "SUM" or "AVE" are applied to that range).

- Report generation in a manual system can be tedious, error prone and poorly designed. Automated systems will have a series of pro forma, ready-to-use reports or reports can be designed and stored for future use. The format of the report can be easily changed as can the presentation style used (e.g. tables, graphics.)

- Quality of output in a manual system depends on the user (e.g. handwriting). With automated systems, it is consistent (e.g. LaserJet output).

- Incidence of errors will be higher in manual systems because they are operated by humans. Provided the program of the automated system contains no programming errors and has not been corrupted, the system will work error free every time. In addition, controls will operate in automated systems to prevent, detect and correct any errors which may be made by the operator in inputting data.

- Making corrections in a manual system often will involve the data being crossed out and new data entered. There will be a limit on the number of times this process can take place. In addition, reports may need to be rewritten to eliminate errors.

Internal Control and Security

FOCUS

This session covers the following content from the *ACCA Study Guide.*

C. Accounting and Reporting Systems, Controls and Compliance

6. Internal controls, authorisation, security and compliance within business

a) Explain internal control and internal check.

b) Explain the importance of internal financial controls in an organisation.

c) Describe the responsibilities of management for internal financial control.

d) Describe the features of effective internal financial control procedures in an organisation, including authorisation.

e) Identify and describe the types of information technology and information systems used by the business organisation for internal control.

f) Identify and describe features for protecting the security of IT systems and software within business.

g) Describe general and application systems controls in business.

Session 14 Guidance

■ **Note** that *Session 13* considered specific accounting systems, cycles and controls. (See the COSO and APB definitions in prior sessions.) This session deals with the overarching concept of internal control and provides context for the controls dealt with in *Session 13*.

■ **Learn** the definition of internal control (s.1) and **know** the detail of the four components of internal control (1.2).

(continued on next page)

VISUAL OVERVIEW

Objective: To describe the basic concepts of internal control and security of information systems.

```
                    ┌─────────────────────────────────┐
                    │          INTERNAL CONTROL        │
                    │  ─────────────────────────────── │
                    │   • Role                         │
                    │   • Components                   │
                    │   • Alternative Categories       │
                    │   • Control Risk                 │
                    └─────────────────────────────────┘
                        /                        \
    ┌──────────────────────────┐    ┌──────────────────────────┐
    │  COMPUTER INFORMATION    │    │      DATA SECURITY       │
    │         SYSTEMS          │    │  ──────────────────────  │
    │  ──────────────────────  │    │   • Threats              │
    │   • Risks                │    │   • Physical Risks       │
    │   • General IT Controls  │    │   • Environmental Risks  │
    │   • Application Controls │    │   • Unauthorised Access  │
    │   • IT-Based Solutions   │    │   • Hacking              │
    │                          │    │   • Viruses              │
    │                          │    │   • Encryption           │
    │                          │    │   • Software Audit Trail │
    └──────────────────────────┘    └──────────────────────────┘
```

Session 14 Guidance

■ **Understand** the difference between preventive, detective and corrective controls (s.1.3).

■ **Recognise** the difference between general IT controls and application controls (s.2) and the various types of threat to data security (s.3).

■ **Understand** the value of encryption (s.3.7) and software audit trails (s.3.8) in preventing and detecting threats.

1 Internal Control

Definition

Internal controls—actions taken by management to enhance the likelihood that established objectives and goals will be achieved. Management plans, organises and directs the performance of sufficient actions to provide reasonable assurance that objectives and goals will be achieved. Thus, control is the result of proper planning, organising and directing by management.

—Institute of Internal Auditors

*Commentary

*Internal check is more specifically concerned with detecting errors and irregularities. It involves one employee independently checking routine transactions that are handled by another employee.

1.1 Role

▦ Internal auditors focus on all business controls in operational cycles, not just those related to financial statements.

▦ External auditors focus on prevention, detection and correction of material misstatements in the financial statements rather than classifying controls according to any particular cycle.

1.2 Components

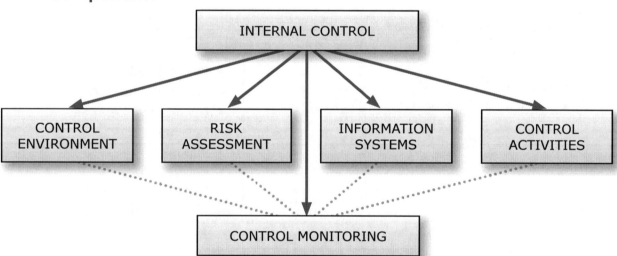

1.2.1 The Control Environment

▦ Consists of the attitude, awareness and actions of an organisation's board of directors and management.

▦ Sets the tone of an organisation, influencing the control consciousness of its management and employees.

▦ Provides discipline and structure which serve as the foundation for effective internal control.

▦ Reflects the organisational culture of honesty and ethical behaviour created by governance and management, supported by appropriate controls to prevent and detect fraud and error, through:

  • Communication and enforcement of integrity and ethical values.

  • Cascade effect (i.e. following management's example).

  • Commitment to competence (e.g. only those with the appropriate skills and knowledge are considered for each position).

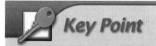

Key Point

The directors are responsible for establishing and maintaining internal financial control.

- Participation by those charged with governance:
  - independent from the entity and management;
  - experienced and prepared to be a sounding board for management;
  - prepared to work with, but stand up to, management;
  - demanding and challenging of management decisions;
  - access to documents and information as required;
  - effective interaction with internal and external auditors; and
  - operation of "whistle-blower" procedures, independent of management.
- Management's philosophy and operating style (including approach to risk management and application of accounting policies).
- Organisational structure (e.g. open and transparent or closed and opaque).
- Assignment of authority and responsibility (e.g. clearly defined).
- Human resource policies and practices (e.g. commitment to best practice in recruitment, training, appraisal, counselling, progression, compensation and remedial actions).
- A strong control environment may help reduce the risk of fraud. However, the elements of the control environment must be considered collectively (e.g. enforcement of ethical values together with appropriate recruitment policies for financial reporting staff will not mitigate aggressive earnings reporting direction by senior management).

1.2.2 Risk Assessment Procedures

- How management identifies **business risks**, as well as how management decides to address those risks and review the results.

- Business risks arise from the way the entity is managed, its operating environment, products, customer base, employee base, ownership, legal and regulatory regimes and the very fact that it operates in a dynamic and adaptive environment.

- There are many classifications of business risk, including: liquidity, interest rate, foreign exchange, procurement, production, brands, reputation, human resources, treasury, information systems, legislation, regulation, and legal liabilities.*

Definition

Business risk—risk that the entity fails to achieve its objectives and execute its strategies.

Commentary

*Good corporate governance embraces a strong risk management process.

Example 1 Business Risks

Suggest FIVE business risks that may affect the preparation of published financial statements.

1.2.3 Information Systems and Control Activities

■ Information systems and control activities were discussed in detail in *Session 13*. Additional considerations are:

- Transactions may be standard (e.g. transactions generated in the normal course of business—sales, purchases, depreciation) or non-standard (e.g. asset impairment, bad debt write-off). How the information system deals with both standard and non-standard transactions (e.g. raising and authorising journal entries) must be understood.

- The information system also must be able to deal with errors and incorrect processing. Is a suspense account used and regularly checked and cleared? Is it possible to override the system or bypass controls? If so, how does management deal with such matters?

- Management must be able to demonstrate that it understands the individual roles and responsibilities of those in the information system.

- Individuals in the system must also understand their roles and responsibilities and how they relate to others in the system.

- The means of reporting exceptions to a higher authority must be clear and unambiguous. This includes reporting channels to management, those charged with governance (e.g. audit committee) and external authorities (e.g. regulators).

1.2.4 Monitoring Controls

■ Without monitoring control systems and receiving feedback on the performance of those controls, the entity's management will have no idea if a control, while still operating, is effective.

■ Monitoring processes assess the design and operation of controls on a timely basis to determine effectiveness and take necessary corrective actions for changes in conditions.

■ Ongoing monitoring activities include regular management and supervisory activities, such as:

- checking that activities such as bank reconciliations are carried out;

- producing reports when expected and carrying out required actions (e.g. follow-up on exception reports);

- ensuring customers pay amounts as stated on their statements or following up on overcharge complaints;

- external regulators reporting on aspects of the internal controls relating to regulations (e.g. financial services);

- internal audit assessing internal control effectiveness and business risk procedures;

- external audit generating management letters and reports; and

- discussing business activity and management accounts at monthly board meetings and challenges by non-executive directors and those charged with governance.

1.3   Alternative Categories

1.3.1   Preventive Controls

■ These controls are designed to prevent a particular risk from happening. Authorisation, segregation of duties, recruiting, training, supervision, passwords and validation are examples of preventive controls.*

*Authorisation may be general (e.g. up to a specified monetary amount) or specific (e.g. for items of capital expenditure).

1.3.2   Detective Controls

■ Detective controls are designed to detect, rather than to prevent, errors should they occur. Examples include reconciliations, exception reporting, physical counting of assets, supervision and quality controls.

1.3.3   Corrective Controls

■ Corrective controls aim to minimise or negate the effect of errors. Examples include follow-up procedures, management action, security backups of data, re-training and contingency planning.

1.4   Control Risk

■ Because of the inherent nature of internal control, there will always be some **control risk**. No internal control system, no matter how well-designed and operated, can provide management with conclusive evidence that objectives have been reached. Only reasonably high, not absolute, assurance can be achieved.*

Control risk—risk that a material error could not be prevented or detected and corrected by the internal control system.

*A determined fraudster will always find ways around control systems. In some cases, the very presence of controls establishes a challenge to "beat the system".

Example 2   Inherent Limitations

Identify FIVE potential limitations within an internal control system.

---

2 Computer Information Systems

2.1 Risks

■ Because of the pervasive nature of information systems in the vast majority of organisations, computer information systems (CIS) present a whole series of particular business risks:

- Reliance on systems or programs which are inaccurately processing data (e.g. programming error resulting in all like transactions being incorrectly processed), processing inaccurate data (e.g. incorrectly captured or transferred from a previous process) or both.

- Unauthorised access (hacking) to transaction data which may result in destruction, corruption or changes to that data, particularly where multi-access (internal and/or external) is allowed to the database. For example:
  —recording of unauthorised transactions;
  —recording transactions which have not occurred; or
  —inaccurate recording of transactions.

- IT personnel gaining unauthorised access privileges resulting in a breakdown of the IT segregation of duties (e.g. a program analyst gaining access to a programme being modified by a programmer).

- Unauthorised changes to data in master files (e.g. adding non-existent employees; changing salary details).

- Unauthorised changes to systems or programs (e.g. a programmer making unscheduled/unauthorised changes to a program).

- Inappropriate controls in the systems development life cycle (e.g. failure to adequately test each development stage resulting in a program which does not meet user requirements).

- Lack of appropriate system changeover procedures to ensure completeness and accuracy of transferring data from an old system to a new system.

- Inappropriate, or lack of, manual intervention (e.g. failure to act on error reports produced by a system).

- Failure by management or IS personnel to make necessary changes to systems or programs when required (e.g. updating to meet customer needs or upgrading software to maintain competitive advantage).

- Potential loss of data or inability to access data as required (e.g. system crash, denial of service attack, prolonged downtime).

- Automatic initiation or execution of transactions (e.g. interest/discount calculations). Authorisation may not be documented but is implicit in management's acceptance of the design of the system.

- The audit trail of the transactions may be fragmented, in that it may exist only for a short time.

■ Because of the specialised nature of CIS, two sets of control procedures have been developed in the overall control framework—general controls and application controls.

2.2   General IT Controls

 **Definition**

General IT controls—Policies and procedures which apply across many applications and support the effective functioning of application controls by helping to ensure the continued operational integrity and security of data and information systems.

■ **General IT controls** aim to establish a framework of overall control and commonly address the business and control risks noted above. For example, controls over:
  - the data centre and network operations;
  - system software acquisition, change and maintenance;
  - development of computer applications;
  - access security;
  - system acquisition, development and maintenance.

■ There are various classifications of general controls:

Administration Controls

  - Segregation of duties** between development (analysts and programmers), maintenance (librarian) and operation.
  - Logical access controls (e.g. passwords)** to enter systems.
  - Computer log of program changes (independent review by IT manager).
  - Restricted physical access** (e.g. to computer room).
  - Firewall and virus update protection.
  - Regular file copying ("dumping").
  - Job scheduling.
  - Backup power resources.
  - Disaster recovery procedures.
  - Maintenance and insurance.

    ** Often classified as Physical controls

Systems Development Controls

  - Standard procedures and documentation—including feasibility study and systems specification with flowcharts or data flow diagrams.
  - System and program testing (test and actual data). Usually pilot operation.
  - File conversion—requires a complete printout and check of file contents before setting up operational master files.
  - Acceptance and authorisation procedures (e.g. by a responsible official of the project steering committee).
  - Training of user staff.

■ Alternatively:

GENERAL IT CONTROLS				
ORGANIZATION AND MANAGEMENT	**APPLICATION SYSTEMS DEVELOPMENT**	**COMPUTER OPERATION**	**SYSTEMS SOFTWARE**	**DATA ENTRY AND PROGRAM**
• Policies and procedures • Segregation of incompatible functions (e.g. preparing input, programming)	• Testing, conversion, documentation • Restricted access	• Authorisation—personnel and programs • Processing errors are detected and corrected	• Authorisation and testing • Restricted access to utilities which may not leave an audit trail	• Authorisation structure • Off-site backup • Recovery procedures

2.3 Application Controls

Definition

Application controls—manual or automated procedures which typically operate at a business process level. Can be preventive or detective in nature and are designed to ensure the integrity of the accounting records and information. Relate to procedures used to initiate, record, process and report transactions or other financial data.

■ **Application controls** provide reasonable assurance that all transactions are authorised, recorded and processed completely, accurately and on a timely basis.

INPUT	PROCESSING	OUTPUT	MASTER FILE
• Passwords (to terminals) • Validation checks • Verification checks • Batch totals • Error investigation and feedback procedures • Document counts	• Check digits • Reasonableness ("range") checks • Existence checks • Mismatch reports ("file no data" or "data no file") • Sequence checks • Format checks • "Run-to-run" controls to ensure no data lost	• Checking control totals • Investigating rejected items • Reviewing accounts and trial balances	• Periodic print-out of standing data and comparison to independent control totals and data • Authorisation of master file standing data updates • Exception reporting (and authorisation) of all changes made to standing data

■ Alternatively as two types of classification:

1. Transaction controls, which aim to ensure:

- completeness;
- accuracy; and
- validity.

2. File controls, which aim to ensure:

- file continuity;
- asset protection, for example:
  — keys, security-coded entry;
  — approval and recording;
  — data security (e.g. library) procedures.

2.4 IT-Based Solutions

In addition to the information systems general and application controls described above, there are many and varied IT-based solutions for enhancing internal control.

2.4.1 Computer Assisted Audit Techniques (CAATs)

- CAATs are a series of interrogation and analysis tools used by internal or external auditors to check that programmed controls in the system operate as intended; for instance, valid data is processed while invalid data is rejected (error trapping) and an exception report is generated.

- In addition, the data produced by a system can be analysed and an audit trail established and followed (e.g. all despatches made during the day can be identified from inventory records, matched with the sales price from the price data base for each item and the total sales calculated for that day. This will then be compared with the recorded sales total for that day. Any difference should be investigated).

2.4.2 Embedded Controls

- Embedded controls are electronic controls which check whether some other control has functioned as intended. They effectively build in redundancy/dependency. Because of the expense of such systems, they would be used only where 100% reliability was crucial.

2.4.3 Intelligent Control Systems (Neural Networks)

- These often are used in banks and other financial institutions. Their development was initially driven by legal requirements for identifying money-laundering transactions or transactions which could potentially relate to money-laundering activities.

- Such systems have evolved into what are now called **neural networks**. Such networks provide predictive fraud detection for credit, debit and private-label cards, as well as retail fraud, e-commerce and money laundering.

3 Data Security

3.1 Threats

- Information security protects the interests of those who rely on information, information systems and communications systems that deliver the information, from harm resulting from hacking, operational error, sabotage and other threats.

- Information privacy is the right of an individual to participate in decision-making regarding the collection, use and disclosure of information personally identifiable to that individual. It is the restriction of knowledge to authorised persons.

- Security and privacy are closely related and it may be difficult to determine whether a particular risk relates to security or privacy. What is clear, however, is that security relates to the whole of the system, whereas privacy only relates to the data held in the system.

- Threats to information systems may arise from:
  - intentional or unintentional acts; and
  - internal and external sources.

▓ Examples include:

- Technical conditions (e.g. program bugs, disk crashes)
- Natural disasters (e.g. fire, flood)
- Environmental conditions (e.g. power surges)
- Human factors (e.g. lack of training, errors, omissions).

3.2 Physical Risks

Physical risks threaten the physical elements of the system—the hardware, software and computer facilities, such as buildings.

▓ Typical risks include:

- Fire
- Flood
- Weather
- Natural disaster
- Terrorist attack
- Accidental damage
- Deliberate damage
- Theft.

Control examples for physical risks include:

▓ Fire systems and procedures:

- Inert gas extinguishing system (not water-based)
- Fire doors
- Heat resistant safes
- Fire prevention and safety rules.

▓ Locating hardware away from sources of risk:

- Heat and water pipes (check ceiling ducting and floor above)
- Under flight paths near airports
- Earthquake zones or below river levels.

▓ Regular building maintenance:

- Checking for faulty electrical circuits
- Fire systems maintenance
- Lagged piping (e.g. insulating pipes to prevent corrosion, freezing, heat loss, etc).

▓ Training of all staff in computer security and safety procedures:

- Attitude (e.g. integrity, carefulness, security aware)
- Strong security culture in the organisation.

▓ Staffing arrangements:

- Authorisation for access and change routines to programs
- Segregation of duties (programmers should not have access to live programs)
- Thorough vetting of job applicants before being employed
- Sensitive staff banned from premises when sacked (and security passes withdrawn/disabled)
- Risk analysis on sensitive staff (e.g. to identify low morale, poor motivation, those who potentially bear a "grudge").

▓ Physical access controls:

- Security guards
- Time controls (e.g. only allowed access between certain times)
- Electronic door locks (PIN, card or bio data entry).

▓ Theft control:

- High-risk systems physically attached to secure points (e.g. laptops chained to a fixed point)
- ID marking—company logo, inventory tag and tracking
- Regular inventory checks.

▓ Regular testing of fail-safe systems:

- "Pull the plug" to see what happens
- Testing of recovery plans.

3.3   Environmental Risks

▓ A number of risks to computerised systems relate to the environment in and around the location of the hardware:

- Temperature
- Humidity
- Power supply
- Spillage and accidental damage.

▓ The best way to control these risks is to isolate the computer system from the outside world by placing it in a specially designed computer room or building. Obviously, this is possible for a large central computer, but not for PCs.

▓ Control examples include:

- Heating and air-conditioning systems
- Smoothed power supplies
- Uninterruptible power supplies (UPS)
- Banning drinks and food in computer areas
- Training-in procedures, awareness and damage limitation.

3.4   Unauthorised Access

▓ The logical access system is the system of facilities developed and maintained to protect data or software from the potential threats of unauthorised access.

▓ Risks include:

- Errors in data
- Falsification of data
- Loss of data
- Disclosure of information to unauthorised individuals.

▓ Access must be limited to those with the appropriate authority through:

- Physical access controls
- System passwords
- Usage logs (usually computer generated)
- Storage of diskettes and tapes in secure locations.

3.5   Hacking

▓ Hacking is deliberate, unauthorised access to a system and data in that system.

▓ The term originally described the activity of individuals who saw systems security as a challenge and wished to show that they were able to breach whatever security was in place. It is now a term used to also describe the criminal activity of stealing (also includes reading) or changing data or any other aspect of a system (e.g. changing programs, adding additional routines).

■ Hacking usually takes one of two forms:

1. **Authorisation attack**—password cracking usually involves computer programs that repeatedly send potential passwords generated from a dictionary, number generator or other sources until the right password is found.

2. **Trapdoor/backdoor attacks**—utilising existing weakness in the program code of the system. Sometimes these are deliberately programmed into the system by the programmer, who can, for example, bypass the password system at a later date.

3.5.1   Threats of Hacking

✗ Data corruption including alteration of, and addition to, data.

✗ Introduction of viruses.

✗ Access to sensitive data.

✗ Access to password files and the password generation code.

✗ Loss of system's operational ability.*

3.5.2   Prevention Procedures

✔ Physical security.

✔ Logical security.

✔ System logs and audit trails.

✔ Sentinels ("watchdog" programs which check for unusual activity).

✔ Data encryption.

✔ Strong quality control and risk analysis procedures in developing programs and websites

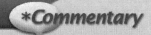

Commentary

*Many of the alterations by hackers made to organisations' websites are due to the poor programming and security features of the Web pages and sites which allow access to the system behind the Web pages.

3.6   Viruses

■ A virus is a rogue program which spreads throughout a computer system, usually with the aim of causing inconvenience or, worse, destroying and altering data, disrupting processing and corrupting memory systems.

■ A virus may be implanted in the system by an employee (e.g. a programmer) or by infection from an outside source, most notably from files and e-mails downloaded from the Internet.

■ The extent of damage caused is limited only by the ingenuity of the virus programmer.

■ Types of viruses include:

● **Boot sector**—runs every time the system is booted (started).

● **File/execute**—infects a program file so each time the program is executed, so is the virus.

● **Overwriting/duplicating**—overwrites programs so the program no longer operates, or adds to a program or file so eventually the storage capacity is fully used.

● **Trojan**—embodied in a host program which appears to be carrying out a normal function, while the Trojan virus carries out a totally different function often unbeknown to the user.

● **Worms**—viruses which "burrow" through the system, usually over networks using the system's distributed resources.

- **Logic bombs**—a traditional programmer's virus, usually hidden in a normal program, activated on the occurrence of a particular event (e.g. reaching a certain account balance).
- **Time bombs**—same concept as a logic bomb, except that the trigger event is a time or date (e.g. on Friday the 13th).

■ Virus attacks can be prevented or minimised through:
- Installation of "sentinels" (e.g. virus detection programs) which check all vulnerable files on boot-up of the system or all files imported to the system (e.g. through discs, sticks, the Internet, e-mails). Such programs can only detect known viruses and must be constantly updated.
- A strongly enforced organisation policy on the use of external programs and the Internet.
- Quality control procedures and segregation of duties over accessing, developing and amending computer programs.

3.7 Encryption

■ The principle of encryption is to make any intelligible data unintelligible. Encrypted data can be read only by using the decryption key.

■ This process prevents unauthorised access to, or understanding of, transmitted or stored data.

■ Areas in which encryption technology is being used include:
- **Authentication**—the ability of each party through the transmission of the data to verify each other.
- **Message integrity**—the ability to detect whether the message has been read or altered in any way.
- **Electronic signatures**—a digital code attached to a message to verify the origins and contents of a message. Enables the recipient to check who sent the data and that it was not altered after transmission.

3.8 Software Audit Trail

■ A record of significant data about each transaction. For example: audit record, user and terminal identifications, the time and date of the transaction, transaction type (e.g. despatch), quantities and values, cross-references to related transactions (e.g. invoice).

■ The software audit trail records information about online transactions so the transaction and its backward and forward paths can be inspected and verified by third parties (e.g. internal auditors, system analysts).

■ Audit trails enable:
- any unusual transaction or events (e.g. fraud) to be investigated, often by producing a log of activity or exception report;
- sensitive data to be monitored;
- errors to be investigated by tracing back through the system via each stage of the transaction process;
- user interface problems to be identified; and
- systems to be thoroughly tested during project development and routine maintenance (both paper based and audit software).

Summary

- Internal controls assist management in meeting organisational goals by preventing, detecting or correcting threats to data accuracy and security.

- The control environment consists of the attitude, awareness and actions of the board and management and determines the control consciousness of employees.

- A suspense account should be regularly checked and cleared to ensure error trapping and correction.

- General controls and application controls help management deal with risks in the CIS environment.

  - General controls apply across many applications and can be classified as systems development controls (system structure) and administration controls (system access, protection and monitoring).

  - Application controls operate at a business process level and are designed to ensure the integrity of the accounting process and data. These can be classified as input, processing, output and master file processes. Alternatively, application controls can be grouped into transaction controls and file controls.

- Embedded controls check whether some other control functioned as intended.

- Information security relates to the system as a whole; information privacy relates to data held in the system. Threats may arise from intentional or unintentional acts as well as coming from internal or external sources.

- Encryption and software audit trails may be used to help secure data.

- Control risk describes risk of the internal control system failing to prevent, detect or correct a material error.

Session 14 Quiz

Estimated time: 15 minutes

1. List the FIVE elements of internal control. (1.2)

2. Explain the concept of "the control environment". (1.2.1)

3. Describe the difference between general IT controls and application controls. (2.2, 2.3)

4. Describe THREE examples of controls for computer physical risks. (3.2)

5. List FIVE control examples applicable to environmental risks. (3.3)

6. List FOUR methods of preventing unauthorised access to data systems. (3.4)

Study Question Bank

Estimated time: 40 minutes

Priority		Estimated Time	Completed
MCQ14	Internal Control and Security	40 minutes	

EXAMPLE SOLUTIONS

Solution 1—Business Risks

- *Changes in regulatory or operating environment*. Changes in the regulatory or operating environment can, for example, result in changes in competitive pressures and significantly different risks. Such risks have to be identified and their impact quantified.

- *New personnel*. Potential risk will depend on their seniority or position. They may have a different focus on understanding and applying internal control; they will need to learn new processes and may attempt to change or ignore existing controls.

- *New or upgraded information systems*. Significant and rapid changes in information systems can change the risk relating to internal control (e.g. previous controls may no longer be effective, new controls are not enacted). The change process in itself is a significant risk in that data may not be correctly converted or the new system does not function as intended.

- *Rapid growth*. Significant and rapid expansion of operations can strain controls and increase the risk of a breakdown in controls (e.g. overtrading, strained gearing and loss of direction).

- *New technology*. Incorporating new technologies into production processes or information systems may change the risk associated with internal control.

- *New business models*, *products or activities*. Entering into business areas or transactions with which an entity has little experience may introduce new risks associated with internal control.

- *Corporate restructurings*. Restructurings may be accompanied by staff reductions and changes in supervision and segregation of duties which may change the risk associated with internal control. Management time spent on restructuring and making every effort to ensure it works means that less time can be spent on running other areas of the business.

- *Expanded foreign operations*. The expansion or acquisition of foreign operations carries new and often unique risks which may affect internal control, for example, additional or changed risks from foreign currency transactions.

- *New accounting pronouncements*. Adoption of new accounting principles or changing accounting principles may affect risks in preparing financial statements, especially in relation to recognition, measurement and disclosure requirements.

Solution 2—Inherent Limitations

- Cost of internal control should not exceed benefits derived.
- Non-routine transactions may not go through the normal processes.
- Human error/machine/IT breakdown.
- Use of inexperienced or untrained staff.
- Collusion by employees or management (to circumvent controls).
- Abuse of responsibility (e.g. management overriding internal control).
- Changes in conditions or deterioration in compliance.
- Poor monitoring.

Business Fraud

FOCUS

This session covers the following content from the *ACCA Study Guide.*

> ### C. Accounting and Reporting Systems, Controls and Compliance
>
> **5. Financial systems, procedures and related IT applications**
> c) Explain why it is important to adhere to policies and procedures for handling clients' money.
> **7. Fraud and fraudulent behaviour and their prevention in business**
> a) Explain the circumstances under which fraud is likely to arise.
> b) Identify different types of fraud in the organisation.
> c) Explain the implications of fraud for the organisation.
> d) Explain the role and duties of individual managers in the fraud detection and prevention process.
> e) Define the term money laundering.
> f) Give examples of recognised offences under typical money laundering regulation.
> g) Identify methods for detecting and preventing money laundering.
> h) Explain how suspicions of money laundering should be reported to the appropriate authorities.

Session 15 Guidance

■ **Know** the difference between fraud and error and the differences in the responsibilities of management and external auditors (s.1).

■ **Recognise** fraud risk factors and give typical examples of fraud in various financial systems (s.2, s.3).

(continued on next page)

VISUAL OVERVIEW

Objective: To describe the potential for fraud and fraudulent behaviour in a business and the types of fraud which can be carried out.

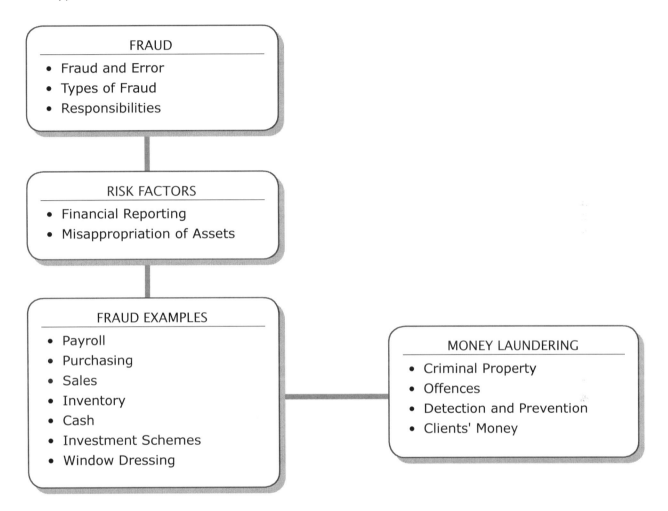

FRAUD
- Fraud and Error
- Types of Fraud
- Responsibilities

RISK FACTORS
- Financial Reporting
- Misappropriation of Assets

FRAUD EXAMPLES
- Payroll
- Purchasing
- Sales
- Inventory
- Cash
- Investment Schemes
- Window Dressing

MONEY LAUNDERING
- Criminal Property
- Offences
- Detection and Prevention
- Clients' Money

Session 15 Guidance

■ **Note** that section 4 is detailed but very important. Ensure that you fully **understand** how to detect and prevent money-laundering offences (s.4).

1 Fraud

1.1 Fraud and Error

Definition

■ A distinction should initially be made between **fraud** and **error**, from the business perspective.

■ Examples of error include:

- A mistake in gathering or processing data used to prepare reports.
- An incorrect accounting or processing estimate arising from oversight or misinterpretation of facts.
- A mistake in the application of accounting principles relating to measurement, recognition, classification, presentation or disclosure.

■ Fraud, however, involves three basic factors:

1. Motivation—incentive or pressure to commit fraud.

2. Opportunity—an advantageous chance to do so.

3. Dishonesty—some rationalisation of the act.

■ The individuals carrying out the fraud may be:

- involved in management or charged with governance (i.e. "management fraud");
- employees (i.e. "employee fraud"); or
- third parties acting alone or in collusion with management and/or employees.

> **Error**—an *unintentional* mistake made in the business through carelessness or ignorance.
>
> **Fraud** (in business)— the *intentional* act of deception, misrepresentation or concealment of information to obtain an unjust or illegal removal of funds or assets from a business or the intentional misrepresentation of financial position or outcomes.

Example 1 Fraud or Error

Classify each of the following as either "fraud" or "error".

Solution

Description	Fraud/Error
(a) Alteration, falsification or manipulation of accounting records or documents.	
(b) Accidentally applying inappropriate accounting policies.	
(c) Collusion.	
(d) Mathematical or clerical mistakes in collecting or processing accounting data.	
(e) Unintentional misapplication of accounting policies.	
(f) Misappropriation of assets (i.e. theft).	
(g) Oversight or misinterpretation of facts resulting in an incorrect accounting estimate.	
(h) Purposefully recording transactions without economic substance.	
(i) Suppression of effects of transactions from records or documents.	

1.2   Types of Fraud

In a business context, there are two basic forms of fraud:

1. Fraudulent reporting (e.g. management information, financial statements).

2. Misappropriation of assets (e.g. theft of cash, theft of inventory, wilful misuse of assets).

1.2.1   Fraudulent Reporting

■ Misstatements or omissions of amounts or disclosures intended to deceive users of financial statements, motivated, for example, by pressures to achieve earnings target, share price, bonus targets or avoiding bank default. Includes:

- Deception (e.g. through manipulation, falsification, forgery or alteration) of accounting records or supporting documents.*

- Misrepresentation, or intentional omission, of significant information.

- Deliberate misapplication of accounting principles affecting the measurement, recognition and disclosure of elements of financial statements.

*A good example of deception is the "rogue traders" at banks attempting to cover up and conceal their true trading positions.

1.2.2   Misappropriation (Theft) of Assets

■ Often, individuals are motivated by "living beyond their means". Examples of theft include:

- **embezzlement**—fraudulent conversion of property by a person in a position of trust;

- **swindling**—fraudulently obtaining property through a false pretence;

- **larceny**—stealing physical assets (e.g. inventory) or intellectual property (e.g. copying CDs);

- **conversion**—using an entity's tangible assets for personal benefit; and

- **fraudulent misrepresentation**—entering fake employees onto the payroll or causing the business to pay for goods and services not received.

■ Theft may be, but is not necessarily, concealed by falsified records or documents.

1.3   Responsibilities

1.3.1   Management

■ Primary responsibility for prevention *and* detection of fraud and error lies with management and those charged with governance. This includes responsibility to develop, implement and monitor an appropriate code of ethics.*

■ Those charged with governance must ensure that the appropriate risk management procedures and internal control are in place and operate. This includes compliance with applicable laws and regulations and the use of internal audit to monitor controls.

*Those charged with governance oversee management. Management creates the control environment. The respective responsibilities of those charged with governance (if any) and management may depend on the entity, voluntary codes, legal requirements, etc.

■ Management must place a strong emphasis on fraud prevention as well as establish and embed a culture of honesty and ethical behaviour throughout the organisation. The auditors (external and internal) and those charged with governance must consider the potential for management override of internal control and the use of inappropriate influence over the financial reporting process (e.g. aggressive earnings management).

Example 2 Management Override

Give FIVE techniques which could be used by management to override internal controls.

1.3.2 Other Employees

■ All employees should be fully aware of the fraud risks and the consequences of committing fraud on the company, on other employees and on themselves.

■ They should be embedded with a moral and ethical obligation not to carry out fraudulent activities, not to seek opportunities to do so nor to encourage others (internally and externally) to do so.

■ Whistle-blowing should be openly encouraged and each employee should know how the system functions and whom to approach with concerns.

1.3.3 Auditors

■ Auditors are not responsible for preventing fraud or errors and therefore cannot be held liable for them, although they may have a responsibility to report discovered fraud. External and internal audit procedures should, however, act as a deterrent.

■ The auditors (internal and external) should consider the risk of material misstatement arising from fraud and error when:
  - planning and performing their work programme and procedures; and
  - evaluating and reporting on their findings.

■ Error is more likely to be detected than fraud because fraud is ordinarily accompanied by acts specifically designed to conceal its existence. For example:
  - collusion;
  - forgery;
  - deliberate failure to record transactions; or
  - intentional misrepresentations to the auditor.

■ However, auditors should plan and perform their work with an attitude of professional scepticism, recognising that conditions or events may be found which indicate that fraud or error may exist.

■ Professional scepticism is an attitude which includes a questioning mind and a critical assessment of audit evidence rather than accepting audit evidence at face value. It requires questioning whether information and audit evidence suggest a material misstatement due to fraud.

■ Areas to consider should at least cover:

- how and where the entity's financial statements may be susceptible to material misstatement due to fraud;
- how management could perpetrate and conceal fraudulent financial reporting and how assets of the entity could be misappropriated (by management and employees);
- the known external and internal factors affecting the entity which may create a pressure for fraud or provide the opportunity for fraud to be perpetrated;
- management's involvement in overseeing employees with access to cash or other assets susceptible to misappropriation;
- any unusual or unexplained changes in behaviour or lifestyle of management or employees;
- how unpredictability will be incorporated into the nature, timing and extent of the audit procedures to be performed;
- whether certain types of audit procedures are more effective than others;
- any allegations of fraud which have come to the auditor's attention; and
- the risk that management could override controls.

2 Risk Factors

2.1 Financial Reporting

2.1.1 Incentives

Risks may arise from incentives and/or pressures. For example:

■ Negative effects on financial stability or profitability due to political, economic, social, technological, industry or entity operating conditions (basically PEST risk factors).

■ External third parties (e.g. investment analysts, banks, credit rating agencies) put significant pressure on management to, for instance, meet forecasts.

■ An entity's poor financial performance places management under personal financial pressure (e.g. personal guarantees of entity debt).

■ Those charged with governance place management under pressure to meet financial targets, including sales or profitability incentive goals (includes pressure on operating personnel from management).

■ Potential loss of management financial incentives (e.g. bonuses) for failing to meet a particular goal.

2.1.2 Opportunities

Other fraud risk arises from opportunities. For example:

- Ineffective monitoring (e.g. poor oversight of the board by those charged with governance or of the CEO by the board).
- A complex or unstable organisational structure (e.g. rapid turnover of senior employees, opaque management structure with unclear lines of responsibility, or unnecessarily complex corporate structure).
- Deficient internal control components (e.g. lack of monitoring, lack of understanding or high turnover of key control staff).

2.1.3 Attitude and Rationalisation

Risks of individuals justifying fraudulent actions may arise due to:

- Ineffective communication of high ethical values (or the communication of poor ethical values) by management.
- Failure by management or those charged with governance to take appropriate action for breaches of the entity's rules and regulations (e.g. fraudulent expense claims, inappropriate use of company assets).
- Known history of violations of laws and regulations which have not been identified or corrected by higher authorities.
- A need to maintain key performance indicators (e.g. earnings per share).
- A need to minimise corporate taxation.
- Failing to correct known ineffective material internal controls.
- A lack of distinction between personal and business transactions.

Example 3 Fraud Risk Factors

Suggest examples of risk factors for each of the following incentive/pressure categories:

(a) **Financial stability or profitability is threatened by economic, industry or entity operating conditions.**

(b) **External third parties (e.g. investment analysts, banks, credit rating agencies) put significant pressure on management.**

(c) **The entity's poor financial performance places management under personal financial pressure.**

2.2 Misappropriation of Assets

2.2.1 Incentives and/or Pressure Arising From:

- Management or employees with financial problems (e.g. debts, divorce, drugs).
- Deterioration of employee/employer relationship (e.g. expected or known redundancy, expected or actual negative changes in remuneration and benefits, expectations on promotions and benefits not met).
- Threats against an employee or significant others if they don't perform the fraud insisted upon by a third party.

2.2.2 Opportunities Arising From:

- The type of assets controlled (e.g. large volumes of cash, easily convertible assets such as bearer bonds, diamonds, computer chips and precious metals, and other assets with high external demand).
- Poor internal control environment (e.g. inadequate segregation of duties or independent checks).
- Inadequate control of senior management expenditures (e.g. travel and other reimbursements).
- Inadequate oversight of employees responsible for assets (e.g. inadequate supervision of remote locations).
- Inadequate recording, tracking and physical reconciliation of assets.
- Inadequate system of authorisation and approval of transactions (e.g. purchasing and asset disposals).
- Inadequate physical safeguards over cash, investments, inventory or fixed assets.
- Lack of mandatory vacations for employees performing key control functions (e.g. minimum of two weeks and preferably over at least one month at the end of the control period).
- Inadequate management understanding of, and controls over, information technology (e.g. a programmer is able to change a program and misappropriate company property).
- Inadequate management understanding of complex processes carried out by employees (e.g. derivative trading).

2.2.3 Attitude and Rationalisation Through:

- Lack of respect for internal control over misappropriation of assets (e.g. ability to overriding existing controls).
- Tolerance of petty theft by management (e.g. stationery, scrap metal, use of company systems for private gain).
- Following the lead of others (e.g. "what is good for management is good for us"). Suggesting that if management carries out fraud, why not others?

Example 4 Organisation Size

The size, complexity and ownership characteristics of a business have a significant influence on the consideration of relevant fraud risk factors.

Required:

Suggest THREE fraud risk factors which apply to a large (e.g. listed) business which do not apply or are less important for a smaller (e.g. unlisted) business.

---

3 Fraud Examples

The following are just a few examples of the basic, unsophisticated frauds which have been carried out in businesses.

3.1 Payroll

■ Falsified timesheets, expense claims and work done; overstated figures entered into payroll records (e.g. by payroll staff); and fictitious employees (e.g. employees do not exist, but are paid).

3.2 Purchasing

■ Examples include:

- Bid fixing (e.g. cartels), kickbacks and inducements (e.g. "brown" envelopes).
- Connected companies (e.g. bogus companies used to inflate purchase costs).
- Middlemen (e.g. unclear why necessary, usually to inflate eventual costs).
- Dummy suppliers (payments made for goods and services not received).
- Advance fees (e.g. once received, the seller disappears).
- Short deliveries (hoping the goods-received system is poor).
- Invoicing for goods or services not delivered (e.g. inclusion in a non-existent trade directory).
- Substandard products (e.g. charged for high-quality products but low-quality ones are delivered).

3.3 Sales

■ Examples include:

- Diversion of customers (e.g. customers directed to companies connected with key employees).
- Bogus goods and services paid for but not delivered.
- Kickbacks.
- Under-billing (e.g. suppression of sales invoices in return for a kickback).
- Under-ringing (cash sales equivalent of under-billing).
- Bad debt write-offs (e.g. writing off a debt for a fee).
- Counterfeit goods.
- Teeming and lading is probably the most famous of the sales-based frauds. It involves the theft of cash or cheque receipts, usually from (credit) customers being covered up by subsequent receipts of cash or cheques.

  For example, a cheque from customer A is misappropriated, but covered by the receipt of cash from Customer B. This leaves a balance on B's account. This is covered by a cheque received from customer C, etc. The balancing item may then be written off by the fraudster as a bad debt, or a false credit note issued. In most cases, a fraudster who suspects detection will resign and disappear.

▨ Long firm fraud (here today, gone tomorrow) is another favourite. The fraudster sets up an account with the target company, initially buying small quantities and setting a good credit history. The size of the orders slowly increases as does the credit limit. Then a significant "one-off" order is requested to meet the demand of a "special customer". Credit is granted and the goods are delivered; the fraudster disappears, leaving a bad debt.

3.4   Inventory

▨ Theft of basic goods, theft of valuable scrap, over-valuation.

3.5   Cash

▨ Easily misappropriated cash, forged cheques, electronic transfers, manipulation of bank reconciliations (beware those prepared on spreadsheets), stolen PIN on charge cards.

3.6   Investment Schemes

▨ An interesting fraud which seems to come up on a regular basis and plays on an individual's naivety or greed. Usually referred to as a Ponzi scheme, after the fraudster who first carried it out.

▨ The fraudster initially pays very high returns (to establish the scheme), but the returns are paid out of new capital receipts. When sufficient funds have been collected by the fraudsters, or when the new funds cease to appear, the fraudster disappears.*

3.7   Window Dressing

▨ Window dressing is a common fraud carried out at year end on financial statements to make them appear healthier than what they really are.

▨ Simply, window dressing involves changing the timing and cut-off of key transactions to improve the financial position. For example:

  • recording after-date sales as sales made just before year end;
  • recording false sales before year end and issuing credit notes after year end;
  • issuing cheque payments before year end to reduce liabilities, but not sending out the cheques until after year end (usually done to improve the liquidity ratio).

*Commentary

*Bernard Madoff carried out the world's largest Ponzi scheme from the 1970s to 2008. It is estimated that $65 billion is missing from client funds. In 2009, at the age of 71, he was sentenced to 150 years in prison.

4 Money Laundering

4.1 Criminal Property

> ### Definition
>
> **Money laundering**—the process by which criminals attempt to conceal the true origin and ownership of the proceeds of their criminal activity, thus allowing them to maintain control over the proceeds and, ultimately, providing a legitimate cover for their sources of income.

- Descriptions of **money laundering** typically include possessing, concealing or in any way dealing with the proceeds of any crime ("criminal property").
- It also includes:
  - an attempt or conspiracy or incitement to commit such an offence;
  - aiding, abetting, counselling or procuring the commission of such an offence; or
  - an act which would constitute any of these offences.
- Criminal property includes, for example:
  - the proceeds of tax evasion;
  - a benefit obtained through bribery or corruption;
  - benefits obtained, or income received, through the operation of a criminal cartel; and
  - benefits (in the form of saved costs) arising from a failure to comply with a regulatory requirement, where that failure is a criminal offence.*

> ### *Commentary
>
> *Details on the UK Bribery Act can be found at:
> www.justice.gov.uk/guidance/docs/bribery-act-2010-guidance.pdf.

4.2 Offences (Under UK Legislation)

4.2.1 Principal Offences

- Failure to appoint a money laundering reporting officer (see s.4.3.2).
- Failure to implement internal procedures to comply with the legislation, including the provision of training.
- Failure to verify the identity of all new clients before commencing a business relationship.
- Obtaining, concealing, retaining or investing funds or property (or assisting another to do so) if members know or suspect or have reasonable grounds to know or suspect that those funds or property are the proceeds of criminal conduct or terrorist funding.
- Failure to report any knowledge or suspicion (see following) as soon as practicable that money-laundering activities are being carried out or suspected ("a suspicion report").
- Doing or disclosing anything which might prejudice an investigation into money-laundering activities (e.g. "tipping off").
- Proceeding with a transaction without the consent of the relevant authority following the submission of a suspicion report.

- Failure to comply with a direction of the relevant authority not to proceed with a transaction or business relationship.
- Failure to maintain records in accordance with legislative requirements.

4.2.2 Fiscal Offences

- Tax-related offences are not in a special category. Tax evasion is a crime, the proceeds of which can be laundered in the same way as those from drug trafficking, terrorist activity, theft, etc.
- Offences may relate to:
  - direct tax (e.g. income tax or corporation tax); or
  - indirect tax (e.g. VAT).
- Tax-evasion offences, which fall within the definition of money laundering, include:
  - under-declaring income; and
  - over-claiming expenses.*

*An action carried out abroad by a UK citizen is relevant if the action would be an offence in the United Kingdom.

4.2.3 Knowledge or Suspicion

- Knowledge is likely to include:
  - actual knowledge;
  - shutting one's mind to the obvious;
  - deliberately refraining from making inquiries; and
  - deliberately deterring a person from making disclosures.
- Suspicion is not defined in existing legislation. Case law and other sources, however, indicate that it is more than speculation but falls short of proof or knowledge.
- There is no *de minimis* limit to consider. Reports must be made irrespective of the value of the benefits obtained, or the seriousness of the offence.

4.2.4 Tipping Off

- The offence of tipping off occurs when an individual who has knowledge or suspicion makes a disclosure to a third party (e.g. the suspected individual or entity) which is likely to prejudice a terrorism or money-laundering investigation.
- There is no need for the investigation to have commenced or a report to have been made—the fact that the suspected individual is warned is sufficient.
- In certain cases, non-disclosure and non-action may be effective tipping off (e.g. not carrying out a client's instructions related to a money-laundering operation).
- Where the action required *is* a money-laundering offence, permission must be obtained from the appropriate authorities before taking the action.
- Fear of tipping off should not prevent professional accountants from discussing money-laundering matters with clients on a non-specific basis. Not doing so, when requested, may amount to tipping off.*

*Any undue delay in carrying out a client instruction or not responding to a request to discuss money-laundering matters may result in tipping off.

4.3 Detecting and Preventing

- The following obligations are designed to assist ACCA members, in practice or commerce, in detecting and preventing their organisations from being used for money-laundering purposes:

  - putting into place internal controls and policies to ensure compliance with legislation;
  - appointing a money laundering reporting officer (MLRO);
  - establishing/enhancing record-keeping systems for all transactions;
  - maintaining systems for verification of clients' identities;
  - establishing internal suspicion reporting procedures; and
  - educating and training all staff in the main requirements of the legislation.

- It is an offence **not** to comply with these obligations and failure to comply can lead to penalties.

4.3.1 Internal Controls and Policies

- Internal controls and policies should be established:

  - to ensure that anyone who suspects money laundering knows how to report this to their MLRO; and
  - to provide the MLRO with the means to judge the reasonableness of the suspicion and thereby assess which suspicions should be reported to the appropriate authority.

- Client and customer acceptance procedures should include:*

  - identification procedures; and
  - gathering information such as:
    - —the client/customer's expected patterns of business;
    - —its business model; and
    - —its source of funds.

*"Customer due diligence" procedures.

- Controls over clients' money and transactions passing through any client account, with particular attention to the:

  - identity of the client;
  - commercial purpose of the transaction; and
  - source and destination of the funds.*

> ***Commentary***
>
> *Control over client money and transactions passing through a client account are of particular importance to accountants and solicitors, as money passed through their client accounts may be used to legitimise the money and frustrate the audit trail.

- Sound policies should also be developed to avoid giving advice and other services to a money launderer.

4.3.2 Money Laundering Reporting Officer (MLRO)

- The MLRO should have a suitable level of seniority and experience (e.g. a principal of an accountancy firm).

- Alternative arrangements (e.g. appointing a deputy) must be made when an MLRO will be unavailable for a period of time to meet the requirement to file reports as soon as reasonably practicable.

- The requirement to appoint an MLRO does not apply to sole practitioners with no employees or associates.

- The MLRO is responsible for:
  - receiving and assessing money-laundering reports from colleagues; and
  - making reports to the appropriate authority on a standard disclosure form.

- It may be appropriate for MLROs to take responsibility for ensuring that individuals are adequately trained (see following).

4.3.3 Record Keeping

- All client identification records together with a record of all transactions, in a full audit trail form, must be maintained.

- Records of transactions must be kept in a readily retrievable form for at least five years following the completion of the transaction (or series of transactions).

- Businesses must have controls to ensure that records are not inadvertently destroyed by one department (e.g. where another is still within a five-year period).

- Client/customer verification records must be retained throughout the period of the relationship and for five years after termination of the relationship.

- ACCA's *Rules of Professional Conduct* "Retention of books, files, working papers and other documents" also apply.

4.3.4 Client Identification

- Verifying the identities of all clients/customers is mandatory.

- Verification must be achieved and documented before any transaction is undertaken. A transaction cannot commence with the intention and expectation of fulfilling this obligation at some later date.

- Sufficient knowledge of a client/customer must be obtained (and kept up to date) to identify unusual and/or suspicious activity.*

*ACCA members must obtain evidence of identity for all clients where:
- an ongoing business relationship is to be established; or
- the total value of any transactions is not known at the outset; or
- "occasional transactions" (i.e. outside the business relationship) are valued at over €15,000.

4.3.5 Typical Identification Procedures

▓ For an individual, organisations should obtain official documents with a photograph establishing the client's full name and permanent address (e.g. driving licence or passport supported by a recent utility bill).

▓ For the entity, organisations should obtain the certificate of incorporation, registered address and a list of shareholders and directors from the Registrar of Companies.

▓ Organisations should check the names of all new clients against lists of known terrorists and other sanctions information such as can be found at:

- the financial sanctions section of www.bankofengland.co.uk (Bank of England information on terrorist organisations); and
- www.treasury.gov/resource-center/sanctions (US Treasury listing of known terrorists).

*Services which involve handling clients' money may be considered to represent a higher than normal risk and so require a higher level of KYC and identification procedures.

4.3.6 Banking and Clients' Money

▓ The Charter for the European Professional Associations in Support of the Fight Against Organised Crime (1999) requires practicing firms to verify client identity when handling client money. Firms with clients' money bank accounts (see s.4.4) denominated in foreign currencies should take particular care. (This is not a new requirement.)*

4.3.7 Suspicion

▓ It is impossible to define suspicion. A suspicious transaction or situation often will be inconsistent with the client's known legitimate business or personal activities.* The key to recognition is to undertake "customer due diligence".

*There is no obligation to quantify the certainty of suspicion in a potential money-laundering scheme.

▓ Examples of potentially suspicious transactions include:

- unusually large cash deposits;
- frequent exchange of cash into other currencies;
- transactions where the counterparty to the transaction is unknown;
- activity inconsistent with normal business activity;
- activity involving offshore business arrangements with no clear business purpose.

4.3.8 Reporting

▓ Members are legally required to report knowledge or suspicions of money laundering to the appropriate authority (e.g. MLRO, police or customs officer).

▓ It is a criminal offence not to do so.

▓ There are no *de minimis* concessions. The obligation to report is irrespective of:

- the amount involved; or
- the seriousness of the offence.

*This could mean that particular work for a client has to stop until consent is given, which may result in effectively tipping off the client.

▓ Standard disclosure forms for full and abbreviated disclosures are downloadable from www.nationalcrimeagency.gov.uk.

▓ If a client requests a money-laundering offence, then a *written* request for consent must be made to the appropriate authority. No action which could be considered an offence must take place for a period of seven working days unless consent is given.*

■ In such circumstances, legal advice must be sought quickly.

■ If no response is received within the seven working days, it is deemed that the consent requested has been given and the business is entitled to proceed.

4.3.9   Educating and Training All Staff

■ Relevant individuals must be provided with training on:

- how to report to the MLRO;
- how to identify clients;
- how to recognise and deal with situations that may involve money laundering;
- the main money-laundering offences; and
- the business's procedures to forestall and prevent money laundering, including identification, record keeping and reporting procedures.

■ Training should enable businesses to establish a culture of compliance.

■ Training should be documented to demonstrate compliance. It does not need to be performed in-house.

■ Effective methods of training may include:

- attending conferences, seminars and courses run by external organisations; and
- participation in computer-based training courses.

4.4   Clients' Money

■ As previously mentioned (see *Session 13*), client money is simply money held by an organisation on behalf of a client (e.g. a solicitor or accountant pending instructions from that client). It is not money belonging to the firm and cannot be counted as an asset of the firm.

■ The holder of client money acts as an agent to the client in relation to that money.

■ In general, controls and procedures must be in place to ensure that:

- All partners, directors and employees are fully aware of the relevant client money procedures and accounting.
- All relevant laws and regulations (e.g. ACCA Code of Ethics and Conduct on client money) are applied and followed.
- Client money and other client assets are kept separately from personal or firm assets (e.g. in a separately designated bank account with limited access requiring two signatories).
- Client money is used only for the purpose for which it is intended following the receipt of written authorisation from the client.
- Any transaction involving client money must be fully supported by relevant documentation and authorisation.
- Client money and any income, dividend or gains generated by that money is regularly accounted for to the client (e.g. regular statements); and
- Client money transactions are independently reviewed to identify suspicious transactions which may be money laundering.

Summary

- Fraud is an intentional act of deception, misrepresentation or concealment; error is unintentional (a mistake). Fraud involves motivation, opportunity and dishonesty.

- While auditors bear no responsibility for preventing fraud or error, the audit procedures may help act as a deterrent.

- Fraud is more difficult for an auditor to find than error, because fraud typically includes some act of concealment. Auditors should conduct their programme with an attitude of professional scepticism.

- The conditions which lead to increased risk of fraud generally include incentives or motivation and justification by the fraudster.

- Money laundering occurs when criminals conceal the true origin and ownership in an attempt to provide legitimate cover for their sources of illegitimate income.

  - It includes possessing, concealing or dealing in any way with the proceeds of a crime (criminal property), or conspiracy and incitement, aiding the criminal, etc.

  - Thus, criminal property includes proceeds of tax evasion, benefits obtained by bribery or corruption and benefits arising from failure to follow a regulatory requirement.

- Knowledge and even suspicion of money laundering should be immediately reported; there is no minimum amount or an offence which is too small.

  - Policies should be in place to avoid counselling a money launderer.

  - Certain firms must have a money laundering reporting officer (MLRO) who takes responsibility for prevention, detection and, in some cases, training.

- No transaction may be undertaken until client identity can be verified.

- Client money should be segregated to prevent commingling.

  - Transactions involving client money should be supported by appropriate documentation.

  - Balances and transactions should be regularly reported to clients and independently reviewed to identify suspicious transactions.

Session 15 Quiz
Estimated time: 15 minutes

1. Explain the difference between fraud and error. (1.1)
2. True or false? Auditors are responsible for detecting all fraud. (1.3)
3. List the THREE elements in fraud risk factors. (2.1)
4. Explain the workings of a Ponzi scheme. (3.6)
5. Define "money laundering". (4.1)
6. Explain the role of the MLRO. (4.3)
7. Describe the controls which should be in place over client money. (4.4)

Study Question Bank
Estimated time: 25 minutes

Priority		Estimated Time	Completed
MCQ15	Business Fraud	25 minutes	

EXAMPLE SOLUTIONS

Solution 1—Fraud or Error

(a) Alteration, falsification or manipulation of accounting records or documents. — Fraud

(b) Accidentally applying inappropriate accounting policies.* — Error

(c) Collusion. — Fraud

(d) Mathematical or clerical mistakes in collecting or processing accounting data. — Error

(e) Unintentional misapplication of accounting policies. — Error

(f) Misappropriation of assets (i.e. theft). — Fraud

(g) Oversight or misinterpretation of facts resulting in an incorrect accounting estimate. — Error

(h) Purposefully recording transactions without economic substance. — Fraud

(i) Suppression of effects of transactions from records or documents. — Fraud

Commentary

*If accounting policies are inappropriately applied intentionally and not out of ignorance, then fraud would apply.

Solution 2—Management Override

- Recording fictitious journal entries, particularly close to the end of an accounting period, to manipulate operating results or achieve other objectives—such entries may need to be reversed out in the following period.

- Inappropriately adjusting assumptions and changing judgements used to estimate account balances (e.g. aggressive application of accounting policies).

- Omitting, advancing or delaying recognition in the financial statements of events and transactions which have occurred during the reporting period (e.g. recognising revenue not yet earned).

- Concealing, or not disclosing, facts which could affect the amounts or disclosures recorded in financial statements (e.g. product liability suits, related-party transactions).

- Engaging in complex transactions which are structured to misrepresent the financial position or financial performance of the entity (e.g. off balance sheet financing and the use of special-purpose entities).

- Altering records and terms related to significant and unusual transactions.

Solution 3—Fraud Risk Factors

Financial Stability or Profitability Is Threatened

- High degree of competition or market saturation, accompanied by declining margins.
- High vulnerability to rapid changes, such as changes in technology, product obsolescence or interest rates.
- Significant declines in customer demand and increasing business failures in either the industry or overall economy.
- Operating losses making the threat of bankruptcy, foreclosure or hostile takeover imminent.
- Recurring negative cash flows from operations or an inability to generate cash flows from operations while reporting earnings and earnings growth.
- Rapid growth or unusual profitability especially compared to that of other companies in the same industry.
- New accounting, statutory or regulatory requirements.

External Third Parties Putting Significant Pressure on Management

- Profitability or trend-level expectations of investment analysts, institutional investors, significant creditors or other external parties, particularly expectations which are unduly aggressive or unrealistic, including expectations created by management in, for example, overly optimistic press releases or annual report messages.
- Need to obtain additional debt or equity financing to stay competitive, including financing of major research and development or capital expenditures.
- Marginal ability to meet exchange listing requirements or debt repayment or other debt covenant requirements.
- Perceived or real adverse effects of reporting poor financial results on significant pending transactions, such as business combinations or contract awards.

Poor Financial Performance Places Management Under Personal Financial Pressure

- Significant financial interests in the entity.
- Significant portions of their compensation (e.g. bonuses, stock options and earn-out arrangements) being contingent on achieving aggressive targets for stock price, operating results, financial position or cash flow.
- Personal guarantees of debts of the entity.

Solution 4—Organisation Size

- Ineffectiveness of those charged with governance and/or the internal audit function. A small (unlisted) business is unlikely to need a separate governance function as it will be owned by members of the management team.

- Lack of enforcement or monitoring of a formal (written) code of conduct. The ethical approach of management and the culture of the organisation are very often set by example. The business probably will be small enough such that executive management has day-to-day contact with other managers and a significant number of employees.

- Domination of management by one individual. In a small business this is very often the case, but does not automatically mean high risk. By itself it does not mean a failure to display and communicate an appropriate attitude regarding internal control. BUT it could be a potential weakness, as there is the opportunity for management override. Assessment of the management integrity is critical.

- An ineffective budgeting system. In a smaller business, management will be able to exercise very close day-to-day monitoring of financial and other transactions. Because of management's closeness to the core transactions of the business, there will be very little, if anything, going on that they do not know about.

- Appear to be outside the normal course of business.

Leadership, Management and Supervision

FOCUS

This session covers the following content from the *ACCA Study Guide.*

D. Leading and Managing Individuals and Teams

1. Leadership, management and supervision

a) Define leadership, management and supervision and explain the distinction between these terms. ☐

b) Explain the nature of management: ☐

    i) scientific/classical theories of management—Fayol, Taylor

    ii) the human relations school—Mayo

    iii) the functions of a manager—Mintzberg, Drucker

c) Explain the areas of managerial authority and responsibility. ☐

d) Explain the situational, functional and contingency approaches to leadership with reference to the theories of Adair, Fiedler, Bennis, Kotter and Heifetz. ☐

e) Explain leadership styles and contexts: using the models of Ashridge, and Blake and Mouton. ☐

Session 16 Guidance

■ **Learn** the definitions, and **understand** the difference between leadership and management (s.1.1) and how the role of a supervisor relates to management (s.1.2). Apply the same approach to authority, responsibility and delegation (s.1.3). The rest of the session deals with the key theories of management and leadership.

(continued on next page)

VISUAL OVERVIEW

Objective: To describe the differences between leadership and management and to consider a number of relevant theories on management and leadership.

```
                    ┌─────────────────────────────┐
                    │  LEADERSHIP, MANAGEMENT      │
                    │       AND SUPERVISION        │
                    │  • Leadership v Management   │
                    │  • Supervisors               │
                    │  • Authority, Responsibility │
                    │    and Delegation            │
                    └─────────────────────────────┘
```

MANAGEMENT THEORY	LEADERSHIP THEORY	MODELS AND THEORISTS
• Need for a Framework	• Approaches	• Blake and Mouton
• Classical Theory	• Quality, Trait and Personality Theories	• Ashridge Management College
• Taylor	• Style Theories	• Fiedler
• Fayol	• Contingency Theories	• Adair, Action-Centered Leadership
• Human Relations Theory		• Bennis
• Mayo		• Heifetz
• Modern Theories		• Kotter
• Drucker		
• Mintzberg		

Session 16 Guidance

■ **Recognise** the key differences between classical management theory (s.2.2), human relations theory (s.2.4) and modern theories (s.2.6).

■ **Know** the approaches to leadership theory (s.3.1) and pay particular attention to the classification schemes developed by Blake and Mouton (s.4.1), and Ashridge Management College (s.4.2). All of these must be fully understood as any one of them could be examined.

1 Leadership, Management and Supervision

1.1 Leadership v Management

■ By definition, leadership is to lead, management is to manage. People are led, but tasks are managed.

■ Because leadership is about influencing behaviour in a particular direction, it is not the same thing as management.

■ Management may be concerned with ensuring that things remain as they are and that a plan is followed and correctly executed.

■ However, leadership is an aspect of management. Good managers must also be leaders, but it does not follow that natural leaders have to be good managers. Leaders can overcome management deficiencies by putting together a team of good managers and then leading that team.

■ Management is a "job". Managers are appointed. Their "job" involves tasks requiring logic, structure, analysis and control. For example:
  - Planning and budgeting
  - Organisation and staffing
  - Monitoring and decision-making
  - Following the rules

■ Leadership is more a quality. Leaders evolve or emerge, usually by popular choice or by necessity.

■ Leadership involves people rather than things. For example:
  - Providing a sense of direction
  - Communicating a vision
  - Inspiring and motivating individuals
  - Voicing the aspirations of the group
  - Creating good teams
  - Setting an example

■ Leadership concerns, *among other things*:
  - moving people from point A to point B;
  - improving performance; and
  - changing the way things are done.

■ Leadership requires effective motivational strategies, communication skills, delegation and interpersonal skills.

1.1.1 Leadership

■ "The activity of influencing people to strive willingly for group objectives." —*Terry*

■ "The capacity to translate vision into reality." —*Bennis*

■ "The art of motivating a group of people to act towards achieving a common goal." —*Ward*

■ Simply put, leadership is about "getting others to follow." —*Peter Drucker*

■ It is about "influence—nothing more, nothing less." —*John C. Maxwell*

1.1.2 Management

▧ "To forecast and plan, to organise, to command, to co-ordinate and to control." —*Fayol*

▧ Deciding what should be done then getting other people to do it. —*Stewart*

▧ A practice rather than a science or a profession so there are no precise solutions, and the ultimate test of management is achievement and business performance. —*Drucker*

▧ General management is at least the sum of its parts ... the general manager must have a working knowledge of all functional aspects of management plus the integrative skills needed to help functional managers work together. —*Financial Times*

1.2   Supervisors

▧ Although **supervision** is a management activity, supervisor often refers to junior management dealing with day-to-day and internal matters of the organisation.

▧ Supervisors typically conduct some smaller portion of a management responsibility. Part of their role is often being at the "coal face" doing the operational work, or an aspect of the work, themselves.

▧ Higher levels of management are further removed from the "coal face" and deal with the tactical and strategic (longer-term, internal and external) management of the organisation.

1.2.1 Duties and Responsibilities

▧ Being responsible for managing a group of people and deciding on, and agreeing on, courses of action to be implemented by the group.

▧ Allocating tasks to and organising the work of the group or team for whom they are responsible.

▧ Liaising with other individuals and groups as the manager of the group, team or resource.

▧ Supervising the work of subordinates and being accountable for achieving the objectives set in an effective and efficient way.

▧ Inducting newly appointed employees into their group.

▧ Maintaining discipline (e.g. ensuring that people keep good time, meet deadlines, carry out the tasks assigned to them or that they observe satisfactory regulations.

▧ Handling personnel problems and settling grievances.

▧ Training and conducting performance appraisals of supervised employees.

▧ Dealing with unsatisfactory performance.

▧ Ensuring that all employees under their control are technically up to date with the requirements of their work.

▧ Keeping higher management and group employees informed.

▧ Conveying to and interpreting for higher management the feelings and views of employees.

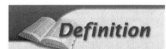

Definition

Supervision—the act of overseeing; inspection; superintendence; oversight. It is the authoritative control to watch over an activity or task being carried out by somebody and ensure that it is performed correctly.

1.2.2 Functions

- **Planning**—preparing schemes or schedules for achieving targets set by either themselves or higher management.

- **Organising**—allocating tasks, and arranging and delegating work and resources to enable the realisations of a plan.

- **Controlling**—ensuring that the workers' performance in terms of cost, quality and quantity of output matches the plan, if necessary by correcting deviations.

- **Communication**—keeping all concerned adequately informed.

- **Problem solving and decision-making**—handling day-to-day difficulties and problems and deciding what needs to be done to ensure the effective performance of the supervised staff.

- **Motivating and maintaining discipline**—encouraging people to give their best within the rules which govern their employment.

Example 1 Quality of Service

Identify TEN personal skills required by a manager in the organisation of work.

1.3 Authority, Responsibility and Delegation

- Without authority, responsibility and delegation:
  - formal organisations could not exist; and
  - only the chief executive would have responsibility and authority, so nothing would get done.

- Management is the act of getting things done (accomplishing objectives) through the work of other people and it cannot succeed without authority, responsibility and delegation.

- Of necessity, the manager has to give some of the work to subordinates.

- Management cannot delegate completely the tasks and authority for planning, co-ordinating, controlling, organising and monitoring; to do so would be to abdicate the management role.

1.3.1 Authority

- **Authority** directly relates to someone's position in an organisation, as an individual or as part of a team. Authority will usually be conferred by a higher authority or, as in the case of many governments, by the people.

- Authority should be sufficient to permit discharges of duties for which the individual is accountable.

- Classifications include:
  - Organisational—arising from the office/position held by an individual.
  - Personal—arising from a person's intelligence, experience or moral worth.
  - Charismatic—charm, leadership, personal qualities.
  - Traditional—elders, parental, armed forces.
  - Legal/rational—law, courts, police or common sense.

Definition

Authority—the right to do something or have something done. It is the right to give orders and the power to exact obedience.

—*Fayol*

1.3.2 Responsibility

▓ Being responsible implies accountability to those who give authority. **Responsibility** and the authority to carry out a task can be delegated. Responsibility (and accountability) for completing a task cannot be delegated.

▓ Directors have the owners' authority to run the organisation, but retain responsibility (accountability) for running an organisation on the owners' behalf.

▓ The directors delegate tasks to managers and grant authority to carry out those tasks. If the managers get it wrong, the directors are still ultimately responsible.

▓ Similarly, managers grant authority and delegate the responsibility to carry out any tasks assigned. However, they do not delegate responsibility to ensure the task is completed; that responsibility stays with the manager.

Responsibility— obligation to use delegated authority for the purpose delegated and to be accountable for performance.

Example 2	Responsibility and Authority

Give an example of the impact of giving responsibility without the necessary authority.

1.3.3 Power

▓ Categories of **power** include:

- **Legitimate or position**—associated with a particular job or position in a hierarchy. This is often equivalent to authority.
- **Legal**—title of ownership, court order.
- **Resource**—control over limited and valued resources, money, information.
- **Charisma**—sheer force of personality to influence and motivate other people.
- **Obligatory**—because a favour is owed.
- **Expert**—having knowledge and expertise required by others.
- **Physical**—physical force, coercion, punishment. May not be up front in organisations, but often is an undercurrent.
- **Negative**—the power to disrupt just by withholding cooperation.

Power—ability to exert a positive influence over objects, persons or situations.

1.3.4 Delegation

▓ **Delegation** implies:

- **authority** to delegate the work to others;
- an expected **initiative** by those to whom the work is delegated; and
- **confidence** that the subordinate can do the job successfully.

Delegation—achieving results by empowering (transferring authority) and motivating others (usually at lower levels in a hierarchy) to carry out tasks for which the delegator is ultimately accountable to a specified level of performance.

1.3.5 Advantages of Delegation

✔ **Gets the work done**—an essential aspect of the manager's work. The manager cannot do it all.

✔ **Use of specialists**—managers may need to delegate tasks for which they do not have specialised knowledge.

✔ **Flexibility**—being able to delegate as and when necessary ensures a quick response to situations (rather than having to refer to a higher authority or disrupting prepared schedules).

✔ **Relief of stress**—relieves work pressure on managers.

✔ **Job satisfaction**—delegating interesting jobs increases employees' enjoyment and employers can encourage better work.

✔ **Training**—"doing" is a very effective training method. Increasing delegation makes training a general day-to-day activity.

✔ **Management succession**—new managers get to know the routine and become accustomed to the advantages and disadvantages of advancement.

✔ **Performance evaluation**—subordinates can be tested under actual conditions before being permanently promoted.*

*Commentary

*Continuous testing becomes accepted as a matter of routine.

1.3.6 When to Delegate

▣ Generally, routine jobs and decision-making should be delegated if:

- the subordinate can do them as well as, as quickly as and as cost-effectively as the manager;
- the experience will contribute to the development of the subordinate; and
- it helps to complete the job.

▣ Supervisory functions (e.g. responsibilities to organise and provide for the development of staff, plan work, check work performance, etc) should not be delegated.

Example 3 Delegation

Identify SEVEN reasons why managers are reluctant to delegate.

---

2 Management Theory

2.1 Need for a Framework

▣ Management theory provides a framework for studying organisations in order to better forecast the behaviour of organisations. Future insight may result in:

- more influence over future events; and
- less disturbance.

▣ Management theory attempts to describe practice and behaviour in organisations and, thus, assists in understanding the principles underlying the management process. Some early theories continue to serve as the building blocks for modern models.

▦ There are many classifications and sub-classifications of management theory. The main ones are:

- Classical/scientific (the technical-rational school of thought)
- Human relations (part of the behaviour school of thought)
- Modern.

2.2 Classical Theory

▦ Incorporates the formal, bureaucratic and scientific approaches, which hold that by improving the organisation, structure efficiency and productivity are increased.

▦ There is a need to:

- understand the organisation's purpose and identify general objectives;
- clarify responsibility levels;
- define and grade duties, resulting in hierarchy and delegation;
- maintain specialisation; and
- coordinate, which requires exercise of authority, unity of action and discipline.

▦ Criticisms of the classical approach include:

- ✗ Emphasis is on technical requirements—"organisations without people".
- ✗ Does not take account of personality factors.
- ✗ People have very limited control over their work environment.
- ✗ Simplistic models of motivation.

2.3 F.W. Taylor

▦ Frederick Taylor (1856–1917) was a manager at the Bethlehem Steel Works in Pennsylvania in the United States at the beginning of the 20th century. He formed his theory of scientific management after making the following observations working at the steel mill:

- "Soldiering"—workers banding together to do as little work as possible. They felt that improving efficiency would eliminate jobs.
- "Rules of thumb"—management had no clear procedures for organising work so different managers had different requirements for performing the same job.
- "Perverse incentives"—workers were concerned that work performed at a faster pace would lead to a higher standard without any increased compensation for the productivity improvement.

▦ Taylor's concepts of scientific management increased productivity in the workplace by:

- standardising tools;
- reengineering work processes for maximum efficiency; and
- motivating workers to perform.

- He was considered the "father" of scientific management and developed a "machine theory model":

  - All work processes can be (scientifically) analysed into discrete, component tasks.

  - Each component can, through "time and motion" studies, be organised to produce the most efficient working method.

  - Requires efficient coordination and control methods (leaving little discretion for employee control over working methods).

  - Workers need to be scientifically selected and trained.

  - Workers must cooperate to ensure that tasks are carried out as prescribed.

  - Incentives motivate workers to obtain the highest possible output ("rational-economic needs" concept of motivation).

  - There is "one best way" to perform each task.*

*Technically, there may be an optimal method of performing a task, but should this method be insisted on?

- Merits of Taylor's work included:

  ✔ Higher wages through increased productivity.

  ✔ Workers are assigned tasks they are capable of doing.

  ✔ Physical strain reduced by eliminating "wasteful" movements.

- Criticisms of Taylor's work included:

  ✗ Rationalising production processes tends to de-skill the workers and leads to boredom.

  ✗ Theory was based on a theme of inefficiency.

  ✗ Workers who are not good at a particular task are assumed to be best at some other task.

  ✗ The workers themselves may often develop "informal" ways which are personally more efficient for them.

  ✗ There is no "one best way" suited to every worker.

2.4   Henri Fayol

- Henri Fayol (1841–1925) was a contemporary of Taylor's, writing about the same time in France. Fayol's focus was on administration rather than on production. Often described as "the father of modern management," his principles are still considered relevant by modern theorists.*

*Fayol spent his entire career in the mining industry.

- Activities in an industrial undertaking, according to Fayol, can be divided into six main groups:

  - Technical activities (e.g. production, manufacturing, adaptation)

  - Commercial activities (e.g. buying, selling, exchange)

  - Financial activities (e.g. obtaining money, using money)

  - Security activities (e.g. protection of property and persons)

  - Accounting activities (e.g. inventory, financial statements, cash flows, costing)

  - Managerial activities (e.g. forecasting, planning, organising, commanding, coordinating and controlling).

▦ Management activities were further expanded on in five categories:

1. **Planning and forecasting**—deciding what needs to be achieved and planning to do so. Involves determining objectives, strategies, policies, programmes and procedures.

2. **Organising**—providing the business with raw materials, equipment, capital and manpower required for its functioning.

3. **Commanding**—motivating and leading. Giving instructions to subordinates to carry out tasks, leading by example, communicating clearly and basing judgements on regular audits. A leader's thorough knowledge of personnel creates unity, energy, initiative and loyalty and eliminates incompetence.

4. **Coordinating**—harmonising and balancing all the functions and activities of the business. Fayol recommended weekly conferences for department heads to solve problems of common interest.

5. **Controlling**—identifying weaknesses and errors by setting targets, receiving feedback and ensuring targets are achieved by conforming activities with plans, policies and instructions.

▦ The mechanistic aspects of management described by his work are still a popular basis for analysing management.

▦ The main criticism of this approach is its generality. It disregards:

✗ the level of management (e.g. strategic, tactical or operational);

✗ their specialism (e.g. production, IT, personnel);

✗ the type of organisation (e.g. public or private);

✗ the environment in which it operates (e.g. regulated or nationalised industries); and

✗ what managers actually do (e.g. when they plan).

2.5 Human Relations Theory

▦ This was developed in reaction to the failure of the classical perspective to:

● recognise that people are human, not machines;

● consider that people work in groups; and

● realise that businesses react with their external environment.

▦ Sole concentration on the scientific and technical aspects of management had led to managers failing to realise that being considered a small cog in a big machine was demoralising for workers.

▦ Increased productivity was therefore sought through meeting the psychological and social needs of workers (i.e. humanising the work organisation) rather than just through pay.

▦ A main theorist in this area is Elton Mayo.

2.6 Elton Mayo

- Elton Mayo (1880–1949) was a researcher from the Harvard Business School. His findings from studies conducted at the Western Electric Company led management theory in a new direction.

- Mayo conducted a variety of experiments on improving productivity in the Western Electric Hawthorne factory in Illinois.

2.6.1 Phase 1: Lighting Experiments

- The first phase of his study was inconclusive. Mayo attempted to find a relationship between the intensity of light in the workplace and productivity. However, this led him to further experiments from which he formed his ideas.

2.6.2 Phase 2: Relay Experiments

- Hawthorne management selected several workers (who assembled telephone relay switches) and asked them to select more workers to form the experimental groups. These groups were taken into a different room in the facility where a series of changes to the work environment were made and output measured. Additionally, facilitators were on hand to receive feedback and answer questions from the workers.

  - 5-minute breaks were given—output increased.
  - 10-minute breaks were given—output increased further.
  - Free hot lunch was given—output increased further.
  - The work day was shortened by half an hour—output increased further.

- Finally, all the benefits were removed and the workers returned to their previous 48-hour work week. Strangely, output reached its highest level.

2.6.3 Mayo's Conclusions

- Social structures among workers have more influence over output than management.

- The workers formed a team and control came from within the team.

- A manager's focus on job satisfaction rather than job efficiency can increase output.

- Replacing the "bossy" supervisor with a friendly facilitator (who listened to and engaged the workers in two-way communication) increased motivation.

- Further research established the basis for the human relations school of management:

  - Employee behaviour depends primarily on the social and organisational circumstances of work.
  - Leadership style, group cohesion and job satisfaction are major determinants of the outputs of the working group.
  - Employees work better if they are given a range of tasks to complete.
  - Informal standards set internally by a working group influence employee attitudes and perspectives more than formal standards set by management.

2.6.4 Criticisms of Mayo's Experiments

✗ The experiments were poorly documented.

✗ People tend to perform better when acting as the subject of any experiment (this was later dubbed "the Hawthorne Effect").

✗ The results could not be scientifically reproduced.

2.7 Modern Theories

▨ An organisation does not exist in a vacuum. It interacts with its environment, being open and dynamic to an ever and rapidly changing environment.

▨ Modern theories take the basis of older theories (e.g. classic and human relations) and update them into the current business environment—risk management, multicultural environment, corporate social responsibility, sustainability, rapid change, information and knowledge management.

▨ Because of the diverse range of cultures with which modern organisations operate, or which operate within one organisation, modern management must recognise that there is "no one best approach" and that management depends on a contingency approach with many varying factors. What works best one day may not be best the next day.*

> ***Commentary**
>
> *Two modern theorists in the contingency approach area are Peter Drucker and Henry Mintzberg.

2.8 Peter Drucker

▨ Peter Drucker (1909–2005) is considered by many to be the "father of modern management" (in relative terms).

▨ He considered that:

- the manager of a business had one basic function— economic performance;
- the role of the manager in the context of the organisation and the employees becoming as one, bound by information and knowledge;
- the impact of information technology would result in flatter management structures;
- workers would tend to become self-managing, especially professional classes; and
- decision-making would be decentralised as knowledge and information becomes available throughout an organisation.

▨ Drucker's five main categories of management include:

1. **Objective setting**—deciding what the objectives of a business should be, then quantifying achievement targets for each objective and communicating priorities to people in the organisation.

2. **Organising work**—dividing tasks and responsibilities into jobs, integrating them into a formal structure and selecting people for the positions.

3. **Motivating employees**—finding out what motivates employees, providing incentives and informing them what is required of them, showing how they fit in to the overall picture.

4. **Job measurement**—establishing objectives (for the firm and the individual worker), comparing and analysing actual performance with those objectives and communicating results with explanations to employees (and superiors).

5. Developing people—including managers. Drucker once said that managers bring out what is best in employees, or they stifle them. They strengthen employee integrity or corrupt them.*

2.9 Henry Mintzberg

■ Henry Mintzberg (1939–) challenges the basic assumption that managers are above the routine demands of day-to-day work. He observed that the behaviour of managers often contrasts with the traditional view of managerial behaviour:

* **High-volume, high-speed work**—little free time often means that they are not always able to be reflective, systematic planners.

* **Variety, fragmentation and brevity**—managers lack time to become deeply involved in a wide range of issues and will rapidly shift their attention from one issue to another. Work is often disjointed and discontinuous.

* **Routine humdrum**—managers do have routine chores to perform and do not leave it all to supervisors or juniors.

* **Issue preference (current, ad hoc, specific)**—managers prefer current, up-to-date (not necessarily certain) information and pay less attention to historical, routine information.

* Complex web of **interactions and contacts** (e.g. clients, associates, peers, secretaries, government, press and other external officials)—management cannot be reduced to a science or an art. Managerial processes cannot be scientifically analysed or codified by a body of theory.

* Strong preference for **verbal media**—greater flexibility, less effort, faster response.

* **Control of the agenda**—successful managers control their personal agendas and have their own information channels and networks.

■ He suggests that in their daily work, managers fulfil three types of managerial roles:

1. Interpersonal

2. Informational

3. Decisional

2.9.1 Interpersonal

■ Figurehead—represents the organisation to others, performs symbolic duties both internal and external.

■ Leader—innovates, motivates, sets examples, provides time and help, hires, fires, trains, builds teams, facilitates team working and fosters employee commitment and loyalty.

■ Liaison—develops a network of contacts external to the vertical chain of command through which information and favours may be exchanged for mutual benefit.

2.9.2 Informational

■ Monitor—receive, review and grade internal and external sources of information, environmental monitoring.

■ Disseminator—ensures that appropriate information is given to the right people at the right time.

■ Spokesperson—presents the organisation's view to the outside world, handles PR, lobbying activities.

*Commentary

*Like Fayol, Drucker believed that employees are not just resources to control but that management also involves interpersonal skills. Drucker, however, integrated the modern theories of motivation and communication.

*Commentary

*This "leading" role relates to the manager's formal position and associated authority.

*Commentary

*Informational managers have contact with all staff and extensive external networks.

2.9.3 Decisional

- Entrepreneur—innovates, introduces new concepts and change management.

- Disturbance handler—responds to the unexpected, makes decisions based on the effect of the disturbance.

- Resource allocator—deals with limited resources to enable objectives to be achieved. He ensures that scarce resources are appropriately used.

- Negotiator—deals with internal and external events and mediates on conflicts between groups in an organisation.

> ***Commentary**
>
> *Decision-making is vital to the stability, growth and future of organisations. Managers must understand how decisions affect all stakeholders and competitors.

3   Leadership Theory

3.1   Approaches

- Definitions of leadership vary. Key elements appear to be persuasion, securing a willing commitment to shared goals, creating direction, energising others and orientation to change.

- "Management" and "leadership" often are confused and used interchangeably.

- Management, while requiring a complex skill set, involves more mechanistic skills which can be taught. The jury is out on whether the motivational and communications skills required for effective leadership are native to particular individuals or also can be taught.

Example 4   Channel Tunnel

Identify the manager and leader from the following scenario: A Eurotrain travelling between Paris and London comes to a halt because of a power failure in the middle of the Channel Tunnel. The backup power systems also have failed. Passengers are beginning to panic.

Example 5   Leadership Skills

Describe the skills required of a leader.

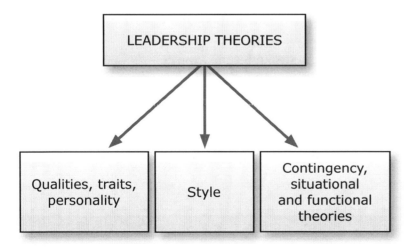

LEADERSHIP THEORIES

- Qualities, traits, personality
- Style
- Contingency, situational and functional theories

3.2 Quality, Trait and Personality Theories

▨ This approach focuses largely on the personal qualities desirable in leaders:

- **Intelligence**—should be above average.
- **Initiative**—independence and inventiveness, the capacity to perceive a need for action and the urge to do it.
- **Self-assurance**—implies self-confidence.
- The **"helicopter factor"**—ability to rise above the particulars of a situation and analyse it objectively in relation to the surrounding context; seeing the "big picture".

▨ Other essential qualities might include enthusiasm, sociability, integrity, courage, imagination, determination, aggression, appearance, interpersonal skills and energy. These can be sub-grouped as being physical traits, personality traits and social traits.

▨ This approach poses questions such as:

- How do you identify and locate such qualities?
- Is the possession of such qualities a necessary and sufficient condition for effective leadership?
- Can you train for courage or determination?

▨ These theories have largely been discredited and rejected by more modern theorists. They argue that:

- The assumption that certain qualities are necessary for leaders has never been substantiated.
- The list of traits is too broad, varied and often contradictory.
- Leadership is too complex to be boiled down to just a list of qualities—the leadership situation must be taken into account.
- People with these traits do not necessarily become good leaders.

3.3 Functional and Style Theories

▨ As the early researchers ran out of steam in their search for traits, they turned to what leaders did—how they behaved (especially towards followers). They moved from leaders to leadership—and this became the dominant way of approaching leadership in organisations in the 1950s and early 1960s. Different patterns of behaviour were grouped together and labelled as styles.

▨ Based on the view that leadership is an interpersonal process. These theories emphasise the functions and style of leaders.

▨ A wide variety of management styles exist and the different theories attempt to classify styles and find the most effective style for a manager/leader to adopt.

▓ Theories include the Ashridge Management College Model and Blake and Mouton's Managerial Grid (see later in this session). As with all functional and style theories, they tend to centre on four main styles:

1. **Concern for task**—leaders emphasise the achievement of concrete objectives. They look for high levels of productivity and ways to organise people and activities to meet those objectives.

2. **Concern for people**—leaders perceive their followers as people (e.g. needs, interests, problems and needs for development). Employees are not the classic units of production, costs or a means to an end.

3. **Directive leadership**—characterised by leaders making decisions and expecting subordinates to follow their instructions.

4. **Participative leadership**—leaders share decision-making (to various degrees) with their subordinates.

▓ As with trait theories, researchers began to question whether the same style would be appropriate in all situations. Researchers began to realise that who leaders are working with and the environment in which they operate were as important as leadership style.

▓ Researchers developed the contingency approach to leadership after concluding that style theories do not consider all variables which contribute to effective leadership.

3.4   Contingency Theories

▓ Contingency theories consider contexts in which leadership is exercised and the need for leadership changes from situation to situation (i.e. there is no right way to lead which will fit all situations).

▓ Many of the theories still contain elements of style theory, but on the basis that the style needed would change with the situation. Particular contexts thus would demand particular forms of leadership.

▓ Contingency theorists include Fiedler, Adair, Bennis and Heifetz.

▓ Three factors began to emerge from the various contingency theories:

● The relationship between the leaders and followers. Liked and respected leaders are more likely to have the support of others.

● The structure of the task. If the goals, methods and standards of performance for a task are clear, then leaders will be better able to exert influence.

● Position power. If an organisation or group confers powers on the leader for the purpose of getting the job done, then this may well increase the influence of the leader.

4 Models and Theorists

4.1 Blake and Mouton

▧ Basically a style theory, but later developed by W. J. Reddin (1987) into a contingency theory model.

▧ Robert Blake and Jane Mouton (Ohio State Leadership Studies) observed that leaders typically have concern for both production (or the task) and people.

▧ These concerns were recognised to be independent (i.e. a leader could be stronger on one and weaker on the other, stronger on both, weaker on both, etc).

▧ They devised a series of questions, the answers to which enabled them to plot these two basic leadership dimensions on a Managerial Grid.

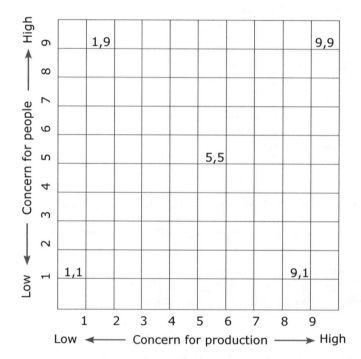

▧ A person who scores 7 on "concern for production" (the x axis) and 5 on "concern for people" (the y axis) is known as a 7,5 leader. The extreme cases shown on the grid are:

● **1,1—Management Impoverished***—the manager exerts the minimum possible effort required to get the job done. The manager is basically lazy, showing little interest in staff or the task.

● **1,9—Country Club Management**—the manager is thoughtful and attentive to people's needs but pays very little attention to achieving results. Although this leads to a convivial atmosphere, little "work" is actually achieved.

● **9,1—Task (Authority-Compliance) Management***—the manager concentrates on production and arranges work to minimise human interference. Workers' needs are virtually ignored.

*This "evade and elude" style is also called "Indifferent".

*This "produce or perish" management style is dictatorial.

- **5,5—Middle of the Road Management**—adequate performance and attempts to provide satisfactory morale within the team. The manager balances the task in hand with motivating employees to achieve these tasks. Sometimes referred to as a "dampened pendulum" approach.

- **9,9—Team Management**—the manager integrates the two areas to foster working together and high production to produce true team leadership. Such managers lead committed employees who identify themselves with the organisational aims.

4.2   Ashridge Management College

- This model presents a continuum of manager/non-manager behaviour, the two extremes being:

  1. Boss-centred (i.e. manager power and influence)

  2. Subordinate-centred (i.e. non-manager power and influence)

- Four main styles of management were identified between two extremes of directive behaviour versus supportive behaviour:

  1. Tells (autocratic)

  2. Sells (persuasive)

  3. Consults (consultative)

  4. Joins (democratic)

- Depending on the task in hand, the decisions to be made, the understanding of the employees by the manager, the manager will change styles to achieve the objective.*

*Commentary

*Note that some modern theorists have taken the basics of the Ashridge model and developed them into a contingency theory continuum.

4.2.1 Tells

- Manager announces a decision which employees accept.

- Advantages include:

  ✔ Quick decisions can be made when required.

  ✔ Most efficient type of leadership for highly routine or programmed work.

- Disadvantages include:

  ✘ Communications are downwards from manager to employees.

  ✘ Feedback not allowed or encouraged. May be possible that instructions will be misunderstood.

  ✘ Compliance from employees is only required. Initiative and commitment is not encouraged.

  ✘ Some employees may refuse point-blank to accept the decision.

4.2.2 Sells

- Manager makes decisions, but believes that subordinates have to be motivated to accept them and correctly carry out their instructions.

- As employees are aware of the decisions and the reasons why, they may be more committed and possibly be able to deal with unforeseen circumstances as the manager will have explained his intentions.

- However, communications are still one-way and some employees still may refuse to accept the decisions. Initiative and commitment from employees may be lacking.

4.2.3 Consults

■ The manager confers and listens to subordinates' proposals, then makes a decision taking subordinates' views into account.

■ In this approach, subordinates are involved in the decision-making process and may feel motivated through having contributed to the final decision. In addition, an agreed consensus, if reached, encourages the subordinates to fully accept the decision.

■ Employees also will be able to input their specific expertise.

■ Disadvantages are:

✗ it may take some time to consult, obtain views and reach a decision;

✗ unless a full consensus is agreed, some employees may feel that their views were ignored and thus become demotivated; and

✗ consultation by the manager does not always mean that they have not already made their mind up and are just going through the motions.

4.2.4 Joins

■ Manager and subordinates make the decision on the basis of joint consultation and consensus.

■ This process can produce a high level of motivation and commitment, plus the advantages noted above for the consultative position.

■ It is possible that taking this approach could undermine the manager's authority and create an involved decision-making process; a compromise may have to be reached to get a decision and move on.

4.3 Fred E. Fiedler

■ Fred E. Fiedler (1922–) is a leading advocate and researcher of contingency theories whose studies into the relationship between leadership style and the effectiveness of the work group identified two styles of leader:

1. Psychologically distant managers (PDMs)

2. Psychologically close managers (PCMs)

4.3.1 PDMs

■ Formalise roles and relationships in the team and maintain distance from their subordinates.

■ Are usually withdrawn and reserved in their interpersonal relationships, despite having good interpersonal skills.

■ Prefer formal communication and consultation methods rather than seeking informal opinion (i.e. use the formal system rather than a mix of formal and informal).

■ Judge subordinates on the basis of performance.

■ Are primarily task-orientated.

4.3.2 PCMs

■ Do not seek to formalise roles and relationships with superiors and subordinates as they prefer informal contacts to, for example, regular formal staff meetings.

- They are more concerned with maintaining good human relationships at work than ensuring that tasks are carried out efficiently.
- Are people centred.
- Fiedler concluded that a structured (or PDM) style works best when the situation is either very favourable or very unfavourable. A favourable situation occurs in situations in which:
  - the leader is liked, trusted and powerful; and
  - employee tasks are clearly defined and unambiguous.
- On the other hand, a supportive (or PCM) style works best when the situation is moderately favourable/unfavourable or neutral to the leader. Thus he intimates that the leader can be either people-oriented or task-oriented but not both.
- He further suggested that group performance would be contingent on the appropriate matching of leadership styles and the degree of favourableness of the group situation for the leader.*

Commentary

*Fiedler found that leaders of the most effective work groups actually tend to be PDMs.

4.3.3 Leadership Effectiveness

- Fiedler further developed his contingency theory in *A Theory of Leadership Effectiveness* (1967), in which he argued that the effectiveness of the work group depended on the situation. The leadership situation is made up of three key variables:

  1. **Leader/member relations**—based on the leader's view of the favourableness or unfavourableness of the work group.

  2. **Task structure**—the extent to which the leader is able to define and control the group's activities.

  3. **Leader position power**—the degree of formal authority/responsibility allocated to the position.

4.4 John Adair, Action-Centred Leadership

- The Action-Centred Leadership Model was devised by John Adair (1934–), a renowned leadership theorist. This model uses three overlapping circles to depict the interdependence of the separate functions of team, task and individual.

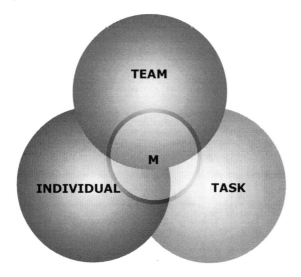

(Action-centered leadership: Adair)

■ Ideally, the manager balances getting the task completed, keeping the team working as one and ensuring that individual members of the team work to their best abilities.

■ But this is contingent on the situation. Should the situation require, the manager may place greater emphasis on elements of one area or apply appropriate weights to elements in all three.

■ Use the analogy of a football team—if two players dislike each other, the whole team suffers and the task (i.e. winning) may not be completed.

■ Team functions include:
- establish and maintain standards;
- build team spirit, encourage, motivate, lead;
- develop team dynamics and work methods to ensure cohesiveness;
- establish channels of communication (intra- and extra-team);
- train the team;
- monitor team performance;
- maintain order and discipline;
- plan for team member succession (e.g. changes in a company board);
- change the membership to reflect environmental changes; and
- ensure continuity of function.

■ Task functions include:
- define the task and set objectives;
- establish a plan to achieve objectives;
- assign responsibilities;
- allocate resources;
- establish control procedures with feedback;
- monitor progress and performance against the plan; and
- reassess the plan, responsibilities, resources, etc to achieve objectives (this could easily mean new objectives are established).

■ Individual functions include:
- recognise and help with personal problems;
- develop and train the individual;
- identify the individual's strengths and weaknesses;
- maximise strengths and minimise weaknesses;
- praise (and reward) good performance; and
- balance the requirements of the individual versus the team

4.5 Warren Bennis

■ Transformational leadership, related to Warren Bennis (1925–2014), motivates through identification with the leader's vision—pulling rather than pushing others on.

■ According to Bennis:
- Managers do things right, meaning transactional leadership (e.g. administer, maintain, focus on systems and controls and the short-term view, ask how and when and keep an eye on the bottom line). • Leaders "do the right things", meaning transformational leadership (e.g. innovate, develop, focus on people, inspire, create trust, ask what and why and have a long-term view and an eye for the horizon).

- Bennis identified four common competences of leadership:
  1. Focus—attention to a compelling cause or vision.
  2. Meaning—the ability to communicate.
  3. Trust—through consistency and honesty.
  4. Self—awareness of personal strengths and weaknesses.
- He also considered that leaders should:
  - constantly remind people why their work is important;
  - create an atmosphere of trust;
  - encourage curiosity and risk in the organisational culture; and
  - foster an atmosphere of hope and believing.
- Typical transformational leadership behaviours, as identified by Bass from the work by Bennis, are:
  - **Idealised influence (attributed and behaviour)**—leaders have high standards of moral and ethical conduct, are held in high personal regard and engender loyalty from followers.
  - **Inspirational motivation**—leaders have a strong vision for the future based on values and ideals. They stimulate enthusiasm, build confidence and inspire followers using symbolic actions and persuasive language. Idealised influence and inspirational motivation are highly correlated and are sometimes combined to form a measure of charisma.
  - **Intellectual stimulation**—leaders challenge organisational norms, encourage divergent thinking and encourage followers to develop innovative strategies.
  - **Individual consideration**—leaders recognise the unique growth and developmental needs of followers as well as coaching followers and consulting with them.

4.6 Ronald A. Heifetz

- One of the major challenges faced by leaders is the implementation of change. Both Heifetz (1961–) and Kotter considered the role of leadership in change management.
- Heifetz (1994) researched the role of leaders in implementing change in society, in which authority is strictly limited and goals are unclear. He considered the differences between leadership and authority and between technical answers and adaptive work.
- Leadership is what individuals do in mobilising other people in organisations or communities. Heifetz referred to this as adaptive work as opposed to technical work.
  - **Adaptive work**—required when the problem cannot be solved with existing skills and knowledge and requires people to make a shift in their values, expectations, attitudes or habits of behaviour. This is often required to ensure organisational survival.
  - **Technical work**—the application of current knowledge, skills and tools to resolve a situation.
- Heifetz found that people believe authority figures should maintain equilibrium and provide direction. They expect those in authority to come up with answers which result in little change and to shield them from (painful) reality, disorder and disorientation.

■ People expect those in authority to control conflict. Therefore, authority figures may hesitate to see conflict as a source of creativity and a necessary component of adaptive change.

■ True leaders recognise the need for change, rather than decide to do nothing and just maintain the norms.

■ He identified two resources available to the leader when change was necessary:

1. The capacity to manage the "holding environment"—the conflicts and stresses of adaptive work.

2. The use of attention—leadership could be defined as getting people to pay attention to tough problems which they would wish to avoid facing. The leader with authority already has people paying attention to what they do and say; therefore, the leader's attention can be more easily directed towards key challenges.

■ Change leadership requires a learning strategy. A leader has to engage people in facing the challenge, adjusting their values, changing perspectives and developing new behaviour.

■ Heifetz formulated four principles for bringing about adaptive change:

1. Recognising that change requires an adaptive approach and understanding the values that need to be shifted and the issues to be resolved to make the change possible.

2. Understanding that adaptive change will cause unhappiness in the people being led and that adaptive change requires the right level of stress to be applied— too little stress and people do not appreciate the need for change; too much stress and there will be no "buy-in".

3. Keep focused on the real issue of succeeding with the change. Do not spend too much time on stress-reducing distractions.

4. Ensure that the people who need to make the change take responsibility and face the reality of doing the work of change for themselves. Leaders provide the direction, posing well-structured questions, rather than offering definite answers.

4.7 John Kotter

■ Many consider Harvard Business School Professor John Kotter (1947–) to be the world's foremost authority on leadership and change.

■ He developed an eight-step change model:

1. **Create urgency**—inspire people to move, make objectives real and relevant.

2. **Form a powerful coalition**—get the right people (identify the leaders throughout the organisation) in place with the right emotional commitment and the right mix of skills and levels.

3. **Get the vision right**—get the team to establish a simple vision and strategy; then focus on emotional and creative aspects necessary to drive service and efficiency.

4. **Communicate the vision for buy-in**—involve as many people as possible, communicate the essentials simply, and appeal and respond to people's needs. De-clutter communications and make technology work for rather than against you.

5. **Remove obstacles**—empower action, enable constructive feedback and support from leaders, and reward and recognise progress and achievements.

6. **Create short-term wins**—set achievable goals (e.g. "bite-size" chunks) and a manageable number of initiatives. Finish current stages before starting new ones.

7. **Build-up on the change**—do not let up; foster and encourage determination and persistence. Encourage ongoing progress reporting; highlight achieved and future milestones.

8. **Make change stick**—reinforce the value of successful change via recruitment, promotion and new change leaders. Embed change into the culture at all levels.

Where the leader meets resistance, Kotter suggests five actions to bring the resistors on board:

1. **Participation and involvement**—aims to involve employees, usually by allowing some input to decision-making, so they are more likely to support necessary changes to be made. "Ownership" will encourage effective commitment to the change.

2. **Education and communication**—aims to keep employees informed, usually through presentations and discussion groups, about the reasons for the required change. This approach relies on the belief that communication about the benefits of change to employees will result in acceptance of the needed changes.

3. **Facilitation and support**—basically through training and counselling. Many employees may need help to overcome their fears and anxieties about change.

4. **Manipulation and co-optation**—the information disseminated emphasises the benefits of the change. Involves covert attempts to sidestep potential resistance.

5. **Negotiation and agreement**—enables those parties with opposing interests to bargain. Usually leads to compromise, then agreement.

Summary

- Leaders have followers; managers have subordinates.

- A modern organisational culture requires individuals who can lead a team as well as manage them towards achieving the organisation's goals.

  - Leaders communicate, motivate and influence.

  - Managers forecast, plan and organise resources to achieve goals.

  - Supervisors manage tasks delegated to them by managers, delegate them further to employees, and inspect performance.

- Authority is the right to give orders and exact obedience. It may be granted based on the organisational role of the individual or from intelligence, charisma, law or tradition.

- Responsibility is the obligation to use delegated authority for the delegated purpose and to be accountable for performance. Responsibility, unlike authority, cannot be delegated.

- Delegation implies authority to delegate the work, expectation of initiative by those delegated the work and confidence in the subordinate to successfully complete the job.

- Management theory attempts to describe practice and behaviour in organisations to assist in understanding the principles underlying the management process. The main classifications are:

  - Classical/scientific—Emphasis on technical aspects of managing tasks to the exclusion of human resources. (Taylor, Fayol, etc)

  - Human relations—Increases productivity by meeting workers' psychological and social needs. (Mayo)

  - Modern (contingency)—Various aspects of both approaches may be appropriate depending on the situation. (Drucker, Mintzberg)

- Leadership theories typically will be categorised as:

  - Traits—qualities such as intelligence, initiative, self-assurance and an ability to see the big picture.

  - Style—the ability to focus on tasks versus the ability to deal with people.

  - Contingency—the application of the appropriate style and traits for a given situation.

- Ashridge Management College presents a continuum of manager/non-manager behaviour summarised as autocratic, persuasive, consultative and democratic.

- Blake and Mouton developed a theory which divides management styles based on the degree of concern for production and concern for people.

Session 16 Quiz

Estimated time: 15 minutes

1. Define "leadership". (1.1.1)

2. Define "authority". (1.3.1)

3. Identify who evolved the "machine theory" model of management. (2.3)

4. Describe a "style theory" of leadership. (3.3)

5. Describe who would be "management impoverished". (4.1)

6. Explain the Ashridge Management College continuum. (4.2)

7. List the EIGHT steps in Kotter's change management model. (4.7)

Study Question Bank

Estimated time: 45 minutes

Priority		Estimated Time	Completed
MCQ16	Leadership, Management and Supervision	45 minutes	

EXAMPLE SOLUTIONS

Solution 1—Quality of Service

- Planning, scheduling and resource allocating
- Time management
- Problem solving
- Decision-making
- Delegating
- Negotiating
- Dispute handling and arbitration
- Briefing
- Supervising
- Reviewing
- Appraising
- Motivating
- Training and coaching
- Communicating (including written and verbal reports, presentations, etc)
- Listening
- Interviewing

Solution 2—Responsibility and Authority

- If responsibility to carry out a task is given, but not the appropriate authority, then the task will not be completed.

- The sales director delegates the task of coordinating sales budgets from all of the organisations' divisions while he spends a week in hospital. However, when his subordinate contacts each division, they refuse to give the necessary information as they only have the authority to give it to the sales director. The director had not delegated the authority, although he had made his subordinate responsible for getting the information in his absence.

Solution 3—Delegation

- "No one can do it better than me."
- What is the need to? They are OK.
- They enjoy doing the work themselves.
- They "have no time to think".
- It takes too much valuable time.
- The subordinate may do a better job than me.
- They believe it is too risky.

Solution 4—Channel Tunnel

- **Management:**

  As the train and passengers are in danger, the duty controller will be calling the emergency services, halting any train about to enter the tunnel, informing his bosses, and attempting to find out what caused the power failure (i.e. following the emergency procedures).

- **Leadership:**

  A passenger, realising that people are beginning to panic, talks calmly to them, reassuring them, informing them of the safety features of the tunnel and what to do in such an emergency. The passenger will be establishing facts (any medical personnel, old people, young children, people afraid of the dark), finding means of lighting, opening the train doors and organising the passengers so they may be led to the nearest emergency exit.

Solution 5—Leadership Skills

- Taking ultimate responsibility, "the buck stops here".

- Making sound and timely decisions.

- Knowing "the job".

- Knowing their own strengths and weaknesses.

- Team building and development.

- Setting achievable goals.

- Being visible and available to the team.

- Setting an example for others to follow.

- Keeping everybody informed.

Recruitment and Selection

FOCUS

This session covers the following content from the *ACCA Study Guide.*

D. Leading and Managing Individuals and Teams

2. Recruitment and selection of employees

a) Explain the importance of effective recruitment and selection to the organisation. ☐

b) Describe the recruitment and selection processes and explain the stages in this process. ☐

c) Describe the roles of those involved in the recruitment and selection processes. ☐

d) Describe the methods through which organisations seek to meet their recruitment needs. ☐

e) Explain the advantages and disadvantages of different recruitment and selection methods. ☐

Session 17 Guidance

- **Note** that recruitment is often considered being about getting sufficient numbers of appropriate candidates "through the door", with selection being the process of selecting the best of them. Relate this session to your own practical experience as much as possible.
- **Understand** the role of the key players (s.1).
- **Know** the advantages and disadvantages of internal versus external recruiting (s.2). Section 2 also looks in more detail at effective recruitment and provides you with an overview on defining the vacancy, defining the job, defining the person and attracting the right person by way of different media or internally.

(continued on next page)

VISUAL OVERVIEW

Objective: To describe the recruitment and selection process.

```
┌─────────────────────────────────────┐
│   RECRUITMENT AND SELECTION          │
│            PROCESS                   │
│  • Importance                        │
│  • Key Stages                        │
│  • Roles and Responsibilities        │
│  • Ineffective Recruitment           │
│  • Success Criteria                  │
│  • Decision-Making                   │
└─────────────────────────────────────┘
```

```
┌──────────────────────────┐      ┌──────────────────────────┐
│  EFFECTIVE RECRUITMENT   │      │       SELECTION          │
│  • Define the Vacancy    │      │  • Selection Process     │
│  • Job Analysis          │      │  • Choosing a Candidate  │
│  • Job Description        │      │                          │
│  • Person Specification   │      │                          │
│  • Appropriate Applicants │      │                          │
└──────────────────────────┘      └──────────────────────────┘
```

```
┌──────────────────────────┐      ┌──────────────────────────┐
│    SELECTION METHODS     │      │   SELECTION INTERVIEWS   │
│  • Pre-selection         │      │  • Importance            │
│  • Applicant References  │      │  • Purpose               │
│  • Selection Methods     │      │  • Conducting an Interview│
│  • Application Forms/CVs  │      │  • Key Skills Required    │
│  • Psychometric Tests     │      │  • Ineffective Interviewing│
│  • Assessment Centres     │      │                          │
│  • Job Simulation         │      │                          │
└──────────────────────────┘      └──────────────────────────┘
```

Session 17 Guidance

■ **Recognise** the differences and approach to job analysis, job description and person specification (s.2).

■ **Understand** details of the selection process, including selection methods (s.3, s.4) and interviews (s.5). Any part of this can be examined, so it needs to be fully understood.

1   Recruitment and Selection Process

1.1   Importance

> **Definition**
>
> **Recruitment**—searching for, raising interest of and obtaining interviews with potential job candidates in sufficient numbers and quality to satisfy the job requirements.
>
> **Selection**—predicting which candidates will make the most appropriate contribution to the organisation now and in the future.

Recruitment and **selection** is basically about finding the right person in terms of skill, disposition and motivation for the job.

1.1.1.   Costs of Wrong Decisions ("Recruitment Errors")

- "Productivity shortfall" (difference between the output of an effective and an ineffective employee).
- Costs associated with high labour turnover:
  - Direct costs (e.g. advertising, search fees, interviews).
  - Overtime during staff shortages.
  - Start-up time and costs (e.g. induction, training, supervision).
  - "Downtime" arising from disruption.
  - Relocation expenses.
  - Joining bonus/leaving payoff.
  - Unquantifiable costs (e.g. of low morale).
- Lowering morale (e.g. if new staff members do not "get on" with other staff).
- Loss of revenue and customer goodwill (e.g. if new staff members upset customers).
- Loss of strategic direction and market credibility (e.g. wrong CEO appointed).
- Cost of undoing any damage done and getting it right.

1.1.2   Benefits of the Right Decision

- Sustained teamwork and cooperation.
- Stable workforce/boardroom.
- Seamless progression.
- Better morale and increased work performance.
- Greater customer satisfaction.
- Strategic goals achieved and increased market credibility.

1.2 Key Stages

- Although many organisations have formal recruitment and selection policies and procedures, others regard this area as a non-core activity dealt with on an ad hoc basis (as and when the need arises).
- However, in broad terms, recruitment and selection concerns:
  - defining the job vacancy/person required (including "job analysis");
  - attracting appropriate applicants;
  - assessing candidates;
  - choosing a candidate; and
  - evaluating the success, or otherwise, of the process.
- Other stages (e.g. induction) may also be considered as part of the recruitment and selection process.

1.3 Roles and Responsibilities*

1.3.1 Senior Managers

- Plan human resources to meet the organisation's long- and short-term strategic objectives.
- Draw up job descriptions and candidate profiles for senior positions.
- Conduct final interviews and appoint candidates for senior positions.

*Commentary

*Great care must be taken by those responsible for recruitment and selection that the process is free of any discrimination (see *Session 18*).

1.3.2 Personnel Officers

- Draw up a recruitment and selection policy for the organisation.
- Provide recruitment and selection advice to senior/line managers.
- Help senior/line managers carry out job analysis and draw up job descriptions and person specifications.
- Place advertisements (e.g. with agencies and on the corporate website).
- Design documentation (e.g. job analysis forms, job application forms).
- Screen job applications and select candidates for interviews.
- Conduct first interviews and select candidates for the next stage.
- Keep personnel records and appropriate employee statistics (e.g. retention rates, staff turnover, absenteeism).
- Monitor adherence to recruitment and selection policies.
- Monitor adherence to legislative requirements (e.g. relating to equal opportunities).

1.3.3 Line Managers/Supervisors

- Carry out job analysis and draw up job descriptions.
- Identify and/or authorise vacancies.
- Conduct interviews.
- Appoint candidates (for less-than-senior positions).

1.3.4 External Agents/Recruitment Consultants

▪ Advise on job descriptions and/or person specifications.

▪ Supply details of suitable candidates already in their database.

▪ Design and run advertisements (in national, local, trade or specialist press or on the Internet).

▪ Screen applicants (e.g. through dedicated response call centres).

▪ Provide individual and group exercises and psychometric profiling.

▪ Administer and interpret psychometric profiling.

▪ Interview candidates and recommend a short list.

▪ Provide executive search and management selection services.

▪ Facilitate "rapid response"/"fast turnaround" advertising.

1.4 Ineffective Recruitment

▪ The importance of recruitment and selection has been described as "finding the right person (in terms of skill, disposition and motivation) for the job". Unless these criteria are achieved, the recruitment process may be ineffective.

▪ There are many reasons for ineffective recruitment. Some of these include:

✗ Poor human resource planning (e.g. an unnecessary position is created).

✗ Inadequate job analysis, leading to incorrect job description (e.g. does not mention 60% travel requirement).

✗ The person specification does not match the actual criteria required for the job (e.g. ability to program in a high-level language when an object-oriented language is required).

✗ Inappropriate methods used for job advertising (e.g. only advertising internally when external advertising may result in better-qualified candidates).

✗ Failure to obtain all necessary documentation (e.g. job application forms, CVs, references, certificates of competence and skill level).

✗ Poor shortlisting of candidates (e.g. person specification not used as a basis to shortlist candidates).

✗ Inadequate selection procedures (e.g. selection only based on a single interview when a practical demonstration of ability also is required).

✗ Poor interview technique (e.g. lack of preparation, no structure, inadequate evaluation, inappropriate interviewer).

✗ Failure to follow up from the interview (e.g. does not get back to preferred candidate quickly enough to prevent them from joining another company).

✗ Failure to meet the promises made in the interview or the terms and conditions of employment (e.g. new employee becomes demotivated and leaves).

✗ Failure to ensure a correct "culture fit" between the new employee and the organisation (e.g. new employee cannot adapt to the methods/people of the organisation and subsequently leaves).

1.5   Success Criteria

1.5.1   Evaluation

▦ The success, or otherwise, of the recruitment and selection process should be evaluated (both quantitatively and qualitatively) in terms of:

- ▪ effectiveness—in distinguishing suitable candidates;
- ▪ efficiency; and
- ▪ fairness—includes, but is not limited to, providing equal opportunities.

▦ At the individual level, the number of incidences of errors, accidents or complaints may identify weaknesses in the recruitment and selection process. Action can then be taken to rectify such weaknesses.

▦ Success criteria also can be used to forecast future recruitment needs, timing and budgets.

1.5.2   Effectiveness Measures*

▦ Retention rates (e.g. of the new student intake in September, 90% are still employed three months later).

▦ Stability index for all, or for groups of, employees (use with retention rate) =

$$\frac{\text{Number of employees with} > \text{one year's service}}{\text{Number employed one year ago}} \times 100\%$$

▦ Staff turnover (i.e. the rate at which employees *who have to be replaced* leave) =

$$\frac{\text{Leavers replaced}}{\text{Average no. of employees}} \times 100\%$$

▦ Promotion rates or periods.

▦ Levels of absenteeism.

1.5.3   Efficiency Measures

▦ Average cost per new appointment.

▦ Time to recruit (e.g. from placing advertisement to conducting interviews and filling the vacancy).

▦ Offer-acceptance rate.

*Commentary

*Where an organisation has more than one interviewer or recruitment process, the measures for effectiveness could also be used to assess interviewer and overall process effectiveness.

1.6 Decision-Making

- In its basic form, decision-making is the process of making informed choices.

- Throughout the recruitment and selection process, decisions are always being made. For example:
  - Is the vacancy necessary?
  - What criteria should be used to define the vacancy/person to fill it?
  - What method of attracting the right applicants should be used?
  - What criteria should be used for screening applicants?
  - Which applicants should be rejected/accepted?
  - Which selection methods are best for the situation?
  - What criteria are used to select the best candidate?

- Whenever a decision is to be made, the basic skills required are the ability to:
  - Recognise that a decision needs to be made.
  - Obtain an understanding of the situation.
  - Gather relevant information.
  - Identify and evaluate alternative courses of action.
  - Select the preferred option.
  - Communicate the decision and control the consequent actions.
  - Review the outcome of the decision made.

- The decision-maker must avoid:
  - Blinkered vision.
  - False justification and manipulation of the facts.
  - The "halo" effect (e.g. making a decision to please a boss or disagreeing with the views of a subordinate).

2   Effective Recruitment

2.1   Define the Vacancy

2.1.1   Authority

■ Authorisation is required to confirm that a vacancy exists and that the vacancy meets the needs of the company.

■ Alternatives should be considered (e.g. redistribution of workloads).

■ Before a position is created, the cost of new personnel needs to be weighed against the benefits of increased/improved output.

■ Consider form of employment:

   ● Permanent contract—full/part time.

   ● Temporary contract—full/part time.

   ● Job sharing (e.g. full-time telephone operator position covered by two part-time employees).

   ● Outworking (e.g. home worker under contract).

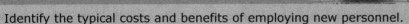

Example 1   Costs and Benefits

Identify the typical costs and benefits of employing new personnel.

2.1.2   Define the Job

■ Traditionally the "job description", based on the "job analysis" (see following).

■ Accountability statements (the results for which the job holder is responsible)—presented as a concise, bullet-pointed list.

2.1.3   Define the Person

■ Traditionally the "person specification" (see below).

■ May form the basis of a job advertisement.

2.1.4   Terms and Conditions of Employment

■ Some will be negotiable and not finalised until the selection stage.

■ Considerations include:

   ● Salary (e.g. band).

   ● Hours of work and holidays.

   ● Benefits.*

*Commentary

*For example, company car, private healthcare, pension contributions, share options.

2.2 Job Analysis

The process of **job analysis** concentrates on what job holders are expected to do.

2.2.1 Purpose

- To provide a realistic set of objectives for the requirements of the job (set out in the job description) and the person to do it (set out in a person specification).

> **Definition**
>
> **Job analysis**—the process of collecting, analysing and setting out information about the content of jobs in order to provide the basis for a job description and data for recruitment, training, job evaluation and performance management.
>
> —*Armstrong*

- May also be used to develop appropriate job training programmes, to establish measurement criteria for performance appraisal and to assess the relative worth and compensation (salary) of each job.

2.2.2 Importance

- It provides the framework on which to draw up any recruitment advertisement.
- It provides the guidelines against which the suitability of applicants will be assessed.
- How each applicant matches up against the person specification can be used to:
  - screen them out (i.e. not invite them to an interview); or
  - identify specific strengths or weaknesses which can be explored during their interview.

2.2.3 Information Obtained

- Purpose of job.
- Job content—duties and tasks involved.
- Accountabilities—results for which the job holder will be held accountable.
- Performance criteria—the minimum knowledge, skills and abilities required.
- Tools and equipment required—laptop, welding torch, protective clothing, etc.
- Responsibilities—for other employees, money, equipment.
- Organisational factors—reporting to line or senior managers.
- Developmental factors—"fast-track" programmes.
- Environmental factors—health and safety issues.

> **Example 2 Job Content of an ACCA Tutor**
>
> Specify the job content you would expect to identify during the job analysis investigation of a full-time ACCA tutor.

2.2.4   Stages in Job Analysis

Stage 1: Obtain all the necessary relevant and appropriate documentation.

Stage 2: Ask managers about the purpose and more general aspects of the job, its main activities and the responsibilities involved.

Stage 3: Ask the jobholders the same questions (because perceptions may differ).

Stage 4: Observe the job holders at work.

Stage 5: Correlate information and cross-check for consistency.

Stage 6: Prepare job description and job specification.

2.3   Job Description

Definition

- **Job descriptions** are particularly useful for tasks of a repetitive nature and where staff turnover is high.

- They can be highly specific because of the detail in the job (e.g. for machine operators, pilots) or fairly general (labourer, consultant).

> **Job description**—sets out the purpose of a job, how it relates to the organisation, the job holder's accountabilities/tasks and lines of reporting.

2.3.1   Purpose and Use

- Job descriptions define the job and describe the relationship of the job to other jobs in the organisation, to the job holder's position in the organisation and to the organisation's strategic objectives.

- They also provide:
  - Information for the person specification (see below).
  - The basis for:
    - legal contracts of employment;
    - staff appraisal and development;
    - redesigning the job; and
    - identifying health and safety issues.

2.3.2   How Prepared

- Information about duties and responsibilities obtained from manager, current job holder, colleagues, observer, etc.
- "Exit" interviews with leavers.

2.4 Person Specification

2.4.1 Content

▪ An appropriate and well-chosen set of categories should encompass the required range of abilities.

▪ Too many categories in the specification will be daunting to those who use it; too few will mean vagueness.

▪ Rodger's Seven-Point Plan or Fraser's Five-Point Grading is often used for the initial framework.

Person specification
—"sets out
the education,
qualifications,
training, experience,
personal attributes
and competences a
job holder requires
to perform his job
satisfactorily."

—*Armstrong*

2.4.2 Comparing With the Job Description

Matching

JOB DESCRIPTION	PERSON SPECIFICATION (RODGER)
• Job title • Place of work • Reporting to whom? • Responsible for subordinates? • Purpose of position • Key duties • Objectives/targets	(1) Physical attributes (2) Attainments (education/ training) (3) General intelligence (e.g. IQ) (4) Special aptitudes (analysis/ design) (5) Interests (practical and social) (6) Disposition (manner) (7) Background (circumstances)

2.4.3 Problems With the Seven-Point Plan

✗ Certain aspects of disposition are cultural and may be misinterpreted (e.g. eye contact may be regarded as disrespectful).

✗ Care must be taken in setting some attributes (e.g. age, gender) as these may be set on grounds other than job performance and thus result in discrimination.

✗ It is difficult to measure general intelligence.*

✗ It gives little attention to factors identifying future potential.*

2.4.4 Five-Point Grading

▪ An alternative to Rodger's Seven-Point Plan (above) is Fraser's Five-Point Grading, which considers:

1. Impact on others (e.g. appearance, demeanour, speech).

2. Acquired knowledge and qualifications.

3. Innate abilities (e.g. mental agility) which can be tested and assessed.

4. Motivation (which is difficult to assess as often specific to an individual).

5. Adjustment (i.e. emotional stability, tolerance, etc).

*A criticism of IQ (Intelligence Quotient) is that it measures the ability to take IQ tests rather than intelligence.

*In some organisations, consideration is also given to the individual's ability to progress to the next promotion level.

2.4.5 Preparation

▓ The person specification is an extrapolation from the job description.

▓ Care should be taken to ensure that it is realistic.*

▓ Each feature (within a category) can be classified as:

   ● essential (e.g. integrity in accountants);

   ● desirable (e.g. patience for teachers); or

   ● contra-indicated, that is, actively disadvantageous (e.g. obesity in a fitness instructor).

*Avoid unrealistic ideals or basing the person specification on the present incumbent whose qualifications exceed what is actually required.

2.4.6 Purpose and Use

▓ The person specification describes the "perfect" person to do the job.*

▓ It may include:

   ● difficulties (e.g. airline staff dealing with distressed passengers); and

   ● distastes (e.g. auditors attending inventory counts in refrigeration units and abattoirs).*

*The "perfect" person for a job, as described by the person specification, may not exist.

*Tedious tasks may also be "distasteful" (e.g. filling in time sheets). Difficulties and distastes are not necessarily one and the same—difficulties may be seen as an attractive challenge.

▓ The person specification:

   ● Can be condensed to provide the job advertisement.

   ● Enables pre-selection and screening of candidates for the actual interview.

   ● Provides a framework and checklist for collecting information for a selection interview plan.

   ● Provides the basis for further training/experience.*

*Candidates know the essential/desirable requirements for a job before applying.

2.5 Attracting Appropriate Applicants

2.5.1 Sources of Applicants

It is always essential to carefully consider the sources of potential applicants to ensure that the best candidates are presented.

▓ Existing internal employees (promotion/transfer):

   ● Self-applicants

   ● Internal advertising

   ● Recommended by line manager

   ● Succession planning

▓ Via existing contacts:

   ● Personal enquiries

   ● Previous unsuccessful applicants

   ● Former employees

   ● Current employee contacts

▨ External contacts:
- Professional and union referrals (keep registers of members in the job market)
- Job centres (e.g. provided by Department of Employment)
- Temporary agencies
- Schools and career centres
- University "milk round" and careers and advisory services
- Business schools
- Government training schemes
- Sponsorship and work experience schemes
- Consultants (may specialise in professional/managerial positions e.g. "headhunters")

▨ Media advertising:
- Websites (e.g. company and/or agency)
- Press (i.e. local/national papers, trade/professional journals)
- Radio (usually local "commercial" stations)
- TV and cinema (e.g. armed forces)
- Billboards/posters
- Exhibitions, recruitment fairs
- DVD, e-media, hardcopy (e.g. brochures)
- Open days

2.5.2 Relative Advantages and Disadvantages

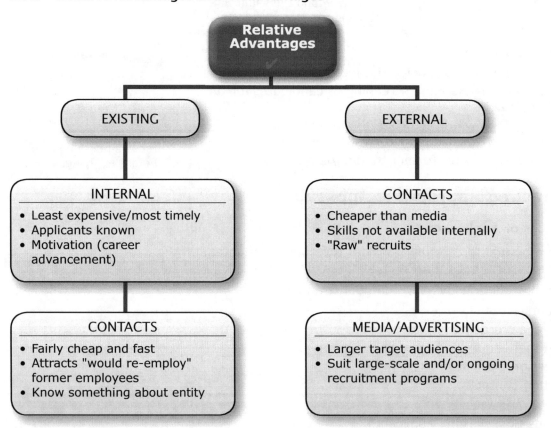

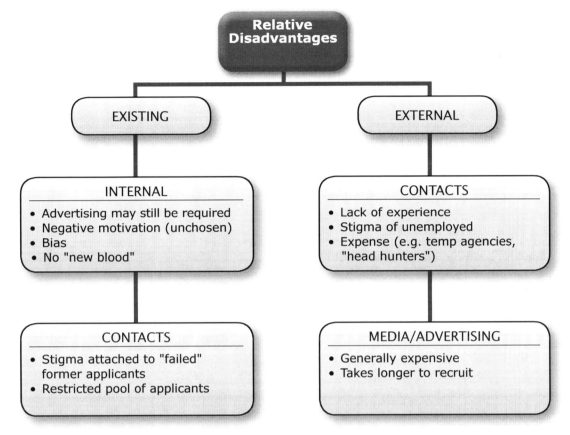

2.5.3 Documentation

■ For internal applicants, their details and experience will have already been documented in personnel records.

■ Most media advertisements (for external applicants) request a curriculum vitae (CV) or a completed job application form. Contact details will be given to apply for an application form or to obtain further information.

■ Information packs (specific detail about the job and the company) sent to applicants who request a job application form give them the opportunity not to proceed further.

2.5.4 Job Application Form/Curriculum Vitae

■ Traditionally emphasise qualifications and work experience.

■ Application forms are formal in their requirements and are mainly used for jobs where the applicant's experience and background are likely to be limited.

■ CVs are free-form and are more commonly used for senior positions where the experience of the candidate will be much more varied.

■ In some cases, personality questionnaires also will need to be completed.

3 Selection

3.1 Selection Process

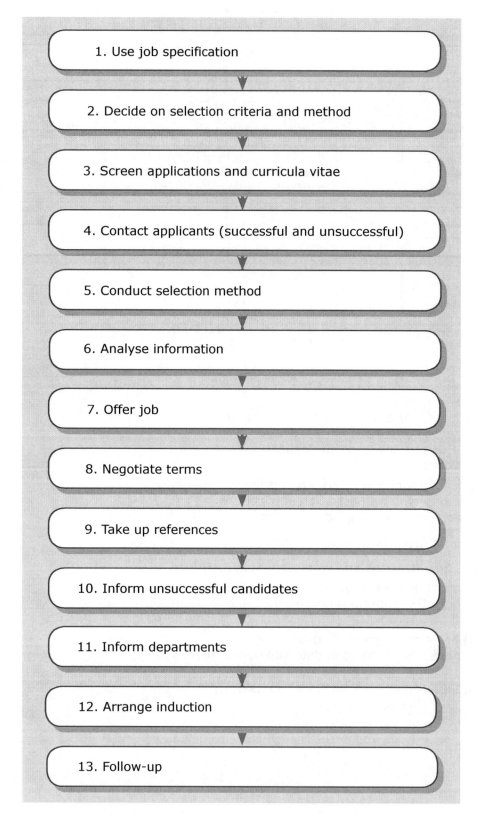

1. Use job specification

2. Decide on selection criteria and method

3. Screen applications and curricula vitae

4. Contact applicants (successful and unsuccessful)

5. Conduct selection method

6. Analyse information

7. Offer job

8. Negotiate terms

9. Take up references

10. Inform unsuccessful candidates

11. Inform departments

12. Arrange induction

13. Follow-up

3.2   Choosing a Candidate

- Candidates should be assessed against the person specification criteria—not against each other.
- Consider not only formal qualifications and ability to do a particular job but also:
  - potential for development and future promotion; and
  - flexibility/adaptability to change (e.g. new procedures, place of work, technology used).
- Candidates may be graded, for example, as:
  - Outstanding (could raise questions as to why candidate is applying—too good?)
  - Above average (has ability to progress to next promotion level?)
  - Average (e.g. meets desired criteria)
  - Below average (e.g. meets minimum criteria)
  - Reject
- If there are too many suitable candidates, the screening criteria can be strengthened (e.g. only select those applicants rated "above average" for the next stage).
- If there are too few suitable candidates, then the job and person specifications should be reviewed (e.g. salary is too low).

4   Selection Methods

4.1   Pre-selection

- Categorise applicants (based on their CVs or application forms) according to their suitability. Consider:
  - availability (e.g. now or six months); how urgent is it to fill the vacancy?
  - reasons for "gaps" in employment record; could be due to "rest at Her Majesty's pleasure" (i.e. prison), although that may not itself exclude a candidate;
  - education (e.g. subject/class of degree, school examination record);
  - professional qualifications (e.g. ACCA);
  - past work experience (e.g. "at least three years of laser cosmetic systems");
  - past employers (some companies will not employ ex-employees of competitors in sensitive positions); and
  - out-of-work activities (to indicate qualitative characteristics and skills).
- Notify unsuitable applicants that they have not been successful, unless they have been advised that no response by a specified date means unsuccessful.
- Start with most suitable "probable" candidates.
- "Fall back" on "possibles" if necessary.

4.2   Applicant References

■ It is common for up to three references to be obtained for shortlisted candidates (past employer and character references), either:*

- when they have been selected for interview;
- to follow up interviews; or
- when a candidate has been selected (either as a "formality" or the job offer is conditional on receipt of satisfactory references).

■ Checking references should be undertaken only with the candidate's permission and with careful timing. It is possible that the applicant's current employer does not know the applicant is seeking new work.*

■ References (or testimonials) usually concern character and suitability to carry out the job applied for (may also include a medical report).

■ References should corroborate and add to the knowledge already gained about a candidate.

■ References may be written (e.g. using a standard form) or oral.

■ Their usefulness depends on the honesty and personality of the person giving the reference and why the candidate listed them.

4.3   Selection Methods

■ The following methods are not all mutually exclusive:

- Selection interviews—most popular/widely used
- Application forms/curricula vitae ("CVs")
- Psychometric tests
- Assessment centres
- Job simulation/work sampling
- Other (e.g. graphology—analysis of handwriting; astrology)

4.4   Application Forms/Curricula Vitae (CVs)

4.4.1   Application Form Content

■ A job application form requests relevant information about the applicant in a standard format. Avoid obtaining information not relevant to the job (e.g. gender, age, date of birth, nationality) unless necessary (e.g. for work permit requirements) or in a separable part of the form relating to equal opportunities monitoring.

■ Forms may vary in design depending on the level of the job being sought (e.g. an application form for a manual job will require less detail than a form for a manager's job).

■ The basic sections in a job application form are:

- Personal information (e.g. full name, address, telephone, languages, etc).
- Education (e.g. name of school/college/university, dates attended, examinations, results and awards, etc) if relevant to the job; otherwise do not ask, especially dates attended (as it may discriminate on the basis of age).
- Trade or professional qualifications (ensure that asking for the date of qualification is relevant, otherwise possible age discrimination).

*The term *candidate* means anyone suitable for the position. Before proceeding with selection methods, however, many organisations find it necessary to shortlist the most suitable candidates to fit the time allotted for interviewing or for other reasons. The shortlist, then, is a selection of the most suitable candidates.

*Refusal by a candidate to supply references should put the firm on guard.

- Employment history (e.g. employer, dates of employment, position held, description of duties, achievements in position, reason for leaving. Again, care should be taken re dates as this may lead to age discrimination.).
- Leisure interests and activities if relevant to the job.
- Further information (sub-headings may vary and only if relevant to the job).
- Details of referees.
- Confirmation statement.
- A separable sheet requesting monitoring information for equal opportunities and diversity monitoring (e.g. age, date of birth, gender, disabilities, nationality, ethnic origin).*

*Care must be taken to ensure that the information requested on the application form is, under data protection principles and discrimination law, relevant and not excessive for purpose (e.g. asking for nationality is irrelevant unless work permit and visas are required).

4.4.2 Relative Merits

✔ Aids pre-selection (screening) of applicants (e.g. to interview or reject).

✔ Inconsistencies and omissions by applicant identified.

✔ Easy to compare candidates.

✔ Focuses on areas of interest to candidates.

✔ Provides useful information as basis for an interview.

✔ It can be cost-effective to choose a successful candidate without an interview process (e.g. when recruiting from "overseas").

✔ Provides base data/permanent record for entry into personnel system.

4.4.3 Disadvantages

✗ Can easily be made up (e.g. false education results, qualifications, interests).

✗ Cannot give guarantee of future performance (e.g. poor correlation between predicted and actual job performance).

✗ Cannot confirm subjective qualitative criteria (e.g. ability to motivate).

✗ May not allow applicant to fully express himself.

4.4.4 Curriculum Vitae

- The CV covers the same areas as a job application form (e.g. personal, education, employment record, interests, etc) but is not of a standard form. The writer decides the format and what to say.

- CVs are usually required for higher-level appointments (e.g. managers, directors) where the work experience of the applicant is likely to be far more varied and cover far more facets than those of a general worker.

- At higher levels of employment, the emphasis is much more on what skills the applicant has and what they have achieved in past positions, rather than on education.

- Because the CV is not of a standard form it is more difficult to review, but it will give more specific information than an application form.

4.5 Psychometric Tests

4.5.1 Examples

```
            ┌─────────────────────────┐
            │    SELECTION TESTS      │
            │  OR PSYCHOLOGICAL TESTS │
            └─────────────────────────┘
```

INTELLIGENCE TESTS	APTITUDE TESTS	ATTAINMENT TESTS	PERSONALITY QUESTIONNAIRES
• Thinking abilities ("mental capacity")	• Innate skills (e.g. verbal reasoning, numeracy)	• Existing knowledge and skills (e.g. typing)	• Traits important to job but not covered by other tests

4.5.2 Qualitative Characteristics of a Good Test

■ Sensitive measuring/discriminates well among candidates.

■ Standardised.

■ Reliable application (i.e. always measures the same skill when applied to different candidates at different times).

■ Relevant application (i.e. it measures what it is intended to measure).

■ Valid (i.e. test will measure characteristics required for job).

4.5.3 Advantages

✔ Reduces subjectivity in choosing successful candidates.

✔ Provides additional evidence of a candidate's suitability/ unsuitability.

✔ Can establish a candidate's practical ability, performance and other characteristics not covered by interview.

✔ Can also be used in making decisions about internal promotions and transfers.

4.5.4 Disadvantages

✗ Supplements rather than replaces interviews.

✗ Interpreting results may require the skills of a consultant psychologist—therefore costly.

✗ Avoiding bias can be difficult.

✗ May not take into account cultural background.

✗ Some tests may be open to faking (e.g. personality questionnaires).

✗ Tests that are not workplace based may not be good indicators of what will actually happen in a practical situation.

4.6   Assessment Centres

4.6.1   Features

- Use more than one technique.
- More than one trained assessor.
- Overall assessment is made later—not during observation.
- Use pre-tested simulation exercises.
- Test skills relevant to job.
- May incorporate interview and other testing procedures.

4.6.2   Typical Programme

- Duration: One day.
- Introduction, aim of programme.
- Appropriate psychological tests.
- Aptitude/intelligence tests.
- Interviews.
- Group and individual exercises.
- Work-based exercises.
- Debriefing/closing session.

4.6.3   Use

- Increasingly used by larger employers, in selecting managers and graduate trainees (i.e. where all candidates have broadly the same educational and work experience backgrounds) in financial services, distribution and leisure industries.

- Group exercises, usually central to assessment centres, are commonly used in selecting management trainees or other staff where sociability (with other staff, customers, suppliers, etc) is considered particularly important.

- Certain group exercises also will determine a candidate's ability to persuade, lead and participate as a team member.

4.7   Job Simulation/Work Sampling

- Job simulation—"role play" interviews and "in-tray" exercises designed to simulate a work situation. May be incorporated into the assessment-centre process.

- Work sampling—spending an agreed time in the organisation to carry out a task.

- Peer rating—candidates together for a period of time may be asked to rate each other. This may be used in assessment centres also.

Definition

Assessment centre— a place where a small group of participants undertakes a series of tests or exercises under observation, with a view to evaluating skills and competences, suitability for particular roles and potential for development.

5 Selection Interviews

5.1 Importance

▓ Regarded as the most important aid to choosing a candidate.

▓ Interviews can take into account physical features, mannerisms and aspects of personality (e.g. sociability) not easily assessed by other means.

5.2 Purpose

▓ Interviews are used to assess a candidate's suitability for the job. They mainly concentrate on the personal qualities of an individual.

▓ Single interviews—clerical/manual staff.

▓ Multiple interviews—managerial positions.

▓ May be one, two or more interviewers.

5.3 Conducting an Interview

5.3.1 Who Is Involved

▓ Most interviews are face-to-face and conducted by one or more:
  • Personnel officers
  • Line managers/supervisors
  • Team members
  • External agents/consultants
  • Executives/partners.

▓ The more senior the position, the more senior the interviewers.

5.3.2 Panel Interviews

▓ Each interviewer has an interest in the appointment and may be allocated an area for questioning.

▓ Although a panel reduces risk of bias (discrimination), it tends to be more formal and intimidating than a one-to-one interview.

5.3.3 Interview Approach

The interview can take many forms but, as a guide, the interviewer should:

Be prepared:	• Have a detailed knowledge of the organisation. • Know the job description and job specification. • Completely review the job application. • Plan the interview and the questions to ask. • Anticipate questions a candidate may ask and have answers ready. • Obtain all other relevant information you or the candidate may need. • Arrange the location (seating/facilities).
Welcome the candidate:	• Initial courtesies (includes being on time). • Brief explanation of the interview format. • Attempt to relax the candidate. • Show enthusiasm.
Control the interview:	• Keep to the plan. • Ensure that all relevant points are brought out by yourself and from the candidate. • Cover aspects in a logical order. • Keep check on the time. • Encourage the candidate to talk. • Check understanding. • Show interest in the candidate.
Close the interview:	• Allow the candidate an opportunity for last questions or to clarify any point. • Explain the next steps in the process (including when a decision will be made). • Exchange final courtesies. • Ensure that the candidate leaves with a positive impression of the firm (they will tell others of their experience).
Final steps:	• Make appropriate notes and rank for suitability. • Operate procedures for notification.

5.4   Key Skills Required

▨ Presentable, interested, friendly and well prepared.

▨ Good people skills (e.g. ability to get on with people, be positive with candidate).

▨ Good questioning skills (e.g. open questions give candidates more opportunity to "chat" than closed questions, whereas the timing of closed questions is easier to monitor and control).

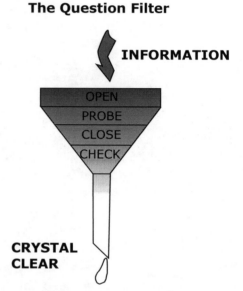

The Question Filter

- Open questions (e.g. "What made you decide to qualify as an accountant?").

- Probing questions (e.g. "Tell me more about the influence your sister had on your becoming an accountant").

- Closed questions (e.g. "When did you qualify?").

- Reflective, checking comments and questions are useful in clarifying understanding. (e.g. "Let me just check—so you passed all your exams at the first attempt?").

- Leading questions should be avoided (e.g. "Meeting deadlines is crucial to this job. Are you good at meeting deadlines?"—The answer will always be "yes").

Ask the right questions and all becomes clear

▨ Listening skills (e.g. concentrate on and understand what is being said, do not let thoughts wander, identify areas for further questioning).

▨ Couching/persuasion skills (e.g. encouraging candidate to talk about themselves, being able to move on in interview without being abrupt or rude).

▨ Understand body language (e.g. nervous posture/gestures, eye contact, facial expressions).

▨ Analysis (e.g. being able to correlate verbal and written information, identify consistencies and gaps in the information given).

5.5   Ineffective Interviewing

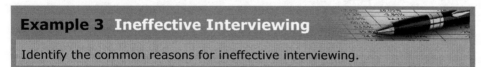

Example 3   Ineffective Interviewing

Identify the common reasons for ineffective interviewing.

Summary

- Making the wrong decisions about a new hire can have far-reaching and costly effects on an organisation.
- The key steps in recruitment and selection involve:
  - defining the job vacancy/person required (including "job analysis");
  - attracting appropriate applicants;
  - assessing candidates;
  - choosing a candidate; and
  - evaluating the success of the process.
- Those responsible for recruitment and selection must take care not to discriminate against protected classes of the labour pool.
- Senior managers plan human resource sourcing to meet strategic objectives.
- Personnel officers develop the structure of the process and monitor policy adherence.
- Line managers and supervisors determine qualifications which meet the job requirements.
- External recruitment professionals may be hired to provide specific services.
- The organisation should measure effectiveness, efficiency and fairness of the process.
- To determine the type of person to be recruited, the organisation must determine the type and authority of the position.
- A job analysis will be used to develop a job description which becomes the basis for recruitment—a person specification.
- Interviews are considered the most important method of choosing a candidate.

Session 17 Quiz
Estimated time: 15 minutes

1. List the FIVE key stages of recruitment and selection. (1.2)
2. Distinguish between recruitment and selection. (1.1)
3. Define job analysis. (2.2)
4. List the SEVEN elements of Rodger's person specification plan. (2.4.2)
5. Explain the major differences between an application form and a curriculum vitae. (4.4)
6. Explain the concept of an assessment centre. (4.6)
7. List the FIVE stages in a typical selection interview process. (5.3)

Study Question Bank
Estimated time: 35 minutes

Priority		Estimated Time	Completed
MCQ17	Recruitment and Selection	35 minutes	

EXAMPLE SOLUTIONS

Solution 1—Costs and Benefits

Typical Costs
- Advertising
- Management time
- Recruitment fees
- Salaries and related costs
- Additional supervisory costs
- Training and development
- Additional equipment, space and facilities

Typical Benefits
- Increased output
- Improved quality of product/service
- Improved quality of life for employees
- Reduction in outsourcing costs
- Competitive advantage
- Legal requirement (e.g. teacher-pupil ratios)

Solution 2—Job Content of an ACCA Tutor*

*Purpose of job—to prepare students for the professional examinations of the ACCA.

- Prepare (word process), for publication:
  - course notes and handouts;
  - study guides and course overviews;
  - monitoring tests and solutions;
  - mock exams, solutions and marking schemes; and
  - revision notes.
- Update course notes and handouts to reflect current best practice and requirements.
- Prepare presentation notes ensuring all aspects of the Course Overview covered.
- Agree with Administration Director courses plan for each diet and ensure workload and travel arrangements are appropriate.
- Travel (by boat, train or plane) to exotic locations (anywhere in the world) in agreement with courses plan.
- Ensure on arrival at course location all material is correct (attendance lists, assessments, course notes and handouts, overhead or multimedia projector).
- Present course material through lecture and examples, following Course Overview.
- Coach students, as required, through examples and practice questions.
- Carry out daily administration—student signing-in sheets, report absentees.
- At the end of each course, hand out and collect assessment forms.
- Be professional at all times.
- Keep up to date on technical and ACCA matters.
- Prepare for and present webinars.
- Prepare visual and audio materials for e-publishing.

Solution 3—Ineffective Interviewing

- Organisation and/or interviewer do not appear professional to candidate.
- Interviewer has insufficient time to prepare (e.g. due to other work commitments).
- Interviewer has pre-conceived view/prejudices of candidate.
- Interview is interrupted (e.g. by phone ringing) or cut short.
- Physical discomfort (e.g. too cold, too hot, sunlight in candidate's eyes).
- All points on the interview plan are not covered (e.g. because time is not controlled).
- Interviewer does more talking than listening and/or candidate is not encouraged to ask questions.
- Negative approach (e.g. decision is based on reasons why candidate is not suitable rather than on positive attributes).
- "Self-image" recruitment (e.g. candidate is chosen because he has similar values and is a "clone" of interviewer).
- Candidate feels that he has not been given a fair hearing.

Equal Opportunities and Diversity

FOCUS

This session covers the following content from the *ACCA Study Guide.*

D. Leading and Managing Individuals and Teams

2. Recruitment and selection of employees

f) Explain the purpose and benefits of diversity and equal opportunities policies within the human resources plan. ☐

g) Explain the practical steps that an organisation may take to ensure the effectiveness of its diversity and equal opportunities policy. ☐

Session 18 Guidance

■ **Note** that discrimination and equal opportunities are important topics for managers in real life. The implications of getting it wrong or doing it incorrectly can have legal and financial implications.

■ **Understand** the difference between equal employment opportunities (legally required) and workplace diversity (ethically, morally and financial desirable) (s.1).

■ **Know** the forms of discrimination (s.2.1).

(continued on next page)

VISUAL OVERVIEW

Objective: To describe the meaning and application of equal opportunities and management of diversity.

```
┌─────────────────────────────────┐
│            DIVERSITY            │
│  ─────────────────────────────  │
│     • Development               │
│     • Research                  │
└─────────────────────────────────┘
                 │
                 │
┌─────────────────────────────────┐
│          DISCRIMINATION         │
│  ─────────────────────────────  │
│     • Forms of Discrimination   │
│     • Equal Opportunities       │
│     • Equal Pay                 │
│     • Sex Discrimination        │
│     • Sexual Harassment         │
│     • Orientation and Religion  │
│     • Disability                │
│     • Age                       │
└─────────────────────────────────┘
                 │
                 │
┌─────────────────────────────────┐
│  MANAGING DIVERSITY AND EQUAL   │
│           OPPORTUNITIES         │
│  ─────────────────────────────  │
│     • Managing Diversity        │
│     • Establishing Policy       │
│     • Equal Opportunities       │
└─────────────────────────────────┘
```

Session 18 Guidance

■ **Recognise** best practices in managing diversity and equal opportunities (s.3).

■ **Be aware** if equal opportunities and diversity are of lesser relevance in your country, make sure you understand what is standard in Europe. You cannot use the excuse that "we do not do it that way in my country".

1   Diversity

1.1   Development

Diversity—a range of things.
Workplace diversity—acknowledgement of and tolerance for differences within and between groups of people in the workplace.

■ Equal employment opportunities under the law and **workplace diversity** are both tied into business ethics and CSR; developments in equal opportunities have been driven forward by legal requirements whereas **diversity** is still a more ethics-oriented issue.*

*Equal employment opportunities law against discrimination based on race, disability, gender, religion and belief, sexual orientation and age has been in place for many years. Diversity will be subject to regulation in the UK when the Corporate Governance Code is updated.

■ Equal opportunity initiatives are grounded in developing a level playing field for all people by ending or reducing discrimination against particular groups and improving fairness in the workplace through the application of law. As seen with corporate law and regulations, from a business and moral perspective, such initiatives will have a limit to their success.

■ Currently, best practice in corporate governance and CSR are driving the concept of diversity in an organisation's workforce to achieve a business, ethical and moral advantage.

■ Harnessing diversity in the workplace will theoretically create a productive environment in which everyone feels valued, their talents are fully utilised and organisational goals are met.

■ People's differences can be many and varied, visible and non-visible (e.g. background, culture, personality, politics, family structure, health, values and work style).

1.2   Research

■ Research has found that culturally diverse teams were more creative than homogenous teams and contributed more effectively to meeting organisational goals. Thus, there is a business case (as well as the moral and ethical case) for diversity, although coping with it would be much harder than simply managing equal opportunities to meet legal requirements.

▨ By analysing organisations which actively pursue a diversity programme (and do not just pay it lip service), researchers have shown that the application of a diverse workforce:

- increases competitive advantage—diversity ensures that a company has employees who come from all parts of society and who are and who look, act, think like and relate to the company's potential customers;
- enables the company to relate much more closely to its markets and meet changing consumer demands and emerging niche markets;
- improves effectiveness and efficiency by maximising the human resource potential;
- increases creativity and innovation;
- broadens the range of employee skills;
- improves working relationships in an atmosphere of trust and inclusion;
- improves customer relations and service to similarly diverse customers;
- enables recruitment from a wider, diverse labour pool, thus enhancing the skills and abilities the company can choose;
- enhances the company's reputation among job seekers; and
- decreases recruitment and turnover expenditures of time and money.

Key Point

The main differences between diversity and equal opportunities are:

Diversity	Equal Opportunities
• Voluntary (at this point)	• Government initiated
• Productivity driven	• Legally driven
• Qualitative	• Quantitative
• Opportunity-focused	• Problem-focused
• Inclusive	• Targeted
• Proactive	• Reactive

2 Discrimination

The areas of discrimination covered in this session are:

▨ equal opportunities;

▨ equal pay; and

▨ gender, colour, race, disability, sexual orientation, religion and age.

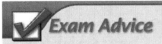

Exam Advice

The examiner does not expect you to know the detail of the UK legislation on work-based discrimination, equal opportunities and diversity. Every jurisdiction will have varying laws on these topics. You will, however, be expected to know the general principles and good practice, using the UK as an example.

2.1 Forms of Discrimination

- **Direct discrimination**—where one interested party is treated less favourably than another.
- **Indirect discrimination**—when a policy or practice appears to be fair in writing, but in practice actually discriminates against an individual or group of individuals. Such a policy has the effect of discriminating although it may not overtly intend to do so.
- **Victimisation**—a form of discrimination against an individual who is penalised for giving information or taking action in pursuit of a claim of discrimination.
- **Harassment**—use of threatening, intimidating, offensive or abusive action, language or behaviour; includes verbal, physical, mental or threatened bullying.

2.2 Equal Opportunities

- Equal employment opportunities exist when there is no unfair discrimination (against gender, colour, ethnic origin, disability, orientation, religion and age) in relation to:
  - access to jobs;
  - employment terms and conditions;
  - promotion prospects;
  - training opportunities;
  - remuneration; or
  - termination of employment.
- Employers should only take into account ability, experience and potential when deciding who the best person is for a position, unless it is obvious that a particular individual is required for the position (e.g. a female nurse dealing with female patients).

2.2.1 Advantages of an Equal Opportunities Policy

✔ A sound business case often can be made for having an equal opportunities policy.
✔ Compliance with relevant legislation and codes of best practice.
✔ Legally, ethically and morally justified and a CSR reporting requirement (see *Sessions 9* and *26*).
✔ Assures a wide and deep "gene pool" to attract and retain the best talent.*

*Commentary

*A survey of the UK's listed companies noted that the majority of company boards were "male, pale and stale". This was considered to be a distinct competitive disadvantage in that the boards did not reflect the environment in which they operated, particularly in relation to their customer base.

✔ Ensures that the organisation's employees and managers reflect the composition of its operating environment (e.g. customer and local communities).
✔ Being able to demonstrate best practice and a non-discriminatory attitude if taken to court by an employee claiming discrimination.

2.2.2 Circumvention

▨ Some organisations may only pay "lip service" to the requirements and do the absolute minimum necessary. For example:

- ● Publish extensive equal opportunity policy documents (e.g. in CSR and sustainability reports) in order to be seen to be good, but in practice do very little.

- ● Deliberately establish or create reasons and situations to ensure discrimination "via the backdoor" (e.g. creating reasons in a job interview, which may or may not be justifiable, for not hiring a particular individual).

- ● Create a work environment which forces an individual to resign (e.g. work colleagues take a dislike and refuse to work with or talk to the individual).

- ● Apply a policy selectively (e.g. to workers and low-grade managers, but not to middle managers or executives) so there is no representation of certain groups at higher levels.

Illustration 1 Discriminatory Selection

An investigative journalist (who was non-white) applied for the same job using two different names. Her employment experience and education were the same on both application forms but on one form, her name implied that she belonged to an ethnic minority and, on the other, her real name implied that she was a white national. She was invited for an interview under her real name, but under the ethnic minority name, she was rejected.

When the interviewer saw that she was non-white, he spent most of the interview time giving the impression that the job was not right for her.

In addition, a white female colleague (who applied with similar, comparable education and experience) also was invited for an interview. She was offered the job.

The subsequent publicity was very damaging to the reputation of the company (which publicly promoted an equal opportunities environment). The directors sacked the interviewer because his discriminatory attitude was at fault rather than the firm's policy. A number of the firm's current and past employees, however, went public and made it clear that the non-discrimination policy was a sham and that the directors actively encouraged indirect discrimination.

2.3 Equal Pay

▨ Under such legislation, any person is entitled to the same remuneration and conditions of service as another who:

- ● is doing similar work; or
- ● is doing work which is of a similar value as judged under a job evaluation exercise.

2.3.1 Job Evaluation

▦ If a job evaluation exercise has not been undertaken, any employee has the right to apply to an industrial tribunal for an order that a job evaluation be performed.

▦ The job evaluation must use analytical methods to compare jobs done by other employees with regard to:

- skills attached to the post; and
- demands made on the individual.

▦ The tribunal's decision (e.g. to increase wages, re-grade jobs, etc) is legally binding.

2.3.2 Measuring Equal Value

▦ Even if two jobs differ in content, a claim for equal pay can be made if the jobs have equal value (in terms of the skills, etc, required to undertake them).

▦ The benchmark for determining equal value is whether the jobs are equivalent in terms of the demands made on the employee.

▦ The legislation offers examples of possible similar and dissimilar demands made on the workers undertaking two hypothetical jobs. These are reproduced below.

Examples of similar demands:

Job α

▦ Responsible for contact with customers.

▦ Lifts heavy weights occasionally.

▦ Diagnoses equipment faults.

▦ Checks inventory levels and orders replacements.

▦ Uses fax and stamping equipment.

▦ On feet most of day.

Job β

▦ Responsible for staff.

▦ Lifts small weights regularly.

▦ Analyses written reports.

▦ Checks work done by subordinates and allocates tasks.

▦ Uses a PC.

▦ Has to concentrate on numbers.

Examples of dissimilar demands:

Job λ

▦ Drives a van.

▦ Sweeps up.

▦ Decides shift rosters.

Job μ

▦ Examines customer complaints.

▦ Chooses fabric for new designs.

▦ Responsible for packing and despatch.

Illustration 2 Equal Value Jobs

In the UK's equal pay framework, examples of "equal value" job pairings are:
- Factory nurse and skilled fitter.
- Secretary and scientific assistant.
- Administrator and data analyst.
- Seamstress and forklift truck driver.
- Quality controller and technical trainer.
- Catering assistant and driver.

2.4　Sex Discrimination

▓ It is illegal to discriminate in the workplace on the basis of sex (gender) in the areas of recruitment, job selection, terms and conditions of employment, training, promotion and pay (including the form of fringe benefits and redundancy pay and pensions).

▓ Though originally introduced because of unfair treatment of women, in recent years the UK legislation has been used successfully by males to sue employers because of discrimination against them in favour of women.

▓ Equal opportunities based on sex discrimination led to some interesting cases and judgments. For example:

- Age limits placed on promotion prospects can be judged as sex discrimination because women who start a family are naturally on leave and may not return to work until after they have exceeded the age limit.

- As part-time workers are mainly female, to offer only limited or no retirement and health benefits to part-time workers may be considered sex discrimination.

- Some jurisdictions have a lower retirement age for women than for men. This may be considered sex discrimination.*

*Commentary

*The difference between retirement ages in the UK (women 60, men 65) was challenged in the courts by a group of men arguing sex discrimination and asking that the retirement age for men be set at 60. Although the court agreed with the men's sex discrimination claim, the government has instituted a policy which raises, in the first stage, the retirement age of everyone to 65 in a series of steps. The second stage will be to raise it further to 68.

- Schools or universities for students of one gender would be practicing sex discrimination, as it is unlawful to segregate the sexes in places of work without reasonable justification. In some jurisdictions, however, specific laws are in place where the sexes are not allowed to mix for cultural or religious reasons.

- The UK military services have, over recent years, allowed women to join and serve in front-line fighting Army units, to train and fly as fighter pilots in the RAF and to serve aboard Royal Navy ships (and submarines) as ratings and officers because of the threat that sex discrimination claims could be made.

2.5　Sexual Harassment

▓ Unwelcome sexual advances, requests for sexual favours and other verbal or physical conduct of a sexual nature constitute sexual harassment when this conduct explicitly or implicitly affects an individual's employment, unreasonably interferes with an individual's work performance or creates an intimidating, hostile or offensive work environment.

▓ Sexual harassment at work threatens the victim's confidence and self-esteem. It can stop a person from working effectively, undermines their dignity and can affect their health and happiness. Such actions can easily become a health and safety matter.

▓ Sexual harassment can occur in a variety of circumstances, including but not limited to:

- The victim as well as the harasser may be a woman or a man. The victim does not have to be of the opposite sex.
- The harasser can be the victim's supervisor, an agent of the employer, a supervisor in another area, a co-worker or a non-employee (e.g. a customer or supplier).
- The victim does not have to be the person harassed but could be anyone affected by the offensive conduct.
- Unlawful sexual harassment may occur without economic injury to the victim.
- The harasser's conduct must be unwelcome and made known to the harasser by the victim.*

*Commentary

*A difficulty faced by many employers is that many people respond to situations in different ways. What may seem like an innocent action or remark to one person may be deemed offensive by another, and the law often sides with the victim rather than the perpetrator. This is particularly the case when the harassment concerns an abuse of power (e.g. a worker being harassed by a manager).

▓ Sexual harassment can take many forms, broadly categorised as verbal, non-verbal or physical.

2.5.1 Verbal

▓ Comments about appearance, body or clothes.

▓ Indecent remarks.

▓ Sexually explicit jokes.

▓ Questions or comments about one's sex life.

▓ Requests for sexual favours.

▓ Sexual demands made by someone of the opposite or the same sex.

▓ Promises or threats concerning a person's employment conditions in return for sexual favours.

2.5.2 Non-verbal

▓ Looking or staring at a person's body.

▓ Display of male or female sexually explicit material, such as calendars, pin-ups or magazines.

2.5.3 Physical

▓ Physically touching, pinching, hugging, caressing or kissing.

▓ Sexual assault.

▓ Rape.

2.6   Sexual Orientation and Religious Beliefs

- Employers cannot discriminate on the basis of an individual's sexual orientation or religion.

- Employers can be held responsible for conduct (including harassment) deemed offensive in regard to an individual's sexual orientation or religion.*

> ***Commentary**
>
> *Employers should not prevent staff from taking absence for religious holidays.

2.7   Disability

- UK legislation makes it illegal for employers to discriminate against disabled individuals:
  - in deciding whom to interview, whom to employ or in terms of an employment offer;
  - in the terms of employment and the opportunities for promotion, transfer, training or other benefits, or by refusing the same;
  - by dismissal or other disadvantages.

- The employer has a duty to make reasonable adjustments to working arrangements or to the physical features of premises where these constitute a disadvantage to disabled people (e.g. easy access for wheelchairs).

2.8   Age

2.8.1   Impacts

- Age discrimination occurs when someone treats a person less favourably because of that person's age and uses this as a basis for prejudice against, and unfair treatment of, that person.

- Age discrimination in employment can:
  - affect anybody regardless of how old they are;
  - reduce employment prospects for older people, younger people and parents returning to work after a period of full-time child care;
  - favour people ages 25 to 35; or
  - prevent the full consideration of abilities, potential and experience of employees.

2.8.2   Factors to Be Considered by Employers

- Age, age-related criteria or age ranges should not be used in advertisements other than to encourage applications from age groups which do not usually apply. Where this is the case, it should be clearly stated and made clear that all age ranges will be treated the same. Failure to do so will be considered as positive discrimination (i.e. favouring one age group over others) and is unlawful.*

> ***Commentary**
>
> *Words such as mature, young, energetic, dynamic and graduate, as well as age-specific messages (e.g. 10 years' experience preferred), must be very carefully used as they are age related.
>
> Photographs of employees must avoid creating an image which would exclude or alienate certain age groups—a fair balance must be obtained overall.

- Interviewers and those concerned with selection must not be subjective on the basis of physical characteristics and unfounded assumptions. They must ensure that their decisions are based on objective criteria, relevant to the job and merit. The age regulations make it unlawful to base decisions on appearance or perceived age, whether older or younger.

- An individual's age should not be used to make judgements about abilities or fitness. Where such a judgement is required, an occupational health or medical practitioner should be consulted. Age should not be used as a factor in physical test requirements.

- Pay and terms of employment should not be based on age but should reflect the value of individual contributions and standards of job performance.

- All employees should be eligible for training and development regardless of age, even when they are nearing a benchmark retirement age (e.g. 65).

- When considering promotion, criteria cannot be based on age, only merit.

- Redundancy cannot be based on age (e.g. last-in, first-out), as this usually means the youngest employees are made redundant first. Similarly, decisions cannot be based on minimising the cost of redundancy, as this implies that workers who have been with the firm the longest and (probably) are older would stay, with the youngest going first. Redundancy must be based on job-related criteria and applied fairly.

- Forced retirement of those below the benchmark retirement age (e.g. 65) is **illegal.** Requests by those approaching retirement age to continue in a job must be carefully considered by employers. If an employer refuses to continue employment when the individual is still physically and mentally able to continue (and the job is still available), this will be considered discrimination.

3   Managing Diversity and Equal Opportunities

3.1   Managing Diversity

- Managing diversity includes:
  - ensuring the opportunity for all employees to maximise their potential, self-development and contribution to the organisation;
  - meeting the needs of a diverse workforce; and
  - reflecting the labour market and customers in the diversity of the workforce.

- People from different backgrounds can bring fresh ideas and perceptions, which can increase production efficiency and improve products.

- Practical issues and steps to achieve workplace diversity may include:
  - Building and maintaining teams in culturally and/or ethnically diverse work groups.
  - Providing support for different family situations of the workforce (e.g. child care and flexitime).
  - Ensuring that career opportunities are attractive and available to all members of the workforce.
  - Promoting a work atmosphere of tolerance for cultural differences.
  - Communicating with customers and employees to make sure their diverse needs are met.

3.2 Establishing Diversity Policy*

3.2.1 Overall Strategy

*Commentary

*The Chartered Institute of Personnel and Development (CIPD) provides a series of "tips".

- Ensure that initiatives and policies have the support of the board of directors and senior management.
- Consider managing diversity as a continuous process of improvement rather than a one-off initiative.
- Develop a diversity strategy to support the achievement of business goals, including ways of addressing the diverse needs of customers.
- Focus on fairness and inclusion, ensuring that merit, competence and potential are the basis for all decisions about recruitment and development.
- Keep up to date with the law and review policies through checks, audits and consultation.
- Address work-life balance challenges in ways that take account of employee and organisational needs and offer suitable choices and options.
- Encourage ownership and discourage risk aversion, aiming to create an empowering culture so that decisions are not passed upwards without good reason.
- Design guidelines for line managers to help them respond appropriately to diversity needs, as they are vital change agents, but give them scope for flexible decision-making.
- Link diversity management to other initiatives such as Investors in People and total quality management.
- Consider individual working styles and personal preferences in the context of national cultures in which the firm operates.

3.2.2 Workplace Behaviour

- Introduce a value system based on respect and dignity for all.
- Aim to describe the desirable behaviours to gain positive commitment.
- Make clear that everyone has a personal responsibility to uphold the standards.
- Introduce mechanisms to deal with all forms of harassing, bullying and intimidating behaviour.
- Make clear that discriminatory behaviour will not be tolerated, is regarded as contravening the values of an organisation and will be treated as a serious disciplinary matter.

3.2.3 Communication

■ Develop an open culture with good communication channels based on open dialogue and active listening.

■ Use different and accessible methods such as newsletters, in-house magazines, notice boards and intranets to keep people up to date about diversity policies and practices.

■ Consult people for ideas.

3.2.4 Training

■ Build diversity concepts and practices into management and other training and team-building programmes to increase awareness of the need to handle different views, perceptions and ideas in positive ways.

■ Consider skills-training and awareness-raising programmes about diversity to help people work together better in a diverse environment.

■ Include diversity issues in induction programmes so that all new employees know about the organisation's values and policies.

■ Train line managers about diversity, aiming to help them understand the issues and drive them into organisational and operational policies and practices.

3.2.5 Measure, Review and Reinforce

■ Regularly audit, review and evaluate progress and keep qualitative data to chart progress and show business benefits.

■ Use employee surveys to evaluate initiatives, to learn whether policies are working for everyone and to provide a platform for improvement.

■ Track actions to learn whether they have had the intended results and make appropriate changes if necessary.

■ Include diversity objectives in job descriptions and appraisals and recognise and reward achievement.

■ Benchmark good practice against other organisations and adopt and adapt relevant ideas where appropriate.

■ Network with others inside and outside your organisation to keep up to date and to share learning.

■ Celebrate successes and use failures to identify learning opportunities.

3.3 Equal Opportunities

■ Equal opportunities requirements must be thoroughly managed, not only to ensure that they are recognised and implemented but also to ensure that they are practical and effective in operation.

3.3.1 Buy-in

■ Ensure that all senior managers are fully aware of the need to follow not only the letter, but the spirit, of equal opportunities. If they are not seen to be applying the spirit of the legislation rather than simply complying with requirements, employees will not take any policy statements seriously.

■ Establish a board-level working party (which should reflect the diversity of the workforce) to produce a draft Policy Statement and Code of Best Practice for all areas of equal opportunities.

3.3.2 Review

▨ Audit all the organisation's current policies, practices and procedures, even those not labelled "personnel", to identify all areas that relate to equal opportunities.

▨ Establish areas that meet, exceed or fail to meet current legislation requirements. Update as necessary to ensure that all functions meet or exceed legal requirements.

▨ Produce a policy statement and codes of best practice for all employees.

3.3.3 Policy

▨ Implement policy as part of an approach to diversity and inclusion.

▨ Use only objective criteria essential for satisfactory performance and ensure that these can be objectively justified.

▨ Communicate policy to all managers and employees and offer training where necessary.

3.3.4 Stance and Key Actions

▨ Undertake regular audits to ensure that best practice is always used in all areas of equal opportunity.

▨ Management should challenge any form of discrimination used by employees.

▨ Educate and train all staff about the implications of any form of discrimination.

▨ Embed diversity and equal opportunities into the culture of the organisation.

▨ Include discrimination offences and disciplinary procedures into every employee's terms and conditions of employment.

▨ Ensure that "whistle-blowing" channels are open and used.

▨ Monitor key profiles (e.g. age, gender, ethnic origins, disabilities) to ensure that discrimination is not being practiced.

▨ Record all processes, monitoring, incidents and action taken, as such information may be needed if a court case arises.

Example 1 Advert Discrimination

Consider the following advertisement from the viewpoint of discrimination.

> "Attractive, young, blonde females required for duties as barmen. Must be available to work at 30 minutes' notice between the hours of 11.30 a.m. and 11.30 p.m."

List the possible ways this discriminates.

Summary

- Equal employment opportunities were established under law in the 1960s. These laws refer to discrimination based on race, sex, national origin, disability, age and sexual orientation.

- Forms of discrimination include direct and indirect discrimination, victimisation and harassment.

- Discrimination may be in relation to access to jobs, employment terms and conditions, promotion prospects, training opportunities, remuneration or termination of employment.

- Discrimination with regard to pay may occur when workers performing similar functions, or judged to be of similar value, do not receive the same pay and terms.

- Firms should perform a job evaluation in order to establish the pay and terms for each position.

- Workers who feel discriminated against based on pay and benefits may request a tribunal to intervene, and the tribunal may require a job evaluation, and may re-grade jobs and increase wages for the position.

- Even jobs with different content may be considered similar if they require the same skills, etc required to undertake them.

- Although an organisation's policies do not overtly discriminate, the firm may be found to discriminate if the effect of its policies is discriminatory.

- Sexual harassment can take many forms, broadly categorised as verbal, non-verbal and physical.

- Workplace diversity refers to the acknowledgement of and tolerance for differences within and between groups of people in the workplace. Although not yet required by law, a body of research indicates a business case for a diverse workplace.

Session 18 Quiz

Estimated time: 15 minutes

1. Explain the concept of "diversity". (1)

2. Give FIVE advantages of a diverse workforce. (1.2)

3. Briefly describe FOUR forms of discrimination. (2.1)

4. List FIVE factors an employer may use which could discriminate against a current or potential employee. (2.3, 2.8)

5. Describe why an organisation should establish a diversity policy. (3.2)

Study Question Bank

Estimated time: 15 minutes

Priority		Estimated Time	Completed
MCQ18	Equal Opportunities and Diversity	15 minutes	

EXAMPLE SOLUTION

Solution 1—Advert Discrimination

- "Attractive" implies particular physical characteristics.
- "Young" implies a particular age limit.
- "Blonde" implies particular races.
- "Female" denotes no males (despite the fact that they will be called "barmen").
- The notice period and timing implies preference for individuals who would not have family commitments.

Session 19

Individuals, Groups and Teams

FOCUS

This session covers the following content from the *ACCA Study Guide.*

D. Leading and Managing Individuals and Teams

3. Individual and group behaviour in business organisations
a) Describe the main characteristics of individual and group behaviour.
b) Outline the contributions of individuals and teams to organisational success.
c) Identify individual and team approaches to work.

4. Team formation, development and management
a) Explain the differences between a group and a team.
b) Explain the purposes of a team.
c) Explain the role of the manager in building the team and developing individuals within the team.
   i) Belbin's team roles theory
   ii) Tuckman's theory of team development
d) List the characteristics of effective and ineffective teams.
e) Describe tools and techniques that can be used to build the team and improve team effectiveness.

5. Motivating individuals and groups
d) Explain how reward systems can be designed and implemented to motivate teams and individuals.

Session 19 Guidance

■ **Note** that this session starts by looking at the individual and a person's behaviour as an individual (s.1).
■ **Understand** the effect on the individual as part of a group (s.2).
■ **Recognise** how formal groups become teams which need to be developed and managed (s.3).

(continued on next page)

VISUAL OVERVIEW

Objective: To describe the characteristics of individual and group behaviour and the formation and success of teams.

```
                    ┌─────────────────────────────────┐
                    │          INDIVIDUALS            │
                    │  • Characteristics              │
                    │  • Behaviour                    │
                    │  • Roles                        │
                    │  • Contribution to Work         │
                    │    Performance                  │
                    └─────────────────────────────────┘
           ┌──────────────────────┐      ┌─────────────────────────────┐
           │       GROUPS         │      │           TEAMS             │
           │  • Characteristics   │      │  • Characteristics          │
           │  • Individuals       │      │  • Purposes                 │
           │    Within Groups     │      │  • Composition              │
           │  • Formality         │      │  • R.M. Belbin              │
           └──────────────────────┘      └─────────────────────────────┘
                                          ┌─────────────────────────────┐
                                          │      TEAM DEVELOPMENT        │
                                          │  • Stage 1: Forming          │
                                          │  • Stage 2: Storming         │
                                          │  • Stage 3: Norming          │
                                          │  • Stage 4: Performing       │
                                          └─────────────────────────────┘
                                          ┌─────────────────────────────┐
                                          │        TEAM BUILDING         │
                                          │  • Successful Teams          │
                                          │  • Issues                    │
                                          │  • Tools                     │
                                          │  • Barriers                  │
                                          │  • Effective v Ineffective   │
                                          │    Groups                    │
                                          └─────────────────────────────┘
                                          ┌─────────────────────────────┐
                                          │   PERFORMANCE AND REWARDS    │
                                          │  • Considerations            │
                                          │  • Measures of Performance   │
                                          │  • Rewards                   │
                                          └─────────────────────────────┘
```

Session 19 Guidance

■ **Remember** that not all teams develop at the same speed and might never mature but might be stuck in any of the stages. So it often falls to the manager to build teams (s.5).

■ **Understand** how to measure team performance and reward teams and individual members of teams (s.6).

■ **Be prepared** to be given a small scenario from which you will need to identify, for example, one of Tuckman's stages of team development or one of Belbin's team roles.

1 Individuals

1.1 Characteristics

■ Individuals are unique and, in systems terms, open and adaptive. At a basic level, individuals seek to satisfy physiological, safety and security needs (Maslow's primary needs). Once basic needs are satisfied, individuals seek social activity and self-fulfilment (e.g. within a group).

■ An individual can achieve a level of success without the assistance of informal or formal groupings, but such success will be limited. The complexity of modern organisations implies that no one individual can bring resources that will satisfy all of the requirements of an organisation.

■ Individuals, as individuals, may follow their own set of rules (within the framework of the law).

1.2 Behaviour

There are many factors that drive an individual's **behaviour** at work. These include:

> **Definition**
>
> **Behaviour**—the relationship between two (or more) individuals, groups and their environment. It is the potential and expressed capacity for physical, mental and social activity between humans.

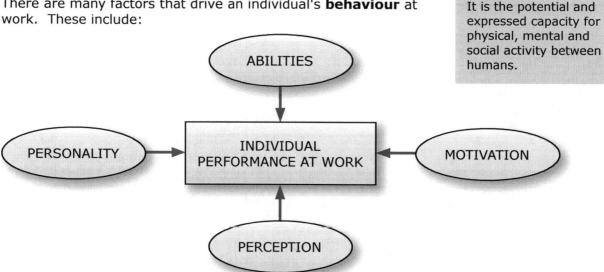

■ **Abilities**—relate to aptitude (i.e. the physical or mental capacity to perform tasks) and learning (i.e. the acquisition of abilities via training or experience). This is related to intelligence, although intelligence is a much wider and more complex subject.

■ **Motivation level**—concerned with the driving forces, such as values, beliefs, attitudes, needs and goals, which channel behaviour.

■ **Personality**—an individual's characteristics and behaviour patterns. Personality traits (e.g. compulsive, practical, unsociable and reflective) tend to stay relatively constant and thus describe personality types (e.g. introvert, extrovert).

■ **Perception**—the selection and arrangement of stimuli into meaningful patterns based on attitudes and experience. Perception depends on the context of the event, the individual, their selectivity, needs and previous experiences.

> **Definition**
>
> **"Halo effect"**—a cognitive bias in which one trait of a person (or thing) influences an overall judgement of that person (or thing).

1.3   Roles

▓ Role theory suggests that the behaviour of individuals in any given situation is in accordance to other people's expectations of how they should behave.

▓ Concepts of role theory include:

- **Role set**—the group of people with whom the focal person (with the focal role) interacts (e.g. tutor and students). Individuals need to be aware of the role set they inhabit at any given time in order to behave appropriately for that role.

- **Role definition**—combines the role expectations of the role set (e.g. a tutor and students will have ideas about what the role of a tutor should be).

- **Role signs**—indicates the role at that time to avoid confusion of others in the role set (e.g. uniform, style of work dress, "labels" such as name plates and size of office or desk, etc).

- **Role ambiguity**—Uncertainty of role (in the minds of either the focal person, or a person in their role set) about, for example, scope of responsibility, advancement opportunity, work evaluation, performance expectations, how friendly to be.

- **Role incompatibility**—arises when the expectations of members of the role set (or the focal member) are opposing as features of the same role (e.g. incompatibility on ethical issues between company policy and standards (to be carried out in a role) and an individual's personal or professional standards).

- **Role conflict**—arises when a person has to perform one or more roles in a situation (e.g. a career woman being expected to be the stereotypical male businessman).

1.4   Contribution to Work Performance

▓ Individuals are needed to perform various roles in organisations, groups and teams.

▓ For example, in team discussions and decision-making, there will be:

- a proposer—originator of ideas;
- clarifiers, supporters and builders;
- defenders, blockers and antagonists;
- experts; and
- all-rounders.

2 Groups

Definition

Group—a collection (two or more) of similar items. The term is usually applied to humans (e.g. a group of people). Technically, two people who interact with each other are sufficient to form a group.

Organisation (as a group)—in behavioural terms, "a collection of rights, privileges, obligations, and responsibilities that are delicately balanced over time through conflict and conflict resolution."

—*Laudon*

2.1 Characteristics

■ **Groups** will have certain characteristics which individuals may not.

■ For example:

* Identity (e.g. membership, sense of sharing, common activities).
* Purpose (e.g. common aims and objectives).
* Leadership (formal or informal).
* Accepted behaviour (e.g. norms of activity, output, productivity, relationships, dress, language—loyalty evolves from accepted behaviour).
* Communication channels.
* Personality and a sense of identity different from those of any individual in the group.
* Forming groups necessitates planning and organising on the part of the **organisation** and employee. Work planning is much easier once effective groups and teams are formed.

2.2 Individuals Within Groups

■ Each individual in a group will bring their own set of skills.
. To complete a particular task usually requires a range of skills.

■ The CEO of an international vehicle manufacturer cannot develop the organisation's strategy on his own. He will have strong skills in some areas, but not in others. As CEO, he is the leader of the executive management team. Between them, they will have all the skills necessary to develop the strategy.

■ A fitter on the production line will not have all the skills necessary to build a car. He will be part of a production team (operational group).

■ In a group, individuals are subservient to the rules of the group and follow group behaviour. By doing so, the achievement of a group is often far greater than what the individual could achieve alone. The individual's share of success from the group, therefore, is greater than any single individual's success.

■ Clearly, groups are relevant to both individuals (socially) and businesses (commercially) and so are widely used.

◼ Categories of individual behaviour in a group (such behaviour would not be shown as a group behaviour, unless all or the majority of the group members showed the same) include:

- solidarity/antagonism;
- agrees/disagrees;
- gives/asks for suggestions, opinions, information;
- bringing in/shutting out;
- clarifying, summarising;
- attacking/defending;
- stating difficulties;
- asking questions; and
- checking understanding.

Example 1 Individuals in Groups

Suggest THREE reasons why individuals are drawn into groups.

2.3 Formality

2.3.1 Informal

◼ Necessary for the successful operation of the organisation provided they do not transgress or conflict with the formal procedures and controls of the organisation.*

◼ Include workplace "cliques", workplace networks, corridor meetings, lunch groups, drinking buddies, etc. They have a constantly fluctuating membership and structure.

◼ Three types of informal relationship:

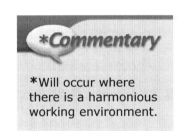

Commentary

*Will occur where there is a harmonious working environment.

1. Horizontal (e.g. two or more employees of similar seniority, but in different departments, share and seek information that does not come to them through the normal communications channel).

2. Ad hoc—similar to horizontal relationships, but the employees are not usually of the same seniority or grade.

3. Leap frog (line bypass)—occurs where there is a need to bypass immediate supervision/management (e.g. because of indecisiveness or information not available).

◼ Should not commit superiors without consultation on questions of policy, control or decisions affecting other groups.

◼ In some organisations, informal relationships are specifically prohibited by the organisation (e.g. Chinese walls established, for example, between an investment bank and a corporate finance department within the same financial firm).

◼ The presence of groups is often a major part of these informal relationships.

◼ A group may be formed specifically to deal with an ad hoc situation, or a group/relationship which exists for a formal purpose can be exploited to tackle an urgent project informally.

◼ In this way, informal social groups (important to employee culture) can exist as a sub-group in a large formal group as well as exist as separate entities.

2.3.2 Formal

- Consciously structured by organisations.

- They are usually task orientated and as such become teams (a group of people who share common objectives and need to work together to achieve them, have a leader and, usually, a distinct culture, status and style).

- Examples include appointed work groups, project teams, a board of directors, committees and a car assembly team.

3 Teams

3.1 Characteristics

- The main difference between a **team** and a group is the formality with which the participants interact with each other and the task to be achieved.

- A team is often referred to as a formal group. It will have specific goals, usually with specific roles for different members of the team but aiming to achieve a collective goal.

- A group, however, is just a collection of people with something in common (e.g. being in the same place at the same time or having a shared interest). Rather than a collective objective, members of a group are mainly concerned with their own interests.

Definition

Team—a small number of people with complementary skills who are committed to a common purpose, performance goals and approach for which they hold themselves accountable.

3.2 Purposes

The main purpose of a team is to achieve an objective in the most effective and efficient way by combining the strengths of individuals working together—as a team.

3.2.1 Identifying Strengths and Weaknesses

- Working in a team can mean a greater use of individual strengths—the collective skills of more than one person.

- Well-balanced teams will ensure that weaknesses are minimised.

3.2.2 Evaluating Opportunities and Threats

- Teams will be able to identify and evaluate opportunities and threats far more quickly and effectively than an individual.

- May be to an individual's benefit (e.g. being part of a team ensures greater work opportunities), to the team's benefit or to the organisation's (e.g. the board will be better than the CEO on his own).

3.2.3 Control

- The fear of "letting the side down" is a powerful motivator.

- Used to control the performance and behaviour of individuals.

- Management use teams to control work by defining responsibilities and delegating as appropriate.

3.2.4   Creative Thinking, Discussion and Decision-Making

- Brainstorming ("think tank")—the more brains, the more ideas; the broader the range of possibilities, the greater the chance of success.
- Group discussion provides greater depth of thought (wisdom) than individual thinking.
- When problems arise, information (external and internal) needs to be gathered, structured, evaluated and a decision made.
- Individuals who have been party to a decision are more likely to accept that decision based on their personal commitment to the choice.

3.2.5   Communication, Coordination and Integration

- Teams provide a framework for members from the same or different parts of the organisation to coordinate and integrate their efforts.
- Potentially complex (from the human perspective) and time-consuming procedures can be avoided.

3.2.6   Social and Emotional Support

- Maslow's hierarchy of needs includes social activity, ego and esteem and self-actualisation. Being a member of a team provides these requirements.
- Emotional support (encouragement, belonging, sharing difficult work, sounding board) is provided in the framework of a team.

3.2.7   Education and Instruction

- A team structure will quickly educate and instruct team members.
- New ideas and practices can be quickly accepted (or rejected).
- Team members will find it easier to keep up to date.

3.3   Composition

3.3.1   Nature of the Team

- There are two basic approaches to organising teamwork—multi-skilled teams and multi-disciplinary teams.
- Multi-disciplinary teams
  - Team members have different skills and specialisms.
  - Skills, experience and knowledge can be pooled or exchanged.
  - Increase members' awareness of objectives and targets.
  - Aid coordination and cooperation between different sections of the organisation.
- Multi-skilled teams
  - Team members can perform more than one task.
  - Allocation of resources and timing is flexible.

3.3.2 Team Requirements

▓ Team members should be good at getting things done and establishing good working relationships. Particular characteristics should therefore be evident in a team:

- Technical specialist skills—a team might exist to combine expertise from different departments.
- Power—team members may have influence.
- Access to resources—a team member may have access to a particular resource required by another team member.
- The personalities and goals of the individual members of the team—will help to determine the group's culture and goals.
- The blend of the individual skills and abilities of its members.

3.4 R.M. Belbin

R. Meredith Belbin drew up a list of the most effective character mix in a team. This involves nine necessary roles which should ideally be balanced and evenly "spread" in the team.*

3.4.1 Chairman Coordinator

▓ Presides and coordinates.

▓ Focuses on the team's objectives.

▓ Delegates work appropriately.

▓ Balanced, disciplined, objective, mature and good at working through others.

▓ Average in terms of intellect or creative ability.

3.4.2 Shaper

▓ Highly strung, dominant, extrovert, passionate about the task.

▓ A spur to action, drive and courage to overcome obstacles.

▓ Readiness to challenge inertia, complacency and ineffectiveness.

▓ Provides the necessary drive to ensure that the team keeps moving and does not lose focus or momentum.

▓ May easily provoke and irritate others and be impatient.

3.4.3 Plant

▓ Individualistic and introverted.

▓ Thoughtful and thought-provoking.

▓ Intellectually dominant, knowledgeable and imaginative.

▓ Good at solving problems in unconventional ways.

▓ Source of ideas and proposals, but often "up in the clouds".

▓ Can be forgetful or scatty.

3.4.4 Monitor-Evaluator

▓ Analytically (rather than creatively) intelligent.

▓ Sober, unemotional, prudent.

▓ Dissects ideas and spots flaws.

▓ Provides a logical eye and makes impartial judgements where required.

▓ Weighs the team's options in a dispassionate way.

▓ Brings team down to earth.

▓ Lacks inspiration or the ability to motivate others.

▓ Possibly aloof and tactless, but necessary.

*Commentary

*Belbin noted that people often display a mix of characteristics, so it is not necessary for teams to have exactly one member representing each type. Her experiments showed that teams consisting of one type, or a limited number of types, fared badly against role-balanced teams.

3.4.5 Resource Investigator

- Popular, sociable, extrovert, relaxed.
- A capacity for generating new contacts; a team's link to the outside world.
- Responds to a challenge.
- Not an originator of ideas, but adds value to the ideas of others.
- Will lose interest fairly quickly.

3.4.6 Implementer (Company Worker)

- Conservative, dutiful, predictable.
- Organising ability, scheduling, planning.
- Can plan a practical, workable strategy and carry it out as efficiently as possible.
- Practical common sense, turning general ideas into specifics.
- Trustworthy and efficient.
- Lack of flexibility, unresponsive to unproved ideas.
- Not a leader, but an administrator.

3.4.7 Team Worker

- Most concerned with team maintenance and social aspects.
- Helps the team to "gel".
- Supportive, understanding, diplomatic, popular.
- Ability to respond to people and situations.
- Uses versatility to identify the work required and complete it on behalf of the team.
- Uncompetitive and indecisive at moments of crisis.
- Sometimes, contribution may only be noticed in their absence (e.g. tend to work in background).

3.4.8 Finisher Completer

- Most effectively used at the end of a task.
- Painstaking, orderly, conscientious, anxious.
- Chivvies the team to meet deadlines.
- Attends to details; perfectionist.
- Urgency and follow-through are important.
- Will "polish" and scrutinise the work for errors.
- Applies high standards of quality control.
- Tendency to worry about small things.
- Reluctance to "let go".
- Not always popular.

3.4.9 Specialist Expert

- Single-minded, self-starting, dedicated.
- Passionate about learning in their own field.
- High level of concentration, ability and skill.
- Tendency to prioritise their own expertise over the team's progress.
- Only interested in their own discipline, overlook the "whole".

4   Team Development (Tuckman)

It may take some time for a group of people who do not know each other to become effective as a team. Bruce W. Tuckman described four stages through which groups proceed to team development.

4.1   Stage 1: Forming

- No more than a collection of individuals seeking to define the purpose of the group and how it will operate.
- Each individual wants to impress his personality on the group.
- Members will be trying to find out about each other and the aims and norms of the team.
- Members are wary about introducing new ideas.
- Objectives being pursued may as yet be unclear and a leader may not yet have emerged.
- May be time-wasting: the team as a whole will not be used to its autonomy.

4.2   Stage 2: Storming

- This frequently involves more or less open conflict between team members.
- Infighting usually revolves around control and dominance and/ or values and principles.
- Sub-grouping into alliances and cliques may occur. This can easily upset any balance in the team and make it difficult for the team to work together.
- Team members will closely watch an appointed leader/manager to assess the role. Trust and respect must be earned from both sides. The manager's leadership, persuasion, negotiation and conflict resolution skills will be tested at this stage.
- There may be changes agreed in the original objectives, procedures and norms established for the team.
- If the team is developing successfully and already has a good blend of personality types (Belbin), then the team can set more realistic targets as trust between the team members increases.

4.3   Stage 3: Norming

- A period of settling down.
- Team members begin to experiment and test reactions as the norms become established.
- Procedures will evolve which enable methodical working to be introduced and maintained.
- There will be agreements about work sharing, individual requirements and expectations of output.
- Approaches to decision-making, behaviour, trust and openness are established.
- Mutual support develops and the team members begin to meld and place team priorities over personal ones.
- Good team managers will ensure that this period is as harmonious as possible. They have in-depth insight to team dynamics.

- This period is shortest when team members are specialists who have worked in similar roles in other teams with similar cultures and expectations or are at the operational level (e.g. work groups) with defined, basic roles.

- Teams formed from the top management of organisations often take the longest to progress through this stage because the subjective, high-risk and complex nature of their work demands exemplary cooperation and understanding.

4.4   Stage 4: Performing

- The team sets to work to execute its task and operate to its full potential.

- The difficulties of growth and development no longer hinder the group's objectives.

- Team relationships have been resolved, roles established, strengths and weaknesses identified and accounted for, communication improved and working methods refined.

- The collective drive is external (to achieve the task) rather than internal (self-destruction).

- The team has become effective.*

Example 2   Dorming
Suggest the characteristics of a team in the "dorming" stage.

> *Commentary*
>
> *A fifth stage, **dorming**, has been identified by John Adair. Some writers also consider that a "mourning/adjourning" stage should be added where the team sees itself as having fulfilled its purpose and will shortly be disbanded or move on to another task.

5   Team Building

5.1   Successful Teams

Successful teams display:

- **Unity of purpose.** Each team member is fully aware of the purpose (objectives) of the team and his role in the team.

- **Understanding and interaction.** This implies well-established verbal, written and non-verbal (physical) communication between members of the team.

- **Cohesiveness of actions.** Team members tend to think and act broadly the same.

- **Shared standards.** Over time, team members develop their own set of behavioural rules; a team code of conduct.

- **Acceptance of a leader.** All teams must be led. The team leader may be an automatic selection when the team is formed or may come to the fore as the team develops. The team leader is fully accepted by all the team members.

5.2 Team-Building Issues

- Team identity:
  - individual team members feel part of the team; and
  - are recognised as part of the team.
- Team solidarity:
  - team members are loyal to the team and each other;
  - will excel "beyond the call of duty" for the sake of the team; and
  - requires good management to control inter-member competition and conflict and ensure fairness.
- Team objectives:
  - are accepted and shared; and
  - receive team members' willing and effective cooperation in achieving them.

5.3 Team-Building Tools

Woodcock ("Team Development Manual") refers to the "building blocks (tools) of effective teamwork". Basically, if these tools are applied to the team then overall performance will improve.

5.3.1 Balanced Roles

- Blend of different talents, abilities and personalities.
- Gaps may be identified and therefore filled.
- Team members must be suitably qualified.

5.3.2 Clear Objectives and Agreed Goals

- Involve the team members in developing objectives and goals.
- Ensure that personal and team objectives converge as much as possible.
- Emphasis on results required (outcomes) rather than on work to do (processes).
- Review on a regular basis and update.

5.3.3 Openness and Confrontation

- Encourage constructive views.
- Encourage full communication and feedback.
- Develop self-awareness and willingness to ask for help.
- Discourage ridicule or retaliation.
- Do not avoid unpleasant issues.

5.3.4 Support and Trust

- Support is "to strengthen by assistance".
- Listen, praise, appreciate, encourage and deal with real issues.
- Trust must be built over time (but can be destroyed in seconds).
- Honest dealing, pragmatism, predictability and loyalty.

5.3.5 Cooperation and Conflict

- Cooperation is working together.
- Team members share knowledge, experience, etc.
- No hidden agendas.
- Conflict is usually inevitable in teams.

- Positive conflict is being open, honest, putting personalities aside and solving problems.

- Negative conflict can quickly destroy any trust built up in the team. The manager must act as counsellor to quickly eliminate the reasons for negative conflict.

5.3.6 Sound Procedures

- Teams are formed to achieve objectives.

- To do so requires effective procedures and methods.

- All team members must know, understand and accept the procedures.

- Depending on the nature of the team, all should be involved in establishing procedures.

- Establishing procedures involves decision-making.

5.3.7 Appropriate Leadership

- The team leader may be the same individual throughout the life of the team or until the objective has been achieved.

- Leadership may change between team members as the tasks required to be completed by the team also change.

- Leaders must adapt their style (telling, selling, participation or delegation) to suit the team and objective.

- Whoever the leader is, that individual must be recognised as "the best of the best" and respected for their leadership skills by the rest of the team.

5.3.8 Regular Review

- Constructive feedback is essential to keep on target, build up trust and support in the team and to improve individual and team performance in the future.

- Review and feedback can be internal, carried out by the team manager or as a peer review, at regular intervals (e.g. when "milestones" or critical success factors have been reached).

- An external review also can be used (e.g. consultants, feedback from other departments, customer surveys, secret shopper, etc).

5.3.9 Individual Development

- For the team to progress, individual members must also progress.

- New or improved personal or technical skills can be trained.

- In multi-skilled teams, members can learn from each other.

- Personal and managerial skills can be developed by observation.

- Development is also self-fulfilment, being content, in tune with life.

- The manager must be aware of individual development requirements.

- Room must be made in a team for individuals to develop inwardly as well as outwardly.

5.3.10 **Sound Inter-Group Relations**

■ Team members are subsystems of the team.

■ Team members must be on good terms with each other.

■ Each team is a subsystem of the organisation.

■ Teams need to work together for the good of the organisation.

5.3.11 **Good Communications**

■ Individuals, teams and organisations need information.

■ Information must be given, received, understood and acted on.

■ Team members who know the following are far more likely to be effective in their team than those who do not:

- What is happening.
- Why it is happening.
- When it is happening.
- Where it is happening.
- How it is happening.
- Who it is happening to.

Example 3   Sound Inter-Group Relations

Applying the building-blocks concept, list the actions which could be taken to ensure sound inter-departmental relations within an organisation.

5.4   Barriers to Team Building

There are many reasons why a particular function may not be achieved. If the characteristics for successful teams are known, then unsuccessful teams will display the opposite characteristics. For example:

✗   Unbalanced roles.

✗   Confused objectives; tasks forced on team members without agreement.

✗   Unconstructive and confrontational group culture; no feedback.

✗   Insincere praise, appreciation or encouragement; trust is broken.

✗   Uncooperative team members, hidden agendas, self-interest.

✗   Procedures distrusted by team members; lack of involvement in decision-making.

✗   Lack of, or poor, communication.

✗   Inappropriate leader.

✗   Non-existent review and individual development.

5.5   Effective v Ineffective Groups

Effective Groups	Ineffective Groups
✔ Informal, relaxed atmosphere.	✗ Bored or tense atmosphere.
✔ Much relevant discussion with a high degree of participation.	✗ Discussion dominated by one or two people and often irrelevant.
✔ Group task or objective clearly understood and commitment to it obtained.	✗ No clear common objective.
✔ Members listen to each other.	✗ Members tend not to listen to each other.
✔ Conflict is not avoided, but brought into the open and dealt with constructively.	✗ Conflict is either avoided or is allowed to escalate into open warfare.
✔ Most decisions are reached by general consensus with a minimum of formal voting.	✗ Simple majorities are seen as sufficient basis for group decisions, which the minority have to accept.
✔ Ideas are expressed freely and openly.	✗ Personal feelings are kept hidden and criticism is embarrassing.
✔ Leadership is not always with the chairman, but tends to be shared as appropriate.	✗ Leadership is provided by the chairman (by implication, tending to be rather autocratic).
✔ The group examines its own progress and behaviour.	✗ The group avoids any discussion about its own behaviour.

6   Performance and Rewards

6.1   Considerations

- The team's performance determines the outcome of the project/task performance.
- Individual and team objectives must be set.
- Measurement criteria must be agreed with each team member and the team as a whole.
- Individual performance will be measured against job descriptions.
- Team performance will be measured against the task specification.

6.2   Measures of Performance

- Output and use of assets (i.e. productivity).
- Budgetary measures (e.g. time and cost constraints).
- Quality control (e.g. no more than x% of product must be rejected).
- Time and motion ratings.
- Increase in market share.
- Participation and team interaction.
- Satisfaction enjoyed by group members.
- Increase in team and individual knowledge and experience.

Care must be taken when considering effectiveness. A team target may be to cut production costs by 25%. In doing so, the team uses inferior materials and meets the objective—but maintenance and repair costs increase.

6.3   Rewards

- May be categorised as:*
    - **Extrinsic** (e.g. salary, bonus, promotion).
    - **Intrinsic** (e.g. achievement, recognition, advancement, job satisfaction).
    - **Personal** (e.g. salary, bonus, benefits, recognition, job satisfaction, achievement, promotion).
    - **Team** (e.g. bonus, benefits, recognition).
- Personal rewards must be seen to be fair by the team as a whole.
- Personal rewards should be benchmarked against personal attributes rather than team attributes (although these may play a part in individual achievement).
- Team rewards and how such rewards will be distributed should be agreed with the team.
- The method of sharing (e.g. a bonus) must be deemed fair and in relation to the effort by each team member. (A common method is to distribute as a % of salary—this does, however, ignore the contribution towards achieving the task by each individual member).
- The process of making the reward must be transparent e.g. personal rewards voted on by the team members (worker of the month) or generally recognised as an outstanding contribution.

*Commentary

*Extrinsic and intrinsic rewards are discussed in detail in *Session 20*.

Summary

- Individuals seek to satisfy physiological, safety and security needs; once these basic needs are satisfied, individuals seek social activity and self-fulfilment.

- *Role theory* suggests the behaviour of individuals in any given situation is in accordance to other people's expectations of how they should behave.

- Groups have characteristics such as identity, purpose, formal or informal leadership, communication channels and norms of behaviour.

- Groups allow individuals to access skills of other individuals.
  - Formal groups are sanctioned by organisations.
  - Informal groups are not consciously sanctioned and typically will be horizontal, ad hoc or leap frog.

- Teams are small numbers of people with complementary skills who commit to a common purpose and hold themselves accountable. Teams always have more formality and, thus, structure.

- Belbin's mix of effective team characteristics includes:
  - a coordinator (chairman);
  - a shaper who spurs the group to action;
  - a plant who solves problems in unconventional ways;
  - a monitor-evaluator to make impartial judgements;
  - an investigator;
  - an implementer who administers for the team;
  - a team worker to hold the team together;
  - a finisher; and
  - an expert (specialist).

- Stages of teamwork often include forming, storming, norming, performing (and some have suggested dorming and mourning/adjourning).

- Successful teams should have balanced roles, clear objectives, openness, trust, cooperation and conflict, sound procedures, appropriate leadership, regular review, individual development, sound inter-group relations and good communications.

- Team rewards may include extrinsic (salary, bonus), intrinsic (recognition) and may be rewarded either personally or as a team. Methods of sharing a team reward must be deemed fair and related to each member's effort.

Session 19 Quiz
Estimated time: 20 minutes

1. Explain the concept of "role theory" and list SIX roles. (1.3)
2. Explain what is meant by "a team". (3.1)
3. State the characteristics of Belbin's "monitor-evaluator". (3.4)
4. Briefly describe the FIVE stages of team development. (4)
5. List FIVE characteristics of successful teams. (5.1)

Study Question Bank
Estimated time: 45 minutes

Priority		Estimated Time	Completed
MCQ19	Individuals, Groups and Teams	45 minutes	

EXAMPLE SOLUTIONS

Solution 1—Individuals in Groups

- A preference for smaller units rather than large (a crowd).
- The need to belong and be appreciated.
- Familiar surroundings, sounds and other members.
- Common interests, social group and objectives.
- The particular activity carried out by the group.
- Available resources within the group.
- Greater power.

Solution 2—Dorming

- A "sixth sense" is developed in the team. Team members know what other team members are doing. Trust is implicit. The team is mature.
- However, there is a danger that team members (and therefore the team) become complacent and go into auto-pilot with no fresh energy or attention focused on the task (even if it changes).
- Efforts are devoted primarily to maintaining the team itself—a social function rather than an objective function.
- In some cases, the team takes on an air of self-satisfaction and superiority ("group think"), moving further away from reality and rejecting anything that does not conform to the members' requirements.

Solution 3—Sound Inter-Group Relations

The organisation is considered to be the team; each department in the organisation, a team member.

A number of ideas can be used in more than one building block.

Not all ideas will be applicable to all organisations. Each organisation must select those which are appropriate to its culture to fully develop sound inter-group relations.

- **Balanced roles**

    Each department should be established for a specific reason by the organisation's board. Specific functions (e.g. HR, production) should be controlled by their respective departments (i.e. "stick to the knitting"—*Peters*). Overlap and conflict of interest should be avoided.

- **Clear objectives and agreed goals**

    The board will set the strategic (long-term) objectives for the organisation as a whole. As the board will consist of directors responsible for each department (e.g. finance director, sales director, etc), the strategic objectives would have been discussed and agreed.

    Each individual department's objectives also would have been discussed and agreed at board level. Directors will then be responsible to ensure that their teams (in each department) are fully aware of their tasks and objectives, the objectives of the other departments and how all objectives meld to achieve the strategic objective.

- **Openness and confrontation**

    The directors must be open and constructive in their views of each other's departments. Ridicule or retaliation at board level will feed down to each department, causing relationships between departments to break down.

    Managers and supervisors of each department should be able to meet on a regular and needs basis. This could be through formal meetings or informal gatherings (e.g. shared canteens, social clubs, organised events).

- **Support, trust, cooperation and conflict**

    Every opportunity should be taken by the directors for departments to work together (cooperate) on projects, even if as observers or by being kept informed of what is happening.

    Cross-departmental teams can be formed (e.g. the Alpha bike team involving all departments in the Alpha bike project). This ties in all departments into the success of the project and eliminates any territorial feeling (e.g. "the project was our idea, why should we involve your department?").

    Share knowledge management between all departments to ensure that knowledge from all departments is open.

    A disputes procedure should be established across all departments to arbitrate inter-departmental disputes which cannot be resolved. The directors and managers must ensure that departments do not perceive that there are winners and losers; only the organisation should be a winner.

- **Sound procedures**

    No one department should be favoured in any way by a given procedure. All should be considered equal. Procedures should be discussed by all departments and approved by the board to ensure consistency of application. This ensures that all departments have ownership of the procedure and will thus be more willing to accept the procedure.

- **Appropriate leadership**

  At the board level, new directors will be jointly agreed by the current directors. (In partnerships, it is common that all partners must agree).

  Most companies also have a policy for current managers to participate in the decision to hire new managers and senior managers, regardless of what department they are in.

  This reduces the possibility of appointing new managers/directors considered inappropriate by their peers.

  Regular review of each department's performance will be carried out at the board level. Ideally this should be fed down to and between individual departments (e.g. monthly newsletters, for open review and discussion).

- **Individual development**

  Although this implies it means an individual, it can also apply to each department being aware of what the others do. This can be achieved by:

  - job experience programmes (e.g. working in another department for a short while);
  - joint training courses (e.g. working as a team);
  - joint meetings;
  - regular presentations by each department (e.g. developments in the last six months in the R&D department); and
  - promotion and movement between departments.

- **Good communications**

  Communication between departments can be formal or informal. The formal level will cover board meetings, manager meetings, employee meetings, newsletters, use of intranets and extranets. The informal level will be opportunities to meet on a regular basis (e.g. rest areas, joint canteens, social clubs, coffee areas, etc).

Motivating Individuals and Groups

FOCUS

This session covers the following content from the *ACCA Study Guide.*

D. Leading and Managing Individuals and Teams

5. Motivating individuals and groups

a) Define motivation and explain its importance to the organisation, teams and individuals.

b) Explain content and process theories of motivation: Maslow, Herzberg, McGregor and Vroom.

c) Explain and identify types of intrinsic and extrinsic reward.

d) Explain how reward systems can be designed and implemented to motivate teams and individuals.

Session 20 Guidance

■ **Note** that this is a **highly examinable** area with many key theories.

■ **Know** the theorists, the distinction between content and process theories and the link between rewards and motivation.

(continued on next page)

VISUAL OVERVIEW

Objective: To define motivation and consider motivation theories.

```
                        ┌─────────────────────────┐
                        │        MOTIVATION        │
                        └─────────────────────────┘
                            /                \
                           /                  \
   ┌──────────────────────────┐     ┌──────────────────────────┐
   │   THEORIES OF MOTIVATION  │     │      PRACTICAL TOOLS      │
   │                           │     │                           │
   │  • Types of Theory        │     │  • Financial Motivators   │
   │  • Content Theories       │     │  • Non-financial Motivators│
   │  • Process Theories       │     │  • Management Involvement │
   │  • McGregor               │     │  • Rewards and Motivation │
   │                           │     │  • Feedback               │
   └──────────────────────────┘     └──────────────────────────┘
```

Session 20 Guidance

■ **Recognise** differences between content theories (s.2.2) which ask, "**What** are the things that motivate people?" (Maslow, Herzberg), and process theories (s.2.3) which ask, "**How** can people be motivated?" (Vroom, McGregor).

■ **Understand** the importance of management involvement in preventing demotivation (s.3.3) as well as the differences between extrinsic and intrinsic rewards (s.3.4).

1 Motivation

Definition

Motivation—the combination of internal and external factors which stimulate desire and energy in people to seek a different state of being. It is the energiser of behaviour and catalyst of all action. In the work environment, motivation creates interest in and commitment to a job, role or subject and stimulates persistent effort to attain a goal.

▓ **Motivation** is about influencing organism behaviour. The need to motivate humans to work has provoked much interest from which a number of ideas, theories and models of motivation have emerged.

▓ In the work environment, motivators are forces which:

- induce individuals to perform; and
- influence human behaviour.

▓ Motivation is a continuous inner process which stimulates, sustains and regulates behaviour towards a specific goal or end. It is:

- all those inner tensions or the needs described as hopes, wishes, desires, fears, or intentions which activate and move people;

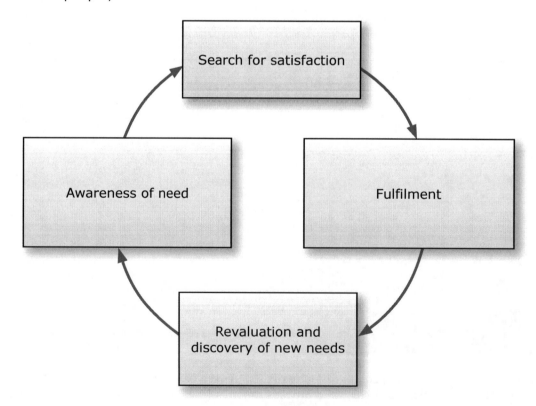

● the will, urge, drive or compulsion to do something, to achieve goals—eat, drink, seek shelter, throw a punch, run a marathon, become an accountant, produce more and better goods at lower cost.

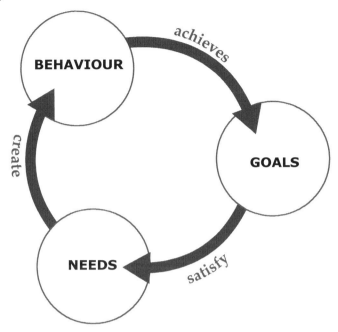

2 Theories of Motivation

2.1 Types of Theory

■ **Motivation theory** describes motivation based on employing identified motivating factors.

■ **Content (needs) theory** focuses on what stimulates, sustains and regulates good directed behaviour (i.e. what particular things motivate people).

■ **Process theory** attempts to explain and describe how people start, sustain and direct behaviour aimed at satisfying needs or reducing inner tension.

■ Content and process theories have been used by management thinkers and practising managers in efforts to motivate work.

2.2 Content Theories

■ Content theories suggest that the urge to commit time and energy to tasks depends on the work or task itself and the rewards gained from completion.

■ The nature of content theories suggests that each person is motivated by the same factors and, in some theories, to the same degree by those factors.

2.2.1 Maslow's Hierarchy of Needs

■ Maslow proposed that people have a complex set of needs which may be arranged in a hierarchy (order of priority) to be satisfied sequentially. This is usually depicted in the form of a pyramid:

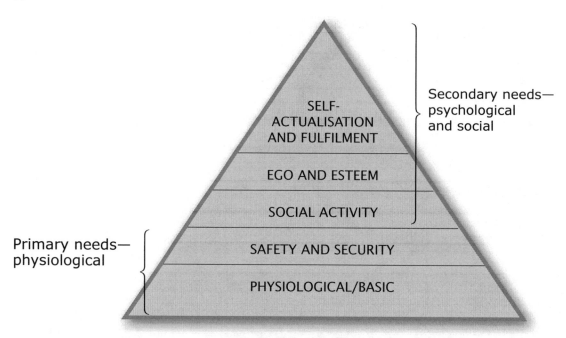

- **Physiological**—need for food, liquid, shelter, sleep, etc, that is no longer needed for a while once satisfied.
- **Security**—need for predictability and order.
- **Social**—need to belong, to be accepted by others.
- **Esteem**—need for achievement, status, respect and recognition by others.
- **Self-actualisation**—realising full potential for self-development.

■ Comments on Maslow's theory include:

- A satisfied need does not motivate. When a need has been satisfied, another need emerges to take its place, so people are always striving to satisfy some need.
- The need interactions of most people are complex, with a number of needs affecting the behaviour of each person at any one time.
- In general, primary needs must be satisfied before secondary needs are activated sufficiently to provoke motivated behaviour.
- There are more varied ways of satisfying secondary needs than there are of satisfying primary needs.

2.2.2   Herzberg's Two-Factor Theory

▦ In the 1950s, Herzberg published research based on a survey of 200 accountants and engineers about events at work that had removed or provided job satisfaction.

▦ Herzberg started with the proposition that each work situation has some satisfying and some dissatisfying features. He concluded that factors that satisfy come from a totally different area in the work situation from those which dissatisfy.

▦ Herzberg's contention is that man has two sets of needs:

- "**Maintenance**" or "**hygiene**" needs—associated with the side of man's nature that wants to avoid pain. These primary determinants of job *dissatisfaction* are *extrinsic* aspects of the job.
- "**Motivation**" needs—which man has for satisfying his desire for achievement, recognition and growth. These primary determinants of job *satisfaction* are *intrinsic* aspects of the job.

▦ **Hygiene** factors are workplace conditions (factors) which the survey suggested should be present, maintained and undisturbed to prevent dissatisfaction:

- company policy;
- supervision;
- salary;
- relationship with peers/subordinates;
- working conditions;
- status; and
- security.

▦ If any of these factors decrease, the employee may become demotivated. If they increase, then the employee may be motivated, until the increase becomes the accepted norm. If the factors then return to their original level, the employee may become demotivated.

▦ Motivators are factors contributing to high levels of job satisfaction and personal growth:

- achievement;
- recognition;
- work itself;
- responsibility;
- advancement; and
- growth.

■ Herzberg also identified three approaches that management can follow in attempting to improve staff satisfaction and motivation.

1. **Job enrichment**—a deliberate, planned process to improve the responsibility and challenge of a job (e.g. delegation or problem solving).

2. **Job enlargement**—widening the range of jobs and so developing a job away from narrow specialisation.

3. **Job rotation**—planned rotating of staff between jobs to alleviate monotony and provide a fresh job challenge. It may take two forms:

   —transferring employees to another job after a period of time to provide a new interest and challenge and to bring a fresh person to the job being vacated;

   —as a form of training, with trainees spending a shorter period in each job before being moved on.

2.3 Process Theories

■ Process theory and process models of motivation depart from the assumption in content theories that everyone responds in much the same way to motivating pressures and that there is, therefore, one best way to motivate everybody.

■ Process theory seeks to explain how motivation occurs given an individual's *personal* needs and goals.

■ Process theories propose that, when going through a conscious decision process, various factors are taken into consideration in determining the level of effort expended on a task.

2.3.1 Vroom

■ Victor Vroom considers that people will expend effort if they believe:

• in the worth of the goal; and

• that there is a reasonable chance that performing the task will lead to achievement of the goal:

- The expectancy model states that motivation (strength of an action) is (=) a product (×) of how much one wants something (the "reward value" or "valence" reflecting preference and priority in personal goals) and one's estimate of the probability that a certain action will secure it ("expectancy").

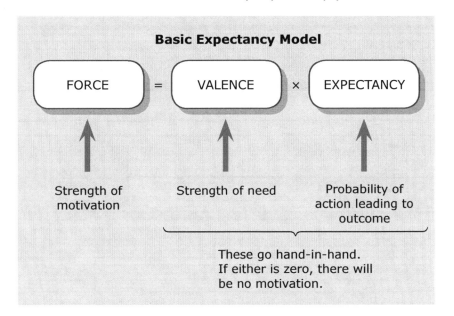

Basic Expectancy Model

FORCE = VALENCE × EXPECTANCY

Strength of motivation

Strength of need

Probability of action leading to outcome

These go hand-in-hand. If either is zero, there will be no motivation.

- The refinement and extension of the basic model aimed to identify the influences on a person's job performance and job satisfaction and took into account such factors as the:
  - value of the reward for effect;
  - perceived effort—reward relationship;
  - energy expended to perform a task;
  - individual's ability and personal traits;
  - individual's perceptions of a work role;
  - characteristics of performance;
  - nature of the rewards available (intrinsic or extrinsic); and
  - perceived equity of rewards and satisfaction (the individual's internal state).

- Recommendations to management that go with this model include:
  - Discover what outcome each employee values most.
  - Define the desired or required performance (i.e. explain what constitutes "adequate performance" necessary to achieve a goal).
  - Ensure that the desired levels of performance are achievable.
  - Link the outcomes desired by employees to the specific performance desired by management.
  - Ensure that the overall motivation strategy avoids conflict (e.g. between the positive expectations it seeks to create and other factors in the work situation).
  - Make outcome or rewards sufficiently attractive to motivate the desired level of performance.

2.3.2 Porter and Lawler

■ A more complex extension of Vroom's process theory of motivation, which takes into account a wide range of factors to determine effort (or motivation).

Exam Advice

This model is **not examinable** but provided as an aid to understanding the relationships between effort and rewards.

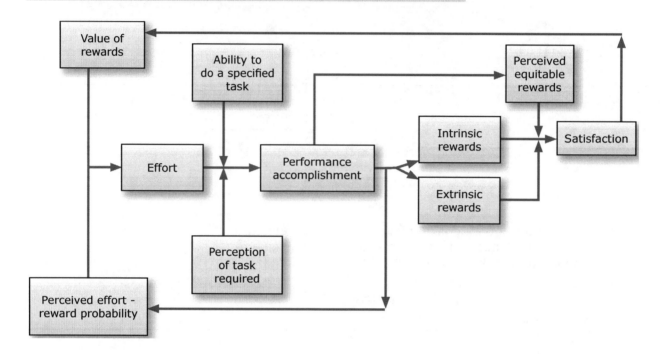

2.4 McGregor

■ Douglas McGregor, a psychologist, challenged some of the assumptions managers make about people in organisations. He proposed a range of behaviour patterns between two extremes called "Theory X" and "Theory Y".

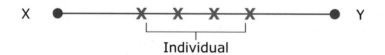

■ Both theories have essentially the same aim, that management should organise the elements of productive enterprise (money, people, equipment) in the interest of economic ends.*

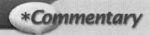

*Commentary

*Note that both Maslow's and McGregor's theories are relevant to management theories and leadership styles.

2.4.1 Theory X

- People are managed by directing, motivating and controlling them and modifying their behaviour to fit the organisation's needs.

- People are motivated mainly by money* and anxiety about their security.

- Most people must be coerced, controlled, directed and threatened, otherwise they would be passive and resistant to organisational needs.

- People must be forced or bribed to put in the right effort.

- The average person:
  - lacks ambition;
  - dislikes work;
  - avoids work;
  - avoids responsibility;
  - wants to be led;
  - is self-centred;
  - resists change;
  - seeks security;
  - is gullible and not very bright; and
  - is mainly motivated by money.*

2.4.2 Theory Y

- Management must arrange organisational conditions and methods of operation so people can achieve their own goals by directing their efforts towards business goals.

- People are not by nature passive or resistant to organisational needs, but have become so as a result of experience in work organisations and industrialisation.

- Motivation, the potential for development and the capacity for assuming responsibility are present in all people.

- The expenditure of physical and mental effort in work is as natural as rest or play.

- Commitment to task is a function of rewards available.

- The average person:
  - accepts responsibility;
  - learns to seek responsibility; and
  - will exercise self-direction towards accepted goals.

- Imagination, ingenuity and creativity are widely distributed.

- Intellectual potential is only ever partially utilised.

---

*Commentary

*One of the great (and unresolved) debates concerns the role of money as a motivator. The arguments can be considered, but conclusions must be drawn on an individual basis.

---

3   Practical Motivation Tools

3.1   Financial Motivators

- Summary of financial motivation theories:
  - Maslow—money satisfies basic needs directly and higher needs indirectly.
  - Herzberg—hygiene factor, unless salary implies status.
  - Vroom—depends on how much you need it.

- Payment by results (in terms of commission or piece-rates) or performance-related pay is therefore appropriate in the right circumstances.

3.2 Non-financial Motivators

- Various non-financial tools are available to motivate staff:
  - Participation.
  - Environment.
  - Job design:
    - enrichment (e.g. greater variety, challenge, responsibility);
    - enlargement (e.g. increase the number of operators);
    - rotation (e.g. exchange of jobs to break monotony).
  - Social factors.
  - Opportunity for self-development.

3.3 Management Involvement

- Management must effectively use all available resources to ensure that the operational, departmental and organisational goals are achieved.

- Ensuring that all employees are motivated to work to their optimum performance is not a straightforward task. Each employee is unique and will therefore have a personal set of motivators (process theory).

- Ideally, the manager must identify personal motivators and apply them in congruence with the organisation's goals.

Example 1 Motivating Staff

Describe SIX ways in which management can motivate staff.

3.4 Rewards and Motivation

- To management, motivation is about encouraging extra performance from employees by controlling their work environment.

- Management's control of the employee's environment will be seen as a motivator (by the employee) only if the environment meets the employee's needs. Such control may be through rewards for past efforts or as incentives to encourage improved future performance (or to maintain a high level of future performance).

3.4.1 Criteria

- Rewards offered to employees may be extrinsic or intrinsic. Child has outlined six criteria for rewards, whether extrinsic or intrinsic. The rewards must:

  1. Encourage people to fill job vacancies and to stay in their job (i.e. not leave).

  2. Increase the predictability of employees' behaviour, so that employees can be depended on to carry out their duties consistently and to a reasonable standard.

  3. Increase willingness to accept change and flexibility. (Changes in work practices are often "bought" from trade unions with higher pay.)

  4. Foster and encourage innovative behaviour.

5. Reflect the nature of jobs in the organisation and the skills or experience required. The reward system should therefore be consistent with seniority of position in the organisational structure and should be considered to be fair by all employees.

6. Motivate (increase commitment and effort).

3.4.2 Extrinsic Rewards

▓ Extrinsic rewards are not within the control of the employee.

Example 2 Extrinsic Rewards

Identify SIX groups of extrinsic rewards, giving examples.

▓ Extrinsic rewards may not always be motivators, but the lack of such extrinsic rewards may be considered demotivators. Many aspects of pay and related benefits rewarded with particular jobs are expected with such jobs (e.g. managers have cars, pensions, healthcare, etc).

▓ Money rewards do not satisfy many of Maslow's needs (e.g. physiological, security, esteem and self-actualisation).

▓ Research has shown that pay will be able to "buy off" the lack of other factors (e.g. poor working conditions) only up to the point where the employee considers "enough is enough". Such points are dependent on the cost which each employee is prepared to pay to forego other factors for higher pay.

3.4.3 Intrinsic Rewards

▓ Although made available by the organisation, intrinsic rewards are unique to each employee and, thus, under each employee's control. For example:
  - companionship;
  - achievement;
  - status and recognition;
  - job interest;
  - participation; and
  - responsibility.
▓ Factors which affect intrinsic rewards include job:
  - design;
  - enrichment (e.g. vertical enhancement);
  - enlargement (e.g. horizontal enhancement); and
  - rotation.

3.5   Feedback

▓ Feedback allows an employee to assess performance against a standard. Such feedback provides an opportunity for the employee to adjust performance.

▓ Constructive feedback occurs when the employee considers the feedback to be of benefit and becomes motivated to implement recommendations made in order to improve.

Summary

- Motivation theory describes motivation based on employing identified motivating factors.

- Content theory focuses on particular things which motivate people.

- Process theory attempts to expand content theory by determining each *individual's* motivators rather than relying on a standard set of motivators.

- Content theories such as Maslow's hierarchy or Herzberg's two-factor theory suggest that the urge to commit time and energy to tasks depends on the work or task itself and the rewards gained from completion.

- Herzberg identified three approaches to improve staff satisfaction and motivation:

  - job enrichment, which addresses improving the responsibility and challenge of a job;

  - job enlargement, which addresses increasing the scope of the job itself; and

  - job rotation, which involves either a) transferring employees after time in a position to increase interest, or b) spending a shorter period in each job before moving on.

- Process theories propose that various factors are taken into consideration in determining the level of effort expended on a task.

- Vroom proposed that workers must believe in the worth of the goal and in a reasonable probability of success in order to justify expending effort.

- Vroom's recommendations include ensuring that success is achievable; defining adequate performance to succeed; linking organisational success to employee rewards; and making sure the system motivates and does not cause conflicts.

- McGregor proposed a continuum in which management believes that workers:

  - are lazy and must be motivated by a carrot-and-stick approach (Theory X); or

  - seek fulfilment in their work and must simply be directed in their efforts towards the organisation's desired outcomes (Theory Y).

- Extrinsic rewards typically will be controlled by management; intrinsic rewards are created within each employee and must be discovered by management.

Session 20 Quiz
Estimated time: 15 minutes

1. Briefly explain the difference between the content and process theories of motivation. (2.1)
2. List the stages of Maslow's hierarchy of needs. (2.2)
3. Explain the differences between McGregor's Theory X and Theory Y. (2.4)
4. List SIX intrinsic rewards. (3.4)

Study Question Bank
Estimated time: 35 minutes

Priority		Estimated Time	Completed
MCQ20	Motivating Individuals and Groups	35 minutes	

EXAMPLE SOLUTIONS

Solution 1—Motivating Staff

- Recognise and meet their needs as far as possible.
- Recognise that employees are human and have feelings.
- Delegate decision-making and responsibility as far as possible.
- Monitor performance and give constructive feedback on performance—praise is as important as criticism.
- Ensure aims are clear—do not confuse then criticise.
- Be available, be consistent.
- Be sincere.
- Follow through.

Solution 2—Extrinsic Rewards

- Wages, salary.
- Pensions, life insurance, private healthcare.
- Bonuses, performance-related pay and like rewards.
- Payment of employee expenses, season ticket loans, crèches.
- Working conditions.
- Training opportunities (e.g. ACCA, MBA).
- A car, mobile phone, home computer, etc.

Training and Development

FOCUS

This session covers the following content from the *ACCA Study Guide.*

D. Leading and Managing Individuals and Teams

6. Learning and training at work

a) Explain the importance of learning and development in the workplace. ☐

b) Describe the learning process: Honey and Mumford, Kolb. ☐

c) Describe the role of the human resources department and individual managers in the learning process. ☐

d) Describe the training and development process: identifying needs, setting objectives, programme design, delivery and validation. ☐

e) Explain the terms "training", "development" and "education" and the characteristics of each. ☐

f) List the benefits of effective training and development in the workplace. ☐

Session 21 Guidance

■ **Note** that training and development contain a wide range of examinable topics and can be linked with appraisal and performance management.

■ **Understand** the overall purpose and importance of training as well as the difference in approach between training and development (s.1).

■ **Recognise** the different schools of thought regarding how people learn. Make sure that you know the difference between behaviourist psychology and the cognitive approach and study the learning styles according to Honey and Mumford, and Kolb (s.2).

(continued on next page)

VISUAL OVERVIEW

Objective: To explain the importance of training and development within organisations.

```
                    TRAINING, DEVELOPMENT AND
                            EDUCATION
                    • Purpose
                    • Concepts
                    • Importance
                    • Approach
                    • Benefits
                    • Other Factors
```

```
        LEARNING PROCESS                    NEEDS ANALYSIS
    • Learning Styles                   • Stages
    • Behaviourist Learning             • Techniques
    • Cognitive Psychology              • Meeting Training Needs
    • Honey and Mumford                 • Development Plan
    • Kolb
    • Effective Learning
    • Barriers
```

```
            PLAYERS
    • Management
    • Employee
    • Training Manager
```

```
            METHODS
    • On-the-Job Training
    • Demonstration, Instruction
      and Coaching
    • Internal Courses
    • External Courses
    • College-Based Courses
    • Others
    • Training and Development
      Evaluation
```

Session 21 Guidance

■ **Know** the roles of the key players (s.3).

■ **Understand** various training methods, which can be divided into off-the-job education/training and on-the-job training (s.4), as well as training needs analysis, which represents a systematic approach to training (s.5).

1 Training, Development and Education

1.1 Purpose

To ensure that the organisation meets current and future operational, departmental and organisational goals and objectives through immediate improvement of work-related performance (training) and the longer-term ability of individuals to show improvement (development).

1.2 Concepts

1.2.1 Training

> **Definition**

"The planned and systematic modification of behaviour through learning events, programmes and instruction which enables individuals to achieve the level of knowledge, skills and competence to carry out their work effectively."

—Armstrong

"The systematic analytical based designing of methods and media so as to enable an individual or group to learn predetermined knowledge and/or processes against predetermined objectives and apply it to a required standard."

—Robin Good

- **Training** takes place continually with the aim to equip employees with skills necessary to achieve short-term objectives.

- It should change behaviour, improve specific knowledge or skills and show benefits in the short-term through, for example:

  - on-the-job training and instruction—employee learns by doing the work under guidance;
  - simulation—employee learns by doing examples of work to be performed on the job;
  - demonstrations—employee is shown how to do the work and then applies principles at a later date;
  - work shadowing—employee follows another employee to see how the work is done;
  - internal and external courses—formal lectures, exercises, case studies, discussion groups);
  - self-study—reading, study tapes, interactive video/CD; and
  - self-learning—doing the work and learning from mistakes made.

- Training is not usually specific to an individual; many employees will pass through the same training programme.

1.2.2 Development

> **Development—**the growth or realisation of a person's ability
> and potential through the provision of learning and educational
> experiences.

▩ Achieves long-term goals, emphasises "personal" growth
of employee, is tailored to meet the specific needs of an
individual and concentrates on general skills rather than
specific skills.

▩ **Development** has longer-term horizons than training and is
usually geared towards promotion and personal skills (e.g.
leadership, time management). It involves training on specific
skills over a period (e.g. time management course which is
then put into practice by the employee).

▩ In a professional context, continuing professional development
(CPD) is the means by which members of professional
associations maintain, improve and broaden their knowledge
and skills, and progress the personal qualities required in their
professional lives. Development aims "to improve personal
performance and enhance career progression", which arguably
is much wider than just formal training with courses.

1.2.3 Education and Learning

> **Education—**the knowledge or skill obtained or developed by a
> learning process.
> **Learning—**the process of acquiring knowledge through experience,
> which leads to a change in behaviour.

▩ An individual who is "educated" is regarded as being in
possession of certain knowledge or skills and has gone
through a particular process to acquire them. This involves
learning (e.g. theory) and training (e.g. practical application).

▩ **Education**, especially university and professional education
and successful completion of examinations, can thus be
considered essential for professional development but is
only one part (perhaps the starting point) of the professional
development process.

1.3   Importance

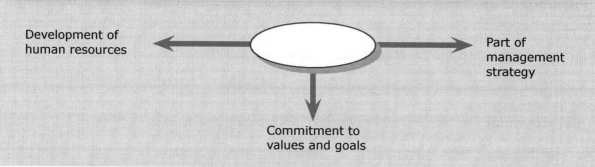

- A strategic and coherent approach to training and development of employees to ensure a continuing contribution to securing a competitive advantage
- Involves all levels of management and employees

Development of human resources

Part of management strategy

Commitment to values and goals

- Current and future organisational, departmental and operational objectives are effectively and efficiently met.
- Continuous improvement of the performance of the organisation, its employees and teams.
- Employees maximise their potential and growth within the organisation.
- Whatever method of training and development is chosen, it should be:
  - relevant to the employee's job;
  - part of the employee's development plan;
  - of interest to and motivating for the employee; and
  - cost effective.

1.4   Approach

- Organisations often incorporate training and development in their strategic plan.
- Identify the skills, knowledge, competences and attitudes required for the organisation to achieve its objectives.
- Identify the training and development activities required to ensure that the skills, knowledge, competences and attitudes are available for the benefit of the organisation.
- Execute actions necessary to achieve relevant training and development.

1.4.1 Training Approach

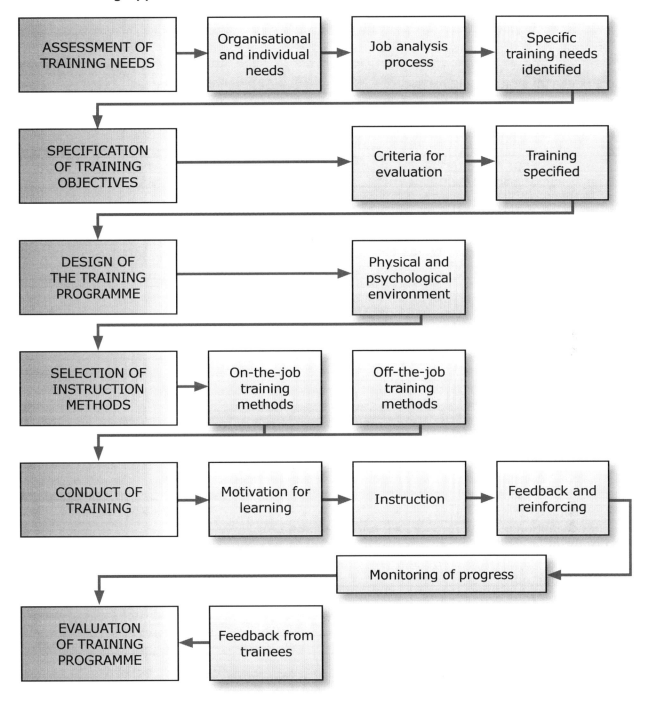

1.4.2 Development Approach

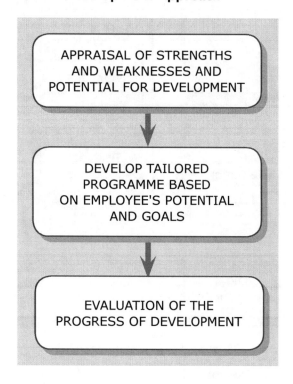

```
┌─────────────────────────────────┐
│   APPRAISAL OF STRENGTHS        │
│   AND WEAKNESSES AND            │
│   POTENTIAL FOR DEVELOPMENT     │
└─────────────────────────────────┘
                │
                ▼
┌─────────────────────────────────┐
│   DEVELOP TAILORED              │
│   PROGRAMME BASED               │
│   ON EMPLOYEE'S POTENTIAL       │
│   AND GOALS                     │
└─────────────────────────────────┘
                │
                ▼
┌─────────────────────────────────┐
│   EVALUATION OF THE             │
│   PROGRESS OF DEVELOPMENT       │
└─────────────────────────────────┘
```

1.5 Benefits

1.5.1 To the Organisation

✔ Ensures that the organisation is able to compete effectively in its marketplace.

✔ Allows the organisation to be open and adaptive (e.g. change management).

✔ Indoctrination of corporate culture and motivation for organisational goals.

✔ Maintains skills required to meet strategic, tactical and operational objectives.

✔ Provides a resource of appropriate expertise.

✔ Allows for succession planning.

✔ Provides employee multi-skill flexibility.

✔ Enhances existing skills.

✔ Greater cost effectiveness (e.g. less supervision, less waste).

✔ Higher productivity.

✔ Lower absenteeism (e.g. because of accidents or boredom).

✔ Lower staff turnover.

✔ Enhances reputation in the local community and with potential recruits.

✔ Enhances reputation with alumni (e.g. staff who leave may refer business).

1.5.2 To the Employee

> **Example 1 Benefits to Employee**
>
> Identify FIVE benefits of training and development to the employee.

1.6 Other Factors

- Training and development cannot be considered to cover all aspects of the organisation/employee relationship. Many other factors must also be taken into consideration.
- For example:
    - personal factors—age, gender, physique, education, aptitude;
    - domestic circumstances—married, divorced, children, location;
    - job factors—environment, space, machinery, methods, hours;
    - work group—work mates, peer group, personalities;
    - organisation factors—type, pay, conditions, attitudes;
    - conflict of values—home life, lack of free time, ethics; and
    - situational stress—deadlines, redundancies, recession.

2 Learning Process

2.1 Learning Styles*

- Learning styles categorise how people learn.
- Training and development opportunities need to reflect learning styles, particularly in group situations.

2.2 Behaviourist Learning

- This type of learning concerns stimulus response. It concentrates on the relationship between stimuli (inputs through senses from the environment) and the reaction to such stimuli.
- "Learning" is the formation of new connections between a given stimuli and response, based on repeated experience (e.g. conditioning, reinforcement).
- Adjustment is made based on the results of a response:*
    - successful and rewarding—do it again;
    - unsuccessful or unpleasant—avoid or change.
- Trial-and-error learning and reward-punishment forms of motivation work on this basis.

*There are two basic schools of psychology concerning learning theory—the behaviourist school and the cognitive school.

*Learners may seek feedback and use it to automatically control their performance (i.e. modify their behaviour).

2.3 Cognitive Psychology

■ This school considers that learning is basically information processing; knowledge is information that can be used to modify or maintain previous behaviour.

■ The human mind not only takes in sensory information, but also organises, interprets and rationalises it in order to make a decision about future behaviour.*

■ Learning uses feedback on the results of past behaviour, as well as from other sources, to make rational decisions about whether to maintain successful behaviours or modify unsuccessful behaviours (in order to achieve goals).

■ Concepts such as motivation, objectives and feedback are important in cognitive learning theory.

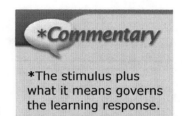

*Commentary

*The stimulus plus what it means governs the learning response.

2.4 Honey and Mumford

■ Identified four learning styles: theorists, reflectors, activists and pragmatists.

2.4.1 Theorists

■ Wish to fully understand basic principles.
■ Are analytical.
■ Are intellectual.
■ Are averse to practical, hands-on type training.
■ Prefer programmed, structured, theoretical training given by like-minded individuals.

2.4.2 Reflectors

■ Are observers.
■ Are thoughtful before taking action.
■ Need to be self-paced.
■ Cannot be rushed or ill-informed.
■ Will produce well-researched and thought-out conclusions.
■ Tend to be slow.
■ Will ask questions but try to avoid any other form of participation.

2.4.3 Activists

■ Practical and participative.
■ Flexible and optimistic.
■ Prefer hands-on experience, rather than theory.
■ Like the pressure of new situations.
■ Rush into situations and then become easily bored.

2.4.4 Pragmatists

■ Will only participate if they can see the relevance.
■ Quickly learn new skills through on-the-job training.
■ Prefer learning outcomes which involve improvement.
■ May easily disregard undeveloped learning opportunities.

2.5   Kolb

- Developed the experiential learning cycle:*

  - **Concrete experiences**—an action, participation, doing something;
  - **Observation**—perception of processes undertaken in carrying out the action;
  - **Reflection**—analyse and evaluate what was done in the processes, perhaps with a third party;
  - **Formation of abstract concepts and generalisations**— understand the end result of the action and how the processes contributed in a positive or negative way to the result; *and*
  - **Applying/testing**—employing the concepts in new situations, which will then lead to new concrete experiences.

*Commentary

*Basically, the experiential learning cycle is the concept of self-learning, learning by experience, learning on the job and self-development.

2.6   Effective Learning

- Individuals learn:
  - if they want to (must be of interest);
  - if they need to (must be motivating);
  - through relation to past, present or future experiences;
  - by putting into practice what they have been taught;
  - with appropriate help and guidance; and
  - in informal and non-threatening environments.

2.7   Barriers

✗ No corporate employee development strategy.

✗ Ineffective corporate culture.

✗ No individual development programmes.

✗ "Job for life" mentality.

✗ "Change blindness."

✗ Limited individual horizon and boundary.

✗ Lack of individual motivation and positive mental attitude.

✗ Peer pressure and group mentality.

✗ Inappropriate training and learning techniques.

✗ Trainer is not fully prepared.

✗ Training environment is not conducive to learning.

3 Players

3.1 Management

▓ Senior management facilitates development of employees in corporate strategy.

▓ General management establishes and fosters a learning and development culture.

▓ Managers and supervisors may:
  ● determine training needs of their departments and teams;
  ● identify their subordinates' competence gaps;
  ● design personal development programmes with individuals;
  ● assist with programme selection and design;
  ● identify opportunities for on-the-job learning;
  ● disseminate relevant information to employees;
  ● motivate and encourage subordinates to undertake training;
  ● evaluate the effect of training and development; and
  ● appraise and counsel individual employees.*

*In "open cultures", it is not unusual for subordinates to also assess training opportunities for their immediate manager.

▓ Where managers and supervisors provide training (e.g. on the job):
  ● sufficient time and resources must be made available;
  ● "train the trainer" programmes must be available; and
  ● interpersonal skills also must be enhanced.

▓ Interpersonal skills required include:
  ● coaching;
  ● counselling;
  ● appraisal;
  ● motivational;
  ● mentoring;
  ● listening;
  ● persuasion; and
  ● presentational (i.e. prepare and present a training session).

3.2 Employee

▓ Modern training and development thought, together with cultural change, place greater emphasis on the responsibility of the individual to identify their own training and development requirements.

▓ De-layering, especially within middle management, has resulted in fewer opportunities for vertical development.

▓ A "job for life" is no longer feasible in the majority of organisations.

▓ Employees who require work for life must be prepared to learn new skills to ensure continued job opportunities.

▓ Multi-skilling is now considered essential for personal job progression.

▓ The pace and the impact of technological change require that employees continually reassess their skills and development requirements.

3.3   Training Manager

▓ The training manager is a specialist appointed to manage the training and development function in the organisation's human resources strategy.

▓ The training manager has many roles and responsibilities.

3.3.1   Coordinating

● Coordinating training and development between departments.
● Ensuring a consistent application of the training strategy.
● Liaising with all departments on training requirements.
● Arranging training courses.
● Maintaining a central training resource (e.g. course material, equipment, records, external course programmes and consultants).

3.3.2   Developing (Usually in Cooperation With Other Managers)

● Analysing training needs.
● Identifying current skills gaps.
● Designing and delivering training programmes.
● Assisting managers (and others) to deliver training programmes.
● Analysing feedback from courses and development programmes.
● Providing feedback to course owners and presenters.
● Modifying programmes to reflect feedback.
● Running "train the trainer" programmes.

3.3.3   Researching

● Critically evaluating and developing the training strategy.
● Advising the board on training and development matters.
● Identifying new and future skills required by the organisation.
● Keeping up to date with training developments and technology.

4   Methods

4.1   On-the-Job Training (Practical)

▨ Training given in the normal work situation in the attitude/knowledge/skill behaviour pattern appropriate to a task or job. It encompasses:

- **Induction**—when a new employee joins a department and is given a brief overview of the department, rules and regulations, the organisation and their role. The induction process is continued by utilising one or more of the methods noted below.

- **Work experience**—an employee is seconded to another department or organisation to obtain detailed knowledge and experience of the work carried out. Such experience can then be used in the employee's original position.

- **Job rotation**—an employee is given several jobs in quick succession to gain a broad understanding of an organisation.

- **Demonstration/instruction**—employee is shown how to carry out a simple task.

- **Coaching**—working with an employee to prepare for a job which involves several tasks over a period.

4.2   Demonstration, Instruction and Coaching

▨ The employee basically is told how to do a job, is shown how to do the job and then allowed to do the job.

▨ Coaching implies a closer, longer-term relationship between the trainer and the trainee, especially where the job is complicated, involves many separate tasks and will take a long time to complete or for the necessary skill level to be obtained (e.g. audit assurance training).

▨ The trainer must be well prepared and skilled in the techniques of:

- briefing;
- supervising;
- reviewing; and
- appraising.

4.2.1   Advantages

✔ Training is relevant to the employee's day-to-day activity.

✔ Opportunities are afforded for the employee to make mistakes.

✔ Training and learning can be carried out at the employee's pace.

✔ Difficult jobs can be broken down into tasks.

4.2.2   Disadvantages

✗ Poor interpersonal skills of the trainer.

✗ Trainer and employee may have a personality clash.

✗ Trainer may be inappropriate (e.g. does not know job).

✗ Bad habits of trainer may be passed on to employee.

✗ Insufficient time is allocated to the training.

✗ Employee is left to "sink or swim".

Example 2 The Coaching Cycle

Suggest FIVE stages in the coaching cycle.

4.3 Internal Courses (Formal)

▓ Usually run by an internal training department using training staff or specialist staff within the organisation.

4.3.1 Methods Used

▓ **Formal lectures**—used to give factual information through one-way presentation allowing little opportunity for participation, usually resulting in a low retention rate (especially if boring).

▓ **Group discussions**—good at generating ideas and solutions, but require a good chairperson to ensure that all is equal and that the discussion does not go off track.

▓ **Demonstrations**—add interest and allow for deliberate errors to be made, but are no substitute for real-life experience and may not be taken seriously.

▓ **Simulations**—the task is learnt through the use of a model or mock-up. Mainly used in training for hazardous or high-risk areas. Trainees may view the exercise as artificial.

▓ **Role-play exercises**—useful for developing interpersonal skills, but require careful planning, tactful feedback and must be seen to be fair and relevant by participants. Often participants find the situations embarrassing and difficult to role play.

▓ **Case studies**—useful to reinforce (or test) general principles previously taught. Employees may be required to develop solutions and learn new principles. Can be time consuming for the learning obtained and may be considered a game by some.

4.3.2 Advantages

✔ Designed to meet the general requirements of the employees and the firm.

✔ Presented by individuals who know the practical aspects of the job.

✔ Can call on external experts to present relevant sessions.

✔ Can be organised to suit the work pattern of the employees.

✔ Easy to link learning to the workplace and therefore reinforce.

✔ Enable employees to meet other members of the organisation at a similar stage of development.

4.3.3 Disadvantages

✗ May not meet all of the specific requirements of an employee.

✗ May be too early or too late to be of maximum benefit.

✗ Training department presenters may not have the practical background.

✗ Specialists may not have the necessary presentation skills.

✗ External specialist may not understand the culture of the organisation.

✗ May not be cost effective for a small number of attendees.

✗ No exposure to the external environment—all in-house.

4.4 External Courses (Formal)

▓ These are similar in nature and method to internal courses.

4.4.1 Advantages

✔ Can be used to plug gaps in internal training.

✔ Access to resources not available or economically viable within the organisation.

✔ Able to exchange ideas with other people from different organisations.

✔ Courses may be held on a regular basis; therefore, a number of employees can attend over time (i.e. less disruption due to employee absence).

✔ Held away from the workplace. Therefore no disruptions are caused by interruptions from work.

✔ Useful to broaden general knowledge of a subject.

✔ One employee or a small group could attend, then disseminate knowledge throughout the organisation through internal training.

4.4.2 Disadvantages

✗ Cannot be tailored to suit the exact requirements of the employee.

✗ Presenters will not have specific knowledge of the organisation.

✗ Employees are required to identify reinforcement opportunities in the workplace.

✗ Employees may consider the course to be a "jolly" (e.g. away from work for a few days, staying in hotels, etc). Although motivational, no improvement in skills may be obtained.

4.5 College-Based Courses

▓ Usually used for "further education" (e.g. to obtain a relevant qualification).

▓ Types of courses include:

● **Day release**—usually one day a week for formal study.

● **Night school/weekends**—attend for one or more evenings or at weekends during employee's own time.

● **Block release**—formal study in a set programme, usually for a number of days at a time.

● **"Sandwich" courses**—work and study rotation over a number of years (e.g. three months' college, three months' work experience, say, over two years).

● **Full-time sponsorship**—attend college/university for a full-time course while on the organisation's payroll. May involve on-the-job training during vacations.

▓ The type of course (or combination) chosen can suit the organisation's and employee's needs and personal requirements.

▓ Courses are usually theoretical in nature and the lecturers may lack practical experience.

▓ Courses which lead to national examinations set at fixed times in a year (e.g. June and December) may be disruptive to the organisation (e.g. employees are not available in peak work periods).

▓ Prolonged periods of employee illness may mean training is deferred (perhaps for up to one year).

4.6 Others

- **Distance learning**—self-study of material—books, videos, CDs, TV broadcasts—with progress examinations and, perhaps, college-based modules or revision course.
- **Computer-based training**—interactive CD, discussion forums on the Internet, webcasts, videos, etc.

4.7 Training and Development Evaluation

- Training and development must be cost effective and assist in meeting the strategic objectives of the organisation.
- The effectiveness of the training must be measured against the training objectives.

4.7.1 Observation of Reactions During Training

- How did the employees respond during and just after the training programme—Stimulated? Bored? Attentive? Asleep?
- Observation is an inexact approach to assess the training and employees during training as it is difficult to match against quantitative objectives. Perhaps the employees are happy because they are spending time away from their work.

4.7.2 On Course Testing

- Can be used at the end of, or during, the training to assess what has been learnt and understood.
- May be paper based, computer based, practical exercises, simulations or observed exercises.
- Only tests one's understanding in the environment of the training programme. Does not test the transfer of skills, knowledge or attitude to the workplace or job.

4.7.3 Course Assessments/Questionnaires

- Used to obtain (from the employee) immediate feedback on the perceived value of the course.
- Very difficult for employees to assess usefulness of training to their workplace and job because they have not yet tried to apply the learning to their work situation.
- Useful to obtain employee's impression of the quality of material, presentation and methods used on the course.

4.7.4 Follow-Up Questionnaires/Interviews/Discussion Groups

- Used to assess the impact of training on the workplace and job after the employee has had the opportunity to put into practice what was taught (e.g. two months later).

4.7.5 Job Performance Measurement

- The effect of the training can be measured directly through the changes made by the employee in carrying out the job.
- Appropriate means of measurement will need to have been established when the training objectives were set.

- May take the form of:
  - random observation of the employee carrying out his duties over a period (e.g. improved technique to ensure a safer operation);
  - measurement of, for example, improved productivity (e.g. higher throughout, fewer rejected products, completing work within budget);
  - review of customer complaints over a set period (say six months);
  - review of absenteeism records for a set period;
  - regular appraisal made by immediate superior and (if 360-degree appraisal is used) by subordinates (usually the best way of assessing interpersonal skills); and/or
  - self-appraisal.

4.7.6 Individual Progression

- Individual progression in an organisation is often directly linked to the level of training and development given to individuals.

- It is essential that a personal development plan is established, critical success factors set and performance indicators established (see *Session 22*).

- The training and development provided needs to be sufficient to ensure the most effective progression. It is possible that if too much is given too quickly, the result will be negative progression and a poor cost benefit.

- Note that other factors (e.g. favouritism) also may play a part.

4.7.7 Operational, Departmental and Organisational Results

- The successful achievement of operational, departmental and organisational goals and objectives (for many companies) relies on an effective policy of staff training and development.

- It is generally accepted that organisations which are supportive of staff training and development recoup the costs of such support through an improved bottom line.

- There are, however, many other factors which affect the results of organisations and the direct impact of training and development cannot always be easily measured (but reduced staff turnover, lower absenteeism, for example, are easily measured).

- Qualitative measures have to be considered and an appropriate cost/benefit analysis carried out (usually at board level).

5   Training Needs Analysis

5.1   Stages

Definition

Training needs analysis—the systematic investigation of an organisation, its aims, objectives, procedures and the capabilities of its personnel in order to identify specific requirements for training and recommend training strategies, plans and training provisions to satisfy those requirements.

▓ Basically:
  ● where are we now—current results, knowledge and skills;
  ● where do we want to be—desired results, knowledge and skills; and
  ● how do we get there—action required.
▓ Specifically:
  ● fully understand the organisation and its business strategy;
  ● understand the job through the job description and personnel specification;
  ● identify changes required in the job or the job holder's performance;
  ● determine the essential skills, knowledge and attitudes required;
  ● access the current level of skills, knowledge and attitude ("ska");
  ● identify the deficient areas (e.g. the "ska" gap); and
  ● develop an appropriate action plan to address the situation.

5.2   Techniques

▓ Desktop reviews of job analysis reports and procedure manuals.
▓ Formal or informal interviews of individuals or groups.
▓ Observation at the organisational, departmental and operative levels.
▓ Questionnaires.
▓ Diaries and log sheets (may take time to complete and may be inaccurate).
▓ Appraisal and performance reviews.
▓ Review of critical incident reports, accident records, breakdown records (such incidents are often caused by poor training or lack of training).
▓ Employee training and attitude surveys (e.g. ask employees what training they require).

5.3 Meeting Training Needs

▨ Needs can be either **individual or group, reactive or proactive**. There may also be **no need** for training, whereby alternative action can be taken.

5.3.1 Individual v Group Needs

▨ Individual needs may relate to:
- induction training;
- introductory training at a basic level;
- progressive training (i.e. as part of a development programme);
- corrective training (e.g. to eliminate mistakes made);
- reinforcement training (e.g. to remind of particular policies); or
- update training (e.g. on new procedures, use of new technologies).

▨ Group needs relate to:
- collective behaviour training;
- the external environment (e.g. customers, suppliers, etc); and
- the internal relationships between group members.

5.3.2 Reactive v Proactive Needs

▨ Reactive needs:
- Weaknesses already exist and action needs to be taken.
- Relate to a specific training need.
- Indication of a difference between performance and organisational objectives and expectations.

▨ Examples of reactive needs include:
- poor job technique;
- reduction in quality of product;
- increasing labour turnover;
- machine breakdowns due to misuse;
- increasing grievances;
- increasing absenteeism;
- increasing customer complaints;
- poor supervision and management practices; and
- insufficient briefing when delegating.

▨ Proactive needs:
- Long-term approach.
- Deal with anticipated changes in the future.
- Relate to development, as longer term.

▨ Examples of proactive needs include:
- change management;
- future introduction of new products and processes;
- future legislation;
- long-term succession planning; and
- technological changes.

5.3.3 No Need

▨ Examples where training and development may not be appropriate include:

- poor recruitment (e.g. the wrong people are being employed);
- inappropriate equipment (e.g. incorrect tools, old and worn out);
- poor job design (e.g. incorrect analysis of job and requirements);
- personal problems (e.g. poor health that is not work related);
- personality conflicts (training may not solve this problem); and
- lack of motivation (counselling will be required to identify why).

5.4 Development Plan

▨ Personal to each employee.

▨ Analyses current skills, knowledge and attitude.

▨ Identifies strengths and weaknesses.

▨ Agrees to goals to remove weaknesses in current job.

▨ Agrees training is required to achieve goals.

▨ Identifies potential opportunities for growth.

▨ Sets goals for growth.

▨ Draws up the development plan to achieve goals, incorporating critical success factors, performance indicators, feedback and appraisal checks.

Summary

- Training takes place continually to immediately equip employees with the skills necessary to achieve short-term objectives and may take the form of:
  - on-the-job instruction;
  - simulation;
  - demonstration;
  - work shadowing;
  - internal and external courses; and
  - self-study.

- Development has a long-term focus and involves the growth or realisation of a person's ability through provision of learning and educational experiences.

- Education is the act or process of acquiring general knowledge, developing the powers of reasoning and judgement, and of general intellectual preparation.

- An employee's development process will involve:
  - appraisal of strengths and weaknesses including potential for development;
  - a tailored program based on the employee's potential and goals; and
  - periodic evaluation of progress.

- Training and development, including education, result in operational benefits, lower staff costs and reputational benefits.

- Learning styles categorise the methods by which people learn:
  - *Behaviourists* believe in a stimulus-response learning (conditioning).
  - *Cognitive learning theorists* believe that the human mind organises, interprets and rationalises information.

- Honey and Mumford identified four learning styles: theorists, reflectors, activists and pragmatists.

- Kolb developed the experiential learning cycle of concrete experiences, reflective observation, abstract conceptualisation and active testing/experimentation.

- Management roles in the training process include coordinating, developing and researching.

- Training and development evaluation includes observation of reactions during training, on course testing, course assessments, follow-up communications, job performance measurement, individual progression and organisational results.

- Training needs analysis determines the nature and type of training, development and education which the organisation should undertake to retain or improve its strategic advantage. The results of the training needs analysis will then become the foundation for the organisation's development plan.

Session 21 Quiz
Estimated time: 25 minutes

1. Explain the difference between training and development. (1.2)
2. List the SIX stages of a training approach. (1.4)
3. Describe Honey and Mumford's reflector learning style. (2.4)
4. List the methods of training. (4.1–4.6)
5. Define "training needs analysis". (5.1)

Study Question Bank
Estimated time: 40 minutes

Priority		Estimated Time	Completed
MCQ21	Training and Development	40 minutes	

EXAMPLE SOLUTIONS

Solution 1—Benefits to Employee

✔ Increased job satisfaction.
✔ Improved work methods.
✔ Enhanced skills, knowledge and abilities.
✔ Greater "saleability" to current or future employer (e.g. promotion opportunities).
✔ Psychological well-being (e.g. a feeling of value to the organisation and peers).
✔ Enhanced motivation.
✔ Achievement of personal goals.

Solution 2—The Coaching Cycle

■ Identify what is required to be learnt and set objectives.
■ Identify the employee's strengths and weaknesses.
■ Plan an appropriate training and development programme. This should include appropriate critical success factors and performance indicators together with feedback mechanisms.
■ Implement the programme and adjust as it progresses to take into account new learning and development opportunities.
■ Review and maintain the employee's progress on a regular basis (e.g. receive feedback on progress and adjust the training and development programme as necessary).

Performance Appraisal

FOCUS

This session covers the following content from the *ACCA Study Guide.*

D. Leading and Managing Individuals and Teams

7. Review and appraisal of individual performance
a) Explain the importance of performance assessment.
b) Explain how organisations assess the performance of human resources.
c) Define performance appraisal and describe its purposes.
d) Describe the performance appraisal process.
e) Explain the benefits of effective appraisal.
f) Identify the barriers to effective appraisal and how these may be overcome.

Session 22 Guidance

■ **Note** that this session describes the benefits of performance appraisal and assessment, and how the organisation appraises and assesses the human resource function's role in the process. This integrates with *Session 21* on learning and development, because appraisals are one method to assess the need for additional training or development to meet the performance criteria established by the needs analysis.

■ **Recognise** the need for the organisation to assess competencies (s.1). These form the basis of areas which will be benchmarked as to performance.

(continued on next page)

VISUAL OVERVIEW

Objective: To understand the concept of competence and the role of the appraisal process in the development of individual skills.

```
                    ┌─────────────────────┐
                    │                     │
                    │    COMPETENCIES     │
                    │                     │
                    └─────────────────────┘
                              │
                    ┌─────────────────────┐
                    │ PERFORMANCE ASSESSMENT│
                    │  • Purpose           │
                    │  • Benefits          │
                    │  • Effective Appraisal│
                    │  • Pay Review        │
                    └─────────────────────┘
                       /              \
```

PERFORMANCE ASSESSMENT
- Purpose
- Benefits
- Effective Appraisal
- Pay Review

FORMS OF APPRAISAL
- Methods
- Types of Assessment
- Assessment Centre

APPRAISAL PROCESS
- Steps
- Management Skills
- Preparation
- Location of Interview
- Conducting the Interview
- Closing Procedures
- Follow-Up
- Feedback
- Barriers

Session 22 Guidance

■ **Understand** the purpose of performance measurement and how it benefits employees and the organisation (s.2).

■ **Know** the forms of appraisal, including various methods and types (s.3) and **understand** the steps in the appraisal process (s.4).

1 Competencies

■ Competencies should be:

- objectively defined (e.g. management as a competency is too broad—there are many aspects of management);
- defined as simply as possible (e.g. easily understood);
- capable of linking together to cover the whole range of skills and abilities required to carry out a job (e.g. management);
- business related; and
- measurable or capable of being objectively assessed.

■ Actual skills and abilities required for each competence can be measured and appraised against a standard:*

- personnel specifications;
- recruitment;
- position definition;
- personal development programmes;
- assessment for qualifications;
- appraisal assessments.

Definition

Competencies—skills and abilities required to successfully carry out a particular function.

*Commentary

*To apply for the ACCA designation, students must demonstrate practical competencies as described in the Practical Experience Requirement (see *Session 23*).

2 Performance Assessment

2.1 Purpose

■ Assessment appraisals are used to:

- assess past performance;
- help improve current performance;
- set performance objectives;
- assess training and development needs;
- aid the personal development of the employee;
- assess salary levels;
- assess future potential (e.g. promotion or multi-skilling);
- assist in career planning; and
- provide a forum for the airing of grievances, work-related or personal problems.

Definition

Performance appraisal—the process by which a manager evaluates the work of an employee, by comparison with preset targets or standards, and provides feedback which shows where improvements are needed and why.

2.2 Benefits

✔ Builds a relationship between the employee, manager and organisation.

✔ The organisation obtains standard information on which to compare all employees.

✔ Allows the manager to objectively review, discuss and compare employee performance using standard appraisal procedures and guidelines rather than relying on hearsay from other sources.

✔ Improves communication between managers and employees.

✔ Constructive help can be offered to the employee based on the appraisal.

✔ Provides feedback to senior management via the employee's immediate supervisor about the job and competencies of the employee.

✔ Maintains performance levels by identifying and correcting problems before they become serious.

✔ Ensures that the employee negates weaknesses and builds on strengths at the earliest opportunity.

✔ Acts as a check on the effectiveness of recruitment and training.

✔ Establishes a database of actual and potential performance as a basis for manpower planning.

✔ Focuses on the needs of the business.

✔ Ensures that the employee's goals are congruent with those of the organisation.

✔ The appraiser also is being appraised through their skill and ability to carry out an appraisal.

2.3 Effective Appraisal Features

Example 1 Features of Effective Appraisal

Identify FOUR features of an effective appraisal.

2.4 Pay Review

▨ The performance appraisal should be a frequent event; the pay review usually being conducted once a year.

▨ From the viewpoint of the organisation, many factors other than performance determine the *amount* of reward which can be afforded.

▨ Additional effort by the employee should be rewarded, usually by extra remuneration.

▨ By conducting the performance appraisal and salary review together:

● salary is inevitably the dominating factor;

● until the employee hears about the salary, nothing else will be considered;

● if the employee is unhappy with the salary increase, it can easily be taken as an unintended negative reflection on performance;

● money dominates the discussion rather than the review of past, present and future performance and development recommendations.

▨ Ideally, performance appraisal and salary review should have sufficient time between them to allow the employee to put into place any improvement considered necessary by the performance appraisal. In other words, employees will have time to modify their performance *before* receiving a poor salary review.

▨ In performance-related pay schemes, the pay review also will incorporate an appraisal. In such cases, additional performance appraisals should be held at various times throughout the year to concentrate solely on performance and development.

3 Forms of Appraisal

3.1 Methods

3.1.1 Open Assessment (Blank Sheet Approach)

- Manager writes a free-form report about the employee.
- Strengths (and weaknesses) can be stressed without constraint.
- Requires good report writing skills.
- Expressed in manager's own terms.
- Impossible to compare employees as no structure is imposed.
- Very difficult to assess changes compared to previous reports.
- Cannot be constructively analysed.
- The assessment is entirely subjective.

3.1.2 Guided Assessment

- Manager is required to address specific headings in the report.
- Guidelines are used to explain the headings and how they should be interpreted (e.g. what does "client working relationship" mean).
- Although placing a structure on the report, the strengths and weaknesses are broadly similar to those for open assessments.

3.1.3 Rating Scales (Grading)

- Competencies identified for a job are given a rating (1 = poor; 5 = excellent; or high, average, low) based on the employee's performance and the general expected performance for an employee at that level (e.g. 3 = satisfactory).
- Forms are easy to complete and may not involve too much thinking on behalf of the manager.
- Tendency to rank everybody as "average".
- Can be subjective, in that each manager will have his own concept of each grade.
- Schemes which arrive at the sum total of all grading to assess the overall performance do not describe the employee's performance.
- Best combined with written elements covering, for example, strengths, weaknesses and recommended action.

3.1.4 Critical Incident Rating

- Ratings are based on recordings and observations by managers of successful and unsuccessful employee behaviour when carrying out the job.*
- Individual employees are then graded based on their behaviours.
- The appraisal concentrates on critical behaviour and actual incidents, rather than general aspects of the job.
- As for rating scales, the sum of the ratings does not provide an overall performance measure.

*Commentary

*"Successful" means meets or exceeds the benchmark.

3.1.5 Peer Comparison

■ All employees in the assessment group (e.g. all assistant managers) are compared with each other.

■ Even with small groups, this can take some time.

■ Employees may resent being directly compared with their peers as part of their appraisal feedback.

■ Difficult to compare peer grading between different departments (e.g. an audit with a tax assistant manager or sales with a marketing manager).

3.1.6 Peer Ranking

■ The same approach as for peer comparison, except that all members of a group are ranked by performance.

■ May be easy to rank at the extremes, but very difficult in the middle.

■ Ranking objectively may be difficult, as different employees will have different strengths and weaknesses.

■ Assumes a normal distribution of competence, which may not be the case.

■ What the employee has actually done and the improvements made since the last review can easily be overlooked.

3.1.7 Management by Objectives (MBO)—Results Oriented

■ Performance is reviewed against defined and agreed tasks and standards.

■ As each employee has agreed to the standards to be achieved, they are able to monitor their own performance.*

■ Targets will be relevant to the job and the employee.

■ May assist in motivating the employee.

■ Targets must be achievable, otherwise they will be ignored.

■ One disadvantage is that the system may concentrate on only a few aspects of the job and ignore all other aspects.

*Commentary

*This effectively makes the manager a coach.

3.2 Types of Assessment

3.2.1 Top-Down

■ The traditional approach, manager to subordinates.

3.2.2 Bottom-Up (Upward Appraisal)

■ Subordinates appraise their managers.

■ Subordinates are in an ideal position to assess the competencies required to manage them.

■ As a manager manages a number of employees, a consensus of the actual capabilities of the manager can be formed, thus avoiding the potential biases of top-down appraisal.

■ Feedback from a subordinate can be given directly to the manager by the subordinate, and can be given anonymously (or directly) from higher management.

■ There is always the fear of reprisals and vindictiveness from the manager.

■ Subordinates may not understand the role of the manager to give an objective opinion.

3.2.3 Sideways Appraisal

■ Given by the customers of the employee.*

3.2.4 360-Degree Appraisal

■ Combines down, up and sideways appraisals.

■ Recognises that some roles cannot be fully appraised unless all sides are seen and considered.

■ Appraisals are carried out by the employee's immediate boss, peer workers, their subordinates and external customers.

■ Provides a fuller assessment of the employee and a more effective development plan.

■ May provide surprising results if conflicting views are given by the appraisal groups. This will require specific counselling to establish why the views diverge.

■ The appraisal system can only be effective in open organisations where employees are prepared to accept and act on constructive criticism.

Commentary

*Customers in a sideways appraisal may be internal or external and the appraisals are often obtained through "customer satisfaction" reports.

3.2.5 Self-Appraisal

■ The employee carries out a self-evaluation of own strengths and weaknesses. This saves the manager's time.

■ Employee motivation may be improved because of increased responsibility.

■ In flat organisations (i.e. with few managerial levels), employees are expected to be responsible for driving their own development. Self-appraisal is a key managerial competence.

■ Because self-appraisal is ongoing, set times for appraisal are unnecessary and the employee development program can be on a rolling basis.

■ Many schemes combine this method with another (e.g. a manager and subordinate fill out the same form, ranking against competence criteria, compare results and then discuss during the appraisal interview). Emphasis is placed on areas in which they sufficiently disagree to establish why they disagree and to agree on appropriate action.

Example 2 Disadvantages of Self-Appraisal

Identify FOUR disadvantages of self-appraisal.

3.3 Assessment Centre

■ Groups of individuals are assessed over a number of days. Several methods of assessment and appraisal are combined.

■ Apart from its use in recruitment (see *Session 17*), the assessment centre approach may be used to appraise potential managers and is a common method of officer/ specialist selection in the armed forces.

4   Appraisal Process

4.1   Steps

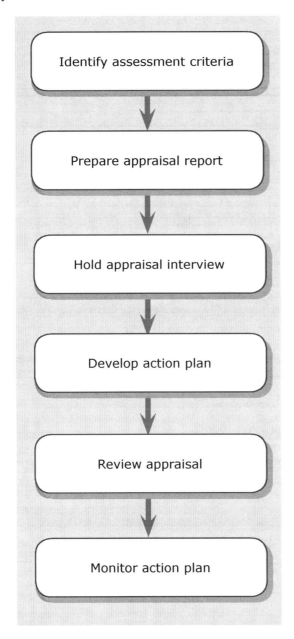

4.2   Management Skills Required

▓ Broadly, interpersonal skills are required. For example:

  • Listening (e.g. the 70% rule)
  • Questioning (open, checking, closed)
  • Non-verbal (e.g. body language of self and appraisee)
  • Counselling
  • Coaching
  • Goal setting
  • Persuasion
  • Assertiveness.

- Combinations of skills will be required depending on the style of the appraisal.
    - "Tell and sell" (more formal)—mainly assertiveness and persuasion.
    - "Tell and listen" (semi-formal)—emphasis on listening, questioning, non-verbal.
    - MBO approach (can be relaxed and informal)—more or less all with the emphasis on coaching.

4.3 Preparation

4.3.1 Identify the Objective of the Interview

- For example:
    - tell and sell (e.g. annual pay review);
    - tell and listen (e.g. semi-annual performance reviews); or
    - coaching (e.g. on-the-job assessment).

4.3.2 Arrange Interview

- Arrange a convenient time and location with the employee.
- Ensure that the employee is fully aware of the purpose of the interview and what it will cover.
- Ensure that the employee receives all necessary documentation in sufficient time to allow the person to fully prepare. For example:
    - up-to-date job description;
    - copy of the action plan and goals set after the last appraisal; and
    - completed assessment/self-assessment form.
- Confirm arrangements with each employee in writing.
- Schedule interviews, making sure that sufficient time is allocated to each interview; that there is sufficient time between interviews to complete notes; and that each interview is treated appropriately and fairly.

4.3.3 Pre-interview Preparation

- Review the employee's file, including job description, personnel specification, job skills, training, job experience, qualifications, etc.
- Review the employee's last appraisal, notes, development plan and goals.
- Determine progress made since the last review, including goals, performance indicators reached (why and why not) and contributory factors not under their control (discuss with other managers as necessary).
- Review the employee's self-assessment form (if system used), identify differences and consider why they arise.
- Obtain all necessary documentation to be used during the interview (including items to be given to the employee).
- From the information obtained, prepare an interview plan.

4.3.4   Interview Plan

▓ Identify the objectives of the interview—what is to be achieved.

▓ Note the approach and order of topics to be covered.

▓ Note the questions to be asked and facts to be ascertained.

▓ Make sure that the review covers the entire period since the last review and not just recent events.

▓ Draft a summary, development plan, training requirements, tasks, etc. These may need to be changed in the light of the interview.

▓ Where the interview is to be highly structured (e.g. tell and sell), then an agenda can be used. Where the interview is less structured, the interview plan will need to be flexible.

4.4   Location of Interview

▓ The location and environment of the interview should be appropriate for its objectives—relaxed but formal for tell and sell, relaxed and informal for counselling and coaching sessions.

▓ In general, the manager should ensure:

 ● an appropriate environment (e.g. temperature, humidity, ease of access, free from interruptions, low noise levels, private);

 ● that the employee is not made to feel uncomfortable (e.g. directly facing sunshine, uncomfortable chair, physical barriers between them, lack of refreshments and appropriate breaks); and

 ● that the employee has access to necessary resources.

4.5   Conducting the Interview

▓ Get into the right frame of mind—"clear the desk".

▓ Welcome the employee, relax and establish rapport.

▓ Make clear that you are meeting to review the employee's performance and to assist in developing the employee over the next measurement period.

▓ Ensure that the employee fully understands what the appraisal is about and that they have all the documentation and information they need.

▓ Lead into the main aspects of the review as quickly as possible.

▓ Progress through the interview plan, applying appropriate interpersonal skills as required:

 ● listening (70/30 rule);

 ● questioning (open, seek rather than give information, assumption-free, not leading, simple);

 ● coaching (seeking the solutions together, with the emphasis on the employee); and

 ● body language (relaxed, truthful, honest, open).

▓ Ensure that the interviewee is involved and feels involved in the process.

▓ Encourage the employee to self-analyse and develop solutions through the use of open questions and coaching.

▓ Ensure that the employee's aspirations and ambitions are realistically achievable (i.e. not impossible).

4.6   Closing Procedures

▓ Summarise what the appraisal has covered.

▓ Give the employee opportunity to react, question and add additional information.

▓ Agree on future goals, the action required and who is responsible for it happening in the form of a written development plan.

▓ Set dates by when the actions should be completed.

▓ Ensure that the employee leaves the appraisal knowing what the manager and organisation feels about their strengths and weaknesses. The employee must also be fully aware of development expectations and likely progress within the organisation.

4.7   Follow-Up

▓ The manager should write a formal report on the appraisal if it is not done during the review.

▓ A copy should be given to the employee for his agreement.

▓ Whatever action was promised by the manager or the employee during the appraisal should be implemented quickly rather than waiting for the next appraisal (which in some cases may be 12 months later).

▓ A manager who delegates an action agreed on in the appraisal must still ensure that the action takes place.

▓ Appraisals should be ongoing.

4.8   Feedback

▓ Feedback requires comparing a system's output with a benchmark or standard and adjusting the input or the process as necessary to ensure that the output meets the standard.

▓ Managers require feedback about how their subordinates are performing to ensure that the organisation achieves operational, departmental and strategic objectives.

▓ Employees need constructive feedback to ensure that they can correct any inappropriate action and be motivated towards continuous improvement.

▓ Constructive feedback is essential to learning and developing a sense of achievement, both strong motivators. Anything less will be demotivating.

▓ The appraisal interview provides an opportunity for general feedback to an employee, but in some situations (e.g. in day-to-day operations) it may be too late (good information needs to be on time). Ideally, evaluation will be an informal process of continuous appraisal with immediate feedback.

■ Feedback can be formal (direct) or informal (via a third party). Workplace examples include:

- praise;
- constructive criticism;
- direct answers to questions;
- physical reactions to questions or different situations;
- gossip;
- budgetary analysis; and
- strike action by employees to a proposal or action by management.

4.9 Barriers to Effective Appraisal*

■ Considered unnecessary by management (e.g. something that has to be done because it was agreed with the trade union) or just a form-filling exercise (e.g. meets the requirements of quality control).

■ Seen as confrontational by both or either parties.

■ Considered a one-way process by management informing an employee of their judgement and the required action to be taken.

■ No more than a "friendly chat"—life continues as normal.

■ Inappropriate measurement criteria (e.g. poor job description, irrelevant competencies and personnel specification).

■ Dislike by employee (e.g. nervous).

■ Manager is ill-prepared, has insufficient or incorrect facts.

■ Manager is subjective or biased and has already "written the final report".

■ Manager dislikes having to give constructive criticism or writing the report (e.g. considers the findings as extremely critical rather than constructive).

■ Employee is held responsible for factors outside of their control.

■ Insufficient time is allocated to the appraisal.

■ Insufficient time is allowed for the employee to prepare.

■ May only be carried out once a year. Targets very quickly become out of date.

■ Employee is unwilling to accept constructive criticism and development assistance.

■ Lack of follow-up and failure to take action agreed at appraisal.

■ System may be inflexible (e.g. "one tool for all" approach).

*"Now my friend, as the appraisal system is a cooperative, constructive, communication process, I will let you know what I have been told is wrong with you, and then you will let me know what else is wrong with you."

Summary

- In order to determine an employee's value, an organisation must define:
  - the competencies required of the employee to successfully execute against the firm's objectives; and
  - the positions within the organisation which will be responsible for executing each component of the objective.
- Performance appraisals are required to ensure that employees meet the needs of their position.
- Forms of appraisal include open assessment, guided assessment, grading, critical incident rating, peer comparison, peer ranking and management by objectives (MBO).
- Assessment can be accomplished as top-down, bottom-up, sideways, 360-degree or self-appraisal.
- Assessment centres may be used to measure performance and provide appraisal, much as they are used to select employees in the hiring process.
- Appraisers must identify the criteria, prepare an appraisal report, hold the appraisal interview, develop an action plan, review the appraisal and monitor the employee's development plan.
- Appraisers should prepare for the interview by identifying the objective, arranging the interview, assembling data, developing the interview plan, ensuring an appropriate environment, conducting the interview, closing the process, following up and providing feedback to the employee.

Session 22 Quiz
Estimated time: 25 minutes

1. List SIX areas where assessment appraisals are used. (1)
2. List the benefits of appraisals. (2.2)
3. Describe the rating scales method of appraisal. (3.1)
4. List the SIX steps in the appraisal process. (4.1)
5. Describe the barriers to an effective appraisal. (4.9)

Study Question Bank
Estimated time: 25 minutes

Priority		Estimated Time	Completed
MCQ22	Performance Appraisal	25 minutes	

EXAMPLE SOLUTIONS

Solution 1—Features of Effective Appraisal

| F |requent | Regular and appropriate for the employee's job. |

F requent   Regular and appropriate for the employee's job.

F actual   Based on targets and measurable performance citing factual examples, not subjective traits.

F irm   Improvement can only start when failure is recognised.

F air   Uniform appraisals in different areas of the company. No bias from single appraiser.

Solution 2—Disadvantages of Self-Appraisal

✗ Employees may not be the best judges of their own performance.

✗ Employees may be too close to the work they carry out in order to be able to stand back and give an objective assessment of their strengths and weaknesses (or just incapable of doing so).

✗ Employees may just wish to develop personal skills without taking into account the organisation's objectives.

✗ If carried out as a joint appraisal with their manager, employees may deliberately understate or overstate rankings in order to tie in with those they expect to receive from their manager.

Personal Effectiveness

FOCUS

This session covers the following content from the *ACCA Study Guide.*

E. Personal Effectiveness and Communication in Business

1. Personal effectiveness techniques

a) Explain the importance of effective time management. ☐

b) Describe the barriers to effective time management and how they may be overcome. ☐

c) Describe the role of information technology in improving personal effectiveness. ☐

2. Consequences of ineffectiveness at work

a) Identify the main ways in which people and teams can be ineffective at work. ☐

b) Explain how individual or team ineffectiveness can affect organisational performance. ☐

3. Competency frameworks and personal development

a) Describe the features of a "competency framework". ☐

b) Explain how a competency framework underpins professional development needs. ☐

c) Explain how personal and continuous professional development can increase personal effectiveness at work. ☐

d) Explain the purpose and benefits of coaching, mentoring and counselling in promoting employee effectiveness. ☐

e) Describe how a personal development plan should be formulated, implemented, monitored and reviewed by the individual. ☐

4. Sources of conflict and techniques for conflict resolution and referral

a) Identify situations where conflict at work can arise. ☐

b) Describe how conflict can affect personal and organisational performance. ☐

c) Identify ways in which conflict can be managed. ☐

Session 23 Guidance

■ **Understand** the need for organisational effectiveness and how an employee's personal effectiveness integrates with organisational goals (s.1).

■ **Recognise** the difference between competence and competency (s.2.2) and formulation of a personal development plan (s.2.3).

(continued on next page)

VISUAL OVERVIEW

Objective: To describe personal development, time management, coaching, mentoring, counselling and conflict and their application within the business environment.

PERSONAL DEVELOPMENT
- Meaning
- Competency and Competence
- Development Plan

INFORMATION SYSTEMS
- Office Systems
- Time Management
- World Wide Web
- Videoconferencing
- Mobile Devices
- Tablets

COACHING AND MENTORING
- Coaching
- Mentoring

PERSONAL EFFECTIVENESS
- Need for
- Management by Objectives

TIME MANAGEMENT
- Need for
- Time-Wasters
- Managing Time
- Summary

CONFLICT
- Meaning
- Concepts
- Impacts
- Symptoms
- Sources
- Management
- Strategies

COUNSELLING
- Need for
- Counselling Process
- Interviews
- Counselling Sessions
- Confidentiality
- Potential Pitfalls

Session 23 Guidance

■ **Know** time management techniques, time-wasters and reasons for procrastination (s.3) as well as how information systems have become time management tools (s.4).

■ **Understand** the difference between coaching and mentoring (s.5) and counselling (s.6), and understand how conflict can be a positive or a negative for the organisation (s.7).

1 Personal Effectiveness

1.1 Need for Effectiveness

■ "The organisation is only as good as its people". It cannot achieve its objectives without effective input from its employees. The more effective (and efficient) the input from employees, the greater the effectiveness of the output of the organisation.

■ As the cumulative effectiveness of employees affects overall effectiveness of the business, personal ineffectiveness can lead to failure to achieve business objectives:*

- At the **operational** level, to have a material effect on the business objectives would probably require group ineffectiveness rather than individual ineffectiveness (e.g. a general lack of training resulting in poor-quality output and low morale).

- At the **strategic** level, the individual ineffectiveness of one director (e.g. the CEO) would be a disaster for the operation of the business as a whole.

Commentary

*This session, together with previous sessions, details how to run a business effectively (e.g. teams, management, recruitment, training and motivation). Ineffectiveness considers the negative aspects of what has already been covered.

1.2 Management by Objectives (MBO)

■ The concept of Management by Objectives (MBO), devised in 1954 by Peter Drucker and developed by John Humble in the 1960s, provides a framework for involving staff at all levels in improving the effectiveness of the organisation.

SENIOR MANAGEMENT DEVELOP
ORGANISATION AIMS

↓

FUNCTIONAL OR SUB-SYSTEM OBJECTIVES
ARE DEVELOPED TO COMPLEMENT THESE

↓

UNIT OR DEPARTMENTAL MANAGERS BREAK DOWN
THEIR OBJECTIVES AND ALLOCATE TO STAFF

↓

INDIVIDUAL OBJECTIVES ARE SET AS PART
OF THE PERFORMANCE APPRAISAL PROCESS

↓

INDIVIDUAL PERFORMANCE IS REVIEWED AGAINST
INDIVIDUAL OBJECTIVES
(Also during the appraisal process)

■ Achievement of individual objectives contributes directly to the achievement of organisational objectives. The realisation by an employee that they contribute improves motivation and effectiveness.

■ Embedded with this is the realisation that failing to achieve an objective through low performance effectiveness may cause the organisation to fail to achieve its objectives.

2 Personal Development

2.1 Meaning

 **Definition**

Personal Development Planning—"A structured and supported process undertaken by an individual to reflect upon their own learning, performance and/or achievement and to plan for their personal educational and career development."

—*Higher Education Academy*

■ Personal development embraces a range of approaches to learning which connect:

● planning—an individual's goals and intentions for learning or achievement;

● doing—aligning actions to intentions;

● recording—thoughts, ideas and experiences in order to understand and evidence the process and results of learning; and

● reflection—reviewing and evaluating experiences and the results of learning.

■ Personal development is concerned with taking responsibility for your own learning; being committed to changing yourself; and taking action to bring about change rather than relying on others to teach you. The underlying fundamental principle is that you, as an individual, wish to change.

■ Personal employment-based development objectives include:

● improving performance in the current work environment;

● improving work skills and competencies;

● planning career development and progression; and

● acquiring transferable skills and competencies.

■ A similar approach can be taken in developing life objectives and in achieving a work-life balance.

■ A number of objectives may arise from a formal appraisal of your work (e.g. need to improve time management). Others may be identified through how you feel, your reactions to certain events and comments made by colleagues, customers, friends and family.

2.2 Competency and Competence

2.2.1 Explanation

- Competency (plural *competencies*) may be defined as the behavioural and technical skills that individuals must have or acquire to perform effectively at work. Competency focuses on personal attributes (e.g. analytical skills, critical thinking, report writing, interpersonal skills and attitudes).

- Competence (plural *competences*) is a broader, work-based concept which describes requirements to effectively perform a job (e.g. brief an audit team, review an audit file, prepare a bank reconciliation, prepare a tax return).*

*Modern practice has been to merge the terms competency and competence. This session uses the term "competency framework" based on the wording in ACCA's F1 Study Guide.

2.2.2 Competency Framework

- A competency framework lists and defines each competency (such as problem solving or people management) required by individuals working in an organisation or part of an organisation.

- The framework brings together all of the various competencies required of an individual in a given position of the organisation.

- Its aim is to ensure that employees possess relevant and up-to-date skills which allow them to undertake their roles effectively and efficiently.

- As discussed in *Session* 22, competencies in the framework should be:
  - objectively defined;
  - simply defined;
  - linked together;
  - business related; and
  - measurable.

- CIPD (see *Session 18*), in its Competencies Toolkit, suggests the following steps to check framework effectiveness:
  - **Communicate the purpose**—ensure that employees understand the purpose of determining competencies. If they don't understand how behaviours contribute to personal and organisational success, there is little point in updating or developing the framework.
  - **Identify key themes**—even if staff members understand the purpose of the framework, it still needs to support the organisation's goals, values, business plans, etc. If people aren't all working towards these aspirations then some individual efforts are likely to be diversions from organisational success.
  - **Get conditions right**—the organisation's procedures need to support the framework and the culture. Resourcing and management structures must also be supportive. If conditions inhibit desirable behaviours, then change the conditions or change the behaviours.

- **Tackle the root cause**—as well as goals and conditions, behaviour is also influenced by underpinning characteristics (knowledge, skills and attitude). One underdeveloped characteristic, such as communication skills, can affect many different behaviours. If managers don't understand this distinction they may focus on trying to improve the behaviour without tackling the root cause.

- **Keep it simple**—there are two key elements to ease of use—language and structure. However "perfect" the framework, if it's too complicated, long or detailed, then it won't be used. The language has to be meaningful to the people who use it.

- **Train, don't blame**—once the structure has been finalised, make sure that everyone who uses the framework is trained in how to use it. A framework is a tool and, as with any tool, will fall into disuse or fail to meet its full potential if not properly understood.*

*Refer to ACCA's competency framework and the related PERs. In addition, review IFAC's (www.ifac.org) International Education Standard 3 (IES 3) *Professional Skills and General Education* and IES 8 *Competence Requirements for Audit Professionals*.

Exhibit 1   PROFESSIONAL SKILLS

The following is an extract from the Professional Skills section of IES 8 *Competence Requirements for Audit Professionals*.

42. **The skills requirement in the education and development program for audit professionals should include:**

   (a) Applying the following professional skills in an audit environment:
   - (i)   identifying and solving problems;
   - (ii) undertaking appropriate technical research;
   - (iii) working in teams effectively;
   - (iv) gathering and evaluating evidence;
   - (v)   presenting, discussing and defending views effectively through formal, informal, written and spoken communication; and

   (b) Developing the following professional skills at an advanced level in an audit environment:
   - (i)   applying relevant audit standards and guidance;
   - (ii) evaluating applications of relevant financial reporting standards;
   - (iii) demonstrating capacity for inquiry, abstract logical thought and critical analysis;
   - (iv) demonstrating professional scepticism;
   - (v)   applying professional judgement; and
   - (vi) withstanding and resolving conflicts.

In the context of the professional accountant, the IES frameworks:

- provide clear guidance to professional qualifying bodies, tuition providers and employers on how to develop and assess competence and maintain and update these competences during the member's working life;

- establish defined, consistent and current standards or attributes required to undertake professional roles competently, which are transferable from one context of the role to another;

- add value in the workplace by allowing a gap analysis between actual performance levels and the defined standards to better target relevant training and development programmes at those who need it; and

- employers and business organisations that support and engage with their employees in training and development will benefit from more effective, efficient and motivated employees who will contribute to increased performance, productivity and profitability.

2.3 Personal Development Plan

A personal development plan (PDP) is a clear progressive action plan for an individual which incorporates a wide set of developmental opportunities, including formal training.

The concept of the personal development plan is one which enables employees to link their development needs with those of the organisation and thus to motivate them and to improve morale.

As a PDP is going to involve change from a current situation, the detail of the current position must first be identified and analysed.

2.3.1 Step 1: Analyse the Current Situation

Reviewing the current job analysis (job description and personnel specification) will provide a detailed list of the skills, knowledge and experience required.*

Against each of the required skills, separate assessments (e.g. high, medium, low or 5, 4, 3, 2, 1) of personal effectiveness and the significance of each skill to the job can be applied. For example:

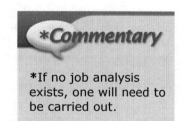

*If no job analysis exists, one will need to be carried out.

Required Skill	Significance	Personal Effectiveness
(1) Leading and participating in meetings		
(2) Briefing staff		
(3) Motivating staff		
(4) Etc.		

- A comparison of the two assessments will highlight key areas requiring attention (e.g. if briefing staff is ranked as high significance but medium/low effectiveness, then the employee requires further personal development in that area).

- An alternative analysis of current and required skills is the personal SWOT (Strengths, Weaknesses, Opportunities and Threats) analysis using an interest/aptitude and performance (IAP) matrix.

- The IAP matrix maps out those skills which are liked against those which are disliked and then sub-analysed into those which are done well against those which are not done well.

	Low	**High**
High	**Likes** *but does not do well*	**Likes** *and does well*
Low	**Dislikes** *and does not do well*	**Dislikes** *but does well*

APTITUDE & INTEREST (vertical axis, High / Low)

PERFORMANCE (horizontal axis, Low / High)

- This approach is useful as it can more easily incorporate the employees' individual interests, as well as the skills and knowledge of the job, into the assessment with the view of including them into the actual role.

- Those matters identified as "does not do well" should be further analysed to identify the specific reasons for "not doing well" (may involve the traditional approach to SWOT analysis) which can then be used as the basis for the development plan.

- By carrying out a gap analysis or similar exercises on where the employee needs to be within some period, the next grade or the next job, the gaps and deficiencies between the current and future requirements can be identified.*

*Commentary

*In businesses, the most common way of identifying strengths and weaknesses is through a formal appraisal, in particular the use of self-appraisal methods.

2.3.2 Step 2: Set Performance Goals

- Having identified the deficiencies in the current skills and the development needs, establish the objectives of the PDP.

- Objectives should be SMART or SMARTER:
  - **S**pecific
  - **M**easurable
  - **A**greed/Attainable
  - **R**ealistic
  - **T**ime-bounded
  - **E**valuated
  - **R**eviewed.

2.3.3 Step 3: Develop an Action Plan

■ Having established the objectives, the manager and employee should determine the best way of achieving them by researching relevant resources, learning opportunities, and learning and development methodologies.

■ The cost/benefit of each method must be assessed and the correct priority applied.

■ The action plan will contain:

● the SMART objective(s);

● the learning and development approaches to achieve each objective; and

● the monitoring and review action required, including how the success of the plan will be measured.*

Commentary

*PDPs are exactly that—personal. Each will thus be different. Although some elements may fit with the firm's objectives, a PDP which emphasises, for example, what will need to be done to advance to a higher-level job with a different firm obviously will not be appropriate for the current firm.

3 Time Management

3.1 Need for

■ Time is a resource which managers must manage to be successful. Unlike other resources, time cannot be made or bought.

■ The ability to control and use time effectively is the most important single management skill.

■ Poor time usage results in:

● Missed deadlines, late appointments, forgotten tasks, indecision, lack of delegation.

● Recurrent crises, constant interruptions, poor thinking, chaotic desk, poor meetings.

● Discourtesy, bad temper, aggressiveness, over-tiredness, high staff turnover.

● Domestic strife, stress.

Definition

Time management —the process of allocating time to tasks in the most effective manner.

3.2 Time-Wasters

■ In his article, "Time Thieves: The 11 Biggest Time-wasters Revealed", Dr Donald Wetmore identified certain activities/ non-activities as being the biggest time-wasters in modern business life.

Example 1 Time-Wasters

Describe FIVE time-wasters.

3.3 Managing Time

3.3.1 Goal Setting

■ Goals are important to ensure that tasks are completed. Applying the SMART concept that goals are measurable and time bound is essential. Once a goal is established an action plan can be made to set out how the goal will be achieved and the resources needed to ensure that it can be achieved.

3.3.2 Planning

▦ Most time management boils down to effective planning, which will ideally take place weekly and daily.

▦ Planning helps to:

- decide how to make effective use of time;
- allocate the week and day ahead; and
- work proactively rather than reactively.

▦ In planning, urgent and non-urgent tasks must be identified. The A-B-C, 1-2-3 Priority System (Alan Lakein) is a common method in which:

- **A** priority = high-value goals (important activities);
- **B** priority = medium-value goals (less-important activities);
- **C** priority = low-value goals (unimportant); and
- the urgency of the task is graded using 1, 2, 3.

▦ As the week progresses, the daily plan will be used to reassess and update the activities allocated to that day in the weekly plan.

▦ Advantages of weekly and daily planning and creating to-do lists include:

- identifying ways in which to manage time more effectively; and
- minimising risk.

▦ By managing time appropriately, urgent matters may disappear altogether and if they do re-surface then planning will make them less urgent and easier to deal with.

▦ Tips on planning include:

- Do not make the planning list too long (e.g. do not set an impossible number of tasks to complete in a day).
- Ensure balance between the easy tasks and the hard tasks. Do not avoid the hard just to complete the easy.
- Focus attention on important tasks as well as the urgent ones.
- Some tasks are fixed; for example, scheduled meetings. It is important to ensure that any preparation work for these meetings is scheduled as a high priority and that all other tasks fit around these fixed commitments.

3.3.3 Prioritising

▦ Managing time effectively, and achieving the things that need to be achieved, means spending time on things that are important and not just urgent. To do this, and to minimise the stress of having too many tight deadlines, it is crucial to distinguish clearly between what is urgent and what is important.

▦ The A-B-C, 1-2-3 approach to prioritising was discussed above. The Time Management Grid which follows categorises events according to their importance and urgency:

- Important activities lead to achieving goals.
- Urgent activities demand immediate attention and are usually associated with the achievement of someone else's goals, or with an uncomfortable problem or situation that needs to be resolved.

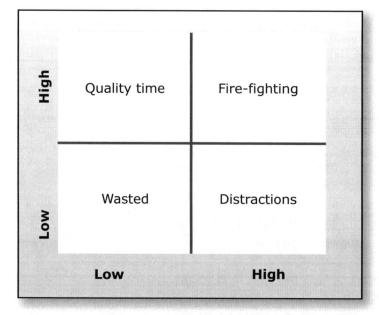

URGENCY

- **Fire-fighting**—important matters have to be dealt with urgently. Because of poor management, they may have moved across from being important but not urgent, and thus take up the limited resource of time.

- **Quality time**—important but not urgent events that can be allocated sufficient time. They must be completed before they become urgent to avoid having too little time to spend on them and diminishing effectiveness.

- **Distractions**—urgent but not important tasks; however, they have to be dealt with (e.g. incoming telephone calls). Good time management techniques can minimise their distraction (e.g. call transfer to a secretary).

- **Wasted**—essential to minimise such activities (e.g. some meetings and travel).

3.3.4 Procrastination

- Procrastination can come about in a number of ways:

  - **Paralysis by planning**—the planning process is drawn out to avoid confronting an issue. For example, by arranging meetings to discuss the issue—or better still, organise a committee to investigate.*

  - **Perfectionism**—this may delay tackling other problems. Perfection may not be required or cost-effective to achieve.

  - **Boredom**—boring jobs are very easy to delay.

  - **Hostility**—where the task is not liked, or the delegator is not liked, there is a strong temptation to delay.

  - The "**Deadline high**"—where jobs are deliberately left to the last minute for the adrenaline rush.

- Recognise when procrastination is happening, identify the reason why and eliminate.

- Avoid by setting deadlines by which goals should be achieved.

- Avoid "deadline high" procrastination by setting intermediary goals that must be achieved.

*Forming a committee to deal with an issue is often a (cynical) way to ensure that nothing gets done while giving the impression of action.

3.3.5 Managing Interruptions

▓ Interruptions are a fact of life. The key to dealing with interruptions is to recognise if they are important, urgent or both and act accordingly.

▓ Techniques which can be used include:

- Divert the telephone—but avoid this being a 24/7 exercise;
- Arrange "open time" so staff will know when you will be available that day (can do by e-mail or instant messaging explaining why you are not available);
- Avoid automatic e-mail downloading—only download and deal with at set times;
- If somebody comes into the office, stand up with an arm outstretched and walk towards the door—they will follow. Identify if urgent, important, etc and act accordingly. Once they are out of the office, it will be difficult for them to come back in. Once they are in and seated, it will be difficult to get them out.

3.3.6 Saying "No"

▓ Not saying no when necessary can lead to over-commitment, stress and uncompleted tasks.

▓ The approach to saying "no" includes:

- Identifying goals and priorities.
- Identifying who the ultimate boss is and who can support.
- Being assertive, fair but firm.
- Explaining the reasons why and giving viable alternatives if possible.
- Explaining the consequences if you were to say "yes".

3.3.7 Paperwork

▓ A lot of time-wasting occurs shuffling papers from one pile to another.

▓ When paper (including e-mails) is received one of the following should be done immediately:

- act on it;
- file it;
- delegate it to someone else; or
- throw it away; delete junk e-mails and throw away junk mail as soon as it is received. If there is no justification for keeping, bin it.*

Commentary

*Dealing with paperwork is sometimes referred to as the ABCD in-tray management—**A**ct on it immediately; **B**in it if worthless, irrelevant or unnecessary; **C**reate a plan if necessary to come back to it; or **D**elegate it.

4 Information Systems

- There are probably very few areas in information technology and systems which have not had an effect on personal development and effectiveness.*

- The following sections provide an overview of a number of areas in IS which have increased the effectiveness and development of individuals.

4.1 Office Systems

- Word processing, spreadsheets, databases, graphics and e-mail.*

- Apart from the designed use of these systems increasing the effectiveness of those who use them, the programs are also used for rudimentary (basic level) lists, diaries and scheduling.

- E-mail has had a significant effect on personal effectiveness, but it needs to be carefully managed.

4.2 Time Management Systems

- These systems include personal time management diary systems through to sophisticated factory time recording and management systems.*

4.3 World Wide Web

- The Web is a vast resource for personal effectiveness and productivity. Just search "personal development plan" as an example to establish the resources available to assist in making a PDP (e.g. fact sheets, questionnaires, videos, blogs, podcasts).

4.4 Videoconferencing

- As the speed and quality of Internet connections continue to improve, the use of videoconferencing is increasingly more common. Significant savings on time and costs can be made, although other aspects (e.g. social contact, physical inspections) will not be available.

4.5 Mobile Devices

- Mobile devices include phones, personal organisers and dictaphones.

- Even the most basic mobile phones include calendar, diary, camera and other important time management functionality. Many of the high-end phones incorporate a jotter function to allow handwritten notes to be entered directly into the system.

- Many dictaphones incorporate flash technology with voice recognition software allowing the recording to be downloaded to a PC for use, for example, in word processing.

4.6 Tablets

- The functionality and power of a laptop, but without the keyboard (input is via a touch screen and stylus) or the weight. Effectively the business standard for executives and other employees.*

Commentary

*Session 24 considers management information systems. All the systems discussed in that session, especially the use of database systems, have significant effects on the personal effectiveness of users in the business.

*Examples of more specialised systems include Microsoft Project Manager, Lotus Notes and collaborative tools aimed at saving significant time while managing activities and projects.

*Search the Internet for "time management systems" to see the range available.

Commentary

*Just ask the question, "How did people work 20, 10 or even 5 years ago without the 'www', smartphones and tablets?"

5 Coaching and Mentoring

5.1 Coaching

> **Definition**
>
> **Coaching**—"developing a person's skills and knowledge so that their job performance improves, hopefully leading to the achievement of organisational objectives. It targets high performance and improvement at work, although it may also have an impact on an individual's private life. It usually lasts for a short period and focuses on specific skills and goals."
>
> —*CIPD*

▓ **Coaching** features include:
- A non-directive form of development.
- Focus on improving performance and developing individuals' skills.
- Focus on achieving specific objectives.
- A one-to-one basis.
- Emphasis on performance at work although personal issues may be discussed.
- Activities that serve both organisational and individual goals.
- Provisions of feedback on both personal strengths and weaknesses.

▓ Coaching is a skilled activity which should be delivered by people trained in this specialised field.

▓ Examples of situations where coaching is a suitable development tool include:
- Helping competent experts develop better interpersonal/ managerial skills.
- Developing an individual's potential and providing career support.
- Developing a more strategic perspective after a promotion to a more senior role.
- Handling conflict situations so they are resolved effectively.

▓ Stages in a coaching approach include:
- Identifying learning objectives.
- Developing a systematic learning and development programme.
- Taking opportunities to broaden knowledge and experience.
- Considering strengths and weaknesses.
- Providing feedback.

5.2 Mentoring

▣ In the workplace, **mentoring** usually means that a more experienced colleague provides not only technical support but also moral and life support for the development of a more junior or inexperienced member of the staff.

▣ It also may be considered a form of apprenticeship, whereby an inexperienced learner learns the tricks of the trade from an experienced colleague, backed up with off-site training.

▣ Mentoring is used specifically and separately as a form of long-term, tailored development for an individual which brings benefits to the organisation. The characteristics of mentoring:

* Essentially a supportive form of development.

* Focuses on helping an individual manage his career and improve skills.

* Personal issues can be discussed more productively unlike in coaching, where the emphasis is on performance at work.

* Providing protection through creating a sense of acceptance and belonging through counselling and friendship.

* Advice with administration, project development and pointing in the right direction.

* Aims at both organisational and individual goals.

> **Definition**
>
> **Mentoring**—"the long-term passing on of support, guidance and advice."
>
> —*CIPD*

6 Counselling

6.1 Need for

▣ Effective **counselling** is in an organisation's interests as it demonstrates commitment to and concern for employees and supports employees (e.g. in taking responsibility for their career development).

▣ It helps to prevent underperformance through:

* reduced labour turnover and absenteeism; and

* increased employee commitment.

▣ Identifies organisational policy and practice which may contribute to the employees' problems and the need for change.

> **Definition**
>
> **Counselling**—the process of helping people clarify their thoughts, feelings and behaviour; identify and accurately define problems; find solutions; or learn to live with a situation.

Example 2 Counselling Situations

"Listening to grievances" is an example of a counselling situation. Suggest FIVE other situations in which a need for counselling may arise.

6.2 Counselling Process

▣ **Recognition and understanding**—managers should be aware that the initial problem raised may be just the "tip of the iceberg" (e.g. an employee with a trivial work-related problem mentions, "By the way—my wife wants a divorce").

▣ **Empowering**—enabling an employee to recognise his problem or situation and encouraging him to express it.

▣ **Resourcing**—managing the problem. Includes deciding who is best able to act as counsellor (e.g. an outside specialist or the employee's line manager).

6.3   Interviews

6.3.1   When Used

▦ For present employees of the company.

▦ To give advice and information and to discuss problems.

6.3.2   Preliminaries

▦ A counselling interview tends to be unstructured.

▦ Little preparatory work may be necessary or possible because the interviewer's role is mainly to react to the interviewee.

▦ However, in appraisal or grievance interviews, the counsellor may decide to follow a particular line before seeing the employee.

6.3.3   Interviewing Skills

▦ Open questioning.

▦ Active listening (probing, interpreting and supporting).

▦ An open mind.

▦ Sincerity and interest.

▦ Remember that the aim is to help the employee to help himself.

▦ Powers of observation—to note behaviour which may be symptomatic of a problem.

▦ Sensitivity to different beliefs and values.

▦ Impartiality—to refrain from giving advice.

▦ Empathy—to appreciate that the problem from the individual's perspective may seem overwhelming.

6.4   Counselling Sessions

▦ May involve:
  - giving advice;
  - encouraging a change in behaviour;
  - discussing a new problem;
  - helping someone take a difficult decision;
  - accepting a situation which cannot be changed; and
  - altering someone's perceptions of an issue.

▦ Aim is not to impose solutions but to induce people to realise for themselves how to overcome difficulties and take appropriate decisions.

▦ Should always be held in private and without interruption.

6.4.1   Non-directive Counselling*

▦ The counsellor assumes:
  - Only the one being counselled can define accurately his own problems.
  - Encouraging the person to talk is the most effective way of getting to the heart of a problem.
  - Solutions to problems will not be implemented unless the person being counselled wholeheartedly agrees with solutions which emerge from the interview.

***Commentary**

*Aims to understand and explain events rather than seek immediate change or remedy.

6.4.2 Directive Counselling

▓ The counsellor takes the initiative and suggests how to solve a problem by:

- outlining the implications and possible consequences of various courses of action;
- suggesting a range of solutions to be considered; and
- charting a path towards the correct decision.

▓ The person being counselled is encouraged to rely on expert knowledge and experience while gradually responding to the counsellor's words and advice. Ultimately, however, the person being counselled makes the final decision.*

Commentary

*Counsellors should believe that the individual has the resources to solve his own problems, albeit with passive or active help.

6.5 Confidentiality

▓ In some situations, an employee cannot be completely open unless they are assured of confidentially.

▓ However, certain information (e.g. about fraud or harassment) once obtained by the organisation may require action.

▓ Therefore, it must be made known to employees when their comments will be passed on to a relevant authority and that the information will be treated in confidence.

6.6 Potential Pitfalls

▓ Taking notes at an inappropriate moment.

▓ Not liking the individual.

▓ Repeating problems.

▓ Taking sides.

▓ Internal and external distractions.

▓ Becoming personally involved.

7 Conflict

Definition

Conflict—friction or opposition resulting from actual or perceived differences or incompatibilities.

7.1 Meaning

▓ **Conflict** situations encompass both opposing behaviour and incompatible goals (e.g. strike or trade union action).

▓ One or both of the parties may be drawn or forced into the confrontation.

7.2 Concepts

7.2.1 "Happy Family" (Traditional) View

▓ A healthy organisational climate is reflected by:

- complete harmony in working relationships;
- loyalty (to employees and employers);
- common commitment to organisational goals and objectives; thus
- relatively easier achievement of those goals and objectives.

▓ Usually characterised by a lack of:

- friction;
- unnecessary duplication of effort;
- frustration; and
- conflict.

- Conflict is seen as dysfunctional (inefficient, ineffective and disruptive); it arises from:
  - poor communication and understanding;
  - personality clashes; or
  - the work of agitators.
- It is disruptive and unnatural and thus represents deviant behaviour which needs to be controlled and changed.
- Conflict situations can result in excessive emotional or physical stress.

7.2.2 The Radical Perspective/Conflict View (Karl Marx)

- Conflict is inevitable due to competition for:
  - limited resources;
  - status; and
  - rewards.
- Conflict is an inherent feature of organisations related to power and politics.*

7.2.3 Interactionist Perspective/"Evolutionary" View

- Conflict is a positive force and necessary for effective performance.
- It raises awareness of the need to change in framework of control.
- The legitimate pursuit of competing interests can balance and preserve social and organisational arrangements.
- A minimum level of conflict:
  - generates self-criticism, change and innovation; and
  - helps prevent apathy or too great a tolerance for the status quo.*

*Commentary

*Conflict is a feature of the unequal nature of organisational life and a natural part of the class struggle. It is not necessarily a bad thing. It can be constructive in bringing about change.

*Commentary

*A good manager doesn't try to eliminate conflict but keeps it from wasting energy.

7.3 Positive and Negative Effects of Conflict

Positive	Negative
✔ Generates better ideas.	✗ Feeling defeated and demeaned.
✔ Invites new approaches.	✗ Distances people.
✔ Provides new solutions to old problems.	✗ Develops a climate of mistrust and suspicion.
✔ Recognises individual's views.	✗ Myopic view of own (narrow) interests.
✔ Clarifies power relationships.	✗ Builds up resistance rather than teamwork.
✔ Stimulates interest and openness.	
✔ Reduces hostility.	✗ Distracts from task.
✔ Tests capabilities (of ideas and people). "Win-win" situations.	✗ Puts people on the defensive.
	✗ Increases employee turnover.

7.4   Symptoms of Conflict

▨ Managers may first become aware of potential conflict through one or more of the following symptoms:

- Poor communications (e.g. withholding and/or distorting information)
- Interpersonal rivalry (e.g. fault-finding in the work of others)
- Inter-group rivalry and jealousy (e.g. "empire-building")
- Low morale and frustration
- Widespread use of arbitration
- Appeals to higher authority
- Inflexible attitudes towards change
- Greater use of the informal organisation (e.g. bypassing formal channels of communication and decision-making).

7.5   Sources of Conflict

▨ Attempting to treat the symptom may exacerbate the conflict. Managers must identify the sources of the conflict and treat the root causes.

▨ Differences between corporate and individual goals are a major source of conflict.

▨ Other conflicts may arise between:

- departments and groups (e.g. due to conflicting goals);
- the formal and informal organisation (e.g. poor communication systems);
- manager and employee (e.g. due to inappropriate leadership style);
- individual and job (e.g. due to stress, illness); and/or
- individuals (e.g. due to personal relationships).

7.5.1   Limited (Scarce) Resources

▨ Most organisational resources are limited—individuals and groups compete for their share (e.g. capital budget allocation).

▨ The greater the limitation, the greater the potential for conflict.

▨ Potential for conflict is intensified when profits and/or revenues fall.

7.5.2   Departmentalisation and Specialisation

▨ Departments tend to be insular—concentrating on achieving their own goals.

▨ Cooperation with other departments is a frequent source of conflict.

▨ Different outlooks and departmental organisational structures are a potential source of conflict:

- A research and development department is most likely to be concerned in the long run with results and operating in a dynamic environment with an organic structure.
- A production department may be more concerned with the short term (e.g. quality control and delivery schedules) and operating in a more stable environment with a bureaucratic structure.

7.5.3 The Nature of Work Activities

- There is greater potential for conflict:
  - when a person's or department's work depends on that of another; and
  - when departments have to work together on a task.
- If reward and punishment systems are perceived to be based on keeping up with performance levels, then the potential for conflict is even greater.

7.5.4 Role Conflict

- A role is the expected pattern of behaviours associated with a particular position in the structure of the organisation (e.g. "manager" role).
- Actual behaviour may not be consistent with the role due to:
  - role incompatibility (not suitable for the role); or
  - role ambiguity (not understanding the role).

7.5.5 Inequitable Treatment

- Unjust treatment in the operation of personnel policies and practices or in reward and punishment systems.
- The perception of inequity may motivate action, including changes in productivity, to restore equity.

7.5.6 Violation of Territory

- Examples of "territory" include:
  - areas of work (e.g. geographical);
  - types of clients dealt with;
  - physical environment (office space, desk, etc); and
  - boundaries of authority.
- Jealousy may arise through status being attached to territory and the "perks" that go with it.
- A new manager can create bad feelings (e.g. of suspicion or resentment).
- "Empire-building" by one department, or individual, encroaching on the work of others.

7.5.7 Environmental Change

- Change in demand.
- Increased competition.
- Government or other intervention.
- New technology.
- Change in social values.

7.5.8 Personal Differences

- Some differences in goals, attitudes and feelings are inevitable because people are so diverse.
- Differences in perception; that is, different people attach different meanings to the same thing.

7.6   Managing Conflict

▨ Denial/withdrawal (i.e. "sweeping it under the carpet")—
conflict may:

  ● "blow over" if trivial; or

  ● become unmanageable if underlying causes are not identified.

▨ Suppression—seeks to preserve working relationships despite minor conflicts.

▨ Dominance—creates lingering resentment and hostility in "win-lose" situations.

▨ Compromise—is inevitable in any organisation made up of different individuals.

  ● Individuals tend to exaggerate their positions to allow for compromise.

  ● Compromise is seen to weaken the value of the decision, perhaps reducing commitment.

▨ Negotiation—the interaction of two or more parties who:

  ● initially have different objectives;

  ● consider they need to be jointly involved in an outcome; and

  ● seek to resolve their differences (by the use of argument and persuasion) in order to achieve a mutually acceptable solution.

▨ Integration/collaboration:

  ● Individuals must accept the need to modify their views for the sake of the task.

  ● Group effort must be seen to be superior to individual effort.

▨ Encourage cooperation—joint problem solving sets goals for all teams/departments to follow.

7.7   Strategies

Many strategies exist for turning conflict into competition or agreement.

7.7.1   Environmental ("Ecological") Strategies

▨ Create conditions in which individuals are better able to interact cooperatively with each other. For example:

  ● Agree common objectives.

  ● Reinforce "team spirit" through culture.

  ● Provide feedback on progress.

  ● Provide adequate coordination and communication mechanisms.

  ● Sort out territorial/role conflicts in the organisational structure.

7.7.2   Regulation Strategies

▨ Provide arbitration to settle disputes.

▨ Establish detailed rules and procedures for conduct by employees.

▨ A liaison/coordination officer or committee.

▨ Use confrontation, or inter-group meetings, to thrash out differences.

▨ Separate conflicting individuals/departments.

▨ Ignore the problem, if it is genuinely likely to "go away".

Summary

- ■ Organisations need skilled people to effectively and efficiently meet objectives. Therefore, it makes sense to develop employees to their full potential.

- ■ Personal development planning involves skills required for the current job as well as for horizontal or vertical positions which the employee could potentially inhabit.

- ■ Time is a scarce resource. Managerial success depends on the manager's ability to control and use time effectively.

- ■ Most time management techniques use some formulation of goal setting, planning and prioritising, with special attention to avoiding time-wasters and procrastination.

- ■ Coaching is targeted toward immediate resolution of a performance issue.

- ■ Counselling is oriented towards getting an employee to open up to an underlying problem creating a performance issue.

Session 23 Quiz

Estimated time: 25 minutes

1. Define "personal development". (2.1)
2. Briefly describe the THREE stages in determining a personal development plan. (2.3)
3. List TEN time-wasters. (3.2, 3.3)
4. Explain the difference between coaching and mentoring. (5.1, 5.2)
5. List the necessary interviewing skills required by a good counsellor. (6.3)
6. Explain the difference between directive and non-directive counselling. (6.4)

Study Question Bank

Estimated time: 20 minutes

Priority		Estimated Time	Completed
MCQ23	Personal Effectiveness	20 minutes	

EXAMPLE SOLUTIONS

Solution 1—Time-Wasters

- **Poor planning**. People don't plan to fail but a lot of people fail to plan. Without weekly and daily plans you will not be prioritising how to spend your time to deal with what should be done, rather than what is "nice" to do.
- **Crisis management**. Sometimes referred to as "fire-fighting". Crisis management, for the most part, is poor time management and is about being reactive rather than proactive (controlling a potential problem before it has a chance to happen).
- **Procrastination**. Putting off tasks until unavoidable. "Procrastination is the thief of time" (Edward Young (1683-1765)). Although planning is critical, actually doing what has been planned is more critical.
- **Interruptions**. Many interruptions are a necessary evil of business life, however many should not be entertained. Always plan time for the unexpected, but make sure that what is unexpected deserves the time of day.
- **Not delegating**. "If you want a job done well you better do it yourself" is often a complete fallacy. Leverage critical time through others and don't allow the things that can be delegated to waste time.
- **Unnecessary meetings**. Most meetings are a complete waste of time creating no economic benefit. They are just a planned ritual. Before a meeting ask, "Is it really necessary?" If it is, then meet but take action as a result of the meeting and not let it be a time bandit.
- **The "shuffling blues"**. Basically shuffling paper from one pile to the next (or e-mail files between folders) without taking any action other than to move it to the next pile. Keep a clean desk, empty your in-box, empty your to-do box and delete the deleted e-mail folder.
- **Poor physical setup**. Not having the things needed frequently within arm's reach and having a lot of the things you rarely need close by causes wasted time retrieving what is most frequently needed.
- **Poor networking**. Good-quality relationships with others are often a significant time saver on the basis that if "you do not know, you know somebody else who does".
- **Bad attitude**. Dwelling on problems rather than solutions and involving others unnecessarily, thus wasting their time. The truth is that 85% of them really do not care and cannot or would not help you; the other 15% are actually glad it is not happening to them.
- **Negative people**. Some people are the "life of the party" and some people would kill the party, if allowed. A lot of time can be spent (wasted) listening to whinges and complaints rather than focusing on what needs to be done. But then, as with crisis management and dealing with the unexpected, it may be part of the job description. If so, the negatives must be managed to minimise the damage.

Solution 2—Counselling Situations

- Handling disputes.
- Assisting people undergoing excessive work-related stress.
- During appraisals.
- Following change, such as promotion or relocation.
- On redundancy or dismissal.
- Dealing with employees accused of improper behaviour or other disciplinary situations.

Information Within Business

FOCUS

This session covers the following content from the *ACCA Study Guide.*

E. Personal Effectiveness and Communication in Business

5. Communicating in business

c) Explain how the type of information differs and the purposes for which it is applied at different levels of the organisation: strategic, tactical and operational. ☐

d) List the attributes of good-quality information. ☐

Session 24 Guidance

■ **Note** that this session looks at the role of information and how this role has changed from that of simply recording transactions and providing accounting information to strategic analysis.

■ **Know** that the basis for designing information systems is organisational requirements.

■ **Understand** the differences among structured, unstructured and semi-structured requirements (s.1.1). Make sure that you understand the difference in a practical context.

(continued on next page)

VISUAL OVERVIEW

Objective: To describe and examine the forms and sources of information required by organisations and the main features of information systems used by organisations.

```
┌─────────────────────────────────────────┐
│         INFORMATION REQUIREMENTS          │
│  • Organisational Requirements            │
│  • Data and Information                    │
│  • Qualities of Information                │
└─────────────────────────────────────────┘
                    │
┌─────────────────────────────────────────┐
│       MANAGEMENT INFORMATION              │
│            REQUIREMENTS                    │
│  • Management Structure                    │
│  • Strategic Management                    │
│  • Tactical Management                     │
│  • Operational Management                  │
└─────────────────────────────────────────┘
                    │
┌─────────────────────────────────────────┐
│           INFORMATION SYSTEMS             │
│  • General Categories                      │
│  • Transaction Processing Systems          │
│  • Office Automation Systems               │
│  • Knowledge Work Systems                  │
│  • Expert Systems                          │
│  • Management Information Systems          │
│  • Decision Support Systems                │
│  • Executive Support Systems               │
└─────────────────────────────────────────┘
```

Session 24 Guidance

■ **Learn** the *qualities of information* (s.1.3). **Recognise** the correspondence between information requirements at the strategic, tactical and operational levels (remember Anthony) and the types of systems that can deliver information needs (s.2, s.3).

■ **Make sure** that you can answer questions in terms of the different types of information systems organisations will need to provide different levels of information in a range of functional areas. Look particularly at the many examples provided and relate to your own job environment.

1 Information Requirements

1.1 Organisational Requirements

▓ Information is required throughout the organisation to support:

- development of strategies and achievement of goals;
- decision-making at all levels in the organisation;
- planning, coordination and control of strategies as well as processes;
- communication throughout, as well as outside, the organisation; and
- analysis of internal and external factors and visualisation.

▓ Anthony's hierarchy (see *Session 6* as well as s.2 of this session) implies a broad range of requirements for internally and externally sourced information throughout organisations.

▓ In considering the broad range of information and its uses, one useful classification is that of structured, unstructured and semi-structured information requirements.

1.1.1 Structured Requirements

▓ Most or all variables are known and decision-making is routine, therefore requiring little judgement. Structured requirements are highly suitable for computerisation. For example, quality inspection, inventory control and re-ordering, discounting sales price of products based on sale by date, depreciation, analysis of financial data based on predetermined rules (e.g. ageing, debt collection periods, gearing, liquidity ratios).

▓ Structured information requirements:

- can be planned in advance and are often repetitive;
- are precise, as they are often based on clear, predefined rules;
- are frequently objective, with little or no scope for the exercise of judgement; and
- are often automated, as they are easily programmed.

1.1.2 Unstructured Requirements

▓ Unstructured requirements depend on intuition or judgement and the solutions are not clear-cut. Unstructured requirements are usually not highly suitable for formal computerisation (e.g. how to respond to a hostile takeover bid, hiring of managerial staff, expanding into new markets, developing new products, reorganising the company).

▓ Unstructured information requirements (i.e. decisions):

- are often unplanned because they are unique. Particularly at the strategic level, unstructured decisions will relate to a set of circumstances the organisation has never faced (and may never again);
- may be intuitive and rely on the professional judgement of the decision-maker;
- have few or no rules, as the decision was unpredictable; and
- are subjective, as they often relate to situations in which outcomes are uncertain.

1.1.3 Semi-Structured Requirements

Semi-structured requirements involve a mix of standard solution
procedures (structured) and individual judgement (unstructured).
Such requirements are difficult to program, though some of the
structured elements of the requirement may be computerised
(e.g. capital investment appraisal).

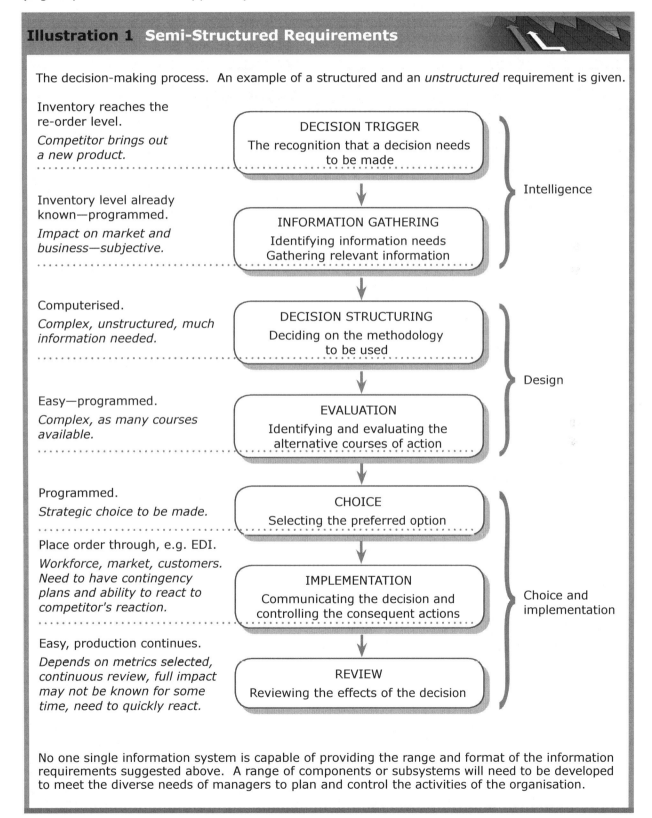

Illustration 1 Semi-Structured Requirements

The decision-making process. An example of a structured and an *unstructured* requirement is given.

Inventory reaches the re-order level.
Competitor brings out a new product.

DECISION TRIGGER
The recognition that a decision needs to be made

Inventory level already known—programmed.
Impact on market and business—subjective.

INFORMATION GATHERING
Identifying information needs
Gathering relevant information

} Intelligence

Computerised.
Complex, unstructured, much information needed.

DECISION STRUCTURING
Deciding on the methodology to be used

Easy—programmed.
Complex, as many courses available.

EVALUATION
Identifying and evaluating the alternative courses of action

} Design

Programmed.
Strategic choice to be made.

CHOICE
Selecting the preferred option

Place order through, e.g. EDI.
Workforce, market, customers. Need to have contingency plans and ability to react to competitor's reaction.

IMPLEMENTATION
Communicating the decision and controlling the consequent actions

Easy, production continues.
Depends on metrics selected, continuous review, full impact may not be known for some time, need to quickly react.

REVIEW
Reviewing the effects of the decision

} Choice and implementation

No one single information system is capable of providing the range and format of the information requirements suggested above. A range of components or subsystems will need to be developed to meet the diverse needs of managers to plan and control the activities of the organisation.

1.2   Data and Information

▓ Directors, managers and workers require information to make decisions.

▓ Information is data that has been processed so that it has a meaning and enables improved decision-making.

▓ To be useful, data must be captured, processed and presented in a form that can be easily understood. The more structured the data, the easier it will be to provide meaningful information.

Data—numbers, letters and symbols that relate to facts, events and transactions.

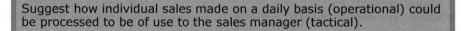

Example 1   Sales Data

Suggest how individual sales made on a daily basis (operational) could be processed to be of use to the sales manager (tactical).

1.3   Qualities of Information

Information should have certain qualities in order for a receiver to understand a situation and make a decision. Although each quality is relevant, its nature will vary depending on the level of management using that information.

1.3.1   Time Period

▓ Can be historical, current or forecast:

● Strategic management will focus on current and planning horizon data for strategy formulation but will use all information (e.g. summarised historical information for trend analysis and comparison to budgets, current information on competitors, forecasts of market growth prospects).

● Tactical management will mainly use near future, current and near past (e.g. yearly budget projections, delivery scheduling, budget variance analysis).

● Operational management is usually only interested in current and near past information (e.g. inventory levels, credit limits, bank account balances, payables, receivables).

1.3.2   Timeliness

▓ Information should be available when needed to reach a decision. If too late, it will be discarded or ignored; if early, it could be misleading as the underlying data may have changed when the decision is made.

▓ Operational information must usually be immediately available (real time) although strategic information need not always be timely, as an immediate decision may not always be needed. Note, however, that an opportunity to purchase additional resources (e.g. another company) or to gain a competitive advantage typically will be time sensitive.

1.3.3 Relevance

▨ Information provided should enable the recipient to make a decision. It must be related to the information needs of the user for a specific situation. Information which is not needed should be omitted, regardless of its "interest" value. Irrelevant information wastes time and may lead to incorrect decisions.

▨ Information systems may provide the same information, in the same format, to all managers. Much of the information they receive may relate to aspects of the business for which they are not responsible. Such information should be filtered or made on an exception basis (e.g. when things go wrong) so as to provide relevant information.

▨ At a strategic level, information usually needs to be formatted to an executive summary with the detail available if needed. Greater detail will be more relevant at the tactical and operational levels.

▨ However, the relevance of certain information, especially that relating to the organisation's environment, may not always be immediately clear.

▨ The highly structured and programmable nature of decision-making at the operational level requires objective, quantifiable information.

1.3.4 Accuracy

▨ Information can be precise or approximate, but should be reported in a form which is sufficiently correct for the intended purpose.

▨ Financial information should be reported to an appropriate level of precision.* Calculations should be correct and totals correctly added.

Commentary

*For example:

Management accounts are usually exact, $0.00, as management needs to know exact income, costs, quantities and values.

Budgets, as they predict the future, will usually be rounded to $000 or even $m (e.g. $0.453m).

Annual financial statements are usually rounded to $m or even $b; users do not need to know the exact figures (which would detract from the clarity of the statements). If the exact figure is required by statute, however, this must be given (e.g. directors' remuneration).

■ Factual data should be supported by notes as required to clarify its meaning.

■ Inaccurate, poorly captured or incorrectly processed data results in information which may be unacceptable to the user (i.e. garbage in, garbage out).

■ Although "accuracy" implies that information should be *free* from error, this need not be the case. The concept of materiality applies to all information, not just accounting records. Information should be accurate enough for the recipient to make the right decision at the right time.

■ Data capture methods which are more accurate than basic keyboard entry include:

  • bar codes, although this depends on accurate data input;
  • electronic point of sales (EPOS), often incorporated with …
  • electronic funds transfer at the point of sale (EFTPOS);
  • optical mark reading;
  • optical character reading (i.e. scanners);
  • magnetic stripe cards and smart cards;
  • touch screens (accurate if correct menu choice made); and
  • voice recognition (improving in reliability).

1.3.5 Completeness

■ Systems should provide enough of the right type of information to make required decisions. How detailed the information will be depends on the user's needs, but it should be free from material omission.

■ Strategic managers often need to make assumptions, extrapolate data, be subjective and sometimes use their "best guess" because the information they require may not be available for several months if not years or is commercially sensitive (e.g. relating to a competitor). They may therefore need to make decisions without all of the desired information.

■ Monthly management accounts may not be complete without comparative information and future predictions, for example, to enable a manager to make a decision on buying levels.

■ An operational inventory re-order decision, for example, could not be made without all the in and out inventory movements having been recorded.*

*Commentary

*Note that setting the re-order level would be a tactical rather than operational decision.

1.3.6 Conciseness

■ Only the information needed should be provided. Information should be clear, sufficiently detailed, yet as brief as possible and still be informative to support the decision being made (e.g. executive summaries and exception reporting).

■ A balance must be reached between complete, relevant and concise information. Complete information may lead to information overload and obscure relevant facts; concise information may lead to insufficient information.

■ Some information systems do not produce concise information because they standardise the output for a wide range of managers, thus producing pages of zero entries. They also provide all available information rather than concentrating, for example, on large adverse variances as in exception reporting.

1.3.7   Understandability

▨ Clear information results in better understanding and allows better decisions. This includes the conscious decision not to take any action, if appropriate. Information which assumes knowledge the recipient does not have may not be fully understood.

▨ This implies that the information must suit the user. Use of technical jargon to impress the user may cause confusion. The relationship between statistical data presented in a tabular format may not be fully understood until presented in a graphical form (e.g. a pie chart).

1.3.8   Confidence

▨ The information provided must be trusted by the user. The user will not use information which has a track record of being frequently wrong or misleading.

▨ Reliable sources of data, data capture, processing and related controls will improve confidence in the information, as will actual results agreeing with the data where the information was predictive in nature.

▨ Where the information has been derived, disclosure of how the derivation has been carried out will improve confidence in the information.

1.3.9   Channel

▨ Information should be appropriately delivered and presented for the user to ensure that it is easy to use. This implies full or summary detail, order (in a predetermined sequence), presentation (e.g. narrative, numerical, graphic, video, audible) and media (e.g. hard copy, electronic, letter, memo, e-mail, e-chat, telephone, SMS).

▨ Strategic managers may prefer, for example, short, paper-based "executive" summaries or a touch screen graphical interface which supports drilling down to the detailed data.

▨ Operational managers may require detailed formal reports, either screen-based or hard copy. They also may require screen-based graphical presentation or audible warning tones when an action is required (e.g. when a bar code is not correctly read).

1.3.10 Volume (Noise)

▨ Basically, information overload. If too much information is received too quickly, the receiver will not be able to sort out what is required to make a decision. This is especially problematic if an immediate decision has to be made.*

▨ Filtering is being specific about what is required. Using key words on searches and exception reporting reduce overload.

*Commentary

*Airbus provides information to pilots electronically through video screens. Successive redesigns of the Airbus flight information systems have resulted in irrelevant information being removed from the screens during emergencies. Only information required by the pilots to make decisions in an emergency (e.g. engine damage) is displayed.

1.3.11 Cost Benefit

■ Whatever the cost of capturing data, processing data and delivering the information, the benefit of using that information must outweigh the costs. Although costs may relate to a monetary value, the time taken to capture, process, deliver, understand and use the information also will have a "cost".

■ In most cases, a quantifiable value can be placed on the use of information. In other cases, this may not be possible. The ultimate test may be that without information the organisation may cease to function, but at what cost?

■ In addition, making the wrong decision through poor-quality information can also be very costly (e.g. missed opportunities and inappropriate decisions resulting in going concern problems).

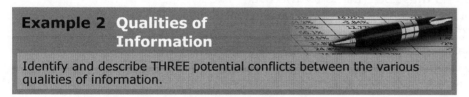

Example 2 Qualities of Information

Identify and describe THREE potential conflicts between the various qualities of information.

2 Management Information Requirements

2.1 Management Structure

■ The Anthony hierarchy is a common categorisation of organisational levels:*

Commentary

*See *Session 6*.

2.2 Strategic Management

■ A board of directors and executive committees typically control the overall strategic planning process. They develop the organisation's mission statement, strategy and overall goals together with the strategies of the separate business units. They also monitor the strategic and operational performance of the organisation.

■ Information is therefore required to:
  ● enable strategic planning;
  ● assess whether the plan is being achieved in practice;
  ● identify when the plan needs changing and how it should be changed.

2.2.1   Strategic Decisions

▦ Strategic decisions:

- affect the whole organisation;
- are often subjective because the future cannot be known;
- may be based on a number of different scenarios;
- are proactive rather than reactive;
- relate to the strategic horizon, which may be 5 years, 20 years or on a rolling basis;
- have a higher level of risk than other decisions because of the unpredictable factors on which they are based (e.g. the future PEST environment);
- are usually complex;
- are unlikely to be recurring; and
- provide the framework and guidance for tactical decision-making.

▦ Examples of strategic decisions include:

- The use of resources to meet objectives.
- Expansion policies, target markets to be addressed, target market penetration.
- Reorganisation strategies.
- Succession planning.
- The specification of required profit levels, return on investment.
- Defining the organisation's policy on quality standards.

2.2.2   Strategic Information

▦ Information required at the strategic level usually has the following characteristics:

- Often prepared on an ad hoc basis.
- Mostly unscheduled (especially external information).
- Summarised so performance can be judged at the highest level, but capable of detailed analysis if required.
- Required infrequently.
- Forward-looking for planning (rather than control).
- Emphasis placed on external, but includes internal to compare performance and products with competitors.
- Wide in scope so as not to narrow the options available.
- Quantitative (past) and qualitative (forward-looking).

2.3   Tactical Management

▦ Tactical managers develop short- to medium-term objectives, plans, policies, procedures, budgets and schedules for their operational units to enable implementation of the organisation's strategic plans.

▦ Information is therefore required to:

- allocate resources; and
- monitor the performance and use of those resources.

2.3.1   Tactical Decisions

▓ Tactical decisions:

- implement the requirements of the strategic plan;
- affect significant parts of the organisation;
- are based on internal and external information;
- are usually based on financial analysis;
- use a mix of qualitative and quantitative data;
- are related to the short and medium term;
- are often recurring processes, although in different contexts (e.g. setting quality standards for different departments); and
- provide the rules for operational decision-making.

▓ Examples of tactical decisions include:

- Allocation of a resource budget and the acquisition of that resource.
- Utilisation of a resource (e.g. staff scheduling).
- Determining pricing levels, discounts, credit limits, re-order levels, etc.
- Setting manufacturing quality standards and the design of a quality control methodology.

2.3.2   Tactical Information

▓ Information required at the tactical level is usually:

- generated primarily from internal sources;
- concerned with business units or activities (sales, marketing, finance, etc);
- fairly detailed to allow manipulation of alternative scenarios and sensitivity analysis;
- prepared routinely (e.g. management accounts and variance analysis);
- relevant to the short and medium term; and
- based primarily on quantitative factors.

2.4   Operational Management

▓ Operational managers direct the use of resources and the performance of tasks according to procedures, set routines, budgets and schedules established at the tactical level.

▓ Information is required to ensure that specific operational tasks are performed as intended.

2.4.1   Operational Decisions

▓ Operational decisions:

- affect day-to-day routine operations;
- are immediate or very short-term;
- are basically concerned with control rather than planning;
- have a low level of risk/uncertainty as they are derived from set rules and procedures;
- are often repetitive;
- can easily be programmed;
- use internal information; and
- follow rules set by tactical decision-making.

▦ Examples of operational decisions include:

    ● Rejection of materials that do not meet specified quality requirements.

    ● Destroying food that has exceeded its "sell-by date".

    ● Electronic submission of data on completion of a specified event.

    ● Re-ordering inventory when the volume in stock reaches the re-order level.

2.4.2 Operational Information

▦ Information required at the operational level usually has the following characteristics:

    ● Very detailed (sometimes even raw data), so specific decisions can be made about individual cost or revenue drivers.

    ● Based on internal quantitative data to ensure full control.

    ● Based on data relating to the past or present, supporting decisions relating to the short-term future.

    ● Relevant to the immediate term.

    ● Task- or routine-specific.

    ● Prepared as often as required (e.g. based on daily delivery schedules, monthly salary run).

3   Information Systems

3.1   General Categories

▦ Although new information systems are developed frequently, they broadly fall into one of six general categories:

    1. Executive support systems (ESS)

    2. Transaction processing systems (TPS)

    3. Office automation systems (OAS)

    4. Knowledge work systems (KWS)

    5. Decision support systems (DSS)

    6. Management information systems (MIS).

▦ These six categories broadly serve the three general management levels of an organisation as suggested by Anthony, plus an additional level (knowledge and data workers) which has evolved through the development of IS:

> **Exam Advice**
>
> Although types of information systems are not directly referred to in the FAB/F1 syllabus, they are a fundamental part of how information is delivered and applied at the different levels of an organisation (which is in the syllabus). As an understanding of these systems is assumed knowledge for later papers (e.g. P3 *Business Analysis*), types of information systems are included here for completeness.

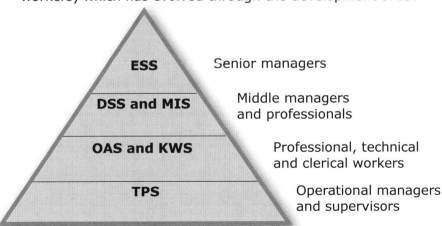

3.1.1   Operational Systems

▨ Assist in day-to-day management of the basic activities of the organisation by tracking the individual transactions that occur in an organisation.

▨ Provide structured, programmable information and enable routine enquiries to be made and answered.

▨ Information in these systems will be easily available, current and accurate.

3.1.2   Knowledge Systems

▨ Help knowledge and data workers develop and design new products and services.

▨ They collect (harvest), store, organise and distribute information and knowledge throughout the organisation; perform administrative tasks; and control the flow of paperwork.

3.1.3   Management Systems

▨ Designed for the monitoring and controlling of the organisation's activities (i.e. other systems) by middle management through use of standard reports or, more often in an information intensive environment, by exception reporting. In addition, at a higher level, they support the decision-making and administrative functions of middle management.*

3.1.4   Strategic Systems

▨ Assist senior managers with long-term strategic planning and need to reflect the way senior managers work (i.e. flexible, unstructured, ad hoc).

▨ A primary area of activity for such systems will be environmental monitoring. This involves identifying changes in an organisation's political, economic, social and technological environment and the effect of those changes on the organisation.

*Commentary

*Included in this category are Decision Support Systems which support the non-routine decision-making (e.g. what-if analysis and modelling required of middle managers).

3.2   Transaction Processing Systems (TPS)

▨ A TPS processes daily data resulting from business transactions, updates operational databases and produces business documents.

  ● Highly structured, producing standard outputs (i.e. detailed reports, listings and summaries) from transaction and event inputs.

  ● Limited processing capabilities (e.g. sorting, listing, merging, updating) and will therefore only support highly structured decisions which rely on standardised information provision.

  ● Adds little value to the data processed.

▨ There are two main types of transaction processing:

  1. Batch processing, in which individual transactions are gathered together and stored for later entry into the computer system.

  2. Real-time processing, in which the transaction is processed as soon as it is captured.

3.3   Office Automation Systems (OAS)

▓ An OAS is designed to increase the productivity of office, data and information workers and all other employees and managers who need to handle and manage documents, scheduling and communication.

▓ User-friendly systems (e.g. Windows, touch screens, tablets, speech recognition) have resulted in core office support (i.e. word processing, messaging, diary, graphical presentations) being carried out by many of the managers themselves.

▓ The introduction of affordable PDAs (personal digital assistants) and smart phones which incorporate work organisation software, diaries, e-mail and Internet access with wireless/Wi-Fi telecommunication have extended the capabilities of OAS to virtually all employees of an organisation. Increasingly, such systems collaborate directly with a broader range of OAS.

3.4   Knowledge Work Systems (KWS)

3.4.1   Terminology

▓ A **knowledge work system** (KWS; also referred to as a knowledge management system—KMS) facilitates creation, integration and dissemination of (new) business knowledge within and throughout an organisation.

▓ A **knowledge worker** (often classified as professional and/or technical employees) is an employee who is primarily charged with creating new information and knowledge (e.g. engineers, designers, researchers, doctors, lawyers, professional accountants and scientists).

▓ A **data worker** is an employee who tends to process information and knowledge rather than create information and knowledge.

▓ Although the key input to knowledge-based systems tends to come from the "professional" employee, new knowledge can come from any employee. For example, an operational worker may draw on her experience of a process to develop a new innovative process; her experience and knowledge is input into the system to be accessed by her fellow workers.

3.4.2   Features

▦ Features of a typical KWS will include:

- **Power**—because of the nature of knowledge work, the software, hardware and other systems need to be very powerful to give knowledge workers the required capability, capacity, flexibility and speed.

- **Specialised software tools**—enable knowledge creation and integration into the business environment. Software will include powerful graphics and analytical models together with groupware and intranet management software.

- **User-friendly interface**—knowledge workers will use the system as a tool to enable them to do their work. Such tools should not waste the time of users and should allow users to be effective and efficient.

- **Communication links**—knowledge workers often require links to external specialist data/knowledge bases, usually via the Internet.

- **Standard software**—includes word processing, e-mail, voice mail, scheduling and basic document handling.

3.5   Expert Systems

3.5.1   Description

▦ Knowledge-intensive computer programmes which capture and codify the expertise of a human in limited domains of knowledge. This knowledge can then be accessed and interrogated by non-experts through following a programmed structure of key questions to obtain an appropriate answer and the reasons/logic behind the answer.

▦ The core of an expert system is the knowledge base, the codified knowledge of the expert. This contains the facts and concepts and the relationships between them. Many expert systems can be purchased as specific packages

▦ For an expert system to be of value to an organisation:

- the expertise to be codified must be capable of being well defined—objective, not subjective;

- problem resolution should be capable of being logically defined following a set of tried and tested rules and procedures;

- the investment and maintenance of the system must be cost beneficial, saving both company time and the cost of hiring expensive experts; and

- reduced errors, reduced training time, improved decisions, improved quality and service are expected.

3.5.2 Examples of Expert Systems

▦ There are many examples of expert systems in daily use which many people do not recognise as such. For example:

- Photocopy control panels allowing the operator to fix common faults (e.g. jammed paper).
- Problem-solving programs ("wizards") incorporated into software issued with computer-based systems.
- Train ticket selection covering journey, time of day, age (e.g. children, pensioners), discounts (e.g. families).
- Telephone or website customer service systems which direct the customer to the appropriate assistant to answer their enquiries (e.g. "Press 1 to ..., 2 for ..., 3 for ...").

▦ Other systems cover more technical rule-based areas such as law, taxation, banking, insurance, medicine, production, quality control and air-traffic control.

3.6 Management Information Systems (MIS)

3.6.1 Description

▦ An MIS is a set of formalised procedures designed to provide managers at all levels with appropriate information from internal and external sources to enable timely and effective decisions for planning and controlling the activities for which they are responsible.

▦ An MIS supports structured decisions at the operational and tactical levels. It is also useful for basic planning purposes of senior managers.

▦ An MIS provides managers with manager-determined information for monitoring day-to-day performance, maintaining coordination and providing background information about the entity's operations.

▦ Reports may be made on a template basis (i.e. regular management accounts) and variance analysis or on an exception basis (i.e. show all inventory items with less than seven days production capacity).

▦ MIS structures are relatively rigid and therefore more suitable to a stable environment. Analytical powers are limited and reports are usually generated as a standard set.

▦ Report details are mainly drawn from information captured and input by the TPS and incorporated into MIS reports which are then made available to managers on a regular basis (i.e. weekly, monthly, etc). The bulk of information provided relates to past performance, particularly towards the end of the budget year or period.

▦ By incorporating Web browsers, managers have some flexibility in accessing external sources of information as well as internal TPS databases, customising reports and on-demand information rather than scheduled reports.

▦ MIS information will also include regular reports generated externally, received by organisational e-mail, incorporated with internal information and then distributed to relevant managers over the intranet (i.e. Accountancy Business Updates, e-Commerce News).

3.6.2 Examples of MIS

> **Example 3** **MIS**
>
> Suggest typical uses of MIS in the following functions:
>
> **(a) Manufacturing**
>
> **(b) Retail**
>
> **(c) Services**
>
> **(d) General**

3.7 Decision Support Systems (DSS)

3.7.1 Description

- A DSS helps managers make decisions, use their own judgement and insights and work in ill-defined areas. It supports decision-making in semi-structured and unstructured situations through the use of databases, analytical models and data analysis tools (model bases).

- Enables managers to focus on the real business problems by gathering, summarising and analysing information relevant to a particular decision area.

- Does not make decisions for the manager, but assists them through the decision-making stages in semi-structured situations (i.e. not easily specified in advance), by providing both internal and external information (structured) and evaluating various options (unstructured).

- Is not concerned with routine processing of transactions, record keeping or producing standard reports. For example, a typical sales MIS will produce sales reports based on product, salesperson, accounts, sales region, etc. A DSS, however, would allow the sales director, incorporating results from market research, to test the potential effect of changing a number of variables (e.g. price, promotions, discounts, commission) on metrics (e.g. market share, contribution) and rank the scenario outcomes.

▓ May be as simple as a spreadsheet packaged application that allows the user to develop his own models and variables (i.e. sales, production and profit forecasts using what-if and sensitivity analysis) or a complex bespoke system using, for example, linear programming, multiple regression forecasting or capital budgeting present value, unique to the individual organisation (e.g. treasury systems, capital investment appraisal or engineering analysis).

▓ Most likely to be used at the middle-manager and professional level for tactical decision-making. But can be used at all levels, for example, to assist in planning.

3.7.2 DSS Structure

▓ Typically, a more complex DSS usually consists of:

* Tools which can condense huge volumes of data drawn from internal as well as external sources and then analyse that data (e.g. data warehousing and data-mining, and the use of online analytical processing).

* Sophisticated problem analysis options for:

— what-if analysis (effect on an output if variables are changed);

— sensitivity analysis (effect on an output if one variable is continuously changed by a small increment);

— scenario analysis (complex what-if analysis, for example, for a change in government).

▓ User-friendly input and output interface, which allows users to easily change assumptions, ask new questions, input new data and obtain clearly understood results.

▓ Statistical, financial and simulation capabilities to ensure quick development of models.

3.8 Executive Support Systems (ESS)

3.8.1 Description

▓ An ESS, sometimes referred to as an Executive or Enterprise Information System or EIS, provides managers with tactical and strategic information for monitoring operating results and general business conditions of the environment.

▓ The executives of an organisation need access to a wide range of internal and external data which will allow them to make complex, unstructured decisions relating to the organisation as a whole.

▓ Senior managers will need internal (e.g. from MIS and TPS) and external (e.g. Internet) executive summaries which enable them to ensure that the organisation's critical success factors are being achieved, to monitor competitors, to monitor the environment (environmental scanning) and to identify opportunities/threats and forecast trends.

▓ ESS were designed to overcome the inflexibility of MIS (e.g. fixed format reports at fixed times from fixed sources—not the way senior managers work). They help managers find the information they need, whenever they need it and in the most appropriate format. They provide a general computing and communications environment rather than providing any fixed application or specific capability.

3.8.2 Primary Features

- Flexibility allows managers to use the system as an extension of their own thinking and work methodologies without the need to address specific problems or have solutions imposed on them.

- Ability to gather and display complex data in a simplified form. The sources of information which a senior manager uses are numerous, in different formats and subject to rapid change.

- Ease of use through point-and-click technology, graphical and tabular displays. This allows information to be quickly assimilated by the manager and allows quick movement between information sets (e.g. between windows).

- Use of templates which are defined by, and can be easily changed by, the user to display information from many sources on one screen. For example, a sales and trend analysis by value and by product for each region and in total would be produced from each region's monthly management accounts, compared to external information downloaded from a trade confederation source and all displayed on one screen.

- Analytical facilities which allow data to be analysed, compared and trends identified.

- "Drill down" facilities which allow investigation of the data behind a piece of information on a selective basis (e.g. into the MIS or TPS database to specifically show the makeup of sales for each region separately). This data would be shown, for example, in a separate window with the system allowing quick comparison of and movement between windows.

- The use of Web browser technology to link related internal or external (Internet and extranet) information (e.g. news reports, direct links to financial market databases).

Illustration 2 General Electric

All of General Electric's senior managers have a constantly updated view of their areas of operations as well as for the enterprise as a whole. The system, referred to as a "dashboard", compares performance metrics (e.g. systems performance, response times, sales or margins, against set targets and will alert the senior managers if any variance exceeds a predetermined limit). Action can then be taken by the manager.

Illustration 3 PepsiCo

ESS systems at PepsiCo allow managers to see how each of their product lines are selling in any store or location, in any country, in any sub-division of that country, in any town, in any customer's particular store in that town, at any time. This information can be presented to managers in whatever form or combination they wish.

Illustration 4 Intelligent Search Engines

Many organisations use ESS incorporating AI (artificial intelligence) and other intelligent search engines to carry out environmental scanning of, for example:

- their competitors' websites, many of which will display organisation charts, customer lists, product lists, press releases, details of speeches given by executives, new executives, etc;
- news agency sites; and
- government sites (e.g. patent registries, statutory report filings).

The information obtained can then be analysed to provide ideas of new products, changes in strategy, potential mergers, etc.

Lauden and Lauden have diagrammatically shown the relationship of information systems to each as:

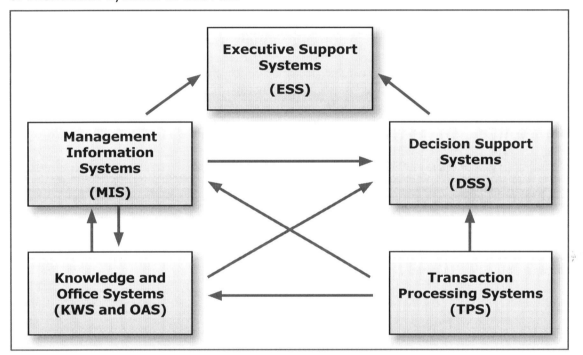

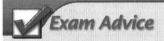
Exam Advice

As the syllabus requires you to "identify the different sources of internal and external information", consider throughout this Study Text the forms of internal and external information and their sources (e.g. PEST, control systems, business risk, fraud, stakeholders, sales, purchases, cash, etc).

24-**19**

Summary

- Structured information can be planned and is repetitive, precise, frequently objective and usually automated. It is highly suitable for computerisation.

- Unstructured requirements are unique, intuitive, unpredictable and subjective. They are not as suitable for computerisation.

- Semi-structured information combines qualities of the two.

- Information must have certain qualities for it to be useful to the receiver for decision-making. These qualities include an appropriate time period, timeliness, relevance, accuracy, completeness, conciseness, understandability, confidence, channel, volume, and cost benefit.

- Decision-makers will have different information needs based on the area of responsibility and level within the company.

  - Strategic management will tend to make fewer, longer-reaching decisions which are non-recurring and usually complex.

  - Tactical managers use near- and intermediate-term information to allocate resources and monitor performance and use of resources.

  - Operational managers make many routine decisions which are usually not that complex and are based on decision frameworks established by tactical managers.

 Session 24 Quiz
Estimated time: 15 minutes

1. Briefly explain the difference between structured and unstructured information requirements. (1.1)

2. Explain the difference between data and information. (1.2)

3. Describe how information can be timely, relevant and accurate. (1.3)

4. State FOUR characteristics of strategic information. (2.2)

 Study Question Bank
Estimated time: 20 minutes

Priority		Estimated Time	Completed
MCQ24	Information Within Business	20 minutes	

EXAMPLE SOLUTIONS

Solution 1—Sales Data

- Volume and value of sales units made (e.g. by product grouping, geographical area).
- If the sales are related to the use of a loyalty or discount card (e.g. supermarkets), analysis can be carried out based on the gender, age, location and other information provided by the card holder.
- Growth or decline in particular markets.
- Identification of trends for particular products which could be matched to specific events (e.g. weather, day of the week, national holidays, concerts, sports).
- Overall increasing or decreasing demand for particular products.

Solution 2—Qualities of Information

1. Timeliness and accuracy—the greater the accuracy required, the more time which may be needed to collect and process the data.
2. Timeliness and cost—the longer it takes to generate information, usually the greater the cost of doing so.
3. Completeness and conciseness—conciseness can be "yes" or "no" but the required information will be incomplete.

Solution 3—MIS

(a) Manufacturing—sales summaries, production summaries, inventory levels, inventory ageing analysis, output levels, receivable balances in arrears.

(b) Retail—sales by department, sales by product, inventory levels, supplier purchase turnover.

(c) Services—summaries of work and costs per client, total fees per client, profit per client.

(d) General—basically, summary information of whatever is held on a database (i.e. by manager, by department, by location, by firm) which can be sorted and ranked by field or by given criteria.

Communication Within Business

FOCUS

This session covers the following content from the *ACCA Study Guide.*

E. Personal Effectiveness and Communication in Business
5. Communicating in business
a) Describe methods of communication used in the organisation and how they are used. ☐
d) Explain a simple communication model: sender, message, receiver, feedback, noise. ☐
e) Explain formal and informal communication and their importance in the workplace. ☐
f) Identify the consequences of ineffective communication. ☐
g) Describe the attributes of effective communication. ☐
h) Describe the barriers to effective communication and identify practical steps that may be taken to overcome them. ☐
i) Identify the main patterns of communication. ☐

Session 25 Guidance

■ **Appreciate** that communication contributes to the success of any organisation by describing who is doing what and how. As you use communication every day, most of this session should be familiar, although you may not recognise its context.

■ **Read** through the whole session a number of times until you have placed the specifics into life context. Also realise that some communication applications (e.g. recruitment and selection) have already been covered in other sessions.

(continued on next page)

VISUAL OVERVIEW

Objective: To describe communication and the skills of effective communication.

```
                    ┌─────────────────────────────────┐
                    │     EFFECTIVE COMMUNICATION      │
                    │  • Communication Process         │
                    │  • Importance                    │
                    │  • Attributes                    │
                    │  • Barriers                      │
                    │  • Flow and Direction            │
                    └─────────────────────────────────┘
                         /                    \
        ┌──────────────────────────┐   ┌──────────────────────────┐
        │   COMMUNICATION MEDIA     │   │       PRESENTATION        │
        │  • Written Methods        │   │  • Methods                │
        │  • Oral Methods           │   │  • Formal Report          │
        │  • Non-verbal Behaviour   │   │  • Letters and Memoranda  │
        │  • Communication Skills   │   │  • Oral Presentations     │
        └──────────────────────────┘   └──────────────────────────┘
                    │
        ┌──────────────────────────┐
        │     COMMUNICATION         │
        │       PATTERNS            │
        │  • Circle                 │
        │  • Chain                  │
        │  • "Y"                    │
        │  • Wheel                  │
        │  • All-Channel            │
        └──────────────────────────┘
```

Session 25 Guidance

■ **Understand** the difference between qualities of information (*Session 24*) and attributes of effective communication (s.1.3).

■ **Know** the media which facilitate communication (s.2) and the appropriate methods for various media (s.3).

■ **Recognise** that communication patterns (s.4) can easily be examined in the form of a short scenario.

1 Effective Communication

1.1 Communication Process

■ **Communication** involves encoding and transmitting an idea through a communication channel which will be received and decoded at the other end of the communication channel.*

■ The communication channel may be subject to various types of external influences, called "noise", which can interfere with the transmission.

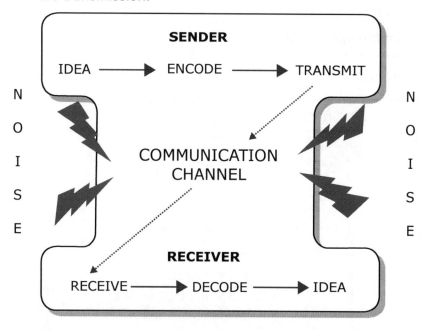

Definition

Communication— sending and receiving information between different parties through written, oral and non-verbal mediums.

Commentary

*"Idea"—may be an attitude or desired action.

■ Encoding may be oral, written or non-verbal.

■ The communication channel (or medium) transmits the message from sender to receiver (e.g. e-mail, telephone conversation, letter).

■ Distortion—in the coding and decoding stages, it may result from the language or medium used (e.g. part of a Cyrillic message can be lost in an e-mail).

■ Noise hinders communication and may render it ineffective. "Noise" may be:

• **physical**—air traffic;

• **lost**—in the post;

• **social**—personality "clashes" or cultural difference;

• **psychological**—due to anger, frustration or fatigue; or

• **poor quality**—a bad communications line or speaking "in jargon" unintelligible to the receiver.

■ As communication is a two-way process, the sender will need feedback to determine whether a message has been received and understood.

1.2   Importance

1.2.1   In Organisations

▩ Providing information:
- for budgetary planning and control;
- for decision-making; and
- about the environment.

▩ Exchanging information with suppliers and customers.

▩ Encouraging participation and motivating individuals.

▩ Inter-departmental coordination.

▩ Communicating decisions.

▩ Maintaining interpersonal skills and relationships.

1.2.2   To Managers

▩ Announcing plans or strategies.

▩ Giving instructions and providing information.

▩ Receiving information.

▩ Exchanging ideas.

▩ Comparing actual results against a plan.

▩ Prescribing rules or procedures.

▩ Communicating job functions.

1.3 Attributes of Effective Communication—the 7 Cs

▩ Not to be confused with the attributes of good-quality information (see *Session 24*), the 7 Cs are:
   1. Completeness
   2. Conciseness
   3. Consideration
   4. Concreteness
   5. Clarity
   6. Courtesy
   7. Correctness.

1.3.1   Completeness

▩ A message is complete when it contains all the facts needed by the receiver for the response desired by the sender.

1.3.2   Conciseness

▩ Conciseness is getting the message through in the fewest possible words, keeping in mind all the other qualities of effective communication. A concise message is complete without being wordy and is only repeated to reinforce.

1.3.3   Consideration

▩ Keeping the receiver in mind while preparing the message defines the quality of consideration. Put oneself in the place of the receiver (empathy); apply integrity and ethics.

1.3.4   Concreteness

▩ Being concrete is being vivid, definite and specific rather than obscure, vague and general. Use specific and accurate words, facts and figures.

1.3.5 Clarity

■ Clarity means getting the message through in an accurate manner understandable to the listener.

■ Choose short, familiar, conversational words.

■ Construct effective sentences and paragraphs.

■ Achieve appropriate readability (through headings and transitions) and "listenability".

■ Include examples, illustrations and other visual aids when desirable.

1.3.6 Courtesy

■ Courtesy means to think about the receiver's reaction and feelings. It involves respect and concern for others which leads to the polite use of words and gestures.

■ Be sincerely tactful, thoughtful and appreciative.

■ Omit expressions which will irritate, hurt or belittle the receiver.

1.3.7 Correctness

■ The correct use of grammar, spelling and punctuation.

■ Use the right level of language and presentation.

■ Maintain acceptable writing mechanics.

■ Choose non-discriminatory expressions.

1.4 Barriers to Effective Communication*

■ Individual bias and selectivity.

■ Differences (e.g. higher regard to a manager's view).

■ Emotional barriers.

■ Language barriers (e.g. use of technical jargon or colloquialism).

■ Inappropriate method of communication (formal or informal).

■ Technical faults in the communication media.

■ Poor listening skills.

■ Poor timing (e.g. too late to be of use).

■ Contradiction of verbal and non-verbal signs (mixed message).

■ Suspicion or lack of trust.

■ Information overload.

■ Selective reporting or withholding of information.

■ "Edited highlights".

■ Location.*

*Communication problems arise from three main sources—the transmission mechanism, interpersonal issues and misunderstanding.

*Many of the above can result in misunderstanding—which in itself can cause communications to break down.

1.5   Flow/Direction of Communication

▦ Vertical:

   ↓ Management communicates policies, plans, information and instructions down the chain of communication.

   ↑ Employees communicate ideas, suggestions, comments and complaints up the chain of communication.

▦ Horizontal (or lateral):

   ←→ Inter-departmental meetings and cooperation between similar groups (e.g. managers).

     Can be:

- Formal (e.g. to coordinate work in a group); or
- Informal (e.g. to provide emotional/social support).

▦ Diagonal:

   ↖↘ Inter-departmental communication by people of different ranks (e.g. between IS managers and production department shop-floor engineers).

2   Communication Media

2.1   Written Methods

2.1.1   Examples*

- Minutes of a meeting
- Letters/memos/faxes
- Post-it (repositionable) notes
- Bulletins/circulars/newsletters
- Notice board
- Brochures
- E-mail
- Budgets.

Commentary

*The choice of medium used in communication depends on factors such as urgency, permanency, complexity, sensitivity and cost.

2.1.2   Skills Required

- Correct spelling
- Suitable vocabulary
- Correct grammar/syntax
- Good writing, word processing
- Suitable style.

2.1.3   Advantages and Disadvantages

✔ Advantages—more permanent, less liable to misinterpretation, aid memory, duplicable, a source of reference.

✗ Disadvantages—may be slow, less timely feedback.

2.2   Oral Methods

2.2.1   Examples

▨ Telephone/teleconferencing/videoconferencing
▨ Conversations
▨ Interviews/meetings
▨ Public meetings
▨ Intercom
▨ Recorded messages/answer phone/voicemail.

2.2.2   Skills Required

▨ Clear pronunciation
▨ Suitable vocabulary
▨ Correct grammar/syntax
▨ Fluency
▨ Body language when "face to face" (e.g. videoconference)
▨ Expressive delivery.

2.2.3   Advantages and Disadvantages

✔ Advantages—more immediate (usually). Often enhanced by non-verbal behaviour. Also feedback and flexibility.

✗ Disadvantages—noise, informality, less permanence, no ability to reference (unless recorded).

2.3   Non-verbal Behaviour

▨ Examples include:
  • Actions
  • Body language—mannerisms and gestures
  • Dress
  • Facial expression
  • Gesture
  • Tone of voice
  • Proximity
▨ Non-verbal behaviour (e.g. body language) can be used to create a desired impression. It will confirm or reinforce a verbal message or even contradict it. As body language can be difficult to control, it can often betray the real intentions of individuals.*

> ***Commentary**
>
> *We speak with our voice but communicate with our body.

2.4   Communication Skills

2.4.1   In Sending Messages

▨ Selecting and organising material, collecting thoughts, constructing sentences, arguments, etc.
▨ Judging the effect of the message on the individual recipient in the given situation.
▨ Choosing appropriate language and medium.
▨ Flexibility/adaptability—being responsive, responsible, diplomatic, tactful, more or less formal as required by the situation.
▨ Using non-verbal signals to support the spoken message.
▨ Seeking and interpreting feedback.

Example 1 Methods of Communication

Suggest and justify a suitable method for communicating the following to employees of a company.

Solution

	Suitable Method	Justification
(a) A hostile bid has been made to take over the company.		
(b) De-recognition of the trade union representing most of the employees.		
(c) Staff canteen is to be replaced with vending machines.		
(d) A fatal accident in the workplace.		
(e) Suspension of a director pending a police inquiry into alleged fraud.		
(f) A pay freeze		
(g) Introduction of a share option scheme.		

2.4.2 In Receiving Messages

▨ Active reading—understanding content, recognising superfluous information, evaluating relevant information.

▨ Listening:
- Preparing to listen
- Being and looking interested
- Concentrating on the message
- Avoiding distractions
- Keeping an open mind
- Asking for repetitions of parts of the message
- Distinguishing the "gist" from the detail
- Asking for clarification
- Making notes on key points
- Using memory-retention techniques (e.g. mind-mapping).

▨ Interpretation:
- Perceiving underlying meaning—is too much being read into the message?
- Recognising non-verbal messages—do they confirm or contradict the spoken message?

▨ Use questioning skills to draw out the required information.

▨ Provide feedback.

3 Presentation

3.1 Methods of Presenting Information

- Formal report
- Letter/memorandum
- Oral presentation
- Meetings.

3.2 Formal Report

The typical layout of a formal report:

- Title page—outline, author, date and recipient(s).
- Table of contents—an indexed reference.
- Introduction—purpose of report and terms of reference.
- Executive summary—overall summary including conclusions and recommendations.*
- Body of report—sectioned with headings (usually numbered) and sub-headings.
- Conclusions and recommendations.
- Appendices—supporting details.

*Commentary

*"BLOT" approach— Bottom Line on Top

3.3 Letters and Memoranda

- Contents may be similar to a formal report, but the format will be different.

3.3.1 Letters

- Sent to people in other organisations.
- Features:
  - Address of sender
  - Your Ref/Our Ref
  - Date
  - Name and address of recipient
  - Dear Sir/Mr ... ("salutation")
  - Title heading
  - "Yours faithfully" or "Sincerely".

3.3.2 Memoranda

- Sent to people in the organisation.*
- Features:
  - Company Name
  - MEMORANDUM
  - To:
  - From:
  - Date:
  - Subject:

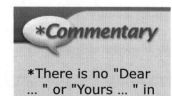

*Commentary

*There is no "Dear ... " or "Yours ... " in a memo.

3.4   Oral Presentations

3.4.1   Key Elements

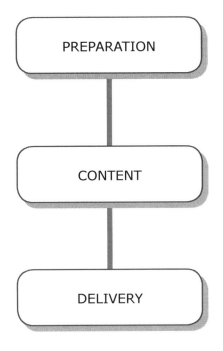

■ Assemble facts and ideas based on the audience and their needs.
■ Consider the environment of the presentation.
■ Develop suitable visual aids.

■ Decide what to include/leave out.
■ Prepare any handouts/course notes.
■ Practice, practice, practice.

■ Use appropriate language.
■ Maintain eye contact.
■ Enthusiasm.
■ Be yourself.
■ Be prepared for questions.

3.4.2   Visual Aids

Advantages

✔ Visual impact.
✔ High retention.
✔ Add interest.
✔ Facilitate understanding.

Disadvantages*

✗ Restricted in the amount of information they can convey.
✗ Receiver may remember the "picture" rather than the message.
✗ Used as a substitute to the speaker (i.e. speaker just repeats the visual content).
✗ May be a "language" barrier.

*There can easily be a tendency to "PowerPoint" everything in a presentation. PowerPoint should enhance and add value to the presentation, not become the presentation.

4 Communication Patterns

A communication network channels information between people. The design of a communication pattern for an organisation will depend partly on the organisation's structure.

4.1 Circle

▪ Each person can communicate directly only with two others*:

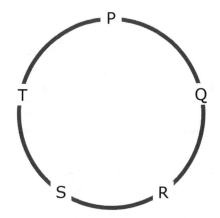

*Commentary

* Not all group members can communicate directly with the group leader or co-ordinator.

4.2 Chain

▪ People at the ends of the chain have only one person with whom to communicate.

▪ The leader cannot know whether the last member receives the correct information; there is no direct feedback to confirm whether the original message has been lost or distorted.*

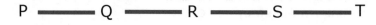

*Commentary

* Members of the same group (i.e. S and T) can communicate with each other. Members of different groups can only communicate through the leader.

4.3 "Y"

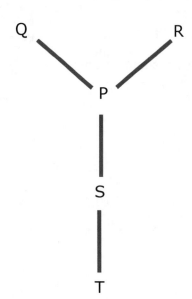

4.4   Wheel

▦ Each person must go through the leader to get a message to a third person.

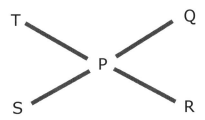

Example 2 Communication Networks

Consider the four network patterns above.

(a)   Identify who you think leads each group.

(b)   Rank the patterns (best to worst) in terms of:

   (i)   speed of problem solving;

   (ii)   level of job satisfaction.

4.5   All-Channel

▦ Combines all the above

▦ In comparison with wheel and circle:
   ● wheel solves simple problems quickest;
   ● all-channel is better for complex problems.

▦ Under pressure to get results, the all-channel system tends to fall into a wheel pattern.

Summary

- Communication involves a sender encoding and transmitting an idea through a communication channel, which is received and decoded at the other end.

- Noise describes anything which hinders communication.

- The original sender of the communication needs feedback to determine whether a message has been received and understood.

- Effective communication requires that the message be complete, concise, considerate, concrete, clear, courteous and correct.

- Barriers to effective communication arise from the transmission mechanism; issues between the sender and receiver; or misunderstanding the message.

- Choice of communication media usually depends on urgency, complexity, sensitivity, cost and the need for permanency.

- Written communication is less likely to be misinterpreted, is duplicable and may be used as a source of reference rather than trying to precisely remember the communication.

- Oral is more flexible and can provide the dimensions of demeanour as well as simple testimony. It may, however, lack permanence and may be subject to later disagreement as to substance.

- Body language can confirm or contradict a verbal communication.

- Key elements of a message involve preparation, content and delivery.

- Visual aids should enhance rather than become the presentation.

- In cases in which information is complex, a distributed processing (all-channel) network may be desirable over a centralised network.

Session 25 Quiz
Estimated time: 10 minutes

1. Describe the communication process. (1.1)
2. List TEN barriers to effective communication. (1.4)
3. State the requirements to be a good listener. (2.4)
4. State FOUR advantages and FOUR disadvantages of visual aids. (3.4.2)
5. Explain the concept of communication patterns, giving examples. (4)

Study Question Bank
Estimated time: 30 minutes

Priority		Estimated Time	Completed
MCQ25	Communication Within Business	30 minutes	

EXAMPLE SOLUTIONS

Solution 1—Methods of Communication

	Suitable Method	Justification
(a) A hostile bid	Open meeting of staff	Allows questions. Can present a "united front". Nothing in writing.
(b) Trade union derecognition	(1) Notice board, then (2) Staff meeting	Quick (reduces gossip time). Allows questions.
(c) Vending machines	Newsletter	Factual Considered management response
(d) Fatal workplace accident	(1) Notice board, then (2) Staff meeting, then (3) Circular	Quick—to put an end to rumours. Generates a feeling of togetherness. Precise response about changes in working practices.
(e) Suspension of a director	E-mail to all staff	Targeted at those who "need to know".
(f) Pay freeze (i.e. 0% pay rises)	Meeting	Very personal. May affect people's motivation.
(g) Share option scheme	Memo	Needs accuracy. Complex issues need time to read and understand.

Solution 2—Communication Networks

(a) P in "Y" and the wheel; P or T in the chain; anyone could be the leader in the circle.

(b) (i) Wheel (best), Y, chain, circle (worst)
(ii) Circle (best), chain, Y, wheel (worst)

Session 26

Ethics and Ethical Behaviour

FOCUS

This session covers the following content from the *ACCA Study Guide.*

F. Professional Ethics in Accounting and Business

1. Fundamental principles of ethical behaviour

a) Define business ethics and explain the importance of ethics to the organisation and to the individual.

b) Describe and demonstrate the following principles from the IFAC (IESBA) code of ethics, using examples.

   i)   Integrity   iv) Confidentiality

   ii) Objectivity   v)   Professional behaviour

   iii) Professional competence

c) Describe organisational values which promote ethical behaviour using examples.

   i)   Openness   iv) Respect

   ii) Trust   v)   Empowerment

   iii) Honesty   vi) Accountability

d) Explain the concept of acting in the public interest.

2. The role of regulatory and professional bodies in promoting ethical and professional standards in the accountancy profession

a) Recognise the purpose of international and organisational codes of ethics and codes of conduct, IFAC (IESBA), ACCA, etc.

b) Describe how professional bodies and regulators promote ethical awareness and prevent or punish illegal or unethical behaviour.

c) Identify the factors that distinguish a profession from other types of occupation.

d) Explain the role of the accountant in promoting ethical behaviour.

e) Recognise when and to whom illegal or unethical conduct by anyone within or connected to the organisation should be reported.

3. Corporate codes of ethics

a) Define corporate codes of ethics.

b) Describe the typical contents of a corporate code of ethics.

c) Explain the benefits of a corporate code of ethics to the organisation and its employees.

4. Ethical conflicts and dilemmas

a) Describe situations where ethical conflicts can arise.

b) Identify the main threats to ethical behaviour.

c) Outline situations at work where ethical dilemmas may be faced.

d) List the main safeguards against ethical threats and dilemmas.

VISUAL OVERVIEW

Objective: To explain why morals, ethics and ethical behaviour are important to the organisation, the professional accountant and the individual.

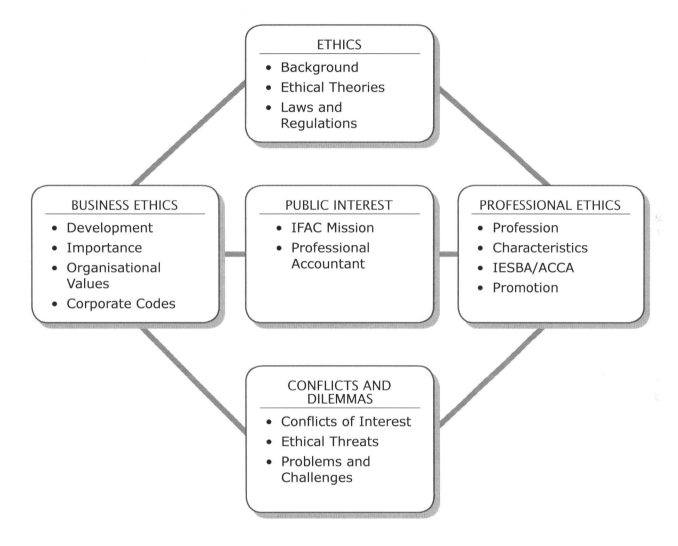

Session 26 Guidance

■ **Understand** the different approaches and groupings of ethical theories (s.1).

■ **Recognise** the link to business culture from *Session 7* (s.2).

■ **Understand** the fundamental principles in ACCA's code of ethics (s.3). Note that independence is *not* a fundamental principle, but to be objective requires that professional accountants in assurance services are independent of their clients.

■ **Know** the ideas behind public interest (s.4) and conflicts, dilemmas and threats (s.5). These areas must not be neglected even though they are at the end of the Study Text for this paper.

Ethics

1.1 Background

> ### Definition
>
> **Morality**—"the norms, values and beliefs embedded in social processes which define right and wrong for an individual or a community."
> —*Crane and Matten*
>
> **Ethics**—the study of morality; analysis of right and wrong and development of rules and principles which determine right and wrong for any situation (ethical theories).

- **Morality** refers to a code of conduct adopted by individuals within a particular environment and a set of agreed rules for *right* and *wrong*.*

- **Ethics** is concerned with the methods by which conduct should be judged right or wrong. It is about how individuals and groups conduct their lives within an externally or internally imposed moral code, how they behave towards each other based on their interpretation of the applicable moral code and the influences placed on them which determine their beliefs.

- Ethics examines the application of moral principles to a situation.

*Kaler (1999) suggests that morality is foremost a social phenomenon (as humans constantly need to establish the rules and arrangements for living together) and that it is all about harm and benefit (right and wrong are primarily about avoiding harm and providing benefits).

1.2 Ethical Theories

- Because ethics is often a personal/cultural/environmental factor, ethical theories sit between two extremes:

   1. Ethical **absolutism**—eternal, universally applicable moral principles. Right and wrong are objective qualities that can be rationally determined and do not change regardless of the person/culture/environment.

   2. Ethical **relativism**—context dependent and subjective. What is morally unacceptable by one person/culture/environment may be totally acceptable by a different person/culture/environment.

- "Traditional" theorists tend towards absolutism whereas "modern" theorists tend towards relativism.

- **Pluralism** accepts that although different views exist on morality, a consensus on basic principles and rules in a certain context can, and should, be reached. This is effectively a midway between the two potential extremes.

1.2.1 Normative Ethics

- Involves arriving at *one* set of moral standards that regulate right and wrong conduct; i.e. how people *ought* to behave. The focus is on deriving a set of foundational principles, or a set of good character traits, regardless of the situation or environment.

▓ The key assumption in normative ethics is that there is only one ultimate criterion of moral conduct (e.g. "Do unto others as you would have them do unto you"). Effectively, it is establishing a benchmark of proper behaviour (e.g. "you should not lie"; "you should not kill").

▓ Many normative principles are already enshrined within laws and regulations (e.g. ACCA's Code of Ethics and Conduct).

1.2.2 Deontological Ethics

▓ Based on the concept of duty. Duty theories base morality on specific, foundational principles of obligation (e.g. an obligation to tell the truth, not to harm others, to improve ourselves, to improve the lives of others).

▓ Concerned with the application of universal ethical principles, in order to arrive at rules of conduct. It originates from the Greek word *deon*, meaning duty or obligation.

▓ Often referred to as non-consequentialist ethical theories as they are obligatory, irrespective of the consequences which will follow. An action can only be considered right or wrong when the moral basis for taking that action is known.

1.2.3 Teleological Ethics

▓ A consequentialist approach, meaning that whether a decision is right or wrong depends on the consequences or outcome of that decision. So long as the consequences of the action taken are more favourable than unfavourable, then the action can be considered morally right. Derives from the Greek word *teos*, meaning *end,* because the end result of the action is the sole determining factor of its morality.*

*Commentary

*The atomic bomb was developed by US and British scientists who had significant moral doubts as to its use because of the large number of people who would be killed. They only continued developing the weapon because the alternative, invading Japan, would have resulted in far higher deaths than the use of the bomb.

▓ May be sub-divided into three areas:

1. **Egoism**—an action is morally right if the consequences of that action are more favourable than unfavourable *only* to the person taking that action.*

2. **Altruism**—an action is morally right if its consequences are more favourable than unfavourable to everyone *other* than the person taking that action.

3. **Utilitarianism**—an action is morally right if the consequences of that action are more favourable than unfavourable to *everyone*.

*Commentary

*Egoism is often considered as the "what is best for me" approach and may be considered as the "ethics of the thief" in that they can justify (to themselves) their actions (e.g. "robbing the rich to give to the poor" or "robbing the poor to make the rich richer"). Utilitarianism is sometimes taught as the "what is best for the greatest number" approach, as it applies to society as a whole. This does, however, leave the question, "What about the rest?" that is, "the greatest harm for the minority".

1.2.4   Instrumentalist Ethics

■ The application of ethical principles to further other objectives rather than as an end in themselves (normative approach). The use of the ethical principles enhances other prospects (e.g. profits) and would thus be applied; if they did not add value, they would not be acted on.

1.3   Laws, Regulations and Ethics

■ The primary source of regulating behaviour of individuals and businesses is the law. Although many laws are based on ethical principles, they have been developed into very detailed codes of procedures and penalties if such procedures are broken or not followed.

■ Individuals and businesses may also be subject to regulations laid down by specific regulatory bodies (e.g. local government, banks, charities, auditors). Again, these codify the required behaviour of individuals, businesses and their managers.

■ By breaking laws and regulations, the individual would be considered to act not only unlawfully but also unethically and below the deemed standard. In many cases, acting unethically usually means that a law or regulation has also been broken.

■ However, in many cases the laws and regulations are often considered to be the minimum requirements expected of members of society. This is of particular relevance in areas of an emerging and rapidly developing nature such that laws and regulations cannot keep up with society's expectations.

■ Ethical behaviour represents the highest level of behaviour that society expects. Individual and business behaviour goes beyond that of just meeting laws and regulations (instrumental approach) and in some cases may even exceed society's expectations (normative approach).

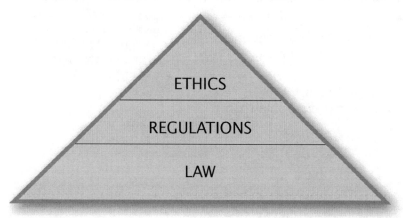

2 Business Ethics

2.1 Development

■ Early business organisations were primarily owner-managed and unincorporated (e.g. sole traders and merchant guilds). As such, morals and **business ethics** applied directly to the individual owners.

■ In the late 1800s, incorporated enterprises were afforded the status of being separate legal bodies (14th Amendment to the US Constitution; *Salomon v A Salomon & Co Ltd*) and as such were held separately accountable from their owners and managers.

■ As international trade increased, many organisations started to take on a global perspective; that is, not only did they export to and import from other countries, but they also initially established representative offices, then built manufacturing facilities and acquired other entities in those countries. In doing so, the managers of the entities had to deal with different cultures, values and morals.

■ The growth of such organisations had direct implications for the local community (e.g. employment, local suppliers, local environment) and in some cases for national governments (e.g. major contributor of taxes, major employer and trainer).

■ Because of this growth, businesses became ever more integrated into local societies and, just as morals and ethics developed for individuals and groups to follow, so the corporate citizen is expected to develop and apply appropriate moral and ethical procedures in parallel. Thus developed business ethics.

■ Operating in the global environment also means that a global eye is placed on an organisation's activities, and stakeholders increase and take a much more active interest in the organisation.

■ The last decade has seen a substantial increase in the scrutiny of the roles and actions taken by corporations as "good corporate citizens" (e.g. ethical behaviour, social responsibility and sustainability). This implies that activities in one location can easily be compared to those of another location and that organisations must now not only consider local ethical standards but also the application of their best moral and ethical practices across all of their operations.

■ All of this is having a significant effect on how corporations are being governed in a "CNN world" and the necessary widening of the directors' vision to consider all affected by the company and who can affect the company.*

Definition

Business ethics—the application of ethics to business behaviour.

"The study of business situations, activities and decisions where (moral) issues of right and wrong are addressed."
—*Crane and Matten*

*Commentary

*"CNN world" describes the ease with which corporations are held to account by publicly airing their actions/inactions (e.g. use of child labour, poor treatment of workers in developing nations).

It may take 20 years to build up a good reputation, but only 20 seconds for bad publicity through the global media to destroy it. Reputation risk is now being taken very seriously.

2.2 Importance

The application of business ethics is important to an organisation for several reasons:

- Organisations' power and influence on society create potential for significant economic damage/benefit to individuals and communities.
- Stakeholder demands for greater accountability and ethical practice.
- Few managers have previously received formal business ethics training and thus need to acquire the skills to recognise ethical dilemmas and how to correctly manage the associated risks.*

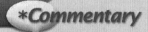

*Commentary

*The professional accountant in business has a crucial role in managing ethical dilemmas in that the accountant, management and the executive board are potentially the only ones to have had formal training and experience in ethics. In the US, it was not until after the Enron saga that business schools included formal ethical training in their MBA programmes.

- Good moral and ethical practice must be seen as a driver for organisational and stakeholder wealth, profitability and resource management rather than a cost.
- An ethically sound company showing good corporate governance suggests a well-run business.
- There are a growing number of "ethically sound" investment and fund management companies which will invest only in ethically sound companies.
- The public profile of a company will be enhanced by sound ethical principles.
- Recruiting and retaining staff is easier if the working environment promotes ethical behaviour.
- Managing risk is easier if moral and ethical practice is driven from the top (management and the board) and embedded throughout the organisation.

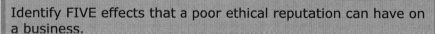

Example 1 Impact of Poor Ethics

Identify FIVE effects that a poor ethical reputation can have on a business.

2.3 Organisational Ethical Values

- The key concepts of corporate governance (see *Session 9*) are the foundation for the organisational values which promote ethical behaviour.

- A key driver of organisational values will be the board demonstrating such values and embedding them in the organisation's culture so that they become second nature to all employees.

- Any organisation which espouses such values to the marketplace will attract stakeholders who relate to those values (e.g. good university graduates will want to be employed by the organisation and customers will have faith in the goods and services provided).

2.3.1 Openness

- The ease with which employees and other stakeholders are able to make meaningful analysis of an organisation's culture, actions, economic and non-financial fundamentals.

- A measure of how good management is at making necessary regulatory and voluntary information available in a candid, accurate and timely manner to all relevant parties.

- Includes company management developing the appropriate culture at strategic and operational levels.

- Reflects whether employees, investors and other stakeholders obtain a true picture of what is happening inside the company.

2.3.2 Integrity and Trust

- Integrity requires management and employees to be open, straightforward and honest in all professional, business, personal and financial relationships. This implies honesty, fair dealing and truthfulness.

- Integrity is fundamental for strong corporate governance. The perceived integrity of the entity, the actions taken by the management and employees, and external and internal reports and information will be determined by the integrity of those involved.

- Individual integrity describes a person of high moral value who observes a steadfast adherence to a strict moral code or ethical code. The virtue of the individual rather than the ethics of the action is emphasised—integrity provides the necessary ethical framework.

- As in many situations in life, trust is vital in corporate governance. Integrity provides the necessary ethical framework to engender trust.

2.3.3 Honesty

- Honesty and probity are fundamental to corporate governance. They cover integrity, honour, virtue and fair dealing.

- Honesty implies that the organisation, management or employees do not mislead anyone on any matter. At a higher level, the chief executive provides all appropriate information to fellow executive directors and NEDs.

2.3.4 Respect

- Respect is based on principles of right and wrong. A person shows respect by caring about principles, people and property. To respect is to care, and to care shows respect.

- Respect is more than a feeling; it is an ethical obligation. For example, an extract from a code of ethics cautions employees:

  - We treat employees, customers and all people with respect at all times.

  - We protect company assets and use them wisely.

- Ethics requires respect for moral principles. Ethical success depends on understanding the profound effect respect has on ethics and character.*

Commentary

*Is it respectful to abuse company equipment because it's not yours? Is it respectful to others to make them clean up your messes or finish your unfinished work? Is it respectful to take inventory or equipment for your own use because no one will miss it? The question of respect applies to almost every kind of workplace ethics problem.

2.3.5 Empowerment

- Empowerment is the process of enabling or authorising autonomous thinking, behaviour, action and control over work and decision-making.

- It aims to increase an employee's discretionary decision-making authority either by direct authority from management or through self-awareness and actions in the culture of an organisation.

- Driven by competitive demand for quick, efficient and effective service and increased returns, organisations empower employees to use their judgement, creativity and ideas in pursuit of enhanced organisational performance and stakeholder satisfaction.*

- Empowerment functions best in an open, trusting, honest and respectful organisational environment.

- Simple examples include:

  - On a production line, any worker can stop the line if they become aware that quality has declined or if they spot a fault in a production item.

  - Shop assistants can deal directly with customer complaints and warranties.

  - Software engineers inform customers directly concerning potential bugs in a software product.

  - Project stakeholders have a direct input into project decision-making.*

Commentary

*Employees may be reluctant to accept self-empowerment and only react when told that they can do so.

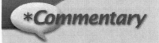

Commentary

*Richard Branson takes a simple approach to empowerment. Happy employees make the customer happy. Happy customers return with new customers and spend more money. This increases profits and opportunities for investment and development.

2.3.6   Accountability

▪ In the context of management, accountability involves acknowledgment and assumption of responsibility for actions, products, decisions and policies encompassing the obligation to report, explain and answer for resulting consequences.

▪ Drs Kishore Raga and Derek Taylor of Nelson Mandela Metropolitan University, South Africa, consider that "Accountability is the fundamental prerequisite for preventing the abuse of power *(of individuals, government, organisations and corporates)* and for ensuring that power is directed towards the achievement of efficiency, effectiveness, responsiveness and transparency."

▪ In the context of ethical behaviour, accountability is an accepted norm. Being ethical implies that you would not abuse your power, you would accept responsibility for your actions and would be accountable to those stakeholders your actions affect. It also implies that the stakeholders affected by decisions and actions are involved in and considered by the decision-making process.

▪ With the organisation as a whole, it will be ultimately accountable to its stakeholders (be they shareholders, employees, customers, local communities) for its decisions and actions. Where such decisions and actions are considered to be unethical, the organisation will (at some stage) be held accountable to explain and make good any damage caused by those actions.

2.4   Corporate Codes of Ethics

▪ Under the Sarbanes-Oxley Act (2002), a **code of ethics** is defined as:

"A codification of standards that is reasonably designed to deter wrongdoing and to promote:

(i)   honest and ethical conduct, including the ethical handling of actual and apparent conflicts of interest;

(ii) full, fair, accurate, timely and understandable disclosure in reports and documents filed with or submitted to the SEC;

(iii) compliance with applicable laws, rules and regulations;

(iv) prompt internal reporting of code violations to an appropriate person; and

(v)   accountability for adherence to the code."

Definition

Code of Ethics— a set of principles within an organisation which guides decision-making and conduct.

Benefits of a code

✔ To define accepted/acceptable behaviours.

✔ To promote high standards of practice.

✔ To provide a benchmark for members to use for self-evaluation.

✔ To establish a framework for professional behaviour and responsibilities.

✔ As a vehicle for occupational identity.

✔ As a mark of occupational maturity.

■ The code may be a requirement of law and regulation (e.g. Sarbanes-Oxley, SEC) or voluntary (e.g. as part of an overall corporate social responsibility programme).*

*Commentary

*The effectiveness of any code will depend on the extent to which it is supported. It is crucial for codes to be fully endorsed and acted on by senior management as well as embedded in the entity's culture.

It is also essential that breaches of the code (whether identified internally or externally) can be reported and acted on. An appropriate whistle-blowing procedure should be actively promoted, usually with anonymous reporting to a senior non-executive director (e.g. on the audit committee).

■ There are two main types of a code of ethics:

1. **Stakeholder-based**—i.e. setting out organisational commitments and staff guidance based on relationships with different stakeholders; and

2. **Issues-based**—offering guidance formulated on issues of concern to the firm.*

■ All codes should start with:

- A preface or introduction (signed by the chairman or CEO or both)—it should set out the purpose, mention important values and explain the leadership commitment.

- Purpose, values and impacts of the business—goods/ services provided, the nature of the business, locations, etc. Thereafter the content will differ according to its type.*

2.4.1 Stakeholder-Based Content

■ **How to use the code**—its purpose, relevance, audience and context. Describe tools or sources of support and summarise the ethical decision-making framework.

■ **Employees**—policies on working conditions, recruitment, development and training, rewards, health and safety, equal opportunities, diversity, retirement, redundancy, discrimination and harassment and use of company assets by employees.

■ **Customer relations**—the importance of customer satisfaction and fair dealing in all agreements, quality, pricing and after-sales service.

■ **Shareholders and lenders**—how their investment is protected and proper return made. A commitment to accurate and timely communication on achievements and prospects.

■ **Suppliers**—prompt settlement of amounts due. Cooperation to achieve quality and efficiency. No bribery or excess hospitality accepted or given.

■ **Society or the wider community**—compliance with the "spirit" of laws, not just "the letter". Obligations to protect and preserve the environment. Staff involvement in local affairs. Policy on sponsorship, education and charitable giving.

*Commentary

*Some codes are hybrids of the *stakeholder-based* and *issue-based* codes.

*Commentary

*The best way to fully understand the broad range and content of the various codes of ethics/conduct is to read through examples. Many organisations' codes can easily be found on the Internet by searching, for example, for "Nike code of ethics conduct".

- **Implementation and reinforcement**—how issued and used and how to get advice. How and to whom to report breaches of the code. Awareness raising illustrations and training programmes.
- **Assurance, reporting and reviews**—measuring effectiveness, annual reporting to the board and updating procedures.

Exhibit 1 JOHNSON & JOHNSON

The following is an excerpt from Johnson & Johnson's credo (www.jnjcanada.com/explore-our-company).

We believe our first responsibility is to the doctors, nurses and patients, to mothers and fathers and all others who use our products and services. ...

We are responsible to our employees, the men and women who work with us throughout the world. ...

We are responsible to the communities in which we live and work and to the world community as well. ...

Our final responsibility is to our stockholders. ...

2.4.2 Issues-Based Content

- Competition
- Bribery and corruption
- Gifts and entertainment
- Conflicts of interest
- Use of company assets
- Information security
- Political contributions
- Human rights standards
- Environmental responsibilities
- Health and safety
- Discrimination
- Work/home balance issues
- Other issues.

Example 2 Other Issues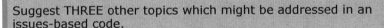

Suggest THREE other topics which might be addressed in an issues-based code.

Exhibit 2 ISSUES-BASED CODE

The following are extracts from the Borealis Ethics Policy (www.borealisgroup.com/en/company/sustainability/our-position/ethical-business).

How We Compete—Borealis is committed to vigorous, lawful, straightforward and ethical competition. We ensure that our business practices fully comply with the competition laws wherever we do business.

Gifts and Hospitality—Provided that an employee uses good judgment and moderation and that the employee's objectivity is not influenced, gifts of a nominal value or modest and reasonable hospitality to further a business relationship are generally acceptable.

The Application of Human Rights Standards in our Business—We seek to increase awareness of human rights issues throughout the organisation worldwide. We take seriously any allegations that human rights are not properly protected within our sphere of influence or that we may be complicit in violations.

Safeguarding Important Information—All employees must take appropriate steps to protect confidentiality and respect confidential information belonging to others.

Our Environmental Responsibilities—As a part of our commitment to Responsible Care®, we strive to be a leader in the environmental performance of our operations and our products throughout their life cycle.

Exhibit 3 CONTENTS OF SAMPLE CORPORATE CODES

The following examples demonstrate the different content contained in various corporate codes.

Vodafone (www.vodafone.com)
- Introduction
- Relevant Officers
- Honest and Ethical Conduct
- Disclosure
- Compliance
- Reporting and Accountability
- Waivers
- Other Policies and Procedures
- Enquiries

BP (www.BP.com)
- Message from Group Chief Executive
- Commitment to integrity
- Health, safety, security and the environment
- Employees
- Business partners
- Governments and communities
- Company assets and financial integrity

Marks & Spencer (www.marksandspencer.com)
- Values
- Customers, Employees, Shareholders, Suppliers
- Environment
- Legislation and Regulation
- Charitable Donations
- Fraud and Financial Reporting
- Innovation
- Consequences
- Employee's Responsibilities—Guidance and Whistle-blowing
- What to do, Reporting, Code of Ethics Acceptance Form.

3 Professional Ethics

3.1 Profession

▪ The oldest recorded use of the word profession, "avowal or expression of purpose," implied religious and moral motives to dedicate oneself to good end.

▪ By the 16th century, "profession" had been extended from its original religious connection and was used for all three of the university-educated occupations—divinity, law and medicine—all of which held high status.

▪ All three professions were concerned with the well-being of individuals obliged to put their trust in members of these occupations if they wished to consult with them. The requirement of trust led to the development of ethical standards and a commitment to provide a service for the public good.

▪ The Industrial Revolution created new skilled occupations (e.g. actuary and engineer), thus the idea of professions as a disciplined group of individuals who adhere to high ethical standards and uphold themselves to, and are accepted by, the public as possessing special knowledge and skills in a widely recognised, organised body of learning derived from a high-level education and training, and who are prepared to exercise this knowledge and these skills in the interest of others.

▪ Thus the modern concept of profession began to evolve.

▪ Examples of modern professions include:
- Health related—doctors, dentists, physiotherapists, psychiatrists and pharmacists.
- Non-health related—architects, engineers, veterinarians, surveyors, lawyers, accountants and teachers.

Definition

Profession—an occupation, vocation or career requiring specialised knowledge and extensive training which usually has a professional association, ethical code and process of certification or licensing.*

***Commentary**

*Inherent in the definition of "profession" is the concept that social responsibilities should take precedence over other considerations.

3.2 Characteristics

▪ There have been many attempts to define a profession through its characteristics:
- Expertise—including specialised knowledge and skill.
- Responsibility—to perform a service that is essential to society.
- Corporateness—a collective sense of unity which originates from the lengthy discipline and training necessary for professional competence, the common bond of work and the sharing of a social responsibility. This sets the professional member apart from laymen.

▪ Another model specifies six characteristics:

1. An intellectual technique.

2. An application of that technique.

3. A long period of training.

4. An association of members.

5. Enforced standards and a statement of ethics.

6. A body of intellectual theory.

■ Although more than 20 elements have been defined, two characteristics are essential:

1. Prolonged specialist training in a body of abstract knowledge.

2. A service orientation.

■ In the accounting profession that body of theory includes:

- accounting standards (e.g. International Financial Reporting Standards);
- auditing standards (e.g. International Standards on Auditing); and
- ethical standards (e.g. IESBA *Code of Ethics for Professional Accountants*).*

■ The International Ethics Standards Board for Accountants (IESBA) distinguishes a profession by certain characteristics, including:

- mastery of a particular intellectual skill, acquired by initial training and then lifelong continuous education;
- adherence by its members to a common code of values and conduct established by its administrating body, including maintaining an outlook which is essentially objective; and
- acceptance of a duty to society as a whole, usually in return for restrictions in use of a title or in the granting of a qualification.

*Commentary

*In the UK, the professional bodies of accountants (e.g. ACCA, ICAEW, ICAS, ICAI, CIMA) have been lobbying the government for many years to recognise the word "accountant" as one to be reserved only for use by professionally qualified accountants. At present anyone can set themselves up in business and use the word "accountant" (e.g. a turf accountant is a bookmaker, traditional taking bets on horses raced on turf). They cannot, however, refer to themselves as being "chartered accountants" (e.g. Chartered Turf Accountant) as this term is reserved for specific professional accountants. (The "C" in the initials of the bodies above stands for "Chartered".)

■ According to IESBA's *Code of Ethics for Professional Accountants*, the objectives of the accountancy profession are:

- to work to the highest standards of professionalism;
- to attain the highest levels of performance; and
- generally to meet the public interest requirement (see later).

■ These objectives satisfy four basic needs:

1. Credibility—society needs credibility in information and information systems.

2. Professionalism—individuals need to be clearly identifiable by clients, employers and other interested parties as professional persons in the accountancy field.

3. Quality of services—there is a need for assurance that all services obtained from a professional accountant are carried out to the highest standards of performance.

4. Confidence—users of the services of professional accountants should be able to see, as well as feel confident, that they are governed by a framework of professional ethics.

3.3   IESBA/ACCA Code of Ethics

▦ The International Federation of Accountants (IFAC) is committed to protecting the public interest by developing high-quality international standards, promoting strong ethical values, encouraging high-quality practice and supporting the development of all sectors of the profession around the world.

▦ IFAC strives to serve the public interest through the development of standards in the areas of auditing, education, ethics and public sector financial reporting by:

 ● advocating transparency and convergence in financial reporting;

 ● providing best practice guidance for professional accountants employed in business; and

 ● implementing a membership compliance program.

▦ A central pillar of IFAC and its member bodies (e.g. ACCA) is the *Code of Ethics for Professional Accountants* developed by the International Ethics Standards Board for Accountants (IESBA). The code sets the standards of conduct to be followed and states the fundamental principles that should be observed by professional accountants.

▦ All members of IFAC are required to implement ethical codes which, as a minimum, require the same standards as that of the IESBA code.

3.3.1   Fundamental Principles

▦ The IESBA Code of Ethics provides five fundamental principles:

 1. Integrity

 2. Objectivity

 3. Professional competence and due care

 4. Confidentiality

 5. Professional behaviour

▦ It also provides a conceptual framework to assist all students and members in applying the principles, regardless of the areas of work undertaken or stage of qualification.

▦ **Integrity**—straightforwardness and honesty in performing professional services. This implies fair dealing and honesty (e.g. members will not mislead clients, they will inform clients when they believe that the client's actions are illegal, they will not overcharge clients nor charge for work not carried out, they will ensure that clients fully understand the consequences of the work being undertaken and they will decline to work for clients they believe to be providing misleading information or attempt to limit the scope of the work carried out).

▦ **Objectivity**—fairness, without prejudice or bias, conflict of interest or influence of others to override professional or business judgements.

Exam Advice

The code also deals with many other areas (e.g. conflicts of interest, second opinions, fees, marketing, disciplinary matters) which are mostly outside of the scope of the F1 paper, but will be examined in F8 *Auditing and Assurance* and P7 *Advanced Auditing and Assurance*.

 **Key Point**

A member's objectivity must be beyond question because objectivity strikes to the heart of whether the professional will act in service to an ideal higher than personal benefit. Objectivity can only occur when the professional is, and is seen to be, independent of interests that could compromise integrity.

■ **Professional competence and due care**—a continuing duty to maintain a level of professional knowledge and skill so that a client (or employer) receives competent services based on current developments in practice, legislation and techniques. Professional accountants must be diligent and apply technical and professional standards when providing professional services. This implies that work must only be accepted on the basis that the member has skills and knowledge necessary to do the work; consultation is always sought on contentious issues; checklists are conscientiously completed and not just on the basis of "ticking the box" (which implies a lack of integrity); and the appropriate standards are always applied when performing work.

■ **Confidentiality**—respect for confidentiality of information acquired as a result of professional and business relationships. Such information must not be:*

   ● disclosed to third parties without proper and specific authority unless there is a legal or professional right or duty to disclose (e.g. it is a legal requirement to report suspicion of money laundering directly to the authorities and not to discuss such suspicions with the client); or

   ● used for the personal advantage of the professional accountant or third parties (e.g. insider dealing).

*Commentary

*Confidentiality means that the audit team of client A can only discuss client A with other members of the current audit team. They cannot discuss client A with anybody else.

■ **Professional behaviour**—compliance with relevant civil and criminal laws and regulations, adherence to applicable codes of conduct (e.g. ACCA Code of Ethics and Conduct) and avoidance of any action which may discredit the profession (e.g. cheating in an ACCA Exam or any other examination, assisting a client in breaking the law, getting into a fight with a client, suggesting that another professional accountant is not professional, misleading or unprofessional advertising, failing to deal with professional and client correspondence promptly). Members must behave with courtesy and consideration towards all with whom they come into contact in a professional capacity.*

*Commentary

*It would be unprofessional, for example, for a firm to advertise using the slogan, "We are the best, better than all the rest," or to use the Tina Turner song with a similar lyric as the background music when telephone callers are placed on hold.

Illustration 1 Unprofessional Personal Behaviour

Many years ago, a student accountant finally managed to pass his last professional examination after having failed it many times. Afterward, he spent that night in various London nightclubs. In the early hours of the next morning he was making his way across a park, somewhat under the influence of alcohol. He was confronted by a small dog which took a dislike to him—the dog ended up in a stream. The dog's owner, an elderly woman, was obviously very upset by this, especially as she also was pushed into the stream. The student was arrested, appeared in court and fined. This came to the notice of his professional body, which subsequently banned him from membership for 10 years because of his "unprofessional behaviour".

3.3.2 Independence

- Although independence can be considered to be a "state of mind", it is important that the professional accountant, when providing assurance services (e.g. an audit), is seen to be independent beyond any doubt.
- Threats to independence include:
  - High level of fees compared to total income of the professional (e.g. income from any one client exceeding 15% of the professional's total income is perceived to be a potential threat).
  - Gifts and hospitality which can only be accepted when the gift/hospitality is clearly insignificant (e.g. a bottle of less expensive, non-collectible champagne at the New Year).
  - Partners or their firm cannot make a financial investment in the client (e.g. shares). If any staff hold such investments they must not be part of the engagement team.
  - Where a partner is a close family member of senior management, the firm cannot provide any assurance service to that entity. Where staff are close family members, they cannot be part of the engagement team.

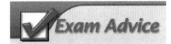

Exam Advice

The ACCA Code of Ethics and Conduct is covered in detail in F8 *Audit and Assurance*.

3.4 Promotion and Enforcement

■ The International Accounting Education Standards Board (IAESB) is an independent standard-setting board in IFAC.

■ The Ethics Education Framework as developed by the IAESB is a four-stage learning continuum to be applied by all professional accountants throughout their careers.

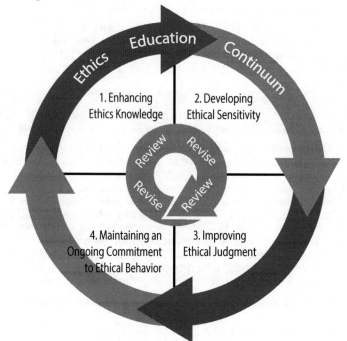

- Ethical **knowledge**—obtaining an understanding of the fundamental theories and principles of ethics, virtues and individual moral development.

- Ethical **sensitivity**—applying the knowledge to the work environment, to enable ethical threats to be recognised.

- Ethical **judgement**—applying knowledge and sensitivity to form reasoned and well-informed decisions.

- Ethical **behaviour**—continuous believing in, applying and acting on ethical principles.

■ Ethical sensitivity and ethical judgement require professional accountants to develop:

- the ability to recognise an ethical threat or issue;

- an awareness of alternative courses of action leading to an ethical solution; and

- an understanding of the effects of each alternative course of action on stakeholders.

■ Doing so improves professional judgement by sharpening ethical decision-making skills through the application of ethical theories, social responsibilities, codes of professional conduct and ethical decision-making models (EDMM).

■ When faced with an ethical dilemma (e.g. when asked to "turn a blind eye" to a falsified expenses claim made by an executive director) under the ACCA's Code of Ethics and Conduct, professional accountants should consider:

- the relevant facts;

- the ethical issues involved;

- related fundamental principles;

- established procedures of the firm;

- the action that can be followed and the probable outcome;

- alternative courses of action and their consequences; and

- internal and external sources of consultation available (e.g. ethics partner; audit committee).

■ If a significant conflict cannot be resolved, consulting legal advisers and/or ACCA should be considered. Such consultation can be taken without breaching confidentiality.

■ If, after exhausting all possibilities, the ethical conflict remains unresolved, members should, where possible, refuse to remain associated with the matter creating the conflict.

■ Where the professional accountant is found to be involved in unethical behaviour, this is usually reported to their professional body (e.g. ACCA), which will then investigate the matter and apply appropriate sanctions if necessary.*

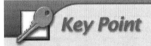
*Commentary

*Reporting unethical behaviour may be made, for example, by another professional accountant, fellow worker, client or a general member of the public. If the behaviour involves legal proceedings, then this may be reported by the police or the courts.

The sanctions which can be applied can range from a "slap on the wrist" reprimand, to a possibly substantial fine through to removal from the members' register (thrown out of the institute). In all cases, if found to have been in breach of the ethics code, the costs of the case will have to be paid by the accountant.

■ Financial regulators and the police (the Serious Fraud Office in the UK) may be involved for violations such as money laundering or proceeds of crime. A guilty verdict will automatically bar the accountant from professional membership for at least 10 years and a custodial sentence is usually applied.

4 Public Interest

4.1 IFAC Mission

Key Point

IFAC's mission is "The worldwide development and enhancement of an accountancy *profession* with harmonised standards, able to provide services of consistently high quality in the *public interest.*"

■ A distinguishing characteristic of a profession is acceptance of its responsibility to the public. The accountancy profession's "public" consists of:

  ● clients;
  ● governments;
  ● employers and employees;
  ● investors and lenders;
  ● the business and financial community; and
  ● others who rely on professional accountants to maintain the orderly functioning of commerce.

■ There is no one objective or legal definition of **public interest**. It is subjective and can mean different things to different groups of people.

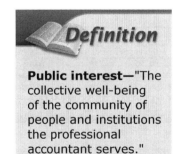
Definition

Public interest—"The collective well-being of the community of people and institutions the professional accountant serves."
—IFAC (2003)

■ It often has been used as an excuse to cross the boundary between private matters and public interest (e.g. publishing photographs of famous people in a private situation on the basis that they have no right to a private life as they always seek publicity and therefore everything they do is "in the public eye" and of public interest).

■ Politicians and governments are significant users of the phrase "in the public interest", but many would cynically suggest that what this really means is "in our own interests".

Illustration 2 Editorial Guidelines

The following is from the British Broadcasting Corporation's editorial guidelines:

"There is no single definition of public interest, it includes but is not confined to:

■ exposing or detecting crime

■ exposing significantly anti-social behaviour

■ exposing corruption or injustice

■ disclosing significant incompetence or negligence

■ protecting people's health and safety

■ preventing people from being misled by some statement or action of an individual or organisation

■ disclosing information that assists people to better comprehend or make decisions on matters of public importance.

There is also a public interest in freedom of expression itself.

When considering what is in the public interest we also need to take account of information already in the public domain or about to become available to the public."

Note that even here, the meaning of "people" and on "public importance" can be questioned.

Illustration 3 Madoff Scandal

Madoff Scandal, 2008

Bernard Madoff ran an investment company which was effectively a pyramid (Ponzi) scheme. At the time of its collapse in December 2008, it was estimated that some $65 billion had been lost, making it the world's largest fraud (so far).

Investigators have noted that a number of European banks had refused to invest with Madoff, after carrying out their own due diligence, as they were unable to "reverse engineer" his investments (i.e. understand how he was able to pay out the high returns he was making and claiming). They did not, however, consider reporting their concerns to the authorities as they were not required to do so and considered it a private matter concerning their individual clients and therefore not a "public interest" matter.

Ironically, the Securities and Exchange Commission, which regulated Madoff, failed to follow through on a number of complaints from a number of actual Madoff investors. The earliest recorded complaint found by investigators (so far) was made in 1999.

4.2 The Professional Accountant

- Clearly a professional accountant's responsibility is not exclusively to satisfy the needs of an individual client or employer. The standards of the professional accountant are heavily determined by the public interest, for example:

  - independent auditors help to maintain the integrity of financial statements presented to financial institutions in support of loans and to stockholders for raising capital;

  - financial executives serve in various financial management capacities in organisations and contribute to efficient and effective use of resources;

  - internal auditors provide assurance about a sound internal control system which enhances the reliability of the external financial information of the employer;

  - tax experts help to establish confidence and efficiency in, and the fair application of, the tax system; and

  - management consultants have a responsibility towards the public interest in advocating sound management decision-making.

- The accountancy profession's public relies on professional accountants for sound financial accounting and reporting, effective financial management and competent advice on a variety of business and taxation matters.

- The attitude and behaviour of professional accountants in providing such services affect the economic well-being of their community and country.

Illustration 4 Economic Growth

Research carried out by Abdolmohammadi and Tucker has shown that many factors can be associated with economic growth in a given country or region. Their recent studies have shown four elements to be of particular importance:

- the legal system;
- the banking system;
- an active stock market; and
- rigorous accounting standards.

Countries with greater numbers of accountants and auditors per capita have greater wealth per capita.

This implies the importance placed by society in such countries on the role of professional accountants as well as the ability of professional accountants to influence and generate economic growth for that country.

---

5 Conflicts and Dilemmas

5.1 Conflicts of Interest

▦ Where ethical conflicts and dilemmas arise, they primarily are in the guise of **conflicts of interest.**

▦ Crane and Matten suggest that conflicts of interest occur when a person's or organisation's obligation to act in the interests of another is interfered with by a competing interest which may obstruct the fulfilment of that obligation.

▦ Conflicts of interest may be:

- Personal v employer—being required to act in an unprofessional way because of a threat to promotion or loss of employment; acting in a particular way to protect the interests of a family member or friend; or disagreement over a particular ethical stance taken by the employer.

- Client v member—giving a client bad advice in order to earn more fees or referring a client to a particular agent, regardless of the client's needs, because that agent provides a greater commission or other benefit to the member.

- Client v client—acting for two clients who are major competitors.

▦ Key requirements to avoid conflicts of interest include:

- Members should place clients' and public interests before their own.

- A firm should not accept or continue an engagement in which there is or is likely to be a significant conflict of interest between the firm and the client.

- Any financial gain which accrues or is likely to accrue to the firm as a result of the engagement (other than properly earned fees, etc) will *always* amount to a significant conflict of interest.

- The firm's work should be managed to avoid the interests of one client adversely affecting those of another.

- Where the acceptance or continuance of an engagement would, even with safeguards, materially prejudice the interests of any client the appointment should not be accepted or continued.

▦ Accounting professionals maintain their objectivity through a combination of impartiality, intellectual honesty and a freedom from conflicts of interest.*

> **Definition**
>
> **Conflict of interest—** "a situation that has the potential to undermine a person's impartiality or objectivity and, thus, integrity because of possible divergence between that person's self-interest and a professional or public interest."
>
> —*Crane and Matten*

> ***Commentary***
>
> *Following the WorldCom and Enron scandals, the collapse of Arthur Andersen (AA) and the introduction of the Sarbanes-Oxley Act (2002), many accountancy firms divested themselves of their consultancy divisions. Many commentators considered that for auditors to also provide consultancy and other services was a clear conflict of interest. Many believed that AA, in particular, "turned a blind eye" to accounting irregularities at WorldCom and Enron for fear of losing the client and lucrative consultancy fees, thus acting unethically and in breach of IFAC's (now IESBA's) Code of Ethics.

Example 3 Potential Conflicts

Identify the potential conflicts with fundamental principles in each of the following situations:

(a) You have been asked to prepare an audit client's financial statements following the sudden departure of their finance director.

(b) You are a financial accountant in a manufacturing company. Your finance director has instructed you to falsify inventory records so that the true age of slow-moving items is concealed.

Commentary

*Do not forget the director's fiduciary duties.

- In the majority of cases, conflicts of interest for directors, managers and other employees revolve around ethical issues and, for professional accountants, around issues of independence as well.*

5.2 Ethical Threats

- An ethical threat arises when an individual, or an organisation, is presented with an option that requires them to violate their ethical code or standards. Their action would be a breach of the ethical culture of the organisation.

- Causes of ethical threats and failures include:
  - Cultural differences resulting in different expectations and practices.
  - Opportunities where ethical problems are not reported or discovered.
  - Lack of opportunities for rectification due to lack of resources.
  - Failure to recognise the ethical dimensions of situations, lack of ethical sensitivity.
  - Lack of understanding of the issues and consequences.
  - Rationalisation of unethical behaviour as part of the embedded culture.
  - Inability to withstand pressures from management, peers or outside interests.
  - Absence of leadership in organisations.
  - Lack of ethical education and knowledge.
  - Lack of effective corporate governance.

- Possible safeguards include:
  - general control mechanisms in risk functions, such as codes of conduct, rules and regulations;
  - peer review, external reviews and self-review processes;
  - disciplinary procedures including guidelines and hearing procedures;
  - ethics awareness, education and development initiatives;
  - promotion of an understanding between ethics and standards among employees;
  - enforcement of the code of conduct; and
  - mentoring support, especially for young employees and those whose cultural background is not the same as that at the head office.

▦ Examples of conflict of interest and other ethical issues in the general context of an organisation include:

- misuse of power—creating unfair terms and conditions of supply through the power of being a buyer);
- preferential treatment—providing special benefits to loyal customers or key suppliers;
- gifts, bribes or hospitality—may be requested/ordered by superiors or by suppliers/customers or offered by suppliers to secure business;
- negotiating tactics, lying, being "economical with the truth", misleading, non-disclosure, deception.
- industrial espionage—burglary, hacking, bugging, "trashing trash" (i.e. searching through a competitor's rubbish);
- "dirty tricks"—black advertising, stealing customers, predatory pricing, sabotage, forcing competitors out of business;
- collusion and cartels;
- endangerment—continuing to sell a product known to be or is potentially unsafe;
- misleading—marketing or other communications targeting vulnerable consumers;
- puffery—product information indicating a product is better than it really is;
- price manipulation—inflating, price fixing, deceptive pricing, or other deceptive pricing (e.g. showing air ticket prices on a website before taxes when the price of a ticket is doubled if VAT, landing and other taxes are added); and
- illegal activity—knowingly breaking the law and/or regulations to gain an advantage.

▦ Most of these will have conflict-of-interest ramifications as the employees involved, if not professional accountants, will be professionals in other trades and subject to codes of ethics which conflict with their professional codes of conduct (e.g. the Chartered Institute of Purchasing and Supply, the Chartered Institute of Marketing, the Chartered Quality Institute and the Chartered Institute of Public Relations).*

***Commentary**

*Search the Internet for "chartered institutes" to appreciate how many potential professional bodies there are and therefore how many codes of ethics and conduct exist.

Example 4 Buyer

Identify the most likely ethical threats faced by a company's procurement director purchasing heavy industrial equipment from overseas.

5.3 Problems and Challenges

▨ Organisations operate in an open, dynamic and ever-changing global environment. There are many ethical pitfalls and traps awaiting the unwary. The following are just a small sample of the types of ethical challenges which face organisations, their managers and employees.

5.3.1 Generally Accepted Practice

▨ Some organisations have "generally accepted practices" which amount to theft or misuse of company assets but are tolerated by management as part of "tradition", "culture" or "something to keep the employees happy".

▨ Examples include:

- use of business phones/computers for private activity;
- claiming for expenses not incurred (e.g. taking a friend to lunch and then claiming it as "potential client entertainment");
- holding lavish private parties and inviting a few business friends, then putting the entire expense through company accounts as business entertainment;
- inflating mileage claims; and
- taking time away from the desk and being covered by colleagues (e.g. signing the missing individual into the organisation's staff system as if they were working).

5.3.2 Setting Precedent

▨ Ethical principles and organisational codes of ethics must be applied to all regardless of their position in the organisation. If the belief in "one rule for them and a totally different one for us" takes hold in an organisation, the moral and ethical structure of that organisation will collapse.

▨ Once a precedent has been set in applying a code of ethics (e.g. an employee was sacked for unethical use of company assets) then the same principles must be applied should a senior manager breach the same rules.

5.3.3 Gifts and Hospitality

▨ As discussed, giving and receiving gifts can create many ethical issues. In some cases, doing so would be considered accepting/giving a bribe while in other cases, not to do so may be considered an insult.

▨ In addition, it is not uncommon for some organisations to be asked by other organisations or individuals for "consultancy or arrangement fees" to ensure that "the process flows smoothly" (often referred to as "grease money").

5.3.4 Conflicts of Interest*

▪ Conflicts of interest arise when an individual or organisation has competing professional or personal interests that make impartial and independent judgement difficult. The individual or corporation is in a position to exploit a professional or official capacity in some way for personal or corporate benefit rather than follow a fiduciary or legal duty (e.g. to maximise the wealth of shareholders and not to make a secret individual profit).

▪ A conflict of interest can exist even if no unethical or improper act results, as it will still create an appearance of impropriety which can undermine confidence in the person or organisation.

▪ Many organisational codes of conduct require individuals to identify potential conflicts of interest and report them to an appropriate official. They would then withdraw to prevent the conflict.

Commentary

*Nepotism, for example, may be perfectly acceptable in some cultures but unacceptable in others.

5.3.5 Insider Dealing

Definition

Insider dealing—"The process where individuals use, or encourage others to use, information regarding a company, which is not generally available, to deal for their own financial advantage (other than in the proper performance of their own job)."
—*UK Financial Services Authority (FSA)*

▪ In some cultures, insider dealing is not considered to be unethical. In others, it is specifically illegal.

5.3.6 Equal Opportunities and Discrimination

▪ International companies have to pay particular attention to different cultural approaches to equal opportunities and discrimination (e.g. in some countries women are not allowed to mix with men in the workplace).*

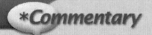

Commentary

*Bank trading rooms are notorious for sex discrimination. Many claims for millions have been made and won by women who were subjected to sexual discrimination (e.g. not promoted) or harassment from male colleagues and bosses.

Summary

- Moral principles arise from a set of agreed rules for right and wrong.

- Ethics is the study of *how* conduct should be considered right or wrong based on the agreed moral principles.

- Absolutism argues that right and wrong derive from a universally applicable moral standard.

- Relativism sees right and wrong as context dependent and subjective.

- Normative ethics judges morality based on an ultimate criterion of moral conduct.

- Deontological ethics judges morality based on duty; that is, obligation regardless of outcomes.

- Teleological ethics approaches morality from the consequences of the outcome.

- Ethical stance determines to some extent how an organisation is viewed by the public and, ultimately, how its decisions affect shareholder wealth. Ethical principles include openness, integrity and trust, honesty, respect, empowerment and accountability.

- A code of ethics is a set of principles which guides decision-making and conduct.

- Codes may be voluntary as part of a CSR programme or a requirement of law as SOX.

- A profession usually requires specialised knowledge and process of certification or licensing, and has an association which has developed a code of ethics.

- The IESBA Code of Ethics specifies integrity, objectivity, professional competence and due care, confidentiality and professional behaviour.

- Ethical dilemmas typically involve conflicts of interest and other ethical threats which require disobedience to an ethical code or standards of conduct.

- Conflicts of interest arise when an individual or organisation has competing professional or personal interests which make impartial and independent judgement difficult.

Session 26 Quiz
Estimated time: 30 minutes

1. Distinguish between morality and ethics. (1)
2. Explain the difference between the absolutism and relativism approaches to ethics. (1.2)
3. Suggest FOUR ways in which ethics can be embedded in an organisation. (2.3)
4. List the FIVE fundamental principles of the ACCA's Code of Ethics and Conduct. (3.3)
5. Explain the concept of "the public interest". (4.1)
6. Give FIVE examples of a potential conflict of interest for the professional accountant. (5.1)
7. Define insider dealing. (5.3.5)

Study Question Bank
Estimated time: 30 minutes

Priority		Estimated Time	Completed
MCQ26	Ethics and Ethical Behaviour	30 minutes	

EXAMPLE SOLUTIONS

Solution 1—Impact of Poor Ethics

- Suppliers not wishing to be connected with the organisation.
- Customers boycotting the organisation's products.
- Inability to recruit high-quality employees, including managers and directors, although a potential CEO may see the situation as an appropriate challenge to "turn the organisation around".
- Increased costs and time taken away from managing the organisation because of bad publicity.
- Increased attention from pressure and lobbying groups.
- Increased monitoring by regulatory bodies, including external auditors, resulting in increased costs.
- Loss of market value due to lower investor confidence in the organisation.
- Increased cost of borrowing.

Solution 2—Other Issues

- Political lobbying
- Speaking out/whistle-blowing
- Executive pay
- Harassment and bullying in the workplace.

Solution 3—Potential Conflicts

(a) Preparation of Financial Statements

There is a conflict with the fundamental principle of "objectivity" (i.e. fairness, without prejudice or bias, conflict of interest or influence of others to override professional or business judgements).

Preparation of financial statements is a management responsibility. Therefore, if an auditor were to undertake this task he would be responsible to management/acting in a management capacity. The auditor could not then be impartial in discharging his responsibility to make an independent report on financial statements to the shareholders.

(b) Falsification of Records

There is a conflict here with several fundamental principles:

- Integrity—such falsification is clearly dishonest.
- Professional competence and due care—to follow the finance director's instruction presumably would result in a material overstatement of inventory. The financial accountant would be professionally negligent to be complicit in this.
- Professional behaviour—dishonesty and negligent actions may clearly discredit the profession.

Solution 4—Buyer

■ The purchasing department, closely followed by the sales department, are considered prime departments for fostering ethical abuse. They primarily are very commercially minded and largely unconcerned with ethics.

■ In its code of ethics, the International Chartered Institute of Purchasing and Supply states that members should:

- Maintain the highest possible standard of integrity.
- Reject any business practice which might reasonably be deemed improper.
- Never use personal authority for personal gain.
- Optimise the use of resources for which they are responsible.
- Provide the maximum benefit to their employers.
- Comply with both the spirit and the letter of the law of their home country and of the country of the supplier.
- Declare any personal interest which may affect or be seen to affect their integrity.
- Respect the confidentiality of any information received as part of their duties.
- Never use any information received as part of their duties for private gain.
- Give honest and clear information to others in the course of their duties.
- Accept no business gift unless clearly of very low intrinsic value (e.g. diaries and calendars).
- Not allow themselves to be influenced or perceived to be influenced in making business decisions as a consequence of accepting hospitality. Hospitality should be managed openly, with care and not greater than the employer is able to reciprocate.

■ Typical situations arising in the buying function include:

- The differences in firm and national cultures. It is not unusual for organisations operating in a particular culture to offer "incentives" to buyers or for buyers to elicit similar as part of the "normal way of doing business".
- Being offered direct or indirect bribes by the supplier, often through the use of "kickbacks" and "rebates".
- Being offered excess entertainment and other "inducements".
- Being asked to fix bids through providing favoured suppliers with confidential information about the business or other bids received.

Index

D

E

F

G

H

Q

R

ACCA

F1/FAB ACCOUNTANT IN BUSINESS

STUDY QUESTION BANK

For Examinations from September 2017 to August 2018

No responsibility for loss occasioned to any person acting or refraining from action as a result of any material in this publication can be accepted by the author, editor or publisher.

This training material has been prepared and published by Becker Professional Development International Limited: www.becker.com/acca

STUDY QUESTION BANK – ACCOUNTANT IN BUSINESS (F1/FAB)

CONTENTS

MCQ 1 – THE BUSINESS ORGANISATION

1.1 **Which items best describe an organisation?**

A	Working together, collective goals, controlled performance
B	Team work, clear rules, collective goals
C	Synergy, clear roles, accepted leader
D	Defined hierarchy, clear objectives, formal rules (2 marks)

1.2 **Which of the following best describes public sector entities?**

A	Traded on the stock market
B	Include charities and NGOs
C	Owned by the government
D	Have the objective of influencing government policy (2 marks)

1.3 A cooperative (collective) would be characterised as _____, while Microsoft would be a _____ company.

Which words correctly complete this sentence?

A	a not-for-profit organisation, public sector
B	a charity, profit driven
C	meeting the needs of its members, publicly traded
D	an NGO, listed (2 marks)

1.4 A computer company has identified that there is demand for a lower-cost laptop to be included in its product range.

Which two departments would most likely be tasked with achieving this?

A	Purchasing, Research and Development
B	Research and Development, Marketing
C	Marketing, Manufacturing
D	Purchasing, Direct service provision (2 marks)

1.5 **Which elements characterise the concept of "service"?**

A	Varied, tangibility, imperishable
B	Consistency, tangibility, simultaneity
C	Tangibility, inconsistency, simultaneity
D	Variability, simultaneity, perishability (2 marks)

1.6 Marketing is a process which identifies, anticipates and satisfies customer needs profitably.

Is this statement true or false?

A	True
B	False (1 mark)

1.7 The main decision under "place" a marketing manager has to take when reviewing the marketing mix is whether to sell directly or indirectly to customers.

Is this statement true or false?

A	True
B	False (1 mark)

1.8 **What are the elements of the purchasing mix?**

A   Price, quality, promotion, place
B   Promotion, price, distribution, place
C   Quantity, quality, price, delivery
D   Quantity, quality, place, delivery   (2 marks)

1.9 According to Professor Kotler, the key elements of a marketing concept are _____ , _____ , _____ , _____ and _____.

Which five words, in correct order, complete this sentence?

A   needs, demands, wants, value and satisfaction
B   needs, advantage, products, transactions and relationships
C   quality, quantity, price, markets and products
D   needs, products, value, exchange and markets   (2 marks)

1.10 Your company is providing accountancy services for small and medium sized enterprises. You are heavily dependent on your employees.

Which three Ps do you have to add to the ordinary four Ps of the marketing mix?

A   Productivity, processes and physical evidence
B   Production, processes and physical evidence
C   People, processes and physical evidence
D   People, processes and procurement   (2 marks)

1.11 Market segmentation involves dividing a broad market into distinct subsets of consumers, businesses or countries in order to design and implement strategies to target them.

Is this statement true or false for the production function?

A   True
B   False   (1 mark)

(19 marks)

MCQ 2 – STAKEHOLDERS IN BUSINESS ORGANISATIONS

2.1 The bi-directional nature of stakeholders means that stakeholders can affect both the achievement of an organisation's objectives and how an organisation uses its resources.

Is this statement true or false?

A   True
B   False   (1 mark)

2.2 In a publicly traded company, the shareholders rely on the independent auditor to verify financial statements prepared by management. This reduces _____.

Which phrase best completes the sentence?

A   monitoring costs
B   stakeholder dissatisfaction
C   the agency problem
D   shareholder conflict   (2 marks)

2.3   **The bank and shareholders are part of which group of stakeholders?**

A   External
B   Internal
C   Unrecognised
D   Connected   (2 marks)

2.4   **Which of the following best describes the activities of a company lobbyist?**

A   Attempts to influence legislation on behalf of a company
B   Attempts to influence a company's objectives
C   Searches for specialist employees on behalf of a company
D   Takes direct action against the activities of a company   (2 marks)

2.5   The tax authority of a city has little interest in the affairs of a chain of car dealerships except that it pays tax. However, if the company's taxes are incorrectly paid or paid late the authority can charge high penalties.

According to Mendelow, what should the car dealership do?

A   Keep the tax authority satisfied
B   Treat the tax authority as a key player
C   Keep the tax authority informed
D   Put minimal effort into dealing with the tax authority   (2 marks)

2.6   A community action group has been formed in response to a planned shopping mall in the center of the city's historic district. The development company has hired a public relations firm to attempt to influence public opinion in their favour.

Which of the following best describes the situation?

A   Grassroots lobbying
B   Agency conflict
C   Lobbyist actions
D   Stakeholder conflict   (2 marks)

(11 marks)

MCQ 3 – THE BUSINESS ENVIRONMENT

3.1   **Which of the following is a source of supra-national legal authority?**

A   City of Stockholm
B   Government of Indonesia
C   European Union
D   State of California   (2 marks)

3.2   **Which of the following best relates to data protection?**

A   The idea that individuals have rights if an entity holds information about them
B   A company policy that requires data security (e.g. passwords on computers)
C   Laws that are enacted to punish hackers, identity thieves, and other cyber criminals
D   Software to thwart hackers (e.g. anti-virus and firewall software)   (2 marks)

3.3 When completing an application form to purchase financial services from a bank, you are requested to check/tick a box if you wish to receive details of other products sold by the bank and their associates.

Which principle of data protection does this example refer to?

A   Data should be processed in accordance with the rights of the individual
B   Data shall be adequate, relevant and not excessive
C   Personal data shall not be kept longer than necessary
D   Personal data shall be processed fairly and lawfully   (2 marks)

3.4 A company sold an old computer at an auction with a customer database still on the hard drive. This computer did not have a password or any database security features enabled.

The company has violated the principles of which of the following?

A   Data protection only
B   Data security only
C   Data protection and data security
D   Data safety, data security and data protection   (2 marks)

3.5 Job descriptions, discipline policies and instructions on the use of equipment are all tools that management can use to promote health and safety in the workplace.

Is this statement true or false?

A   True
B   False   (1 mark)

3.6 David was standing on his chair to shout good news about gaining a new client to the rest of his colleagues. He fell off the chair and broke his arm.

Who is responsible for the accident?

A   David's company
B   The chair manufacturer
C   David
D   Both David and David's company   (2 marks)

3.7 **According to social and demographic trends which of the following best describes countries where death rates fall while birthrates remain unchanged?**

A   Developing counties
B   Post-industrial countries
C   Fully developed countries
D   Pre-industrial societies   (2 marks)

3.8 **When the workforce is aging, which of the following statements is true?**

A   The cost of that workforce will be lower
B   The cost of that workforce will remain constant
C   The cost of that workforce will be higher
D   The additional costs of that workforce will be covered by the government (2 marks)

3.9 **Which of the following best describes the term "carbon footprint"?**

    A   The impact an organisation's use of sustainable power has on the environment

    B   A measure of the emission of greenhouse gases by organisations or individuals

    C   The effect on the reserves of oil and gas from manufacturing, transportation and power generation

    D   Prehistoric footprints from extinct, large land animals captured in carbon-based fossils   (2 marks)

3.10 The information systems (IS) strategy should drive the business strategy as IS is often the most expensive function in a business.

    Is this statement true or false?

    A   True
    B   False   (1 mark)

3.11 A logistics company has developed a unique extranet website for its customers - they can choose the method of delivery to match their carbon footprint, see exactly where their shipments are at any time on a map of the world and the route it is taking.

    What is the potential competitive advantage?

    A   Growth
    B   Cost leadership
    C   Strategic alliance
    D   Differentiation   (2 marks)

3.12 **Which of the following is a disadvantage of outsourcing IS?**

    A   A key resource will be dealt with by an external provider
    B   Enables management to concentrate resources on key activities
    C   Risk management and planning is more assured
    D   Cost effective for smaller entities   (2 marks)

3.13 Michael Porter's Five Forces model is used to determine the profit potential of an individual business.

    Is this statement true or false?

    A   True
    B   False   (1 mark)

3.14 **The number and quantity of new entrants in an industry depends on which one of the following?**

    A   Switching costs of suppliers
    B   The profit potential of the industry
    C   Barriers to entry
    D   The threat of substitute products   (2 marks)

3.15 For supermarkets, _____ is/are _____ because of their relative size compared to suppliers.

Which words, in order, best complete this sentence?

A   barriers to entry, high
B   the threat of substitute products, low
C   the bargaining power of customers, high
D   the power of buyers, high   (2 marks)

3.16   Which list includes Porter's Generic Strategies?

A   Differentiation focus, price focus, cost focus
B   Cost leadership, cost focus, price leadership
C   Market leadership, marketing focus, differentiation
D   Cost leadership, differentiation, niche focus   (2 marks)

                                                                 (29 marks)

MCQ 4 – THE MACRO-ECONOMIC ENVIRONMENT

4.1   What does the study of macro-economics concern?

A   Individual firms
B   Large firms
C   The economy
D   Private sector firms   (2 marks)

4.2   Which of the following is a list of macro-economic policy objectives?

A   Full employment, economic growth, price stability
B   Balance of payments, interest rates, full employment
C   Price stability, exchange rates, balance of payments
D   Interest rates, limited inflation, full employment   (2 marks)

4.3 Gross Domestic Product (GDP) is calculated as _____ + _____ + _____ + _____.

Which words correctly complete this sentence?

A   Consumption, investment, government spending, net exports
B   Consumption, savings, investment, government spending
C   Consumption, investment, taxation, net exports
D   Consumption, savings, taxation, net exports   (2 marks)

4.4   "The Paradox of Thrift" correctly refers to which of the following?

A   If tax rates increase then consumption with decrease
B   If consumption increases then savings will decrease
C   If tax rates increase then savings will decrease
D   If savings increases then consumption will decrease   (2 marks)

4.5   Supply side economics is usually associated with the work of whom?

A   Adams
B   Keynes
C   Friedman
D   Marx   (2 marks)

4.6 **What was the initial impact of the subprime banking crisis (crunch) of 2007/08?**

- A Inflation
- B Lack of liquidity
- C Unemployment
- D Stagflation (2 marks)

4.7 Orders are declining, inventory levels and prices are falling with redundancies increasing.

What stage of the business trade cycle is described above?

- A Depression
- B Recession
- C Recovery (1 mark)

4.8 Carlos works in commercial fishing in Spain. He, and many like him, is unemployed due to greatly reduced catch numbers and strict government regulations.

Which type of unemployment best describes this situation?

- A Real wage
- B Seasonal
- C Frictional
- D Structural (2 marks)

4.9 **Which of the following are key elements of fiscal policy?**

- A Taxation, interest rate adjustments
- B Government spending, taxation
- C Demand-side policies, adjusting the money supply
- D Government expenditure, central bank policy (2 marks)

4.10 **Which of the following best describes a "supply-side" approach to economic recovery?**

- A Low tax rates, limited government spending, de-regulation
- B Increased government spending, low tax rates, support of depressed industries
- C Increase in public works projects, temporary budget deficits, low tax rates
- D Increased regulation, support of depressed industries, increase in public works projects (2 marks)

(19 marks)

MCQ 5 – THE MICRO-ECONOMIC ENVIRONMENT

5.1 **Which of the following statements about price elasticity are correct?**

- (1) It is defined as the % change in price divided by the % change in demand
- (2) An item which has an elasticity greater than one is price sensitive
- (3) An item which has an elasticity of less than one is said to be inelastic
- (4) If demand for an item is inelastic and its price falls, total revenue will decrease

- A 1 and 2
- B 2 and 4
- C 1 and 3
- D 3 and 4 (2 marks)

5.2 **Which of the following commodities has a high income elasticity of demand?**

  (1) A commodity that has substitutes
  (2) A commodity that has no substitutes
  (3) A commodity on which a high fraction of income is spent
  (4) A commodity which is necessary

  A 1 only
  B 3 only
  C 1 and 3
  D 2 and 4   (2 marks)

5.3 **Which of the following is micro-economics NOT concerned with?**

  A Consumers
  B Firms
  C Aggregate demand
  D Industries   (2 marks)

5.4 **Which of the following most strongly relates to an imperfect market?**

  A Many sellers, many buyers, no barriers to entry
  B Monopoly, oligopoly control
  C Many sellers, many buyers, imperfect information
  D Selling price set by market, no barriers to entry (2 marks)

            (8 marks)

MCQ 6 – ORGANISATIONAL STRUCTURE

6.1 Melissa is the owner of a property management business. She is actively involved in the work of her eight employees.

  Which structure best describes Melissa's business?

  A Matrix
  B Entrepreneurial
  C Tall
  D Hybrid   (2 marks)

6.2 Paul works as a desktop-publishing specialist in an advertising agency. Paul creates layouts for print-related advertising campaigns for the 8 Account Managers and the Art Director he supports. He also works closely with the agency's 5 Art Managers and their Creative Director.

  Which structure best describes this section of the advertising agency?

  A Entrepreneurial
  B Product based
  C Service oriented
  D Matrix   (2 marks)

6.3   A French logistics company has acquired similar businesses in Bulgaria, Romania and Ukraine in support of its expansion strategy. This has resulted in wider spans of control and a shorter scalar chain.

  A   True
  B   False   (1 mark)

6.4   **Which is a potential disadvantage of decentralisation?**

  A   Duplication of resources
  B   "One-size-fits-all" decision making
  C   Restricted career development
  D   Overloaded senior management   (2 marks)

6.5   **Which of the following would most likely occur after a company completes the outsourcing of its IT department?**

  A   Decentralisation of its local offices
  B   Longer scalar chains in the company
  C   Less specialisation in the company
  D   A narrower span of control for production managers   (2 marks)

6.6   **Which of the following statements is correct?**

  A   Scalar chain tells you the levels of management in a company
  B   Span of control tells you the levels of management in a company
  C   The "grapevine" is part of an organisation's formal structure
  D   Outsourcing will lead to a more bureaucratic company structure   (2 marks)

6.7   **Which of the following is a characteristic of the formal organisation?**

  A   Driven by lateral communication
  B   Bottom up
  C   Based on professional networks
  D   Top down   (2 marks)

6.8   **Which of the following is most likely to be a disadvantage in an informal organisation?**

  A   Innovation is inhibited
  B   Decrease in motivation
  C   Increase in bureaucracy
  D   Spreading of rumors   (2 marks)

6.9   Supervisors are part of the tactical workforce.

  Is this statement true or false?

  A   True
  B   False   (1 mark)

6.10 Due to heavy snowfall, a number of employees have phoned their manager to say they cannot make it to the office and are unlikely to do so for at least a week. The manager reallocates work priorities between the available staff.

What level of organisational planning is the manager using?

    A   Strategic

    B   Tactical

    C   Operational   **(1 mark)**

(17 marks)

MCQ 7 – ORGANISATIONAL CULTURE

7.1 **Influences on a company's culture include which of the following?**

    A   Communication style, rules, reward systems

    B   Rituals, dress code, control systems

    C   Control systems, organisational structure, power structures

    D   Age of the company, power structures, management style   **(2 marks)**

7.2 **Which of the following are the three levels of Schein's culture model?**

    A   Espoused values, basic assumptions, artefacts

    B   Artefacts, core values, hidden assumptions

    C   Basic assumptions, values, rules and regulations

    D   Company policy, organisational structure, employee values   **(2 marks)**

7.3 Natalia works in the purchasing department of a large furniture production company. She and her three colleagues report to the department manager, have clear job descriptions and use a customised computer system to do their work.

Which of Handy's cultures best describes Natalia's department?

    A   Task

    B   Role

    C   Person

    D   Power   **(2 marks)**

7.4 In the Santiago branch of an international law firm, senior managers enjoy luxurious perks, including expensive company cars, extravagant offices, and other benefits. Their colleagues in other branches do not receive such generous benefits-in-kind.

Which of Hofstede's cultural models most closely describes this situation?

    A   High person culture

    B   High individuality

    C   High power-avoidance

    D   High power-distance   **(2 marks)**

7.5 "Explicit" culture describes the belief that a company's culture naturally emerges over time as individuals transform themselves into groups.

Is this statement true or false?

    A   True

    B   False   **(1 mark)**

7.6 A portrait of the senior partner hangs in the office reception. Inscribed on the portrait are the firm's corporate values and beliefs.

Which of Schein's cultural levels does this best represent?

A   Level 1 artefacts and creations
B   Level 2 espoused values
C   Level 3 basic assumptions and values   (1 mark)

7.7 **When is culture most likely to be a liability?**

A   When culture increases consistency of good behaviour
B   When management is competent
C   When the environment is dynamic
D   When culture reduces ambiguity   (2 marks)

(12 marks)

MCQ 8 – COMMITTEES IN THE BUSINESS ORGANISATION

8.1 Standing committees are often formed to deal with temporary issues (e.g. a project steering committee).

Is this statement true or false?

A   True
B   False   (1 mark)

8.2 **Which of the following is an advantage of a committee?**

A   No one individual is held responsible for the decision
B   Procedural matters take time
C   More experienced members might have more influence   (1 mark)

8.3 **Which of the following is the best skill set required by a good chairman?**

A   Tactful, ability to organise, good language and grammar skills
B   Organised, good note taking ability, full understanding of procedures
C   Understanding of procedures, firmness, impartiality
D   Firmness, impartiality, ability to organise   (2 marks)

8.4 With a committee, the number of members should be _____ and _____.

Which words, in correct order, best complete this sentence?

A   large, possessing good communication skills
B   at least three, not more than eight
C   balanced, highly skilled
D   carefully considered, balanced   (2 marks)

(6 marks)

MCQ 9 – GOVERNANCE AND SOCIAL RESPONSIBILITY

9.1   Corporate governance can be defined as the way in which an organisation is regulated and monitored.

Is this statement true or false?

A   True
B   False   (1 mark)

9.2   Which of the following is considered best practice under Corporate Governance?

A   Split roles of CEO and Chairman, audit committee, remuneration committee
B   External audit, split roles of CEO and Chairman, audit committee
C   Professionally qualified risk manager, ethics committee, audit committee
D   Finance director to chair audit committee, combined role of CEO and chairperson, external audit   (2 marks)

9.3   Which of the following relates to a rules-based system of corporate governance?

A   A company should follow the spirit of the law
B   Comply or explain approach if rules are not followed
C   Market decides the penalty for breaking the code
D   Code is embedded in the laws of the country   (2 marks)

9.4   Which of the following factors is often a factor of corporate scandals?

A   Separate CEO and Chairman
B   Segregation of duties between key personnel
C   Lack of oversight
D   Overly strict internal controls   (2 marks)

9.5   Which of the following best describes corporate social responsibility?

A   Impacts on society, maximising shareholder wealth, behaving responsibly
B   Philanthropic values, legal values, true and fair financial statements
C   Ethical behaviour, economic development, quality of life
D   Establishing charities, quality of life, sustainable accountability   (2 marks)

9.6   Which of the following is a benefit of a remuneration committee?

A   Reduces the conflict of interest between NEDs and executive directors
B   Ensures fair salary for all employees
C   Ensures employment law for operational staff (e.g. minimum wage) is followed
D   Reduces the agency problem   (2 marks)

9.7   Which of the following best describes sustainable development?

A   Development that will not compromise the needs of future generations
B   Development that will always meet the needs of the present
C   Development that will always maintain a fixed state of harmony
D   Development that is expected to continue in the foreseeable future   (2 marks)

(13 marks)

MCQ 10 –ACCOUNTING AND FINANCE

10.1   **Which activity is concerned with recording and classifying transactions?**

    A   Management accounting
    B   Cost accounting
    C   Financial accounting
    D   Bookkeeping   (2 marks)

10.2   The marketing department in a major building materials supply company needs information on product profit margins before executing a new pricing strategy.

    Who in the company would investigate and provide this information?

    A   Treasury department
    B   Financial accountant
    C   Management Accountant
    D   Bookkeeper   (2 marks)

10.3   **Which function ensures that a business has sufficient funds, in the appropriate currencies, to meet operational, financial and strategic objectives?**

    A   Financial accounting
    B   Treasury
    C   Management accounting
    D   Planning and budgeting   (2 marks)

10.4   **Which is the correct transaction flow?**

    A   Transactions – daybooks – ledgers – financial statements
    B   Transactions – ledgers – control accounts – financial statements
    C   Primary transactions – summarised transactions – daybooks – financial statements
                                                                        (1 mark)

10.5   A manufacturing group has transferred its car manufacturing operations to an emerging economy. The Board of Directors has chosen this location because of lower production costs, availability of a skilled workforce and tax incentives, over a five year period, that the government is offering to manufacturing companies employing more than 500 employees.

    What tax strategy is this company using?

    A   Tax avoidance
    B   Tax harmonisation
    C   Tax mitigation
    D   Tax evasion   (2 marks)

                                                                        (9 marks)

MCQ 11 – EXTERNAL AND INTERNAL AUDIT

11.1   Internal auditors are not required to consider fraud.

    Is this statement true or false?

    A   True
    B   False   (1 mark)

11.2 **Which one of the following is a key difference between internal and external audit?**

 A   Internal report to shareholders, external report to directors

 B   Internal are independent of the company, external are often employed by the company

 C   Internal report on systems, controls and risks, external on financial statements

 D   Internal must have an ACCA qualification, external need a BA and MA qualification   (2 marks)

11.3 Internal auditors have an unavoidable _____ problem.

 Which word correctly completes this sentence?

 A   Loyalty
 B   Competence
 C   Independence   (1 mark)

11.4 External audit is required by _____ to form an opinion on the _____ of financial statements.

 Which words, in order, correctly completes this sentence?

 A   management, true and fair
 B   law, true and fair view
 C   law, fair and firm view
 D   management, fair and frequent view   (2 marks)

11.5 **Which one of the following contains three of the four elements in an assurance relationship?**

 A   Responsible party, intended user, regulator
 B   Government, practitioner, subject matter
 C   Intended user, subject matter, practitioner
 D   Practitioner, responsible party, tax authorities   (2 marks)

11.6 **Which one of the following would internal audit most likely be expected to report on?**

 A   success of a marketing campaign
 B   design of a POS-campaign
 C   competence of a director
 D   design and implementation of the most efficient combination of manual and automated controls   (2 marks)

11.7 **Which one of the following are most important aspects of the assessment of the professional proficiency of internal audit?**

 A   Due professional care, competence, co-ordination and communication

 B   Due professional care, competence, continuing education and compliance with standards

 C   Due professional care, competence, co-ordination, human relations

 D   Due professional care, competence, communication and friendliness   (2 marks)

11.8 Companies listed on one of the major stock exchanges in the EU (Frankfurt, London, Paris) are legally obliged to appoint internal auditors.

Is this statement true or false?

A   True
B   False   (1 mark)

11.9 **Which of the following are the two main features of internal audit?**

A   Appraisal and independence
B   Appraisal and service
C   Independence and internal control
D   Independence and service   (2 marks)

(15 marks)

MCQ 12 – REGULATORY ENVIRONMENT OF ACCOUNTING

12.1 In most jurisdictions, "accountant" is a reserved term, but "auditor" is not.

Is this statement true or false?

A   True
B   False   (1 mark)

12.2 Regulatory financial reporting is usually controlled by legislation, supra-national bodies, accounting standards, and/or GAAP.

Is this statement true or false?

A   True
B   False   (1 mark)

12.3 **Which are the two main international accounting organisations that have a direct impact on the accounting professional?**

A   IASB, ACA
B   ACCA, IFAC
C   IFAC, IASB
D   ACCA, ICAEW   (2 marks)

12.4 **The development of IFRS is a closed process and, as such, public observers are not admitted at meetings.**

A   True
B   False   (1 mark)

12.5 A professional accountant miscalculates a client's tax liabilities, resulting in a tax investigation and fine on the client.

With which one of the following can the client register a complaint?

A   Taxation authorities
B   The police
C   The Financial Reporting Council
D   The accountant's professional body   (2 marks)

12.6 **Which one of the following is an objective of the International Accounting Standards Board?**

A   To be the sole provider of financial reporting standards
B   To monitor the application of financial reporting standards
C   To bring about the convergence of national accounting standards
D   To issue all reporting, auditing and ethical standards   (2 marks)

12.7 **For at least how many years (under best practice) should accounting records be kept for listed companies and for other companies?**

A   Six and three years respectively
B   Nine and six years respectively
C   Indefinitely for listed and three years for other
D   Indefinitely for both   (2 marks)

(11 marks)

MCQ 13 – FINANCIAL SYSTEMS AND PROCEDURES

13.1 A system is a group of interacting, interrelated or interdependent elements in place to support a framework of policies and procedures.

Is this statement true or false?

A   True
B   False   (1 mark)

13.2 To ensure that _____ achieve their objectives, _____ should be formally developed by management to be applied in each system.

Which words, in correct order, correctly complete this sentence?

A   Procedures, policies
B   Policies, procedures
C   Polices, plans
D   Systems, policies and procedures   (2 marks)

13.3 **Which of the following stages of a purchase cycle are in the correct order?**

A   Purchase order, purchase requisition, goods received, payment made
B   Purchase requisition, purchase order, goods received, payment made
C   Purchase order, goods received, purchase requisition, payment made
D   Purchase order, payment made, goods received, purchase requisition   (2 marks)

13.4 The overall objective of _____ is to ensure all goods and services dispatched are correctly _____ and processed.

Which words, in correct order, correctly complete this sentence?

A   Sales, invoiced
B   Logistics, handled
C   Marketing, researched
D   Payroll, managed by people   (2 marks)

13.5 In a classic inventory system, regular inventory counts take place and require computerised systems. In contrast, in a perpetual inventory system, annual inventory counts take place the same day of every year.

Is the above statement true or false?

A True
B False (1 mark)

13.6 **Which of the following contains a correct list of inventory categories?**

A Work-in-progress, incomplete goods, finished goods
B Un-processed materials, finished goods, processed materials
C Raw materials, work in progress, finished goods
D Uncompleted goods, finished materials, goods held for resale (2 marks)

13.7 John carries out a credit check on an order before giving authorisation to the warehouse manager who carries out a final check on the order and the goods. All internal documentation, except the order, is pre-numbered in sequential order.

Which transaction cycle does this describe?

A Purchases
B Wages
C Sales
D Cash (2 marks)

13.8 **What does the term "ghost employee" mean?**

A Employees who are on annual leave
B Employees who are clocked in by other employees
C Employees who "fade away" when required to work overtime
D Individuals on the payroll who are not employed by the company (2 marks)

13.9 **Which one of the following sets are control activities?**

A Authorisation, segregation of duties, cut-off
B Performance reviews, physical controls, accuracy
C Authorisation, information processing, segregation of duties
D Performance reviews, recorded assets, cut-off (2 marks)

13.10 **"What if analysis" is most commonly used with which of the following software packages?**

A Spreadsheets
B Database management systems
C Word processing
D Graphics presentation (2 marks)

13.11 **What is the key role of accounting in purchasing?**

A To compare prices
B To choose suppliers
C To maintain margins
D To procure raw materials and services (2 marks)

(20 marks)

MCQ 14 – INTERNAL CONTROL AND SECURITY

14.1 **Which one of the following are all components of an internal control framework?**

A Control environment, governance and management functions, sharing of information

B Control environment, risk assessment, control activities

C Governance and management functions, administrating and accounting controls, control activities

D Governance and management functions, control activities, functional activities

(2 marks)

14.2 **What does the mnemonic "CAVE" stand for?**

A Communication, attention, value for money, expertise
B Concise, accurate, valid, economic
C Complete, accurate, valid, existence
D Correct, available, valid, existence (2 marks)

14.3 The main factors that will be reflected in an organisation's control environment are the philosophy and operating style of the directors and management.

Is this statement true or false?

A True
B False (1 mark)

14.4 **Which one of the following contains business risks that may affect the production of financial statements?**

A Rapid growth and changes in the regulatory environment
B New products and experienced personnel
C Corporate restructuring and outsourcing
D Increase in transactions and established information systems (2 marks)

14.5 An accounting system consists of _____, _____ and _____ to enable _____ , _____. and _____of the records and information necessary to satisfy reporting objectives.

Which words, in correct order, correctly complete this sentence?

A infrastructure, processes, data; initiation, material, reporting
B software, data, information; reporting, accountability, audit
C physical environment, computer systems, people; recording, reporting, accountability
D hardware, procedures, controls; translate, initiate, transfer (2 marks)

14.6 **Which one of the following correctly categorises authorisation, segregation of duties and passwords?**

A Corrective controls
B Detective controls
C Preventive controls (1 mark)

14.7 When an employee is leaving her workplace, she is responsible for turning on the alarm system for the whole office.

To which one of the following categories does this control belong?

A	Reliance	
B	Unauthorised access	
C	Segregation of duties	
D	Physical control	(2 marks)

14.8 Application controls typically operate at a business level. They can be _____ or _____ in nature and are designed to ensure the _____ of the accounting records and information.

Which words, in correct order, correctly complete this sentence?

A	integrative, detective, objectivity	
B	preventative, detective, integrity	
C	preventative, detective, initiative	
D	detective, manipulated, integrity	(2 marks)

14.9 **Application controls on data input include which one of the following?**

A	Validation checks	
B	Existence checks	
C	Dumping data	
D	Range checks	(2 marks)

14.10 The purpose of encryption is to make any intelligible information unintelligible.

Is this statement true or false?

A	True	
B	False	(1 mark)

14.11 **Which of the following contains the most examples of risks to data?**

A	Hardware and software error, human error, deliberate actions	
B	Hardware and software error, human error, regular testing	
C	Deliberate actions, unintended actions, "pull the plug", authorised access	
D	Human error, deliberate actions, unintended actions, regular maintenance	
		(2 marks)

(19 marks)

MCQ 15 – BUSINESS FRAUD

15.1 A rigorous system of control will prevent and eliminate all fraud and errors.

Is this statement true or false?

A	True	
B	False	(1 mark)

15.2 Misappropriation of assets is _____ .

Which word, in correct order, correctly completes this sentence?

A   fraud
B   error
C   misinterpretation   (1 mark)

15.3 **In a business context, what are the two basic forms of fraud?**

A   Fraudulent reporting and misappropriation of assets
B   Theft of cash and theft of inventory
C   Misuse of assets and theft of cash
D   Misstatements of disclosures and deliberate misapplication of accounting principles
                                                                           (2 marks)

15.4 **Which of the following is a "skimming" fraud?**

A   Diversion of major customers
B   Window dressing
C   Unusual discounts
D   Small amounts are diverted from a large number of transactions   (2 marks)

15.5 Window dressing is a common ____carried out at the ___ of a year on financial statements to make them appear _____ than what they really are.

Which words, in order, correctly complete this sentence?

A   error, end, healthier
B   fraud, end, healthier
C   fraud, beginning, healthier   (1 mark)

15.6 **Which of the following is NOT a problem for obtaining audit evidence that might indicate fraud?**

A   Differences between accounting records and third party confirmations
B   Proper cost and management accounting systems
C   Unreasonable time pressure from management
D   Lack of response by management to enquiries   (2 marks)

15.7 **Which of the following is a risk factor regarding financial stability?**

A   Significant financial interest in the entity
B   Overly optimistic press releases and annual reports
C   Personal guarantees of debts of entity
D   Significant decline in customer demand   (2 marks)

15.8 Olga is a loan application supervisor at a major bank. Her best friend drives a top-of-the-range sports Mercedes. Olga is very jealous as her friend who, although not as attractive as Olga, always seems to get the best men. Olga believes the car attracts them. Her manager is currently ill and is not expected to return to work for at least six months. Olga has been asked to continue her work and take on her manager's loan authorisation responsibilities without any oversight from other managers. She is not paid any extra for doing so.

Which one of the following lists the factors that place Olga as a high fraud risk?

A	Greed, jealousy, opportunity	
B	Pressure, ability, lack of controls	
C	Incentive, opportunity, rationalisation	
D	Position, desire, power	(2 marks)

(13 marks)

MCQ 16 – LEADERSHIP, MANAGEMENT, SUPERVISION

16.1   Leadership is a quality; management is a job.

Is this statement true or false?

A	True	
B	False	(1 mark)

16.2   Management, according to Fayol, is to _____, _____, _____, _____and_____ .

Which words correctly complete this sentence?

A	communicate, plan and forecast, organise, command, control	
B	co-ordinate, plan and forecast, organise, command, control	
C	co-ordinate, plan and forecast, motivate, command, control	(1 mark)

16.3   Mintzberg suggested that managers in their daily work fulfil three types of managerial role – interpersonal, informational and decisional.

Which one of the following correctly describes one of these categories?

A	Interpersonal: Disturbance-handler, leader, spokesperson	
B	Informational: Figurehead, disseminator, monitor	
C	Decisional: Resource allocator, liaison, entrepreneur	
D	Interpersonal: Figurehead, leader, liaison	(2 marks)

16.4   **Which one of the following best describes the main role of a supervisor?**

A	Liaison officer between management and workforce	
B	Getting involved in day-to-day work and help solve problems	
C	Training and conducting appraisals	
D	Allocating tasks to the right people to ensure that these tasks are performed effectively and efficiently	(2 marks)

16.5   Authority is the ability to do something, power is the right to do something or have something done.

Is this statement true or false?

A	True	
B	False	(1 mark)

16.6   **Which of the following are the three types of authority a manager usually has?**

A   Charismatic, traditional, legal
B   Line, staff and functional
C   Direct, indirect and delegated
D   Resource, expert and charisma   (2 marks)

16.7   **What is the most effective management/leadership style suggested by Blake and Mouton?**

A   9,1
B   9,9
C   1,1
D   1,9   (2 marks)

16.8   Four main styles of management were identified by the Ashridge Management College within two extremes of directive versus supportive behaviour.

These are best described by which one of the following?

A   Tell, autocratic, participative, democratic
B   Democratic, autocratic, pragmatic, diplomatic
C   Tell, sell, consult, join
D   Objective, decisive, visionary, pragmatic   (2 marks)

16.9   Maxim is the manager of a call centre. McKinsey has advised him that by reorganising his teams to complete highly specific tasks the call centre will be able to increase the throughput of work significantly, as well as increasing the number of sales calls made to the public. The reorganisation is unpopular with many workers, who feel that their jobs will become boring and repetitive.

The proposal to reorganise the work of the call centre utilises principles put forward by which school of management thought?

A   The human relations school
B   The modern school
C   The classical/scientific school
D   The administrative school   (2 marks)

16.10   Fiedler focuses on two styles of leaders taking the relationship between leadership styles and the effectiveness of the work group into consideration.

Which of the following describe these two styles?

A   PDMs and PDLs
B   PDMs and PCMs
C   PLMs and PLLs
D   PDLs and PCLs   (2 marks)

16.11 ABC is an old, well-established company having to deal with the current economic crises. Profits are falling due to less export orders and the use of old technology. Many employees have been with the company for the past 20 years and do not understand why they should now change and learn new things. They blame the past unsuccessful months on management.

According to Heifetz which sort of change is necessary in this situation?

A   Transformational
B   Fundamental
C   Technical
D   Adaptive   (2 marks)

16.12 **Which of the following is implied by delegation?**

A   "No one can do it better than me"
B   "I enjoy doing the work myself"
C   The person delegating has the authority to do so
D   The manager delegating the work has no confidence in his subordinates   (2 marks)

(21 marks)

MCQ 17 – RECRUITMENT AND SELECTION

17.1 You have recently been employed as your firm's first human resources manager. One of your initial tasks will be to devise a recruitment and selection plan for junior and middle management.

Which one of the following best describes the stages of recruitment and selection?

A   Advertising a position, assessment of application, notifying the candidates

B   Identifying/defining requirements, attracting potential employees, selecting candidates

C   Setting recruitment and selection objectives, advertising a position, selecting candidates

D   Setting recruitment and selection objectives, attracting potential employees, setting interview and test dates   (2 marks)

17.2 **What does a person specification describe?**

A   The number of people needed for job vacancies
B   Attributes of a person ideal to fill a position
C   Main tasks and responsibilities involved in a job
D   Performance results of a job holder   (2 marks)

17.3 A company urgently needs a CFA-qualified analyst but has neither the internal resources nor a large budget for advertising.

Which one of the following would be the most appropriate recruitment medium?

A   recruitment agency
B   advertisement in a large, nation-wide newspaper
C   advertisement on national TV
D   recruitment fairs   (2 marks)

17.4 A job description sets out the total requirements of a job – its purpose, how it relates to the organisation, the jobholder's accountabilities/tasks and lines of reporting. It may also cover the physical, social and economic factors that affect the job.

Is this statement true or false?

A True
B False (1 mark)

17.5 **In measuring the success, or otherwise, of the recruitment and selection process, which two performances measures could be used?**

A Effectiveness and speed
B Fairness and speed
C Effectiveness and efficiency
D Efficiency and staff turnover (2 marks)

17.6 **A person specification typically includes which of the following detail?**

A Place of work and key duties
B Purpose of position and reporting responsibilities
C Job title and purpose of position
D Education and competencies (2 marks)

17.7 **According to research, what selection method is the most reliable predictor of job performance?**

A Personality and intelligence tests
B References
C Work sampling
D Interviews (2 marks)

17.8 Personality and cognitive tests are more reliable predictors of job performance than interviews.

Is this statement true or false?

A True
B False (1 mark)

17.9 Assessment centres are specialised locations where a small group of participants who undertake a series of test and exercises under observation with a view to the assessment of their skills and competencies, suitability for particular roles and potential for development

Is this statement true or false?

A True
B False (1 mark)

17.10 **Which of the following is more likely to play an inappropriate role in selection?**

A Personality and attractiveness
B Appearance and behaviour
C Race and gender
D Hygiene and performance (2 marks)

(17 marks)

MCQ 18 – EQUAL OPPORTUNITIES AND DIVERSITY

18.1 Maria has offered to give evidence at the "Inspectorate for workers" on behalf of a colleague who is claiming that she has been passed over for promotion because she is a woman. Over the following weeks, her boss repeatedly denies her requests for work breaks because she is having "time off" at the inspectorate, although he has usually granted them before.

Which of the following describes the discrimination that Maria has been subjected to?

A   Indirect discrimination
B   Direct discrimination
C   Harassment
D   Victimisation   (2 marks)

18.2 It is generally legal and acceptable to use age limits or phrases that imply restrictions (such as "recent graduate") in job advertisements.

Is this statement true or false?

A   True
B   False   (1 mark)

18.3 **Diversity is about which one of the following?**

A   Equal opportunity for all staff to contribute to the company's objectives
B   Treated with respect regardless of their age, ethnicity or background
C   Acknowledged and respected for their differences in the workplace
D   Encouraged to adopt to the company's culture   (2 marks)

18.4 Equal opportunities legislation usually means that employers must ensure that stable same sex partnerships are treated the same as married couples, dress codes are sufficiently flexible to allow for religious expression and staff are not prevented from taking absence for religious holidays.

Is this statement true or false?

A   True
B   False   (1 mark)

18.5 **Discrimination in which one of the following areas is most likely to be illegal in respect of disabled individuals?**

A   Favouring people in the age group 25 to 35, providing access for wheelchairs, paying disabled people more money

B   Allowing for active participation of disabled people, providing disabled people with special training, accepting a lower level of skills and competences

C   Deciding who to interview, who to employ, who to promote and who to dismiss
                                                                                  (1 mark)

18.6 Sexual harassment is any unwanted conduct of a sexual nature, or based on sex, affecting dignity of women at work.

Is this statement true or false?

A   True

B   False   (1 mark)

(8 marks)

MCQ 19 – INDIVIDUALS, GROUPS AND TEAMS

19.1 You are the manager of the Alpha team. A "sixth sense" has developed in the team with members knowing what others are doing in the team. Trust is implicit. The team is mature.

At what stage of team development is the Alpha team?

A   Performing

B   Norming

C   Storming

D   Dorming   (2 marks)

19.2 **In which order does a team normally progress through Tuckman`s stages?**

A   Norming, forming, storming, performing

B   Performing, storming, forming, norming

C   Forming, norming, storming, performing

D   Forming, storming, norming, performing   (2 marks)

19.3 In a project team, Olga is the person everyone turns to with their problems and team conflicts, knowing that she will respond to them, listen, understand, mediate and be diplomatic.

Which of Belbin's team roles does Olga fulfil?

A   Implementer

B   Team worker

C   Finisher

D   Resource Investigator   (2 marks)

19.4 **Which of the following statements best describes the purpose of a multi-disciplinary team?**

A   Team members have different skills, work in different departments and can perform more than one task

B   Team members can perform more than one task and are flexible

C   Team members know their objectives, can perform more than one task and are flexible

D   Team members have different skills, work in different departments and can be pooled or exchanged.   (2 marks)

19.5 Cohesive teams generally take more risky decisions than the same individuals working separately.

Is this statement true or false?

A   True
B   False   (1 mark)

19.6 There are many factors that drive a person`s behaviour at work.

Which of the following contains two of the more critical factors?

A   Perception and motivation
B   Understanding and work performance
C   Motivation and interests
D   Attitude and behaviour   (2 marks)

19.7 High labour turnover is a characteristic of effective teams.

Is this statement true or false?

A   True
B   False   (1 mark)

19.8 Role ambiguity is the same as role uncertainty.

Is this statement true or false?

A   True
B   False   (1 mark)

19.9 **Which one of the following identifies a difference between a group and a team?**

A   The members negotiate their personal roles and positions
B   The members work in cooperation
C   Members always agree with other members
D   Decisions are taken by members through consensus   (2 marks)

19.10 "Leap frog" occurs when there is a need to bypass colleagues of the same seniority.

Is this statement true or false?

A   True
B   False   (1 mark)

19.11 **Who described the "team building tools" of effective teamwork?**

A   Belbin
B   Tuckman
C   Maslow
D   Woodcock   (2 marks)

19.12 In the annual Six Nations rugby tournament England, France, Ireland, Italy, Scotland and Wales play a series of games to determine which team is the best.

At what stage of development is each of the teams?

A   Storming
B   Performing
C   Norming
D   Dorming   (2 marks)

19.13 For team rewards to be effective, the team must have certain characteristics.

Which one of the following contains such appropriate characteristics?

A   Distinct roles, maturity, targets, performance measures
B   Task specification, measurement criteria, group think, lack of communication
C   Distinct roles, maturity, targets, unbalanced roles
D   Task specification, measurement criteria, insincere praise   (2 marks)

(22 marks)

MCQ 20 – MOTIVATING INDIVIDUALS AND GROUPS

20.1 **Which of the following does not fit into Maslow's hierarchy of needs?**

A   Love/social
B   Safety
C   Enrichment
D   Esteem   (2 marks)

20.2 **Which statement best shows the difference between content theory and process theory?**

A   Process theories explain which variables affect motivation; content theories explain how the variables affect it

B   Content theories address the effects of cognitive dissonance; process theories address workplace activities

C   Content theories address workplace comfort; process theories address workplace activities

D   Content theories explain which variables affect motivation; process theories explain how the variables affect it   (2 marks)

20.3 According to Herzberg, an encouraging leadership style is a motivator factor

Is this statement true or false?

A   True
B   False   (1 mark)

20.4 A reward is given for some _____, an incentive is an _____ of a reward.

Which words, in correct order, correctly complete this sentence?

A   Contribution, success
B   Success, offer
C   Offer, success   (1 mark)

20.5 **Which one of the following describes a "horizontal" extension of a job to increase task variety?**

    A   Job description
    B   Job evaluation
    C   Job enlargement
    D   Job enrichment   (2 marks)

20.6 **Which of the following are wholly "intrinsic rewards"?**

    A   Performance related pay and companionship
    B   Achievement and private health care
    C   Job interest and share schemes
    D   Responsibility and job interest   (2 marks)

20.7 **What type of motivation theory is used by the expectancy model?**

    A   Process theory
    B   Needs theory
    C   Content theory
    D   Equality theory   (2 marks)

20.8 **According to McGregor, Theory Y people are motivated by which of the following?**

    A   Money and security
    B   Money and achievement at work
    C   Interpersonal relationships and recognition for good work
    D   Interpersonal relationships and tight control   (2 marks)

20.9 A fast food chain supplies its franchises with detailed manuals that describe the exact processes employees should follow to accomplish daily tasks like preparing burgers, coffee, French fries and salads. Additionally, each franchise must install cameras to monitor both sales and supply areas to ensure employees are not slacking.

The head office of this chain clearly adheres to which set of assumptions about human motivation?

    A   Collectivism
    B   Individualism
    C   Theory X
    D   Theory Y   (2 marks)

20.10 Employees are impacted by both external and internal forces of motivation.

Which one of the following statements is appropriate?

    A   It is more important to understand internal forces than external forces of motivation
    B   Less important to understand internal forces than external forces of motivation
    C   It is important to understand both forces of motivation
    D   The need for motivation is seldom recognised by any manager   (2 marks)

(18 marks)

MCQ 21 – TRAINING AND DEVELOPMENT

21.1 Research has shown that one reason for employee dissatisfaction with their employer is the lack of training and development opportunities. The failure of many companies to establish a training and development strategy is a specific determining factor in not attracting or keeping good employees.

Is this statement true or false?

A   True
B   False   (1 mark)

21.2 Med likes to "get his hands dirty" doing something practical rather than listening to his manager instructing him from a procedures manual. His motto is "don't worry, be happy".

Which one of Honey and Mumford's learning styles is best suited to Med?

A   Theorist
B   Activist
C   Pragmatist
D   Relativist   (2 marks)

21.3 **Which one of the following best describes Kolb's experiential learning cycle?**

A   The development and use of a knowledge and skills database
B   Learning on-the-job and coaching
C   Life-long learning
D   Concept of self-learning and learning by experience   (2 marks)

21.4 Training and development needs arise from _____

Which words, in correct order, correctly complete this sentence?

A   meeting the organisational and individual needs identified in a SWOT analysis
B   a structured and methodical approach to knowledge and skill acquisition
C   the organisation's business plan, corporate plan or human resource plan.   (1 mark)

21.5 Training is a learning process that involves the acquisition of knowledge, sharpening of skills, concepts, rules, or changing of attitudes and behaviours to enhance the performance of employees.

Is this statement true or false?

A   True
B   False   (1 mark)

21.6 Training is an event; development is a process.

Is this statement true or false?

A   True
B   False   (1 mark)

21.7 **How can companies make their training needs analysis more effective?**

    A   Focus on what people are failing to do

    B   Understand current skills, look forward to desired outcomes to meet objectives and skills required, identify and train for the skills gaps

    C   Focus on those who are not doing so well, "catching up" with how the best of the team already performs

    D   Focus on remedial training   (2 marks)

21.8 The equation "required level of competence minus present level of competence" describes _____

    Which of the following correctly completes this sentence?

    A   training objectives
    B   training outcome
    C   training stages
    D   training needs   (2 marks)

21.9 Induction is the _____ whereby a person is formally _____ and _____ into an organisation.

    Which words, in correct order, correctly complete this sentence?

    A   process, integrated and welcomed
    B   process, introduced and integrated
    C   method, integrated and welcomed
    D   product, introduced and integrated   (2 marks)

21.10 **Which one of the following is an advantage of on-the-job learning?**

    A   minimises risk
    B   allows focus on learning
    C   supports practical application
    D   focuses on standardisation of trainings   (2 marks)

21.11 **What learning style would a person prefer and learn best from on-the-job training using project work or job instruction?**

    A   Theorist
    B   Reflector
    C   Pragmatist
    D   Activist   (2 marks)

21.12 **When designing an equal opportunities training program which of the following is most likely to be considered?**

    A   Comparable worth
    B   Those traditionally discriminated against
    C   Disparate success
    D   Reverse discrimination   (2 marks)

(20 marks)

MCQ 22 – PERFORMANCE APPRAISAL

22.1   Appraisals allow managers to objectively review, discuss and compare the performances of employees, help the organisation to obtain standard information and to provide a forum for the airing of grievances, work related or personal problems.

Is this statement true or false?

A   True
B   False   (1 mark)

22.2   The term assessment centre does not refer to a physical place, instead it describes an approach.

Is this statement true or false?

A   True
B   False   (1 mark)

22.3   **Which one of the following contains two features of an effective appraisal?**

A   Fair and flexible
B   Fair and frequent
C   Frequent and honest
D   Honest and objective   (2 marks)

22.4   The first steps of an effective appraisal process are _____ and _____.

Which words, in correct order, correctly complete this sentence?

A   Communicating standards and discussing results
B   Establishing performance standards and measuring actual performance
C   Establishing assessment criteria and preparing appraisal report
D   Establishing performance standards and providing feedback   (2 marks)

22.5   Conducting an appraisal interview requires certain skills.

Which one of the following describes best appraisal interview skills?

A   Staying focused on key information and fully involving the appraisee in the appraisal process

B   Enhancing trust and mutual support in the working relationship

C   Dealing with objections and disagreements

D   Confront poor performance in a constructive manner   (2 marks)

22.6 On your first assignment at your new firm, you reported to the senior partner. At the end of the assignment you asked the partner for a formal appraisal review. "You did OK. As a small firm, we quickly get to know the strengths and weaknesses of our staff. We do not consider an appraisal system necessary."

Which one of the following is most likely to be an overall benefit of an appraisal?

A   Assists realising personal aspiration

B   Establishes reward and remuneration levels

C   Focuses on the needs of a business through ensuring that employer's goals and those of the organisation are congruent.

D   Develops skills and expertise   (2 marks)

22.7 **Which one of the following appraisal methods involves the appraiser and appraisee completing similar assessment forms then comparing their notes?**

A   Peer comparison
B   360-degree appraisal
C   Self-appraisal
D   Top-down appraisal   (2 marks)

                                                                                                        (12 marks)

MCQ 23 – PERSONAL EFFECTIVENESS

23.1 As a personal development plan involves the change from a current situation, the details of the current position must first be identified and analysed.

Is this statement true or false?

A   True
B   False   (1 mark)

23.2 When a manager is carrying out an assessment of an employee, they need to identify _____ and _____ of that employee.

Which words, in correct order, correctly complete this sentence?

A   interests and hobbies
B   effectiveness and significance
C   strengths and weaknesses   (1 mark)

23.3 **The biggest time-waster in modern business life is which one of the following?**

A   Learning from others
B   Poor planning
C   Creating a plan
D   Using "waiting" and "travelling" time creatively   (2 marks)

23.4 **Which of the following contains the core objectives of the coaching process?**

A   Developing a person's skills to help him/her succeed in the job

B   High performance and improvement within a short period of time

C   Exchange of knowledge and sustained partnering relationship

D   High performance and improvement through developing a person's skills and knowledge to achieve organisational objectives   (2 marks)

23.5 **Which of the following outlines the stages of a counselling process?**

A   Recognition, understanding, empowering and resourcing

B   Dealing with issues such as lack of experience or technical knowledge necessary to fulfil the job requirements

C   Looking at how much time could be made free by completing the project to set deadlines

D   Interview, counselling session, knowledge transfer, establishing a relationship

    (2 marks)

23.6 Counselling often deals with issues such as "listening to grievances".

Is this statement true or false?

A   True

B   False   (1 mark)

(9 marks)

MCQ 24 – INFORMATION WITHIN BUSINESS

24.1 **Which of the following relates to structured information requirements?**

A   Intuitive requirements, judgemental, easily programmable

B   Precise, require professional judgement, subjective

C   Easily programmable, routine, objective

D   Subjective requirements, objective programming requirements, intuitive   (2 marks)

24.2 **Which of the following best describes the qualities of information?**

A   Time period, programmable, channel

B   Cost benefit, materiality, strategic

C   Manageable, confidence, historic

D   Relevance, conciseness, volume   (2 marks)

24.3 Karl works in a logistics company. He uses a handheld scanner to individually scan the barcodes on pallets as they arrive in the warehouse.

What type of system does Karl use?

A   Transaction Processing System

B   Expert Database System

C   Management Information System

D   Knowledge Work System   (2 marks)

24.4 Point & Click Camera is a major camera dealer in Paris. On their website, customers have the option of using a "wizard" feature to help them choose a camera. The wizard asks a series of linked questions and then presents the best three options for the customer.

Which term best describes this section of the website?

A   Transaction Processing System
B   Decision Support System
C   Management Information System
D   Knowledge Work System   (2 marks)

24.5 An oil company produces an internal report using an executive information system. This report provides information regarding oil production by region, current and forward spot prices for different petroleum products, updated key performance indicators (KPI) for the past 12 months and estimated KPI for the next 12 months together with summaries of press reports related to their company and competitors. The Board of Directors receives this report before their quarterly meetings.

According to Anthony's Hierarchy, this report provides _____ information.

A   Strategic
B   Tactical
C   Operational   (1 mark)

24.6 Unstructured information is required for regular, routine decision making. However, it needs to be further summarised or sorted in a report to be useful.

A   True
B   False   (1 mark)

24.7 **Who among the following managers use Management Information Systems most extensively?**

A   Senior managers
B   Middle managers
C   Operational managers
D   Technology managers   (2 marks)

24.8 **Which level of managers requires information that uses a mix of quantitative and qualitative data and may be used to set the rules for operational decision making?**

A   Senior managers
B   Executive managers
C   Operational managers
D   Middle managers   (2 marks)

(14 marks)

MCQ 25 – COMMUNICATION WITHIN BUSINESS

25.1 Good communication is effective and efficient – it achieves the communicator's objective for communicating (effective) without unnecessary waste of resources (efficient).

Is this statement true or false?

A True
B False (1 mark)

25.2 The choices below are various stages in a typical communication process. Which one is the second stage?

A Receiving a message
B Encoding a message
C Choosing an appropriate channel (medium)
D Decoding a message (2 marks)

25.3 In addition to timely and trusted, which one of the following are also two attributes of effective communication?

A Volume and noise
B Accuracy and material
C Trust and confidence
D Relevant and volume (2 marks)

25.4 Communication is the oxygen of an organisation; without communication the organisation could not survive.

Is this statement true or false?

A True
B False (1 mark)

25.5 When management communicates policies, plans, information and instructions we talk about _____ or _____ communication.

Which words, in correct order, correctly complete this sentence?

A diagonal or inter-departmental
B lateral or formal
C vertical or downwards
D horizontal or informal (2 marks)

25.6 The choice of a medium used in communication depends on which factors?

A Urgency and cost
B Complexity and vocabulary
C Good writing, typing and suitable style
D Sensitivity and fluency (2 marks)

25.7 **Which of the following is a suitable method for communicating that a hostile bid has been made to take over the company?**

A	Notice board
B	E-mail to all staff
C	Open staff meeting
D	Memo

(2 marks)

25.8 **Which communication pattern (communication network) is the quickest way to reach a conclusion?**

A	"Y" and "wheel"
B	"Y" and "all-channel"
C	"Wheel" and "circle"
D	"Wheel" and "chain"

(2 marks)

(14 marks)

MCQ 26 –ETHICS AND ETHICAL BEHAVIOUR

26.1 Ethical absolutism means that right and wrong are subjective and context dependent.

Is this statement true or false?

A	True
B	False

(1 mark)

26.2 The directors of a firm are discussing the introduction of a code of ethics. The creative director will support the introduction of a code so long as it can be demonstrated that it will lead to increased profits. One of the non-executive directors pointed out that having the code would identify the company as having ethical principles and that it was the right thing to do, regardless of the outcome.

Which ethical theories are the creative director and non-executive director applying?

	Creative director	*Non-executive director*
A	Normative	Instrumental
B	Deontological	Teleological
C	Teleological	Deontological
D	Instrumental	Normative

(2 marks)

26.3 Sasha, an audit assistant for BA & Co, a firm of certified chartered accountants, reports to the ethical partner that his wife works as the personal assistant to the research and development manager at a new client. The partner informs Sasha that this would be a breach of the ACCA Ethical Code and that he will not be assigned to the audit of that client.

What breach of the ACCA code is the partner referring to?

A	Integrity
B	Objectivity
C	Confidentiality
D	There is no breach

(2 marks)

26.4 It was OK for Robin Hood to steal from the rich and give to the poor.

What is this statement an example of?

A   Ethical conflict resolution
B   Normative ethics
C   Teleological ethics
D   Absolutist ethics   (2 marks)

26.5 **Which of the following items are included in the ACCA Code of Ethics?**

A   Due care, integrity, professional behaviour
B   Honesty, accountability, professional integrity
C   Due Process, professional accountability, honesty
D   Integrity, independence, professional competence   (2 marks)

26.6 Irina is the senior costing accountant (ACCA qualified) at a listed international engineering company. During her review of a contract to build a dam, she notices that some of the costs appear to be higher than she would have expected. There are also a number of cost items that do not normally appear in tenders for building dams. When she enquires of the CEO, she is told not to worry as this is the first of a new type of dam that requires extra costs. She is also told that when the contract is signed, it will mean that her annual bonus would be double that of the previous year. She is pleased to hear this as her mother needs to have a very expensive operation.

Which of the following actions would be the most appropriate for Irina to now take?

A   Resign
B   Report the CEO to the police
C   Discuss the matter with the firm's audit committee
D   Give her approval to the contract and take no further action.   (2 marks)

26.7 **A "professional" is characterised by which of the following?**

A   Mastering skills, professional association, code of ethics
B   Certification, annual examination, continuous development
C   Code of conduct, minimum salary, certification
D   Annual testing, minimum salary, code of conduct   (2 marks)

26.8 **Why does the professional accountant have a special role in promoting ethical behaviour throughout business?**

A   They are seen as the guardians of company finances
B   They are often the only person on a board that belongs to a profession
C   They undertake a long period of training
D   Ethics is inter-linked with financial probity   (2 marks)

(15 marks)

MCQ 1 – THE BUSINESS ORGANISATION

Item   Answer   Justification

1.1   A   A contains the most general descriptors related to an organisation. "Teamwork", "synergy", "accepted leader" are elements of teams, rather than organisations.

1.2   C   "Public Sector" relates to government. This should not be confused with "publicly traded" which means that the company is listed on a recognised stock exchange and can sell its shares to the general public. An entity in the "public sector" would normally not have shares.

1.3   C   Microsoft is not a public sector business. A cooperative is not defined as an NGO or a charity.

1.4   A   The marketing department would have already identified the need; the manufacturing department would build it to the determined specifications with direct service provision dealing with after sales service and maintenance. Therefore, purchasing and R&D would work together in designing the system and sourcing the necessary components at the appropriate price.

1.5   D   Service provision characteristics include variability, intangibility, perishability, simultaneity and ownership.

1.6   A   True. As described by the Chartered Institute of Marketing.

1.7   A   True. How the product is distributed (i.e. logistics of storage and transportation). How the product is placed in front of the customer.

1.8   C   Not to be confused with the marketing mix – product, price, promotion, place.

1.9   D   Needs also covers wants and demands. Value covers satisfaction and quality. Exchange relates to transactions and relationships.

1.10   C   People – corporate culture, motivation, attitude, skills, commitment. Process – procedures, capacity, speed, access. Physical evidence – environment, facilities, packaging, brochures, business cards.

1.11   A   True (Kotler). Segmentation allows an organisation to treat similar customers in similar ways, while distinguishing between dissimilar customer groups.

MCQ 2 – STAKEHOLDERS IN BUSINESS ORGANISATIONS

Item   Answer   Justification

2.1   B   False. Bi-directionality in this case means "to affect" and "to be affected by" the organisation. The statement given is uni-directional in that both elements relate to the business only. The effect on the stakeholder is not given.

2.2   C   "Agency problem" refers to the inherent conflict of interest between a company's owners and its managers. The managers may wish to pursue their own interests rather than those of the shareholders. The auditor carries out an independent audit of the financial statements produced by the directors for the shareholders and reporting on their "truth and fairness". The auditor also acts as a deterrent to the directors perpetrating any fraud as the auditor is required to perform procedures with a reasonable expectation of detecting fraud and material error.

2.3   D   Connected stakeholders, although external, will usually have a contractual right that "connects" them to the business. Other examples include suppliers, customers, auditors, trade unions.

> **Tutorial note:** *External stakeholders do not have such connections with the business (e.g. no contractual rights). They include governments, local communities and pressure groups. Internal stakeholders are intimately related to the organisation (e.g. employees, directors). Unrecognised stakeholders are exactly that – groups not recognised as having stakeholder rights.*

2.4   A   A lobbyist acts on behalf of an organisation usually for or against particular or proposed legislation. So a company lobbyist acts in the interests of the company that engages their services.

> **Tutorial note:** *Do not confuse "lobbyist" with "activists" who act against a company. As an example, Greenpeace engages lobbyists to support or derail particular environmental legislation (e.g. the building of a third runway at London Heathrow airport) and takes action directly against companies (e.g. the occupation of oil rigs due to be sunk in the North Sea or harassment of whaling ships).*

2.5   A   So long as the car dealership pays its taxes on time and for the correct amount, the tax authority will take little interest in its activities, apart from occasional visits to check the books and records. The tax authority does, however, have high power (being supported by legislation) should there be a need to use it. If the tax authority starts to take a keen interest in the activities of the business, it can quickly become a key player.

2.6   D   The company, its shareholders, employees, potential customers, the local community and the action group are all stakeholders in the project. Their different needs are in conflict (certainly the company and the community action group). There appears to be no conflict between the directors and shareholders, thus no agency problems. Lobbying would be part of the actions taken by each of the stakeholder groups in support of their conflict.

MCQ 3 – THE BUSINESS ENVIRONMENT

Item   *Answer*   *Justification*

3.1   C   A supra-national body is outside of a national jurisdiction. In the EU, the legal systems of national governments are supplemented by various laws and regulations issued by the EU. (The UN and WTO are other examples.)

3.2   A   Concerns the potential damage and injury that can be caused to individuals by the misuse of their personal data.

3.3   D   Completing and signing a form containing personal data gives authority for that data to be lawfully processed for the purpose indicated on the form. Checking the box gives authority for that data to be used for other (stated) purposes and by other (stated) entities.

3.4   C   Data protection has been breached as the data may be used for unauthorised purposes. Data security concerns protecting the integrity of the data – this has been breached as the data was not deleted before the computer was sold nor was it encrypted.

| 3.5 | A | True. A formal health and safety policy/manual; job descriptions; design of work systems; regular training and instruction of employees; communication to employees (e.g. notice boards); disciplinary procedures; health and safety officers; employee counselling and management responsibility (e.g. attitude) are all tools to promote health and safety. |

3.6   C   Standing on his chair is not required by his job and his chair is not designed for this activity.

Tutorial note: *If he had been encouraged to do so by his manager, then his employer would be liable.*

3.7   A   Post-industrial countries are in the process of switching to service industries – birth rates tend to fall significantly. Fully developed countries have low birth rates and low death rates. Pre-industrial countries have high birth rates and high death rates, thus the population is generally static.

3.8   C   In any given job, employees who have been doing that job for a long period of time tend to be paid at a higher rate that employees just starting the same job. This usually reflects higher skill levels, experience, customer orientation and loyalty.

3.9   B   There are various definitions, for example "The total set of GHG (greenhouse gas) emissions caused directly and indirectly by an individual, organisation, event or product". All have a similar theme based on the emissions of greenhouse gases. Environmental, ecological and social footprints are similar measures.

Tutorial note: *See www.footprint.wwf.org.uk to calculate a personal footprint.*

3.10   B   False. The overall strategy that drives a business is the business strategy. All other functions are used to ensure the success of that strategy. Thus IS strategy must be embedded within the business strategy to achieve the business strategy.

3.11   D   "Unique" means distinguishing itself from its competition – differentiation.

3.12   A   B, C and D are all advantages of outsourcing.

3.13   B   False. The model relates to an industry and a market as a whole.

3.14   C   Players already in the market will attempt to make it more difficult for new entrants to enter their market. Barriers to entry include high capital costs, economies of scale, product differentiation, limit on distribution channels, regulations, supplier and customer loyalty.

3.15   D   Supermarkets (as an industry) take a significant proportion of a suppliers' production. Many of the suppliers to individual supermarket chains are relatively small and depend very heavily on the continued buying of their product by the supermarket.

3.16   D   Developed from the five forces model – cost leadership, differentiation and focus (or niche).

MCQ 4 – THE MACRO-ECONOMIC ENVIRONMENT

Item	Answer	Justification

4.1   C   Macroeconomics is the field of economics that studies the behaviour of the aggregate economy through considering economy-wide elements (e.g. changes in (un)employment, national income, rate of growth, gross domestic product, inflation and price levels).

4.2   A   A fourth objective is the acceptable balance between exports and imports at any given time.

Tutorial note: The other choices contain the tools required to achieve policy objectives (e.g. interest rates, exchange rates).

4.3   A   GDP is the total market value of all final goods and services produced in the country in a given period of time (usually a calendar year). Remember that the balance of payments represents the difference between imports and exports.

4.4   D   With a given amount of income, as people save more, they will naturally have less to spend. This will mean less demand for goods and services, thus business activity will decline. Therefore the "paradox of thrift" (as phrased by John Maynard Keynes).

4.5   C   Milton Friedman (University of Chicago) is associated with supply side economics.

4.6   B   The banking crisis that flowed through from the subprime crisis was initiated because banks stopped lending to each other in fear that any loans would not be repaid. This resulted in a halt to institutional and private lending.

4.7   B   The classic signs of recession. Usually official when GDP is negative for two or more consecutive quarters.

4.8   D   As there has been a change in the "structure" of the industry (i.e. lower fish stocks and reduced catch quotas) unemployment is referred to as structural unemployment.

Tutorial note: Real wage unemployment occurs when workers require wage rates to remain high even though the supply of workers is greater than the demand for them. Seasonal changes with the seasons (e.g. weather, fruit picking, building). Frictional arises due to inefficient communication to the available workers about the job.

4.9   B   Action by the government to achieve economic objectives through the use of the fiscal instruments of taxation, public spending and the budget deficit or surplus. Interest rates, money supply and central bank are elements of monetary policy.

4.10   A   Focus on creating the right conditions in which private enterprise can flourish and thereby raise the capacity of the economy to provide the output demanded. The private sector, being driven by the profit motive, is deemed to be more efficient at providing the output required than the public sector. The others contain elements of managing the demand for goods and services.

MCQ 5 – THE MICRO-ECONOMIC ENVIRONMENT

Item Answer   Justification

5.1   D   Only 3 and 4 are true.

5.2   C   Where a cheaper substitute is readily available, if the price of a commodity increases, buyers will switch to the substitute (reducing the demand for the commodity). High fraction of income indicates luxury commodities. As income increases so demand will proportionately increase greater than the increase in income. If the price of the luxury commodity increases, and income remains static, its demand will drop. Essentials have low elasticity (0 to +1). Buyers will strive to obtain the commodity as it is perceived they cannot survive without it.

5.3   C   A, B and D relate to the definition of microeconomics. C is a macro term.

5.4   B   A characterises a perfect market. C & D contain elements of both perfect and imperfect markets. Only B (without further information) directly relates to an imperfect market.

MCQ 6 – ORGANISATIONAL STRUCTURE

Item Answer   Justification

6.1   B   Entrepreneurial structures usually mean that the owner of the business works with and alongside the employees of the business.

6.2   D   Team work, projects and reporting to different people are elements of a Matrix structure. Paul does not have one direct manager as he reports to two separate directors.

6.3   B   False. Fayol referred to the vertical arrangement of direct authority as the "scalar chain". Therefore, a bigger group of companies (all things being equal) will result in a larger scalar chain in the power vertical of the group.

6.4   A   The others are disadvantages of centralisation.

6.5   C   Outsourcing IT will result in the company no longer having specialisation in IT.

6.6   A   Span of control relates to the number of subordinates reporting to a manager. The "grapevine" is an informal means of communication. Outsourcing may result in little change to a bureaucratic company structure or it will reduce the bureaucracy.

6.7   D   Formal organisations are led by the CEO with a board of directors. Thus control and communication is normally top down.

6.8   D   The others are potential disadvantages of the formal organisation.

6.9   B   False. Supervisors are part of the operational workforce. They manage at the "coal face" – that is, as well as managing small working groups they also carry out similar work.

6.10   C   Reorganising daily tasks is an operational matter.

MCQ 7 – ORGANISATIONAL CULTURE

Item	Answer	Justification
7.1	C	The others contain specific examples of culture (e.g. rituals, dress code, control systems, power structures).
7.2	A	Hidden assumptions, rules and regulations, company policy and organisational structure are not specific to any one of Schein's levels.
7.3	B	Her job is continuous, effectively bureaucratic; therefore not task orientated. The organisation does not exist to serve individuals within it; thus not a person culture. There is no indication in the scenario that the organisation is driven by a central source of power – the scenario basically describes the traits of a role culture.
7.4	D	The scenario indicates that there are more powerful groups in the company and that an inequality exists, which (without any other indications) is endorsed by those other offices.
7.5	B	False. The opposite term is correct: "implicit"
7.6	A	Although the portrait has the firm's values inscribed on it, it (in itself) is an artefact. It is part of the physical environment.
7.7	C	When the business environment is open and dynamic, the culture of the business also needs to be open and dynamic. If it cannot respond to change, the business is at a disadvantage. The other options all positively affect culture (i.e. as an asset).

MCQ 8 – COMMITTEES IN THE BUSINESS ORGANISATION

Item	Answer	Justification
8.1	B	False. Standing committees deal with long term issues. Temporary issues are usually handled by an "ad hoc" committee.
8.2	A	The others are disadvantages.
8.3	C	The others contain skills required of company secretary rather than the chairman (e.g. organising ability, note taking, understanding procedures, writing and grammar, organising).
8.4	D	Committees can, in theory, be of any size. But the larger they are, the more unwieldy they become. Smaller, usually means a lack of ideas and possibility that that all necessary areas will not be discussed. If all members of a committee are highly skilled, the skill set of the committee will be biased and unbalanced.

MCQ 9 – GOVERNANCE AND SOCIAL RESPONSIBILITY

Item	Answer	Justification
9.1	B	False. Corporate governance concerns direction and control by the board of directors. Regulation and monitoring would be carried out by an external body under specific rules and regulations (e.g. the UK's Financial Services Authority).

9.2	A	External audit is dealt with through legislation. Risk managers and an ethics committee are at the discretion of the board. Audit committee members must be independent (the FD would not be). Most codes do not recommend that the role of the CEO and Chairman be combined.
9.3	D	All the others are elements of a principles-based system.
9.4	C	All of the others are indicators of strong systems. Lack of oversight may imply weak board control of the CEO or weak oversight by a regulatory authority.
9.5	C	CSR is the continuing commitment to behave *ethically* and *contribute to economic development* while *improving the quality of life* of the workforce and their families as well as of the local community and society at large. It refers to all the effects a company may have on society and the need to deal with those effects on all stakeholders in a responsible way.
9.6	D	The remuneration committee (which consists of independent NEDs) aims to establish a rewards policy that attracts, retains and motivates directors to run the company successfully and to design remuneration packages that align their interests with those of the shareholders.
9.7	A	Sustainability is defined as development that meets the needs of the present without compromising the ability of future generations to meet their needs.

MCQ 10 – ACCOUNTING AND FINANCE

Item	*Answer*	*Justification*
10.1	D	The basic classification and recording of actual transactions in monetary terms. Bookkeeping provides the underlying data that is used in financial, cost and management accounting.
10.2	C	Management accounting is the process of identification, measurement, accumulation, analysis, preparation, interpretation and communication of financial information that is used internally by management to formulate policies, plan, forecast, direct, evaluate, analyse, make decisions and control the business.
10.3	B	Treasurers are responsible for the management of money in a business. They also deal with financing, foreign currency and taxation.
10.4	A	Transactions are recording in the day books, which are summarised for posting to the ledgers (control accounts are kept in the ledgers). A trial balance is then extracted from the ledgers and the financial statements prepared.
10.5	C	The company is perfectly entitled to take the tax incentive offered as it is both within the letter of the law and the spirit of the law (to attract new employers). Many tax avoidance schemes, although within the law, are not in the spirit (e.g. using an unconnected vehicle) and taxation authorities are increasingly rejecting them. Tax evasion is illegal.

MCQ 11 – EXTERNAL AND INTERNAL AUDIT

Item	Answer	Justification
11.1	B	False. Internal audit is defined as "an independent, objective assurance and consulting activity designed to add value and improve an organisation's operations. It helps an organisation accomplish its objectives by bringing a systematic, disciplined approach to evaluate and improve the effectiveness of risk management, control, and governance processes". This includes considering the risk of fraud.
11.2	C	External report to shareholders, internal to directors (or audit committee). External must be independent, internal cannot be independent as they are employees. External must be suitably qualified (e.g. ACCA), internal may be qualified or by experience.
11.3	C	See above.
11.4	B	External audit is a statutory requirement to report on the financial statements in terms of truth and fairness.
11.5	C	The four elements are: a responsible party, the subject matter, the intended user and a practitioner.
11.6	D	Control systems are core to the work of internal audit. They would not be designing and implementing systems, but they would be reviewing the design of systems (e.g. to ensure they meet objectives and have appropriate controls in place) and testing system and control operation.
11.7	B	Look out for words like compliance.
11.8	B	False. It is advisable to do so (e.g. the UK Combined Code) but there is no law that requires companies to do so.
11.9	A	See above re definition.

MCQ 12 – REGULATORY ENVIRONMENT OF ACCOUNTING

Item	Answer	Justification
12.1	B.	False. Accountant, professional accountant, tax accountant, etc are not reserved terms. Auditor is reserved and requires the appropriate professional qualification, training and continued development.
12.2	A	True (e.g. Companies Acts, IFAC, IFRS and US GAAP).
12.3	C	ACA, ACCA, ICAEW are members of the IFAC and base their rules on those of the IFAC.
12.4	B	False. It is an open process and the public observers are allowed.
12.5	D	The first level of complaint would usually be to the accountant. Should the client gain little satisfaction, the next stage would be to complain directly to the accountant's professional body (e.g. the ACCA).

| 12.6 | C | Other objectives are: to develop, in the public interest, a single set of high quality understandable and enforceable global accounting standards and to promote the use and rigorous application of those standards. |

| 12.7 | A | Under UK law, six and three years are the minimum periods for accounting records to be kept. |

MCQ 13 – FINANCIAL SYSTEMS AND PROCEDURES

Item	*Answer*	*Justification*
13.1	B	False. A system is a group of interacting, interrelated, or interdependent elements forming a complex whole. It is an organised assembly of resources and procedures united and regulated by interaction or interdependence to accomplish a set of specific functions. Policies and procedures support systems.
13.2	D	A policy is a plan, a set of coherent decisions, a course of action or guiding principle intended to influence and determine decisions. It may be a specific programme consisting of desired objectives and the means to achieve them.
		Procedures are a set of established forms or methods for conducting the affairs of an organised body such as a business, club, or government. They are standard, detailed steps that prescribe how to perform specific tasks taken to accomplish an end.
13.3	B	Purchase requisition from the department must come first.
13.4	A	The standard objective of a sales system.
13.5	B	False. In the classic inventory system, inventory is counted and valued at the end of every year. In a perpetual (continuous) inventory system computer based control and valuation is at the centre of the system. Inventory quantities and values are maintained. The records are checked counting high value items inventory on a regular basis (e.g. every month) and low value items less frequently (e.g. every three months). All items must be counted at least once per year.
13.6	C	IAS 2 *Inventories* and generally-accepted accounting principles (GAAP).
13.7	C	An order is received from a customer. A pre-numbered despatch note will be raised and sent to the warehouse with the order after the credit controller has checked the customer's credit. A pre-numbered sales invoice will be raised with a copy sent to the customer and to the sales ledger for posting to the customer's account.
13.8	D	Employees on the payroll who do not exist and are therefore paid for a service that they have not provided.
13.9	C	Control activities (to ensure that the control objective can be achieved) are generally grouped into five areas – authorisation, performance reviews, information processing, physical controls, segregation of duties.
13.10	A	Although database management systems can be used, the most common approach is to use a spreadsheet.
13.11	C	Other roles include providing suppliers with financial detail about the firm, preparing overall financial budgets, advising on the economic viability of settlement discount terms and advising purchasing of the most economical way of settling with suppliers.

MCQ 14 – INTERNAL CONTROL AND SECURITY

Item	Answer	Justification
14.1	B	Control environment, risk assessment, information systems, control activities and control monitoring.
14.2	C	Authorised (Valid - **V**) transactions are promptly recorded (Complete - **C**) in the correct (Accurate - **A**) amount in the appropriate (**A**) accounts in the proper (Correct Cut-off – **C**) accounting period and that recorded assets exist (Existence – **E**).
14.3	A	True. Control environment relates to the governance and management functions – attitude, awareness and actions.
14.4	A	Look for risks that may lead to financial statement errors.
14.5	C	Physical and hardware infrastructure, software, people, procedures and data to initiate, record, process, report and maintain accountability.
14.6	C	Designed to prevent a particular risk happening. Also includes training, supervision and validation. Detective controls are designed to detect errors should they happen (e.g. reconciliations, exception reporting) and corrective controls aim to minimise or negate the impact of errors (e.g. backups, contingency planning, management action).
14.7	D	Other examples include passwords, placing key assets in secure locations, comparing and reconciling actual to book.
14.8	B	Manual or automated procedures that typically operate at a business process level. Can be preventative or detective in nature and are designed to ensure the integrity of the accounting records and information. Relate to procedures used to initiate, record, process and report transactions or other financial data.
14.9	A	Other examples include passwords, verification, batch totals, error investigation and document counts. Existence and range checks are subsets of validation.
14.10	A	True. The principle of encryption is to make any intelligible data, unintelligible – which can then only be read by using the decryption key. This process prevents unauthorised access to, or understanding of, the data being transmitted or stored.
14.11	A	Covers physical risks, environmental risks, unauthorised access, hacking, viruses.

MCQ 15 – BUSINESS FRAUD

Item	Answer	Justification
15.1	B	False. Control systems have inherent weaknesses (e.g. they can be overridden or just not operated). No control system can be 100% perfect and in most cases, humans are involved.
15.2	A	Misappropriation is a deliberate act. It is not error.
15.3	A	B, C and D are examples of A.
15.4	D	Skimming meaning taking off a bit at the top – think of "skimmed milk".

15.5	B	Simply, window dressing involves changing the timing and cut-off of key transactions to improve the financial position. For example, recording after-date sales as sales made just before the year end, recording false sales before the year end and issuing credit notes after the year end, issuing cheque payments before the year end to reduce liabilities, but not sending out the cheques until after the year end (usually done to improve the liquidity ratio).
15.6	B	"Proper" implies they are correct and could be used as a basis for reconciling to the financial statements. All the others (A, C & D) could result in insufficient audit evidence being obtained.
15.7	D	Implies potential for reduced profits, lower bonuses, targets not being met and eventually going concern risk.
15.8	C	Sometimes referred to as dishonesty, motivation and opportunity. Olga wants to have a Mercedes so she can attract the "good" men and be as good as, if not better, than her friend. Taking on her manager's responsibilities without any oversight provides her with the opportunity to obtain the necessary money without anyone being aware. As she is not being paid any extra for the additional responsibility, she is justifying her actions as being such a reward.

MCQ 16 – LEADERSHIP, MANAGEMENT, SUPERVISION

Item	Answer	Justification
16.1	A	True. Leadership is to lead – organisations, people, providing a sense of direction, visionary, motivating, establishing the culture. Management is to manage – tasks, plans, operations, resources.
16.2	B	Fayol divided industrial activities into six groupings: technical, commercial, financial, security, accounting and managerial. Managerial was further sub-divided into five categories.
16.3	D	Interpersonal – figurehead, leader, liaison. Informational – monitor, disseminator, spokesperson. Decisional – entrepreneur, disturbance handler, resource allocator, negotiator.
16.4	D	Supervision is the act of overseeing; inspection; superintendence; oversight. It is the authoritative control to watch over an activity or task being carried out by somebody and ensure that it is performed correctly.
16.5	B	False. It is the other way around.
16.6	B	A and D: not every manager is a charismatic person, C: is only a description of various forms of authority.
16.7	B	9,9 Team Management. The manager integrates concern for people and concern for task to foster working together and high production to produce true team leadership. Other areas are 1,1 Management Impoverished, 1,9 Country Club Management, 9,1 Task (Authority-compliance) Management and 5,5 Middle of the Road Management.
16.8	C	Tell is an autocratic style, sell is persuasive and join is democratic.
16.9	C	Incorporates the formal (bureaucratic) and scientific approaches that take the view that efficiency and productivity are increased by improving the organisation structure.

16.10   B   A leading advocate and researcher of contingency theories, his studies into the relationship between leadership style and the effectiveness of the work group, identified two styles of leader: PDMs = psychologically distant managers and PCMs = psychologically close managers.

16.11   D   Adaptive work is required when the problem cannot be solved with existing skills and knowledge and requires people to make a shift in their values, expectations, attitudes or habits of behaviour. This is often required to ensure organisational survival.

16.12   C   Achieving results, by empowering (transferring authority) and motivating others (usually at lower levels in a hierarchy) to carry out tasks, for which the delegator is ultimately accountable, to a specified level of performance. With A and B the manager would not delegate. With D the manager should not be delegating.

MCQ 17 – RECRUITMENT AND SELECTION

Item   *Answer*   *Justification*

17.1   B

17.2   B   Sets out the education, qualifications, training, experience, personal attributes and competences a job holder requires to perform the job satisfactorily.

17.3   A   A specialist agency is likely to have a database of currently available, suitably qualified, individuals.

17.4   A   True. The key stages of recruitment and selection cover defining the vacancy and person required, attracting applicants, assessing candidates, choosing a candidate and evaluating the process.

17.5   C   Fairness (e.g. equal opportunities) is also a measure but not speed and staff turnover.

17.6   D   A person specification sets out the education, qualifications, training, experience, personal attributes and competences a job holder requires to perform the job satisfactorily. A, B and C are contents of a job description.

17.7   C   Work sampling (i.e. spending an agreed time in the organisation to carry out a task) is the best predictor. (Although it will be difficult to assess a candidate's ability to carry out an audit before they have been trained, for example.)

17.8   A   True. Interviews can be biased. The best solution is a combination of different techniques.

17.9   B   False. The procedures can be undertaken at any location or office and at any time.

17.10   C   Continuous research shows race and gender to be "hidden issues".

MCQ 18 – EQUAL OPPORTUNITIES AND DIVERSITY

Item	Answer	Justification
18.1	D	Victimisation is a form of discrimination against an individual who is penalised for giving information or taking action in pursuit of a claim of discrimination.
18.2	B	False. Age discrimination is, in many jurisdictions (e.g. the UK) illegal. Discrimination laws are designed to prevent anybody being denied a job, training or a promotion because of age. Individuals are also protected from harassment or victimisation because of their age.
18.3	C	Diversity is the acknowledgement and respect of differences within and between groups of people, particularly in the workplace. Harnessing these differences will create a productive environment in which everybody feels valued, their talents are fully utilised and organisational goals are met.
18.4	A	True. Discrimination on the basis of sexual orientation and religious beliefs is usually unlawful in most jurisdictions that have implemented equal opportunities legislation.
18.5	C	These areas also apply to any group and any form of discrimination. Providing wheelchair access, for example, is an employer's duty.
18.6	B	False. Do not forget men. Men can be sexual harassed by women and also other men.

MCQ 19 – INDIVIDUALS, GROUPS AND TEAMS

Item	Answer	Justification
19.1	D	Identified as a fifth stage by Adair to Tuckman's four stages. There is a risk that the team becomes complacent and switches to "auto-pilot".
19.2	D	
19.3	B	The implementer has organising ability, practical common sense and is predictable. The finisher is orderly, conscientious, perfectionist, tendency to worry over small details and is not always popular. The resource investigator is good at finding things, generates new contacts, responds to a challenge, adds value to ideas.
19.4	D	Team members have different skills and specialism; skills, experience and knowledge can be pooled or exchanged; increases members' awareness of objectives and targets; aids co-ordination and co-operation between different sections of the organisation.
19.5	A	True. Group think, sharing responsibility, greater knowledge and understanding of the risks being taken.
19.6	A	Abilities, motivation level, personality, perception.
19.7	B	False. High labour turnover would be an indicator that the team was ineffective.
19.8	A	True. Role ambiguity is the uncertainty of a role in the minds of either the focal person or a person in the role set.

19.9 D Within a team, decisions are usually taken by the team leader.

19.10 B False. "Leap frog" occurs where there is a need to bypass immediate management (e.g. going directly to a senior manager rather through your immediate manager).

19.11 D Belbin relates to team profiles, Tuckman to team development (forming, storming, norming, performing) and Maslow to the hierarchy of needs.

19.12 B As each team is selected from a squad of players, even if team members change from game to game, or are substituted during a game, the team as a whole should still remain at the performing stage. Forming, storming and norming should have taken place during the preparations for the tournament.

19.13 A Group think, lack of communication, unbalanced roles and insincere praise are not characteristics of effective teams and, by extension, effective team rewards.

MCQ 20 – MOTIVATING INDIVIDUALS AND GROUPS

Item Answer Justification

20.1 C Physiological, security, social, esteem and self-actualisation.

20.2 D Content theory focuses on the question of what stimulates, sustains and regulates good directed behaviour (i.e. what particular things motivate people). Process theory attempts to explain and describe how people start, sustain and direct behaviour aimed at the satisfaction of needs or the elimination or reduction of inner tension.

20.3 B False. It is a hygiene factor – take it away and the motivation declines.

20.4 B

20.5 C Widens the range of tasks and so develops the job away from a narrow specialisation.

20.6 D Performance related pay, health care and share schemes are extrinsic in that they are not within the control of the employee. Responsibility and job interest are within the control of the employee.

20.7 A Vroom is an example of the expectancy model (Force = Valance × Expectancy).

20.8 C Money, security, tight control are examples appropriate to Theory X people.

20.9 C The scenario implies tight control and direction.

20.10 C Any aspect that affects the motivation of an employee should be considered.

MCQ 21 – TRAINING AND DEVELOPMENT

Item	*Answer*	*Justification*
21.1	A	Was training and development a key element in your decision to join your firm *(other than pay, of course)*?
21.2	B	False. Activists are practical and participative, flexible and optimistic, prefer hands on experience rather than theory, like the pressure of new situations and often rush into situations, then become easily bored.
21.3	D	Concrete experiences, observation, reflection, abstract concepts and generalisations, applying/testing leading to concrete experience, etc.
21.4	C	The appropriately trained and developed workforce is essential for the effective and efficient execution of the business plan.
21.5	A	True. The planned and systematic modification of behaviour through learning events, programmes and instruction which enables individuals to achieve the level of knowledge, skills and competence to carry out their work effectively.
21.6	A	True. Development is the growth or realisation of a person's ability and potential through the provision of learning and educational experiences.
21.7	B	The systematic investigation of an organisation, its aims, objectives, procedures and the capabilities of its personnel in order to identify specific requirements for training and recommend training strategies, plans and training provision to satisfy those requirements.
21.8	D	The difference represents a competence gap to be filled through a training needs analysis.
21.9	B	Induction aims to make, for example, a new employee as effective and efficient as quickly as possible.
21.10	C	Training given in the normal work situation in the attitude/knowledge/skill behaviour pattern appropriate to a task or job.
21.11	D	See above.
21.12	B	An equal opportunities programme should be designed to make participants aware of those who are traditionally discriminated against as well as the typical actions and procedures that are considered discriminatory.

MCQ 22 – PERFORMANCE APPRAISAL

Item	Answer	Justification
22.1	A	True. This is a basic description of appraisals.
22.2	A	True. Apart from its use in recruitment, the assessment centre approach is very often used to appraise potential managers and is a common method of officer/specialist selection in the armed forces.
22.3	B	Frequent, factual, firm and fair.
22.4	C	Identify assessment criteria, prepare appraisal report, hold appraisal interview, develop action plan, review appraisal, monitor action plan.
22.5	A	Key information will set the objective and scope of the appraisal. Involving the appraisee ensures all matters can be fully discussed and the appraisee can take ownership of appraisal feedback and recommendations – appraisals are not a one-way "tell".
22.6	C	A, B and D will, at various times, be elements of C.
22.7	C	Self-appraisal is where the employee carries out a self-evaluation of their own strengths and weaknesses. It is commonly extended by the manager completing a similar form and then discussing with the employee the similarities and differences between their assessments.

MCQ 23 – PERSONAL EFFECTIVENESS

Item	Answer	Justification
23.1	A	True. If you know where you want to go, but do not know where you are, you do not know the direction of getting there.
23.2	C	Enhance and utilise the strengths, minimise the impact of weaknesses and plan to eliminate.
23.3	B	You do not plan to fail, but may fail to plan. In order of the biggest time wasters, the first is poor planning; second is crisis management (fire-fighting) then procrastination, interruptions, not delegating, unnecessary meetings, shuffling, poor physical setup, poor networking, bad attitude, negative people in that order.
23.4	D	Coaching is "developing a person's skills and knowledge so that their job performance improves, hopefully leading to the achievement of organisational objectives. It targets high performance and improvement at work, although it may also have an impact on an individual's private life. It usually lasts for a short period and focuses on specific skills and goals".
23.5	A	
23.6	A	True. The process of helping people to clarify their thoughts, feelings and behaviour, identify and accurately define problems, find solutions, or learn to live with a situation.

MCQ 24 – INFORMATION WITHIN BUSINESS

Item	Answer	Justification
24.1	C	Structured requirements can be planned in advance, are often repetitive, precise, pre-defined, objective, often automated and easily programmed.
24.2	D	Time period, timeliness, relevance, accuracy, completeness, conciseness, understandability, confidence, channel, volume and cost benefits are all considered to be qualities of information.
24.3	A	The bar code scanner is used to capture data. The scenario does not indicate that there is any added value to the captured data (e.g. it is not being processed in any useful way for management analysis).
24.4	B	The "wizard" is effectively an interactive system linked to a knowledge base that allows customers to see a range of options that matches their criteria (established through a series of questions) and presents appropriate options to the user for their final decision. This is the core of a decision support system.
24.5	A	Strategic. The information is generated by an EIS (generally a strategic tool that allows drill down to tactical and operational information) for the highest level of executive management. Most of the information in the report would relate to updating of strategic decisions.
24.6	B	False. The statement is contradictory. Information, to be useful to the user, would need to be structured to meet the user's needs. Thus the statement that "unstructured information is required for regular, routine decision making" does not make sense.
24.7	C	MIS is used at all levels, including, for example, drill down from EIS. However, it is most extensively used at operational levels meeting the day-to-day requirements of supervisors and operational managers.
24.8	D	Senior and executive managers (are basically the same) require information that is primarily qualitative. They use elements of such data to set tactical requirements and guidelines. Operational managers use information which is predominantly quantitative. They follow the rules and guidelines set by the tactical (middle) managers.

MCQ 25 – COMMUNICATION WITHIN BUSINESS

Item	Answer	Justification
25.1	A	True.
25.2	B	The physical sequence is *idea, encode, transmit, receive, decode*. However the appropriate communication channel needs to be chosen before a message can be appropriately encoded.
25.3	D	Timely, relevant, accurate, complete, concise, understandable, trusted, communication (recipient and channel), volume and cost-benefit. Each of the pairs given in A, B and C are related (e.g. trust and confidence – if you trust a communication source you have confidence in that source).
25.4	A	True. It could also be described as the "life-blood" of the organisation.

25.5 C In addition, vertical implies up or down and thus includes communication from employees. Downwards is the style of authoritarian management.

25.6 A B, C and D do not directly relate to the medium used. In general terms, to deliver communication quickly and directly will incur a higher cost (e.g. e-mail is cheap, but may not be opened; using a courier to ensure the message is delivered into the hands of the recipient and to wait for a reply, is costly).

25.7 C Allows employees to raise concerns and discuss as a group. A, B and D will be used to initiate the meeting.

25.8 A Both have a central figure (e.g. the manager) and the minimum number of channels between players.

MCQ 26 – ETHICS AND ETHICAL BEHAVIOUR

Item Answer Justification

26.1 B False. Absolutism concerns eternal, universally applicable, moral principles. Relativism is context dependent and subjective.

26.2 D Instrumentalist ethics is the application of ethical principles to further other objectives (e.g. to increase profits) rather than as an end in themselves (the normative approach). Teleological ethics is a consequentialist approach (dependent on the consequences or outcome of that decision) and deontological ethics is based on duty and foundational principles of obligation.

26.3 D Sasha is not a partner nor is he a senior member of the audit team. His wife is the PA to the HR Director, who is not part of the finance team nor has any input into financial matters. There is therefore no ethical threat to the independence of BA & Co.

26.4 C Teleological ethics – whether a decision is right or wrong depends on the consequences or outcome of that decision.

26.5 A Integrity, objectivity, professional competence and due care, confidentiality and professional behaviour are the five fundamental principles.

26.6 C As a listed company, whistle blowing procedures would normally be in place as part of good corporate governance. "A" is not an option as this is refusing to accept responsibility for dealing with the matter. Reporting directly to the police would be a breach of employment confidentiality, unless there is an argument for public interest (unlikely). D would be a clear breach of any ethical code that Irina is subject to.

26.7 A A profession is characterised by the development, mastering and examination of specialist skills during a period of training; governance by a professional association; compliance with an ethical code; certification process to practice; continuous development through theory and practical application.

26.8 B As a professional accountant they have a code of ethics at the core of their activities. Most other board members do not belong to any form of professional society.

ABOUT BECKER PROFESSIONAL EDUCATION

Becker Professional Education provides a single solution for students and professionals looking to advance their careers and achieve success in:

- Accounting

- International Financial Reporting

- Project Management

- Continuing Professional Education

- Healthcare

For more information on how Becker Professional Education can support you in your career, visit www.becker.com/acca.

Becker Professional Education
is an ACCA approved content provider